Francis E Jones

June 1954

PELOUBET'S

SELECT NOTES

C-25 PRINTED IN U.S.A.   B. PLOCKHORST

CHRIST TAKING LEAVE OF HIS MOTHER.

FOUNDED BY REV. FRANCIS N. PELOUBET, D.D.

PELOUBET'S
SELECT NOTES

ON THE

INTERNATIONAL BIBLE LESSONS
FOR CHRISTIAN TEACHING.

UNIFORM SERIES

1954

John — Gospel of Divine Love
The Northern Kingdom and Its Prophets
Growth in Christian Living
Wisdom and Worship in Old Testament Literature
(Job, Psalms, Proverbs, Ecclesiastes)

BY

WILBUR M. SMITH, D.D.

Eightieth Annual Volume

BOSTON 16, MASS., U.S.A.
PUBLISHED BY W. A. WILDE COMPANY
131 CLARENDON STREET   BOSTON 16, MASSACHUSETTS
Printed in U.S.A.

CONTENTS.

V

AUDIO-VISUAL SELECTIONS.

This year audio-visual aids are listed with each lesson following The Teacher's Library. Not all lessons lend themselves to the use of this kind of aids. It is not well to use projected materials at every class session, or even as a regular practice. They should never substitute for the adquate preparation of the lesson by the teacher. Sometimes they can be used in the assembly periods where all can share them.

Annotations are included with many of the listings this year, which may be of some help in selection, but they should not be depended upon to take the place of previewing (or screening, as it is called). Selections should be made long enough in advance so that bookings can be made — usually one should make these arrangements a month ahead of the time of showing, and in the case of special materials for holiday seasons more time is recommended.

A number of regional distribution offices have been established in different parts of the country. Most of the major denominations have audio-visual departments in connection with their headquarters or publishing houses. The Church Film Library, 1399 N. Lake St., Pasadena, Calif., serves as West Coast distributor for nine denominations. The Evangelistic Audio-Visual Association, 2342 E. 126th St., Compton, Calif., serves a wider area, but has a more limited stock.

Most public libraries now have the basic tools for films and filmstrips, *Educational Film Guide,* and *Filmstrip Guide* respectively. These give descriptive information, but not sources for borrowing. For a church that wants to purchase tools for selection, the following two are most comprehensive: *Master Guide to Religious and Other Comparable Motion Pictures* and *Master Guide to Religious and Other Comparable Filmstrips*, both published in looseleaf form by Selected Films Release Service in Whittier, Calif., and *Audio-Visual Resource Guide* issued by the Visual Education Fellowship of the International Council of Religious Education. These are not limited to religious materials, but include other related titles that can be used at times. Slides, filmstrips and motion pictures are included, and there is an elaborate outline of organization, which one may use as a guide, if desirable. Whether or not one can go along with the philosophy of religious education underlying these selections, the listings, descriptions and evaluations are often helpful. Every opportunity for training should be seized by those in charge of the audio-visual program, as these materials require special handling and the machinery to project them must be understood and cared for. Showings should be preceded by an introduction and followed by a discussion, to obtain maximum results.

ARNOLD D. EHLERT

BIBLIOGRAPHIES.

For this year's lessons, I am giving special bibliographies only for the History of Israel, the Book of Proverbs, and the Gospel of John. Other portions of Scripture will be given ample bibliographies in the separate lessons.

HISTORIES OF THE HEBREW PEOPLE AND OLD TESTAMENT ARCHAEOLOGY.

WILLIAM G. BLAIKIE: *A Manual of Bible History.* New edition, rev., New York, 1925. Brief; conservative; a good handbook.

FRANK KNIGHT SANDERS: *History of the Hebrews.* New York, 1914. Material excellently arranged for classroom work; more liberal in its views than the volume by Blaikie.

F. J. FOAKES-JACKSON: *The Biblical History of the Hebrews.* 2nd edition, London, 1927.

W. F. BURNSIDE: *Old Testament History for Use in Schools.* 12th edition, Cambridge, 1904; by an outstanding scholar.

CHARLES FOSTER KENT: *The Student's Old Testament.* New York, 1904–1927. 6 vols. Suggestive; material well arranged; marred in places by radical interpretations.

ALFRED EDERSHEIM: *The Bible History.* 7 vols. Though published many years ago, will be found of value.

A. P. STANLEY: *Lectures on the History of the Jewish Church.* 3 vols. Various editions. The most brilliant and fascinating history of the Hebrew people ever written in our language. Every Sunday School teacher should possess this work.

STEPHEN L. CAIGER: *Bible and Spade.* An Introduction to Bible Archaeology. Oxford, 1936. An invaluable handbook, excellently setting forth the confirmations of archaeological discoveries, written in a delightful manner; a book to keep near by; not expensive.

ELMER W. K. MOULD: *Essentials of Bible History.* New York, 1939. 678 pages. The most important recent scholarly survey of the entire field of Biblical history, with over-emphasis upon sociological subjects, and too severely critical in places; packed with information.

IRA MAURICE PRICE: *A Syllabus of Old Testament History.* 14th edition, 1932, 216 pp. *The Dramatic Story of Old Testament History.* 2nd edition, 1935, 471 pp. The former is an outline of the historical data of the Old Testament, with excellent bibliographies. The latter is in narrative form, charmingly written, well illustrated, with a more liberal viewpoint than the earlier works.

GEORGE L. ROBINSON: *The Bearing of Archaeology on the Old Testament.* New York, 1941, 207 pp. One of the best handbooks for the study of the archaeological aspects of the Old Testament we have; well worth purchasing.

J. McKEE ADAMS: *Biblical Backgrounds, a Geographical Survey of Bible Lands in the Light of the Scriptures and Recent Research.* Nashville, Tenn.: Broadman Press, 1934. 481 pp. With good pen and ink maps, and excellent illustrations.

————: *Ancient Records and the Bible, a Survey of Archaeological Evidences.* Nashville, Tenn.: Broadman Press, 1946. 397 pp. With many full-page plates. A volume that will be a valuable addition to any teacher's library.

HENRY PRESERVED SMITH: *Old Testament History.* New York, 1903. In *The International Theological Library.*

EDWARD J. YOUNG: *An Introduction to the Old Testament.* Grand Rapids: William B. Eerdmans, 1949. 414 pp. This is the most important conservative introduction to the Old Testament available in the English language. It is thoroughly up to date, written by a scholar who believes in the inspiration of the Scriptures, and who frankly faces all the important critical problems that confront the serious student of the Old Testament.

JOSEPH P. FREE: *Archaeology and Bible History.* Wheaton, Ill.: Van Kampen Press, 1950. Written by a conservative scholar who has covered the whole field of Biblical archaeology. It is a treasure-house, the result of twenty years of study and teaching.

JACK FINEGAN: *Light from the Ancient Past; The Archaeological Background of the Hebrew Christian Religion.* Princeton University Press, 1946. 500 pp. This volume, with over two hundred illustrations, has been received with great acclaim on both sides of the Atlantic. It is not as Biblical as Dr. Free's work, but covers some extra-Biblical material not in that volume; one supplements the other.

PAUL HEINISCH: *History of the Old Testament.* St. John's Abbey, Collegeville, Minn., 1952. A very scholarly work written by a Roman Catholic; elaborate footnotes; abreast of the most recent scholarship.

COMMENTARIES ON THE GOSPEL OF ST. JOHN.

F. GODET: *Commentary on the Gospel of John.* 2 vols. Trans. from the French, with Notes, by Timothy Dwight, President of Yale College. Masterly, profound, edifying.

MARCUS DODS: *The Gospel of St. John.* 2 vols. The *Expositor's Bible* series. Invaluable, inexpensive.

CHARLES R. ERDMAN: *The Gospel of John.* Philadelphia, 1917. Brief, clear, suggestive.

S. D. GORDON: *Quiet Talks on John's Gospel.* New York, Chicago, 1915.

A. PLUMMER: *The Gospel According to St. John.* The *Cambridge Bible for Schools and Colleges.* Cambridge, 1886.

PAUL HARRISON: *The Gospel of St. John.* Grand Rapids, Michigan, 1932. With helpful light from oriental customs.

GEORGE REITH: *The Gospel According to St. John,* with Introduction and Notes. 2 vols. Edinburgh. In *Hand-books for Bible Classes and Private Students.* In the mind of the editor, the most valuable, illuminating work on John, for its size, in our language; rich notes. This has just been republished recently.

A. T. ROBERTSON: *The Divinity of Christ in the Gospel of John.* New York, London, 1916.

J. C. RYLE: *Expository Thoughts on the Gospels.* 3 vols. Unsurpassed as a devotional commentary.

W. GRAHAM SCROGGIE: *St. John.* London and Edinburgh. In the *Study Hour Series.* Brief, suggestive, good outlines.

MELVIA THOMAS SHELFORD: *The Christ as John Knew Him.* Lectures on the Gospel According to John. New York, 1928.

ROBERT E. SPEER: *John's Gospel: The Greatest Book in the World.* New York, London, 1915. A fine hand-book.

B. F. WESTCOTT: *The Gospel According to St. John.* Originally published 1881 in *The Speaker's Commentary* Series. Many later impressions. In many ways, the greatest commentary on the Fourth Gospel in English.

J. RITCHIE SMITH: *The Teaching of the Gospel of John.* New York, London, 1903. Theological.

JOHN PETER LANGE: *The Gospel According to John.* Revised, enlarged, and edited by Philip Schaff. New York, 1871, and later impressions. Rich, better for those who read the Greek text.

ROBERT LEE: *The Outlined John.* London. Outlines only.

F. N. PELOUBET: *Suggestive Illustrations on the Gospel of John.* New York, 1898. Exceptionally valuable for Sunday school teachers.

ARTHUR W. PINK: *Exposition of the Gospel of John.* 4 vols. Swengel, Pa. Dispensational. In places quite original.

JOHN CALVIN: *A Commentary on the Gospel According to John.* A new translation by William Pringle. Edinburgh, 1847. 2 vols.

A. C. GAEBELEIN: *The Gospel of John.* New York, 1936. 414 pp. By one of the great Biblical expositors of this generation.

R. C. H. LENSKI: *The Interpretation of St. John's Gospel.* Columbus, Ohio, 1931, 1418 pp. One of the great commentaries of this day, the depths of which few have even begun to fathom.

THOMAS WHITELAW: *The Gospel of St. John:* an Exposition Exegetical and Homiletical. 1888, 461 pp.

EVERETT F. HARRISON: *The Son of God Among the Sons of Men.* Boston: W. A. Wilde Co., 1949. This is one of the finest studies of the principal characters of the Gospel of John that has been written. It would prove an excellent text for any minister in the mid-week service.

MERRILL C. TENNEY: *John, the Gospel of Belief.* Grand Rapids: Eerdmans, 1948. A superb piece of work, the best treatment of the subject announced in the title that we have.

viii

BIBLIOGRAPHIES.

EDWYN C. HOSKYNS: *The Fourth Gospel*. London, 1947. This work of 600 pages is the most scholarly, conservative volume on the Gospel of John that has been published for years. It is heavy reading, but ministers especially will revel in its profound discussion of the great themes of the Fourth Gospel.

COMMENTARIES ON THE BOOK OF PROVERBS.

FRANZ DELITZSCH: *Biblical Commentary on the Proverbs of Solomon*. 2 vols. Edinburgh, 1874. Any commentary by Delitzsch on Old Testament books will be found still superb in the interpretation of Hebrew words, and in profound theological and historical exegesis. It is seldom that one turns to him without great profit.

DAVID THOMAS: *The Practical Philosopher: Brief and Suggestive Moral Readings on the Book of Proverbs*. 4th ed., 1885. This great work of 800 pages is very difficult to come upon. I have not used it in *Peloubet's Notes* previously, but have drawn from it extensively in these pages.

JOHN MILLER: *Commentary on the Proverbs*. 2nd ed., Princeton, New Jersey, 1887. A large work of over 600 pages; in many places excellent comments.

E. H. PLUMPTRE: *The Book of Proverbs*, in the *Bible Commentary* series.

OTTO ZÖCKLER in the *Lange Series of Commentaries*. Especially valuable for its comprehensive introduction.

R. F. HORTON: *The Book of Proverbs*, in the *Expositor's Bible*. This volume is divided into subjects rather than chapters as they occur in the Bible, and for such treatment the pages are excellent.

WILLIAM ARNOT: *Laws from Heaven for Life on Earth*. First and second series, London, 1856, etc. This is by all means, to my knowledge, the finest series of expository messages on the Book of Proverbs in the English language. The work is not too difficult to come upon.

H. A. IRONSIDE: *Notes on the Book of Proverbs*. One of the earlier volumes of this well-known expositor, and I have always thought one of his best. Contains many helpful exhortations.

A. R. FAUSSET in the *Jamieson, Fausset and Brown Commentary*. For strict exegesis, this is about the finest.

T. T. PEROWNE, in the *Cambridge Bible for Schools and Colleges*. 1899. Excellent for the exact meaning of each clause.

INTRODUCTION.

HOW THESE OUTLINES CAME TO BE.

The Background Out of Which the Outlines Come.

The International Sunday School Lesson Committee first issued outlines for Uniform Lessons in 1872. Since that date, cooperatively prepared outlines for Sunday School lessons have been made available to publishers of Sunday School lesson materials each year. Though there have been many changes in the framework of the outlines and changes in the general principles upon which they are built, the basic purpose of the outlines has remained the same. This purpose is to offer a plan that will be in line with the principle of uniformity of Bible-study materials for various age groups in the Sunday School and place strong emphasis upon the actual content of the Bible record. The ultimate end sought is the acceptance of the Bible as the very Word of God, and its use in helping growing persons increasingly to know its content and to understand its message in the light of their own experiences and relationships. It seeks to provide for the fruitful study of the Bible as a whole but gives larger place to those portions of the Scripture which afford greatest teaching and learning values.

The outlines here presented are for 1954, in the cycle of 1951–56, inclusive. This cycle is the second developed under the plan for the production of lesson outlines set up by the International Council of Religious Education to take effect with the outlines beginning January 1, 1945, for all age groups from primary through adult. The Committee on the Uniform Series was instructed to develop outlines which would be the basis for a "system of lessons, biblical in content, maintaining the principle of uniformity through including a core of common material and emphasis to be developed in all age groups, but providing for a graded approach through supplemental materials and adaptations within the several age groups."

How the Committee on the Uniform Series Is Set Up.

The committee is made up of persons appointed by their respective denominations, which, although differing in certain elements of faith and polity, hold a common faith in Jesus Christ, the Son of God, as Lord and Saviour, whose saving gospel is to be taught to all mankind. There are approximately seventy members of the committee, representing thirty denominations in the United States and Canada. The committee holds one meeting each year, which usually extends through an entire week of work, and the members of the committee do ad interim work.

The General Plan of Work Under Which the Outlines Are Developed.

The outlines are planned in six-year cycles. In each year of the cycle there is at least one quarter of study on the life and teaching of Jesus and the challenge to commitment to the Christian way of life. In the cycle for 1951–56, a bird's-eye view of the sweep of the whole Bible is provided by a study of "Great Epochs of the Bible." There are quarters of lessons from the call of Abraham to the end of the New Testament story in the Acts. There are distributed through the years so as not to spend too much time consecutively in the study of historical lessons. The wisdom literature of the Old Testament and the prophets are included as well as the New Testament Epistles and Revelation. Lessons on Christian faith and life are provided under such quarterly themes as "Christian Teachings on Human Relations," "The Ten Commandments and the Teaching of Jesus," "Bible Teachings for a Better World," "Growth in Christian Living," and "Christian Teachings." Finally, a quarter is devoted to the study of some selected "Great Passages of the Bible."

Special topical studies such as temperance, world peace, civic responsibility, Christian family life, and the like are included where such studies are directly related to the Bible portions being studied rather than as studies unrelated to the rest of the course. It is the purpose of the committee to provide at least one temperance lesson in every quarter.

xi

INTRODUCTION.

A measure of gradation is provided for in the selection of specific Bible passages for the various age groups, but common Scripture material is chosen for all age groups unless this interferes with meeting the religious needs of the pupils. Christmas and Easter are kept in mind, and, wherever feasible, the Easter material is included in a relationship that will give it climactic value. The phases of the church year are also kept in mind for the help of those churches which wish to give emphasis to them.

What the Outlines Offer.

The outlines here presented include material for every Sunday of the year. They include a general weekly subject, with a basic Scripture block, which is selected for the use of editors and writers in developing lesson materials based upon the outlines. In some cases it is not intended that the entire Scripture block shall necessarily be studied by teachers and pupils, but that the editors and writers may select the material which is to receive detailed treatment.

For each session there is provided a devotional passage selected for use in worship services of church schools using the lessons.

The outlines also include a topic for each age group, a memory selection, and brief suggestions to indicate to editors and lesson writers the particular emphasis the committee had in mind in making the selection of Scripture material. These notes are suggestions and do not propose an official interpretation of the passage.

The Outlines for 1954.

The outlines for 1954 begin with a study of "John — Gospel of Divine Love." The second quarter deals with "The Northern Kingdom and Its Prophets." This is followed by the series, "Growth in Christian Living." The concluding quarter provides a study of "Wisdom and Worship in Old Testament Literature."

Memory Selections.

The New Testament memory selections are from the Revised Standard Version of the New Testament, published by Thomas Nelson and Sons and copyrighted by the Division of Christian Education of the National Council of Churches of Christ in the United States of America. The Old Testament memory selections are from the American Standard Version, also published by Thomas Nelson and Sons and copyrighted by the Division of Christian Education of the National Council of the Churches of Christ in the United States of America. Denominations are free to use any version desired.

xii

PREFACE.

During the last four years, more new versions of the entire Bible and of the New Testament and important works about the Bible have been made available to English readers than probably in any other one four-year period in modern times. I do not here want to discuss the commendable and regrettable features of the new versions but rather to mention some of the more important books about the Bible that have recently appeared with the hope that many teachers will find ways of purchasing some of these volumes. Let us begin with the matter of versions. In 1950, a book appeared by one of the best conservative scholars of Great Britain, F. F. Bruce, entitled *The Books and the Parchments*, a work of 260 pages, which in my opinion is the best scholarly up-to-date concise survey of the whole subject of the original text and later versions now available. There are even chapters here on "The Bible and the Alphabet," "The Targums," and "Lost Books." The volume is available through the Fleming H. Revell Company. The most exhaustive modern study of the English versions of the Bible appeared in 1952, with the title, *English Versions of the Bible*, by Hugh Pope. This work of nearly 800 pages with exhaustive bibliography was written by a Roman Catholic Dominican scholar and consequently, we are sorry to say, there are some very unkind things in this volume regarding Wycliffe and Coverdale but, nevertheless, the book is infinitely superior to any recent work issued by a Protestant. In this country, it is published by the B. Herder and Company of St. Louis.

The latest Bible Dictionary is the one carrying the title, *Harper's Bible Dictionary*, by Madeleine S. Miller and J. Lane Miller, a work of 850 double column pages, published in 1952 by Harpers. For historical, archaeological, and geographical themes, the volume is superior to any other that we have. In Biblical criticism, however, it is liberal and in many of its theological expressions not acceptable by those who believe in the full inspiration of the Scripture. The work is beautifully illustrated.

The best conservative introduction to the Old Testament is the one published by Eerdmans in 1949, *An Introduction to the Old Testament*, by Dr. Edward J. Young of Westminster Theological Seminary. It is indispensable for the serious student of the Old Testament. A good book briefly surveying the prophetical literature of the Old Testament is *Men Spake from God* by Professor H. L. Ellison of the London Bible College, published by the Paternoster Press in 1952. One will not agree with everything in this volume but it is written by a conservative and a scholar who has spent years in the study and teaching of the Old Testament. The two most significant commentaries on New Testament books, as far as I know, that have recently appeared are those that have been published in the new series, *The New International Commentary*, also projected by Eerdmans. In 1951, the volume on Luke appeared by Norval Geldenhuys and in the latter part of the same year, the volume on Acts by Dr. F. F. Bruce, the finest work on this important New Testament book that has appeared in a quarter of a century. The most important one-volume commentary of recent times comes from Roman Catholic scholars, entitled *A Catholic Commentary on Holy Scripture*, published in 1953 by Thomas Nelson. It is the largest one-volume commentary in our language embracing over one and a half million words with an index extending through 240 columns. The book defends the Catholic faith, of course, but it is an important work. I am very happy to announce that by the time this volume of Peloubet's Notes is made available, the Inter-Varsity Christian Fellowship of England, after years of work on the part of many outstanding conservative scholars, will have published what will prove to be the most important one-volume commentary on the Bible from a conservative view-point that has ever appeared in our language. I am saying this after a careful reading of proof sheets. This is exactly the volume we have been waiting for and wanting for many years. In this country, it will be made available through the Wm. B. Eerdmans Company of Grand Rapids.

Two works on separate Biblical subjects that might be called definitive have recently appeared, on subjects far removed one from the other. The first is by my friend Dr. Merrill F. Unger, of Dallas Theological Seminary, *Biblical Demonology*, a volume of 250 pages published by Van Kampen Press of Wheaton, Ill. Dr. Unger began the study of this subject ten years ago, and after submitting a doctoral dissertation on it, he began an even more thorough investigation, with the result that we have now what will be recognized on every hand as the most comprehensive treatment of the difficult subject of demons in the Old and New Testaments thus far published in our language. Thoroughly acquainted with the original biblical languages, Dr. Unger is able to distinguish the meanings of the numerous words used in the Scriptures for supernatural evil powers, and for their various manifestations through human agents on earth. The book also includes a historical survey of the interpretation of demonology itself, and contains chapters on demon possession, magic, divination, and necromancy. The other volume is a work published by Chronica Botanica Company of Waltham, Mass., late in 1952, *Plants of the Bible*, by Dr. Harold N. Moldenke, assisted by Alma L. Moldenke. It is estimated, though I think Dr. Moldenke does not himself say this, that there are 3,500 species of plants to be found from Northern Syria to Sinai, grouped in 850 genera, representing 124 orders. It is generally stated that there are 280 different plants mentioned in the Bible, though not all of them can as yet be identified. This work (I would judge that the text devoted to the description of species embraces about 155,000 words) describes 230 species. The material is arranged alphabetically, according to the Latin name of the species, beginning with *Acacia nilotica*, the scientific term for a form of acacia which some believe was the species of the bush which Moses saw aflame, as recorded in Exodus 3:2–4. The shittim wood, often mentioned in the Old Testament, is another species of acacia, to which our author devotes nearly three pages.

The careful reading of any one of these volumes will greatly enrich a teacher's ministry. We are certainly living in a day when people everywhere seem truly interested in the Bible and Biblical subjects though we must admit that such interest is not in itself a synonym for loyalty to the Christian faith or salvation through Christ, but we can all hope that such an interest will for many lead to a living experience with the Son of God.

WILDE'S BIBLE PICTURE SET

Illustrating the International Bible Lessons for Christian Teaching
Uniform Series for 1954

Sixty pictures printed in black and white on heavy stock 6 × 8
$1.20 postpaid.

(Also sold singly on orders for 20 or more at 2 cents each.)

FIRST QUARTER

Lesson 1
635 The Christ. Bida.
34 Jesus, Twelve Years Old, On His Way to Jerusalem. O. Mengelberg.
Lesson 2
52 Purification of the Temple. H. Hofmann.
Lesson 3
53 Nicodemus' Visit to Jesus. Artist Unknown.
Lesson 4
54 Jesus and the Woman of Samaria. Dore.
Lesson 5
80 Christ Raising the Daughter of Jairus. Gustav Richter.
271 Temperance. E. Burne-Jones.
Lesson 6
83 Miracles of the Loaves and Fishes. Bartolome Esteban Murillo.
Lesson 7
93 "I Am The Light of the World." Holman Hunt.
Lesson 8
593 Christ Healing the Blind Man.
Lesson 9
116 The Good Shepherd. B. Plockhorst.
Lesson 10
118 Raising of Lazarus. Bonifazio II.
Lesson 11
136 Jesus in Gethsemane. H. Hofmann.
Lesson 12
133 Jesus Washes the Disciples' Feet. Brown.
Lesson 13
63 Jesus and His Disciples Going Through Cornfield. Gustave Dore.

SECOND QUARTER

Lesson 1
535 Jesus in Prayer. Alexandre Bida.
Lesson 2
138 Jesus Taken Captive. H. Hofmann.
534 Christ's Entry Into Jerusalem. B. Plockhorst.
Lesson 3
161 Risen Lord and Mary Magdalen. B. Plockhorst.
Lesson 4
656 Jeroboam Making Idols to Worship.
Lesson 5
489 Jeroboam's Calf-Worship Rebuked. Artist Unknown.
Lesson 6
494 Slaughter of the Prophets of Baal. Gustave Dore.
Lesson 7
661 Elijah Denouncing the Crime of Ahab in Naboth's Vineyard.
Lesson 8
504 Prophets. John Sargent.
Lesson 9
662 Elisha Raises the Shunammite's Son. Benj. West.
Lesson 10
756 Amos (From Sargent's Prophets)
Lesson 11
781 Defeat Through Drunkenness.
Lesson 12
683 Hosea (From Sargent's Prophets)
680 "The River that Runneth to Ahava."
Lesson 13
528 The People of Israel Praying God to Send the Messiah. Crimani Breviary.

THIRD QUARTER

Lesson 1
31 Infancy of Christ. H. Hofmann.
Lesson 2
811 The Student Christian.
Lesson 3
800 Timothy Learning the Scriptures.
808 A Page from the Mazarin Bible.
Lesson 4
719 The Soul's Awakening. J. J. Sant.
Lesson 5
810 The Pilgrims Going to Church.
Lesson 6
67 Consider the Lilies. Henry Le Jeune.
Lesson 7
792 Training for Olympic Games.
627 Three Members of a Temperance Society. Herring.
Lesson 8
603 Alms Deeds of Dorcas. W. C. T. Dobson.
Lesson 9
542 St. Christopher Carrying the Child Jesus Across the River. Hans Memling.
Lesson 10
695 "Come Unto Me All Ye That Labor." Carl Bloch.
Lesson 11
460 Paul Preaching at Athens. Raphael.
Lesson 12
647 The Christian Graces. Geo. E. Hicks.
Lesson 13
122 The Way, The Truth and Life. Alexandre Bida.

FOURTH QUARTER

Lesson 1
624 Happy Days of Job. W. C. T. Dobson.
Lesson 2
833 Job and His Friends.
Lesson 3
487 King Solomon. Gustave Dore.
Lesson 4
809 Christ Blessing the Evening Meal. Leon L'Hermitte.
Lesson 5
501 Rebuilding the Temple. Artist Unknown.
Lesson 6
480 David Showing Saul that He had Spared His Life. Gustave Dore.
465 Christ at the Home of Mary and Martha. Eichstaedt.
Lesson 7
438 Young David Rescuing the Lamb. Elizabeth Gardner.
Lesson 8
784 David the Psalmist.
Lesson 9
380 Moses and the Burning Bush. Dore.
Lesson 10
483 Nathan's Parable Against David. Payer.
Lesson 11
653 Last Judgment. Fra Angelico.
Lesson 12
430 Angels' Heads. Sir Joshua Reynolds.
14 The Angels and the Shepherds. B. Plockhorst.
Lesson 13
318 Head of Christ. H. Hofmann.

XV

FIRST QUARTER.

JANUARY 3 — MARCH 28, 1954.

JOHN—GOSPEL OF DIVINE LOVE.

LESSON I. — January 3.

GOD REVEALED IN CHRIST. — John 1; 20:30–31.

PRINTED TEXT, John 1:14–23, 29–45.

Devotional Reading: Hebrews 1:1–9.
Beginner Topic: BABY IN THE TEMPLE.
    Lesson Material: Luke 2:21–40.
    Memory Verse: Surely God is good.   Psalm 73:1.
Primary Topic: FINDING JESUS, THE FRIEND.
    Lesson Material: John 1:35–51; 20:30–31.
    Memory Verse: God . . . loved us and sent his Son.   1 John 4:10.
Junior Topic: JESUS' FIRST FOLLOWERS.
    Lesson Material: John 1:19–51; 20:30–31.
    Memory Verse: God . . . loved us and sent his Son.   1 John 4:10.
Intermediate-Senior Topic: INTRODUCING JESUS.
    Lesson Material: John 1; 20:30–31.
    Memory Verse: These are written, that ye may believe that Jesus is the
    Christ, the Son of God; and that believing ye may have life in his name.
    John 20:31.
Topic for Young People and Adults: GOD REVEALED IN CHRIST.
    Lesson Material: John 1; 20:30–31.
    Memory Verse: These are written, that ye may believe that Jesus is the
    Christ, the Son of God; and that believing ye may have life in his name.
    John 20:31.

1

THE TEACHER AND HIS CLASS.

The **Younger Classes** may be introduced to this lesson by having their attention drawn to an interesting word occurring here three times — *find*. Many packaged breakfast foods are now advertised as having prizes at the bottom of each box. Children enjoy finding these things, or anything they think is of value. In this lesson, finding always implies hunting for something, sometimes for a prolonged period. Here several people are finding their dearest loved ones to tell them that at last they have found the one who is the Messiah of whom the prophets spoke.

The **Older Classes** may be reminded at the beginning of this lesson that there are possibly 620,000,000 people in the world today who are classified as Christians. I am sure that many of them do not pray and read the Bible, and some of them perhaps do not know much about Christ, but these are the latest statistics given in our almanacs. Whatever be the great number of Christians, certainly more adherents than of any other religion in the world, our lesson is the story of how the first few men came to follow Christ. We could call them, therefore, the first true Christians in the world.

THE LESSON IN ITS SETTINGS.

Time. — February A.D. 27.

Place. — Jesus was baptized near Bethabara, otherwise known as Bethany at the Jordan River, on the boundary between Judah and Benjamin.

THE PLAN OF THE LESSON.

SUBJECT: How True Men of God Coming into the Presence of Christ were Immediately Convinced that He was the Promised Messiah and the Son of God.

I. THE PROLOGUE, John 1:1–14.
1. The pre-existent Christ, vs. 1–3.
2. The incarnate Christ, vs. 4, 5.
3. The forerunner of Christ, vs. 6–8.
4. The unrecognized Christ, vs. 9–11.
5. The omnipotent Christ, vs. 12, 13.
6. The glorious Christ, v. 14.

II. THE WITNESS OF JOHN THE BAPTIST TO CHRIST, 1:15–28.
1. His early testimony to the Christ soon to appear, vs. 15–18.
2. His own relationship to Christ, vs. 19–28.
3. His identification of Christ now in their midst, vs. 29–34.

III. CHRIST WINS HIS FIRST DISCIPLES, 1:35–51.
1. Andrew and John follow Christ, vs. 35–40.
2. Andrew brings his brother Peter to Christ, vs. 41–42.
3. Jesus finds Philip, vs. 43, 44.
4. Philip finds Nathaniel, vs. 45–51.

THE TEACHER'S LIBRARY.

The amount of material on this lesson is enormous, and we can refer to only a part of it. First of all, the major lives of Christ are here quite adequate; also the more important commentaries on the Gospel of John, a list of which will be found in the Introduction to this volume. Of course all volumes dealing with the characters of the Gospels will be found helpful for the study of Andrew, Philip, and Nathaniel. I would suggest especially James Jeffrey: *The Personal Ministry of the Son of Man;* W. Boyd Carpenter: *The Son of Man Among the Sons of Men;* Alexander Whyte: *Bible Characters, Joseph and Mary — James the Lord's Brother;* L. R. Scarborough: *How Jesus Won Men;* G. Campbell Morgan: *The Great Physician;* and Everett F. Harrison: *The Son of God Among the Sons of Men.* There are numerous books on John the Baptist, who plays a prominent part in this lesson, particularly those by J. Feather, F. B. Meyer, H. R. Reynolds, and A. T. Robertson.

For sermonic material, the best on our lesson is found in G. Campbell Morgan: *The Westminster Pulpit,* Vol. 2, as follows: verse 14, pp. 265–272; verses 38, 39, pp. 353–360; verses 41, 42, pp. 369–376; verse 43, pp. 377–384; verse 45, pp. 385–392. Also, on verse 29, see F. W. Boreham: *A Bunch of Everlastings,* 39–50; verse 36, Alexander Whyte: *The Walk, Conversation and Character of Jesus Christ Our Lord,* pp. 95–104; verses 43–51, R. C. Trench: *Studies in the Gospels,* 66–82.

AUDIO-VISUAL AIDS.

These passages in John do not cover all the story of John the Baptist, but sections of the following audio-visual aids will be found useful.

FILMSTRIP: "John the Baptist," Cathedral, 35 fr., b&w.

SLIDE SET: "John the Baptist," Church-Craft #11, 8 sl., col., manual. Actual rite of baptism not shown.

SLIDE SET: "The Life of Christ Visualized." Move 4 (The Bible in Pictures), Visser-slides #55–60, 5 sl., col. Includes guide chart. Shows also the descent of the Holy Spirit upon Christ.

JOHN 1:14. And the Word became flesh.

Without a single sentence of redundancy, or a line of repetition, a volume of five hundred pages could easily be written on the first chapter of John's Gospel, the teaching of which we must now compress into thirty minutes. Unless the teacher is to present only a fragment of the chapter, or leave the class confused by the crowding in of too many themes, he will have to determine what he is going to emphasize, and then concentrate on the various aspects of the particular subject he has chosen. The great theme here is Christ, beginning with His eternal existence and coming down to the earliest months of His earthly ministry. This is a chapter of amazing contrasts. The Prologue (vs. 1–14) is probably the most profound single passage in all the Gospels, if not in all the New Testament, and thousands of pages have been written about it: but the account of Jesus and His earliest disciples, beginning with verse 35, is simplicity indeed. The chapter begins with the eternal and omnipotent Christ: but soon we are in the presence of the incarnate Christ and the human Jesus. The prologue is framed in the mould of Greek thinking; but all the interviews with John the Baptist and the early disciples are definitely Hebraic.

I. THE PROLOGUE, John 1:1–14. Even though it is not in the printed text, we must not begin the study of this chapter without having the first verse before us: "In the beginning was the Word, and the Word was with God, and the Word was God." On this Westcott says, "The three clauses contain all that it is possible for man to realize as to the essential nature of the Word in relation to time, and mode of being, and character: He was (1) in the beginning: He was (2) with God: He was (3) God. At the same time these three clauses answer to the three great moments of the Incarnation of the Word declared in verse 14. He who 'was God' *became flesh:* He who 'was with God,' *tabernacled among us* (compare 1 John 1:2): He who 'was in the beginning,' *became* (in time)." Without any further comment on these words, I would like to give the outline developed by Canon Westcott in his superb volume on John's Gospel, from which I shall be frequently quoting in this lesson. His outline is different from mine, and from that which others have drawn up. Verses 2–18 he entitles, "The Word in Relation to Creation," which divides into three parts: the essential facts (2–5); the historic manifestation of the Word generally (6–13); the Incarnation as apprehended by personal experience (14–18). We must confine ourselves here to the first two divisions. Westcott further divides vs. 2–5 as follows: the source of creation in the divine counsel (2); the act of creation (3); the being of things created (4–5). The second section he divides in three parts: the testimony of prophecy represented by John (6–8); the manifestations of the Word (as Light) before the Incarnation (9–10); the coming of the Word to the chosen people consummated at the Incarnation (11–13). This last division is broken down into two parts: national unbelief (11) and individual faith (12, 13).

We are now ready for that which in some ways is the greatest single brief statement of the Incarnation of the Son of God in all the Bible. From Westcott's four great pages on this one verse, I would select the following comments. 14. **And the Word became flesh.** "The personal title *Logos* is used absolutely only in vs. 1, 14 (Rev. 19:13; Heb. 4:12 — *the Word of God*). In 1 John 1:1, the phrase 'the Word of life' is not personal, but equivalent to 'the revelation of the life.' . . . The personal titles 'the Word' and 'the Word of God' must be kept in close connection with the same terms as applied to the sum of the Gospel in the New Testament and with the phrase, 'the word of the Lord' in the prophecies of the Old Testament. The Word, before the Incarnation, was the one source of the many divine words; and Christ, the Word Incarnate is Himself the Gospel . . . The Lord's human and divine natures were united in one Person, as against various forms of Nestorianism, according to which He has a human personality and a divine personality, to which the acts, etc., belonging to the respective natures must be referred. As 'all things *became* through the Word,' so He Himself '*became flesh*.'

15. John beareth witness of him, and crieth, saying, This was he of whom I said, He that cometh after me is become before me: for he was before me.

The first creation and the second creation alike center in Him. By His own will He 'became' that which first 'became' through and in Him. Humanity from the side of its weakness and dependence and mortality is naturally described as 'flesh.' In this respect 'flesh' expresses here human nature as a whole regarded under the aspect of its present corporeal embodiment, including of necessity the 'soul' (12:27) and the 'spirit' (11:33; 13:21; 19:30) as belonging to the totality of man (compare Heb. 2:14). At the same time the word marks the points of connection between man and the material world, so that it has a further significance as presenting in a familiar contrast the spiritual and the material." — *B. F. Westcott.* **And dwelt among us.** Let me here move from Westcott to Dr. G. Campbell Morgan. "He is all I am, but He is all God is. And when I lay this hand of mine upon His hand, I have touched the hand of a man such as I am; but I have taken hold of the might of God. And when I look into the eyes of the Man Who pitched His tent among Galilean fishermen, I have looked into human eyes all brimming with love, but through them I have looked into the very heart of the infinite God. He is the Tent of meeting. I find God in Christ, as nowhere else." — *Dr. G. Campbell Morgan.* (**And we beheld his glory.** "The word 'glory' carries on the parallel between the divine Presence by the Word Incarnate among men. From time to time the Lord manifested His glory in the wilderness (Ex. 16:10; 24:16; 40:34, etc.); in the Temple of Solomon (1 Kings 8:11); and to the prophets (Isa. 6:3; compare ch. 12:41; Ezek. 1:28, etc.; Acts 7:55); and even so Christ's glory flashed forth at crises of His history. It is not possible for us to define exactly in what way this majesty was shewn, by signs, by words, by events. Compare Luke 9:31 f. It is enough that the Evangelist records his own experience. The Son of Man had a glory which corresponded with His filial relation to the Father, even when He had laid aside His divine glory (17:4). — *B. F. Westcott.* **Glory as of the only begotten from the Father**). "This glory of the Incarnate Word is described as being 'glory as of an only son from his father,' a glory, that is, of one who represents another, being derived from him, and of the same essence with him . . . Christ is the One only Son, the One to whom the title belongs in a sense, completely unique and singular, as distinguished from that in which there are many children of God (vs. 12 ff.). The use of the word elsewhere in the New Testament to describe an only child (Luke 7:12; 8:42; 9:38; Heb. 11:17) brings out this sense completely." — *B. F. Westcott.* **Full of grace and truth.** "This fullness of grace and truth does not exhaust the meaning of the 'glory.' In the glory of the Incarnate Word there are two elements, as His one Person unites two natures: in part the glory is unique (in kind and not only in degree) belonging to the God-man and not to the perfect Man; in part it is communicable to men, as Jesus Himself says, 'The glory which Thou gavest me I have given them.' " — *William F. Moulton.*

II. THE WITNESS OF JOHN THE BAPTIST TO CHRIST, 1:15–28. It is difficult to assign a definite chronological sequence to the verses that now follow. Probably Andrews and others are right in affirming that verses 15–18 should be assigned to the earliest ministry of John the Baptist, possibly the summer of A.D. 26, and that between this paragraph and all that follows we are to include the Synoptic accounts of the preaching of John the Baptist (Matt. 3:1–12 and parallels), the baptism of Jesus (3:13–17 and parallels) and the temptation of Jesus (4:1–11) all of which occurred in January, A.D. 27, the remainder of the chapter recording events taking place about February of that year.

1. HIS EARLY TESTIMONY TO THE CHRIST SOON TO APPEAR, vs. 15–18. **15. John beareth witness of him, and crieth, saying, This was he of whom I said, He that cometh after me is become before me: for he was before me.** "The loud cry of the faithful witness has come down through all the years; we seem to hear its echoes

16. For of his fulness we all received, and grace for grace.

17. For the law was given through Moses; grace and truth came through Jesus Christ.

18. No man hath seen God at any time; the only begotten Son, who is in the bosom of the Father, he hath declared *him*.

still. The Baptist clearly refers to witness which he had borne after Jesus appeared; hence the words, 'This *was* he,' — It is unusually difficult to find a rendering that will fully convey the meaning of this verse. As the word 'before' occurs in two members of the verse, the English reader inevitably considers the contrast to be between 'is preferred' (or 'is become') and 'he was.' In reality, 'before' here answers to two different words. A literal translation will show at once the meaning and the difficulty of finding an easy expression of the meaning: 'He that cometh behind me has become in front of me, because He was before me.' Jesus came 'after' or 'behind' John, as coming later in His manifestation to the world. The last words of the verse require further notice. They are not fully represented by 'before me,' as if they contained nothing beyond a comparison of Jesus with the Baptist. The former word is absolute, 'He was first'; the other word is added because a comparison is needed, 'first in regard of me.' " — *William Milligan*.

16. For of his fulness we all received, and grace for grace. Lenski begins his comment on this passage by quoting Colossians 1:19, " 'For it pleased the Father that in him should all fulness dwell.' This is the 'riches' of the Lamb, Revelation 5:12; 'the unsearchable riches of Christ,' which Paul was counted worthy to preach to the Gentiles, Ephesians 3:8; 'the riches of his grace,' Ephesians 1:7. Luther pictures the inexhaustible nature of this fulness: 'This spring is inexhaustible, it is full of grace and truth from God, it never loses anything, no matter how much we draw, but remains an infinite fountain of all grace and truth; the more you draw from it, the more abundantly it gives of the water that springs into eternal life. Just as the sun is not darkened by the whole world enjoying its light, and could indeed light up ten worlds; just as 100,000 lights might be lit from one light and not detract from it; just as a learned man is able to make a thousand others learned, and the more he gives, the more he has — so is Christ our Lord, an infinite source of all grace, so that if the whole world would draw enough grace and truth from it to make the world all angels, yet it would not lose a drop; the fountain always runs over, full of grace.' . . . He is the Giver — we are the recipients, and that is all that we are or could be. It was so with John and his fellow witnesses who directly beheld the Saviour, and are the persons embraced in 'we all'; and it is so still with us who now behold the Savior in the inspired testimony of these original witnesses." — *R. C. H. Lenski*. **17. For the law was given through Moses; grace and truth came through Jesus Christ.** "The law is not undervalued. It was divine. It was a gift of God. It was a gift through the great Lawgiver of whom Israel was proud. But it was a fixed unalterable thing, with definite boundaries, not stretching out into the illimitable and eternal. It could not express unbounded grace and truth, unbounded love, because in its very nature law has limits which it cannot pass. Now, however, there has 'come' (a far higher word than 'was given') a fulness of grace and truth, within which we stand, and which we are to appropriate more and more — vast, illimitable, as is that God who is love." — *W. F. Moulton*. **18. No man hath seen God at any time; the only begotten Son, who is in the bosom of the Father, he hath declared** *him*. "The phrase, 'in the bosom' is used of the closest and tenderest of human relationships, of mother and child (Num. 11:12) and of husband and wife (Deut. 13:6) and also of friends reclining side by side at a feast (compare 13:23) and so describes the ultimate fellowship of love. The exact form of the original words is remarkable. The phrase is not strictly 'in the bosom,' but 'into the bosom'. Thus there is the combination of rest and motion, of a continuous relation with a realization of it. The 'bosom of the Father' is a state and not a place. . . . The word here translated *declared* means in the

5

19. And this is the witness of John, when the Jews sent unto him from Jerusalem priests and Levites to ask him, Who art thou?

20. And he confessed, and denied not; and he confessed, I am not the Christ.

21. And they asked him, What then? Art thou Elijah? And he saith, I am not. Art thou the prophet? And he answered, No.

22. They said therefore unto him, Who art thou? that we may give an answer to them that sent us. What sayest thou of thyself?

Greek, *to declare once and forever*, and is a word used in classical writings of the interpretation of divine mysteries. . . . The knowledge of God, which Christ had as God, He set forth to men as man. Compare Matthew 11:27. Men *hear* from Him that which He *saw*." — *B. F. Westcott.* We could tarry with this verse for the remainder of the lesson.

2. HIS OWN RELATIONSHIP TO CHRIST, vs. 19–28. Thus far John the Baptist has been speaking of Christ only in His glory, eternity, deity, creating activity, incarnation and infinite fullness, and, except for one phrase in verse 15, he has omitted any reference to himself. But now, with all Judea and Galilee being moved by his mighty preaching — recorded not by John but by the Synoptics — with thousands of people confessing their sins, many wonder if this is not the Messiah for whom Israel has been looking, and this question John the Baptist must face. **19. And this is the witness of John, when the Jews sent unto him from Jerusalem priests and Levites to ask him, Who art thou? 20. And he confessed, and denied not; and he confessed, I am not the Christ. 21. And they asked him, What then? Art thou Elijah? And he saith, I am not. Art thou the prophet? And he answered, No. 22. They said therefore unto him, Who art thou? that we may give an answer to them that sent us. What sayest thou of thyself?** The comment of Hoskyns is compact, and full of references, but is very important. "The Jewish authorities, with the approval of the populace in Jerusalem, had put Jesus to death; and the Evangelist knows too well that since that time the Jews had consistently and with great bitterness everywhere opposed and persecuted His disciples (Matt. 28:15). Throughout his gospel the Evangelist therefore uses the phrase 'the Jews' to denote the national rejection of the Christ and especially His rejection by the Jewish authorities (2:18; 5:9, 15–18; 7:13, 15; 9:22; 18:12, etc.) by the Pharisees (4:1; 9:13, etc.) and by the chief priests and the Pharisees (7:32, 45; 11:47, 57; 18:3). . . . In the perspective of the gospel, the Jews are therefore merged in the 'world' (15:18), which, though created by the Word of God, does not receive Him when He comes into the world to His own. Indeed, it is in the open opposition of the Jews that the general, though less self-conscious opposition of the world is most clearly seen. The Baptist not only denies that he is the Christ (compare Acts 13:25) but disclaims all personal authority. . . . It is clearly implied in the New Testament that the two prophets, Moses and Elijah, were associated in popular Jewish expectation with the advent of the Messiah (Rev. 11:3, 6; Mark 9:5, and parallels). The expectation was authorized by Deuteronomy 18:15, 18; compare 1 Maccabees 4:46; 14:41; John 6:14; 7:40 and by Malachi 4:5; compare Ecclesiasticus 48:10; Mark 6:15; 8:28; 9:12. In Acts 3:22 and 7:37, Jesus as the Christ is Himself 'the prophet' who had been promised in Deuteronomy 18:15. John's denial that he is Elijah superficially contradicts Mark 9:12, 13; Matt. 11:14; 17:11, where Jesus declares that John is the Elijah who was to come as the forerunner of the Messiah (the sayings are omitted by Luke, but see Luke 1:17). There is, however, no real contradiction, for it is one thing to be named Elijah by the Christ, but quite another for a man, even for a prophet, to assert it of himself; just as it was one thing for Simon to be named by Jesus Peter, where it would have been quite another had he said of himself 'I am the Rock.' It is therefore too subtle a refinement of exegesis to suppose

23. He said, I am the voice of one crying in the wilderness, Make straight the way of the Lord, as said Isaiah the prophet.

29. On the morrow he seeth Jesus coming unto him, and saith, Behold, the Lamb of God, that taketh away the sin of the world!

that the Evangelist here rejects the identification of John with the Elijah of the Malachi passage, the prophet of the End, in order to assert that he more properly fulfils Isaiah 40:3. There is a similar superficial though unreal contradiction between verse 21b and Matthew 11:9; Luke 7:26." — *E. C. Hoskyns.* 23. **He said, I am the voice of one crying in the wilderness, Make straight the way of the Lord, as said Isaiah the prophet.** John is here quoting Isaiah 40:3. "While he denies emphatically that he is the Christ, he on the other hand acknowledges that he is the one of whom Isaiah spoke as the forerunner of the Messiah. Matthew 3:3; Mark 1:3; Luke 3:4 all interpret Isaiah's word as actually fulfilled in the Baptist and his work. Even without this decisive evidence, no other conclusion can be drawn from the Baptist's answer to the committee of the Sanhedrin. He furnishes this committee with more than they had asked, when they requested: 'What dost thou say concerning thyself?' He supplies them with a divinely inspired statement from the greatest of their own prophets concerning his person and work. Isaiah's words do not merely happen to fit the Baptist's thought, these words constitute the authority for his work." — *R. C. H. Lenski.* Having denied that he is the Christ, though acknowledging that he is the forerunner of the Messiah, John is pressed with another question, Why was he baptizing? John, like Jesus, seems to have an answer upon his lips given by God Himself. "The reply is in two parts, and suggestive rather than explicit. 'I baptize because the form of this baptism shows that, however striking outwardly, it does not belong to the work of the Christ; and still it is designed to prepare for the recognition of the Christ actually present in the midst of you. My work is the work of a servant, and the work of a herald. There is nothing to condemn in my conduct if you consider what my baptism is, and what the Christ's baptism is, and know that He is among you, so that the preparatory rite has a just place.' The Pharisees hear words which might well move them to deeper questionings; but for this they had no heart. It is enough to have discharged their specific duty." — *B. F. Westcott.* We must not forget that it is these very people now receiving specific answers to all their questions who will in less than four years demand that the One of whom John is here speaking be put to death as a blasphemer. The clear testimony of John the Baptist to the Messiahship of Jesus will come up for debate in the last week of Christ's incarnate life, long after John has been put to death, when Jesus faces them with the question, "The baptism of John, whence was it? from heaven or from men?" and they refused to answer (Matt. 21:23–27 and parallels).

3. HIS IDENTIFICATION OF CHRIST NOW IN THEIR MIDST, vs. 29–34.

Up to this point our Lord himself has not appeared in any specific event, though no doubt all of Judea and Galilee were already aware that Jesus was a prophet come from God, and soon they would know Him as the very Son of God. 29. **On the morrow he seeth Jesus coming unto him, and saith, Behold, the Lamb of God, that taketh away the sin of the world!** On this great utterance, repeated again in verse 36, let us first have before us the technical statement of Hoskyns on Christ as the Lamb of God, and then a glorious passage from Alexander Whyte. "No new title or description is here introduced (Acts 8:32; 1 Pet. 1:19; Rev. 5:6, 8, 12; 6:16, 7:9 sqq., 12:11 etc.). The faith of the apostles is authorized by the original and primary witness of John, who declares Jesus to be the property of God, by whose complete obedience the normal sacrifices in the Temple — a lamb without blemish was offered daily both morning and evening (Ex. 29:38–46) and even during the siege of Jerusalem these sacrifices were maintained in spite of very great difficulties — were fulfilled and superseded (2:18–22). The regal authority of Jesus is contrasted with the destructive tyranny of the enemies of God (Rev. 17:14).

30. This is he of whom I said, After me cometh a man who is become before me: for he was before me.

31. And I knew him not; but that he should be made manifest to Israel, for this cause came I baptizing in water.

32. And John bare witness, saying, I have beheld the Spirit descending as a dove out of heaven; and it abode upon him.

33. And I knew him not: but he that sent me to baptize in water, he said unto me, Upon whomsoever thou shalt see the Spirit descending, and abiding upon him, the same is he that baptizeth in the Holy Spirit.

34. And I have seen, and have borne witness that this is the Son of God.

In the development of his narrative the Evangelist shows that the witness of John is applicable to the fulfilment both of the Passover (2:13; 19:35 ff.; Exod. 12:7 ff.; Heb. 11:28) and of the prophecy in Isaiah 53:1 ff. (12:38, compare Luke 22:37; Acts 8:32; Rom. 10:16; 1 Pet. 2:22–25). The verb translated *taketh away* is used frequently by the Evangelist, meaning to take up and remove out of the way (2:16; 11:39; 19:38; 20:2, 13, 15) and so to destroy (10:18; 11:48; 15:2; 19:15, 31). Its use with *sins* as its object is Scriptural (LXX 1 Sam. 15:25; 25:28; Exod. 28:38; 34:7; Lev. 10:17; Mic. 7:18, but not in Isa. 53:4 ff.). Jesus bears the consequence of human sin in order that its guilt may be removed." — *Alexander Whyte*. In his great sermon on this text, Alexander Whyte quotes the famous hymn, "Just as I am without one plea, but that Thy blood was shed for me, and that Thou bidd'st me come to Thee," and adds the following moving paragraph: "Thy *blood*, O Lamb of God, and Thy *bidding*. These are now my two all-prevailing pleas. With these two pleas I shall always come with boldness to the throne of grace. And I am sure that as often as I plead those two pleas I shall never be put to shame. Let us come then. Let us come and let us learn better and better in what way to come. In what way and with what manner of motion. We come, but not by locomotion as in all other cases of coming. We come, but not by removing ourselves out of one place and removing ourselves to another place. We come by a real locomotion, indeed; but it is by the locomotion of the mind and the heart. . . . Look, then, till your heart is affected, and till with your whole heart you come to Him. And come at all times, and come in every way. Come from all your former ignorance and indifference, and come to the intensest interest and anxiety. Come from never thinking a thought about the Lamb of God to thinking about nothing and about no one half so much. Come from seeking your own pleasure in everything to asking what will please Him. Come from taking your own way in everything to taking His way in everything, and your neighbor's way as often and as far as it is His way. Come from a hardness of heart like the nether millstone, to an utter brokenness of heart, and till your head is waters. Come from never taking time to pray in secret, to praying in secret in all places, and at all times. Come like old Bishop Andrews. Come every fourth day of the week from pride to humility, and from envy to pitifulness, and from wrath to patience, and from gluttony to sobriety, and from lasciviousness to purity, and from covetousness to contentment, and from sloth to ready zeal. And in all that, and at the heart of all that, and as the true end of all that, say continually, O Lamb of God, I come." — *Alexander Whyte*. 30. This is he of whom I said, After me cometh a man who is become before me: for he was before me. 31. And I knew him not; but that he should be made manifest to Israel, for this cause came I baptizing in water. 32. And John bare witness, saying, I have beheld the Spirit descending as a dove out of heaven; and it abode upon him. 33. And I knew him not: but he that sent me to baptize in water, he said unto me, Upon whomsoever thou shalt see the Spirit descending, and abiding upon him, the same is he that baptizeth in the Holy Spirit. 34. And

35. Again on the morrow John was standing, and two of his disciples; 36. and he looked upon Jesus as he walked, and saith, Behold, the Lamb of God! 37. And the two disciples heard him speak, and they followed Jesus. 38. And Jesus turned, and beheld them following, and saith unto them, What seek ye? And they said unto him, Rabbi (which is to say, being interpreted, Teacher), where abidest thou? 39. He saith unto them, Come and ye shall see. They came therefore and saw where he abode; and they abode with him that day: it was about the tenth hour. 40. One of the two that heard John *speak*, and followed him, was Andrew, Simon Peter's brother.

I have seen, and have borne witness that this is the Son of God. It is simply impossible in this one lesson to give any detailed exposition of all these verses — and here I must be exceedingly brief. In an older work on John the Baptist, by Feather, is the finest statement I have seen on the concluding verse of this portion of our study. "By the time of John and Jesus, this phrase, Son of God, had come to designate Him who stood out in Jewish thought and hope above the race, and who held such a special relation to Jehovah as the earthly Head of His people, as to justify its limitation to Him. In other words, it was one of the titles of the Messiah. He was especially worthy of that designation who should restore the kingdom to Israel, make the theocracy once more a living fact, and rule in Jerusalem righteously, while all the kingdoms of the earth should be subject to His sway and bring their riches to His feet. King of the Jews, Messiah, and Son of God appear to be synonymous and interchangeable terms." — *J. Feather.* Many will ask what John may have meant by the phrase, "and I knew him not," in verse 33, for it is a difficult passage. Jesus and John were related by family. Milligan says, "The solution of the difficulty is to be found in keeping distinctly before us the official and not personal light in which both Jesus and the Baptist are presented to us here. John does not deny personal knowledge of Jesus, but he does say that up to this time he had not known Him in His messianic character."

III. **CHRIST WINS HIS FIRST DISCIPLES,** 1:35-51. The late Dr. L. R. Scarborough, for many years President and Professor of Evangelism in the Southwestern Baptist Theological Seminary entitles the chapter in which he discusses this portion of the first chapter of John, "Jesus Starts a School of Evangelism." Here was had for the first time, chronologically speaking, the word *disciple*, meaning *a learner*, and then, *a follower*. The first two disciples were, before they ever saw Christ, disciples of John the Baptist. One of these was Andrew, the brother of Simon Peter; and the one not named we may well believe was John, who was to become the Apostle.

1. ANDREW AND JOHN FOLLOW CHRIST, vs. 35-40. **35. Again on the morrow John was standing, and two of his disciples; 36. and he looked upon Jesus as he walked, and saith, Behold, the Lamb of God! 37. And the two disciples heard him speak, and they followed Jesus. 38. And Jesus turned, and beheld them following, and saith unto them, What seek ye? And they said unto him, Rabbi (which is to say, being interpreted, Teacher), where abidest thou? 39. He saith unto them, Come and ye shall see. They came therefore and saw where he abode; and they abode with him that day: it was about the tenth hour. 40. One of the two that heard John *speak*, and followed him, was Andrew, Simon Peter's brother.** We rarely ever discuss Andrew, though often John the Apostle and Simon Peter; so here let us confine ourselves to a study of Andrew. "Andrew was attracted to Bethany beyond Jordan by the preaching of John the Baptist as so many others had been. It is even possible that Andrew and Simon came with the

41. He findeth first his own brother Simon, and saith unto him, We have found the Messiah (which is, being interpreted, Christ).

42. He brought him unto Jesus. Jesus looked upon him, and said, Thou art Simon the son of John: thou shalt be called Cephas (which is by interpretation, Peter).

43. On the morrow he was minded to go forth into Galilee, and he findeth Philip: and Jesus saith unto him, Follow me.

44. Now Philip was from Bethsaida, of the city of Andrew and Peter.

---

crowd that included Philip of Bethsaida and Nathanael of Cana. . . . They are all at Bethany beyond Jordan at the same time when John the Baptist bears his remarkable and stirring witness to the Messiahship of Jesus on two successive days as the Lamb of God that takes away the sin of the world, and as the Son of God (John 1:29–51). Andrew along with the rest felt the pull of John's mission and message. He had come close to the Baptist on one of the days at Bethany, so close that he could hear distinctly the Baptist's striking testimony to Jesus as the Messiah. Andrew has the further distinction of being the first one who followed Jesus as Messiah. That is honor enough for any man." — *A. T. Robertson.* "Our Lord's dealing with him began with His question, 'What seek ye?' We pause to remind ourselves that that is the supreme question in any and every human life. Our Lord did not ask Andrew who he was looking for. There was no need to do that. It was quite evident that he was seeking Jesus. What He did ask him was, why he was doing that very thing. Why are you coming after Me? What is it that you really want? This question to Andrew becomes the more arresting when we remember that the words are the first recorded words of Jesus as He commenced His public ministry. The question was one that plumbed the very deeps of personality. Jesus was drawing him out by driving him in." — *G. Campbell Morgan.*

2. Andrew Brings His Brother Peter to Christ, vs. 41, 42. The very hour that Andrew became convinced that Christ was the Messiah of whom all the prophets did speak, he sought out his brother Peter, who was to become the first of the apostolic group. **41. He findeth first his own brother Simon, and saith unto him, We have found the Messiah (which is, being interpreted, Christ). 42. He brought him unto Jesus. Jesus looked upon him, and said, Thou art Simon the son of John: thou shalt be called Cephas (which is by interpretation, Peter).** "Christ first said to Peter a thing which I am inclined to believe no one understood at the moment except Simon. Notice that Simon did not answer. There is never a word recorded that he said. Do you not see that the very silence of the man is evidence of the fact that he had heard something that astonished him. You may charge me with imagination, but I think I know Simon well, having affinity with him. I know exactly what he had felt before he met Christ. Oh, if I could but gather myself together. Oh, these questionings, these impulses, these volitions that strive and struggle and fail. Oh, if I could be what I would be. If I could be a really strong man. Brought by his brother to the Stranger, Jesus looked into his eyes, looked intently at him so that Peter knew he was seen through and through, and He said, 'Thou art Simon the son of John: thou shalt be called rock.' I think from that moment hope sprang up in his heart. I think it was that word which won Simon. Not merely that he was convinced of the Messiahship of Jesus (I am not sure that he ever was until Caesarea Philippi was reached) but here was Someone who believed in the possibility of realizing him, and Who promised that he should be rock." — *G. Campbell Morgan.*

3. Jesus Finds Philip, vs. 43, 44. **43. On the morrow he was minded to go forth into Galilee, and he findeth Philip: and Jesus saith unto him, Follow me. 44. Now Philip was from Bethsaida, of the city of Andrew and Peter.** "He was the first disciple of whom we are told in the gospel record that Jesus deliberately set about finding him. The story does not suggest an incidental haphazard meeting with a

45. Philip findeth Nathanael, and saith unto him, We have found him, of whom Moses in the law, and the prophets, wrote, Jesus of Nazareth, the son of Joseph.

---

man. He knew him. To Nathanael Jesus said, 'When thou wast under the fig tree, I saw thee.' That was true also of Philip. Christ knew him, knew where he was, knew that he was too slow a man to be in that inner circle of John's disciples. He went after him. 'He findeth Philip' of set purpose, of intimate knowledge, and of definite intention. Notice the next step. He called him. This is the first occasion on which Christ used, so far as the records reveal, that all-inclusive formula which was so often afterwards upon His lips, 'Follow Me.' It was a call to surrender, and a call to obedience. He found this slow man, and He laid upon him the word that indicated the necessity for his surrender and the necessity for his obedience. What is the next thing in order? Jesus sent him out as an apostle, this slow man! On what errand? To represent Him, to carry His message to his own people. When the twelve were first sent out they were forbidden to go to Samaria, or outside the borders of their own national life. Philip was one of those sent out under that first commission. He was sent again under the great commission which overstepped the boundaries of Israel's national life and included Samaria and the uttermost part of the earth." — *G. Campbell Morgan.*

4. PHILIP FINDS NATHANAEL, vs. 45–51. What a wonderful series of lessons in personal work do we have in these verses. This scene in the life of Nathanael is one of the gems in the New Testament, but we cannot tarry with it today. **45. Philip findeth Nathanael, and saith unto him, We have found him, of whom Moses in the law, and the prophets, wrote, Jesus of Nazareth, the son of Joseph.** "Nathanael had expressed his faith as the result of his first contact with Christ. Now the Lord lit the lamp of hope for him as He told him that there were greater experiences yet in store. The vision which had come to Jacob was confirmed to Nathanael in Christ. He, the Son of man, would be the Channel of prayer as typified in the ascending angels, and the Channel of answers as suggested by the descending angels. After the dream, when Jacob awoke, he had said: 'Lo, God is in the place, and I knew it not.' This was to be ratified in the experience of Nathanael through his Lord. In Him he should discover the nearness of God, even though he had been ignorant of it." — *G. Campbell Morgan.*

THE LESSON IN LIFE, LITERATURE, AND ARCHAEOLOGY.

Miss Clara Schlegel, for many years secretary to Dr. James M. Gray while he was President of the Moody Bible Institute, in an article of reminiscence, writes as follows: "On one occasion, when reading a letter from a former student in China received shortly after the martyrdom of John and Betty Stam, Dr. Gray was greatly moved. Bowing his head and covering his face with his hands, he said: 'I do not feel worthy to unloose the shoes of these missionaries. They have given up so much to serve God that I am almost ashamed to read their letters.' The humility and sincerity of his inner life was thus frequently revealed."

A TRUTH FOR THE CLASS TO CARRY AWAY.

The uniqueness of the person and work of Jesus, the Son of God, impels all who are His to make Him known everywhere.

Did the disciples of John the Baptist preach about John the Baptist? What characteristics distinguished each of these first disciples of Jesus? In how many ways in this passage is Christ not only central but different from other men, even the most godly men? How is the first chapter of John's Gospel definitely linked with the final commission of Christ appearing at the conclusion of the Gospel of Matthew? In what ways do these very earliest disciples of Jesus remind us of the Apostle Paul?

11

LESSON II. — January 10.

JESUS USES HIS AUTHORITY. — John 2.

PRINTED TEXT, John 2:1-11, 13-25.

Devotional Reading: Ephesians 1:15–23.
Beginner Topic: BIG BOY JESUS.
   Lesson Material: Luke 2:39–52.
   Memory Verse: I was glad when they said unto me, let us go unto the House of Jehovah. Psalm 122:1.
Primary Topic: JESUS AT A WEDDING.
   Lesson Material: John 2:1–10.
   Memory Verse: Whatsoever he saith unto you, do it. John 2:5.
Junior Topic: JESUS AT A WEDDING.
   Lesson Material: John 2:1–10.
   Memory Verse: Whatsoever he saith unto you, do it. John 2:5.
Intermediate-Senior Topic: FEARLESS FOR GOD.
   Lesson Material: John 2.
   Memory Verse: God is a Spirit: and they that worship him must worship in spirit and truth. John 4:24.
Topic for Young People and Adults: JESUS USES HIS AUTHORITY.
   Lesson Material: John 2.
   Memory Verse: God is a Spirit; and they that worship him must worship in spirit and truth. John 4:24.

THE TEACHER AND HIS CLASS.

The Younger Classes may be introduced to this lesson concerning a miracle of Christ by an illustration from an experience of the editor. Some years ago, during the second World War, I was being entertained at the home of a physician friend, along with a number of other guests, one of whom was an internationally famous chemist from Switzerland, then working for the United States government. During the evening this man showed us some newspaper articles concerning his discoveries in chemistry during the preceding years, and astonishing discoveries they were. As he unfolded some of these fascinating subjects, in a moment of carelessness I exclaimed, "Miracles!" At once he replied, "No, not miracles, just science." He was right, for *no* scientist is performing *miracles*. Science is doing wonderful things, we must acknowledge, but everything done in that field is due to the discovery of certain laws and properties. Jesus performed miracles; that is, He possessed power by which He could bring to bear upon an object influences which man in himself does not possess, that could overcome all laws of nature, that man himself cannot duplicate today. These miracles pointed to his uniqueness, and ultimately to His deity.

The Older Classes, in beginning this lesson, should be directed to the account of the birth of the Christian Church in the second chapter of Acts, and especially to Peter's great sermon in which, setting forth the person, work, death, and resurrection of Christ he uses the phrase (v. 22) "a man approved of God among you by miracles and wonders, and signs which God did by Him in the midst of you, as ye yourselves also know." We are now beginning a study of these miracles which, as signs of Christ's deity, were used in the early church as indisputable testimony to the divine mission and personality of Jesus of Nazareth.

THE LESSON IN ITS SETTING.

Time. — All the events of our lesson took place between February and April A.D. 27.

Place. — The miracle of the changing of water into wine occurred in a lovely village not far from Nazareth, Cana of Galilee. The cleansing of the Temple and the teaching that followed took place in Jerusalem.

———

THE PLAN OF THE LESSON.

SUBJECT: Three Different Responses to the Performing of Miracles By Jesus.

I. The First Miracle of Jesus' Public Ministry, John 2:1–12.

II. Jesus' First Cleansing of the Temple in Jerusalem, 2:13–17.

III. Jesus' First Announcement of His Death and Resurrection, 2:18–22.

IV. Christ's Deep Insight into the Hearts of His Hearers and of All Men, 2:23–25.

———

THE TEACHER'S LIBRARY.

There is a vast amount of material on this lesson, including, first of all, the major lives of Christ, and a magnificent chapter in A. B. Bruce: *The Training of the Twelve;* the principal commentaries on John's Gospel (among which Lenski is here superior to them all), a list of which will be found in the Introduction to this volume. All works on the miracles of Christ

will have helpful chapters, e.g., the volumes by John Laidlaw, R. C. Trench, William M. Taylor, etc., and five great sermons in the first volume of Charles H. Spurgeon: Sermons on Our Lord's Miracles, Nos. 9–13. Above all, there is one volume of exquisite beauty devoted entirely to this subject — Hugh Macmillan: *The Marriage in Cana of Galilee* (London, 1882). See also a good chapter in T. V. Tymms: *The Private Relationships of Christ,* 89 ff.

For sermonic material, on 2:1–5, see G. Campbell Morgan: *The Westminster Pulpit,* Vol. 3, 1–8; on 2:17, the same, Vol. 5, 190–192; on 2:23–25, the same, Vol. 2, 329–336; also, on 2:10, Simcox: *The Cessation of Prophecy,* 98 ff.; on 2:21, Hugh Macmillan: *The Sabbath of the Fields,* 165–189; and on 2:25, J. D. Jones: *Watching the Cross,* 93 ff.

———

AUDIO-VISUAL AIDS.

FILMSTRIP: "The Wedding at Cana," Concordia #C–26, 20 fr., col. Jesus at the wedding at Cana; His conversation with Mary; the changing of water into wine; the faith of the disciples.

SLIDE SET: "The Wedding in Cana," Church-Craft #15, 7 sl., col.

SLIDE SET: "The Life of Christ Visualized," Move 7 & 8 (The Bible in Pictures), Visserslides #74–80, 6 sl., col. Show a guide chart of the route to Cana, the wedding, the wine exhausted and the filling and serving of the wine.

———

John 2:1. And the third day there was a marriage in Cana of Galilee.

I. THE FIRST MIRACLE OF JESUS' PUBLIC MINISTRY, John 2:1–12.
There are approximately thirty-seven specific miracles in our Lord's life, recorded in the four Gospels, in addition to a great many not specifically referred to, indicated by such a phrase as, "He healed many of divers diseases," etc. Only one miracle is recorded in all four Gospels — the feeding of the five thousand. Six miracles are recorded exclusively in John's Gospel. The event we are about to consider is the first miracle recorded in the fourth Gospel, but it is actually the thirteenth in chronological order, preceded by three in Matthew, two in Mark, and seven in Luke, including the healing of the woman with the issue of blood (13:11), a man with dropsy (14:2), the ten lepers (17:11), etc. This took place in a little village of Cana, probably to be identified with the modern city of Khirbet Kana, seven and one-half miles north of Nazareth, and fifteen miles west of Capernaum, where Josephus himself, the Jewish historian, resided for some time. There is no symbolical meaning to the name *Cana.* In the New Testament it is never referred to outside of John's Gospel (see 4:46 and 21:2). I remember, when last in Palestine, being much impressed myself with the simplicity and "openness" of this town, and with the beauty of the church which is supposed to have been built over the site of this miracle, though of course the tradition is of no great value. **1. And the third day there was a marriage in Cana of Galilee.** John is here counting the days from 1:43, when Philip and Nathanael began to follow Jesus. The "third day" after implies the intervening of two nights. The passage which begins at the end of chapter 1 and extends through this miracle is, I believe, the only place in the four Gospels where we have the time of events designated as following one another in *three successive days.* "This wedding must be conceived in the Jewish fashion. In the betrothal bride and groom were pledged to each other in a way

13

2. And Jesus also was bidden, and his disciples, to the marriage.

3. And when the wine failed, the mother of Jesus saith unto him, They have no wine.

4. And Jesus saith unto her, Woman what have I to do with thee? mine hour is not yet come.

5. His mother saith unto the servants, Whatsoever he saith unto you, do it.

that truly made them man and wife, although following this ceremony the two did not at once live together. An interval, longer or shorter, followed, and then the wedding took place. The groom, with his companions, brought the bride, with her companions to the groom's home, and there, without any further pledge, the celebration began, starting toward evening with a feast as grand as possible, and continuing for a week, the couple now living together." — *R. C. H. Lenski.* **And the mother of Jesus was there.** In his Gospel, John never refers to himself, nor to any of his relatives, by name, not even to Mary, who appears here at the beginning as "the mother of Jesus," and again in 19:25. "Mary was not present, like her son, as an invited guest, but as a friend of the groom, or of the bride, or of both, to aid in the feast. Perhaps she was related to one of the couple. This would explain how she knew about the lack of wine, and how she took steps in the matter." — *R. C. H. Lenski.* **2. And Jesus also was bidden, and his disciples, to the marriage.** "The connective adds this statement to the one on Mary, and at the same time indicates that this is a little different. We have no connective with this delicate force in English. The point of difference lies in the verbs: Mary just 'was' there as a matter of course; Jesus 'was invited' in a formal way. The aorist also indicates that the invitation was effective — Jesus accepted. The verb is singular, and thus lifts Jesus into prominence over his disciples: *he* was invited and they too, but not on an equality — they only on account of Jesus." — *R. C. H. Lenski.* These disciples probably included those who were later to be called as apostles. It would seem that already throughout Galilee a number of men were known as the intimate friends of the Master. **3. And when the wine failed, the mother of Jesus saith unto him, They have no wine.** "The Greek words so rendered mean literally, 'Wine having failed.' This circumstance probably shows the poor and humble condition of those to whose marriage Jesus was invited. His acquaintances and those of His mother were not wealthy persons. It throws light on this expression, and indeed on the whole story, to remember that a marriage feast among the Jews was often an affair of several days' duration, and an occasion when many were invited. Consequently it entailed not only much expense, but a considerable consumption of food and wine. **4. And Jesus saith unto her, Woman what have I to do with thee? mine hour is not yet come.** Many reading our Lord's words here will think that Christ was rude in so speaking to his mother, but the great New Testament Greek scholar Westcott well reminds us that "in the original there is not the least danger of reproof or severity in the term. The address is that of courteous respect, even of tenderness; see 19:26, and compare 4:21 and 20:13, 15. At the same time it emphasizes the special relation which it expresses; as here, the contrast between the Divine son and the human mother. The phrase serves to show that the actions of the Son of God, now that He has entered on His divine work, are no longer dependent in any way on the suggestion of a woman, even though that woman be His mother." — *B. F. Westcott.* Concerning His "hour," a phrase frequently found in John's Gospel, see Luke 22:53 and John 7:8. **5. His mother saith unto the servants, Whatsoever he saith unto you, do it.** Mary's word to the servants "means that she is wholly satisfied with her Son's reply. The word here translated *servant* is not the New Testament word generally translated such, meaning *slave*, but *diakonoi*, from which comes our word *deacon*, meaning, *to minister*. These are voluntary assistants come in to help in a friendly way with the work at the wedding feast. They lay hand to what is needed of their own

14

6. Now there were six waterpots of stone set there after the Jews' manner of purifying, containing two or three firkins apiece.

7. Jesus saith unto them, Fill the waterpots with water. And they filled them up to the brim.

8. And he saith unto them, Draw out now, and bear unto the ruler of the feast. And they bare it.

9. And when the ruler of the feast tasted the water now become wine, and knew not whence it was (but the servants that had drawn the water knew), the ruler of the feast calleth the bridegroom,

---

accord, or at the request of those who manage affairs. Jesus was a guest and had no hand in managing affairs." — *R. C. H. Lenski.* **6. Now there were six waterpots of stone set there after the Jews' manner of purifying, containing two or three firkins apiece.** "The water was used for the washing of hands and vessels, as mentioned in Matthew 15:2; Mark 7:3; one of the traditions of the elders, probably resting on the ritual connected with the laver in the Temple Court, and on promises such as Ezekiel 36:5. The word 'purifying' is the same as in 3:25, where it is used in connection with John's baptism; also in Hebrews 1:3, 'purged our sins.' *Firkin (Vierkin* — ¼ of a barrel — 7½ gals.), Greek, *metretes,* holding 8⅞ gals.), rather more than the Jewish measure a Bath. Each would contain, therefore, about 20 gallons less or more." — *George Reith.* **7. Jesus saith unto them, Fill the waterpots with water. And they filled them up to the brim.** "One wonders what the helpers thought while they were filling up those jars. John adds only the little touch, 'to the brim.' Did managing Mary insist on their obeying orders promptly and strictly? Well, they would! Did the helpers smile at each other when they carried all that water to the pots, and crack jokes with each other about this Rabbi who would give the guests this precious water as a new kind of wine?" — *R. C. H. Lenski.* **8. And he saith unto them, Draw out now, and bear unto the ruler of the feast. And they bare it.** "The original word is applied most naturally to drawing water from the well (4:7, 15), and not from a vessel like the waterpot. Moreover the emphatic addition of *now* seems to mark the continuance of the same action of drawing as before, but with a different end. Hitherto they had drawn to fill the vessels of purification: they were charged *now* to 'draw and bear to the governor of the feast.' . . . That which remained water when kept for a ceremonial use became wine when borne in faith to minister to the needs, even to the superfluous requirements, of life." — *B. F. Westcott.* "The steward was the manager of the feast, whether himself one of the guests selected for the office by the groom, or one who did not dine with the rest as a guest, is hard to say. One of his functions is incidentally mentioned, namely that of tasting food and drink before these were offered to the guests. He is named from the *triclina,* couches for three persons each, three of them placed usually on three sides of a low table, for the guests to recline on while dining." — *R. C. H. Lenski.* Out of this text, Spurgeon draws the following principles: "(1) When Christ is about to bestow a blessing He gives a command. (2) Christ's commands are not to be questioned, but to be obeyed, even when they seem trivial to us. (3) Whenever we get a command from Christ, it is always wisdom to carry it out zealously. (4) Our earnest action in obedience to Christ is not contrary to our dependence upon Him, but it is necessary to our dependence upon Him. By our earnest action we are not interfering with Christ but proving our faith in Him, if we work for Him as He bids us work. (5) Our action alone is not successful. If we fill the waterpots with water, He alone can turn it into wine. (6) Although human action in itself falls short of the desired end, yet it has its place and God made it necessary by His appointment. Do the ordinary duties of Christian men and women — things in which there is no power of themselves, but which Jesus Christ makes to be connected with his divine working, and it shall be for your instruction, and your comfort, that you had such work to do." — *Charles H. Spurgeon.* **9. And when.**

15

10. and saith unto him, Every man setteth on first the good wine; and when *men* have drunk freely, *then* that which is worse: thou hast kept the good wine until now.

11. This beginning of his signs did Jesus in Cana of Galilee, and manifested his glory; and his disciples believed on him.

13. And the passover of the Jews was at hand, and Jesus went up to Jerusalem.

---

the ruler of the feast tasted the water now become wine, and knew not whence it was (but the servants that had drawn the water knew), the ruler of the feast calleth the bridegroom, 10. and saith unto him, Every man setteth on first the good wine; and when *men* have drunk freely, *then* that which is worse: thou hast kept the good wine until now. "The moment the triclinarch tasted the wine it flashed into his mind that someone had made a grand mistake in regard to the wine. He hastens to call the bridegroom, and John reports this detail first in order to indicate the actuality of the miracle: water turned into wine; and secondly to indicate the quality of this wine. . . . The triclinarch points out that the bridegroom has made a serious mistake. He has allowed the poor wine to be served first, and kept this excellent wine till the last; whereas everybody, when compelled to use two such qualities of wine, does the reverse. The groom, of course, is even more astonished than his steward, for he knew of no such good wine. . . . The steward cannot mean that the guests are drunk, and therefore this excellent wine will be lost upon them. It is utterly impossible for us to image Jesus present in a tipsy crowd, to say nothing of aiding such carousing by his first miracle." — *R. C. H. Lenski.* 11. **This beginning of his signs did Jesus in Cana of Galilee, and manifested his glory; and his disciples believed on him.** Dr. F. B. Meyer in his beautiful devotional commentary on John's Gospel says that Christ showed forth His glory in the following ways: (1) He demonstrated that true religion is consistent with ordinary life. (2) He taught the beauty of waiting meekly for God. (3) It was His glory to awaken us to see the divine power in the ordinary processes of nature. (4) We see compressed into a single flash the same power that works throughout the wine-lands every summer, transforming the dew and rain into the juices that redden the drooping clusters of the vines. The power needed to raise the dead shows how much is constantly demanded to keep us living. In Him all things consist. (5) It was His glory to show the ascending scale of God's gifts. The devil ever gives his best first, and when the appetite is somewhat palled, he puts on his worse, even to the worst. Gold at the crown, clay at the foot. The Lord Jesus, on the other hand, is always giving something better. That which you know of Him today is certainly better than that you tasted when first you sat down at His board. What will it be to sit at the marriage supper of the Lamb, not as guests, but as the Bride!" — *F. B. Meyer.*

II. **JESUS' FIRST CLEANSING OF THE TEMPLE IN JERUSALEM,** John 2:13–17. Most of Jesus' time was spent in Galilee, but the days in the capital, where the Temple was located, are always marked with episodes of unusual importance. The first time Jesus was in Jerusalem was, of course, when He was presented in the Temple, February, 4 B.C. (Luke 2:22–38); He was again brought to Jerusalem when twelve years of age (Luke 2:45–52). This is the first visit of Jesus to the holy city since He had arrived at manhood. 13. **And the passover of the Jews was at hand, and Jesus went up to Jerusalem.** This is the first time in my editing of Peloubet's Notes that I have used the great work on the Fourth Gospel by the late Edwyn Clement Hoskyns, a volume especially rich in places like this. "Jerusalem at the time of the passover was the appropriate place and occasion for Jesus to inaugurate His mission and explain its significance (compare 5:1; 6:4; 11:55; 18:38, 39; 19:14). In Jerusalem stood the temple of God; and the temple consecrated the city. . . . Here the priesthood and people are tested whether

14. And he found in the temple those that sold oxen and sheep and doves, and the changers of money sitting:

15. and he made a scourge of cords, and cast all out of the temple, both the sheep and the oxen; and he poured out the changers' money, and overthrew their tables;

16. and to them that sold the doves he said, Take these things hence; make not my Father's house a house of merchandise.

17. His disciples remember that it was written, Zeal for thy house shall eat me up.

they seek the things of men, their own things, or the things of God. The Evangelist states that the passover was *of the Jews*, less in order to inform his gentile readers than to contrast Jewish sacrifice with that by which it is fulfilled (1:29, 36; compare 1 Cor. 5:7). Origen comments: 'The passover of the Jews consists of a sheep which is sacrificed, each man taking a sheep according to his father's house; and the passover is accompanied by the slaughter of thousands of rams and goats, in proportion to the number of houses of the people. But our Passover is sacrificed for us, namely, Christ. The contrast between the temple and that which is greater than the temple belongs also to the synoptic tradition (Matt. 12:6–8)." — *E. C. Hoskyns.* **14. And he found in the temple those that sold oxen and sheep and doves, and the changers of money sitting: 15. and he made a scourge of cords, and cast all out of the temple, both the sheep and the oxen; and he poured out the changers' money, and overthrew their tables; 16. and to them that sold the doves he said, Take these things hence; make not my Father's house a house of merchandise. 17. His disciples remember that it was written, Zeal for thy house shall eat me up.** "The word translated *temple* in vs. 14, 15 denotes the whole compass of the sacred enclosure, including the entire aggregate of sacred buildings and courts. Another word, also translated *temple* is used in vs. 19–21 to designate the *sanctuary* (R.V. mg.) which consisted of the Holy Place and the Holy of Holies. Oxen, sheep, and doves were necessary for the prescribed purification before the celebration of the passover ritual (11:55; 2 Chron. 30:18); the presence of money-changers was equally necessary if pilgrims were to be given an opportunity to receive the temple shekels and half-shekels in exchange for foreign currency which, though in ordinary use in the country, was forbidden in the temple. Two different words are used for 'changers of money.' The one (v. 14) is found only in this passage and in literature dependent upon it. The other (v. 15, Mark 11:15; Matt. 21:12) is found in the papyri, and must have been in fairly common use, since the Atticists condemned it as a vulgarism; the word — from which the Greeks got their Kollybos and Cicero his Collybus the money-lender — is of Semitic origin, formed from the same root as Caliph (deputy successor) and means properly one who changes coin of one country for that of another. The scourge (compare Mark 15:15; Matt. 27:26) was made of twisted rushes (*cords*, compare Acts 27:32). Neither the meaning of the words nor the general sense of the passage supports Westcott's judgment that the scourge was used as 'a symbol of authority and not as a weapon of offence.' " — *E. C. Hoskyns.* The action of our Lord in the Temple at this time is an echo of Malachi 3:1–3, but His words are made up of quotations from Isaiah 56:1 and Jeremiah 7:11. "The perception of the disciples at the time — they see no more than that a consuming zeal for the purity of the temple has prophetic sanction (Ps. 69:9) — is contrasted with their later insight (v. 22) and with the irritated questioning of the Jews (v. 18). The word translated *eat up*, in addition to meaning that the mind is strongly moved, suggests also destruction (Rev. 11:5; 20:9). The disciples do not yet understand that the zeal of Jesus must be consummated in His own death or that the purification of which His action is a sign depends upon the sacrifice of His body (19:30; compare 13:4–11; 17:19)." — *E. C. Hoskyns.* John is the only one who records

17

18. The Jews therefore answered and said unto him, What sign showest thou unto us, seeing that thou doest these things?

19. Jesus answered and said unto them, Destroy this temple, and in three days I will raise it up.

20. The Jews therefore said, Forty and six years was this temple in building, and wilt thou raise it up in three days?

21. But he spake of the temple of his body.

---

this cleansing of the Temple; the Synoptics, and not John, narrate for us a cleansing of the Temple during Passion Week (Matt. 21:12–17; Mark 11:17, etc.).

III. JESUS' FIRST ANNOUNCEMENT OF HIS DEATH AND RESURRECTION, John 2:18–22. In the first part of our chapter, Christ manifests His authority in the realm of nature; in the subsequent paragraph, which we have just studied, He manifests His authority over the Temple and the priesthood. He is now about to reveal prophetically, ultimately, actually His power over death. The chapter closes with a statement regarding Christ's profound knowledge of man. **18. The Jews therefore answered and said unto him, What sign showest thou unto us, seeing that thou doest these things? 19. Jesus answered and said unto them, Destroy this temple, and in three days I will raise it up. 20. The Jews therefore said, Forty and six years was this temple in building, and wilt thou raise it up in three days?** Hoskyns has a remarkable paragraph here on the significance of the resurrection of Christ as occurring on the third day, a time factor often on the lips of Jesus, and repeated by the Apostle Paul in 1 Corinthians 15:4. "In the East a clear distinction is made between the third and the fourth day. It is, for example, a widely observed rule in hospitality — it was the practice of Mohammed — for a guest to remain three days with his host (rest-day, drest-day, departure day). To remain longer, to remain on the fourth day, is a very serious matter. . . . Three days may be said to constitute a temporary habitation, the fourth day implies permanent residence. A similar distinction between three days and the fourth day appears also in another connection. It seems to have been a widespread belief among the Jews, a belief of whose existence elsewhere there is evidence, that the soul of a dead man hovered near the corpse for three days hoping to return to the body, but that on the fourth day, when decomposition set in, the soul finally departed. . . . Moreover, quite apart from any popular superstition, three days mark the period during which the ravages of death are not altogether visible. With the fourth day it is different. Martha supposes it impossible for Lazarus to be raised from the dead, because he had been four days in the grave (11:39). Again, the distinction between the third and the fourth day is the distinction between what may be temporary and what must be permanent." — E. C. Hoskyns. No other man in his right mind has ever ventured to use words like these concerning his own resurrection. None of the apostles ever did; no prophet in the Old Testament ever declared that he would rise again on the third day; no great founder of the religions of this earth, except Jesus, has ever dared to use these words. The wonderful fact in relation to this is not simply that Jesus made such a statement, but that on the third day He did rise. Had He not risen, you and I would not be studying His Word today. The fact that He did rise makes Him unique among all the people on earth, the only Saviour of men, and the only begotten Son of God. **21. But he spake of the temple of his body.** "As the temple at Jerusalem, with its marble pavements, its pillared cloisters, its terraced courts, its rich adornment, was one of the fairest spectacles under the sun, so is the human body, designed and built by the Divine skill, worthy of its Creator. Consider those ivory pillars of bone; those alabaster walls of flesh; that many-toned organ of speech; those long corridors of brain and nerve, through which thought and emotion move; those storied archives where memory resides as the custodian of the records of the past: and tell me if you do not see an exquisite beauty and delicacy in the Lord's com-

18

22. When therefore he was raised from the dead, his disciples remembered that he spake this; and they believed the scripture, and the word which Jesus had said.

23. Now when he was in Jerusalem at the passover, during the feast, many believed on his name, beholding his signs which he did.

24. But Jesus did not trust himself unto them, for that he knew all men.

25. And because he needed not that any one should bear witness concerning man; for he himself knew what was in man.

---

parison, as 'He spake of the temple of his Body.' Wherever the religion of Jesus went, men conceived a new idea of the sacredness of the body. Had He not worn it? Had He not carried it through death into the light of Easter, and the glory of the throne? Had He not spoken of it as a temple? The natural instincts could be neither common nor unclean. And it must be possible so to order and rule them as that they should be the willing servants of a holy will and consecrated purpose; not impeding the symmetrical beauty of the loftiest characters, but promoting it; and doing the will of God on earth as it is done in heaven." — *F. B. Meyer.* 22. **When therefore he was raised from the dead, his disciples remembered that he spake this; and they believed the scripture, and the word which Jesus had said.** It is amazing how completely the disciples' comprehension of Jesus changed after the resurrection. They seem to have almost forgotten some words that Christ plainly spoke regarding this coming event, but when it took place, and they remembered His Words, they became more deeply convinced than ever of the truthfulness of their Lord's utterances.

IV. CHRIST'S DEEP INSIGHT INTO THE HEARTS OF HIS HEARERS, John 2:23–25. 23. **Now when he was in Jerusalem at the passover, during the feast, many believed on his name, beholding his signs which he did.** 24. **But Jesus did not trust himself unto them, for that he knew all men.** These are profound words, and they need some consideration. Godet says, "Their faith, to the view of Jesus, was not faith. No doubt it had for its object His revelation as Christ and Son of God; but it rested only upon the external fact of His miracles. The logical relation between this aorist *believed* and the present participle *seeing* is expressed by the conjunction *because*. This faith had nothing inward and moral; it resulted solely from the impression of astonishment produced upon them by these wonders. Signs may, indeed, strengthen and develop true faith, where it is already formed, by displaying to it fully the riches of its object (2:11). They may even, sometimes, excite attention; but not produce real faith. Faith is a moral act which attaches itself to the moral being in Jesus. The last words: 'which He did' depict, indeed, the nature of this faith; it was the material operation which impressed these persons. These miracles were, undoubtedly numerous; allusion is made to them in 4:45. John relates, however, only one of them; so far different is His aim from that of the Synoptics. He wishes only to describe here a spiritual situation. Jesus is no more dazzled by this apparent success than He had been discouraged by the reverse which He had undergone in the temple. He discerns the insufficient nature of this faith." — *F. Godet.* 25. **And because he needed not that any one should bear witness concerning man; for he himself knew what was in man.** I wish it were possible to quote here Dr. Campbell Morgan's entire sermon on this text, preached now nearly fifty years ago. "He knew men of different temperaments: whether it were the retiring, shrinking Philip, having to be called before he followed, and for ever more living, as my friend Mr. Elvet Lewis has beautifully put it, on the edge of the crowd, or whether it was fiery, impetuous Peter. He knew them and dealt with them according to their temperaments. He so spoke in metropolitan Jerusalem, as to arrest the attention of the leaders of the day, men of light and leading, and as to make them say, 'How hath

19

this Man letters, having never learned?' He so spoke to the great crowd of poor people that they heard Him and trusted Him. He won them. He knew men of all ages, men of years, young men, little children, men of all habits. He knew man, and because He knew man, He knew men. If you and I try to study humanity by studying men we shall never understand humanity. If we come to know man in the light of God's revelation we shall know how to deal with men. Here standing in the midst was one who knew them. . . . But this knowledge did not produce hopelessness in Him, for He dealt with men everywhere as being salvable by grace. Sometimes one finds oneself limited, straitened to find words to tell some great truth! So am I now! How shall I tell it? How shall I say what I mean? Thus — He treated men as worth dying for. He looked upon man as possible of being remade through His passion and His death! How a man would like to stay here were he preaching to Christian people rather than to an assembly in which there are those who are seeking Christ. These are the views of humanity which create the evangelistic fervour. Every human face is the outward manifestation of spiritual being. Every human being is in the grip of sin in some form. Every human being can be saved. In the power of these things we dare preach and work. He knew what was in man. What did His knowledge of men produce in the Christ? My first answer is the answer of the whole book. His incarnation is the first result. He expressed God to man through man's own nature. 'No man hath seen God at any time; the only begotten Son, which is in the bosom of the Father, He hath declared Him.' How? By being made flesh. That was the first thing He came to do. That is the burden of my message. If I can see how Christ looked at man, I shall know God's attitude. If I can discover the diversity of His method and learn therefrom, that though I am a lonely man, there being no other like me in the world, having peculiar sins and temptations, so that I cannot be classified, Christ can yet deal with me, I shall know that God can deal with me. The incarnation was not the beginning of a new fact, it was the initiation of a new revelation. When the Word became flesh the eternal nearness of God blossomed into visibility, but the psalmist of the olden day had sung the great truth, Thou knowest me, I cannot escape from Thee. God was ever present, but the fact became patent when the Man of Nazareth took form and substance and shape, so that these very eyes could see, and this very hand could feel, and this life of mine could come to understand. He did that because of His knowledge of man. His knowledge of man compelled Him to express God for humanity that humanity might have knowledge of God." — *G. Campbell Morgan.*

THE LESSON IN LIFE, LITERATURE, AND ARCHAEOLOGY.

In the life of the famous missionary to the Jews, John Wilkinson, is the following anecdote: "Only a few weeks ago I heard a Rabbi in a synagogue in one of the large province towns say to the Jews what amounted to a recommendation to read the New Testament. The Rabbi, while reproving the Jews for holding conversations during the synagogue worship, said, 'I fear you even transact business in the House of God — and such has been the case for centuries past. If you look into the New Testament you will find that the founder of the Christian religion charged the Jews with a similar sin in His day. He said, "Ye have made the House of God a house of merchandise." ' "

A TRUTH FOR THE CLASS TO CARRY AWAY.

As set forth in this lesson, we must ever insist upon the absolute uniqueness and supremacy of Christ. He did things here that no other man could do, and He can do things now for men, in redeeming them, in making them the children of God, in giving to them eternal life, all of which no other person in the world can do.

How does this lesson, relating to the early life of our Lord, throw light upon His statement, made after the resurrection, that all authority had been given unto Him? What authority does Christ now exercise? What is wrong in selling merchandise in the Temple? In how many ways in the ministry of Jesus are the

*subjects of marriage, and bride and bridegroom used? If Christ had all this
authority at the beginning of His ministry, what conclusion do you draw from the
fact that at the same time He predicted the necessity for His death?*

LESSON III. — January 17.

JESUS AND NICODEMUS. — John 3.

PRINTED TEXT, John 3:1-21.

Devotional Reading: 2 Corinthians 5:17-21.
Beginner Topic: JESUS' KIND HANDS.
   Lesson Material: Luke 13:10-17.
   Memory Verse: Jehovah is good to all. Psalm 145:9.
Primary Topic: NICODEMUS TALKS WITH JESUS.
   Lesson Material: John 3:1-21.
   Memory Verse: For God so loved the world, that he gave his only begotten
   Son, that whosoever believeth on him should not perish, but have eternal
   life. John 3:16.
Junior Topic: NICODEMUS TALKS WITH JESUS.
   Lesson Material: John 3:1-21.
   Memory Verse: For God so loved the world, that he gave his only begotten
   Son, that whosoever believeth on him should not perish, but have eternal
   life. John 3:16.
Intermediate-Senior Topic: A CONFIDENTIAL INTERVIEW.
   Lesson Material: John 3.
   Memory Verse: For God so loved the world, that he gave his only begotten
   Son, that whosoever believeth on him should not perish, but have eternal
   life. John 3:16.
Topic for Young People and Adults: THE NEW BIRTH.
   Lesson Material: John 3.
   Memory Verse: For God so loved the world, that he gave his only begotten
   Son, that whosoever believeth on him should not perish, but have eternal
   life. John 3:16.

THE TEACHER AND HIS CLASS.

The **Younger Classes** might be introduced to this lesson by being asked to whom they would go if, while living in the city, they were requested to write a paper on wheat-growing, something which possibly they had never seen. They would go to some authority on wheat, either written articles or a farmer who grows wheat. A man, thinking he had been unjustly treated in a business deal, would go to consult a lawyer, who would know what to do. In our lesson, the outstanding spiritual teacher of Israel of that day found himself troubled about the great question of how to possess eternal life, and to receive help on this, he went to Jesus, who, he must have thought, was a far greater authority on this than anyone else.

The **Older Classes** may be introduced to this lesson concerning regeneration and the need for a change in the human heart by being reminded of two or three statements made by outstanding world citizens about the time of the dropping of the atomic bomb. Dr. Robert M. Hutchins, at that time Chancellor of the University of Chicago, spoke of the "moral, intellectual and spiritual reformation for which the world waits." President Truman, on March 7, 1946, at Columbus, Ohio, said that the present world conditions "call for a moral and spiritual awakening in the life of the individual." Professor Toynbee declared that what we most need at this hour is "a change of heart," and he supplemented this statement with a quotation from the book of Ezekiel, "A new

21

heart will I give you, and a new spirit will I put within you." This is exactly what the Lord is speaking of in this lesson.

THE LESSON IN ITS SETTING.

Time. — Our Lord's interview with Nicodemus occurred in April, A.D. 27.

Place. — As far as we know, the interview with Nicodemus took place in Jerusalem. Aenon, where John was baptizing, has not been definitely located, but it was probably on the Jordan near the boundary of Galilee and Samaria.

THE PLAN OF THE LESSON.

SUBJECT: What Christ Said about the Conditions which Make Us Acceptable to God and Guarantee our Possession of Eternal Life.

I. CHRIST'S CONVERSATION WITH NICODEMUS, John 3:1–15.
   1. The interview is begun by Nicodemus, vs. 1, 2.
   2. The discussion regarding the new birth, vs. 3–8.
   3. The bewilderment of Nicodemus, v. 9.
   4. Christ's teaching about "heavenly things," vs. 10–15.

II. ETERNAL LIFE FOR MAN IS THROUGH CHRIST ALONE, 3:16–21.

III. JOHN THE BAPTIST'S FINAL TESTIMONY TO THE PRE-EMINENCE OF CHRIST, 3:22–36.

THE TEACHER'S LIBRARY.

In addition to the principal commentaries on John's Gospel, and many of the more important lives of Christ, there are a number of excellent chapters on the character of Nicodemus; e.g., Everett F. Harrison: *The Son of God Among the Sons of Men*, 65–74; James Hastings: *The Greater Men and Women of the Bible*, Vol. 5,

pp. 378–384; G. Campbell Morgan: *The Great Physician*, 35–72; A. T. Robertson: *Some Minor Characters of the New Testament*, 1–12; F. A. Noble: *New Testament Conversions*, 351–369; A. B. Davidson: *The Called of God*, 249–271; James Jeffrey: *The Personal Ministry of the Son of Man*, 47–50; W. Boyd Carpenter: *The Son of Man Among the Sons of Men*, 187–208; George Matheson: *Representative Men of the New Testament*, 109–130; J. G. Greenhough in *Men of the New Testament*, 131–140; Alexander Whyte: *Bible Characters, Joseph and Mary — James the Lord's Brother*, 36–45; Adolph Saphir: *Conversion Illustrated by Examples Recorded in the Bible*, 189–216; J. D. Jones: *The Hope of the Gospel*, 126–138; and L. R. Scarborough: *How Jesus Won Men*, 59–71, 195–199. I am acquainted with three books, all of an earlier date, devoted entirely to the subject of Nicodemus: Joseph Grierson: *Earthly and Heavenly Things* (Edinburgh, 1859); J. N. P. Otts: *Jesus and Nicodemus* (Philadelphia, 1867) and John T. Reid: *Jesus and Nicodemus*.

On the subject of the new birth, see G. Campbell Morgan: *The Spirit of God*, 213–225; R. A. Torrey: *Fundamental Doctrines of the Christian Faith*, 206–214; J. Ritchie Smith: *The Teaching of the Gospel of John*, 236–240; F. B. Meyer: *Five "Musts" of the Christian Life*, 9–20; and a great article, "Regeneration" in Hastings: *Dictionary of Christ and the Gospels*, Vol. 2, pp. 485–489.

Sermonic material is vast, and for that reason, I am going to give only the meagerest references. On verse 8 there is a great sermon by H. P. Liddon in *University Sermons*, 2nd series, 79–97; on verses 14, 15, see Robert M. Edgar: *The Philosophy of the Cross*, 145–159, and a sermon, seldom seen today, by Martin Luther on verses 16–21 in *Sunday Half-Hours with the Great Preachers*, 429–443.

AUDIO-VISUAL AIDS.

FILM: "Nicodemus — Being Born Again" (Episode IV in the series The Search for Christ), Illustrate, Inc., 12 min., sd., b&w. A series of drawings showing a boy and his guardian seeking Jesus, but never quite catching up to him, and always hearing what He has done from others. Simple and slow enough for the younger children.

FILM: "Born Twice," Grace Films, 21 min., sd., col. An exposition of Scripture, presenting the new birth.

SLIDE SET: "Nicodemus," Church-Craft #16, 6 sl., col.

The principal theme of our lesson today is the New Birth, as set forth by Jesus at the beginning of His ministry, in a profoundly significant conversation with Nicodemus. This subject is generally discussed under the heading of *regeneration*, so that perhaps a brief discussion of that word might begin the study today. *Regeneration* is made up of two words. The word *generate* means to begin something, to commence something, to give birth to something, from which comes our word *generation*. Incidentally, the first four letters of this word, *gene*, is that very important term in modern biology, which represents the basic factor of biological life. The prefix *re* means *again*, so that *regeneration* means *to be born again*. The English word occurs in Matthew 19:28 and Titus 3:5. The Greek word there is

JOHN 3:1. Now there was a man of the Pharisees, named Nicodemus, a ruler of the Jews.

2. The same came unto him by night, and said to him, Rabbi, we know that thou art a teacher come from God; for no one can do these signs that thou doest, except God be with him.

3. Jesus answered and said unto him, Verily, verily, I say unto thee, Except one be born anew, he cannot see the kingdom of God.

palingennesia, in which again the idea of birth, or genesis, is prominent. The Latin version translates this by our English word *regeneration*. In 1 Peter 1:23, we have the phrase, "to be born again," which in the Greek is *anagennao*. Here again is a form of the Greek word genesis. In the Latin, this is *regenerare*. Therefore, we really have two words in the New Testament implying a new birth. One refers to individuals, and the other to the great regeneration of the world yet to come. One can hardly conceive of a greater word than this in any language, more hopeful and comprehensive, filled with promise.

I. **CHRIST'S CONVERSATION WITH NICODEMUS, John 3:1–15. 1. Now there was a man of the Pharisees, named Nicodemus, a ruler of the Jews:** "John means us to understand that out of the many who 'believed in the name' of Jesus was one deserving of special attention, not merely as representing a higher class and special culture, but chiefly because, brought by the signs (i.e., Jesus' miracles) to a degree of faith, he was desirous of knowing more; and our Lord's dealings with Nicodemus show how He sought to lead all who were so prepared to a deeper knowledge and higher faith. . . . Nicodemus is described as a Pharisee, and as 'a ruler of the Jews,' — i.e., a member of the Sanhedrin (compare 7:50), the great council of seventy-one which held supreme power over the whole nation. In other passages John uses 'ruler' in this sense (see 7:26, 48; 12:42); here only does he join with it the words 'of the Jews.' " — *William Milligan*. In verse 10, Nicodemus is given a notable title, "the teacher of Israel," "for the whole people listened to what he had to say. **2. The same came unto him by night, and said to him, Rabbi, we know that thou art a teacher come from God; for no one can do these signs that thou doest, except God be with him.** There has been a great deal of discussion as to why Nicodemus came to Jesus by night, and generally the later reference (John 19:38–39) is used to support the idea that he did not want to be seen by those with whom he associated. However, the late Dr. Hoskyns has reminded us that "No doubt learned Jews were in the habit of discussing during the night, and no doubt they recommended it as especially suitable for the study of the law. No doubt also Nicodemus wished to secure solitude in order to converse with Jesus about the deep things of religion. But 'darkness' and 'night' in the fourth Gospel are sinister words (9:4; 11:9, 10; 13:30)." In approaching Christ, Nicodemus makes three significant confessions concerning Him: First, that He is a teacher; secondly, that God sent Him; and thirdly, that He performed supernatural miracles. What these miracles at this time were, we do not know except that at the marriage of Cana of Galilee, recorded in the preceding chapter. **3. Jesus answered and said unto him, Verily, verily, I say unto thee, Except one be born anew, he cannot see the kingdom of God.** Here is one of the most profound statements ever uttered by our Lord. There has been a great deal of discussion concerning an exact translation of the Greek word in the Revised Version here translated *anew*, but in the margin given as *from above*. The Greek word certainly means *from above* in verse 31, and in 1 John 2:29; 5:1, etc. "Notwithstanding these arguments it is probably that *anew* is the true rendering." — *William Milligan*. While it is true that only in this discourse does Jesus specifically speak about regeneration, or being born again, yet we should remember that the New Testament is saturated with the idea. The Apostle John himself speaks of men being born of God (1 John 3:9; 4:7; 5:1, 4, 18); the Apostle Peter refers to the same idea in the word *conversion* (Acts 3:19); the Apostle Paul expresses the idea in the

4. Nicodemus saith unto him, How can a man be born when he is old? can he enter a second time into his mother's womb and be born?

5. Jesus answered, Verily, verily, I say unto thee, Except one be born of water and the Spirit, he cannot enter into the kingdom of God.

6. That which is born of the flesh is flesh; that which is born of the Spirit is spirit.

7. Marvel not that I said unto thee, Ye must be born anew.

8. The wind bloweth where it will, and thou hearest the voice thereof, but knowest not whence it cometh, and whither it goeth: so is every one that is born of the Spirit.

---

phrases "being born alive from the dead" (Romans 6:13), "being a new creature" (2 Cor. 5:17), "putting on the new man" (Col. 3:9, 10), "the washing of regeneration" (Titus 3:5), "being made a partaker of the divine nature" (1 Peter 2:9; 2 Peter 1:4). This idea of being born again is what we might call, radical. Our first birth determines the race in which we are born, the capacities we derive from our parents, the physical bodies in which we will live, and probably, the very temperaments we will display through life, the weak characteristics and the strong factors of our entire human career. In fact, one can say that, humanly speaking, about all a person is going to be is already latent in that little new-born babe. One may have remarkable experiences later, grow and acquire a larger vision, etc., but nothing will ever be able to deliver him from the forces which will dominate him from the time he is born till the time he dies except a new birth. The question arises, What did our Lord mean by "the kingdom of God"? He did not mean the Messianic kingdom. He did not mean a kingdom on this earth. He meant a spiritual kingdom, that in which God rules, in which God's laws are obeyed, and the subjects are God's children. The kingdom of God has a universal scope. It abides forever. To be a member of it is to have the life of God within one's soul; to be outside of it is to be lost forever. Entrance into this kingdom, our Lord said, is not by human effort but by something absolutely supernatural. **4. Nicodemus saith unto him, How can a man be born when he is old? can he enter a second time into his mother's womb and be born? 5. Jesus answered, Verily, verily, I say unto thee, Except one be born of water and the Spirit, he cannot enter into the kingdom of God. 6. That which is born of the flesh is flesh; that which is born of the Spirit is spirit. 7. Marvel not that I said unto thee, Ye must be born anew.** The question of Nicodemus is natural. Second birth is something of which he had never heard before. In answer to the question, our Lord repeats what He had just said, and adds that this new birth is of the Spirit. What is meant by being "born of water" has created a great deal of discussion. The words of William Milligan are helpful. "The words 'water and spirit' are most closely joined, and placed under the government of the same preposition. A little earlier in the Gospel (1:33) we find the same words — not, indeed, joined together as here, but yet placed in exact parallelism, each word, too, receiving emphasis from the context. Three times between 1:19 and 1:33 John speaks of his baptism with water; twice there is a reference to the Spirit (1:32, 33); and in verse 33 John's baptizing with water and our Lord's baptizing with 'Holy Spirit' stand explicitly contrasted. It is very possible that this testimony was well known to others besides John's disciples, to all indeed in Judea who were roused to inquiry respecting the Baptist and his relation to Jesus." — *William Milligan.* Many believe that the water here refers also to the Word of God, and with this I would agree. There is certainly some relationship between what Christ utters here at the beginning of His ministry and what the Apostle Peter, a generation later, writes to the Church, when he speaks of "having been begotten again not of corruptible seed, but of incorruptible, through the word of God" (1 Pet. 1:23). On the word *must*, Hoskyns remarks that this has reference to "the absolute requirement of the will of God, and the

9. Nicodemus answered and said unto him, How can these things be?

10. Jesus answered and said unto him, Art thou the teacher of Israel, and understandest not these things?

11. Verily, verily, I say unto thee, We speak that which we know, and bear witness of that which we have seen; and ye receive not our witness.

12. If I told you earthly things and ye believe not, how shall ye believe if I tell you heavenly things?

---

plural is used because the demand of God is universal." 8. **The wind bloweth where it will, and thou hearest the voice thereof, but knowest not whence it cometh, and whither it goeth: so is every one that is born of the Spirit.** It is not without meaning that the word translated *spirit* and the word translated *wind*, is in the Greek the same word, *pneuma*, from which comes our word *pneumatic*, meaning filled with air, and *pneumatology*, meaning the doctrine of the Holy Spirit. "The wave of air in its origin, course, and issues, is mysterious, invisible, indefinable; but its presence around me and in my surroundings is to be known by practical results, and by them alone: 'Thou hearest the sound, the voice.' The trees of the wood, the waters of the mountain lake, you 'hear the wind' in them and on them; and thus you ascertain its presence there. 'So is everyone that is born of the Spirit'; every one. The divinely mysterious process produces known and observable effects; and its presence, not in the abstract, but here or there, is to be verified by them and by them alone. Regeneration, the coming to be one of the children of God, in John the Apostle's sense, in the Lord's sense, is indeed a 'secret thing' in itself; but its evidences are practical and plain. The Spirit is eternal, divine; but where He effectually works the New Birth, there, in one degree or another, so says the Lord here, you will hear the sound, you will trace results. And what is the sound of the heavenly Wind in the being, in the life? It consists of things which indeed belong to, though they are not the creatures of, the circumstances of the common day: 'love, joy, peace, longsuffering, gentleness, goodness, faithfulness, meekness, self-control.' It consists, in fact of love, love in distribution, heaven-given love to God and to man in God." — *H. C. G. Moule.* 9. **Nicodemus answered and said unto him, How can these things be?** "It is never the way of Jesus to turn aside an earnest seeker. Impossible though it be to explore the mystery of the new birth which rests in the counsels of God, there is profit in being directed to the external means upon which faith must rest if the new birth is to be realized. So the Lord proceeded to point to the one event that sinners must know about and appropriate for themselves if they would become partakers of the divine nature." — *E. F. Harrison.* 10. **Jesus answered and said unto him, Art thou the teacher of Isreal, and understandest not these things? 11. Verily, verily, I say unto thee, We speak that which we know, and bear witness of that which we have seen; and ye receive not our witness. 12. If I told you earthly things and ye believe not, how shall ye believe if I tell you heavenly things?** "Our Lord does not say 'and knowest not'; Nicodemus is not blamed for any want of *previous* knowledge of these things, but because he does not perceive the truth of the teaching when presented to him — and presented, moreover, by One whose right to teach with authority he had himself confessed. It will be observed that Jesus does not answer the 'How' of the preceding question. . . . The sudden transition to the plural 'we know' is remarkable. We cannot suppose that our Lord here joins with Himself the prophets of the Old Covenant, or John the Baptist, or that He is speaking of the testimony of the Father and the Holy Spirit. The key to the plural is found in verse 8. Every one who dwells in the spiritual world of which Jesus has been speaking is a witness to its reality and its wonders. Here then Jesus associates with Himself in this emphatic testimony all who have been born of the Spirit. . . . Nicodemus had at first said 'we know' (v. 2), as rep-

13. And no one hath ascended into heaven, but he that descended out of heaven, *even* the Son of man, who is in heaven.

14. And as Moses lifted up the serpent in the wilderness, even so must the Son of man be lifted up;

15. that whosoever believeth may in him have eternal life.

resentative of others like-minded with himself, who by the signs had been led to faith in the name of Jesus, but were ignorant of His spiritual work. Jesus now contrasts with these another class, consisting of all whom from their own experience could join Him in His testimony to the reality of the spiritual kingdom. The words of Jesus in 9:4 are equally remarkable in their association of His people with Himself. — The two parallel members of this verse bring the truth expressed into bold relief." — *William F. Moulton*. "*Heavenly things* refer to those truths which belong to a higher order, which *are* in heaven, and are brought down thence to earth as they can *become* to men. Such was the full revelation of the Son, involving the redemption of the world and the reunion of man with God, which is indicated in the three following verses." — *B. F. Westcott.* **13. And no one hath ascended into heaven, but he that descended out of heaven, *even* the Son of man, who is in heaven.** Even a child may be expected to ask, If Jesus is the Son of man, and at this time was on earth in Jerusalem talking to Nicodemus, how could He refer to Himself as the one "who is in heaven"? A note in the margin of the Revised Version says that many ancient authorities omit this phrase, but Hoskyns reminds us that it is found "in the vast majority of Greek manuscripts," and no doubt belongs here. A comment by Lenski will be of help here. "This person is God the Son himself, whose coming down in the incarnation is not a mere change of residence. Though he came down, and now speaks to Nicodemus as the Son of man, he remains 'he who is in heaven.' He cannot change his divine nature, cannot lay it aside, cannot cancel even temporarily his divine Sonship, his unity of essence with the Father and the Spirit. . . . The Son of man so described can have this character only because prior to his incarnation he was in heaven; that he is there now, even while speaking to Nicodemus, is the one thing that, so many think, must be eliminated. . . . When the Spirit in the form of a dove came down out of heaven upon Jesus, he did not thereby remove his person and presence from heaven, nor when he was poured out upon the disciples on Pentecost. The same is true of Jehovah when he appeared to Abraham, to Moses in the fiery bush, and when he descended on Sinai, to mention only these." **14. And as Moses lifted up the serpent in the wilderness, even so must the Son of man be lifted up; 15. that whosoever believeth may in him have eternal life.** The reference here is to Numbers 21:9. "In the wilderness, the Israelites, in consequence of their murmurings, were bitten by fiery serpents, and were in imminent danger of death; but the Lord directed Moses to make a serpent of brass, and to put it upon a pole, and whosoever looked upon it lived. So are we all by nature; we are bitten by the old serpent, the devil, and our death is on us. But God arranged it that a cross should be raised on Calvary, and whosoever looks sincerely to Christ crucified begins to live for ever. Into the face of the dying Saviour we are required honestly to look, and that look of faith proves saving. . . . No less valuable instrument suffices for the regeneration of man; no Church, however venerable, nor priesthood, however pretentious, nor baptism, however scrupulously administered, can supply the medium through which the great Spirit acts, — this, in the case of souls capable of thought, is Jesus Christ lifted up in sight of dying man upon His cross!" — *R. M. Edgar.*

II. ETERNAL LIFE FOR MAN IS THROUGH CHRIST ALONE, 3:16–21. The paragraph arrangement in the Revised Version of 1901 is one of its most valuable assets. In this chapter the 36 verses are divided into four paragraphs, the first closing with verse 15. It is almost universally admitted that the entire chapter was not uttered to Nicodemus. Just where the conversation breaks off,

16. For God so loved the world, that he gave his only begotten Son, that whosoever believeth on him should not perish, but have eternal life.

17. For God sent not the Son into the world to judge the world; but that the world should be saved through him.

18. He that believeth on him is not judged: he that believeth not hath been judged already, because he hath not believed on the name of the only begotten Son of God.

---

we cannot dogmatically affirm, but possibly it was at verse 15. A second problem then arises, Are the remainder of the words of this chapter those of Christ, or are they the words of the Apostle John? Here again there is considerable division among scholars. Personally, I believe that verses 16–21 are from the lips of our Lord. I doubt if John could have written these sentences. They seem to come direct from the heart and mind of the Son of God. **16. For God so loved the world, that he gave his only begotten Son, that whosoever believeth on him should not perish, but have eternal life.** This is probably the most famous verse in all the New Testament. It is so often used as the text of a sermon, and we have so frequently commented upon it in other volumes of *Peloubet's Notes*, that I am taking the liberty of passing it by in this lesson with only a brief paragraph. I think Professor Lenski's comment on this inexhaustible passage has not been used in previous volumes. "Even after carefully defining 'love,' no human intelligence can fathom how God could thus love the world. The revelation of this love divides the Christian religion so radically from all others, that no bridge can possibly connect the two. The former is divine, the latter only human. And this love of God is the pinnacle of all his glory, the crown of all his attributes. It makes God supremely attractive to every sinner needing this love, a most efficacious call to trust this love and thus to have all that it gives. . . . The gift was actually made, the aorist marks the past fact. God's own Son sat before Nicodemus at that very moment. Jesus does not use again 'the Son of man' as in verses 13–14. There it fits as describing what he who came out of heaven became here on earth. Here the divine act of love takes us into heaven and shows us the gift of that love as it was when the act of giving occurred. That gift was 'his Son the Only Begotten.' . . . The gift is a unit act, but the purpose attached to it holds till the end of time. The repetition stresses this purpose clause, even as repetition constantly marks emphasis. Jesus virtually says: Note well once more this *fiducia* of believing, this personal singular, this universality, this possession, this wondrous life." **17. For God sent not the Son into the world to judge the world; but that the world should be saved through him. 18. He that believeth on him is not judged: he that believeth not hath been judged already, because he hath not believed on the name of the only begotten Son of God.** "The thought of the last verse is expanded. There it was the gift of God's love that was brought before us; now it is the mission of the Son. To 'may perish' here corresponds 'may judge the world,' to 'have eternal life' answers 'may be saved.' This alone is sufficient to show that the word 'judge,' though not in itself equivalent to 'condemn' has reference to a judgment which tends to condemnation. The Jews believed that Messiah would come to glorify Israel, but to judge the Gentiles; the solemn and emphatic repetition of 'the world' rebukes all such limitations. . . . It may seem hard to reconcile the first part of this verse with 5:22, 27; 9:39; 12:48. We must, however, recognize a two-fold purpose in Christ's coming. He came to save, not to judge the world. He came to judge the world in so far as it will not allow itself to be saved; and this judgment is one that takes place even now (because even now there is wilful unbelief), though it will only be consummated hereafter. . . . So long as the unbelief is persisted in, so long does the sentence which the rejection of Jesus brings with it remain in force against him. The great idea of the Gospel, the

19. And this is the judgment, that the light is come into the world, and men loved the darkness rather than the light; for their works were evil.

20. For every one that doeth evil hateth the light, and cometh not to the light, lest his works should be reproved.

21. But he that doeth the truth cometh to the light, that his works may be made manifest, that they have been wrought in God.

---

division of all men into two classes severed from each other, is very clearly presented here; but no *unchangeable* division is thought of. The separation is the result of deliberate choice; and whilst the choice is adhered to, the severance abides. — As the faith of the believer is faith 'in Him,' faith that brings personal union, the unbelief is the rejection of His Person revealed in all its dignity, the only begotten Son of God." — *William Milligan.* 19. **And this is the judgment, that the light is come into the world, and men loved the darkness rather than the light; for their works were evil. 20. For every one that doeth evil hateth the light, and cometh not to the light, lest his works should be reproved.** In spite of the love, the hope, the promise that radiates from this paragraph, there is also a dark and tragic note here. Men love darkness rather than light, for their deeds are evil. Probably never in the history of the world, at least in modern times, has there been such evil as we have now. Our newspapers seem to be hardly more than a record of evil, apart from deliberations in legislative bodies and announcements of marriages and deaths. The statistics of our criminal reports are steadily rising. Embezzlement is rapidly increasing. The revolt of our youth is creating problems which we have not been able to solve. Here in Los Angeles County in Southern California, eight thousand people pass through the jail every seven days. When we lift our eyes and look across the water to the lands behind the Iron Curtain, we shudder for the evil that is being perpetuated there. The vice in our great cities around the world is nothing less than horrifying. Something is wrong with the human heart; its compass points away from God. This is what Jesus meant. It seems to be more true now than when He was talking to Nicodemus. 21. **But he that doeth the truth cometh to the light, that his works may be made manifest, that they have been wrought in God.** Though practically ignored as such, here is a great verse for a sermon text. A man who loves the truth will come to the light; that is, if he is a seeker after truth, he will come into the presence of God. If he is a hypocrite, he will try to hide behind a skeptical attitude, an agnostic position, a pretense at atheism, or a general religious affirmation with the person of God left out. I believe it can be said without contradiction that the reason most men who know of a living, loving sovereign God, who sent His Son to die for us, do not embrace Him as Saviour and Lord is that they are not seeking the truth and prefer to live in sin.

III. **JOHN THE BAPTIST'S FINAL TESTIMONY TO THE PRE-EMINENCE OF CHRIST,** 3:22–36. The second half of this chapter contains the remarkable final witness of John the Baptist to the absolute pre-eminence of Christ, of whom he was the forerunner. This will be the last time we see John the Baptist until he stands before Herod condemning him for his evil life, as the result of which he is executed. Note how close to the phraseology of John the Apostle, the author of this fourth Gospel, are these wonderfully rich exclamations of John the Baptist. If the text did not explicitly state otherwise, we could well believe they were the words either of Christ himself or of the Evangelist. Inasmuch as this passage does not appear in the printed text, we must give it only the briefest consideration. First of all it would be of value to list the various tributes which John here pays to the Lord Jesus Christ, who was at this time only beginning His public ministry. He is called the Christ, which means the Messiah, and the Bridegroom; He is said to have come from above, from heaven, which is true of no other individual who ever walked this earth; He is the one whom God sent; He is loved by the Father, who gave Him all things; the eternal destiny of all men is determined by Christ — those who receive Him have eternal life and those who do not have the wrath of God abiding on them.

One phrase we might well emphasize here is that of verse 31, "He that cometh from above is above all." The words of Lenski here are unsurpassed. "The heavenly origin of Jesus makes him supreme over all men, who are all wholly of earthly origin. Since the entire contrast from verse 27 on deals with persons, 'above all' must mean not 'above all things,' but 'above all men.' " Christ is above all in the fact that He was pre-existent, before He came to earth, in the divine origin of His incarnate state, in the absolute sinlessness of His life, in His complete victory over all the world, in His absolute power over nature, disease, demons and death, in the truth that He brought to men, in His relationship to God as His only begotten Son, in His resurrection by His own determination, in the fact that He is the Head of the Church, in the assurance that the time is coming when all things will be subjected unto Him, and in the fact that by His death we are reconciled to God. The great characters of history all pale when brought into the glorious light of the pre-eminence of Christ.

THE LESSON IN LIFE, LITERATURE, AND ARCHAEOLOGY.

"On one occasion during the civil war, when Mr. Moody was acting as chaplain, he was awakened one night when he was very tired to go and see a dying soldier. When he began to speak to him about God the soldier said, 'He cannot save me; I have sinned all my life.' And Moody began to think of his mother a long way off, and he thought probably the mother was praying for her boy even then, and he sat up through the night, telling him promise after promise, praying with him, but nothing could avail. At last he read the third chapter of John, how Nicodemus came to the Master. As he read he noticed that the young fellow's eyes became riveted upon him, and he seemed to drink in every syllable. When he came to the words, 'As Moses lifted up the serpent in the wilderness, even so must the Son of man be lifted up; that whosoever believeth in him should not perish, but have eternal life,' he stopped Mr. Moody, and asked 'Is that true?' 'Yes,' Moody said. 'Well,' he said, 'I never knew that was in the Bible. Read it again.' Leaning on his elbow at the side of the cot, he drew his hands together tightly, and when Moody had finished reading he said, 'That is good! Won't you read it again?' Slowly he repeated the passage the third time. When he had finished he saw that the young soldier's eyes were closed, and the troubled expression on his face had given way to a peaceful smile. His lips moved, and as Moody bent over him to catch what he was saying he heard, in a faint whisper, 'As Moses lifted up the serpent in the wilderness, even so must the Son of man be lifted up; that whosoever believeth in him should not perish, but have eternal life.' He opened his eyes and said, 'That is enough. Do not read any more.' The next day Mr. Moody found that he had passed away peacefully with the words of that promise on his lips."

A TRUTH FOR THE CLASS TO CARRY AWAY.

I believe that a lesson like this should be brought to a close in only one way — by the teacher prayerfully, solemnly, lovingly, asking the class if they are personally conscious of having experienced a new birth, and know that they have passed from death unto life. Don't forget the remark of Spurgeon, who once said, "I may not know the day of my birth, but I know I am alive; and I may not know the exact date of my new birth, but I know that I am a child of God."

In how many ways does Christ prove Himself pre-eminent in this lesson? What are some differences between the testimony of Nicodemus to Christ and that of John the Baptist? In how many ways in this one lesson is the love of God revealed? What are some of the consequences in a man's life on this earth of being born again? Did Jesus Himself need to be born again? (Emphatically no.)

29

LESSON IV. — January 24.

JESUS AND THE SAMARITANS. — John 4:1–42.

PRINTED TEXT, John 4:5–9, 25–42.

Devotional Reading: Romans 1:8–16.

Beginner Topic: FRIEND TO A SICK MAN.
    Lesson Material: Matthew 9:1–8; Mark 2:1–12; Luke 5:17–26.
    Memory Verse: The Lord is my helper. Hebrews 13:6.

Primary Topic: A TALK BESIDE A WELL.
    Lesson Material: John 4:1–42.
    Memory Verse: This is indeed the Saviour of the world. John 4:42.

Junior Topic: JESUS HELPS SOME FOREIGN PEOPLE.
    Lesson Material: John 4:1–42.
    Memory Verse: This is indeed the Saviour of the world. John 4:42.

Intermediate-Senior Topic: SEEING IS BELIEVING.
    Lesson Material: John 4:1–42.
    Memory Verse: We have heard for ourselves, and know that this is indeed the Saviour of the world. John 4:42.

Topic for Young People and Adults: CROSSING MAN-MADE BARRIERS.
    Lesson Material: John 4:1–42.
    Memory Verse: We have heard for ourselves, and know that this is indeed the Saviour of the world. John 4:42.

THE TEACHER AND HIS CLASS.

The Younger Classes might be introduced to this lesson by being reminded that, without any preceding warning or notice, the experience of just one hour of a day that otherwise would be no different from any other day, can prove to be the most influential event of our entire life, changing its course and giving us some insight into what the years may have in store for us. When he was a boy, Dr. John Henry Jowett, who became in his day one of the greatest preachers in Great Britain (and America), was one day reading in the library of the town in which he lived, and was observed by a total stranger as he eagerly devoured the pages that were before him. The stranger came over, put his hand on the boy's shoulder, and said that he had been watching him, and that surely God had a great work for him to do. This lifted the lad onto a high plane, and he became the source of unceasing inspiration in the years that followed. So this Samaritan woman, on a day that she thought would be just as dreary and monotonous, just as overcast with sorrow and shame as any other day, unexpectedly met One of whom she had probably never heard before, who not only changed her whole life, in thought and deed, but made her the instrument for a great revival in that town.

The Older Classes might begin this lesson by a discussion on the subject of *conversation*. We used to talk about "the art of conversation," but today that seems to be an all but forgotten subject. We just chatter now, in short sentences that concern insignificant themes. The days pass and we have not said or heard anything of any great importance. I doubt if Jesus ever had ten minutes of conversation with any one in all of Palestine but that He began to talk about the greatest themes, resulting in the transformation of lives, and in truth taking the place of error, and hope in place of despair. This fourth chapter of John's Gospel is the record of one brief conversation that Jesus had with a despised woman, out of which came a revival in a most unexpected place.

THE LESSON IN ITS SETTING.

Time. — December, A.D. 27.

Place. — Jacob's Well, near Sychar in Samaria, not far from the great city of Shechem.

30

THE PLAN OF THE LESSON.

SUBJECT: How a Conversation of Less than an Hour Lifted a Person Living on a Low Level Into Heavenly Places, and Changed a Life of Emptiness into One of Abounding Joy.

I. JESUS' CONVERSATION WITH THE SAMARITAN WOMAN, John 4:1–27.

1. How He came to be at Sychar, vs. 1–6.
2. His request for a drink of water, vs. 7–9.
3. His declaration regarding His ability to give living water, vs. 10–15.
4. His probing of the woman's sinful heart, vs. 16–19.
5. His great assertion regarding the spirituality and worship of God, vs. 20–24.
6. He declares himself to be the Messiah, vs. 25–27.

II. THE REVIVAL IN SYCHAR, John 4:28–42.

1. The woman's testimony concerning Christ, vs. 28–30.
2. The intervening instruction for the disciples, vs. 31–38.
3. The Samaritans and Christ, vs. 39–42.
   a. their initial belief in Him because of the woman's testimony, v. 39.
   b. their request for Christ to abide with them, v. 40.
   c. their subsequent growth in faith, vs. 41, 42.

THE TEACHER'S LIBRARY.

In addition to commentaries on the Gospel of John, which are listed in the Bibliography in the Introduction to this volume, one should consider the question of the Samaritans and the location of Sychar. For this, there are two good articles in James Hastings: *Dictionary of the Apostolic Church,* Vol. 2, "Samaria," 557–560, and "Sychar," 686–687; see also a very vivid description in William M. Thomson: *The Land and the Book,* Vol. 2, pp. 109–146; Gustav Dalman: *Sacred Sites and Ways,* 209–220; A. T. Schofield: *Where He Dwelt,* 65–90 (with some beautiful pictures); and the interesting pages in

W. B. McCrackan: *The New Palestine,* 349–357. For chapters covering the entire episode, see especially R. C. Trench: *Studies in the Gospels,* 83–137; G. Campbell Morgan in the *Westminster Pulpit,* Vol. 3, pp. 25–32; and his volume, *The Great Physician,* 73–80; also A. T. Robertson: *Some Minor Characters in the New Testament,* 94–101; David Gregg: *New Epistles From Old Lands,* 75–96; F. A. Noble: *New Testament Conversions,* 67–83; James Jeffrey: *The Personal Ministry of the Son of Man,* 60–71; Adolph Saphir: *Conversions Illustrated by Examples Recorded in the Bible,* 217–252; A. Kuyper: *Women of the New Testament,* 31–33; W. F. Adeney: *Women of the New Testament,* 85–99; Isaac Williams: *Female Characters of Holy Scripture,* 221–223; H. C. G. Moule: *From Sunday to Sunday,* 147–158; and L. R. Scarborough: *How Jesus Won Men,* 72–87.

For sermonic material, on verses 11 and 20, see John A. Bain: *Questions Answered by Christ,* 140–152; on verses 12–14, G. Campbell Morgan: *Westminster Pulpit,* Vol. 2, pp. 209–216; and H. P. Liddon: *Passiontide Sermons,* 244–258; on verses 23, 24, Andrew Murray: *With Christ in the School of Prayer,* 9–15; and W. G. T. Shedd: *Dogmatic Theology,* Vol. 1, pp. 151–172. For verse 28, see David Gregg: *New Epistles from Old Lands,* 75–96; on verses 36–38, W. M. Taylor: *The Limitations of Life,* 375–399; and verses 4 and 44, F. B. Meyer: *Five "Musts" of the Christian Life.*

AUDIO-VISUAL AIDS.

FILM: "The Woman of Samaria" (Bible Story Pictures), American Bible Society, 15 min., sd., b&w. Follows closely the story in John 4:1–42. Narrated. Jesus' face not seen. Acting slow in places, but useful to show certain details of the story.

FILM: "Woman at the Well" (Living Bible series), Family Films, 13 min., sd., b&w (also available in color). The colored version is brilliant. Jesus is seen in full countenance. There is good depiction of the rulers.

FILMSTRIP: "The Woman of Samaria," Concordia #C–23, 28 fr., col. Includes map of journey. Title captions.

SLIDE SET: "The Life of Christ Visualized." Move 10 (The Bible Visualized), Visser-slides #91, 94, 95, 97, 99, 5 sl., col.

In beginning this lesson, one should, first of all, turn to a map of Palestine showing the divisions of the land during the time of Jesus, where he will discover that this country of Samaria lies between Judea in the south, with its great capital of Jerusalem, and Galilee in the north, where Jesus spent most of His life while on earth. Samaria extended from the Mediterranean Sea to the Jordan River. The Jews occupied Judea, and, along with many Gentiles, thousands of Jewish families lived in Galilee; whereas, no Jews lived in Samaria, for there were centuries of bitterness between them and the Samaritans. The Jew considered himself defiled by going into Samaria; in fact, it could have been a very dangerous journey. The city of Samaria, now called Shechem, was the capital of the Northern Kingdom (1 Kings 16:23, 24) and was once a mighty, rich, and proud city. When the city was destroyed in 721 B.C. and most of the inhabitants were taken in captivity to Babylon, their captors brought into the land a mongrel group, who settled there and inter-married with the Jews, as recorded in 2 Kings 17:24–33. The result of this was not strange to say, that the remaining Israelites became idolators, but

JOHN 4:5. So he cometh to a city of Samaria, called Sychar, near to the parcel of ground that Jacob gave to his son Joseph.

6. And Jacob's well was there. Jesus therefore, being wearied with his journey, sat thus by the well. It was about the sixth hour.

7. There cometh a woman of Samaria to draw water: Jesus saith unto her, Give me to drink.

8. For his disciples were gone away into the city to buy food.

9. The Samaritan woman therefore saith unto him, How is it that thou, being a Jew, askest drink of me, who am a Samaritan woman? (For Jews have no dealings with Samaritans.)

---

rather, there developed here the nucleus of a new race, the Samaritans, who took the Pentateuch for the basis of their religion, who believed that Abraham had offered his son Isaac on their Mount Gerizim, and that actually they were the true worshippers of Jehovah. It is interesting to note that there is a small remnant of the Samaritan race still in existence, living in Shechem, numbering about a hundred and fifty. They still despise the Jews, and the Jews despise them. In Matthew and Mark, we have very little regarding Christ and the Samaritans, but in Luke's Gospel there are a number of references to these people, and here in John's account is this record of Christ's conversation with the Samaritan woman, unique in the four Gospels. What happens here on this day is a token of the universality of the Christian religion, which will be established by the life, death, and resurrection of the Person who is now to talk with this Samaritan woman.

I. JESUS' CONVERSATION WITH THE SAMARITAN WOMAN, John 4:1–27. We read here that Jesus "must needs pass through Samaria," and we ask, What does this *must* mean? Our Lord was on the way to Galilee from Judea. He could have crossed the Jordan and proceeded to Galilee by that longer route. The *must* here no doubt refers to the event now to take place, wholly unknown to everyone else but the Lord Jesus. 5. So he cometh to a city of Samaria, called Sychar, near to the parcel of ground that Jacob gave to his son Joseph. 6. And Jacob's well was there. Jesus therefore, being wearied with his journey, sat thus by the well. It was about the sixth hour. Sychar is no doubt the modern Askar. Jacob's well is one of the truly identified sites of the Gospels, lying in the mouth of the valley separating Mount Ebal from Mount Gerizim, one and one-half miles east of Shechem and about 1100 yards from the traditional site of Jacob's tomb. The well has been visited for centuries, and the water is appreciated by all who come to this spot weary with travel. There is no reference to this well of Jacob in the Old Testament. A similar scene is found in the life of Moses (Ex. 2:15). 7. There cometh a woman of Samaria to draw water: Jesus saith unto her, Give me to drink. 8. For his disciples were gone away into the city to buy food. 9. The Samaritan woman therefore saith unto him, How is it that thou, being a Jew, askest drink of me, who am a Samaritan woman? (For Jews have no dealings with Samaritans.) The woman's surprise in having Jesus make this request is based upon the bitter hatred existing for at least four centuries between Jews and Samaritans. "An Arab writer says, 'The Sheikhs of Nablus and its neighborhood are robbers; their women pretty, but proud; the peasants insolent and quarrelsome.' This witness is true of Nablus and Sebustieh, as travellers often experience even at the present day. It seems always to have been thus, from the time when Simeon and Levi with 'instruments of cruelty' massacred the inhabitants of Shechem, down to the current hour." — *Dr. William Thomson.*

Up to this moment the conversation, somewhat brief, though probably more extended than the writer has felt it necessary to record, is wholly on what we might call an earthly level — concerning drink, thirst, the Jews and the Samaritans. Suddenly Jesus lifts it onto a high spiritual plane, telling the woman that if she only knew what the gift of God was, and if she knew with whom she was talking, and who was asking her for a drink, she would have asked Him for what He could bestow, and He would have given her living water.   The conversation continues and Jesus gradually unfolds to her the meaning of His words — that the water He would bestow would remain to the recipient a well of water springing up unto everlasting life, different from that which Jacob had drawn from the well and his descendants after him.   "We have a magnificent symbolism of this, the life-giving power of these waters, in Ezekiel 47:9 — 'Every thing shall live whither the river cometh'; that is, the river issuing from under the threshold of the House of God (v. 1; compare Rev. 22:1; Joel 3:18; Zech. 14:8). . . . He is Himself the true fountain of Jacob (Deut. 33:28); this name He implicitly challenges as His own. There is only One, who can be what Christ here declares that He is, namely, 'a fountain of living waters' (see Jer. 2:13; 17:13), and that is God.   On the strength of this saying Augustine rightly claims Psalm 36:9, 'With thee is the fountain of life' as fulfilled in Christ, and brings that passage into closest connection with this." — *R. C. Trench.*

The woman do doubt was not fully apprehending what Christ was saying here, just as many Christians today have not fully apprehended these wonderful words of our Lord, but she knows that she is hearing something more gratifying, more vital, more satisfying than anything she has known in her life, so naturally she asks the one with whom she is talking for this water, that she might thirst no longer. As the conversation suddenly rose from the earth into great spiritual heights, it now with equal suddenness descends to earth again.   She has asked for this gift, and may have it freely by grace, but not until something has taken place in her life, for this gift has to do with divine life, with holy living, and there is the sin problem to be dealt with before the gift can be received.   Knowing this, Jesus said to her, "Go, call thy husband, and come hither."   This is the last subject this woman wanted to discuss, for she had been married five times, frequently divorced, and was now living with one who was not her husband, which was as contrary to Samaritan law as it was to the law of the Old Testament.   She knew she was living in sin, and no doubt in that Samaritan village she was a despised, and ill-treated woman.   " 'Go, call thy husband!'   What a train of memory that word evoked! Beneath its spell, she was back long years; again an innocent girl, courted by him in the sunny vineyards of Gerizim; going with him to his home as his loving wife. Then perhaps there came a growing coldness, leading to alienation and dislike, ending in infidelity.   That husband might have died of a broken heart.   She had tried to banish his memory and his face, though they would haunt her. . . .   But why awake such memories?   Why open the cupboard-door and bid that skeleton step down?   Why unsod that grave?   Why lay bare that life-secret?   It could not be otherwise.   The wound must be probed to the bottom and cleansed, ere it could be healed.   There must be confession before forgiveness.   The sin had to be called to remembrance, ere the son could be raised from death by the prophet's hand.   This woman must judge her past sins in the light of those pure eyes, ere she could know the bliss of the fountain opened within the soul. . . .   Go, call thy husband; pay back those dishonest gains; make up that long-standing feud; recall those violent, uncharitable words; summon husband, wife, child, that bright-eyed boy whom you misled, that pure fame you tarnished, that nature, like virgin snow, which you trampled under foot. . . .   Nothing that has ever occurred in our lives has escaped the keen notice of Christ, or been forgotten by Him; and here or hereafter we must hear every detail told with circumstantial clearness by his lips.   But it is a thousand times better to hear it now, when the dread recital may be followed by the loving announcement: 'Thy sins, which were many, are all forgiven thee.'   How we wince when our Lord comes into such close quarters with us! — as the blood-shot eye dreads the light, or the broken limb evades the touch, or the bankrupt hides his ledgers.   Like this woman, we start some old worn-out theological controversy, to put Him off the scent.   There are plenty of people who spend their lives in theological disputes and refinements, because in this way they dexterously

25. The woman saith unto him, I know that Messiah cometh (he that is called Christ): when he is come, he will declare unto us all things.

26. Jesus saith unto her, I that speak unto thee am *he*.

27. And upon this came his disciples; and they marvelled that he was speaking with a woman; yet no man said, What seakest thou? or, Why speakest thou with her?

---

manage to pass muster as religious people; though, all the while, they dread anything like definite appeals to their hearts." — *F. B. Meyer*.

Seeking to avoid further discussion of the matter, the woman simply told the Lord that she had no husband, upon which Jesus so plainly unfolded to her her own past life that she was compelled to exclaim, "I perceive that thou art a prophet." But even yet, she is going to try to escape this embarrassment by talking about religious matters. She does not want to go on discussing her husband, her illicit relationships, or anything else of her private life, with this man, so she introduces the subject of worship of God on the part of the Samaritans, and of the Jews in Jerusalem. Jesus is willing to discuss this, so He continues the conversation along this line, and in so doing, He gives to this woman, a Samaritan, despised, living in known sin, the greatest single statement regarding God that ever passed His holy lips. . . . "Confronted by Jesus, the woman is met by the end and fulfilment of prophecy, that is to say, by the operation of the Spirit of God, and also by the consequent corresponding possibility of the advent of the true and spiritual worship of the Father, which is the fulfilment of both Jewish and Samaritan worship, and which is, in fact, the worship awaited by the Father. There can now be men, real men of flesh and blood, who brought to the truth, must worship God in spirit." — *Dr. Hoskyns*. "God is a Spirit, and they that worship Him must worship in spirit and truth." By this word Jesus admits the woman to the very citadel of the faith. It was more important for her to know whom to worship than where: it would bring her to feel more acutely that whether Jew or Samaritan were right, she was all wrong. The conception of God as Father is the last and greatest revelation. . . . What she needed was a Messiah to save her from sin. And Jesus, with a clearness and directness unparalleled, perhaps because in the woman's mind the idea of the Christ was not mingled and confused with political hopes, disclosed Himself to her (compare 9:37). And here the interview broke off. Who else but the Christ could He be who had presented Himself to her as giver of living waters to quench the thirst of the soul; who had caused her to feel how intense that thirst was, and how vainly she had tried to quench it from troubled springs; who had roused her to a sense of her need and sin, and then had disclosed the fatherly heart of God yearning over this prodigal daughter, and going out in purposes of mercy and love to her? None but Christ can read off to us our inmost heart and life, and then lest we be broken, read off to us the heart of God the Father desiring us, notwithstanding all our sin." — *George Reith*.

25. The woman saith unto him, I know that Messiah cometh (he that is called Christ): when he is come, he will declare unto us all things. 26. Jesus saith unto her, I that speak unto thee am *he*. 27. And upon this came his disciples; and they marvelled that he was speaking with a woman; yet no man said, What seakest thou? or, Why speakest thou with her? Marcus Dods has some fine words here on the need for simplicity in worship. "No doubt that worship may be real and acceptable which is offered in the silence and solitude of a man's spirit; but we naturally utter what we feel, and by the utterance strengthen the feelings that are good, and rid ourselves of the bitterness and strain of those that are painful and full of sorrow. Besides, the Church is, before all else, a society. Our religion is meant to bring us together, and though it does so more effectually by inspiring us with kindliness and helpfulness in life than by a formal meeting together for no purposes of active charity, yet the one fellowship aids the other, as many of us well

28. So the woman left her waterpot, and went away into the city, and saith to the people,

29. Come, see a man, who told me all things that *ever* I did: can this be the Christ?

30. They went out of the city, and were coming to him.

31. In the mean while the disciples prayed him, saying, Rabbi, eat.

32. But he said unto them, I have meat to eat that ye know not.

33. The disciples therefore said one to another, Hath any man brought him *aught* to eat?

34. Jesus saith unto them, My meat is to do the will of him that sent me, and to accomplish his work.

35. Say not ye, There are yet four months, and *then* cometh the harvest? behold, I say unto you, Lift up your eyes, and look on the fields, that they are white already unto harvest.

36. He that reapeth receiveth wages, and gathereth fruit unto life eternal; that he that soweth and he that reapeth may rejoice together.

37. For herein is the saying true, One soweth, and another reapeth.

---

know. . . . But if the words of Christ were not intended to put an end to outward worship altogether, they do, as I have said, form a strong argument for simplicity of worship. No forms whatever are needed that our spirit may come into communion with God. Let us begin with this. As true and perfect worship may be rendered by the dying man, who cannot lift an eyelid or open his lips, as by the most ornate service that combines perfect liturgical forms with the richest music man has ever written. Rich music, striking combinations of colour and of architectural forms, are nothing to God so far as worship goes, except in so far as they bring the human spirit into fellowship with Him. Persons are differently constituted, and what is natural to one will be formal and artificial to another." — *Marcus Dods.*

II. THE REVIVAL IN SYCHAR, John 4:28–42. From the text, it would seem that our Lord never did get the drink of water that He so greatly needed, nor did the woman get the pitcher of water for which she had come to the well. This conversation of less than one-half hour had made something far more imperative for her. She rushed back to the city to report what had happened. **28. So the woman left her waterpot, and went away into the city, and saith to the people, 29. Come, see a man, who told me all things that *ever* I did: can this be the Christ? 30. They went out of the city, and were coming to him.** Strange indeed were these words from this previously despised woman. She was the last person from whom the proud Samaritans ever expected to hear anything on a religious subject, but no doubt her facial expression, and the contrast between what she was saying and what they had heard from her in preceding years persuaded them that she had been talking to some remarkable person at the well, so they went out to see who it was.

With the conversation of Jesus with His disciples, wonderful as the words are, we need not tarry here, but should devote all of our time, it seems to me, to the one main theme of this chapter. **31. In the mean while the disciples prayed him, saying, Rabbi, eat. 32. But he said unto them, I have meat to eat that ye know not. 33. The disciples therefore said one to another, Hath any man brought him *aught* to eat? 34. Jesus saith unto them, My meat is to do the will of him that sent me, and to accomplish his work. 35. Say not ye, There are yet four months, and *then* cometh the harvest? behold, I say unto you, Lift up your eyes, and look on the fields, that they are white already unto harvest. 36. He that reapeth receiveth wages, and gathereth fruit unto life eternal; that he that soweth and he that reapeth may rejoice together. 37. For herein is the saying true, One**

35

38. I sent you to reap that whereon ye have not labored: others have labored, and ye are entered into their labor.

39. And from that city many of the Samaritans believed on him because of the word of the woman, who testified, He told me all things that *ever* I did.

40. So when the Samaritans came unto him, they besought him to abide with them: and he abode there two days.

41. And many more believed because of his word;

42. and they said to the woman, Now we believe, not because of thy speaking: for we have heard for ourselves, and know that this is indeed the Saviour of the world.

---

soweth, and another reapeth. **38. I sent you to reap that whereon ye have not labored: others have labored, and ye are entered into their labor.** These words are probably at the foundation of a similar statement by the Apostle Paul in 1 Corinthians 9:7–10. Jesus himself is sowing and reaping, and exhorts His disciples to immediately become engaged in the same glorious spiritual labor. Lenski has a great passage here. "In the supreme sense Jesus is *the* Sower, for there is no reaping except from his sowing; in fact, before Jesus came, they who reaped did so on the strength of the sowing he was to do. Jesus did some reaping. He had gathered the disciples and other believers, and would gather in these Samaritans. But chiefly Jesus did sowing; he did not leave a field reaped bare to his disciples, but a field thoroughly seeded, fast maturing unto harvest. When we compare the 500 brethren who gathered in Galilee to meet Jesus by appointment after his resurrection, with the 3000, the 5000, and the ever increasing multitude of believers in the next few years, we see indeed that Jesus was the Sower, the disciples the reapers. Yet, looking at the work of those who preceded and who followed Jesus, we see one set of men always enters into the labors of another set. The apostles reaped, but they also sowed, from which their pupils reaped again, and so on down the ages. So we today have entered into other men's labors. Recount their long line, their blessed names, their great exertions! But let the reaper ever be humble, and remember the Sower and the sowers, and not attribute the success to himself. On the other hand, if called to sow, complain not; this hard work is just as necessary, just as blessed as the reaping. Both sower and reaper shall rejoice together. When the sheaves are brought in at last, when the reapers raise the great song of praise, the sowers who began the work that proved so successful shall lead the procession, and so even they shall enter into other men's labor, even that of the reapers who harvested what these reapers sowed. But of them all we shall see not one who does not altogether enter into the labor of Christ." — *R. C. H. Lenski.*

We now return to the closing events of this marvelous interview of Jesus with the Samaritan woman. **39. And from that city many of the Samaritans believed on him because of the word of the woman, who testified, He told me all things that *ever* I did.** I cannot read this without thinking of another verse found in the high-priestly prayer of our Lord recorded in this same Gospel (17:20), "Neither pray I for these alone, but for them also who shall believe on me through their word." Christ here refers to His followers and disciples, but a whole year will pass after the conversation with the woman of Samaria before He calls his disciples. May it not be then that this Samaritan woman was the means of more people receiving Christ as the Messiah and Saviour than any other one person in the entire first year of our Lord's ministry? **40. So when the Samaritans came unto him, they besought him to abide with them: and he abode there two days. 41. And many more believed because of his word; 42. and they said to the woman, Now we believe, not because of thy speaking: for we have heard for ourselves, and know that this is indeed the Saviour of the world.** What a contrast we have here between the Samaritan woman's initial statement, that the Jews have no dealings with the Samaritans, and the condition that was soon prevailing, wherein the Samaritans pled with Christ to stay with them, as a result of which many more believed because of Christ's own teaching.   No doubt the woman now retires from the forefront and Christ himself so teaches that they immediately become convinced He is the Saviour of the world.   "Jesus stands before us today in person in his Word, and we can hear him directly and personally in that Word, as if we had sat among the listeners at Sychar.   We can do this every day; they had him only two days.   They had to hold what he said in their memories; we can examine the inspired written Word as it is fixed for all time.   And thus these believers confess: 'we know.'   Their faith is explicit, not ignorance, the great mark of unbelief, but sound, genuine knowledge, the knowledge that one attains by himself drinking the living water, eating the bread of life, actually being reborn of the Spirit. Argument, science, philosophical reasoning cannot affect such faith; the true believer simply smiles and says, 'I know.'   Only contact with Jesus can work this knowledge of faith (Acts 4:13, 14).   All false faith merely imitates this knowledge of true faith, it thinks it knows and yet does not know (9:24; compare with 9:31–33)." — R. C. H. Lenski.

Dr. F. B. Meyer has a very fine analysis of the contrasts that we find in this chapter: "He is weary; yet he proposes to give rest from heavy burdens and wearisome pilgrimages (v. 15).   He asks for a drink of water; yet He offers to set flowing wells and fountains of water (v. 10).   He is a suppliant for the gifts of another; yet He talks of being able to give with unlimited munificence (v. 14).   He is an obscure stranger; yet He is greater than the venerable patriarch whose name had lingered for long centuries round that spot (v. 12).   He hungers; yet He eats of meat of which no one knows, and finds sustenance in the act of doing the will of his Father (v. 34).   He is surrounded by the signs of sowing time; yet He proclaims that He is amid the joys of harvest (v. 35).   But chief among these contrasts is the one drawn by Himself between the cool, deep, dark depths of Jacob's well, about a hundred and fifty feet below, and the springs or fountains which He was prepared to open up in the heart of this woman, and of whomsoever else He could induce to accept them." — Dr. F. B. Meyer.

THE LESSON IN LIFE, LITERATURE, AND ARCHAEOLOGY.

At the age of thirty-nine, the consecrated missionary, J. Hudson Taylor, founder of the China Inland Mission, lost his beloved wife and companion.   The following days of loneliness he later recalled in these words: "How lonesome were the weary hours when confined to my room.   How I missed my dear wife and the little pattering footsteps of the children far away in England!   Then it was I understood why the Lord had made that passage so real to me, 'Whosoever drinketh of the water that I shall give him *shall never* thirst.'   Twenty times a day, perhaps, as I felt the heart-thirst coming back, I cried to him: 'Lord, you promised! You promised me that I should never thirst.'   And whether I called by day or night, how quickly He always came and satisfied my sorrowing heart!   So much so that I often wondered whether it were possible that my loved one who had been taken could be enjoying more of His presence than I was in my lonely chamber." — J. Hudson Taylor.

A TRUTH FOR THE CLASS TO CARRY AWAY.

Inasmuch as this lesson, for the most part, is but a record of a conversation between Christ and a single individual who at this time was about as bereft of spiritual knowledge and desire as anyone could be, it seems that we have here an excellent illustration of what the Apostle Paul means by the obligation of Christians to edify one another by our very words (Eph. 4:29).   So much of our conversation today is of a trivial, superficial nature.   If our tongues were wholly yielded to God, surely more people with whom we come in contact would be the richer

37

spiritually; and thus we can fulfil Paul's other word, that though we be poor, we make others rich (2 Cor. 6:10).

Do you think that the same results would have occurred if the meeting of Christ and the Samaritan woman had taken place three years before this? What does this lesson teach us about the capacity for the highest spiritual truth in the heart of any member of the human race? What is there about the sincere worship of God that demands the putting away of known sins? How many different tributes are paid to Christ in this lesson? How do you account for what seems the almost total inactivity of the disciples in this great hour?

LESSON V. — January 31.

DOING THE WORKS OF GOD. — John 4:43—5:47. (Temperance)

PRINTED TEXT, John 4:46b–54; 5:2–18.

Devotional Reading: Romans 12:1–13.
Beginner Topic: THE LOST SHEEP.
    Lesson Material: Luke 15:1–7; Matthew 18:12–14.
    Memory Verse: Praise ye Jehovah, for Jehovah is good. Psalm 135:3.
Primary Topic: JESUS HELPS A SICK BOY.
    Lesson Material: John 4:46–53.
    Memory Verse: Jesus of Nazareth . . . went about doing good. Acts 10:38.
Junior Topic: Jesus Helps a Worried Father.
    Lesson Material: John 4:46–53.
    Memory Verse: Jesus of Nazareth . . . went about doing good for God was with him. Acts 10:38.
Intermediate-Senior Topic: JESUS HELPED THE NEGLECTED.
    Lesson Material: John 4:43—5:47.
    Memory Verse: I came that they may have life, and may have *it* abundantly. John 10:10.
Topic for Young People and Adults: FAITH THAT MAKES WHOLE.
    Lesson Material: John 4:43—5:47.
    Memory Verse: I came that they may have life, and may have *it* abundantly. John 10:10.

THE TEACHER AND HIS CLASS.

The Younger Classes might be asked a question, as the teacher begins this lesson, the answer to which could be put on the blackboard: Who do you think is the most important individual of the following group: the man in the circus who swallows a sword, the outstanding orator of a nation, the man who knows the secrets of the atom, the one who can sing most effectively in grand opera, or, one who could bring healing to diseased, suffering mankind? All but the last person mentioned here could not in themselves bring peace and joy to men, for what they do we might call external, superficial. When Jesus came, He healed men, and women, and children, and also taught them about God and the forgiveness of sins. All of this is in our lesson today.

The Older Classes should again be reminded, at the beginning of this lesson, that even now, nineteen hundred years after Jesus has come and gone, His life on this earth is the most discussed, the most thoroughly studied, and the most influential life of all the great characters of history. More books appear in our · language concerning Jesus than are written, during the same period, about Plato, Aristotle, Alexander the Great, Caesar, Cicero, Augustine, Thomas Aquinas, Martin Luther, Napoleon Bonaparte, Karl Marx, and George Washington; put together.

Why is this so? Because of what Jesus claimed to be, what the early Church knew He was, and what millions of His followers since have believed Him to be. This one chapter which we are studying today cannot be matched in any literature in the world outside of the Gospel records.

THE LESSON IN ITS SETTING.

Time. — The healing of the nobleman's son occurred in December, A.D. 27, and the healing of the impotent man, in April, A.D. 28.

Place. — The nobleman of our lesson lived in Cana of Galilee, and Jesus was somewhere in Galilee when the interview with this man took place. The pool of Bethesda was in the city of Jerusalem.

THE PLAN OF THE LESSON.

SUBJECT: How Christ, Even at the Beginning of His Ministry, Revealed Himself as the Only Begotten Son of God, the Messiah of Whom All the Prophets Did Speak.

I. CHRIST'S HEALING OF THE NOBLEMAN'S SON — THOUGH ABSENT FROM HIM, John 4:46b–54.

1. The request of the father, vs. 46b–49.
2. The announcement, vs. 50.
3. The immediate restoration, vs. 51–54.

II. THE HEALING OF THE IMPOTENT MAN — CHRIST BEING PRESENT, 5:1–18.

1. His helpless condition, vs. 1–5.
2. His mood of hopelessness, vs. 6, 7.
3. The command of Jesus, v. 8.
4. The instant cure, v. 9.
5. The questions of the Jews, vs. 10–13.
6. The warning, v. 14.
7. The determination to kill Jesus, vs. 15–18.

III. SOME SUBSEQUENT TEACHINGS OF CHRIST, 5:19–47.

1. The intimate relationship between the Father and the Son, vs. 19–27.
2. The resurrection to come, vs. 28, 29.
3. The four-fold witness, vs. 30–47.
   a. John the Baptist, vs. 30–35.
   b. Christ's own miracles, v. 36.
   c. the Father, vs. 37, 38.
   d. the Old Testament Scriptures, vs. 39–47.

THE TEACHER'S LIBRARY.

For this lesson, all the important commentaries on John's Gospel, and the major lives of Christ will be helpful. Here once again we need the great books on Christ's miracles, especially those by Trench, William Taylor, and John Laidlaw. There are interesting articles on the pool of Bethesda in all the larger Bible dictionaries. Chapters on the two major characters appearing in this lesson will be found in G. Campbell Morgan: *The Great Physician.* There is an excellent chapter on the impotent man in *The Son of God Among the Sons of Men,* by Everett F. Harrison, pp. 90–103; and a good study of the nobleman in James Jeffrey: *The Personal Ministry of the Son of Man,* 72–83.

For sermonic material, on the healing of the nobleman's son, see G. Campbell Morgan in the *Westminster Pulpit,* Vol. 3, pp. 49–56; Alexander Maclaren: *Expositions of Holy Scriptures, St. John 1–8,* pp. 235–245; and, a chapter on the impotent man in G. Campbell Morgan, as above, 57–64. On 5:17, I know of nothing better than the sermon in J. S. Howson: *Meditations on the Miracles of Christ,* 2nd series, 105–122.

On the irregular flow of the water in the pool of Bethesda see Edward Robinson: *Biblical Research in Palestine,* Vol. 1, pp. 505–508.

AUDIO-VISUAL AIDS.

FILM: "A Certain Nobleman," Cathedral, 20 min., sd., b&w, guide (also available in silent form, 30 min.). The local sorcerer fails to heal the sick son, whereupon a slave persuades the master to seek Jesus' help. Figure of Jesus not seen. There is an accompanying filmstrip of the same name.

SLIDE SET: "The Nobleman's Son," Church-Craft #18, 5 sl., col.

In our lesson today we find our Lord performing miracles both in Galilee and in Judea. Here are wonderful deeds, and wonderful words — a perfect illustration of a later reference to Christ as one who was mighty in deed and in word. (Acts 7:22) I can think of no better introduction to our study today than the opening paragraph of the chapter mentioned above by my friend and colleague, Dr. Everett F. Harrison. "Of the seven signs which are mentioned in the Fourth Gospel, four took place in Galilee, and three in Judea. Of the former group, only the feeding of the five thousand had a setting of great publicity. There was no displeasure with Jesus over the performance of these miracles, although the discourse on the Bread of Life which followed the multiplying of the loaves and fishes stirred criticism. Yet even here the result was the fading away of the concourse of people

John 4:46b. And there was a certain nobleman, whose son was sick at Capernaum.

47. When he heard that Jesus was come out of Judaea into Galilee, he went unto him, and besought *him* that he would come down, and heal his son; for he was at the point of death.

48. Jesus therefore said unto him, Except ye see signs and wonders, ye will in no wise believe.

---

which had seemed ready to follow Him, even to the point of making Him a king. When we turn to the signs which took place in Judea, however, we note a distinct and growing hostility to Jesus, which is to be explained in part by the fact that this was the center of Judaism, which resented the claims and activity of the Galilean prophet, and in part by the conduct of Jesus Himself, who seemed deliberately to choose the feast times for His signs, when many would be gathered together, and to go about His miracles in a way calculated to offend the rulers of the Jews."

I. CHRIST'S HEALING OF THE NOBLEMAN'S SON — THOUGH ABSENT FROM HIM, John 4:46b–54. We are now about to study the first of the healing miracles of our Lord, and the first occasion on which Jesus was asked to heal anyone. Students will recall that the conversation with Nicodemus in chapter 3 took place in Jerusalem. Immediately after this, Jesus left Judea to depart into Galilee, making it necessary for Him either to go through Samaria, or, as many Jews did, cross the Jordan and enter Galilee from above the lake. Most of the fourth chapter is occupied with the story of Jesus and the Samaritan woman. At the opening of our lesson, Christ has just arrived in Galilee, in the city of Cana where the first miracle had been performed (John 2:1–11). Twenty-five miles away, in Capernaum, where Christ spent more time during his earthly ministry than in any other place, was a nobleman who had a son near death. He had heard of the healing power of Jesus, and immediately sought him to come and lay His hand upon his son. 46b. **And there was a certain nobleman, whose son was sick at Capernaum. 47. When he heard that Jesus was come out of Judaea into Galilee, he went unto him, and besought** *him* **that he would come down, and heal his son; for he was at the point of death.** The Greek word here translated *nobleman* means "either one born of royal blood, or an official in the service of a king or emperor. Here it is probably intended to refer to an officer in the service of Herod Antipas, Tetrarch of Galilee, who is called a king in Mark 6:14 and Matthew 14:9. It is significant likewise in the fact that whereas the rulers in Jerusalem rejected Jesus, the servant of a purely worldly prince believed with his whole house." — *E. C. Hoskyns.* It is revealing to study the different reasons that men and women came to Christ. "It is one of the strange mysteries of divine grace that 'not many noble, not many wise men, are called into the kingdom,' (1 Cor. 1:26) not because God does not love to aid them as well as the poor; but because, possessing in themselves so much to minister to their purely worldly happiness, they are less impressed with their spiritual state, and consequently less inclined to accept the Saviour's offers. What, then, brought this nobleman to Jesus? What brings most men to Jesus? You have the answer in the Saviour's words: 'They that are whole need not the physician, but they who are sick.' " — *James Jeffrey.* 48. **Jesus therefore said unto him, Except ye see signs and wonders, ye will in no wise believe.** " 'You Galileans,' says Jesus, speaking to the courtier, but through him to His countrymen, 'have received Me in so far as miraculous evidence has left you no choice, but your faith is still only of that weaker sort which leans on the crutch of sensible evidences.' These words cannot be fairly construed into a disparagement of miracles on our Lord's part; that He wrought them unwillingly, or that He counted them of no value. The words . . . are intended to correct the unreasonable tendency of the human heart to demand a surfeit of external

49. The nobleman saith unto him, Sir, come down ere my child die.

50. Jesus saith unto him, Go thy way; thy son liveth. The man believed the word that Jesus spake unto him, and he went his way.

51. And as he was now going down, his servants met him, saying, that his son lived.

52. So he inquired of them the hour when he began to amend. They said therefore unto him, Yesterday at the seventh hour, the fever left him.

53. So the father knew that *it was* at that hour in which Jesus said unto him, Thy son liveth: and himself believed, and his whole house.

54. This is again the second sign that Jesus did, having come out of Judaea into Galilee.

---

witness, to require a king and an amount of evidence for Divine facts that are inconsistent with the Divine methods and detrimental to the spiritual nature. When men have had sufficient evidence to accredit Divine communications, and still refuse to accept these, they violate a law of spiritual knowledge. When they demand additional, reiterated and superfluous evidence, they are showing themselves not wise and cautious, but bigoted and unbelieving." — *John Laidlaw.* 49. **The nobleman saith unto him, Sir, come down ere my child die.** 50. **Jesus saith unto him, Go thy way; thy son liveth. The man believed the word that Jesus spake unto him, and he went his way.** "In a moment he obeyed. In his soul is the birth of confidence. Faith has not come to its full fruition. He has not yet become a disciple of Jesus, is not by any means prepared to stand by the side of Christ as one of His followers; but there is born in his heart a confidence, created by the presence, the personality, the power of Christ. . . . He took Him at His word and went. Not yet intelligent, triumphant faith, compelling him to hand himself over to the Lordship of Christ: but a venture made, and a risk taken, upon a new basis. He came speculatively, out of love for his boy. He goes, hoping, with confidence in his heart. The fact that it was not an action born of an intelligent faith is evidenced by his inquiring of his servants." — *G. Campbell Morgan.* 51. **And as he was now going down, his servants met him, saying, that his son lived.** 52. **So he inquired of them the hour when he began to amend. They said therefore unto him, Yesterday at the seventh hour, the fever left him.** The time element here is exceedingly interesting, and the words of the late Professor Laidlaw are illuminating. "The Jewish day, by which St. John reckons, ended at sunset. No doubt the courtier took his departure as soon as possible when his prayer was answered. The messengers were not despatched from Capernaum till perhaps some hours after the sudden cessation of the fever in the patient, i.e., till it had become clear that he was cured. So the meeting described took place probably not far from Capernaum, and not long after sunset, when the words used would be appropriate enough. When the cortege was met, the father eagerly asked when the son began to amend. They answered that it was not mere amendment, but instantaneous health; and this, in case of fever, proved the preternatural element. The fever had left him suddenly and entirely at the seventh hour on the previous day, that is, at the very hour when Jesus spoke the healing word. Thus was the faith which accepted a word without a sign confirmed by a sign unasked and unexpected." 53. **So the father knew that** *it was* **at that hour in which Jesus said unto him, Thy son liveth: and himself believed, and his whole house.** 54. **This is again the second sign that Jesus did, having come out of Judaea into Galilee.** What a world of difference one decision, or a single event, can make in our lives! The nobleman, at least forty years of age at this time, had lived two-score years without knowing Christ. The illness of his son, and the stories he had heard about Jesus, led him to the decision to give Christ the opportunity to heal the boy. What

JOHN 5:2. Now there is in Jerusalem by the sheep *gate* a pool, which is called in Hebrew Bethesda, having five porches.

3. In these lay a multitude of them that were sick, blind, halt, withered.

5. And a certain man was there, who had been thirty and eight years in his infirmity.

6. When Jesus saw him lying, and knew that he had been now a long time *in that case*, he saith unto him, Wouldest thou be made whole?

---

if he had not started out from his home in Capernaum? What if skeptics had prevailed upon him not to undertake such a journey? What if he had not believed Jesus' assertion concerning his son? "The boy believed, the mother believed, and the rest of the household believed. There you have the story of the turning to Christ of the first entire family. It began almost hopelessly. A nobleman, a king's man, acquainted with the purple, related to the household of Herod Antipas, expecting men to do obeisance to him and do his wishes, in agony about his boy, going, and making a desperate venture, doing a most unusual thing. How does it end? This man has found another King, and has become a King's man in a new sense, and he surrenders and takes his household with him." — *G. Campbell Morgan.* How many millions in the world today have heard about Christ, have read the Gospels, have heard sermons about Him in church, on the radio, have read books about Him, and yet have not believed and received Him as Saviour.

II. **THE HEALING OF THE IMPOTENT MAN — CHRIST BEING PRESENT, 5:1–18.** Christ now returns to Jerusalem, upon the occasion of some great feast in the Jewish calendar. This introduces us to the fourth and major division of the Gospel, extending to the close of chapter 12, immediately followed by the long, detailed account of the events of Thursday and Friday of Holy Week. Contrary to his usual custom, John does not specify what feast this was. Milligan is probably right in saying that, "The indefiniteness of the language here is designed to prevent our resting on the thought of this particular festival as fulfilled in Jesus, and to lead to the concentration of our attention on the Sabbath shortly to be mentioned, which in this chapter has an importance altogether exceptional."

Everywhere that Jesus went, he found sorrow, suffering, hunger, ignorance, prejudice, and too often, death. In the miracle we have just studied, the nobleman comes to Christ; in the account of this miracle, Christ comes to the afflicted one. 2. **Now there is in Jerusalem by the sheep *gate* a pool, which is called in Hebrew Bethesda, having five porches. 3. In these lay a multitude of them that were sick, blind, halt, withered.** The location of this pool has been a subject of wide disagreement, but probably it is the one near the sheep's gate and tower of Antonia, discovered in 1888, near St. Anne's Church, having a five-arch portico. The name means "house of kindness." Those who have both the Authorized and the Revised text before them will note that all of verse 4 is omitted in the latter version. Further reference to this will be made in the "Life and Literature" section of our lesson. 5. **And a certain man was there, who had been thirty and eight years in his infirmity.** "These 'thirty and eight years' answering so exactly to the thirty-eight years of Israel's punishment in the wilderness, have not unnaturally led many, old and new, to find in this man a type of Israel after the flesh." — *R. C. Trench.* "We see Him deliberately picking out a notoriously hard case, perhaps the worst in that whole motley collection of distorted humanity. He did not wait to be spoken to, but took the initiative, asking the man if he wished to be made well." — *E. F. Harrison.* 6. **When Jesus saw him lying, and knew that he had been now a long time *in that case*, he saith unto him, Wouldest thou be made whole?** On the surface, this question seems superfluous. One would naturally think that the man wanted to be made whole, that it was the one thing in life he did want, that for which he had been hoping these thirty-eight years.

42

7. The sick man answered him, Sir, I have no man, when the water is troubled, to put me into the pool: but while I am coming, another steppeth down before me.

8. Jesus saith unto him, Arise, take up thy bed, and walk.

9. And straightway the man was made whole, and took up his bed and walked. Now it was the sabbath on that day.

10. So the Jews said unto him that was cured, It is the sabbath, and it is not lawful for thee to take up thy bed.

And yet, possibly not. Maybe he had been accustomed to being waited on so long, to being free from the burden of supporting a family, that he now preferred this life — we have all seen such cases. Then, he might have been utterly discouraged. Even though he wanted to be made whole, what was the object of talking about it? Having failed to find a cure in thirty-eight years, he has lost hope of ever being well again. No doubt our Lord's question held more meaning than mere physical healing, as we shall soon learn. **7. The sick man answered him, I have no man, when the water is troubled, to put me into the pool: but while I am coming, another steppeth down before me.** On the troubling of the water, we shall have more to say at the conclusion of the lesson. "The very extremity of his need rendered unavailing his repeated efforts to be the first to reach the waters when the mysterious troubling had taken place." **8. Jesus saith unto him, Arise, take up thy bed, and walk. 9. And straightway the man was made whole, and took up his bed and walked.** "With this word of authority there went, no doubt, to complete the impression, the tones of the Speaker and the look — that undescribed and probably indescribable thing, which must have oft shown through the fleshly veil to those who were privileged to behold the Word made flesh. The man felt that this Unknown One was no ordinary being. What would have been mockery from common lips he received as truth and life from those which now opened to bid him rise, and walk. He asked no question. He started no difficulties. He obeyed as his Deliverer bade him, and he was healed in the act of obeying. He took up the little pallet — by this time in all likelihood a wretched mass of rags — on which he had lain so long. In his joy he would most likely have left it there, had not his Healer expressly bidden him bear it. For what purposes is clear. . . . In the helpless sufferer we note openness, trust, and implicit obedience. He rose at a word, when mere nature and sense felt every physical impossibility. He went at a word, when there was almost equal difficulty in the social and religious sphere." — *John Laidlaw.*

The late Professor Laidlaw divides this narrative of the healing of the impotent man into three parts, geographically: at the pool, on the street, in the temple. On his way home, the miraculously healed man is examined by the Jews. **Now it was the sabbath on that day. 10. So the Jews said unto him that was cured, It is the sabbath, and it is not lawful for thee to take up thy bed.** The words of Trench here — we have not used Trench for some time — are concise and illuminating. "By 'the Jews' we understand here, as constantly in St. John, not the multitude, but the Sanhedrists, the spiritual heads of the nation (1:19; 7:1; 9:22; 18:12, 14; compare v. 3; 20:19). These find fault with the man, for had not Moses said, 'In it thou shalt not do any work' (Ex. 20:10) and still more to the point Jeremiah, 'Take heed to yourselves, and bear no burden on the Sabbath days' (17:21); so that they seemed to have words of Scripture to justify their interference and the offence which they took. But the man's bearing of his bed was not a work by itself; it were merely the corollary, or indeed the concluding act, of his healing, that by which he should make proof himself, and give testimony to others, of its reality. It was lawful to heal on the Sabbath day; it was lawful then to do whatever was immediately involved in, and directly followed on, the healing." — *Richard C.*

11. But he answered them, He that made me whole, the same said unto me, Take up thy bed, and walk.

12. They asked him, Who is the man that said unto thee, Take up *thy bed*, and walk?

13. But he that was healed knew not who it was; for Jesus had conveyed himself away, a multitude being in the place.

14. Afterward Jesus findeth him in the temple, and said unto him, Behold, thou art made whole: sin no more, lest a worse thing befall thee.

15. The man went away, and told the Jews that it was Jesus who had made him whole.

Trench. **11. But he answered them, He that made me whole, the same said unto me, Take up thy bed, and walk. 12. They asked him, Who is the man that said unto thee, Take up *thy bed*, and walk? 13. But he that was healed knew not who it was; for Jesus had conveyed himself away, a multitude being in the place.** The very words of the Jews to this restored man are a revelation of the hardness of their own hearts. They have no word of congratulation for the healed man; they do not rejoice with him in his glorious restoration; they do not begin to discuss the possibilities that the one who healed him was Jesus, the Messiah of God. The great issues involved in this miracle are wholly ignored. "Note the malignity and bitterness of their question. It is not, 'Who is He that cured thee?' 'Let us know who is this wonderful and merciful Healer, that we may go with thee to adore Him'; but, 'Who is He that bade thee carry thy bed on the Sabbath?' A more appalling example of the blinding effects of self-righteousness could not well be imagined. . . . They can see no good in One who held different views and followed a different practice. He must be a sinner. He has broken the Sabbath, and no miracle of healing which He may have wrought must weigh for a moment against this judgment." — *John Laidlaw.*

We come now to the third geographical area, the temple. **14. Afterward Jesus findeth him in the temple, and said unto him, Behold, thou art made whole: sin no more, lest a worse thing befall thee.** Ah, here we are face to face with a new word in these healing miracles, something deeper and more deadly than disease, paralysis, leprosy — sin. Though a man may enjoy robust health he is still plagued with this evil thing. "Man's present life is full of the pains and penalties of sin; but these, plainly, in Christ's view, do not exhaust sin's awful and prolific harvest. The righteousness of the principle on which they happen at all in this world prepares for 'eternal sin' an eternal judgment. Besides the general truth of the connection between sin and suffering here vindicated, we have in all likelihood something more special. The case here dealt with by Jesus was one in which disease and sin were mixed up together; where what began as sin remains as disease, and that which is now disease continues to breed sin. . . . Christ shows at once the utmost tenderness for the sufferer and the sternest faithfulness towards the sinner. He lays down also the profound and ever-to-be-remembered law, that the cure in such cases is, at heart, moral and spiritual, not merely physical." **15. The man went away, and told the Jews that it was Jesus who had made him whole.** "It is rather hard to account for the healed man's act of conveying the information to the Jews which they sought, especially if the hostility of the rulers toward Jesus were generally known, as was true later on (9:22). Or did his fear of the rulers more than balance his sense of gratitude to Jesus? Perhaps he entertained hopes that they, too, would seek Jesus in faith and receive a blessing at His hand. The most likely explanation is that he felt a sense of obligation to complete his side of the story before the governing body of his people." — *E. F.*

16. And for this cause the Jews persecuted Jesus, because he did these things on the sabbath.

17. But Jesus answered them, My Father worketh even until now, and I work.

18. For this cause therefore the Jews sought the more to kill him, because he not only brake the sabbath, but also called God his own Father, making himself equal with God.

Harrison. **16. And for this cause the Jews persecuted Jesus, because he did these things on the sabbath.** We find here the seeds of a hatred for Jesus on the part of the Jews which will ultimately lead to their crucifying Him. "Had the Jews been teachable and free from prejudice, had they taken the miracle as the starting point of their reasonings, they would have been prepared to hear the grounds of the claims of Jesus thus to regulate their law." **17. But Jesus answered them, My Father worketh even until now, and I work. 18. For this cause therefore the Jews sought the more to kill him, because he not only brake the sabbath, but also called God his own Father, making himself equal with God.** Canon Howson reminds us that there are three major truths implied in this utterance of Christ: (1) there is an assertion of the Lord's Deity. (2) There is an assertion of His supremacy over Nature, of His upholding all things by His power. By this miracle we see God the Father and God the Son perpetually working. (3) Finally, "if the work of God and of Christ is unceasing, then much dignity belongs to work, and idleness is disgrace and sin."

III. **SOME SUBSEQUENT TEACHINGS OF CHRIST,** 5:19–47. The remainder of this chapter, none of which is assigned to the printed text, forms one of the profoundest passages in all the Gospels, though one seldom studied. An entire book could be written upon these verses alone. There are depths here which I do not intend to fathom in *Peloubet's Notes;* furthermore, no teacher will have time for this if he gives proper consideration to the two miracles. Let me give a suggestive summary of what is here, and then we might turn for a moment to the rich comments of the late Professor Hoskyns in his epochal work on John's Gospel. The passage has three fundamental themes: first, the inter-relationship of the Son and the Father; secondly, the pre-eminence of the Son in His being the source of eternal life for man (vv. 24, 39, 40) and in His alone possessing the power by which the resurrection from the dead will take place (vv. 25, 28, 29); and thirdly, a condemnation of the Jews who were rejecting Him. The first theme might be unfolded as follows: The Son does what the Father does (v. 19); the Son is beloved by the Father (v. 20); the Son bestows life as the Father is the life-giver (vv. 21, 26); all judgment has been given by the Father to the Son (vv. 22, 27, 30); the Son is to be honored as the Father is to be honored (v. 23); the Son has been sent into the world by the Father (vv. 36–38); and the work Christ accomplished on earth was given to Him by the Father. We must limit comment here to that on three clauses. At the end of verse 20 we read, "greater works than these will he show him, that ye may marvel." "The future tense — will show (contrast 3:35) means that the Evangelist is not now speaking of the eternal relation between God and the Logos. He directs the attention of his readers to the historical mission of Jesus. There are greater works than have as yet been recorded, works that involve the final perception of the Son (Rev. 1:1) and constitute Him as the place in history where the final distinction is made between life and judgment. In Jesus the world is confronted by the End." — *E. C. Hoskyns.*

Beginning with verse 37, we have recorded the mutual testimony of the Father and the Old Testament Scriptures. "To the witness of John the Baptist and of the works of Jesus is now added the witness of the Father in the Old Testament Scriptures. . . . The Jews to whom Jesus and His disciples speak have no direct knowledge or vision of God; they neither hear His voice (contrast 14:24) nor see

His form (Deut. 4:12; contrast 1:18; 6:46, 47; 14:9) nor does His word abide in them (contrast 15:7; 1 John 2:14, 24). They do, however, possess the written Scriptures which are the witness of the Father to the Son; and these they persistently misunderstand, for they examine them on the false assumption — the Greek verb translated 'ye think' (v. 39) is used several times elsewhere with this suggestion (v. 45; 11:13, 31; 13:29; 16:2; 20:15; compare Matt. 6:7) — that the written words of Scripture are themselves life-giving." — *E. C. Hoskyns.*

At the conclusion of this chapter, Christ utters a stern note of condemnation for the Jews who are now rejecting Him. "This judgment means that the gulf between Jesus and the Jews is unbridgeable, for the division between them concerns the reality of God. They direct their eyes to God in order that their selfish desires may be strengthened — this is sin; He, in order that every trace of egotism and independent desire may be destroyed — this is righteousness (17:25, 26)." — *E. C. Hoskyns.*

The sentences of this chapter do not only contain beautiful spiritual truths, and reveal the eternal relationship of the Father and the Son, but they carry a message of life and death. We may think what we will of Plato's philosophy, of Caesar's military genius, of the theology of Thomas Aquinas, of the theory of relativity of Einstein, and it will make little difference in this life, and surely no difference in the life to come. But what one does with Christ will determine the eternal destiny of His soul. How we need to ring this out in our preaching and teaching in this day of world crisis.

THE LESSON IN LIFE, LITERATURE, AND ARCHAEOLOGY.

In the discussion of the healing of the impotent man at the pool of Bethesda, I said that at the end of the lesson we would look further at this strange late gloss on the tradition held by the Jews of that day that an angel now and then stirred these waters, at which time they had healing properties. My own opinion is that the passage does not belong in John's own inspired account. It is the only statement in all the New Testament of which I know that can be called mythical. There was, however, a stirring of the waters in this particular pool. Over one hundred years ago, the great pioneer explorer in Palestine, Dr. Edward Robinson, an American Biblical scholar, gave careful attention to this in the first volume of his famous *Biblical Researches in Palestine.* Other writers have also made reference to it. Dr. Robinson himself witnessed the phenomena about which he writes. "As we were preparing to measure the basin of the upper fountain (in the afternoon of April 30) and explore the passage leading from it, my companion was standing on the lower step near the water, with one foot on the step and the other on a loose stone lying in the basin. All at once he perceived the water coming into his shoe; and supposing the stone had rolled, he withdrew his foot to the step; which however was also now covered with water. This instantly excited our curiosity; and we now perceived the water rapidly bubbling up from under the lower step. In less than five minutes it had risen in the basin nearly or quite a foot; and we could hear it gurgling off through the interior passage. In ten minutes more it had ceased to flow; and the water in the basin was again reduced to its former level. Thrusting my staff in under the lower step, whence the water appeared to come, I found that there was here a large hollow space; but a further examination could not be made without removing the steps."

A TRUTH FOR THE CLASS TO CARRY AWAY.

When the Apostle Peter was depicting the Lord Jesus to the Gentile centurion and his household, he remarked that Jesus, anointed with the Holy Spirit and with power, "went about doing good and healing all that were oppressed of the devil." Our lesson today is a perfect illustration of this characterization of Simon Peter. And Christ has continued to do good — saving men, granting them hope, and life, forgiveness and liberty. He asks men today what he asked of the impotent man, "What would ye that I should do for you?" This is the reason we do not have more answers to our prayers — we do not sit down quietly and determine what we need from the Lord. This ministry of Jesus is also carried on by His servants throughout the world, missionaries, especially medical missionaries, Christian teachers — wherever a true servant of Christ goes, there is a good deed performed.

Which of these two miracles would be the more difficult to perform? What differences are there in the attitudes toward Christ of the nobleman, the nobleman's son, the impotent man, and the opposing Jews? Who had the faith in this narrative that brought about these miraculous healings? With all the sick, and impotent, and lame, and blind in Jerusalem on this one day, why do you think that Jesus went down to this particular place where the impotent man was lying?

TEMPERANCE MATERIAL FOR LESSON OF JANUARY 31.

The use of, and expenditure for tobacco and alcoholic beverages in our country is mounting at an alarming rate. In 1951, the total amount of money spent for alcoholic beverages in the United States was $9,150,000,000, as against $2,000,000,000 in 1934. This country in 1951 spent 4.7 times as much money for this as for all religious and welfare activities combined. In that year our nation consumed 83,718,067 barrels of beer, or the equivalent of 17.1 gallons for every man, woman, and child in the United States. In the first six months of 1952, our country manufactured 111,000,000 pounds of tobacco, and for this we spent $2,500,000,000. In 1951, we spent the enormous sum of $4,081,000,000 for cigarettes alone. It is hard to believe that there are 1,300,000 retailers of cigarettes in this country. The Gallup Poll reports that six out of every ten adults in the United States drink beer or other intoxicating beverages either occasionally or frequently.

To these figures should be added one more tragic note. In the State of California alone in 1952, the amount of money passing through pari-mutuel windows at the race tracks was $363,888,458. Of this, $313,000,000 was returned to the betters, but in the State of California in 1952, those betting at the race tracks lost over $50,000,000!

LESSON VI. — February 7.

CHRIST, THE LIVING BREAD. — John 6.

PRINTED TEXT, John 6:3–11, 48–59, 66–69.

Devotional Reading: Galatians 1:15–21.
Beginner Topic: IN A BIG STORM.
 Lesson Material: Matthew 8:18, 23–27; Mark 4:35–41; Luke 8:22–25.
 Memory Verse: The Lord is my helper. Hebrews 13:6.
Primary Topic: A BOY HELPS JESUS.
 Lesson Material: John 6:1–14.
 Memory Verse: Give us this day our daily bread. Matthew 6:11.
Junior Topic: A BOY HELPS JESUS.
 Lesson Material: John 6:1–14.
 Memory Verse: Give us this day our daily bread. Matthew 6:11.
Intermediate-Senior Topic: KEEPING FAITH ALIVE.
 Lesson Material: John 6.
 Memory Verse: I am the bread of life: he that cometh to me shall not
  hunger, and he that believeth on me shall never thirst. John 6:35.
Topic for Young People and Adults: How CHRIST SUSTAINS US.
 Lesson Material: John 6.
 Memory Verse: I am the bread of life: he that cometh to me shall not
  hunger, and he that believeth on me shall never thirst. John 6:35.

THE TEACHER AND HIS CLASS.

The Younger Classes may have this lesson introduced in a very effective but simple way, by having placed before them on the table a portion of a loaf of bread. Let the pupils discuss the origin of this bread — from the flour, back to the wheat growing in the field, and the kernel of wheat that was dropped in the ground. How did the little kernel of wheat planted in the ground ever produce sixty or eighty kernels at the top of the stalk, multiplying itself sixty or eighty times? It drew nourishment out of the soil, chemicals, the very chemicals we need in our bodies to help us grow. When Jesus was on earth, He claimed to be the Bread of Life, by which, of course He meant that which appropriated would give us divine life, spiritual life, eternal life. How this is possible is the main theme of our lesson.

The Older Classes may be introduced to this lesson by an idea which William James, the philosopher, forcefully set forth years ago in his brilliant book, *The Will to Believe.* He pointed out that there are some options in life which are compulsory, and others that can be ignored. An example of the latter can be this: A woman leaving the house in the morning sees an overcast sky, and she has to make a decision whether or not to take an umbrella. She can avoid the decision by remaining at home. A decision that we are forced to make is in regard to food. If we are going to live, we must eat, for there is no other way to maintain life than by eating. Our Lord presents himself in this lesson as the absolute unique source of spiritual life, so that any man who desires this life must receive Christ. He can reject Christ, but thereby he will remain dead in his sins.

THE LESSON IN ITS SETTING.

Time. — April, A.D. 29.

Place. — The feeding of the five thousand took place at Bethsaida, on the Sea of Galilee, and the great discourse on the Bread of Life in the synagogue in Capernaum.

THE PLAN OF THE LESSON.

SUBJECT: Christ's Own Testimony to His Absolute Indispensability for All Who Would Have Eternal Life.

I. THE MIRACLE OF FEEDING THE FIVE THOUSAND, John 6:1–14.
1. Christ's foreknowledge, vs. 1–9.
2. Christ's power, vs. 10, 11.
3. Christ's plan, vs. 12, 13.
4. Christ acknowledged as Prophet, v. 14.

II. THE MIRACLE OF WALKING ON THE WATER, John 6:15–21.

III. CHRIST'S SERMON ON THE BREAD OF LIFE, John 6:22–59.
1. The attending circumstances, vs. 22–25.
2. The true work of God, vs. 26–29.
3. The request for a sign, vs. 30, 31.
4. "I am the bread of life," vs. 32–40.
5. This Bread communicates eternal life, vs. 41–50.
6. This Bread is Christ's flesh, vs. 51–59.

IV. THE TWO GROUPS CONTRASTED, John 6:60–71.
1. Those who departed from Christ, vs. 60–66.
2. Those who confessed Christ, vs. 67–71.

THE TEACHER'S LIBRARY.

All commentaries on John's Gospel of any real value will have helpful material on this lesson. I cannot fail here to emphasize the brilliant though brief chapter on "Christ the Bread of Life," in the volume by Marcus Dods in *The Expositor's Bible.* All books on the miracles of Christ will be found helpful in the study of this lesson.

On Christ the Bread of Life, see G. Campbell Morgan: *Parables and Metaphors of Our Lord,* 289–298; Charles H. Spurgeon: *The Names and Titles of the Lord Jesus Christ,* 555–566; Thomas Marjoribanks: *The Sevenfold I AM,* 85–100; and the article, "Bread," in James Hastings: *Dictionary of Christ and the Gospels.* On the lad who enters into the earlier part of this lesson, see a choice chapter in Joseph Hammond: *The Boys and Girls of the Bible,* Vol. 2, pp. 144–153.

For the exposition of various passages, see Alexander Maclaren: *Expositions of Holy Scripture, St. John 1–8,* pp. 251–279; for verses 5 and 67, G. H. Knight: *The Master's Questions to His Disciples,* 73–79, 185–191; verses 66–68, John Henry Jowett: *God Our Contemporary,* 168–180; verse 68, S. H. Kellogg: *The Past, a Prophecy of the Future,* 95–111; and verse 69, Andrew Murray: *Holy in Christ,* 125–131. The greatest treatment of the theological significance of Christ's teaching here concerning His flesh and blood is in George Smeaton: *The Doctrine of the Atonement as Taught by Christ Himself,* 270–283.

AUDIO-VISUAL AIDS.

FILM: "Basket of Blessing," Evangel Films, 11 min., sd., col.   A lad dreams he was the boy in Christ's day with the loaves and fishes.   Primarily for children.

FILMSTRIP: "Feeding of the Five Thousand," Concordia #25, 37 fr., col.   Background and events of the story.

JOHN 6:3. And Jesus went up into the mountain, and there he sat with his disciples.

4. Now the passover, the feast of the Jews, was at hand.

5. Jesus therefore lifting up his eyes, and seeing that a great multitude cometh unto him, saith unto Philip, Whence are we to buy bread that these may eat?

6. And this he said to prove him: for he himself knew what he would do.

7. Philip answered him, Two hundred shillings' worth of bread is not sufficient for them, that every one may take a little.

8. One of his disciples, Andrew, Simon Peter's brother, saith unto him,

9. There is a lad here, who hath five barley loaves, and two fishes: but what are these among so many?

In studying again this sixth chapter of the Gospel of John, we have before us one of the greatest passages in all the wonderful Word of God.   If we should come upon such a page as this in any other piece of literature in the world, even in the Old Testament, we would be compelled to say that the person who talked like this was beside himself, that he was not only egotistical, but insanely so, for he was claiming honor, titles, and prerogatives that no *mere* human being could ever truthfully claim.   No human being could ever be what Christ claims to be in this chapter — not even Abraham, Moses, Isaiah, or Paul; no Luther, Napoleon, or Einstein.   The person speaking here is not only Jesus the son of Mary, but the eternal Son of God, and what He says about Himself is not true of any other person. This is what lends solemnity to the study of the Scriptures, and gives such deep and eternal significance to any decision man makes concerning Jesus Christ.

I. THE MIRACLE OF THE FEEDING OF THE FIVE THOUSAND, John 6:1–14.   This is the only miracle recorded in the Gospels that is found in all four of these narratives (elsewhere in Matt. 14:13–21; Mark 6:32–44; and Luke 9:10–17).   Though the miracle itself is assigned to the printed text, I believe in this lesson we would do well to give less consideration to this event, which has often come up for study in the International Lessons, and dwell at greater length upon the inexhaustible words of our Lord found at the end of the chapter.   The story is simply told.   For technical matters, we need only to know that two hundred shillings would amount to about thirty dollars, in the early part of our century, and now perhaps fifty dollars.   But fifty dollars worth of food could never feed five thousand people — really, there were more than that, five thousand men, as Matthew tells us, besides women and children (14:21).   3. **And Jesus went up into the mountain, and there he sat with his disciples.   4. Now the passover, the feast of the Jews, was at hand.   5. Jesus therefore lifting up his eyes, and seeing that a great multitude cometh unto him, saith unto Philip, Whence are we to buy bread that these may eat?   6. And this he said to prove him: for he himself knew what he would do.   7. Philip answered him, Two hundred shillings' worth of bread is not sufficient for them, that every one may take a little.   8. One of his disciples, Andrew, Simon Peter's brother, saith unto him, 9. There is a lad here, who hath five barley loaves, and two fishes: but what are these among so many?**

49

10. Jesus said, Make the people sit down. Now there was much grass in the place. So the men sat down, in number about five thousand.

11. Jesus therefore took the loaves; and having given thanks, he distributed to them that were set down; likewise also of the fishes as much as they would.

---

10. Jesus said, Make the people sit down. Now there was much grass in the place. So the men sat down, in number about five thousand. 11. Jesus therefore took the loaves; and having given thanks, he distributed to them that were set down; likewise also of the fishes as much as they would. Frequently in some modernistic quarterlies of our day, the miraculous aspect of this event is treated slightingly, so that when one gets through trying to understand a few subtle sentences, he comes to the conclusion that there was no miracle after all, but merely something just as things happen every day. I would like to go back to Trench's great statement concerning this, more needful now than ever before. "An analogy, and, so to speak, a help to the understanding of this miracle has been found in that which year by year is accomplished in the field, were a single grain of corn multiplies itself, and in the end unfolds in numerous ears; — and, with this analogy in view, many beautiful remarks have been made; as this, that while God's everyday miracles had grown cheap in men's sight by continual repetition, He had therefore reserved something, not more wonderful, but less frequent, to arouse men's minds to a new admiration. Others have urged that here, as in the case of the water made wine, Christ did but compress into a single moment all those processes which in ordinary circumstances He, the same Lord of nature, causes more slowly to succeed one another. But, true as in its measure is this last observation, it must not be forgotten that the analogy is good only to a certain point. For that which finds place in the field is the unfolding of the seed according to the law of its own being. Thus, if the Lord had taken a few grains of corn and cast them into the ground and if, a moment after, a large harvest had sprung up, to this the name of such a 'divinely-hastened process' might have been fitly applied. But with bread it is otherwise; since, before that is made there must be new interpositions of man's art, and those of such a nature as that by them the very life, which up to this point has unfolded itself, must be crushed and destroyed. A grain of wheat left to itself could never, according to the laws of natural development, issue in a loaf of bread. And, moreover, the Lord does not start from the simple germ, from the lifeful rudiments in which all the seeds of a future life might be supposed to be wrapt up, and by Him rapidly developed, but with the latest artificial product. . . . Thus He, all whose works were 'signs' and had a tongue by which they spoke to the world, did in this miracle proclaim Himself the true bread of the world, which should satisfy the hunger of men; the unexhausted and inexhaustible source of all life, in whom there should be enough and to spare for all the spiritual needs of all hungering souls of all ages." — R. C. Trench. The word translated "given thanks" in verse 11 is the Greek word from which comes our eucharist, which in the Church later came to be a technical term for the Lord's Supper, because it was on that occasion that Christ gave thanks (Luke 22:19; 1 Cor. 11:24). The gathering up of the fragments and the subsequent remarks are found only in John's record of this miracle. "The crowd, judging that one who is able to feed them miraculously can also with miraculous power lead them against the Romans, decides to appoint as king the man whom God has manifestly appointed as His prophet. Movements of revolt were most frequent in Galilee, and they were led by men who were supposed to be prophets. . . . In the discourse that follows, the misunderstanding of the Galileans is set forth: treating the miracle merely as an act of feeding (v. 26), they misunderstand the nature of the salvation Jesus brings (vv. 33–35) and of His sovereignty over them (compare 18:36, 37)." — E. C. Hoskyns.

II. THE MIRACLE OF WALKING ON THE WATER, 6:15–21. This miracle, found also in Matthew 14:22–36 and Mark 6:45–56, while significant in itself, does not directly bear upon the subject of Christ the Bread of Life, and so need not detain the teacher in this particular lesson. I think one excellent paragraph from Lenski, which I have never used before, will be adequate for comment on these verses. "The darkness, the hour of night, the storm and danger still in full force, the exhausting battle with the oars, all combined to make the disciples give way to the superstitions still lurking in their minds. What would some who now smile at superstition have felt and said, if they had held an oar in that boat. Mark adds that Jesus was about to walk on past the boat; John reports only his drawing nigh. Jesus was giving the disciples time to recover from their fright, also time to ask him to enter the boat. In trying to imagine Jesus walking on the sea we must not overlook the storm and the raging waves. These howled and dashed about him, but they did not affect him in the least. He was not tossed up and down; his clothes and body were not wet with spray. Before him, as he moved his feet, a smooth, apparently solid path lay, on which he walked as on ordinary ground. He did not move as a specter is supposed to move; no unearthly light played around him, as painters often imagine." — *R. C. H. Lenski.*

III. CHRIST'S SERMON ON THE BREAD OF LIFE, 6:22–59. The preceding miracles had, presumably, taken place on Friday, for the discourse we are now to consider was uttered in the synagogue at Capernaum, and normally, services were held there only on Saturday, the Sabbath. The miracle took place in Bethsaida on the northeast shore of the Sea of Galilee, where a great multitude now gathered to see Jesus, and, failing to find Him, set out for Capernaum on the northwest shore of the lake, confident the Master would be there. Here they began the conversation with Him with the ridiculous question, "When camest thou hither?" It was really none of their concern, and certainly not a matter of importance; but all men who are continually before the public must expect silly questions, and must expect to have the most personal and private aspects of their lives inquired about, discussed, and reported — sometimes falsely. Probably the superficiality of it all was what led Jesus at once to speak a word of rebuke, pointing out that they were following Him because of His ability to satisfy their physical hunger. This leads Him to lift their thoughts from bread for their bodies to that kind of food that endures unto everlasting life. Before He was through speaking, the question arises as to where this might be secured. Jesus replies that this was the purpose of His coming into the world. Now, on a higher level, they ask what they might do to work the works of God. The answer from Jesus is definite: they are to believe on Him, this person standing before them, because He was sent of God to give everlasting life, to provide them with that spiritual bread which their souls needed. In the early part of the day they had hurried everywhere to find Jesus, and now having found Him, and heard these words, they began to doubt, to resist, and to ask for a sign so that they might believe on Him, reminding Him that God had given their fathers bread from heaven in the wilderness (Num. 11:6; 21:5). This does not baffle the Lord. He has the answer: that bread which Moses brought down from heaven did not result in anything more than physical nourishment, and those that ate of it ultimately died; but what He wanted to give them was the "true bread from heaven," and this bread, said He, is the one which cometh down out of heaven and giveth life unto the world. These are glorious sentences. "In that Eastern country in those times, and very largely today in that particular neighborhood, bread as we understand it, made of meal, is primary food. It is always considered so. All other articles of food were looked upon as accessory; permissible, but unnecessary. . . . Go to the East today, and it will be found whether among Arabs, Jews, or other members of that land, they never tread under foot a piece of bread. However soiled it is, however smirched or contaminated, they never put their foot on it. . . . In Genesis 3:10 we find it said, 'In the sweat of thy face shalt thou eat bread.' That did not merely mean an article of food made out of barley or wheat meal; but it meant food; and from there, all the way

48. I am the bread of life.

49. Your fathers ate the manna in the wilderness and they died.

50. This is the bread which cometh down out of heaven, that a man may eat thereof, and not die.

51. I am the living bread which came down out of heaven: if any man eat of this bread, he shall live for ever: yea and the bread which I will give is my flesh, for the life of the world.

52. The Jews therefore strove one with another, saying, How can this man give us his flesh to eat?

53. Jesus therefore said unto them, Verily, verily, I say unto you, Except ye eat the flesh of the Son of man and drink his blood, ye have not life in yourselves.

54. He that eateth my flesh and drinketh my blood hath eternal life; and I will raise him up at the last day.

55. For my flesh is meat indeed, and my blood is drink indeed.

56. He that eateth my flesh and drinketh my blood abideth in me, and I in him.

---

through the Word bread refers to food generally. So it does here. The emphasis is laid upon that peculiar food which was the general source of sustenance in the East. Its sanctity was always remembered, because of its symbolism in the East." — *G. Campbell Morgan.* "What bread is to the body, Christ is to the soul. As the body requires for its support this daily bread of earth, material outside of itself, since it has not the principle of its continuance in itself and is dependent on such supply, so the soul requires for its support Christ, an object outside of itself, not having the principle of life in itself, depending on the fulness which Christ and Christ alone affords to it. Here the analogy fails. For this *true* bread is that which imparts life, as well as sustains it; and in its production we have no hand, as we have with bread of earth, great Divine gift as this last is. Christ is the bread which cometh down out of heaven, ready for use, as was its symbol, the manna. All we have to do is to come and take and eat. . . . The sign of His ability to give is to be sought in this personal relation with Himself, expressed by coming to and believing on Him. Unless we come and believe, we do not know that He is the Bread of God. We must take and eat, and in this personal participation alone is each one certified of the power of Jesus to satisfy spiritual hunger and thirst for evermore." — *George Reith.*

There are great statements in the passages of our lesson not included in the printed text which need careful consideration, but for which we have neither space nor time in class. Rather than break up our printed text into phrases and verses, I think it will be more profitable to include the entire paragraph. **48. I am the bread of life. 49. Your fathers ate the manna in the wilderness and they died. 50. This is the bread which cometh down out of heaven, that a man may eat thereof, and not die. 51. I am the living bread which came down out of heaven: if any man eat of this bread, he shall live for ever: yea and the bread which I will give is my flesh, for the life of the world. 52. The Jews therefore strove one with another, saying, How can this man give us his flesh to eat? 53. Jesus therefore said unto them, Verily, verily, I say unto you, Except ye eat the flesh of the Son of man and drink his blood, ye have not life in yourselves. 54. He that eateth my flesh and drinketh my blood hath eternal life; and I will raise him up at the last day. 55. For my flesh is meat indeed, and my blood is drink indeed. 56. He that eateth my flesh and drinketh my blood abideth in me, and I in him.** The truly profound words of Professor Smeaton here will need to be studied carefully, but they contain the real meaning of these verses. "As the multitude whom our

57. As the living Father sent me, and I live because of the Father; so he that eateth me, he also shall live because of me.

58. This is the bread which came down out of heaven: not as the fathers ate, and died; he that eateth this bread shall live for ever.

59. These things said he in the synagogue, as he taught in Capernaum.

Lord addressed were the same persons who had witnessed His miracle of the loaves, and as they were going up to the passover (v. 4), it is probable that He drew this peculiar style of address from the sacrifice of which they were going to partake. He intimated, in effect, that He was the reality of the sacrifice, that the paschal lamb was but the shadow, and that they must, with much more eagerness than they looked forward to the passover, eat His flesh and drink His blood. The declaration that they must drink His blood must have sounded strange in the ears of a Jewish company, accustomed to look with peculiar awe on blood. But the difficulty is much diminished, when we reflect that they were on their way to offer the paschal sacrifice, and that He virtually said to them, 'I am the substance or reality of that type.' . . . It was not by His incarnation or by His personal appearance alone that He became the Life of the world. He is the resurrection and the life to unnumbered millions of redeemed men (John 11:25), only as He laid down His life that He might take it again (10:17). That He might be in a position to give life to those whose persons were under condemnation and whose natures were alienated from the life of God, He must needs give His flesh for the life of the world (6:51). As the Righteousness and Life, He was able to overcome sin and death: but He must needs subject Himself to the penalty of death by taking on Himself the guilt which had been the cause of separating between God and man. It is as the Lamb of God that He gives life to the world (1:29). Only the Good Shepherd who gave His life for the Sheep (10:15) is in a position to bring back life to those who are dead in trespasses and sins. . . . He commends Himself to us as the eternal life personally considered, as the meritorious cause of life, as the dispenser of life; and he who believes in Him hath everlasting life (John 5:24)." — *George Smeaton.*

There is considerable disagreement among New Testament students as to whether or not these verses are to be referred to later statements uttered at the Lord's Table. One cannot deny that there is great similarity here, but we must not conclude from this passage, as some do, that the elements set forth at the Lord's Table are actually the flesh and blood of Christ, the eating of which will give us everlasting life. We are not to think that Christ is here building up an argument for the Mass and the daily sacrifice of Himself. Marcus Dods has a passage on the necessity for eating the flesh of Christ that is so rich I never tire of reading it. Let us have before us our Lord's own words, followed by the exposition. **57. As the living Father sent me, and I live because of the Father; so he that eateth me, he also shall live because of me. 58. This is the bread which came down out of heaven: not as the fathers ate, and died; he that eateth this bread shall live for ever. 59. These things said he in the synagogue, as he taught in Capernaum.** "Most emphatically does our Lord say that we must 'eat His flesh and drink His blood' if we are to partake of His life. That is to say, the connection between Christ and us must be of the closest possible kind; so close that the assimilation of the food we eat is not too strong a figure to express it. The food we eat becomes our blood and flesh; it becomes our life, our self. And it does so by our eating it, not by our talking of it, not by our looking at it, and admiring its nutritive properties, but only by eating it. And whatever process can make Christ entirely ours, and help us to assimilate all that is in Him, this process we are to use. The flesh of Christ was given for us; by the shedding of Christ's blood, by the pouring out of His life upon the cross, spiritual life was prepared for us. Cleansing from sin and restoration to God were provided by the offering of His life in the

66. Upon this many of his disciples went back, and walked no more with him.

67. Jesus said therefore unto the twelve, Would ye also go away.

68. Simon Peter answered him, Lord, to whom shall we go? thou hast the words of eternal life.

69. And we have believed and know that thou art the Holy One of God.

---

flesh; and we eat His flesh when we use in our own behalf the death of Christ, and take the blessings it has made possible to us; when we accept the forgiveness of sins, enter into the love of God, and adopt as our own the spirit of the cross. His flesh or human form was the manifestation of God's love for us, the visible material of His sacrifice; and we eat His flesh when we make this our own, when we accept God's love and adopt Christ's sacrifice as our guiding principal of life. We eat His flesh when we take out of His life and death the spiritual nutriment that is actually there; when we let our nature be penetrated by the spirit of the cross, and actually make Christ the Source and the Guide of our spiritual life." — *Marcus Dods.*

IV. **THE TWO GROUPS CONTRASTED,** 6:60–71. The result of this discourse was an immediate winnowing of those who were listening. Why some resent the words of Christ and turn from the gospel, and others embrace the message of Christ with joy and fervor, you and I will never know. This is one of the deepest mysteries of history, repeated every day and every year. When some in this group heard the words of our Lord about eating His flesh and drinking His blood, they complained and murmured, and many departed. 66. **Upon this many of his disciples went back, and walked no more with him.** My friend Dr. William Culbertson, President of the Moody Institute, called to my attention a few years ago the fact that three times in the Gospel of John does such a separation as this occur. It is still true — and everywhere increasingly so — that when the atoning work of Christ is mentioned, when the significance of His shed blood is preached, some men turn from the message. In the most elaborate, much-advertised, commentary on the Bible of our day, now coming from the press, the whole theme of blood sacrifice is denounced. The commentators go so far as to say that we must find a new vocabulary to express what Christ came to do, because the modern mind will have nothing to do with the blood of Jesus. Well, even Paul knew "enemies of the cross."

As our Lord saw these men go away, He was no doubt grieved, knowing that unless they came back and received Him, they were lost. He asked the Twelve if they would also leave him. 67. **Jesus said therefore unto the twelve, Would ye also go away.** 68. **Simon Peter answered him, Lord, to whom shall we go? thou hast the words of eternal life.** "Who among all the apostles of modern unbelief will comfort us in sickness and in sorrow, in bereavement and in anguish, if we leave Jesus? I am soon myself to die. Who among them all will stand at my bedside and say, 'I am the Resurrection and the Life'? To whom, in short, shall we turn for strength, for consolation, for satisfaction in all the infinite yearnings of our souls, if we leave Jesus? Can the spirit's thirst be allayed by the prescriptions of philosophy? Can the hunger of the soul after everlasting life be appeased by dry husks of scientific theories? Where, *where* shall we obtain the living water, and the bread which endureth unto life eternal, except at the table of our Father in heaven? And by whom, O Christ, shall we come unto the Father, but by Thee, who with the Holy Ghost art most high in the glory of the Father for evermore!" — *S. H. Kellogg.* 69. **And we have believed and know that thou art the Holy One of God.** "The Holy One of God! in a fulness of meaning that passeth knowledge, in spirit and in truth, Jesus now bears this title. He is now the One Holy One whom God sees, of such an infinite compass and power of holiness, that He can be holiness to each of His brethren.   And even as He is to God the Holy One, in whom He delights, and for whose sake He delights in all who are in Him, so Christ may now be to us too the One Holy One in whom we too may delight, in whom the Holiness of God is become ours.   'We have believed and know that Thou art the Holy One of God,' — blessed they who can say this, and know themselves to be holy in Christ.   In speaking of the mystery of the Holy Trinity, we saw how Christ stands midway between the Father and the Spirit, as the point of union in which they meet.   In the Son, 'the very image of His substance' (Heb. 1:3) we have the objective revelation of Deity, the Divine Holiness embodied and brought nigh.   In the Holy Spirit we have the revelation subjectively, the Divine Holiness entering our inmost being and revealing itself there.   And the work of the Holy Spirit is to reveal and glorify Christ as the Holy One of God, as He takes of His Holiness and makes it ours.   He shows us how all is in Christ; how Christ is all for us; how we are in Christ; and how, as a living Saviour, Christ through His Spirit takes and keeps charge of us and our life of holiness.   He makes Christ indeed to be to us the Holy One of God." — *Andrew Murray.*

THE LESSON IN LIFE, LITERATURE, AND ARCHAEOLOGY.

In the excellent autobiographical volume by James M'Kendrick, *Seen and Heard*, is a most interesting illustration of verse 47 of the text for our lesson today. While evangelizing in Rosehearty, a fishing village in Ireland, the meeting began poorly, so Mr. M'Kendrick went out after the villagers, and soon the number in attendance began to increase.   Some young men, however, started to throw large stones on the roof of the hall.   As the people were leaving that night, the evangelist asked a serious-looking man if he would read John 6:47, which he did.   Mr. M'Kendrick continues, "I said, 'That is the way of salvation.'   He inquired, 'Can I be saved by just believing?'   I asked him to read the verse again, which he did, and added — 'If that is how people are saved, I can be saved now.'   I tried to help him all I could, and there the man truly trusted Christ as his Saviour, and went home to let his wife know of the great change.   Instead of going to bed, he went through the village to tell all his relatives he was saved — urging all to come to the service the following night, and this many did.   In the course of the service he asked opportunity to tell what God had done for him, and he did it with power and sincerity, and others were saved also.   They likewise, in turn, earnestly sought the salvation of their friends and acquaintances, with the result that in a short time the soul's salvation was the prevailing subject of conversation in Rosehearty, and daily some were added to the saved.   The congregation so increased that neither church nor hall could accommodate them."

A TRUTH FOR THE CLASS TO CARRY AWAY.

There is one thing universally agreed upon regarding bread, and that is, it satisfies human hunger.   For this reason Christ took the word to Himself: He satisfies the deepest spiritual needs of the human soul, and will continue to do this throughout eternity.   Through Him we have peace with God, sonship in the family of God, a hope that nothing can destroy, and deliverance from sin and the fear of death.

How many things are said about Christ in this lesson which cannot be said of any other person who ever lived?   Why do you think certain people left Christ this day when He began to speak about the necessity for His death?   Why is not the holy life and heavenly teaching of Jesus sufficient for man's redemption?   In how many ways does Christ here, though He does not use the word, reveal His love for us?   In what ways do founders of modern religions differ from Christ in their utterances concerning themselves?

LESSON VII. — February 14.

"CAN THIS BE THE CHRIST?" — John 7—8.

PRINTED TEXT, John 7:37–52; 8:12–19.

Devotional Reading: Colossians 1:15–23.
Beginner Topic: THE CHILDREN'S BEST FRIEND.
    Lesson Material: Matthew 19:13–15; Mark 10:13–16; Luke 18:15–17.
    Memory Verse: I love thee, O Jehovah. Psalm 18:1.
Primary Topic: PEOPLE WONDER ABOUT JESUS.
    Lesson Material: John 7:1–17, 30–52.
    Memory Verse: Never man so spake. John 7:46.
Junior Topic: PEOPLE WONDER ABOUT JESUS.
    Lesson Material: John 7:1–17, 30–52.
    Memory Verse: Never man so spake. John 7:46.
Intermediate-Senior Topic: FAITH FACES DOUBT.
    Lesson Material: John 7—8.
    Memory Verse: I am the light of the world: he that followeth me shall not walk in the darkness, but shall have the light of life. John 8:12.
Topic for Young People and Adults: JESUS DECLARES HIS DEITY.
    Lesson Material: John 7—8.
    Memory Verse: I am the light of the world; he that followeth me shall not walk in the darkness, but shall have the light of life. John 8:12.

THE TEACHER AND HIS CLASS.

The Younger Classes may be introduced to this lesson, devoted to a record of the growing opposition to Christ and an increasing rejection of His claims, by an illustration, the events of which some of the class may have experienced personally. Several boys may be down at the seashore with sand shovels. When the tide is out, they may build sand houses as high as they can reach, perhaps three or four feet. When the tide comes in and recedes again, the whole mountain of sand will disappear. The sea is so powerful that the sand cannot resist its pulling strength. The same is true of buildings on the seashore, during a storm. So men through the ages have raised mountains of objections to Christ, then a great revival sweeps the land and all these objections seem to crash to the ground, and the tide of His saving grace, His love, His power to deliver from sin and darkness continues to flow.

The Older Classes may have pointed out at the beginning of this study the terrible antagonisms to Christ today. In a long article in the recently published *Soviet Encyclopedia*, His very existence is denied. This week brings news that the Indian government has issued statements claiming that missionary work in India is not altogether advantageous for that land. Ten years ago, eight thousand Protestant missionaries were laboring in China; now there are less than one hundred, and these are in jails or confined under house arrest. At one time in China there were 275 Protestant and Roman Catholic hospitals, two-thirds of the better hospitals of the nation; today all of them are in the hands of the communists. At one time 25 per cent of the people listed in the Chinese *Who's Who* were Christians, and 50 per cent were graduates of Christian schools; today her governors, cabinet ministers, and educators are almost all communists. But Christ is the truth; He is the only Saviour, and He will abide when all objection has gone forever.

THE LESSON IN ITS SETTING.

Time. — The events of the 7th chapter of John occurred in the summer of A.D. 29, and those of the 8th chapter, in October of the same year.

Place. — The discourse in chapter 7 was given in Bethsaida, on the Sea of Galilee, and the events recorded in chapter 8 took place in Jerusalem.

56

FEBRUARY 14.   "CAN THIS BE THE CHRIST?"   JOHN 7:37–52.

THE PLAN OF THE LESSON.

SUBJECT: The Subtle Attempts of the Jews in the Last Six Months of Christ's Ministry to Expose Him as a Deceiver, As an Evil Man, As Possessed with a Demon, and Their Final Determination to Kill Him.

I. THE GREAT DEBATE ABOUT CHRIST AT THE FEAST OF TABERNACLES, John 7:1–53.

1. The journey to Jerusalem, vs. 1–10.
2. The preliminary division of opinion regarding Him, vs. 11–13.
3. The question about the source of His knowledge, vs. 14–19.
4. The question about His origin, vs. 20–30.
5. The mission of the soldiers, vs. 31–36.
6. The continued discussion about His origin, vs. 37–43.
7. The advice of Nicodemus, vs. 44–53.

II. CHRIST THE LIGHT OF THE WORLD, John 8:12–59.

1. The initial assertion, v. 12.
2. The truthfulness of His claims, vs. 13–20.
3. The tremendous importance of believing Christ, vs. 21–30.
4. The origin of disbelief — Satan, vs. 31–47.
5. The pre-existence of Christ, vs. 48–58.
6. The attempt to kill Him, v. 59.

THE TEACHER'S LIBRARY.

For the study of this lesson, the lives of Christ are of practically no value. We do not need sermonic material here, for there must be a grasp of the entire narrative rather than an extended consideration of some few verses. Therefore, the commentaries will prove the best aids for any serious teacher, though even here we may occasionally be disappointed; for example, to these 102 verses, Marcus Dods devotes only 13 pages, though he gives more than that to the opening eighteen verses of chapter 10. For an introductory study, may I suggest A. T. Robertson: *The Divinity of Christ in the Gospel of John*, chapter 3, "The Growing Hatred of Jesus," pp. 65–94, discussing chapters 5–11; William Manson: *The Incarnate Glory*, chapter 5, pp. 126–150, discussing chapters 7–9; and, especially, Merrill C. Tenney: *John, the Gospel of Belief*, pp. 129–151. For detailed exposition, my opinion is that the four best volumes are those by R. C. H. Lenski, George Reith, Milligan and Moulton, and E. C. Hoskyns. In *Questions Answered by Christ*, by John A. Bain, there are three chapters, pp. 166–184, on John 8:25, 33, 53. On John 7:37–39, there are two superb sermons in G. Campbell Morgan: *The Westminster Pulpit*, Vol. 5, pp. 193–212. On Christ the light of the world, see the same, Vol. 3, pp. 353–360; T. Marjoribanks: *The Sevenfold "I Am's" of Christ*, 3–19; and a great sermon by Alexander Maclaren: *Expositions of Holy Scripture, John 1–8*, pp. 319–330.

AUDIO-VISUAL AIDS.

No audio-visual aids discovered.

The preparation of this lesson has been a very unusual experience for the editor. I almost felt that I had never read these chapters before, so new did many of the verses seem to me; and I believe that to many these chapters will come as a new revelation. Of course no teacher can interpret 102 verses in any 30-minute period. In this lesson we should emphasize the major points, and avoid lengthy discussions of difficult problems, the consideration of which would mean that the great lessons of this passage would be lost for lack of time. Robertson well says that, "Nowhere is John more dramatic and powerful than in the swift movement of these chapters. The various elements of the national life move before us as they take various attitudes towards Jesus of Nazareth."

I. THE GREAT DEBATE ABOUT CHRIST AT THE FEAST OF TABERNACLES, John 7:1–53.

1. THE JOURNEY TO JERUSALEM, vs. 1–10. The circumstances which surrounded Christ during this tremendous debate concerning His person are important. The time is that of the Feast of the Tabernacles, the last of three festivals at which the men of Israel were required to present themselves in Jerusalem, beginning late in September or early in October, a harvest festival and a historical memorial of the earliest days of Israel (Lev. 23:39–43). It was a season of great rejoicing. The brethren of Christ urged Him to depart for Jerusalem, with His disciples, for the celebration of this feast, and for the purpose of manifesting Himself to the world, though we are told that his brethren did not even believe that He was the Messiah, the Son of God. To this our Lord replied, "I go not up unto this feast, because my time is not yet fulfilled." Some manuscripts read so that the text is translated, "I go not up *yet* unto this feast," etc. But then we read that when His brethren had departed for Jerusalem, He also went up, not publicly but privately. Did our Lord contradict himself here? The words of Professor Tenney are excellent on this passage. " 'Time (*kairos*) in 7:6 referred to a suitable

hour for public manifestation rather than the date of His death. Verse 30 of the same chapter uses the word 'hour' (*hora*) and connects it with His appointed destiny rather than with the psychological moment for action. If these two terms had different meanings, then any idea of deception is removed from the text. As it stands, Jesus told the brethren that He was not going up to the feast, and then promptly went. No duplicity was involved. He urged His brethren to go since it made no particular difference when they arrived; but in His case, He could appear only at the time appointed by the Father." — *Prof. Merrill Tenney.*

2. The Preliminary Division of Opinion Regarding Him, vs. 11-13. Because of previous experiences, the Jews were led to believe that Christ would be present in Jerusalem at the great feast, and so they were looking for Him. The first words concerning Him are not uttered in His presence, but are spoken by different groups of Jews. The initial criticism (and praise) are general: they will soon become specific. Some are saying that He is a good man: others claim He is a deceiver. I think it would be well to list at this point the various accusations against Jesus which are to be found in this lesson: He leadeth the multitude astray, 7:12; He is possessed by a demon, 7:12; 8:48, 52; His record is not true, 8:13; He is a Samaritan, 8:48. On the other hand, He is called a good man, 7:12; the prophet, 7:40; one who speaks as no man ever spoke before, 7:46.

3. The Question About the Source of His Knowledge, vs. 14-19. We might say that Christ came to carry on a five-fold ministry: to live a perfect example before men; to reveal the truth by His teaching; to bring conviction of sin and a confession of Christ by His preaching; to prove Himself to be the Son of God by His miracles; to die for our sins on the cross, and rise for our justification. Immediately upon arriving at the Temple, Christ begins to teach, and His teaching is so wonderful that the Jews, even those who opposed Him, ask the question, "How knoweth this man letters, having never learned?" "What surprises them, they say, is that a man who has had no proper education should presume to teach in public and palm himself off as one who is versed in scriptural learning. Their question is a general exclamation addressed, not to Jesus, but to the multitude. It charges Jesus with incompetency, with utter lack of proper qualifications for being a great religious teacher. The purpose of the rulers is to discredit Jesus with his audience. The force of their question is: 'This fellow does not know what he is talking about, because he has never studied in any of our Jewish schools.' We meet the same charge today when any man dares to contradict the 'scientific' critics of Christ and the Gospel. At once he is branded by them as an ignoramus, incompetent to speak on these subjects, because he is not one of their guild who has preempted 'scientific' learning, and does not bear the stamp of their approval. The object is to impress the crowd; and the secret object to maintain their own authority by crying down the man who challenges it." — *R. C. H. Lenski.* The word here translated "letters" is the Greek word *grammata*, from which we get our word *grammar*, meaning, the rabbinical study of the Old Testament writings. Jesus' reply is two-fold: first, He received His teaching from God the Father — a great truth frequently emphasized in this Gospel (3:11; 8:26, 28; 12:49; 14:24); secondly, any man can know whether or not He speaks for God if he desires God's will. "No words can more clearly show that the very end of the teaching of Jesus as set forth in this Gospel is not empty speculation but practical righteousness." — *William Milligan.*

4. The Question About His Origin, vs. 20-30. The accusations now become increasingly bitter and diabolical. The Jews go so far as to accuse Christ of being possessed by demons, an accusation brought against Him previously (see Matthew 11:18). Some, deeply impressed with the content and boldness of Christ's teachings, began to ask if this is not the promised Messiah. They seem to answer their own question in reasoning that it could not be, for the origin of the Messiah is wrapped in mystery, but the origin of this man Jesus, all know. "He is a man of Nazareth and has come from Galilee (1:45, 46; 18:5, 7; 19:19; 2:11-13; 4:54; 5:1; 7:9, 10). It is therefore impossible to consider Him seriously as the Messiah. . . .

JOHN 7:37. Now on the last day, the great *day* of the feast, Jesus stood and cried, saying, If any man thirst, let him come unto me and drink.

38. He that believeth on me, as the scripture hath said, from within him shall flow rivers of living water.

No doubt the question of the paternity of Jesus does lie in the background; later it emerges as a clear issue (8:19, 36 ff.; compare 7:42), and, in spite of 1:45 and 6:42, it is precisely the unknown paternity of Jesus that gives the Jews a ground of accusation against Him. . . .   The complete failure of the men of Jerusalem to recognize in Him the Messiah therefore involves their complete ignorance of God (8:19, 54, 55), and their ignorance is contrasted with the knowledge of Jesus who is from God and was sent by Him (compare Matt. 11:27; Luke 10:22), and by implication, with the knowledge of the Christian believers (4:22; 17:25, 26).   Once again the Jews' knowledge that Jesus came from Galilee is denounced as mere knowledge according to the flesh, with which is contrasted the spiritual knowledge that perceives in the man from Nazareth of Galilee, the Messiah of God and the Saviour of the world." — *E. C. Hoskyns.*

5. THE MISSION OF THE SOLDIERS, vs. 31–36.   Utterly confounded by Christ's response to all their questions, and unable to prove any serious charge of deception or falsehood, or illegitimate claims, these men do what many have done before in rejecting the truth of a teacher, they determine to put Christ to death.   In this they fail, for "his hour was not yet come."   Six months would yet elapse before the time ordained of God for His crucifixion.   Nevertheless, soldiers are sent to apprehend Him.   During this time, many in the multitude began to believe on Christ.   "Even though their belief was not as yet intellectual or what it ought to be, as indeed it could be, their moral attitude to him was enough to warrant them being called believers.   "They did not suffer prejudices or appearances to interfere with their judgment.   So they are led on by the Spirit of God." — *George Reith.* The situation prevailing here is exactly that in the world today.   There is a division among men concerning Christ, and were He to come back to any communist-controlled countries, they would attempt to crucify Him again, even as they have already put to death millions of those who confessed His name.

6. THE CONTINUED DISCUSSION ABOUT HIS ORIGIN, vs. 37–43.   37. **Now on the last day, the great *day* of the feast, Jesus stood and cried, saying, If any man thirst, let him come unto me and drink.**   "The last day of the feast was the greatest of all.   According to Jewish tradition, the eighth day was observed as a holy convocation, which marked the conclusion, not only of the Feast of Tabernacles, but of the whole cycle of the festal year.   On each day the ritual included a libation of water which was taken in a golden vessel from the pool of Siloam, and which was offered by the priests as they sang: 'With joy shall ye draw water out of the wells of salvation' (Isa. 12:3). . . .   In place of the physical water He proffered the spiritual; instead of a ritual He offered a reality." — *Merrill Tenney.*   38. **He that believeth on me, as the scripture hath said, from within him shall flow rivers of living water.**   These words from our Lord are probably from a combination of Isaiah 58:11 and Zechariah 14:8.   "His entire mission and work, together with all the blessings he has come to bestow, are the fulfillment of God's ancient promises, which proves beyond question the genuineness of his Messiahship. . . .   That every believer actually attains through Jesus what God promised ages ago by the mouth of his holy prophets is the subjective evidence for the truth of Christianity. . . .   'Living water' is one of the frequent allegorical expressions used in the Scriptures, in which the figurative term is at once expounded by the non-figurative.   We may analyze as follows: the fountain — Jesus ('let him come unto me'); thirsting, coming and drinking, taken together — the inner man; the water — true life; the flowing rivers — life-giving influences for others.   The abundance of the latter is indicated by the plural 'rivers' saving influences in various directions and of differ-

39. But this spake he of the Spirit, which they that believed on him were to receive: for the Spirit was not yet *given;* because Jesus was not yet glorified.

40. *Some* of the multitude therefore, when they heard these words, said, This is of a truth the prophet.

41. Others said, This is the Christ. But some said, What, doth the Christ come out of Galilee?

42. Hath not the scripture said that the Christ cometh of the seed of David, and from Bethlehem, the village where David was?

43. So there arose a division in the multitude because of him.

44. And some of them would have taken him; but no man laid hands on him.

45. The officers therefore came to the chief priests and Pharisees; and they said unto them, Why did ye not bring him?

46. The officers answered, Never man so spake.

47. The Pharisees therefore answered them, Are ye also led astray?

48. Hath any of the rulers believed on him, or of the Pharisees?

49. But this multitude that knoweth not the law are accursed.

50. Nicodemus saith unto them (he that came to him before, being one of them)

---

ent kinds." — *R. C. H. Lenski.* **39. But this spake he of the Spirit, which they that believed on him were to receive: for the Spirit was not yet *given;* because Jesus was not yet glorified.** "John refers, of course, to the free and universal outpouring of the Spirit on all believers in Jesus Christ, begun in outward symbol at Pentecost, and continuing ever since (Eph. 1:13 ff.). Not that the Spirit was nonexistent before, and not that there was absolutely no manifestation of Him hitherto. The statement is a relative one. The end to which all the earthly course of the Lord, reached only through the sufferings and death, was pointing, was 'the glory I had with Thee before the world was' (17:5; see 11:4; 12:16, 23, 27 ff.; 13:31 ff.; 17:1; Heb. 2:9)." — *George Reith.* **40. *Some* of the multitude therefore, when they heard these words, said, This is of a truth the prophet. 41. Others said, This is the Christ. But some said, What, doth the Christ come out of Galilee? 42. Hath not the scripture said that the Christ cometh of the seed of David, and from Bethlehem, the village where David was? 43. So there arose a division in the multitude because of him. 44. And some of them would have taken him; but no man laid hands on him.** The passage referred to here is Micah 5:2, also quoted by the scribes in relation to the wise men coming to Jerusalem (Matt. 2:6). "Time has shown that they really did not comprehend the width of Scripture truth; that they read into it their own narrow notions; or at any rate time has shown that what Scripture did say, even if it did, say precisely as they understood it, it did not say against the opinions, or the man, to which or to whom they were opposed." — *George Reith.* It is true that Christ did come from Galilee, where He had lived all the years of his youth and early manhood, until about thirty years of age. That He was born in Bethlehem, as the prophet said the Messiah must be, seems to be not known to these Jews at this time.

7. THE ADVICE OF NICODEMUS, vs. 44–53. In the midst of the multitude was a man whom we first met in chapter 3, Nicodemus, who came to Jesus by night. **45. The officers therefore came to the chief priests and Pharisees; and they said unto them, Why did ye not bring him? 46. The officers answered, Never man so spake. 47. The Pharisees therefore answered them, Are ye also led astray? 48. Hath any of the rulers believed on him, or of the Pharisees? 49. But this multitude that knoweth not the law are accursed. 50. Nicodemus saith unto**

51. Doth our law judge a man, except it first hear from himself and know what he doeth?

52. They answered, and said unto him, Art thou also of Galilee? Search, and see that out of Galilee ariseth no prophet.

JOHN 8:12. Again therefore Jesus spake unto them, saying, I am the light of the world: he that followeth me shall not walk in the darkness, but shall have the light of life.

---

them (he that came to him before, being one of them) 51. Doth our law judge a man, except it first hear from himself and know what he doeth? 52. They answered, and said unto him, Art thou also of Galilee? Search, and see that out of Galilee ariseth no prophet. The soldiers who were sent to take Jesus now return without their prisoner. When asked the reason for their failure to bring Him, they give a tremendous reply — that they had never heard a man speak as this man Jesus spoke. "The authority, majesty, and power of the speaker held these officers back, contrary to explicit orders; compare Matthew 7:28. They acknowledge that the manner of Jesus is beyond anything ever found in any other man. They are only one step from saying that this manner is superhuman, yea, divine. Much as these officers felt constrained to obey their orders, a stronger influence had come over them — they simply could not and would not lay hands on a man who spoke as this man did. Thus another strange thing appears: the very tools through which the rulers planned to bring Jesus to prison and to death, by making this honest confession, disrupt the unity of the Sanhedrin, and thus cause their own plan to be dropped. The means defeat the end. God often plays with His enemies and makes their schemes ridiculous." — R. C. H. Lenski.

On the testimony of Nicodemus, my friend Dr. Merrill Tenney has an excellent summary. "The reappearance of Nicodemus is difficult to explain unless he afterward became a believer, and reported this story himself. The discussion among the Pharisees must have taken place in private, especially since a scheme to arrest or kill Jesus was being considered. It is hardly conceivable that the Pharisees would have planned the matter openly when Jesus had a large number of sympathizers. Only one on the inside would report this, and he was the only insider who would do it. The weight of Nicodemus' defense was placed upon an impersonal technicality, not upon a warm personal faith. Before casting aspersions upon him because he did not instantly and warmly espouse Jesus' cause, one should remember that he probably stood alone among a group of unscrupulous men who would turn on him at the slightest provocation. He made a plea for fair play, perhaps as a means of trying their temper. . . . His belief was feeble, but genuine. In spite of the depressing rebuff that he received to his humane suggestion of fair play, he remained a loyal though rather passive supporter of Jesus." — Dr. Merrill Tenney.

II. CHRIST THE LIGHT OF THE WORLD, John 8:12–59. I am purposely omitting any discussion of the story of the woman taken in adultery, occupying the first eleven verses of this chapter. Many of our best Biblical scholars, even among the conservatives, believe that this is a late insertion. Furthermore, any comment on these verses would interrupt the main theme of the lesson.

1. THE INITIAL ASSERTION, v. 12. Again therefore Jesus spake unto them, saying, I am the light of the world: he that followeth me shall not walk in the darkness, but shall have the light of life. "With this verse, the proof of the thesis that Christ is the world's Light becomes direct. It is grounded on the plea advanced by Jesus that the believer in Him will not find himself walking in darkness, but will have the light of life (8:12). That is, he will have inward evidence of Divine and eternal things. Christian experience will be to him a path of shining light, shining more and more to the perfect day. . . . In the last analysis, the central truth of Christianity turns on the self-attestation of Jesus: the latter is not a de-

13. The Pharisees therefore said unto him, Thou bearest witness of thyself; thy witness is not true.

14. Jesus answered and said unto them, Even if I bear witness of myself, my witness is true; for I know whence I came, and whither I go; but ye know not whence I come, or whither I go.

15. Ye judge after the flesh; I judge no man.

16. Yea and if I judge, my judgment is true; for I am not alone, but I and the Father that sent me.

17. Yea and in your law it is written, that the witness of two men is true.

18. I am he that beareth witness of myself, and the Father that sent me beareth witness of me.

19. They said therefore unto him, Where is thy Father? Jesus answered, Ye know neither me, nor my Father: if ye knew me, ye would know my Father also.

---

batable matter but a datum. . . . It is clear — and it will become clearer as we proceed — that the arguments handled in this chapter state on the one hand the stock-representations of Judaism against Jesus of Nazareth, and on the other hand the Christian answer. The final stand of Christianity is made on the irrefragable position that Jesus is His own evidence, the True Witness concerning Himself. To desert this ground is to abandon Christianity. Nevertheless, Christ has also the evidence of God, for to know Him is to know the Father. This is matter of experience. He who has surrendered to Christ has no doubt whatsoever that by the same token he is yielding to God." — *William Manson*. On the phrase, "shall not walk in darkness," Meyer has said, "Not in the darkness of ignorance and error; not in the darkness of perplexity and confusion; not in the darkness of joylessness and depression. If any man dares to follow Christ so far as he knows, deliberately sacrificing his own will and way to His, it is simply marvellous how the mists will roll up, the night clouds disperse, and the perplexities which had beset the soul give way as brushwood before the tread of the sportsman. — *F. B. Meyer*.

2. THE TRUTHFULNESS OF HIS CLAIMS, vs. 13–20. 13. The Pharisees therefore said unto him, Thou bearest witness of thyself; thy witness is not true. 14. Jesus answered and said unto them, Even if I bear witness of myself, my witness is true; for I know whence I came, and whither I go; but ye know not whence I come, or whither I go. 15. Ye judge after the flesh; I judge no man. 16. Yea and if I judge, my judgment is true; for I am not alone, but I and the Father that sent me. 17. Yea and in your law it is written, that the witness of two men is true. 18. I am he that beareth witness of myself, and the Father that sent me beareth witness of me. 19. They said therefore unto him, Where is thy Father? Jesus answered, Ye know neither me, nor my Father: if ye knew me, ye would know my Father also. When the Pharisees accused Christ of speaking of Himself falsely, without any external support, He immediately replies with a verse from their own Old Testament scriptures, Deuteronomy 19:15 (see also 17:6), that when two men testify to any fact, it is to be believed, and goes on to insist that what He has said about Himself, God the Father also says. Our Lord accuses these people of ignorance, of knowing not the Father. Professor Tenney has set forth the knowledge of Jesus and the ignorance of the Pharisees in an interesting form:

Jesus		Pharisees	
I know	14	Ye know not	14
I judge no man	15	Ye judge after the flesh	15
I am from above	23	Ye are from beneath	23
I am not of this world	23	Ye are of this world	23

62

"They had judged Him by mere outward appearance, and according to their own merely human thoughts and wishes. Having formed for themselves without patient study of the Scriptures, and thus without the guidance of the Spirit of God, their conception of Messiah and of His kingdom, they rejected Jesus because He did not answer their expectation. But for this, the Divine witness in Him would have reached their hearts. 'I judge no one.' They judged according to their own nature — standing alone, without the guidance of the Father, not taking the Father along with them in judging, and thus not judging 'righteous judgment' (7:24)." — *W. F. Moulton.*

3. The Tremendous Importance of Believing Christ, vs. 21–30. Bishop Ryle begins his exposition of this paragraph with almost the very words I have used elsewhere in this lesson, "This passage contains deep things, so deep that we have no time to fathom them." We should emphasize here one statement of our Lord, "Except ye believe that I am he, ye shall die in your sins." Bishop Ryle says, "These solemn words are invested with peculiar solemnity when we consider from whose lips they came. Who is this that speaks of men dying 'in their sins,' unpardoned, unforgiven, unfit to meet God — of men going into another world with all their sins upon them? He that says this is no other than the Saviour of mankind, who laid down His life for His sheep, — the loving, gracious, merciful, compassionate Friend of sinners. It is Christ Himself! Let this simple fact not be overlooked. . . . Finally, let us never forget that unbelief is the special sin that ruins men's souls. Had the Jews believed on our Lord, all manner of sin and blasphemy might have been forgiven them. But unbelief bars the door in mercy's face and cuts off hope. Let us watch and pray hard against it. One of the strongest sayings ever used by our Lord was this, 'He that believeth not shall be damned' (Mark 16:16)."

4. The Origin of Disbelief — Satan, vs. 31–47. In this paragraph is one of the most oft-quoted utterances of Christ to be found in all the Gospels — "Ye shall know the truth, and the truth shall make you free." This profound statement infuriated the Jews to whom Jesus was speaking, and their anger was so blinding as to cause them to utter one of the strangest falsehoods ever to come from the lips of intelligent men — "We have never yet been in bondage to any man." Well, they were in bondage in Egypt; they were again and again in bondage to the Philistines, as the Book of Judges tells us; they were in bondage in Babylon, and here they are once again under the yoke of a foreign power, Rome. However, Christ was not speaking of political freedom, but of freedom from sin, as He immediately affirms, and it is from this bondage that Christ would set men free. Following up their proud statement that they were Abraham's seed, Jesus informed them that if they were the true children of Abraham, that is, spiritually as well as physically, they would do the works of Abraham. Abraham believed God. Christ came to announce the truth of God, and these men were about to kill Him. "You are doing the works of your father," said the Lord, "but your father is Satan." In verse 44 we come upon the greatest single declaration concerning the devil to be found anywhere in the Word of God. Here Satan is said to be a murderer, to be utterly devoid of the truth, to be a liar and the father of lies; thus, all deception, all false religions, all hatred toward God and God's Son, the antagonism of the world to the Church — all these ultimately derive from the power of this evil one, who at the end of the age will be finally defeated and cast into the lake of fire forever. It is in this passage also that our Lord asserts His own absolute sinlessness. Every phrase here should have extended comment, but we are not able to give it in this lesson. I have often felt that one of the most difficult questions to answer is that which Jesus presents here, "If I say the truth, why do ye not believe me?" "As the sick man is the slave of his disease, so the sinner is the slave of sin; and unless intervention breaks the power of sin, the sinner is doomed." — *Merrill Tenney.* In re-examining these verses, we realize that here are things so profound, and yet so elemental, that the world as a whole knows nothing about them — the deep, unceasing, supernatural conflict that is going on

in the world for the souls of men, the powers that rest upon the heart, and will, and mind, of lost men to keep them from coming to Christ for deliverance, and the greater power, the love, the graciousness, the very deity of the Lord Jesus Christ, drawing men to Him for eternal life and salvation.

5. THE PRE-EXISTENCE OF CHRIST, vs. 48–58. Once again our Lord puts forth a truth about which whole volumes have been written, namely, that of His pre-existence. When the Jews asked Him if He was greater than their father Abraham and the prophets, He gave the astonishing reply, "Your father Abraham rejoiced to see my day, and he saw it and was glad." Of course the Jews retorted that this was impossible, for Abraham had lived nineteen hundred years before that, and Christ was less than fifty years of age. So Christ furthers His remark with an even greater statement, "Before Abraham was born, I am." "In the clearest possible manner Jesus declares, not only His existence before Abraham, but also the essential distinction between His being and that of any man. Man is born, man passes through successive periods of time: of Himself, in regard alike to past, present and future, Jesus says 'I am.' He claims for Himself that absolute, unchanging existence which is the attribute of God alone." — *William Milligan.*

6. THE ATTEMPT TO KILL HIM, v. 59. Carefully note that throughout this long argument, Christ, on the one hand, never ignores the questions of the Jews, while they, on the other hand, instead of believing Him and acknowledging that He is speaking the truth, move on to another question, and another, in a fixed determination not to accept Him. Now, finding themselves utterly baffled by the Lord's great declarations, which they cannot refute, they attempt to put Him to death. Such is often the experience of those who try to reveal truth to those who are determined to abide in the falsehood of the evil one.

THE LESSON IN LIFE, LITERATURE, AND ARCHAEOLOGY.

Dr. Daniel C. Gilman, the famous president of Johns Hopkins University of a previous generation, hesitated for some time before choosing a motto for the new university, an institution which was to prove epochal in the history of American education. Finally he chose Jerome's translation of the phrase in John 8:32, "The truth shall make you free," which in the Latin reads "*Veritas vos liberabit.*"

A TRUTH FOR THE CLASS TO CARRY AWAY.

This lesson might best be concluded with a brief review of those things which mark Christ as infinitely superior to all other men: the very claims He made concerning Himself; His oneness with the Father; His pre-existence; His sinlessness; and the fact that through Him alone men have eternal life, and the promise of resurrection from the dead.

How do you account for the fact that with all the evidence they had, many refused to accept Christ as the Messiah and the Son of God? How many of the characteristics of Satan mentioned by Christ in this lesson are actually revealed in the events of these chapters? In what ways is Christ greater than Abraham, who looms so large in this discussion? If the characters of this lesson were grouped at a trial of Jesus as to those who would defend Him and those who would prosecute Him, who would be on the side of the defense? Has the division of opinion concerning Christ portrayed in this lesson decreased or increased in the centuries that have followed?

LESSON VIII. — February 21.

THE MAN BORN BLIND. — John 9.

PRINTED TEXT, John 9:1-11, 24-38.

Devotional Reading: Ephesians 2:11-22.
Beginner Topic: FRIEND TO ZACCHEUS.
    Lesson Material: Luke 19:1-10.
    Memory Verse: The Lord is my helper. Hebrews 13:6.
Primary Topic: A BLIND MAN SEES.
    Lesson Material: John 9:1-38.
    Memory Verse: Jesus went about all the cities and the villages, teaching
    . . . and preaching . . . and healing. Matthew 9:35.
Junior Topic: A BLIND MAN SEES.
    Lesson Material: John 9:1-38.
    Memory Verse: Jesus went about all the cities and the villages, teaching
    . . . and preaching . . . and healing. Matthew 9:35.
Intermediate-Senior Topic: HAVING EYES THAT SEE.
    Lesson Material: John 9.
    Memory Verse: One thing I know, that, whereas I was blind, now I see.
    John 9:25.
Topic for Young People and Adults: SIGHT FOR MAN'S BLINDNESS.
    Lesson Material: John 9.
    Memory Verse: One thing I know, that, whereas I was blind, now I see.
    John 9:25.

THE TEACHER AND HIS CLASS.

The Younger Classes may be introduced to this lesson by being asked which of their five senses — smell, touch, hearing, taste and sight — they count the most valuable, and which would be the last they would want to give up. Everyone will agree that this would be their sight. Through our eyes we see the beauties of nature; we look upon the faces of loved ones; we read; we do our work in the chemical and physical laboratories; artists paint, women sew, etc. We are about to study an amazing episode, of a man blind from birth having his sight instantly, completely, and permanently restored to him by the power of Christ.

The Older Classes will find here an excellent illustration of the value of personal testimony. I believe that the matter of public testimony *can* be overdone, while, on the other hand, too many Christians do not practice it enough. A born-again Christian ought to have more than a testimony. Saying the same thing every Wednesday night for ten years, gets very monotonous, and ultimately brings little blessing. The testimony is good in a new audience, to neighbors, strangers, and unbelievers, in that it is a witness to what Christ has done; but to Christians gathered together week by week, one should unfold the treasures of the Word of God. The greatest tragedy is that a man should try to speak of the things pertaining to Christ to others when he has had no experience himself. Yet a genuine testimony, given in love, is often more powerful than a sermon.

THE LESSON IN ITS SETTING.

Time. — Fall of A.D. 29.
Place. — Somewhere in the city of Jerusalem.

THE PLAN OF THE LESSON.

SUBJECT: The Testimony of One, No Matter How Humble and Uneducated, Who has had a Real Experience with Christ Cannot be Contradicted by Even the Most Learned Skeptics.

I. JESUS DISCUSSES THE STATE OF THE BLIND MAN WITH HIS DISCIPLES, John 9:1-5.

65

II. JESUS RESTORES SIGHT TO THE MAN BORN BLIND, 9:6, 7.

III. THE UNBELIEVING NEIGHBORS AND PHARISEES REFUSE TO ACKNOWLEDGE THE MIRACLE, 9:8–34.

1. The question of *identity*, vs. 8, 9.
2. The question of *how* his eyes were opened, vs. 10–15.
3. The question of *who* could perform such miracles, vs. 16–23.
4. The clear testimony of the one once blind, vs. 24, 25.
5. The question of *how* is again debated, vs. 26, 27.
6. The one once blind declares his conviction that Jesus is of God, vs. 28–33.
7. He is cast out, though his words could not be contradicted, v. 34.

IV. JESUS IN CONVERSATION WITH THE ONE ONCE BLIND LEADS HIM TO BELIEVE IN HIM AS THE SON OF GOD, 9:35–38.

V. JESUS' FINAL WORDS TO THE PHARISEES, 9:39–41.

THE TEACHER'S LIBRARY.

The major lives of Christ will be found, for the most part, rather unsatisfactory in their treatment of this chapter, and even the larger commentaries on John's Gospel are surprisingly weak here. An excellent exception to this is the profound and searching treatment by R. C. H. Lenski, who devotes 35 pages to this chapter. Even the works on the miracles of Christ are not of great value here, with the exception of the pages in Trench. The best single chapter on the entire episode is in the volume by my friend and colleague, Dr. Everett F. Harrison, *The Son of God Among the Sons of Men*, 117–130. See also F. A. Noble: *Typical New Testament Conversions*, 103–118; G. Campbell Morgan in the *Westminster Pulpit*, Vol. 3, pp. 161–168; and David Gregg: *Studies in John's Gospel*, 148–161.

Sermonic material on the printed text is not very important. On verses 1–5, see G. Campbell Morgan in the *Westminster Pulpit*, Vol. 8, pp. 145–152; on verse 2, J. A. Bain: *Questions Answered by Christ*, 185–190; on verses 35–38, Alexander Maclaren: *Triumphant Certainties*. Above all, see ten sermons by Charles H. Spurgeon, gathered together in the second volume of his *Sermons on Our Lord's Miracles*.

AUDIO-VISUAL AIDS.

FILM: "Blind Beggar of Jerusalem," Cathedral, 25 min., sd., b&w, guide. Follows Biblical account closely. Jesus appears on the screen. Accompanied by filmstrip of the same name.

JOHN 9:1. And as he passed by, he saw a man blind from his birth. 2. And his disciples asked him, saying, Rabbi, who sinned, this man, or his parents, that he should be born blind?

In the four Gospels we find three different occasions on which our Lord opened the eyes of blind men. The first occurred in Capernaum, when two blind men were healed, a miracle recorded only in Matthew 9:27–31; another near Jericho involving two other men, recorded in all of the Synoptics (Matt. 20:29–34; Mark 10:46–52; Luke 18:35–43); and this third miracle of restoration of sight which we are about to study, recorded only in John's Gospel. I believe that before entering upon the lesson itself, it might be well to consider the condition of a man born blind. "To be blind is to lose half of creation. Blindness renders half the works of God meaningless blanks. The heavens are resplendent with shining worlds and twinkling stars and golden clouds, but the blind do not know it. The towering mountains have a majesty and the blooming valleys are robed in beauty and the waterfalls are adorned with flashing rainbows, but the blind do not know it. There is love-light in the eyes of friends and a talking soul in the human face, but the blind do not know it. There is a world of graceful forms and a world of brilliant hues, but the blind do not know it. Blindness shuts out from life the grand and beautiful, the bright and glorious. It makes the universe as black as pitch and as unattractive. The lot of the hero of this story was that of a blind man. He was blind in the dark ages of blindness."

I. JESUS DISCUSSES THE STATE OF THE BLIND MAN WITH HIS DISCIPLES, John 9:1–5. The record of this miracle begins in a strange way. Apparently before the blind man says a word to Jesus — and it would seem he did not even know Jesus was there — even before the Lord speaks to the blind man, this unfortunate beggar becomes the subject of a discussion between Christ and His disciples. **1. And as he passed by, he saw a man blind from his birth. 2. And**

3. Jesus answered, Neither did this man sin, nor his parents: but that the works of God should be made manifest in him.

4. We must work the works of him that sent me, while it is day: the night cometh, when no man can work.

5. When I am in the world, I am the light of the world.

---

his disciples asked him, saying, Rabbi, who sinned, this man, or his parents, that he should be born blind? The question is somewhat ambiguous. If the man was born blind, how could that condition have been brought about by any sin on his part? They certainly were not referring to a state of pre-existence on his part. We must be very careful in making such a statement as this. While all illness, disease, and deformity is the *ultimate* result of the sinful condition of this human race, many men and women are born with handicaps which cannot possibly be accounted for, either by any definite sin on their part, or on the part of their immediate parents, and we ought not to go around saying that a certain condition existing from birth is some judgment of God upon the family. Many sins do have their judgments, but in the matter of physical deformities the ultimate cause no man knows. Our Lord replies to the question with one of the most profound utterances that ever escaped His lips. 3. Jesus answered, Neither did this man sin, nor his parents: but that the works of God should be made manifest in him. 4. We must work the works of him that sent me, while it is day: the night cometh, when no man can work. 5. When I am in the world, I am the light of the world. "The Authorized Version reads at the fourth verse, '*I* must work the works of Him that sent *Me*.' I draw attention to this simply to observe that the value of the teaching is not changed. I accept the consensus of scholarly opinion that the change is warranted. What Jesus really said was, 'We must work the works of Him that sent Me.' In the old rendering the singular pronoun 'I' agreed with the singular pronoun 'Me,' and emphasized the mission of Christ as the Son of God. In the new rendering the plural pronoun 'we' still recognizes the mission of Christ, but suggests the fellowship of His disciples in that mission. Now we come to that which to my own mind is supremely important in an understanding of the statement of Jesus. There are two readings of this text made possible by a change in the punctuation without the alteration of a single word. Let us read the next sentence after changing the period to a comma: 'Jesus answered, Neither did this man sin, nor his parents: but that the works of God should be made manifest in him, we must work the works of Him that sent Me, while it is day.' We immediately recognize that this is a great change. When investigating this matter, knowing my own incompetence in many ways, I submitted the passage with my suggestion to an eminent scholar. In his letter replying to my enquiries, he said: 'He would be an exceedingly bold scholar who would undertake to prove the punctuation be one way or the other on the mere ground of the Greek itself. It seems as if the question would have finally to be decided on doctrinal grounds, for it is plain that the difference in punctuation of the verse would change the meaning altogether. If one reading would be more in spirit with the tenor of Christ's teachings, as seems quite probable, that would be quite naturally preferable.' . . . Let us now attempt to gather up some of the values. The first value is, that the fact that the Son of God is sent to remove disability, is demonstration of another fact, that such disability is not the will of God for men. Said Jesus, He hath sent Me to do His works. What are they? To open those blind eyes! Therefore those blind eyes are not the will of God for a man. I think that discovery is gain, for even in Christian circles we hear a great deal — I was going to say blasphemy, I will amend my word and say nonsense — about suffering being the will of God. Every crippled child is contrary to the will of God; every mentally deficient man or woman is contrary to the will of God; every inefficient being spiritually is contrary to the will of God. There may be a sense in which it is in the will of God that they should continue to suffer disability. That is not a contradiction. I go

6. When he had thus spoken, he spat on the ground, and made clay of the spittle, and anointed his eyes with the clay,

7. and said unto him, Go, wash in the pool of Siloam (which is by interpretation, Sent). He went away therefore, and washed, and came seeing.

8. The neighbors therefore, and they that saw him aforetime, that he was a beggar, said, Is not this he that sat and begged?

9. Others said, It is he: others said, No, but he is like him. He said, I am *he*.

---

into the room where my little child is in bed tossed with fever. It is entirely against my will that my child should be in bed tossed with a fever. My little child says to me, Take me out! I answer, No, darling, you must stay here! Am I contradicting my original intention? God's will is not human suffering and disability, but human perfection, glory and beauty. Yet in that larger discipline of life, the meaning of which will break upon us from the other side, He allows us to remain in circumstances of affliction, the meaning of which is postponed. The deepest fact in the story is that when Jesus opened the blind eyes, He said in the midst of the world's history, God is against all human blindness." — *G. Campbell Morgan.*

II. **JESUS RESTORES SIGHT TO A MAN BORN BLIND,** 9:6, 7. It is interesting to note here that, as in the other miracles of our Lord, very little space is given to the actual miracle, but much is said of its significance. This is true also of Christ's resurrection; in fact, His actual coming forth from the tomb is nowhere described in the New Testament. 6. **When he had thus spoken, he spat on the ground, and made clay of the spittle, and anointed his eyes with the clay, 7. and said unto him, Go, wash in the pool of Siloam (which is by interpretation, Sent). He went away therefore, and washed, and came seeing.** "For the blind man here uses a sign language. The only answer we know for the question, why Jesus proceeded in this fashion (as also in Mark 7:33; 8:23) is that he knew best how to obtain his object. Placing the mud from his own spittle on the beggar's eye-lids lets him know that the healing power comes from Jesus. The beggar is not merely to wash this mud off, for which any place with water would suffice, but to wash it off in the pool of Siloam, which word or name signifies 'the One Sent.' For the beggar to act on this strange command, with nothing but an implied promise, requires some degree of faith, certainly also intended to be aroused by Jesus, as in the analogous case of the ten lepers (Luke 17:14). We may call these effects in the beggar psychological, if we will. Since the beggar is to co-operate in the procedure of his healing by going and washing in that pool, it is idle to deny these effects on the score that they are psychological. . . . Just as Jesus used the Temple as his own Father's house, in which he has a son's rights, so now he appropriates this Temple pool and its waters for his sacred purposes. How the spring and pool originally came to be called 'Siloam' need not be inquired; they now became indeed the spring and pool of Jesus, the One Sent. They were appropriated by him and used in his mission of making manifest the works of God and thus sending out light in the world (vv. 3, 5). We cannot assume that Jesus selected this pool for the beggar's washing without himself being conscious of the meaning of its name. He never acts without the most comprehensive insight. In this instance even the disciples may well have caught the connection: 'Wash in the pool of Siloam — of the One Sent.' Even the beggar afterwards does not say merely: 'Go wash!' but: 'Go to Siloam, and wash!' " — *R. C. H. Lenski.*

III. **THE UNBELIEVING NEIGHBORS AND PHARISEES REFUSE TO ACKNOWLEDGE THE MIRACLE,** 9:8–34.

1. THE QUESTION OF IDENTITY, vs. 8, 9. 8. **The neighbors therefore, and they that saw him aforetime, that he was a beggar, said, Is not this he that sat and**

10. They said therefore unto him, How then were thine eyes opened?

11. He answered, The man that is called Jesus made clay, and anointed mine eyes, and said unto me, Go to Siloam, and wash: so I went away and washed, and I received sight.

begged? 9. Others said, It is he: others said, No, but he is like him. He said, I am he. Here indeed we have the beginning of one of the strangest arguments to be found anywhere in the Scriptures. That the person walking around in their midst could now see, everyone had to admit, but somehow there was a unanimous reluctance on the part of these neighbors to recognize that a miracle had been performed, so they tried to explain the phenomenon some other way. Foolishly, they began to ask whether this man now seeing was the same beggar who had been blind during all the years they had known him! The whole discussion was rather stupid, like so many discussions in philosophy, and it was brought to an abrupt and final end, by the man simply saying, "I am he." He knew he was the man born blind, now seeing, and his testimony could not be contradicted.

2. THE QUESTION OF HOW HIS EYES WERE OPENED, vs. 10–15. From the matter of his identify, the discussion now turns to the method by which this man was healed of his blindness. 10. They said therefore unto him, How then were thine eyes opened? 11. He answered, The man that is called Jesus made clay, and anointed mine eyes, and said unto me, Go to Siloam, and wash: so I went away and washed, and I received sight. Note carefully that there is not one utterance of rejoicing on the part of the neighbors, or the Pharisees, over the fact that the man has had his sight restored. It would seem that this man's interrogators knew the answers to all the questions before asking them. They knew that Jesus was involved in this, and the miracle is so startling and incontrovertible that they are determined to destroy the power of this testimony by some subtle process of reasoning in which to entangle this man. There is no question about the man being in his right mind, for he can recall everything that happened. He is now brought to the Pharisees. "These Pharisees are the only ones who show concern, and even they do not know just what they want; for presently they themselves are divided. These Pharisees do not act as a regular court, either as belonging to the Sanhedrin, or as one of the two lesser courts in Jerusalem, each constituted of twenty-three members, or as rulers of a local synagogue. They act only as an incidental gathering of men of the influential Jewish party, just Pharisees who are bent on making their superior influence felt." — R. C. H. Lenski. The once-blind man now has to go over the entire incident again. The essence of his testimony is this: He was blind from birth; He met a man Jesus, who told him to go to the pool of Siloam and wash; this he did; the result was that he received his sight.

3. THE QUESTION OF WHO COULD PERFORM SUCH MIRACLES, vs. 16–23. Verse 16 opens with "therefore . . . ." What would be a normal sentence following such testimony? That this must indeed be a man from God. That is not what we find here, however. The third problem is now raised, and this time by the Pharisees, who were skilled in theological discussions, and who had a score of worthless reasons for not accepting Christ as the Sent One of God. Realizing that this miracle had been performed on the Sabbath day, they said that settled the question — the one who did this could not be of God. "We cannot be sure whether this is the last day of the Feast of the Tabernacles (7:37), or the next Sabbath. There were seven miracles of mercy wrough on the Sabbath: (1) withered hand (Matt. 12:9); (2) demoniac at Capernaum (Mark 1:21); (3) Simon's wife's mother (Matt. 8:14, 15); (4) woman bowed down eighteen years (Luke 13:14); (5) dropsical man (Luke 14:1); (6) paralytic at Bethesda (John 5:10); (7) man born blind." — A. Plummer. Others said that a man who was a sinner could not possibly perform such a miracle as this, recognizing that such a deliverance from blindness could only be by the power and with the approval of God. So they turned to the blind

24. So they called a second time the man that was blind, and said unto him, Give glory to God: we know that this man is a sinner.

25. He therefore answered, Whether he is a sinner, I know not: one thing I know, that, whereas I was blind, now I see.

26. They said therefore unto him, What did he to thee? how opened he thine eyes?

27. He answered them, I told you even now, and ye did not hear; wherefore would ye hear it again? would ye also become his disciples?

man again, to ask him what *he* thought of the person who had so graciously and undeniably given him his sight. This time we discover that the man's conception of the One who healed him is higher than at first, for he answered: "He is a prophet." "Not yet the Messiah, not yet the Son of God; of these higher dignities of his benefactor the man as yet has no guess; but what he believes Him he boldly declares Him, 'a prophet' — one furnished with a message from above, and attesting that message by deeds which no man could do, except God were with him (John 3:2; 4:19; 6:14). They who asked this cared not in the least for the judgment of the man, but they hoped to mold him into an instrument for their own wicked purposes." — *R. C. Trench.*

4. THE CLEAR TESTIMONY OF THE ONE ONCE BLIND, vs. 24, 25. **24. So they called a second time the man that was blind, and said unto him, Give glory to God: we know that this man is a sinner.** "In all due form, as before a court of law, the beggar is brought in again. Expectantly he faces these Jews who pose as a court, wondering what they had extracted from his parents. It is John who calls him 'the man that was blind' (we would say 'had been blind'). The investigation has ended, the verdict is now handed out, and though it deals with Jesus, is addressed to the beggar. One of the Jews acted as spokesman. 'Give glory to God' is an adjuration (compare Josh. 7:19; 1 Sam. 6:5) to seal as the truth before God the summary of the whole matter, at which these Pharisees have arrived, and to which they demand that the beggar should solemnly assent by assuming the adjuration himself, plus the finding to which it is attached. . . . The Pharisees admit nothing about the healing in their verdict; they do not even say that God wrought it; they ignore it altogether. What they say is this: 'Give glory to God now by telling the truth, and this is the truth, which *we* now positively know — and *we* are the people to know — that this man is an open sinner.' They imply that they have sounded this thing thoroughly, that besides the man's testimony they have heard that of others, and the only correct conclusion of the whole case is what they now state. They count on their superior authority for submission on the part of the beggar." — *R. C. H. Lenski.* **25. He therefore answered, Whether he is a sinner, I know not: one thing I know, that, whereas I was blind, now I see.** We might almost say that this is the key verse of the chapter. "No amount of pretentious contradiction, no badgering by men of higher station, can shake him from this confidence, that though he was blind, he now sees. The rights of personality and the validity of individual experience are widely recognized today. No one is in position to deny what another has claimed for himself unless there is unbalanced mentality or wilful perversion that can be demonstrated. Some types of experience, to be sure, can be labelled delusion when all the factors are broken down. But no one of these qualifying elements or any other is present in this instance. Here is a normal man who has passed through an abnormal experience and is able calmly to appraise it." — *E. F. Harrison.*

5. THE QUESTION OF HOW IS AGAIN DEBATED, vs. 26–27. **26. They said therefore unto him, What did he to thee? how opened he thine eyes? 27. He answered them, I told you even now, and ye did not hear; wherefore would ye hear it again? would ye also become his disciples?** "The tables are being turned. They, as judges, thought to question him, as defendant; he now becomes the judge, and

28. And they reviled him, and said, Thou art his disciple; but we are disciples of Moses.

29. We know that God hath spoken unto Moses: but as for this man, we know not whence he is.

30. The man answered and said unto them, Why, herein is the marvel, that ye know not whence he is, and *yet* he opened mine eyes.

31. We know that God heareth not sinners: but if any man be a worshipper of God, and do his will, him he heareth.

32. Since the world began it was never heard that any one opened the eyes of a man born blind.

33. If this man were not from God, he could do nothing.

34. They answered and said unto him, Thou wast altogether born in sins, and dost thou teach us? And they cast him out.

---

probes them as defendants with telling questions.   God helps his own in the tests to which they are put for Jesus' sake. . . .   He is hardly making only an artful thrust at the Pharisees; his artless simplicity leads him to entertain the thought that possibly these men are willing to change their minds about Jesus." — *R. C. H. Lenski.*

6. THE ONE ONCE BLIND DECLARES HIS CONVICTION THAT JESUS IS OF GOD, vs. 28-33.   The Pharisees have been utterly routed, one might say, in their attempt to confuse this man and to rob Christ of the glory which was rightly His because of the supernatural act He had performed.   The determination of these people that Christ must not be recognized as of God is nothing less than satanic — as all such opposition to Him ever since has been satanic — and there is no other way to account for it.   28. **And they reviled him, and said, Thou art his disciple; but we are disciples of Moses.**   29. **We know that God hath spoken unto Moses: but as for this man, we know not whence he is.**   In dealing with the evidence at hand, all their efforts have failed, so they have to go back to Moses, a person living fourteen hundred years before, and boast that they are his disciples, in contrast with this poor man being a disciple of Christ.   30. **The man answered and said unto them, Why, herein is the marvel, that ye know not whence he is, and *yet* he opened mine eyes.**   31. **We knew that God heareth not sinners: but if any man be a worshipper of God, and do his will, him he heareth.**   32. **Since the world began it was never heard that any one opened the eyes of a man born blind.**   33. **If this man were not from God, he could do nothing.**   "What they intended as a slighting reference to His humble origin became a boomerang as the man born blind turned it right back at them.   These Pharisees were supposed to know. They had already declared with some finality that Jesus was a sinner.   Now it is pointed out to them that everyone knows the obvious truth that God does not hear those who wilfully oppose Him, but He does hear a genuine worshipper, one who truly seeks to do His will.   Warming to his subject, the speaker proceeds to another observation.   No one in the past history of his people had been healed of congenital blindness.   He was not a doctor of the law, but he had searched with the help of others the records of the past to see if they held out even a faint ray of hope for him, and there was none.   Such a cure had never been made.   Now the fact that it has been made upon him by Jesus is all the proof he needs that Jesus must have been heard of God and must have truly sought to honor God." — *E. F. Harrison.*   "The logic in the little lecture is invincible.   It deals with premises which are axiomatic to all Jews.   Hence the conclusion is inevitable." — *R. C. H. Lenski.*

7. HE IS CAST OUT, THOUGH HIS WORDS COULD NOT BE CONTRADICTED, v. 34. **They answered and said unto him, Thou wast altogether born in sins, and dost thou teach us?   And they cast him out.**   "What the disciples thought possible, and

35. Jesus heard that they had cast him out; and finding him, he said, Dost thou believe on the Son of God?

36. He answered and said, And who is he, Lord, that I may believe on him?

37. Jesus said unto him, Thou hast both seen him, and he it is that speaketh with thee.

38. And he said, Lord, I believe. And he worshipped him.

---

what Jesus roundly denied (vv. 2, 3) these Jews make their shameful refuge, namely, that this man's affliction of blindness from his birth proved his wickedness, and that even to the present time. 'In sins' is placed forward for emphasis.'' — R. C. H. Lenski. "This violent putting of him forth from the hall of audience was only the beginning of the things which he should suffer for Christ's sake. Still there was, to use the words of Fuller on this very occasion, this comfort for him, that 'the power of the keys, when abused, doth not shut the door of heaven, but in such cases only shoot the bolt beside the lock, not debarring the innocent person entrance thereat.' " — R. C. Trench.

IV. **JESUS IN CONVERSATION WITH THE ONE ONCE BLIND LEADS HIM TO BELIEVE IN HIM AS THE SON OF GOD,** 9:35–38. **35. Jesus heard that they had cast him out; and finding him, he said, Dost thou believe on the Son of God?** "The emphasis of the pronoun is remarkable and may be contrasted with verse 34. *Dost thou*, the outcast, thou that hast received outward sight, thou that hast borne a courageous testimony, *believe on the Son of Man* — cast thyself with complete trust on Him who gathers up in Himself, who bears and who transfigures all that belongs to man? The thought of 'the Son of Man' stands in true contrast with the selfish isolation of 'the Jews.' The new society, seen here in its beginning, rests upon this foundation, wide as humanity itself." — B. F. Westcott. **36. He answered and said, And who is he, Lord, that I may believe on him? 37. Jesus said unto him, Thou hast both seen him, and he it is that speaketh with thee.** "Did you ever notice how exquisitely beautiful the addition in this text is to the words which He used to the woman of Samaria? To her, He simply said, 'I that speak unto thee am he.' To the man who had only had a pair of eyes that could not see anything for some four and twenty hours, He said, 'Thou hast *seen* Him.' And was not that enough to prove His claim? 'Thou hast seen him.' He gave you the eyes to see; now He has given you the Christ to look at. . . . Be sure of this, that the perception of Christ's real presence, and work with us and on us, which is made ours through faith, is as real, as direct, and I believe a great deal more reliable, than the thing that we call 'sight,' which is secured by the plan of a material beam of light upon nerves that may be diseased, and may carry erroneous messages to the brain." — *Alexander Maclaren.* **38. And he said, Lord, I believe. And he worshipped him.** This man, of course, did not have a full conception of all that the Sonship of Christ involved, for even the Apostles themselves were slow in coming to realize the full meaning of Christ's deity. But this man did believe that Christ had come from God, and He was the Sent One of God, that He was God's prophet, that He was God's Son, that He was doing God's work, that His words were true. A man who believes this much will believe all else that he finds concerning Christ in the Word of God. This man had not yet been trained in the theological formulations of the great creeds of the Church, but he knew Christ to be the Son of God, he loved Him, and bore testimony to Him. The fact that he worshipped Him "shows that his idea of the Son of God includes attributes of divinity. The word for worship occurs elsewhere in this Gospel only in 4:20–24 and 12:20, always of the idea of the worship of God." — A. Plummer.

V. **JESUS' FINAL WORDS TO THE PHARISEES,** vs. 39–41. "We see in these verses how dangerous it is to possess knowledge, if we do not make good use of it. The rulers of the Jews were fully persuaded that they knew all religious truth. They were indignant at the very idea of being ignorant and devoid of spiritual eyesight. 'Are we blind also?' they cried. And then came the mighty sentence, 'If ye were blind, ye should have no sin; but now ye say, We see; therefore your sin remaineth.' Knowledge undoubtedly is a very great blessing. The man who cannot read, and is utterly ignorant of Scripture, is in a pitiable condition. He is at the mercy of any false teacher who comes across him, and may be taught to take up any absurd creed, or to follow any vicious practice. Almost any education is better than no education at all. But when knowledge only sticks in a man's head, and has no influence over his heart and life, it becomes a most perilous possession. And when, in addition to this, its possessor is self-conceited and self-satisfied, and fancies he knows everything, the result is one of the worst states of soul into which man can fall. There is far more hope about him who says, 'I am a poor blind sinner and want God to teach me,' than about him who is ever saying, 'I know it, I know it, I am not ignorant,' and yet cleaves to his sins. — The sin of that man 'remaineth.' Let us use diligently whatever religious knowledge we possess, and ask continually that God would give us more. Let us never forget that the devil himself is a creature of vast head-knowledge, and yet none the better for it, because it is not rightly used. Let our constant prayer be that which David so often sent up in the hundred and nineteenth Psalm, 'Lord, teach me Thy statutes: — give me understanding: — unite my heart to fear Thy name.'' — *J. C. Ryle.*

THE LESSON IN LIFE, LITERATURE, AND ARCHAEOLOGY.

In the second volume of the great life of Hudson Taylor by Dr. and Mrs. Howard Taylor, we are told that in Mr. Taylor's own home in China two texts were hung on the walls of the dining room — "I must work the works of Him that sent me," and "Even Christ pleased not himself." The gifted biographers add, "That 'must' was very real to the missionary household. It was work, real, earnest, self-sacrificing work, that filled the busy days, crowding chapel and guest-hall with friendly hearers."

A TRUTH FOR THE CLASS TO CARRY AWAY.

In this age of increasing antagonism to the person of Christ and the Christian religion, with attempts being made, even in our own country, to reduce Him to the level of other religious leaders, we who are His followers must be sure that we have had a definite experience of miraculous transformation by His power, and then must let the world know what Christ has done for us.

What made the Pharisees so reluctant to acknowledge that this miracle had been performed by Jesus? How many different factors led this formerly blind man to believe that Christ was truly the Son of God? What part did the man himself play in this marvelous restoration of sight? How can religious leaders become actual hindrances to the welfare of the souls of men? Are there some things that we can believe though we cannot tell how these things happen? (Certainly. We can believe that turning a switch will illuminate a room, though we may know nothing about electricity.)

LESSON IX. — February 28.

THE GOOD SHEPHERD. — John 10.

PRINTED TEXT, John 10:1–14, 27.

Devotional Reading: Ezekiel 34:11–16.
Beginner Topic: A BOY'S LUNCH.
  Lesson Material: Matthew 14:13–21; Mark 6:30–44; Luke 9:10–17; John 6:1–13.
  Memory Verse: Praise Jehovah: for Jehovah is good. Psalm 135:3.

Primary Topic: JESUS' STORY OF A SHEPHERD.
　　Lesson Material: John 10:1–5, 11–14.
　　Memory Verse: Jesus went about all the cities and villages, teaching . . . and preaching . . . and healing. Matthew 9:35.
Junior Topic: JESUS' CONCERN FOR ALL PEOPLE.
　　Lesson Material: John 10:1–30.
　　Memory Verse: I am the good shepherd; and I know mine own, and mine own know me. John 10:14.
Intermediate-Senior Topic: THE GOOD SHEPHERD.
　　Lesson Material: John 10.
　　Memory Verse: Other sheep I have, which are not of this fold: them also I must bring, and they shall hear my voice; and they shall become one flock, one shepherd. John 10:16.
Topic for Young People and Adults: CHRIST'S LOVE FOR ALL PEOPLE.
　　Lesson Material: John 10.
　　Memory Verse: Other sheep I have, which are not of this fold: them also I must bring, and they shall hear my voice; and they shall become one flock, one shepherd. John 10:16.

THE TEACHER AND HIS CLASS.

The Younger Classes may be introduced to this lesson by having their attention drawn to a subject which, possibly, they have never thought of specifically, and yet with which they are intimately acquainted — the human voice. Ask the children if their mother, their teacher, near-by neighbor, or perhaps an aunt, were to speak to them from behind a screen, would they be able to identify each one as they spoke their name. Of course they would. Our Lord is speaking here of those who *hear* and *know* His voice, as distinguished from the voice of others. Of course we do not literally hear the voice of Jesus today, but when we read the Gospels and listen to the words that He spoke, we are hearing Him.

The Older Classes may easily enter into this lesson by the teacher's emphasizing the matter of leadership. I am writing this a week before President-elect Eisenhower takes office. We have chosen him as our leader. Now, while he has a cabinet, the House of Representatives, and the Senate, as well as thousands of other people to help him, the thirty-five million people who voted for him as leader thereby expressed their willingness to follow *him* in the difficult days ahead for our nation. In a higher realm, and for all eternity, our Lord is our Leader, our Shepherd, bringing us to God. Most of the 10th chapter of John's Gospel is concerned with this subject.

THE LESSON IN ITS SETTING.

Time. — The first part of our lesson, through verse 21, took place in October, A.D. 29, and the remaining portion, down to verse 40, in December of that year.

Place. — The entire chapter with the exception of the last three verses, records discourses uttered in Jerusalem.

THE PLAN OF THE LESSON.

SUBJECT: Christ's Own Words Concerning His Relationships to Mankind and to God the Father Testify to His Absolute and Eternal Preeminence.

I. CHRIST THE GOOD SHEPHERD, John 10:1–21.
　1. The true shepherd and false shepherds contrasted, vs. 1–6.
　　a. in relation to the sheepfold, 1–3a.
　　b. in relation to the sheep, 3b–6.
　2. Christ the door, vs. 7–9.
　3. The objects of the good shepherd and false shepherds contrasted, vs. 10–14.
　4. The good Shepherd gives his life for the sheep, vs. 16–18.
　5. The division among the people caused by this address, vs. 19–21.

II. CHRIST CLAIMS TO BE ONE WITH THE FATHER, 10:22–39.
　1. The question of the Jews, vs. 22–26.
　2. Christ and his sheep, vs. 27–29.
　3. Christ and the Father, v. 30.
　4. The great debate that followed, vs. 31–39.

THE TEACHER'S LIBRARY.

On the entire subject of shepherd-life in Palestine see Anna F. Mamreov: *A Day with the*

Good Shepherd (1910); Stephen A. Haboush: *My Shepherd Life in Galilee* (1917); W. M. Thomson: *The Land and the Book,* 201–205; and the article by Frank Richards, "Sheep-Shepherd," in James Hastings' *Dictionary of Christ and the Gospels,* Vol. 2, pp. 620–621. On Christ as Shepherd, see three sermons by Charles H. Spurgeon, in his *The Messiah: Sermons on Our Lord's Names and Titles and Attributes,* 255–290; Samuel H. Geisy: *The I AM'S of Christ,* 259–286; T. Marjoribanks: *The Sevenfold "I AM,"* 65 ff.; Ada R. Habershon: *The Study of the Types,* 135–142; David Gregg: *Studies in John's Gospel,* 162–177. On Christ as the Door and the Shepherd, see also, G. Campbell Morgan: *The Parables and Metaphors of Our Lord,* 309–318.

For the passages of our lesson which speak of Christ's death, there is nothing richer than the pages in George Smeaton: *The Doctrine of the Atonement as Taught by Christ Himself,* 319–333, and 368–378. (I am pleased to report that this book, which had become exceedingly scarce, is now available from the recent reprint by the Zondervan Publishing House of Grand Rapids.)

Among the commentaries on John's Gospel, those by Godet, Lenski, and Marcus Dods will be found especially helpful, but let me commend to all teachers the great work by E. C. Hoskyns, *The Fourth Gospel* (London, 1947), one of the greatest books on John's Gospel ever writen — if one wishes a book for study.

It is hardly necessary to mention sermonic material, but on verse 3 there is a good sermon in W. R. Nicoll: *Sunday Evening,* 217–223; on verse 9, A. C. Gaebelein: *The Church in the House,* 132–142; on verse 11, G. Campbell Morgan in *The Westminster Pulpit,* Vol. 4, pp. 297–304; H. P. Liddon: *Easter in St. Pauls,* 312–322; and A. G. Gossip: *The Galilean Accent,* 96 ff.

AUDIO-VISUAL AIDS.

SLIDE SET: "Jesus the Good Shepherd," Church-Craft, 6 sl., col.

FILMSTRIP: "Shepherd's Psalm," R. C. Mitchel Productions, 25 fr., col.

SLIDE SET: "The Shepherd and His Sheep," Visual Education Service (Available from Society for Visual Education), 29 sl., col., with book of the same name. There is also a filmstrip of the same name (61 fr., col., text-on-film). This is from the Bible Books for Small People series.

JOHN 10:1. Verily, verily, I say unto you, He that entereth not by the door into the fold of the sheep, but climbeth up some other way, the same is a thief and a robber.

2. But he that entereth in by the door is the shepherd of the sheep.

Since our lesson includes the great discourse of our Lord in which He identifies Himself as the Good Shepherd of the sheep, it might be well to recall here how frequently this metaphor appears throughout the Scriptures. Israel is referred to as God's flock again and again in the Old Testament, as in Psalm 23; 79:13; 80:1; Isaiah 40:11; Jeremiah 23:1–4. The true Shepherd of Israel, none other than the Son of David, is contrasted with the false shepherds who betrayed the children of Israel in Jeremiah 33, Ezekiel 34 and 37, and Zechariah 11. "In the New Testament this rich and impressive metaphorical language comes to rest with its application to Jesus as the true Shepherd of the people of God (Mark 6:34; 14:27; Luke 12:32; 15:3–7; Matt. 9:35, 36; 15:24; 18:12 sqq., 26:31; Heb. 13:20; 1 Pet. 2:25; 5:4; compare Rev. 12:5; 19:15 in the Greek) and to His disciples as the shepherds who exercise authority in His name (Matt. 10:6; Acts 20:28; Eph. 4:11; 1 Pet. 5:2, 3; compare Rev. 2:27). The activity of the false shepherds reaches its climax both in the opposition of the Jewish authorities to Jesus, and in those false prophets and powerful men who, having broken into the Church, usurp the authority of the true pastors of the sheep (Matt. 7:15, 16; Acts 20:29, 30). This Christian background of language and metaphor, which itself presumes the Old Testament background, is wholly sufficient to account for the form and content of the parable in the Fourth Gospel." — *E. C. Hoskyns.*

I. **CHRIST THE GOOD SHEPHERD,** John 10:1–21. It is a little difficult to divide these verses, though I have tried, once again, to make a new outline. Throughout this section, down to verse 13, the work of Christ as the Good Shepherd is contrasted with the false shepherds, whom the Old Testament so frequently condemns; in fact, the discourse itself begins with a statement concerning those who seek to enter the sheepfold by any other way than the door. 1. **Verily, verily, I say unto you, He that entereth not by the door into the fold of the sheep, but climbeth up some other way, the same is a thief and a robber. 2. But he that entereth in by the door is the shepherd of the sheep.** Before proceeding further

75

3. To him the porter openeth; and the sheep hear his voice: and he calleth his own sheep by name, and leadeth them out.

4. When he hath put forth all his own, he goeth before them, and the sheep follow him: for they know his voice.

5. And a stranger will they not follow, but will flee from him: for they know not the voice of strangers.

in the interpretation of this passage, we should have before us some conception of the meaning of the door in relation to the shepherd. "We must be careful to draw the distinction between the fold and the flock. The fold was a walled or palisaded enclosure, always open to the wind. The very word translated *fold* implies that, the sweeping wind, not a roof, but an enclosing wall. The sheep did not climb the walls. In that country there was only one entry, one door, never two. . . . It was never a gateway in those Eastern folds, never a door on hinges. It was merely an opening. . . . It was my privilege to cross the Atlantic with Sir George Adam Smith. He told me this story. He was travelling in the East one day, and came up to one of those folds, a wall in this case, and there was an opening in the wall. The shepherd was on hand, so Sir George said to him, 'Is that a fold for sheep?' 'Oh yes,' he replied. Sir George then said, 'I only see one way in.' 'Yes,' said the man, 'there it is, there is the door,' pointing to the opening in the wall. Then Sir George said to him, 'But there is no door there'; and to his amazement — for it was naturally said, they were not talking of the New Testament or of Christianity — this shepherd said to him, 'Oh I am the door.' Sir George said his mind went back to John's record. He said to the shepherd, 'What do you mean by calling yourself the door?' To which the shepherd replied, 'The sheep go inside, and I come there and lie down across the threshold, and no sheep can get out except over my body, and no wolf can get in except over me.' " — *G. Campbell Morgan.* The one who climbs up some other way is trying to get at the sheep, which are not his possession, and, stealing them, he will destroy them, as we read in verse 10. I frankly believe that every religious leader in the world who sets up some cult, attempting to lead men and women away from Christ, and pretending to offer them a way of life and hope, apart from Him, is of these thieves and robbers. Dr. Gaebelein has a great sermon on the significance of the door. He speaks first of the door of the ark, in Genesis 7; the blood-marked door, Exodus 12:13; the door of hope, Isaiah 2:15; the door of the Tabernacle, Exodus 26:1; and the shut door, Matthew 25:1–13. **3. To him the porter openeth; and the sheep hear his voice: and he calleth his own sheep by name, and leadeth them out.** Sir William R. Nicoll in a remarkable sermon on this verse identifies the porter, the doorkeeper, with the Holy Spirit. On hearing the porter's voice, we shall have something more to say later. **4. When he hath put forth all his own, he goeth before them, and the sheep follow him: for they know his voice. 5. And a stranger will they not follow, but will flee from him: for they know not the voice of strangers.** The reference here is not to the porter but to the shepherd. May I use here again an illustration from an experience of mine in Palestine some years ago, in the very valley where it is thought David wrote the Twenty-third Psalm. After carefully listening to the shepherds as they called their own sheep, with a strange guttural sound which to us seemed quite simple, I tried to utter the same sound. Instead of being totally indifferent to the new voice, the sheep actually got up and ran away. They not only knew that I was a stranger, and not their shepherd, but they were afraid of me. This is why a Christian, truly saturated with the Word of God, flees from so-called religious teachers who deny the deity of Christ, who are enemies of His Cross, who repudiate supernaturalism, who wish to synthetically unite all different religions into one vast undefined, acceptable mass of various ethical and moral precepts. My friend Mr. Douglas Ober of Baltimore once told me that in discussing this passage with a shepherd, he was told that the only time a sheep will follow a voice not belonging to his own shepherd

76

6. This parable spake Jesus unto them: but they understood not what things they were which he spake unto them.

7. Jesus therefore said unto them again, Verily, verily, I say unto you, I am the door of the sheep.

8. All that came before me are thieves and robbers: but the sheep did not hear them.

9. I am the door; by me if any man enter in, he shall be saved, and shall go in and out, and shall find pasture.

---

is when he is sick. **6. This parable spake Jesus unto them: but they understood not what things they were which he spake unto them.** The Pharisees were *not* seeking the truth, as they constantly claimed to be. They were bound by legalistic chains, they were self-righteous; while they made a pretense of being pious, their own hearts were often wicked. This would not be true of all Pharisees, of course, but the larger number. With Christ before them in a life of absolute sinlessness, uttering words nobler, more heavenly than any heard on earth before, able to perform miracles, going about doing good, after looking Him over, they rejected Him, called Him a blasphemer, and said He was worthy of death. They understood the words Jesus was uttering, but they would not comprehend the truth behind the words, that Christ was the Shepherd. Many people listen to Gospel sermons, expressed in the plainest language, but leave the church having absorbed nothing.

Our Lord now turns from the metaphor of the shepherd to that of the door. **7. Jesus therefore said unto them again, Verily, verily, I say unto you, I am the door of the sheep. 8. All that came before me are thieves and robbers: but the sheep did not hear them.** The identification of "all who came before me" as thieves and robbers has given rise to much speculation. I think the words of Hoskyns are adequate here. "Every claim in the past, or in the present to give life except through Jesus is destructive of life; all who make the claim have been and are thieves and robbers, whom the true servants of God have never followed. In this all-embracing condemnation the Hebrew Patriarchs, Moses, and the Prophets of Israel, are, of course, not included. Their inclusion would contradict the whole tenor of the Fourth Gospel (e.g., 4:22; 5:45-47; 6:45; 7:19; 8:56; 12:38-41) and of every other New Testament document; and moreover, it would mean that the Old Testament Scriptures were in themselves life-giving or claimed to be so. But this is precisely what the Evangelist will not allow. The Jews search the Scriptures because they suppose wrongly that in them they have eternal life — 'and these are they which bear witness of me; and ye will not come to me, that ye may have life' (5:40)." — *E. C. Hoskyns.* **9. I am the door; by me if any man enter in, he shall be saved, and shall go in and out, and shall find pasture.** Now for the first time there enters into this beautiful discourse the word *saved*, one of the greatest words in our language, embracing everything that God longs to do for us through Christ. The verb translated *saved* "means not only to be rescued and delivered, but includes the condition that results, to be safe. Here the context demands the latter, and this whether the shepherd is meant or the sheep. . . . The image is not that of a fold as a refuge to which a sheep may flee for safety, for in the next breath Jesus speaks of going out and finding pasture. Would the sheep then be exposed again? Moreover, the entire conception of a sheep going in and out of a fold at pleasure is wrong. No sheep does that. It is led in by the shepherd and led out by him. Nor does the sheep go out and seek, and perhaps find, pasture for itself. This is not the business of the sheep at all, but that of the shepherd, and he always makes certain of the pasture. All is badly out of line if by 'anyone' we understand a sheep; all is perfectly in line when we understand a shepherd." — *R. C. H. Lenski.*

Our Lord returns now to the matter of these thieves, false shepherds. The last half of this verse has been a favorite text of ministers in every generation, but we

10. The thief cometh not, but that he may steal, and kill, and destroy: I came that they may have life, and may have *it* abundantly.

11. I am the good shepherd: the good shepherd layeth down his life for the sheep.

12. He that is a hireling, and not a shepherd, whose own the sheep are not, beholdeth the wolf coming, and leaveth the sheep, and fleeth, and the wolf snatcheth them, and scattereth *them:*

13. *He fleeth* because he is a hireling, and careth not for the sheep.

---

ought to note that the verse begins with a terrible statement regarding the purpose of the thief. **10. The thief cometh not, but that he may steal, and kill, and destroy: I came that they may have life, and may have** *it* **abundantly.** Ultimately this thief is the devil: Satan has no other object than this, to destroy everything worthwhile in a man's life, and he rejoices in the perishing of every soul. Hospitals, asylums and such institutions are filled with those whom Satan has been destroying — and I do not mean that all sickness and mental troubles are the direct result of Satan's activity, by any means. I spoke at a mission in a near-by city recently, where I had nearly four hundred men in front of me, and on the very faces of many could be seen the marks of these frightful, destroying influences of Satan. Nineteen hundred years of history since Jesus came, present the testimony of millions of lives that to receive Christ is to be the possessor of abundant life, abundance of peace, joy, love, hope, liberty, moral life, spiritual life, life now and life forever — the life that is in Christ. No other person gives this.

11. I am the good shepherd: the good shepherd layeth down his life for the sheep. 12. He that is a hireling, and not a shepherd, whose own the sheep are not, beholdeth the wolf coming, and leaveth the sheep, and fleeth, and the wolf snatcheth them, and scattereth *them:* **13.** *He fleeth* **because he is a hireling, and careth not for the sheep.** We have here another great theme regarding the shepherd. Not only does he know his sheep, and that by name; bringing them to pasture; saving them, and giving them abundant life, but in addition to all this, he declares that he has come to lay down his life for the sheep. This is one of the great statements of Christ concerning His death. "The phrase 'lay down his life' is characteristically Johannine. It denotes the voluntary death of Jesus (15:13; 1 John 3:16) and that martyrdom which is conditioned by faith in Him (13:37, 38). The application of the complementary phrase 'take it again' (vv. 17, 18) to the Resurrection is important for the exegesis of the Washing of the Feet. Whether or no the words 'lay down his life' echo the Marcan 'give his life' (Mark 10:45; Matt. 20:28) the meaning is the same." — *E. C. Hoskyns.* "He in substance says that His death, though a violent one, and necessarily inflicted by other hands, would not be against His will, but His own spontaneous act; that He could ward it off if He pleased; but that He would voluntarily submit to it for the sake of His sheep, and to secure His right to them. When He says that He giveth His life for the sheep, He intimates that, in His capacity as a substitute, and as the High Priest, who was called of God, He would lay down His life for His people, by a voluntary act of self-oblation. And He announces in the sequel, as we shall see, that He had full authority over Himself, and was about to do what was competent to no created intelligence, to none but a divine person, to die for His fellows, or, as He sacerdotally expresses it, to lay down His life for the sheep. . . . 'The good Shepherd giveth His life *for* the sheep.' The phrase indisputably means, for their benefit, for their good. Nor must it be omitted, that when the clause in which this expression occurs, denotes *instead of* — which it frequently does — this latter idea is to be regarded as rather involved in the nature of the transaction, than derived from the preposition itself. When He says, therefore, that He died or laid down His life for the sheep, the phraseology implies that from the nature of the case, He suffered in their room and stead. . . . He thus represents Himself

14. I am the good shepherd; and I know mine own, and mine own know me,

as laying down His life to save theirs from the danger and destruction which inevitably impended, or as dying to separate His sheep from those that were exposed to the destroyer, and ready to be devoured." — *George Smeaton.* **14. I am the good shepherd; and I know mine own, and mine own know me.** Here we should emphasize the precious truth that Christ knows His sheep, and knows all about them. "He knows us, not merely as we seem to be, but as we are. Others look us in the face day by day, and we them. They touch the surface of our real life; perhaps they see a little way below the surface. But 'what man knoweth the things of a man, save the spirit of man that is in him?' (1 Cor. 2:11). What do they know of that which passes in the inmost sanctuary of the reason, of the conscience, of the heart? Nay; do they know much of our outward circumstances; of our trials, our struggles, our exceptional difficulties, or what we deem such? . . . There is One Being Who knows all; upon Whom nothing that passes is lost; to Whom nothing that affects us is matter of indifference. To Him all hearts are open, all desires known; from Him no secrets are hid. . . . Each moment that passes adds something which He has already anticipated; but yet the addition of new details forfeits nothing in the clearness of His comprehensive survey. It is because He knows us thus perfectly that He is able to help us, guide us, feed us, save us, if we will, even to the uttermost." — *H. P. Liddon.* It is very significant that the verb *to shepherd* is also used as a verb for indicating *feeding*, which we can well understand; but it also means in some places *to rule*, and thus it is used in Revelation 2:27; 12:5, and 19:15. This links up with the great theme of what is called in the civilizations of antiquity, and especially in Egypt, the "shepherd kings," and Christ is just this. He is our shepherd who leads us: He is our King who rules us — and that forever.

While it is not in the printed text, I do think we should say a word concerning verse 16, "And other sheep I have, which are not of this fold: them also I must bring, and they shall hear my voice; and they shall become one flock, one shepherd." Some interpret our Lord's words here to mean people who are acceptable to God, even though they have no relationship to the Church of Christ; or, possibly personalities living on other planets, but I am quite sure that Bishop Westcott is correct in saying that, "the flock of Christ is not confined to those enclosed in the Jewish fold, whether in Palestine or elsewhere. Even before His death, He has other sheep who, even if they know Him not, are truly His (11:52). The words are the historic affirmation of the truth set forth in John 1:4 and 9." Verse 18 has profound significance, namely, that Christ offered Himself a sacrifice for sin. No man could slay Him; though the Jews might crucify Him, no one could take His life until the hour came when He was ready to give up that life. It was a voluntary death, and He could bring life back into His body, which you and I cannot do. "The Good Shepherd is not the kind of shepherd that is willing or ready to lay down his life for the sheep, but Jesus, the Master, who had actually done so. Here, as in 2:19, the Resurrection is thought of as an action of Jesus Himself, whereas elsewhere it is referred to as an act of God (Acts 2:24; Rom. 1:4). The Evangelist can use language that seems to attribute independent action to Jesus, only because there was nowhere in His words or actions any independence whatever — I can do nothing of myself (5:30)." — *E. C. Hoskyns.*

As a result of these tremendous sayings, words that had never before passed the lips of any man on earth, there was a violent *division* among the Jews, as there had been before, and has been since. Some said He was demon-possessed, but others declared that such was impossible, for He was opening the eyes of the blind, and a demon-possessed man could never do that.

II. **CHRIST CLAIMS TO BE ONE WITH THE FATHER,** 10:22–39. I believe it is better for the teacher to devote his entire half-hour of instruction to the

27. My sheep hear my voice, and I know them, and they follow me:

shepherding work of the Lord Jesus, and keep to the printed text. We can then give only a word to this concluding section, important as it is. 27. **My sheep hear my voice, and I know them, and they follow me.** There is a truth here so deep that I do not pretend to fully fathom it. The word *hear* in this text means to hear believingly, of course. Many hear the Word of God but reject it. This statement would seem to imply that there are certainly people in the world in each generation toward whom the grace of God is savingly extended. They are Christ's sheep, by choice, and love, and redemption. It is to those who, hearing and believing, He gives eternal life. We should certainly here be free from any mere technical bondage to words and ask ourselves the question, Do we believe that only Christ can give eternal life? Sitting at the breakfast table with a dear friend of mine in London last summer, and looking around at the crowded neighborhood there, I said, "Do you believe that all the people in this neighborhood without Christ are lost forever?" He replied, "I have no other answer but that of the New Testament — they are lost." This truth is also found expressed in 18:37. I am sure that verses 28 and 29 of this text teach nothing less than the comforting fact that when a man is saved by faith in Christ and is born again by a work of the Holy Spirit, is made a member of the body of Christ, and his name is written in the Lamb's Book of Life, nothing will ever be able to take away this divinely bestowed salvation. Since works do not attain salvation, but it is of grace, then works do not forfeit salvation, for God keeps us by grace. In concluding this lesson, let us not overlook the courteous way in which our Lord answers these questions. He was willing to discuss and debate His deity, His divine origin, His supernatural works, His oneness with the Father. Some contend that we should just preach the Gospel and let the Lord do the rest; in other words, we should never argue it, debate it, or carry on a prolonged discussion regarding its merits. A chapter like this contradicts any such statement. Christ gave a reason for His claims, and we should be ready to give a reason for the hope that is within us.

THE LESSON IN LIFE, LITERATURE, AND ARCHAEOLOGY.

The late Professor W. Mackintosh Mackay of Glasgow, in his fascinating book, *The Disease and Remedy of Sin*, gives this testimony of a Highland minister, Rev. Mr. Sage, whose wife had died with her first child, and because of which his faith, and even his reason, seemed to reel. "I lay down wishing that I might die. Then Conscience began to ask, 'Why did I wish to die?' My sorrows at once responded, 'Just to be with Harriet.' But was I so sure of that? If Harriet was in heaven, as I could not but hope she was, was nothing else to be the consequence of death but that I might go to be with her? I was struck dumb! So then, the only reason I wished to die was not to be 'with Christ,' but to be with Harriet. As if Harriet without Christ could make happiness for me! This discovery threw me into a terrible state of despondency. I was perambulating the garden at the time. I betook me to my bedroom and threw myself on my knees to pray; but could not. My spirit was angry, proud and unsubdued. God had deprived me of the object of my dearest affection. Not only so, but He had withdrawn the only source out of which I could draw strength. What a God I had to deal with then! How unlike me! But 'who is a God like unto Thee?' In the sovereignty of the Spirit's influence, that passage — 'I am the door' — glided into my mind without any previous attempt to seek it. Like a light dim at first it gradually brightened. I laid hold of 'the hope set before me.' If I may dare say, I did enter that door even then. At that solemn moment, notwithstanding outward bereavement, I experienced 'all joy and peace in believing.' I was enabled, without a murmur, to resign my beloved Harriet to His keeping."

A TRUTH FOR THE CLASS TO CARRY AWAY.

The characterization of Christ as the true Shepherd is not one given to Him by men. President Eisenhower has been elected to his high office, as have our senators and representatives, but Jesus was never elected to be the Good Shepherd, to lay down His life for the sheep: He came as our Shepherd, and voluntarily laid down His life for us.

How many characteristics of Christ are revealed in this lesson? Why does the human soul need a divine Shepherd? How do you account for the fact that thousands hear the Gospel, and hear Christ presented faithfully, who do not follow the Lord? Who are some of the false shepherds today of whom Christ was speaking then? In how many ways does this exquisite teaching of Jesus illuminate the 23rd Psalm?

LESSON X. — March 7.

THE RAISING OF LAZARUS. — John 11:1-54.

PRINTED TEXT, John 11:20–29, 32–46.

Devotional Reading: Luke 7:11–23.
Beginner Topic: BREAKFAST WITH JESUS.
    Lesson Material: John 21:1–17.
    Memory Verse: Thou art nigh, O Jehovah. Psalm 119:151.
Primary Topic: JESUS HELPS HIS FRIENDS IN BETHANY.
    Lesson Material: John 11:1–46.
    Memory Verse: (Jesus said) I came that they may have life. John 10:10.
Junior Topic: JESUS, THE LORD OF LIFE.
    Lesson Material: John 11:1–54.
    Memory Verse: (Jesus said) I came that they may have life, and may have it abundantly. John 10:10.
Intermediate-Senior Topic: LORD OF LIFE AND DEATH.
    Lesson Material: John 11:1–54.
    Memory Verse: I am the resurrection, and the life: he that believeth on me, though he die, yet shall he live; and whosoever liveth and believeth on me shall never die. John 11:25–26.
Topic for Young People and Adults: LORD OF LIFE AND DEATH.
    Lesson Material: John 11:1–54.
    Memory Verse: I am the resurrection, and the life: he that believeth on me, though he die, yet shall he live; and whosoever liveth and believeth on me shall never die. John 11:25–26.

THE TEACHER AND HIS CLASS.

The Younger Classes might begin this lesson by the teacher's pointing out at once the great chasm that separates the person Jesus, whom we are studying from week to week, and the greatest men now living, or who have lived at any time. I am dictating this lesson between the time of the election of General Eisenhower as President of the United States, and his inauguration in that high office. Now General Eisenhower is a great man, and he is gathering around him some great men, those of the highest calibre. We are going to ask from them, and expect from them, great things. We hope they will bring about a cessation of the war in Korea, that there will be a cleansing of corruption in our government, and a reduction in government expenses. There is one thing, however, for which no one is asking — a miracle. No one is expecting the President-elect to cure the incurable, to make bad men good, to raise the dead. The historical reality of that which we are about to study in the life of Jesus recorded in the life of any modern man would be repudiated.

The Older Classes may be introduced to this lesson with a statement that I heard in Great Britain this summer. Professor Joad, one of England's most distinguished philosophers, sometimes called "the brain trust," participating in a broadcast panel was asked, "If you had the privilege of asking just one question of God Himself, with the promise that you would have an answer, what would that question be?" Instantly Professor Joad replied, "I would ask Him what happened to Christ on the third day after His death." We would not say this of anyone else. Resurrection relates either to Christ's own resurrection, or to the resurrection He accomplished.

THE LESSON IN ITS SETTING.

Time. — January, A.D. 30.
Place. — Home of Mary and Martha in the village of Bethany, on the eastern slope of the Mount of Olives.

THE PLAN OF THE LESSON.

SUBJECT: A Unique Event in the Life of Christ in which His Compassion, His Foreknowledge, His Love and His Power are All Displayed.

I. THE CONFIDENCE IN CHRIST SHOWN BY THE FAMILY OF LAZARUS, John 11:1–10.

II. CHRIST'S CONCEPTION OF DEATH AS SLEEP, 11:11–16.

III. CHRIST'S COMPASSION AND COMFORT FOR THE MOURNING FAMILY, 11:17–32.
1. The worthlessness of artificial comfort, vs. 17–19.
2. Christ's words of hope to Martha, vs. 20–27.
3. Christ's compassion for Mary, vs. 28–32.

IV. CHRIST'S POWER OVER DEATH, 11:33–44.

1. On the way to the grave, vs. 33–37.
2. The command at the grave, vs. 38–40.
3. The prayer at the grave, vs. 41, 42.
4. The miracle at the grave, vs. 43, 44.

V. THE NEW DETERMINATION TO PUT CHRIST TO DEATH, 11:45–54.

THE TEACHER'S LIBRARY.

On Lazarus and the 11th chapter of John's Gospel there is a vast amount of material. All lives of Christ, commentaries on John's Gospel, books that deal with the subject of Gospel miracles, and all volumes that have chapters on the characters of the New Testament will have material of some value on this chapter. Some years ago J. D. Jones devoted an entire volume to these verses, *The Lord of Life and Death*, a remarkable book, but spoiled in part by his belief in the ultimate salvation of all souls, or universalism. Dr. Hugh Macmillan in his exhaustive work, *Our Lord's Three Raisings From the Dead*, devotes 200 pages to this miracle. For Bethany, see J. R. MacDuff: *Memories of Bethany;* J. R. Miller: *Mary of Bethany;* W. M. Clow: *The Idylls of Bethany;* and James Culross: *The House at Bethany.* On Lazarus himself, there is not as much material as one would expect; see, however, A. T. Robertson: *Some Minor Characters in the New Testament*, 177–182; T. R. Williams: *Men of the New Testament*, 195–204; an article by A. Plummer, in James Hastings' *Dictionary of the Bible*, Vol. 3, 85–88; an article by E. H. Plumptre in William Smith's *Dictionary of the Bible*, Vol. 2, 1612–1617; and a characteristically brilliant treatment in Alexander Whyte's *Bible Characters, Joseph and Mary to James*, 78–86.

With all of this material, I think it is not necessary to give a long list of sermons, but would suggest the following: on verses 25, 26, F. W. Boreham: *A Handful of Stars*, 44–56; John J. Gossip: *The Galilean Accent*, 151–160; James Hastings: *Great Texts of the Bible, St. John 1–12*, 464–481; and G. G. Findlay: *The Things Above*, 141–157. There are two chapters on various verses here in G. H. Knight: *The Master's Questions to His Disciples*, 213–226. On verse 39, there is a great deal of material; e.g., G. H. Morrison: *The Wind on the Heath*, 189–197; L. R. Scarborough: *The Tears of Jesus*, 13–24; A. H. Strong: *Miscellanies*, Vol. 2, pp. 310–327, and the article, "Tears," by A. P. Sym in Hastings: *Dictionary of Christ and the Gospels*, Vol. 2, pp. 706–707.

AUDIO-VISUAL AIDS.

FILM: "The Raising of Lazarus," Churchcraft, 13 min., sd., b&w. Presents in detail the events of this remarkable story. A discussion guide is available.

The great German commentator, H. A. W. Meyer has well said of this chapter: "No narrative of the New Testament bears so completely the stamp of being the opposite of a later invention. The very artistic style of representation, which in the account of this last and greatest miracle is most strikingly prominent, is only comprehensible from the personal, profound, and sympathizing recollection which has preserved and cherished, even in its finest traits, the truth and reality of the event with peculiar vivacity, fidelity, and inspiration." — *H. A. W. Meyer*. Canon Westcott, in his epochal commentary on this Gospel, reminds us that the numerous minute touches "mark the fullness of personal knowledge or the impression of an eye-witness, as for example, the relation of the family to Jesus, the delay of two days, the exact following of the Jews and their weeping, the prostration of Mary, the successive phases of the Lord's emotion, and the appearance of Lazarus." — *Canon Westcott*.

There are two men named Lazarus in the New Testament. One is the beggar at the rich man's gate in a parable recorded in Luke 16:19–31, and the other, a brother of Mary and Martha, living in Bethany, who is never referred to apart from this and the next chapter of John's Gospel. There are three miracles of resurrection in our Lord's ministry, apart from His own — the raising of the daughter of Jairus (Matt. 9:18–19, 23–26 and parallels), the raising of the widow's son (recorded only in Luke 7:11–17) and the one we are to study here. This is the greatest of all, because the body of Lazarus had already begun to disintegrate by the time Jesus arrived, and no theory that Lazarus was not really dead can be applied here. If anyone was ever dead, he was. There is nothing fantastic in the entire narrative. If this were being written out of one's imagination, or a tradition of the Second Century, we would have here some words from Lazarus after he rose from the dead, perhaps an account of his experiences during the time of death. The simplicity and the restraint of the narrative bear testimony to its historicity.

I. **THE CONFIDENCE IN CHRIST SHOWN BY THE FAMILY OF LAZA-RUS,** John 11:1–10. The Gospel narratives give one previous occasion in which Jesus was visiting the home of Mary and Martha (Luke 10:41–42), and each night during Holy Week He lodged in this home (Matt. 21:17; Mark 11:11, 19). One can hardly question the conclusion that this home was more of a home for Jesus than any other on earth. His brothers did not believe in Him at this time as the Messiah of God, and other places He visited might not understand Him, but Mary, Martha and Lazarus somehow had a true, deep understanding of the nature and needs of Christ. No doubt everything in the home was arranged so as to please the Lord. I am sure that when He wanted to be left alone, they did just that, and that they did not prod Him with questions day and night. No one in that home, I am quite confident, ever asked Jesus where Cain got his wife, or what was the first and great commandment. Here He was loved, and He gave a deep love in return. Here was rest, restoration of spirit, understanding that can come only from mutual love, renewal of strength for the next day's tasks and burdens. And yet, into this home sickness had come. Don't ever let anyone tell you that some devout child of God is ill because God is displeased with him, or is punishing him, or because there is some sin in his life. God may send sickness for chastisement, but not in every case, and we must be very careful in judging in matters like this. It is easily understood why the sisters sent word to Jesus concerning their brother's illness. They knew He could make Lazarus well with a word, and they knew He was the only one who could do this; and yet, the Lord neither sent word commanding his recovery, nor did He immediately leave for Judea and Bethany, to be at the bedside of His friend. Rather, we read that when the Lord heard this, He remained two days in the same place. Maclaren has some wonderful words on this in one of his great sermons. "We have all of us, I suppose, had experience of desires for the removal of bitterness or sorrows, or for the fulfilment of expectations and wishes, which, we believed, on the best evidence that we could find, to be in accordance with His will, and which we have been able to make prayers out of, in true faith and submission, which prayers have had to be offered over and over and over again, and no answer has come. It is part of the method of Providence that the lifting away of the burden and the coming of the desires should be a hope deferred. . . . But do not let us forget that Heaven's clock is different from ours. In our day there are twelve hours, and in God's a thousand years. What seems long to us is to Him 'a little while.' For two days, eight-and-forty hours, He de-

JOHN 11:20. Martha therefore, when she heard that Jesus was coming, went and met him: but Mary still sat in the house.

21. Martha therefore said unto Jesus, Lord, if thou hadst been here, my brother had not died.

22. And even now I know that, whatsoever thou shalt ask of God, God will give thee.

23. Jesus saith unto her, Thy brother shall rise again.

24. Martha saith unto him, I know that he shall rise again in the resurrection at the last day.

---

layed His answer to Mary and Martha, and they thought it an eternity, while the heavy hours crept by, and they only said, 'It's very weary, He cometh not.' How long did it look to them when they had got Lazarus back? The longest protraction of the fulfilment of the most yearning expectation and fulfilled desire will seem but as the winking of an eyelid when we get to estimate duration by the same scale by which He estimates it, the scale of Eternity." — *Alexander Maclaren.*

II. CHRIST'S CONCEPTION OF DEATH AS SLEEP, John 11:11–16. Passing by the profound and very important words of Christ regarding twelve hours in the day, and walking in the light, which do not directly relate to the printed text, we go on to Jesus' announcement that Lazarus is asleep, and that He is ready now to go to wake him out of his sleep. The disciples understood Him to mean just normal sleep, but Christ meant by this word death itself. He could not have meant ordinary sleep, of course, for He would not expect Lazarus to be sleeping all the days and nights it would take Him to get from where He was in Galilee to Judea. Sleep is elsewhere used in the New Testament as a figure of speech for death (Matt. 27:52; Acts 7:60; 13:36; 1 Cor. 11:30 and 15:6, 18; 1 Thes. 4:13; 2 Peter 3:4). Our word *cemetery* comes directly from a Greek word meaning *a sleeping place.* Eadie, in his commentary on Thessalonians beautifully says regarding sleep, "Sleep implies continued existence, rest and awakening. The sleeper does not cease to be, though he sinks into a kind of unconsciousness; he is often thoughtful and active in dreams, but in this state of insensibility he enjoys repose and then he wakens to fresh activity." Incidentally, there is no hint here in this narrative that someone reported Lazarus' death to Jesus, but yet He knew of it.

III. CHRIST'S COMPASSION AND COMFORT FOR THE MOURNING FAMILY, John 11:17–32. No doubt the two sisters were sitting with the mourners, and being constantly interrupted, at a time when one wants to be alone, by platitudinous expressions of sorrow and attempted comfort. Suddenly news is brought that Jesus has come. The hearts of both women were now moved with expectation, at least with some joy that the glorious Redeemer was with them. Many have known the Lord to come nigh to them in such hours as this. 20. **Martha therefore, when she heard that Jesus was coming, went and met him: but Mary still sat in the house. 21. Martha therefore said unto Jesus, Lord, if thou hadst been here, my brother had not died. 22. And even now I know that, whatsoever thou shalt ask of God, God will give thee.** The statement of Martha is identical with that made by Mary in verse 32. No doubt the sisters had been talking over this matter together and had come to the same conclusion. "Martha's word is neither accusation nor reproach, but deep sorrow and poignant regret. When Lazarus was sick, the sisters longed, 'Oh, if only He were here!' and then they sent Him word, but Lazarus died, and so the regret set in, 'Oh, if only He had been here.' So many sick He had healed, and yet their brother had to die. Who will write the story of these sad, sad 'if's'? And yet Martha is firmly convinced by all that she had seen and heard of Jesus; and her conviction holds in spite of what now seems so dark to her, so hard to explain." — *R. C. H. Lenski.* **23. Jesus saith unto her, Thy brother shall rise again. 24. Martha saith unto him, I know**

84

25. Jesus said unto her, I am the resurrection, and the life: he that believeth on me, though he die, yet shall he live;

26. And whosoever liveth and believeth on me shall never die. Believest thou this?

27. She saith unto him, Yea, Lord: I have believed that thou art the Christ, the Son of God, *even* he that cometh into the world.

28. And when she had said this, she went away, and called Mary her sister secretly, saying, The Teacher is here, and calleth thee.

29. And she, when she heard it, arose quickly, and went unto him.

32. Mary therefore, when she came where Jesus was, and saw him, fell down at his feet, saying unto him, Lord, if thou hadst been here, my brother had not died.

---

that he shall rise again in the resurrection at the last day. **25. Jesus said unto her, I am the resurrection, and the life: he that believeth on me, though he die, yet shall he live;** Surely we have here one of the most glorious statements, full of hope, power, the assurance of eternal life, that ever came from the lips of Christ. Here our Lord utters one of His great "I am's." He is both *the* resurrection and *the* life, and in Him is the assurance that those who believe in Him will be raised from the dead and be the possessors of eternal life. One can say that these are only words. Yes, that is all they are, just words, but in a few moments He would prove that they were also divine promises, stupendous reality, by revealing His power to make resurrection possible. And then, in a few weeks, He himself would rise from the dead and put a glorious seal upon these most comforting words. **26. And whosoever liveth and believeth on me shall never die. Believest thou this?** It is in John's Gospel that we have the fullest teaching of Christ on the subject of life. Here He is not only *the* life, but those who believe in Him shall also have that life, and shall never die. By this of course Christ meant that they would never suffer that aspect of death which proceeds from the wrath of God. Their bodies would deteriorate, but they would live on, waiting for the resurrection of the body. "The resurrection is one manifestation of the Life. It is involved in the *Life*. It is a personal communication of the Lord himself, and not a grace which He has to gain from another. He *is* that which men need. He does not *procure* the blessing for them." — *B. F. Westcott.* **27. She saith unto him, Yea, Lord: I have believed that thou art the Christ, the Son of God, *even* he that cometh into the world.** "To believe is to receive, hold, enjoy the reality and power of what Christ is saying, with all that lies in it of joy, comfort, peace, and hope. In 'I have believed' note the emphatic pronoun. Others have not believed, others have charged Jesus with blasphemy (10:33) for calling himself 'the Son of God' — Martha 'has believed,' has done so this long while, and is believing now." — *R. C. H. Lenski.*

Christian faith and belief in the great truths that relate to Christ should and must, normally, be followed by action. Thus here, Martha seeks out her sister and announces that the Master is come. **28. And when she had said this, she went away, and called Mary her sister secretly, saying, The Teacher is here, and calleth thee. 29. And she, when she heard it, arose quickly, and went unto him.** It is most significant that it was to Martha, supposed by so many to be the less spiritually-minded of the two sisters, that Jesus gave the fullest revelation on this day. **32. Mary therefore, when she came where Jesus was, and saw him, fell down at his feet, saying unto him, Lord, if thou hadst been here, my brother had not died.** The moment Mary came into Jesus' presence, she fell at His feet and uttered the same words that Martha had spoken to Him in the earlier part of the chapter. No doubt the sisters had been discussing what would have hap-

33. When Jesus therefore saw her weeping, and the Jews *also* weeping who came with her, he groaned in the spirit, and was troubled,

34. And said, Where have ye laid him? They say unto him, Lord, come and §ee.

35. Jesus wept.

36. The Jews therefore said, Behold how he loved him!

37. But some of them said, Could not this man, who opened the eyes of him that was blind, have caused that this man also should not die?

---

pened had Jesus been there before the brother died, and the same words were in their minds, and thus on their lips. The whole scene is very natural.

IV. **CHRIST'S POWER OVER DEATH,** John 11:33-44. Up to this time in the narrative, we have had nothing but words — words from Martha, from Mary, and from Jesus. The crisis now approaches. If Jesus is *the* resurrection, can He manifest it by a miracle of resurrection? But now, on this occasion, as He is about to give the greatest proof of His deity up to the time of His own resurrection, He displays in a remarkable way His true humanity, and deep compassion. 33. **When Jesus therefore saw her weeping, and the Jews *also* weeping who came with her, he groaned in the spirit, and was troubled,** "The word here translated *groan* occurs five times in the New Testament, here and verse 38; Matthew 9:30; Mark 1:43; 14:5. In all cases, as in classical Greek to express not sorrow but indignation or severity." — *A. Plummer.* "The *spirit* is the seat of the religious emotions, as the *soul* is that of the natural affections. Thus in 12:27, Jesus says: 'My soul is troubled,' because the foreseeing of His suffering makes His nature shudder, while here and in chapter 13 it is in His *spirit* that He is agitated, because in both cases He sees Himself in immediate contact with evil in its blackest form, and because with a holy horror he feels the nearness of the invisible being who has taken possession of the heart of Judas, and (in our passage) of that of His declared enemies. This parallel throws light on the groaning of Jesus in verse 33. This internal revolution terminated in this sudden and brief question, 'Where have you laid him?' — *F. Godet.* 34. **And said, Where have ye laid him? They say unto him, Lord, come and see.** 35. **Jesus wept.** Hugh Macmillan once said: "I am strongly tempted to do nothing more than repeat the words: for I feel that to comment upon them is to gild the sunshine and paint the lily. . . . The dead are raised to life by no callous philosopher with a hard eye and unfeeling heart; by no magician who simply waves his hand and accomplishes with no cost or effort to himself the mighty miracle; by no God who stands afar off in the heavens and issues His commandments to the dead to rise as He issued His commandment to light to appear at the creation; but by One who is very near with the tender weakness that is more moving and majestic than all our strength, and the sorrowful experiences that are more beautiful and precious than all our gladness." — *Hugh Macmillan.* 36. **The Jews therefore said, Behold how he loved him!** 37. **But some of them said, Could not this man, who opened the eyes of him that was blind, have caused that this man also should not die?** "The miracle done on the man sent to the Pool of Siloam was one that had agitated Jerusalem on one of the Lord's former visits, and it is now remembered. No mention is made by these inhabitants of the capital of the two raisings from the dead which took place in Galilee. These were probably discredited, even if heard of, in Jerusalem. And they now half-insinuate that even the Siloam miracle could not have proved real power, since so little power is shewn by Jesus here in a case where He is believed to have had so much heart and wish to do a good turn. These natural human tears are accepted as evidence that He had no power to do more than weep." — *John Laidlaw.* As far as the Gospel record informs us, this is the only time in the three years of Jesus' ministry that he ever came to a grave. The next grave will be His

38. Jesus therefore again groaning in himself cometh to the tomb. Now it was a cave, and a stone lay against it.

39. Jesus saith, Take ye away the stone. Martha, the sister of him that was dead, saith unto him, Lord, by this time the body decayeth; for he hath been *dead* four days.

40. Jesus saith unto her, Said I not unto thee, that, if thou believedst, thou shouldest see the glory of God?

41. So they took away the stone. And Jesus lifted up his eyes, and said, Father, I thank thee that thou heardest me.

42. And I knew that thou hearest me always: but because of the multitude that standeth around I said it, that they may believe that thou didst send me.

---

own, and the words used to describe that grave are quite similar to those we have here (Luke 23:53). 38. **Jesus therefore again groaning in himself cometh to the tomb. Now it was a cave, and a stone lay against it.** "This, like many other touches in the narrative, indicates the social position of the Bethany family. It was not a common burial-place among many, but like what we call a family vault. These were caverns, partly natural, partly artificial in some rocky hill, probably in imitation of the ancestral cave of Machpelah, to which the Jew looked back with such reverence. These vaults usually had a stone at the entrance, either like a cover or trough-stone, when the cave was vertical, or like a door when it was horizontal, to keep out beasts of prey; often used also as a memento of the dead." — *John Laidlaw*. 39. **Jesus saith, Take ye away the stone. Martha, the sister of him that was dead, saith unto him, Lord, by this time the body decayeth; for he hath been *dead* four days.** All readers of the Gospels and students of our Lord's resurrection are acquainted with the fact that Christ predicted He would rise on the third day, and that it was the third day on which He rose. Even Paul refers to this time element (1 Cor. 15:4). "It appears that in ancient thought the third day was connected with the phenomena of dissolution. Traces of this survive in many religions. Plato suggests a delay of burial for three days to distinguish between apparent and real death. Popular opinion among the Jews held that after death 'the soul hovered above the grave until the third day, desiring to return to the body; but when it sees the appearance change, then it leaves the body altogether. Clearly, then, the significance of the Third Day, to the Eastern mind, as the date of Resurrection, is that it denotes the reality of the Death, and yet the exemption from corruption. It is Resurrection at the earliest moment consistent with the one, and at the latest consistent with the other." — *W. J. Sparrow Simpson*. Everything seems to be against the Lord here, even the resistance of believing hearts. 40. **Jesus saith unto her, Said I not unto thee, that, if thou believedst, thou shouldest see the glory of God? 41. So they took away the stone. And Jesus lifted up his eyes, and said, Father, I thank thee that thou heardest me. 42. And I knew that thou hearest me always: but because of the multitude that standeth around I said it, that they may believe that thou didst send me.** "He puts forth supernatural power to do that which no less power could accomplish; but all the rest — removing the stone beforehand, loosening the grave-clothes afterwards — he bids men do in the ordinary way. No doubt the power which could call Lazarus from the sleep of death included power to rend the rocks, roll away the stone, strip off the grave-bands without human aid. . . . He addresses God by that name in the use of which He had already so offended the Jews. With holy familiarity and boldness, needing no introductory adoration, and using no names of worship, but as a Son in His love and confidence, He says simply, 'Father!' " —

43. And when he had thus spoken, he cried with a loud voice, Lazarus, come forth.

44. He that was dead came forth, bound hand and foot with grave-clothes; and his face was bound about with a napkin. Jesus saith unto them, Loose him, and let him go.

45. Many therefore of the Jews, who came to Mary and beheld that which he did, believed on him.

46. But some of them went away to the Pharisees, and told them the things which Jesus had done.

John Laidlaw. **43. And when he had thus spoken, he cried with a loud voice, Lazarus, come forth.** We cannot help but recall here the earlier teaching of our Lord, that in the last days, at His return, He will call with a loud voice to the dead generally (John 5:25, 28, 29) and they will come forth. The Book of Revelation reveals the risen Lord as one whose voice is as the sound of many waters (1:15). **44. He that was dead came forth, bound hand and foot with grave-clothes; and his face was bound about with a napkin. Jesus saith unto them, Loose him, and let him go.** "The sinner, like Lazarus, is dead, buried, we may say already corrupt and loathsome. Christ comes Himself to the sinner's tomb. He bids, 'Take away the stone.' . . . It is the 'effectual call' of His word and spirit. The man hears, the dead lives, the soul is converted. Then, once more, comes in the use of means. Remove hindrances; explain to the restored soul the way of life more perfectly. Let him use all appointed helps for enlargement and strengthening. Let the living help their new-raised brother — 'Loose ye him, and let him go.' Not to dwell on detail, let us note that the hinge of comparison between the spiritual and the literal resurrection is that the moving power of both is the Divine in the human, God manifest in Jesus Christ." — *John Laidlaw.* Practically all agree that Lazarus at this time did not receive a resurrection body, but that Christ restored to its normal vigor and health the body in which he had been living, and brought back the spirit of Lazarus into that body. While the New Testament does not record it, surely Lazarus died again, and with other believers awaits the return of Christ. How long he lived after this, we do not know. It is a testimony to the veracity of this narrative that there is not one hint of mere inquisitiveness, not a word escapes Lazarus' lips concerning the experiences that were his from the hour his spirit departed from his body until it returned. **45. Many therefore of the Jews, who came to Mary and beheld that which he did, believed on him. 46. But some of them went away to the Pharisees, and told them the things which Jesus had done.** Lenski believes that those who told the Pharisees of what had happened were among the believers, so that "not at second or at third hand, but at first hand the enemies of Jesus obtained the information." "By this stupendous deed so publicly wrought, so universally and undeniably witnessed, Jesus' claim to be the Christ was brought to a climax. Those who opposed His claims had no longer any plausible excuse for doubt — it became hostile denial. They simply resolved not to believe in Him. They would not have Him to be their Messiah, let His claims be ever so clear. His followers were confirmed beyond the possibility of doubt. Their numbers were swelled by remarkable accessions. Many of the eye-witnesses became from that moment faithful disciples. . . . It serves exactly the same purpose in modern thought as it served in the history of its own time. If we would bring any writer or speaker on the character and claims of Jesus to a test, let us see what he makes of the raising of Lazarus. At that point he must either worship Jesus of Nazareth or crucify Him." — *John Laidlaw.*

V. **THE NEW DETERMINATION TO PUT CHRIST TO DEATH,** John 11:47–54. Bishop Ryle in a very practical chapter on this wicked determination of Christ's enemies, says we should observe at least three things in reading these concluding verses: the desperate wickedness of man's heart in refusing to be convinced by overwhelming evidence; the blind ignorance with which God's enemies often act and reason, as here, when they said if they let Christ alone they would be ruined, but if they put Him to death they would be saved, whereas later history showed that by putting Him to death they finally brought down upon them tragedy and ruin; and finally, the importance that bad men sometimes attach to outside ceremony, while their hearts are full of sin, as here, when the Jews went up to Jerusalem before the Passover to purify themselves, when, at the same time, they were ready to do the will of the Pharisees, and to put their own Messiah to a violent death. Of course Caiaphas was not aware of the full truthfulness of what he said in declaring that one man must die for the whole nation. We must understand that the comment in verses 51 and 52 is by John the Apostle, and not a continuation of the speech of Caiaphas.

THE LESSON IN LIFE, LITERATURE, AND ARCHAEOLOGY.

Bayle, in his famous *Dictionary* (Vol. 5, p. 17) tells us that the great philosopher Spinoza once said that "if he could have persuaded himself of the resurrection of Lazarus, he would have broken in pieces his whole system and embraced the ordinary faith of Christians."

A TRUTH FOR THE CLASS TO CARRY AWAY.

With a miracle such as this put before us, with such overwhelming evidence, there comes to my mind something that has given me frequent concern, and has led me to prayer in this regard. Is there not some way in which we can present the evidence for Christ's deity as set forth in the Gospels to some of our leading intellectuals, just to give them the evidence? Many of them have never faced the simple testimony of the Gospels. An intellectual is no better than anyone else, but it would be wonderful if some of these who edit our most famous magazines, head our greatest universities, and lead in the supremely important fields of scientific research today, could be won to Christ as their Lord and Saviour. Let us all pray about this and quietly seek a way to effectively present this evidence.

How many characteristics of Christ can you find in this lesson? In what ways was the death of Christ different from the death of Lazarus? Do you find here any parallels between the burial of Lazarus and the burial of our Lord? How does this chapter illustrate the assertion of the Apostle Paul that Christ brought life and immortality to light through the Gospel (2 Tim. 1:10)? Would you say that the opposition to Christ at the time of our lesson was of the same nature as that of today, and how do you account for this?

LESSON XI. — March 14.

JESUS FACES THE CROSS. — John 11:55—12:50.

PRINTED TEXT, John 12:1–7, 20–32.

Devotional Reading: 1 Corinthians 1:18–31.
Beginner Topic: ANDREW'S NICE NEWS.
   Lesson Material: John 1:35–42.
   Memory Verse: GOD . . . Loved us, and sent His son. 1 John 4:10.
Primary Topic: A GIFT FOR JESUS.
   Lesson Material: John 12:1–8.
   Memory Verse: We love, because he first loved us. 1 John 4:19.
Junior Topic: HONORING JESUS.
   Lesson Material: John 12:1–8, 20–26.
   Memory Verse: We would see Jesus. John 12:21.

Intermediate-Senior Topic: The Great Choice.
    Lesson Material: John 11:55—12:50.
    Memory Verse: He that loveth his life loseth it; and he that hateth his life in this world shall keep it unto life eternal. John 12:25.
Topic for Young People and Adults: Jesus Faces the Cross.
    Lesson Material: John 11:55—12:50.
    Memory Verse: He that loveth his life loseth it; and he that hateth his life in this world shall keep it unto life eternal. John 12:25.

THE TEACHER AND HIS CLASS.

The **Younger Classes** may be introduced to this lesson, parts of which are profound, by a simple question. When the father of the home wishes to present the mother with a bouquet of flowers, on a wedding anniversary, or a birthday, and provided it is spring or summer and they are available, why does he not pick some dandelions, or yellow daisies, or the lovely white flower called Queen Anne's lace, and bring them home, instead of some American Beauty roses or orchids? The reason of course is that they are what we call weeds; they are common. These can be had without any cost or effort, and therefore cannot be symbols or expressions of one's great appreciation of another. Incidentally, *appreciate* comes from the same root as the word *appraise;* our appreciation should in some way express the inestimable value we place upon the love and friendship of another. In this lesson we learn of a friend of Jesus who expressed in an extreme way her great devotion to Christ.

The **Older Classes** should here again have emphasized, as in the lesson on the 10th chapter of John, the significance of the cross of Christ. For myself, I have lately received a new conception of the centrality that the cross of Christ is given in the speeches of Jesus recorded in John's Gospel. We are living in a day when in many pulpits the cross of Christ, in its New Testament meaning, is never referred to. Mohammedanism denies that Jesus died; modernism shrinks from blood atonement; Unitarianism will have none of it. Still, in the mind of Christ, and in the teachings of the Apostles, it is central. How foolish any man is, whatever be his training and wisdom, to take a view of the death of Christ different from that which He took. If Jesus was wrong in His conception of His death, I am more and more convinced that His ministry does not then warrant the attention the Church has given it.

THE LESSON IN ITS SETTING.

Time. — The supper at Bethany was on Saturday evening, after sundown, April 1, A.D. 30. The Triumphal Entry took place on Sunday, and the events from verses 20 through 50, on Tuesday.

Place. — The anointing of our Lord occurred in Bethany, a small town just over the ridge on the eastern slope of the Mount of Olives. All other events took place in Jerusalem.

THE PLAN OF THE LESSON.

SUBJECT: The Abiding Power of the Death of Christ in Relation to Satan, Mankind, the World, and God the Father.

I. The Passover Pilgrims Inquire for Jesus, John 11:55–57.

II. The Contrast of Mary and Judas in the Bethany Home, 12:1–8.

III. The Contrast of Visitors to Bethany and the Chief Priests, 12:9–11.

IV. The Triumphal Entry into Jerusalem, 12:12–19.

V. The Inquiring Greeks, 12:20–33.
    1. Their inquiry is reported to Jesus, vs. 20–22.
    2. Christ talks about the necessity for His death, vs. 23–26.
    3. The voice from heaven, vs. 27–30.
    4. The power of the cross, vs. 31–33.

VI. The Vast Consequences Which Follow Believing in Christ and Rejecting Him, 12:34–50.

THE TEACHER'S LIBRARY.

All commentaries on John's Gospel, and the major lives of Christ, will give great help in the study of our lesson. In addition, there are two magnificent chapters in A. B. Bruce: *The Training of the Twelve* — on the anointing in Bethany, pp. 297–316 (in my mind the greatest single chapter on this passage ever written), and on the coming of the Greeks, pp. 317–325. Also on the appearance of the Greeks, a chapter I have not previously consulted, James Jeffrey: *The Personal Ministry of the Son of Man*, 96–107. On the scene in Bethany there are two beautiful chapters in W. M. Clow: *The Idylls of Bethany*, 107–124, 143–160. Some of the richest pages ever written on certain verses of this chapter that relate to our Lord's death are those by George Smeaton: *The Doctrine of the Atonement as Taught by Christ Himself*, especially on verses 31, 32, pp. 294–300, 304–313. For these verses also see the relevant pages in James Denney's great book, *The Death of Christ*.

On verses 25–27, see Alexander Whyte: *With Mercy and With Judgment*, 126–132; on verses 26 and 32, G. Campbell Morgan in *The Westminster Pulpit*, Vol. 8, pp. 209–216, and Vol. 1, pp. 105–112. On verse 32, there are many great sermons, two of which are found in a volume now seldom seen, Robert M. Edgar: *The Philosophy of the Cross*, 19–34; also one by Marcus Dods, "The Promise of Victory," in an exceedingly rich volume which seems to be known to few, *Missionary Sermons*, 1812–1924, pp. 215–226.

On the metaphor of the grain of wheat, see G. Campbell Morgan: *The Parables and Metaphors of Our Lord*, 324–329.

AUDIO-VISUAL AIDS.

FILMSTRIP: "Mary Annoints Jesus," Concordia No. C–28, 19fr., col. Based on the Matthew account, which has her annointing his head instead of his feet, but most of the other details of the story are the same.

We are now about to enter what has been rightly called the Holy of Holies of John's Gospel, the record of the last week of our Lord's life, generally known as Passion Week, or Holy Week. It is very significant that this Gospel of 21 chapters should devote 7 full chapters, one-third of the book, to this last week. If the remainder of our Lord's public ministry were recorded with the same fullness in this Gospel, we would have a book of 1274 chapters, a great many more than are in the entire New Testament. There seems to be throughout the narrative recording the events of the earlier part of the week an atmosphere of tension, expectancy, and there hovers over all that takes place and all that is being said the realization that the death of Christ is not far away.

I. **THE PASSOVER PILGRIMS INQUIRE FOR JESUS, 11:55–57.** With His approaching death uppermost in the mind of Christ, and surely known to His most intimate friends, and sought for by His enemies, there falls just at this time the Passover season of the Hebrew people, the slaying of the lamb in memory of God's great deliverance of Israel from their enemies as they made the exodus from Egypt. The Apostle Paul calls Christ our Passover. "Do you realize the timeliness of Christ's coming, and the significance of the 'six days' of His sojourn (12:1)? The Passover was the time of the slaying of the lamb, and the offering for the sin of the people. But this Passover was to be the time when the Lamb of God should be slain and the atonement made for the sins of the whole world, which would abolish, as it has done, the sacrifices of Jerusalem. Before that Passover Jesus must finish the work God gave Him to do. Before that Passover the hours of His agony would be undergone. Therefore six days before He suffered the article of death, Jesus, the Lord of Humanity, flesh and blood as we are, tempted in all points as we are, with a heart and a spirit that had their own needs, came to Bethany. Bethany was the place of His preparation." — *W. M. Clow.* How strange to read that many Jews were going up to the Temple to purify themselves, when at the same time a great number of them would unite in murdering the only holy, sinless being that has ever come to this earth. There were many conflicting opinions concerning Christ: many people believed that He was the Messiah; His disciples knew that He was the Son of God; and the Sanhedrin had already decided, in their own minds at least, that He was a blasphemer, worthy of death.

II. **THE CONTRAST OF MARY AND JUDAS IN THE BETHANY HOME, 12:1–8.** We have often considered, in previous years, the significance of this home of Mary, Martha, and Lazarus, in the village of Bethany, where Jesus no doubt found more rest for heart and body than at any other single place on earth. These are not His relatives. They are in comfortable circumstances, though not rich.

91

JOHN 12:1. Jesus therefore six days before the passover came to Bethany, where Lazarus was, whom Jesus raised from the dead.

2. So they made him a supper there: and Martha served; but Lazarus was one of them that sat at meat with him.

3. Mary therefore took a pound of ointment of pure nard, very precious, and anointed the feet of Jesus, and wiped his feet with her hair: and the house was filled with the odor of ointment.

4. But Judas Iscariot, one of his disciples, that should betray him, saith,

5. Why was not this ointment sold for three hundred shillings, and given to the poor?

6. Now this he said, not because he cared for the poor; but because he was a thief, and having the bag took away what was put therein.

The friends in this home knew how to protect Him from the pressure of crowds, from thoughtless intrusion upon His private life. They knew when He wanted to be alone in prayer, and I am sure that they did not spend the hours He was there in asking questions. The home undoubtedly was clean, the conversation wholesome, and here Jesus was revered as both friend and Son of God. **1. Jesus therefore six days before the passover came to Bethany, where Lazarus was, whom Jesus raised from the dead.** The frequent references to death in this chapter deserve a more careful study than we have time for here. The fact that Lazarus was dead is mentioned three times (vs. 1, 9, 17); the burying of Christ is mentioned in verse 7; the determination of the chief priests to put Jesus to death is set forth in verse 10; our Lord refers to death twice in verse 24, to being lifted up on the cross twice in verses 32–34. He interprets the preceding words in referring them to "what manner of death He should die." **2. So they made him a supper there: and Martha served; but Lazarus was one of them that sat at meat with him. 3. Mary therefore took a pound of ointment of pure nard, very precious, and anointed the feet of Jesus, and wiped his feet with her hair: and the house was filled with the odor of ointment.** "The quantity of the ointment was a pound, twelve ounces according to the weight of water. The word translated *ointment* is a general term for any perfume or essence with delightful odor. 'Nard' is the plant which furnishes the essence for the perfume, the finest coming from India. The word translated *pure* derives from a word meaning genuine, as against adulterated preparations. All the Evangelists remark on the value of the perfume. Judas mentions the actual value. The question is asked how Mary came to have so precious a perfume at hand on this occasion. We like to think, in lieu of any other answer, that Mary provided this precious essence long in advance for an occasion of this kind, freely spending her money for the honor of Jesus." — *R. C. H. Lenski.* **4. But Judas Iscariot, one of his disciples, that should betray him, saith, 5. Why was not this ointment sold for three hundred shillings, and given to the poor? 6. Now this he said, not because he cared for the poor; but because he was a thief, and having the bag took away what was put therein.** The approximate price of this perfume would be fifty dollars, a large sum of money at that time. "The words of Judas regarding the use of this money for the poor cover the gravest kind of a charge not merely against Mary, but against Jesus himself. Judas implies that Jesus is robbing the poor; that he is lavishing upon himself what should be devoted to charity; that for his own glorification he allows a waste that is wrong; that his example is harmful to others — and that Judas is the man who knows what is right, proper, charitable, and is not afraid to come out with it! . . . He had charge of the offerings, and thus his little peculations were of sacred money, offerings made to the Lord. This makes his crime blacker. Incidentally we see that Jesus and his disciples had a common purse — what was his was theirs; and Judas,

7. Jesus therefore said, Suffer her to keep it against the day of my burying.

Jesus' familiar friend, who lifted up his heel against him, ate his bread." — *R. C. H. Lenski.* How utterly insincere the words of this man. This recalls to mind a story told concerning that great man of God, the late Dr. William Anderson of the First Presbyterian Church of Dallas, Texas. While on a speaking mission at a southern college some years ago, he set aside certain hours for conferences with the students. One of those who came to see him began to complain about the extravagance of churches in building large edifices, including his own in another city which had cost almost $300,000. "Why," he asked, "should not some of this money go to missions?" Dr. Anderson let him present his case, and then, noticing a very beautiful fountain pen in the hand of the student, he admired it and asked the young man what it cost. He said it was an unusual pen and cost twenty dollars. To this Dr. Anderson replied, "Why did you not buy a five-dollar pen and give the other fifteen dollars to missions?" There is much meaningless talk similar to that of Judas among people today. **7. Jesus therefore said, Suffer her to keep it against the day of my burying.** "When Mary bought and kept the ointment ready, she did this consciously for the very purpose Jesus so clearly states. Let us remember that what Jesus spoke in Galilee (Matt. 16:21); what he told his disciples so plainly at the beginning of his last journey (Matt. 20:17; Mark 10:32–33; Luke 18:31–34) and what he told his enemies in Jerusalem (John 7:33; 8:21–23; 10:11, and 17–18, and what these enemies knew well, Mary must also have known. She knew in addition the threats and plots of his enemies, with which Jesus too had charged them openly (John 5:18; 7:1 and 19; 8:59; 10:31, etc.; 11:53 and 57). The disciples, true enough, did not realize what was so close at hand. But why should not one heart at least realize it? The character of this woman is such that it ought not to surprise us, that where dull-witted men failed, she saw that Jesus was indeed going straight to his death — even to crucifixion, as he himself said." — *R. C. H. Lenski.* "Here I break again Mary's alabaster box that the odour of its ointment may fill this house. Here we would again listen to the Master's praise. Here would we rise up to the lesson which consummates all its teaching. That lesson is that it is possible for men and women so to please God that they shall call forth His praise. It is a great truth that nothing that man can do can justify the sinner before God. Quite apart from our stained memories, our guilty consciences, our blemished lives, we cannot offer our best, and our highest and our holiest, for our own salvation. 'Nothing in my hand I bring' is a line that must never leave our lips. But a humble, believing, adoring soul may greatly please God, and God is not difficult to please. No mother hears her child calling with more joy than God hears your voice in your prayers. No father sees his son's endurance, and his endeavour after a purer life with more gladness than God sees yours. No lover accepts a gift with more delight than God accepts yours — when they are given in love." — *W. M. Clow.* The anointing at Bethany is also found in Matthew 26:6–12 and Mark 14:3–9.

III. **THE CONTRAST OF THE VISITORS TO BETHANY AND THE CHIEF PRIESTS,** 12:9–11. There seems to be in these verses one of the greatest contrasts to be found anywhere in the Bible. Here are multitudes of people coming to Bethany to see Lazarus, whom Jesus had raised from the dead, and Him who had raised him, many of whom were believing on Him; while, at the same time, the chief priests, the ecclesiastical authorities of Judaism who officially ministered in the Temple, were plotting to put Lazarus to death. This is only part of their plot to put Jesus to death. How foolish of men to fight the plans of God.

IV. **THE TRIUMPHAL ENTRY INTO JERUSALEM,** 12:12–19. Inasmuch as this spectacular and significant event is recorded in all four Gospels (see Matt. 21:1–11; Mark 11:1–11; Luke 19:28–44) and we have studied it almost every year, I would like to limit the comment here to one brief paragraph, concerning the word *Hosanna.* "This word is untranslatable into Greek, as the Septuagint

20. Now there were certain Greeks among those that went up to worship at the feast:

21. These therefore came to Philip, who was of Bethsaida of Galilee, and asked him, saying, Sir, we would see Jesus.

22. Philip cometh and telleth Andrew: Andrew cometh, and Philip, and they tell Jesus.

23. And Jesus answereth them, saying, The hour is come, that the Son of man should be glorified.

---

translator recognized by paraphrasing it with 'Save now.' . . . The importance of the occurrence of the word in the narrative of the Triumphal Entry is its marking of the fulfilment of an Old Testament citation and of a ritual practice among the Jews. The reference in verse 15 to Zechariah 9:9 is clear, but the Evangelist does not cite it verbally. He abbreviates it, substituting 'Fear not, daughter of Zion (compare Isa. 44:2 and Zeph. 3:16) for 'Rejoice greatly, O daughter of Zion.' . . . In the sayings of the Rabbis the Hebrew word for 'the world' means 'everybody,' and often has the adjective *whole* added to it." — *E. C. Hoskyns.*

V. **THE INQUIRING GREEKS,** 12:20–32. While the Triumphal Entry of our Lord is recorded in all four Gospels, the event we are now about to study is in the Gospel of John exclusively. Again note the contrast. While the Jews, Israel, the people of the old Covenant, those who had a true priesthood, a true temple, and a true God, are plotting to put the descendant of David, the prophesied Messiah, to death, there come to Jesus some Gentiles, Greeks, desiring to see the Person of whom they had heard so much. 20. **Now there were certain Greeks among those that went up to worship at the feast:** "These Greeks were former idolaters who had accepted the essentials of the Jewish religion and some of its customs and practices, without formally being received into the synagogue by circumcision, which would have made them 'proselytes of righteousness.' They resembled the Ethiopian eunuch, the centurion Cornelius, and others. Many of these proselytes visited the great Jewish festivals. Their purpose was 'to worship at the feast,' like the Jews whose faith they shared. Whether they also went up for purposes of business we do not know; John intimates nothing on that score, rather the contrary. Solomon's prayer at the dedication of the Temple expressly refers to such 'strangers' (see 1 Kings 8:41–43)." — *R. C. H. Lenski.* 21. **These therefore came to Philip, who was of Bethsaida of Galilee, and asked him, saying, Sir, we would see Jesus. 22. Philip cometh and telleth Andrew: Andrew cometh, and Philip, and they tell Jesus.** "One feels, almost instinctively, that there was more than curiosity prompting this request, more than the desire to see the most interesting man of His day. Had that been all they wanted, they might have attained their object without having recourse to the disciples. Jesus came to Jerusalem every day at that time. His route to Bethany was well known. He taught daily in the temple, and could easily have been seen coming and going. It was the desire for a personal interview with Jesus, that they might open their hearts to Him, and might come to know Him better. Not improbably they had heard Jesus spoken of as the Messiah of the Jews. They had perhaps seen deeper into His mission than many of His countrymen. For them the idea of a Jew ruling the world would have had no great fascination, but if they had begun to feel restless, and dissatisfied with their old life, as they must have felt when they became proselytes to the Jewish faith, if they had found in Judaism the rest they expected, if the question had forced itself upon them, how are we to obtain the favour of Jehovah, who cannot look upon sin; if they had been trying to get behind the meaning of the sacrifices and ritual of Judaism, then it might be that this Jesus, whom they had heard spoken of as the Prophet of Nazareth in Galilee, would be able to solve all these questions, and to give rest to their weary souls." — *James Jeffrey.* 23. **And Jesus answereth them, saying, The hour is come, that the Son**

24. Verily, verily, I say unto you, Except a grain of wheat fall into the earth and die, it abideth by itself alone; but if it die, it beareth much fruit.

25. He that loveth his life loseth it; and he that hateth his life in this world shall keep it unto life eternal.

26. If any man serve me, let him follow me: and where I am, there shall also my servant be: if any man serve me, him will the Father honor.

---

of man should be glorified. "The actual day of Jesus' death was not yet come, but 'the hour' or time for his death had now arrived. Yet, strange to say, Jesus calls this 'the hour for the Son of man to be glorified.' In this He sums up everything — the passion as something glorious, the exaltation following, and the future adoration by the hosts of believers the world over and in heaven. Jesus was glorified in the obedience he rendered to the Father even unto the death of the cross, and in the redemption he thus achieved for the fallen world; he was glorified when the Father highly exalted him, giving him a name above every name and seating him at his right hand; he was and is glorified in the work of the Holy Spirit ('he shall glorify me,' 16:14) as it leads thousands to the feet of the Saviour. . . . The glory begins with the passion — Jesus sees how from his passion and death a magnificent vista opens, reaching onward through the ages into all eternity, and it is one shining path of glory. The passive verb ascribes the glorifying act to the Father." — *R. C. H. Lenski.* 24. **Verily, verily, I say unto you, Except a grain of wheat fall into the earth and die, it abideth by itself alone; but if it die, it beareth much fruit.** 25. **He that loveth his life loseth it; and he that hateth his life in this world shall keep it unto life eternal.** "He is illustrating a tremendous truth concerning Himself. Take hold of the figure in simplicity. Imagine that you hold a grain of wheat in your hand, a little thing, a husk on it, but inside the husk is the grain, and the scientists can tell you all the things that are in it. But while you look at that grain, you cannot really see it. O yes, you say, there it is. Philip and Andrew could see Jesus. There He was. The inquiring Greeks could see Jesus. There He was. The grain of wheat, can I see it? Yes, but I cannot see its meaning. I cannot see its possibilities. I cannot see what really lies potentially within the little grain. Would I really see it? Very well then; put it in the ground. . . . All you can see of it is that it dies. . . . Then presently the blade, the ear, the full corn, 30, 60, 100 fold in the ear. But they were all in the little grain you looked at, that was sown. It is not done. Husk it. Get those grains out, 30, 60, 100; and so the process is running on. . . . In great wisdom and perfect understanding He saw they could see Him, but they could not see Him. They could only really see Him as He fell and died; that out of that death of His there should spring life, the life that multiplied, life that grew until the harvests should be gathered in. He would be seen in that way, and that way alone. . . . He went on and applied it immediately to His disciples. 'If any man serve Me, let him follow Me.' Where was He going? He was going to the Cross. Where was He going? He was going to resurrection and triumph. Where was He going? The grain of wheat was going to fall into the ground and die. Where was He going? Through that death life should spring, and harvests should result. 'If any man serve Me, let him follow Me,' and accept that principle. Whether by dying or living, 'where I am, there shall also my servant be; if any man serve Me, him will the Father honour.' " — *G. Campbell Morgan.* 26. **If any man serve me, let him follow me: and where I am, there shall also my servant be: if any man serve me, him will the Father honor.** On this verse there is nothing quite to compare with the words of Dr. G. Campbell Morgan in a sermon preached many years ago. "The word at the center of my text for serving is arresting, not by its sublimity, but by its simplicity. Those of you who are familiar with the Greek

27. Now is my soul troubled; and what shall I say? Father, save me from this hour. But for this cause came I unto this hour.

New Testament will at once remember that the actual word *diakanos*, describes service in a different way to *doulos;* the second word representing the bondslave and describing a relation, while the former word simply refers to one who runs on errands, and describes an activity. In this particular word our Lord therefore laid His emphasis upon an activity. . . . The idea is that of attachment to a person in order to do anything He commands or needs. To be the servant of Him, to serve His interests. No official position is suggested by the word *serve*, or by the word *servant*. It is devoid of all dignity. Not even does it suggest skill or special aptitude or past training. It is the simplest of all words. Upon another occasion our Lord said, 'Pray ye the Lord of the harvest that He send forth labourers into His vineyard,' and the particular Greek word used suggests not the skilled worker, but the labouring man who cannot do anything and therefore may do everything. . . . Service means doing the thing He tells us; telling men that they must be born again; going into a hospital and sitting by the side of sick folk; being content to do the things He says; that is service. To trust, never to doubt the wisdom of His outlook, or the wisdom of His command; to do the thing so apparently useless, that seems to bring no result, and to keep on doing it day by day, week by week, month by month, until the years of life have run out and we seem to have done nothing." — *Dr. G. Campbell Morgan.*

27. **Now is my soul troubled; and what shall I say? Father, save me from this hour. But for this cause came I unto this hour.** "The trouble of soul here announced by Christ is not to be explained by the mere recoil of sinless nature from the approach of death. It is to be explained by supernatural causes — that is, by the divine anger against sin, as it was borne by the substitute of sinners; and the allusion to His death in the previous context seems to have given the occasion for letting in upon His soul, by a special avenue, a sense of the divine wrath. . . . The next words, 'Save me from this hour,' convey, in substance, the same petition that comes before us in the Gethsemane scene. We may suppose one of two explanations. We may either suppose that He does not ask deliverance from the death, but only from the accessories or accompaniments of it, which were so overwhelming, that the horror and anguish seemed to Him insupportable. It will then be a prayer for such a mitigation of the anguish, that He might finish the work of human redemption successfully. Or we may suppose that He prays to be saved from the punitive justice, the cup, or the baptism, within the sphere of which He was now brought. The latter seems the better exposition, though it has far greater difficulties, and brings us up at once to the inscrutable mystery of pure humanity asking with submission, and asking sinlessly, under the stunning sense of present anguish, whether there was no possibility of being saved from that hour. But the next clause points out in what way His mind returned to its rest: 'But for this cause came I unto this hour.' He reverts to the vicarious suffering as the design of His incarnation, as the very end of His coming. . . . This whole scene discovers the two great features of the atonement — sin-bearing and sinless obedience. The exclamation, beyond doubt, is extorted by the pressure of the divine wrath. Nor is this invalidated, in any measure, by the fact that the Scripture represents the Lord Jesus as the object of the divine complacency and love; and the more so, because He laid down His life for the sheep (John 10:17). It is urged by those who have inadequate views of the vicarious satisfaction, that the beloved Son could never be the object of the Father's anger, and therefore, that this exclamation could never arise from any such experience. That objection proceeds on a mistaken view of what is meant and confounds the personal with the official relation of the Son of God. In His personal capacity He was, and could never cease to be, the beloved Son. But in His official capacity He was the substitute of sinners, the sin-bearer and the curse-bearer, who came into the world to put

28. Father glorify thy name. There came therefore a voice out of heaven, *saying*. I have glorified it, and will glorify it again.

29. The multitude therefore, that stood by, and heard it, said that it had thundered: others said, An angel hath spoken to him.

30. Jesus answered and said, This voice hath not come for my sake, but for your sakes.

31. Now is the judgment of this world: now shall the prince of this world be cast out.

away sin by the sacrifice of Himself; and the personal relation in which He stood to the Father lent to the official all its efficacy and value." — *George Smeaton.* Three times during the ministry of our Lord was a voice heard from heaven confirming His utterances and affirming His deity: at the baptism (Matt. 3:17); at the time of the Transfiguration (Matt. 17:5) and here.   28. **Father glorify thy name.** "Reveal to men, and here to Greeks, as the representatives of the heathen world, in all its majesty the fulness of this Thy title shewn in the Son." **There came therefore a voice out of heaven, *saying.*** "The utterance was real and objective, that is, it was not a mere thunder-clap interpreted in this sense; yet, like all spiritual things, this voice required preparedness in the organ to which it was addressed." **I have both glorified it, and will glorify it again.** "The reference is to historic facts in the life of Christ, as, for example, to the signs which He wrought as signs of the Father (compare 5:23; 11:40); or perhaps more especially to the great crises in His ministry, the Baptism (Matt. 3:17) and the Transfiguration (Matt. 17:5), in which His Sonship, and so the Father's character was revealed. This glorification was not a mere repetition but a corresponding manifestation of the Father's glory. The glorification during the limited, earthly ministry to Israel was followed by a glorification answering to the proclamation of the universal Gospel to the world." — *B. F. Westcott.*   29. **The multitude therefore, that stood by, and heard it, said that it had thundered: others said, An angel hath spoken to him.   30. Jesus answered and said, This voice hath not come for my sake, but for your sakes.** "This multitude is part of the pilgrim host come to attend the Passover. They heard the sound from heaven without distinguishing the words. Compare Acts 9:7, where Jesus from his throne of glory speaks to Saul on the road to Damascus, and where likewise only they understand for whom this is intended, while the rest hear only a sound. The question of faith or of its lack should not be brought in as an explanation for understanding the words or for hearing only a sound — Saul certainly had no faith, yet he understood. The understanding reached those for whom it was intended; yet for the rest God wanted the impression of a supernatural manifestation connected with Jesus. The astounding sound coming from heaven was called 'thunder' by those who sought a natural explanation. Perhaps the sound resembled thunder to their ears. Others, nearer the truth, connect the sound with Jesus, and imagine that an angel from heaven has spoken to him. The thunder hypothesis would suit the skeptics of today, who would deem any but a natural explanation of supernatural phenomena 'superstition.' Yet in the clear skies of Palestine thunder is a poor hypothesis, rather on the cheap order of the new wine in Acts 2:13." — *R. C. H. Lenski.*

31. **Now is the judgment of this world: now shall the prince of this world be cast out.** "When in the Temptation the devil showed Him all the kingdoms of the world in a moment of time, and said, 'All this power will I give thee, and the glory of them, for that is delivered unto me,' the Lord did not challenge his statement and charge him with falsehood, but by his silence acquiesced in the proud boast. . . . The world of which we have been speaking is the stratagem by which the devil holds the souls of men in thrall. The world is to Satan what the web is to the spider, the bait to the angler, the lure to the fowler. Very specious and attractive were the appearances and the religious professions of the world; but Christ

32. And I, if I be lifted up from the earth, will draw all men unto myself.

---

tore the veil from it and revealed its true nature, so that we might be no longer cajoled by its appearances. It was needful that He should assume our nature, so as to meet and vanquish the devil on his chosen battleground, and in the race that he had seduced. This is the clue to the Incarnation. This explains the conflict which raged so fiercely throughout the Lord's brief early ministry. . . . In his Ascension our Lord showed that He had acquired as man the power to overthrow and cast out the devil. As a matter of fact, it is probable that he was cast out from the presence-chamber of God, where he had accused Job, and the high priest Joshua, and others of the saints. He was cast out into the heavenly places, where he is still prince of the power of the air, until Christ descends thither with his Church. He shall then be cast out into the earth with great wrath, knowing that his hour has come; and he shall afterwards be cast down into the bottomless pit, and finally into the lake of fire. The Lord's death and ascension did potentially that which He has been realizing actually ever since." — *F. B. Meyer.* **32. And I, if I be lifted up from the earth, will draw all men unto myself.** This reference may be to both the crucifixion and the resurrection. In a book rarely seen today, published in 1874, by Robert M'Cheyne Edgar, *The Philosophy of the Cross*, is an excellent analysis of this. He says first that "Christ crucified is still attracting hostile criticism. The spirit of the age, brethren, is to do, if possible, without the Cross. It is a foolish dream, men suppose, to expect saving power to be exercised through it. . . . And finally, Christ crucified is still attracting loving subjects to His sway. To the Cross of Christ as a rallying-point we are all invited, that we may come under the sway of the crucified Jesus. Under the shadow of His Cross we acknowledge the sovereign power of self-sacrificing and obedient love. We enlist in the army of this King, we feel humbled and inspired as we contemplate His fate, and we resolve to wage war with evil in our hearts and in our world, and to kill it through His Cross. With the weapon of the Cross we feel we can slay any hydra that may confront us, even should it have a hundred heads!" — *R. M. Edgar.*

VI. **THE VAST CONSEQUENCES WHICH FOLLOW BELIEVING IN CHRIST, AND REJECTING HIM,** 12:34–50. Up to this point we have observed a number of persons seeking to behold, to talk with, to listen to the Lord Jesus. The Passover pilgrims inquired for Him; many came to Bethany to see the One who had raised Lazarus from the dead; the chief priests sought Him that they might put Him to death; multitudes followed Him in the Triumphal Entry into Jerusalem; and the Greeks came that they might listen to His teaching. But from this point on, we seem to be in an atmosphere of extreme earnestness, of crisis. Our Lord now uses words which reveal what a man does in relation to Christ as the most important decision he can possibly make. He calls Himself the light and urges men to believe on Him. He announces that belief in Him implies belief in God the Father; that whoever looks upon Him sees God the Father; and that whoever believes on Him is delivered from darkness. The address is solemnly concluded by a warning that all who reject Christ will be judged and condemned on the last day, and a declaration that all He has been saying He has received of the Father, and receiving and believing what He has said will determine the eternal destiny of a man's soul.

THE LESSON IN LIFE, LITERATURE, AND ARCHAEOLOGY.

Some years ago a young man wrote Dr. James M. Gray, who had been President of the Moody Bible Institute for many years, asking, "How do you live a day?" This is a difficult question, and Dr. Gray took a great deal of time in answering it. Part of that reply was as follows: "You noted that my days were lived evenly, and as explaining that I may say, and perhaps I ought to say, that years ago I took

Paul's admonition in 1 Corinthians 10:31 as a life motto, and the measure in which by divine grace I have lived up to it is, I believe, the secret of what you observed. There is also one other Scripture which for a third of a century has gone with it in perceptibly moulding my life. It is the word of our Lord in John 12:26: 'If any man serve me him will my Father honor.' These are two great rules of being for a young Christian believer, whose results are to be coveted above everything else in the world, and I commend them to you."

A TRUTH FOR THE CLASS TO CARRY AWAY.

I believe that the one great question to press here, in whatever way the teacher feels led when the hour for presenting the lesson has come, is this, Does the cross of Christ mean to us what Christ meant it should mean to us: Is what Christ did on the cross as central in our lives as the work He came to do on the cross was central with Him?

Why do you think these Greeks were so eagerly seeking Christ? Who in this lesson might be placed in the outer circle of those drawn to Christ, who in a nearer group, and who were the nearest of all? Why are not men drawn to Christ today? How do you account for the fact that the disciples play such a small part in the events recorded in this chapter? Are there any indications here of the actual deity of Christ?

LESSON XII. — March 21.

THE NEW COMMANDMENT. — John 13—14.

PRINTED TEXT, John 13:3–5, 12–17, 34, 35; 14:21–24.

Devotional Reading: 1 John 4:11–21.
Beginner Topic: AT TIMOTHY'S HOUSE.
  Lesson Material: 2 Timothy 1:1–6; 3:14–17.
  Memory Verse: O give thanks unto Jehovah; for he is good.   Psalm 136:1.
Primary Topic: "LOVE ONE ANOTHER."
  Lesson Material: John 13:1–17.
  Memory Verse: (Jesus said) A new commandment I give unto you, that ye love one another; even as I have loved you.   John 13:34.
Junior Topic: "LOVE ONE ANOTHER."
  Lesson Material: John 13:1–17.
  Memory Verse: (Jesus said) A new commandment I give unto you, that ye love one another; even as I have loved you.   John 13:34.
Intermediate-Senior Topic: THE MARK OF DISCIPLESHIP.
  Lesson Material: John 13—14.
  Memory Verse: A new commandment I give unto you, that ye love one another; even as I have loved you, that ye also love one another.   John 13:34.
Topic for Young People and Adults: JESUS' NEW COMMANDMENT.
  Lesson Material: John 13—14.
  Memory Verse: A new commandment I give unto you, that ye love one another; even as I have loved you, that ye also love one another.   John 13:34.

THE TEACHER AND HIS CLASS.

The **Younger Classes** may be introduced to this lesson by an illustration from the life of the editor. Years ago, one of our nephews, when a small boy, spent one month each summer with us, and many of the things he said then we still remember with pleasure and delight. He liked to have me read to him. In the morning he would come into my study and, after a general conversation, he would inveigle me into making a promise that I would read to him that evening. Sometimes when evening came I would be detained at a committee meeting, or in visitation until late, but he would always remind me that I was to read to him. "Maxie, it is so late, I will read to you tomorrow night," I would say. "But, Uncle Wilbur, you *promised* me," would be the immediate response. That was the end of the argument. I had to keep my word. Promises must be kept. If they are not met, one loses confidence in the person who made the promise, and his influence is gone. Our lesson has to do with some wonderful promises that Jesus made to his disciples and those who would follow Him. His promises that relate to this life have been gloriously kept from generation to generation, and we may be sure that those pertaining to the life to come will be kept with equal fullness.

The Older Classes may be reminded, at the beginning of this lesson that, as in all great literature, and lofty living, there are violent contrasts to be found; they are discovered here and there in the Bible, and nowhere more than in the life of our Lord, as set against the background of his generation. All in the same evening we have, on the one hand, the betrayal of Judas and the denial of Simon Peter, and, on the other hand, the marvelous humility of the Son of God, and His glorious words concerning love for one another, a home with the heavenly Father, the promise of the Holy Spirit and the bestowal of peace.

THE LESSON IN ITS SETTING.

Time. — Thursday evening, April 6, A.D. 30.

Place. — The Upper Room, where the Last Supper was held, and the road to the Garden of Gethsemane, on the slope of the Mount of Olives.

THE PLAN OF THE LESSON.

SUBJECT: The Actions, Warnings, Admonition, and Promises of Christ on the Night Before His Death.

I. JESUS WASHES THE FEET OF HIS DISCIPLES, John 13:1–17.

II. JESUS MAKES TWO ANNOUNCEMENTS CONCERNING TWO OF HIS DISCIPLES, 13:18–30, 36–38.
1. The betrayal of Judas, vs. 18–30.
2. The denial of Peter, vs. 36–38.

III. THE PRIMACY OF LOVE AMONG CHRIST'S DISCIPLES, 13:31–35.

IV. THE WONDERFUL WORDS OF JESUS REGARDING OUR HEAVENLY HOME, 14:1–12.

V. THE PROMISE OF THE HOLY SPIRIT, 14:13–26.

VI. THE BESTOWAL OF PEACE, 14:27–31.

THE TEACHER'S LIBRARY.

The literature on this lesson is enormous. In addition to all the larger commentaries on John's Gospel, and the more complete lives of Christ (which will be only fairly helpful here), such volumes as the following will be valuable: T. D. Bernard: *The Central Teaching of Jesus Christ* (1892); A. E. Garvie: *The Master's Comfort and Hope* (1917); E. R. Hendricks: *Christ's Table Talk*, 83–146; William Evans: *From the Upper Room to the Empty Tomb*. Of course all works devoted to the lives of the apostles will contain useful material for the study of this lesson; also volumes on the teaching of Jesus, especially the great work by G. Campbell Morgan.

On the subject of heaven there is a great amount of literature, some of it not important. The following volumes have passages on the words of our lesson: David Gregg: *The Heaven Life;* Hy Pickering: *Heaven, the Home of the Redeemed;* Edward M. Bounds: *A Place, a City, a Home.*

Two excellent volumes containing chapters on the promise of the Holy Spirit are Andrew Murray: *The Spirit of Christ*, and J. Ritchie Smith: *The Holy Spirit in the Gospels.*

We need not tarry long with sermonic material; in fact, the only verses in the lesson for which there is helpful sermonic material are 13:2–5, for which see John Hutton: *There They Crucified Him*, 44 ff.; J. D. Jones: *The Inevitable Christ*, 105–124; John Henry Jowett: *The Transfigured Church*, 119 ff.; and David Smith: *The Pilgrim's Hospice*, 51 ff.; also 13:13, for which see T. H. Darlow: *Via Sacra*, 67–74; and, 13:34, 35, J. G. Greenough: *Great Texts of the New Testament*, 99 ff.

AUDIO-VISUAL AIDS.

There are aids covering the larger subject of the crucifixion, including in passing the material in this lesson, but it will probably be better to dispense with them here in favor of a thorough discussion of the lesson.

JOHN 13:3. *Jesus*, knowing that the Father had given all things into his hands, and that he came forth from God, and goeth to God;

4. Riseth from supper, and layeth aside his garments; and he took a towel, and girded himself.

5. Then he poureth water into the basin, and began to wash the disciples' feet, and to wipe them with the towel wherewith he was girded.

"Jean Paul Richter says that no day should close without a look at the stars. Certainly no life will ever be great and good, no life will continue to bear about with it the atmosphere and quality of Christ, which does not think, in those solitary moments which come to even the busiest of us, of those grave and happy words spoken of our Lord as fortifying Him on the last night He spent with us, fortifying Him for Gethsemane and the Judgment Hall and Calvary — words in which we are told that on the night in which He was betrayed our Lord reminded Himself that He was come from God, and was going to God, and therein found strength to finish the work which the Father had given Him to do." — *John Hutton.*

I. JESUS WASHES THE FEET OF HIS DISCIPLES, 13:1–17. Practically the entire portion of John's Gospel from the opening of the 13th chapter to the end of the 17th chapter — all to be placed on Thursday evening of Holy Week — consists of the wonderful final discourse of Christ to the inner circle of His disciples. The single exception to this is the act which opens our lesson, Christ's washing of the disciples' feet. Note the tremendous contrast between the first two verses of this 13th chapter — Christ, the obedient servant of God, and Judas Iscariot, the traitor — Judas, possessed of the devil: Christ, obedient to the Father's will; love for others, filling the heart of Christ: treason, filling the heart of Judas. Verses 1 to 3 reveal to us something of the vast omniscience of Christ. These are John's words, not those of our Lord, and one wonders how John came to know the extent of Christ's knowledge. **3. Jesus, knowing that the Father had given all things into his hands, and that he came forth from God, and goeth to God.** "His will and thinking is one with that of the Father. 'He did come out from God' declares his deity, his essential oneness with God. As one who thus came out from God he now goes back to God. . . . He who shares omnipotence with God, in essential oneness with him, now performs an act, in which the very opposite of this divine majesty is brought to view, an act in which divine majesty makes itself the most lowly servant — 'who, being in the form of God, counted it not a prize to be on an equality with God, but emptied himself, taking the form of a servant' (Phil. 2:6–7). Here he took water and washed his disciples' dusty feet; presently he poured out his own blood to wash their sinful souls." — *R. C. H. Lenski.* **4. Riseth from supper, and layeth aside his garments; and he took a towel, and girded himself. 5. Then he poureth water into the basin, and began to wash the disciples' feet, and to wipe them with the towel wherewith he was girded.** The washing of the disciples' feet took place in the Upper Room, where the Lord's Supper was instituted that same night. The account of the Lord's Supper is given by the three Synoptics, but not by John (Matt. 26:20–29, etc.); whereas the washing of the disciples' feet, which occurred immediately preceding the Supper, is recorded only by John. "In the Greek the words 'layeth aside his garments' and the corresponding words in verse 12, 'had taken his garments,' are strikingly significant, since the verbs 'lay aside' and 'take' have been previously used with reference to the death and resurrection of Jesus. 'Therefore doth the Father love me, because I lay down my life that I may take it again' (10:17, 18; compare 10:11, 15; 13:37, 38; 15:13; 1 John 3:16). The girding with the towel marks the action of a slave. . . . The Lord, having thus removed His clothes and assumed the vesture of a slave, undertakes the action of a slave. He poured water into a

12. So.when he had washed their feet, and taken his garments, and sat down again, he said unto them, Know ye what I have done to you?
13. Ye call me, Teacher, and Lord: and ye say well; for so I am.
14. If I then, the Lord and the Teacher, have washed your feet, ye also ought to wash one another's feet.

---

basin, and began to wash the disciples' feet and wipe them with the towel. To wash the feet of their masters belonged to the duties of slaves (1 Sam. 25:41)." — *E. C. Hoskyns.*　Five disciples appear by name in this narrative — Judas Iscariot, Judas (not the Iscariot), Thomas and Philip (beginning of chapter 14), and Peter, who is involved in two episodes recorded here, namely, his strange behaviour when Christ approached him to wash his feet, and his refusal to believe Christ's prediction that he would betray Him that very night.　I am sure that Peter's insistence that Christ should not wash his feet was prompted by his own deep consciousness of his utter inferiority to the Lord Jesus, knowing that, rather, he should be washing Jesus' feet.　To overcome this stubbornness on the part of Peter, our Lord tells him that what was now about to take place was of so mysterious a nature that he would not fully understand it until after the resurrection, at which time many truths concerning Christ would appear in a clearness not known to the disciples during their Lord's earthly ministry; also, they would be participants in the illuminating work of the Holy Spirit.　When our Lord told Peter that if the Redeemer did not wash his feet that night, he would have no part with Him, He was not in any way referring to Peter's salvation through Christ, but rather to his communion with Christ.　"We have been washed — once, definitely and irrevocably, we have been bathed in the crimson tide that flows from Calvary; but we need a daily cleansing.　Our feet become soiled with the dust of life's highways; our hands grimy, as our linen beneath the rain of filth in a great city; our lips — as the white doorstep of the house — are fouled by the incessant throng of idle, unseemly and fretful words; our hearts cannot keep unsoiled the stainless robes with which we pass from the closet at morning prime.　Constantly we need to repair to the Laver to be washed.　But do we always realise how much each act of confession on our part involves from Christ on his?　Whatever important work He may at that moment have on hand; whatever directions He may be giving to the loftiest angels for the fulfilment of his purposes; however pressing the concerns of the Church or the universe upon his broad shoulders — He must needs turn from all these to do a work.　He will not delegate.　Again He stoops from the Throne, and girds Himself with a towel; and, in all lowliness, endeavours to remove from thee and me the stain which his love dare not pass over.　He never loses the print of the nails; He never forgets Calvary and the blood; He never spends one hour without stooping to do the most menial work of cleansing filthy souls.　And it is because of this humility He sits on the Throne and wields the sceptre over hearts and worlds." — *F. B. Meyer.*

Every deed of Christ during His public ministry, extending over three and one-half years, had its immediate physical, material, significance, e.g., the quieting of the waves, the cleansing of the leper, the raising of the dead, the feeding of the five thousand, etc., but it also had a deeper, spiritual, abiding significance.　The cleansing of the leper is symbolic of Christ's cleansing us from sin.　The command to the waves to be still is an expression of his desire that we have peace in our own hearts.　This menial task of washing from the disciples' feet the accumulation of dust from their walk across the city also has its spiritual significance, and this Christ did not want them to miss.　**12. So when he had washed their feet, and taken his garments, and sat down again, he said unto them, Know ye what I have done to you?　13. Ye call me, Teacher, and Lord: and ye say well; for so I am. 14. If I then, the Lord and the Teacher, have washed your feet, ye also ought to**

15. For I have given you an example, that ye also should do as I have done to you.

16. Verily, verily, I say unto you, A servant is not greater than his lord; neither one that is sent greater than he that sent him.

17. If ye know these things, blessed are ye if ye do them.

---

wash one another's feet. 15. For I have given you an example, that ye also should do as I have done to you. 16. Verily, verily, I say unto you, A servant is not greater than his lord; neither one that is sent greater than he that sent him. 17. If ye know these things, blessed are ye if ye do them. Before making any comment on these verses, I must make a confession here. Not until a few days ago, when reading John's Gospel on the train, did I notice this remarkable phrase from the lips of Christ in which He proclaims Himself "the Lord and the Teacher." Some groups in the Christian Church, from early times down to the present, insist that we should make a practice of doing exactly what Christ did, in washing one another's feet. No great objection can be raised to this, but I believe that the view of the larger part of the Church down through the ages is the correct one — that what Christ meant here was that we should ever be willing to be servants of brethren in Christ, to do the menial things, and to manifest a spirit of humility, even as He did.

II. JESUS MAKES TWO ANNOUNCEMENTS CONCERNING TWO OF HIS DISCIPLES, 13:18–30, 36–38.

1. THE BETRAYAL OF JUDAS, vs. 18–30. In studying the four accounts of the last week of our Lord's life, one discovers the amazing fact that Jesus spoke more of the approaching betrayal of Judas than of any other one subject. If I may say this reverently, it seemed to weigh heavily upon His mind. He was more grieved over this coming betrayal than He was disturbed by the thought of the coming agony of the cross. We must condense our comment on this passage, however. It is clear that none of the apostolic group had any premonition at all that one of their number, within a few hours, would betray the Master, and even when He announced that there was a traitor in their midst, none of them seemed to know who it could be. "To the Beloved Disciple Jesus unmasks the betrayer. He will dip a morsel of bread or meat (either meaning of the Greek word is possible) in the dish, and will present it to the disciple who is to betray Him. . . . The moment of his exposure is also the moment when Satan finally takes possession of him wholly (8:44; 13:2; Luke 22:3). . . . His exposure in the presence of the disciples by the Lord Himself provides the opportunity for his complete surrender to the promptings of the Devil. The judgment of Judas is set in the words which follow. The Lord commands him to proceed with his work as quickly as possible. Then he went forth immediately into the darkness. Having surrendered himself to the Prince of this world, Judas is banished from the light, and passes out into the darkness under the judgment of God (3:19; 9:4; 11:10; compare Luke 22:53). Even the Beloved Disciple, who knows the identity of the traitor, does not grasp the imminence of the betrayal. They suppose the urgency of the departure of Judas to be occasioned by some lack of preparation for the Feast, or by the need of some exercise of charity in view of its proximity; and think that, as the treasurer of the society (12:6) he was instructed to make good the deficiency or perform the required act of mercy." — E. C. Hoskyns.

2. THE DENIAL OF PETER, 13:36–38. Not only is Christ burdened with the weight of His approaching death, involving falsehood, brutality, misunderstanding, insults, mockery, the beatings, the scourge commanded by Pontius Pilate, and the crucifixion itself, in addition to the foreknowledge of Judas' betrayal, but He is fully aware that on this very night, Peter, one of the two leaders of the apostolic group, will deny Him. Even Peter was not aware that he was going to do this, and uttered bolder assertions of his loyalty to Jesus this night than did any of the other apostles. John's account of Christ's warning to Peter is slightly different

34. A new commandment I give unto you, that ye love one another; even as I have loved you, that ye also love one another.

35. By this shall all men know that ye are my disciples, if ye have love one to another.

from that of the Synoptics, but the one only supplements the others (see Matt. 26:31–35 and parallels).

III. **THE PRIMACY OF LOVE AMONG CHRIST'S DISCIPLES, 13:31–35.** This chapter, introducing us to the events of Thursday, contains the first part of the long discourse of Jesus to His disciples. It begins with the statement that Christ "having loved His own which were in the world, He loved them unto the end." Before entering into the valley of the shadow of death, our Lord, who was the living embodiment of love for others, gives to His disciples, and through them to the Church in all ages, this great fundamental principle, which, I believe, is not possible to practice apart from the indwelling of the Spirit of Christ. Westcott reminds us that the word here translated "little children" in verse 33 occurs not only here in the Gospels, but is found in the First Epistle of John six times. It is a word "emphasizing the idea of kinsmanship; and the diminutive conveys an expression at once of deep affection and also of solicitude for those who as yet are immature. But using it here the Lord marks the loving spirit of the communication which He makes." — *B. F. Westcott.* **34. A new commandment I give unto you, that ye love one another; even as I have loved you, that ye also love one another. 35. By this shall all men know that ye are my disciples, if ye have love one to another.** "The newness Jesus means is not strange and startling to the disciples, it has a familiar and pleasant look. Jesus has brought a new love into the world, a love not only faultless and perfect as love, but one intelligently bent on salvation for the one loved. Only the disciples know from Jesus what this love is, only they have made the experience of his love; hence this precept is for them alone — it would be useless to give it to the world. So also this love is to be for 'each other' in the circle of the disciples." — *R. C. H. Lenski.* Dr. Meyer reminds us that this is a commandment. "Obviously, then, obedience must be possible. Christ had gauged our nature not only as Creator, but by personal experience. He knew what was in man. The possibilities of our nature were well within his cognisance; therefore it must be possible for us to love one another qualitatively, if not quanitatively, as He has loved us. Do not sit down before this great command and say it is impossible; that were to throw discredit on Him who spake it. Dare to believe that no word of his is vain. He descries eminence of attainment which it is possible for us all to reach: let us surrender ourselves to Him, that He may fulfil in us his ideal, and make us experts in the science of love." "'If you have love among each other' invites a test, expected to be met. Still false disciples will appear, even the world will discover that they are false, by their lack of love. The question is not wholly shut out: Have I this love which Jesus enjoined upon his disciples the night in which he was betrayed? How many Christians show malice, spite, hatred, coldness, enmity to each other? Where no love is, there no discipleship can be." — *R. C. H. Lenski.*

IV. **THE WONDERFUL WORDS OF JESUS REGARDING OUR HEAVENLY HOME, 14:1–12.** On the marvelous sentences of this familiar and oft-repeated passage from the Gospels, whole books could be written, but since none of the verses are assigned to the printed text, we can comment only with irritating brevity. Notice first that what Christ wants for His disciples is an untroubled heart. Our Lord did not anywhere promise the disciples freedom from tribulation and trouble, from the hatred of the world, or even martyrdom. He warned that they might experience all these things, but through it all, nothing was to allow their hearts to be overly agitated. They might suffer, but they were not to fret. Among the great themes in this chapter, the first is that of heaven. While the word *heaven* was often on the lips of our Lord, only here does He speak at some length about actual life in heaven. This is reserved for another book written by John the Apostle, the Book of Revelation, particularly the 21st chapter. Heaven is home for us, because it is our Father's home, and here the followers of Christ are promised "mansions," a word coming out of the Latin from a Greek word meaning "to remain, to abide," used in medieval times of stations on a great road where travelers found refreshment. These mansions are prepared by our Lord for us, and when the time comes for us to occupy them, Christ himself will come back and take us to the Father's house; and thus forever, He said, we shall be dwelling with Him. When my dear friend Dr. Harry Rimmer passed away a few months ago after a long period of suffering, he cried out just before his spirit left the body, almost in a state of unconsciousness, "O, mansions for me!" I have no doubt that he actually saw the mansions here referred to.

Imbedded in this paragraph is one of the most profound statements our Lord ever uttered — "I am the way, and the truth, and the life: no one cometh unto the Father, but by me." In his comparatively recent work, of great value, on the Gospel of John, the late Dr. E. C. Hoskyns has a rich comment. "The road to God is knowledge of the Truth, and regeneration, enlightenment and the possession of Life. Truth and Life are no ideal abstractions. They are present concretely in the incarnate Son of God, who is both the Truth and the Life. He gives the Life which He is (11:25, 43, 44), He reveals the Truth which He is, He offers the Light which He is (1:9; 8:12; 9:7), just as He speaks the Word and provides the Bread which He is (1:1; 8:43; 6:27, 35, 63). Consequently He is the way, as He is the Door (10:7, 9). No man can attain the Father except by perceiving the Truth, and participating in the Life which is revealed to men in His Son." — *Dr. E. C. Hoskyns.* Many will ask how the statement in verse 12 can be true, that those who believe on Christ will do greater works than Christ did. Note that this does not read "greater *miracles*." An illustration of this truth could be the work of the Old Fashioned Revival Hour. In one Sunday afternoon on this program, Dr. Charles Fuller proclaims the Gospel to possibly more people than the Lord Jesus had before Him in all of His sermons in three and one-half years. Some evangelists of modern times have seen a thousand and more people come forward to confess Christ within two hours at a single service. We have no record of anything like this taking place during the earthly ministry of our Lord.

V. **THE PROMISE OF THE HOLY SPIRIT,** 14:13–26. There are many promises in this chapter, but I would here emphasize the one given in the greatest detail. Here are promises of answered prayer, and of the love and indwelling of the Father and Son, but principally our Lord's teaching here relates to the Holy Spirit, whom He would send. First of all we should have before us the titles of the Holy Spirit as given by Christ in this passage. In verses 16 and 26, He is called the Comforter; also in verse 26, the Holy Spirit; in verse 17, the Spirit of truth, a title also found in 15:26. The word here translated *Comforter* is a Greek word *Paraclete*, from two Greek words, *kaleo*, meaning *to call*, and *para*, meaning, *at one's side;* therefore the title of the Holy Spirit here implies that He will be one who will come to our side to aid us, instruct us, defend us. When our Lord says that the Holy Spirit is "another Paraclete," He implies that He Himself was the first Paraclete of the disciples, when walking in their midst. The Latin word is *Advocate,* from which we get our English word *advocate,* referring to one who defends another; in fact, in many European countries, a lawyer is called an *advocat.* The Holy Spirit is called the "Spirit of truth," for He is the one "by whom the truth finds expression and is brought to man's spirit. The Truth is that which the Spirit interprets and enforces." — *B. F. Westcott.* This title is in strong contrast to "the spirit of error" (1 John 4:6). Everywhere in the New Testament the Holy Spirit is not an influence, or an energy, but a Person, none other than the third Person of the Godhead. "There are certain works ascribed to Him in the Bible — the work of creation, the work of regeneration, of teaching, of leading and guiding, of comforting, and of sanctifying men. All these things are ascribed to the Holy Spirit, and are not these to be predicated only of a personal being?

JOHN 14:21. He that hath my commandments, and keepeth them, he it is that loveth me: and he that loveth me shall be loved of my Father, and I will love him, and will manifest myself unto him.

22. Judas (not Iscariot) saith unto him, Lord, what is come to pass that thou wilt manifest thyself unto us, and not unto the world?

23. Jesus answered and said unto him, If a man love me, he will keep my word: and my Father will love him, and we will come unto him, and make our abode with him.

24. He that loveth me not keepeth not my words; and the word which ye hear is not mine, but the Father's who sent me.

Then take the attributes which are ascribed to the Holy Spirit in the Bible, the attributes of holiness, of truth, of goodness, of love; can these things belong to any other than a personal being?" — *James M. Gray.*

In the midst of this teaching on the Holy Spirit is inserted an almost unfathomable statement concerning the love of God for men and the love of the redeemed for God. **21. He that hath my commandments, and keepeth them, he it is that loveth me: and he that loveth me shall be loved of my Father, and I will love him, and will manifest myself unto him. 22. Judas (not Iscariot) saith unto him, Lord, what is come to pass that thou wilt manifest thyself unto us, and not unto the world? 23. Jesus answered and said unto him, If a man love me, he will keep my word: and my Father will love him, and we will come unto him, and make our abode with him. 24. He that loveth me not keepeth not my words; and the word which ye hear is not mine, but the Father's who sent me.** As profound and inexhaustible as this passage is, we can begin to understand, and appropriate, and live its truths by setting forth the fundamental ideas presented to us here. On the one hand, Jesus talks about our loving Him — twice in verse 21, once in verse 23, and once in verse 24 — but the idea is not left suspended. Strange as it may seem, the reality and genuineness of our love for Christ is here made to depend upon our keeping Christ's commandments, keeping his Word, that which Christ had received from the Father and had faithfully communicated to His own. There is an exact parallel to this fundamental principle in Christian life at the conclusion of the Sermon on the Mount, where Christ, setting forth precepts for the life of a disciple, tells His followers that those who would do the things He had commanded would be likened to the man who built his house on a rock, and thus was able to weather all the storms and experiences of life. By "the word" here, Christ means the whole body of His teaching, concerning purity of life, prayer, the absence of resentment, love for one another, the bearing of one's cross, a righteousness exceeding that of the Pharisees, a life free from the entanglements of the world, absolute devotion to Christ the Master, etc. Keeping Christ's word is obeying His word. In conservative circles today I fear that this side of the Christian life is somewhat forgotten. We become so insistent in matters of doctrine, important as they are, that we neglect the teaching on the life one ought to live — the life of peace with one's fellowmen, free from backbiting, unjust criticism, schism, gossip, bitterness, uncleanness, deceit, hypocrisy. If our love for Christ is true, and if obedience to His word is our daily habit, we will be (1) loved of the Father, (2) loved of the Son, (3) indwelt by both Father and Son, and (4) Christ will manifest himself to us. The word *abode* in verse 23 comes from the same root as the word *mansion* at the beginning of the chapter. "Have you not sometimes taken up a daisy, and looked into its little upturned eye, and thought and thought again, till through the gate of the flower you have passed into an infinite world of life, beauty, and mystery? There are moments when even a flower is transfigured before us, and manifests itself to us as a thought of God, a ray of his glory, the frail product of his infinite mind, the wick around which trembles the fire of the Shekinah! Have you not sometimes stood alone amid mountains, glaciers, wooded valleys, and rushing streamlets, till Nature has dropped her vail, and revealed herself in a phase of beauty and a depth of meaning which struck you as altogether unique and singular?   So there are moments in the life of the believer, when Christ, who is ever with us, manifests Himself as He does not to the world.   There is borne in upon the spirit a consciousness that He is near; there is a waft of his breath, a savour of his fragrant dress, fresh from the ivory palaces." — *F. B. Meyer.* On the teaching ministry of the Holy Spirit, which is exceedingly important, see also John 16:13; 1 John 2:20, 27; and 1 Corinthians 1:6–16.

VI. **THE BESTOWAL OF PEACE,** 14:27–31. In this last section, no part of which is assigned for the printed text, I think we need dwell only on this one final gift of the departing Christ — "Peace I leave with you."   Dr. Meyer distinguishes between "peace" and "my peace." "The former refers to the result of his work for us on the cross: 'Being justified by faith, we have peace with God through our Lord Jesus Christ'; the latter refers to *His* indwelling, who is our Peace.   The one He has bequeathed as a legacy to all men: the Testator died, and left in his will a perfect reconciliation between God and man, which is for all who are willing to avail themselves of it; the other is *a gift,* which must be appropriated and used, or it will be ineffectual.   We must have peace *with* God before we can enjoy the peace *of* God.   We must receive the atonement, with all its blessed comfort, before we can enter upon our heritage in Christ Jesus."

THE LESSON IN LIFE, LITERATURE, AND ARCHAEOLOGY.

Miss Constance Padwick in her remarkable Life of the Great Missionary Henry Martyn records the following incident occurring in 1805 when after months at sea the ship at last came to San Salvador.

"Here Martyn went ashore on a new continent and spent one of the sunniest fortnights of his life. 'Nothing but negro slaves' was his first impression, 'very good-natured cheerful looking people.   A slave was sent to gather three roses for me. . . .   A slave in my bedroom washed my feet.   I was struck with the degree of abasement expressed in the act; and as he held the foot in the towel with his head bowed down towards it, I remembered the condescension of our blessed Lord.' "

A TRUTH FOR THE CLASS TO CARRY AWAY.

Hardly any passage in all the New Testament is so important for true conservative, Bible-believing Christians today as the lesson we have just studied.   I happen to know of a church of strongest orthodoxy where during an angry session with the officers and the pastor, one man received a black eye.   The result of this was the exodus of over a hundred members of that church.   The occasion was reported in the city's daily newspapers.   It brought shame to Christians and was a cause of ridicule among unbelievers.   We will draw people to Christ when we become like Christ and there is no power in the world that can draw like love.

In how many ways is Christ here revealed as infinitely superior to all other characters in history?   Are the things Christ promised here as necessary in this atomic age as in the time of Christ?   What are the fundamental differences between Peter and Judas?   How did Christ practise in His own life on earth the admonitions that He here gives to His disciples?   How does this lesson prove that the peace that Christ bestows can reign in the heart no matter how tragic the circumstances of the hour might be?

LESSON XIII. — March 28.

JESUS STRENGTHENS HIS DISCIPLES. — John 15—16.

PRINTED TEXT, John 15:12–19; 16:1–13.

Devotional Reading: Acts 2:1–4, 33, 37–39.
Beginner Topic: NEWS FOR A STRANGER.
  Lesson Material: Acts 8:3–8, 26–40.
  Memory Verse: Jehovah is good to all. Psalm 145:9.
Primary Topic: LIVING AS FRIENDS OF JESUS.
  Lesson Material: John 15:12–17.
  Memory Verse: Ye are my friends, if ye do the things which I command you. John 15:14.
Junior Topic: LIVING AS FRIENDS OF JESUS.
  Lesson Material: John 15:1–19.
  Memory Verse: (Jesus said) Ye are my friends, if ye do the things which I command you. John 15:14.
Intermediate-Senior Topic: THE PROMISED GUIDE.
  Lesson Material: John 15—16.
  Memory Verse: When he, the Spirit of truth, is come, he shall guide you into all the truth. John 16:13.
Topic for Young People and Adults: THE GUIDANCE OF THE SPIRIT.
  Lesson Material: John 15—16.
  Memory Verse: When he, the Spirit of truth, is come, he shall guide you into all the truth. John 16:13.

THE TEACHER AND HIS CLASS.

The Younger Classes might be introduced to this lesson, which begins with the metaphor of Christians being branches of the vine, Christ, and closes with a rich unfolding of the possibility of new life in Christ by the Holy Spirit, with a simple illustration which I take from my boyhood years. Many years ago, before the development of great apple orchards, there were some varieties of apples in the small orchards of country folk that were absolutely worthless for marketing purposes, and not even very suitable for domestic use. One of them, I remember, was called the Lover apple. It was small, bitter, without color. But later, when the finer varieties began to be developed, such as the Northern Spy, the Stark Delicious, etc., I have seen slips from these trees grafted onto a Lover tree twelve or fifteen years old, and in two or three years that formerly almost worthless tree would be producing bushels of Northern Spy or Stark Delicious apples. By nature we are sinful creatures, incapable of attaining the glory of God or fullness of life, but when we become identified with Christ, and His life flows

into us, we begin to bear the fruits of the Holy Spirit and become increasingly like unto the Son of God.

The Older Classes will find in this lesson two contrasting truths: on the one hand, the strange, mysterious, but nevertheless real, constant and deep opposition of the world to Christ, and, on the other hand, the infinite resources for a new, rich, satisfying life available for those who receive the Lord Jesus, and thus become identified with Him. Probably never since the end of the Roman persecutions of Christians in the Fourth Century has there been such opposition to Christianity and its Christ as we see in the world today. This is a time, above all times, when men are classified as to whether they are with Christ or against Him.

THE LESSON IN ITS SETTING.

Time. — The words of these chapters were uttered by our Lord on Thursday evening, April 6, A.D. 30, immediately following the institution of the Last Supper.

Place. — On the way from the Upper Room in Jerusalem to the Garden of

108

Gethsemane on the lower slopes of the Mount of Olives.

3. The work of the Holy Spirit in believers, vs. 12-15.
4. The sorrow of the disciples, vs. 16-22.
5. The privileges of prayer, vs. 23-33.

THE PLAN OF THE LESSON.

SUBJECT: The Mysterious, Wonderful, Enriching Work of the Three Persons of the Godhead in the Inner Life of All Who Receive Christ as Their Saviour.

I. THE VINE AND THE BRANCHES, John 15:1-11.

II. THE COMMANDMENT PERTAINING TO LOVE, 15:12-17.

III. THE OPPOSITION OF THE WORLD TO CHRIST AND CHRIST'S FOLLOWERS, 15:18-25.

IV. CHRIST'S SECOND PROMISE CONCERNING THE HOLY SPIRIT, 15:26, 27.

V. CHRIST WARNS THE DISCIPLES OF COMING PERSECUTION AND DISCUSSES HIS OWN IMMINENT DEATH AND RESURRECTION, 16.

1. In general, vs. 1-6.
2. He speaks of the necessity of His going, vs. 7-11.

THE TEACHER'S LIBRARY.

All of the major commentaries on John's Gospel will be found helpful in the study of this lesson. In addition, there are some volumes devoted exclusively to this last discourse of our Lord recorded only in this Gospel, as T. D. Bernard: *The Central Teaching of Christ* (1892) and a more recent work by Canon H. Leonard Pass: *The Glory of the Father*. All volumes adequately dealing with the great subject of the Holy Spirit will contain chapters on the teachings of Christ on the Holy Spirit found in the verses of our lesson. I would especially commend the relevant pages in J. Ritchie Smith: *The Teaching of the Gospel of John*, 169-174, 281 ff. While it is not a part of the printed text, there is a good chapter on Christ the Vine in G. Campbell Morgan: *The Parables and Metaphors of Our Lord*, 341-347.

For sermonic material on 15:15, 16, see W. M. Clow: *The Evangel of the Straight Gate*, 247-258; G. Campbell Morgan in *The Westminster Pulpit*, Vol. 8, pp. 313-320; Andrew Murray: *With Christ in the School of Prayer*, 178-192; and on verse 8, G. Campbell Morgan: *The Holy Spirit*, 104-109.

AUDIO-VISUAL AIDS.

No audio-visual aids discovered.

On Tuesday of Holy Week, our Lord was speaking primarily to Israel, in terms of sternness, with parables of warning and the great Olivet Discourse; on Wednesday He was in seclusion; on Thursday evening the washing of the disciples' feet took place, the announcement of the betrayal of Judas and of Peter's denial, the institution of the Lord's Supper, and then the long walk of two or three miles from the Upper Room to the Garden of Gethsemane. No man, no matter how great and noble, could ever utter such words as now pass the Saviour's lips. Each sentence deserves hours of meditation. We are here indeed on holy ground. The words which Jesus uttered then are just as vital, just as true, and the life there set forth just as needful and possible today as when Jesus walked with His own.

I. **THE VINE AND THE BRANCHES**, 15:1-11. While this exquisite teaching in metaphor is not assigned to the printed text, we must tarry for a moment with its general truth, for it is the proper introduction to the subsequent teaching of our Lord on this occasion. Note especially the way in which the discourse opens, "I am," and then note how many times in these eleven verses we have the pronoun "I" and "me." All the possibilities of rich, spiritual life, eternal life itself, derive from our relationship to Christ. He is the true Vine. "The vine is not only the main stem. It is part of it, in certain senses it may be the principal part of it; but that is not the vine. In the vine we see diversity: root, main stem, branches, leaves, tendrils, fruit. I am all that, said Christ, I am the vine. In the recognition of diversity there is a declaration of completeness. The completeness of the vine is created by the fact that Christ is all. Where then do we come in? Does that shut us out? Of course not. I am everything, said Christ, main stem, branches, everything; and you are the branches; that is, you are parts of Me. You are as closely united to Me in the essentials and entirety of life as those

109

JOHN 15:12. This is my commandment, that ye love one another, even as I have loved you.

13. Greater love hath no man than this, that a man lay down his life for his friends.

14. Ye are my friends, if ye do the things which I command you.

15. No longer do I call you servants; for the servant knoweth not what his lord doeth: but I have called you friends; for all things that I heard from my Father I have made known unto you.

16. Ye did not choose me, but I chose you, and appointed you, that ye should go and bear fruit, and *that* your fruit should abide: that whatsoever ye shall ask of the Father in my name, he may give it you.

branches are in the vine; and the vine is incomplete without the branches. Our Lord said to these men, Apart from Me, literally, severed from Me, cut off from Me, you can do nothing. And he surely also meant to say, Apart from you, I can do nothing in this world. I must have the branches. But see the wonder of that. To these men our Lord said, You are going to lose Me, and you are troubled; but I am here, I am with you, I come again. I come with the coming of the Paraclete. I come to you uniting Myself to you so completely that you shall be part of Me, and I part of you; for you abide in Me, and I in you. What a figure it is!" — *G. Campbell Morgan.* Even though this is what may well be called the darkest night in human history, and though Christ himself is separated by only a few hours from all the indignities, the insults, the brutalities of His angry and blinded enemies, and within less than twenty-four hours will be upon the cross, He speaks here of His *joy;* and not only that, but He tells us that one of the objects of His entire discourse with the disciples at this time is that His joy might be in them, and that their joy might be full.

II. **THE COMMANDMENT PERTAINING TO LOVE,** 15:12–17. We come now upon a statement of our Lord which almost seems a paradox — the exhortation to love one another, stated as a *commandment.* This is not the first time during the sacred evening that our Lord has uttered such words; we find them in 14:21, 23, 24, in a portion of this chapter not assigned for the printed text (v. 9) and repeated in verse 17. The exhortation is accompanied by two corollary truths: first, the supreme proof of love for another is in giving our life for the one loved; and, secondly, this perfect manifestation of love is found in the work of Christ. Over and over again in the Scriptures, the love of God and the love of Christ are identified with the death of our Lord; e.g., in Romans 5:8, "But God commendeth his own love toward us, in that while we were yet sinners, Christ died for us." **12. This is my commandment, that ye love one another, even as I have loved you. 13. Greater love hath no man than this, that a man lay down his life for his friends. 14. Ye are my friends, if ye do the things which I command you.** In this first half of the chapter there are really three different directions of love — the Father loves the Son, the Son manifests Himself to His own, and we are to love one another as He loved us. Our Lord, even in the matter of love, continues to carry out the deep truths expressed in the metaphor of the vine. As a branch must remain in the vine, receiving life from it, so we are to abide in the love of Christ. How this abiding is to be maintained is clearly set forth — in obeying our Lord's commandments. Upon receiving Christ as Saviour, we acknowledge Him as our Lord, we belong to Him, we are members of His body. As our head controls what our body does, so Christ is to control what the members of His body do. How gracious of our Lord to be that much interested in us, as parents are in training their children.

A new word is introduced by our Lord when speaking of His love for us, and His commandments to us — *friend.* **15. No longer do I call you servants; for the servant knoweth not what his lord doeth: but I have called you friends; for all**

110

17. These things I command you, that ye may love one another.
18. If the world hateth you, ye know that it hath hated me before *it hated* you.

---

things that I heard from my Father I have made known unto you. 16. **Ye did not choose me, but I chose you, and appointed you, that ye should go and bear fruit, and *that* your fruit should abide: that whatsoever ye shall ask of the Father in my name, he may give it you. 17. These things I command you, that ye may love one another.** Dr. G. Campbell Morgan has a magnificent paragraph on this matter of friendship. "A slave was the property of his master; unable to possess, and so having nothing of his own, unable to elect and so unable to do, on his own initiative; a slave was therefore at the disposal of his owner, all his putting forth of energy must be for the increase of the possessions of the one who possessed him; all his choosing must be in accord with the choosing of the one who owned him. The law of the slave's life is that of unquestioning submission, of blind obedience. . . . Christians are still the bondslaves of Jesus. His property, unable to possess or to have of their own, unable to elect save under the compulsion of His choice, or to do save as the doing is the putting forth of energy on His behalf. Christians are still called upon to increase His possessions, and to elect in accordance with His elections. But here we halt. The slave renders unquestioning submission, and blind obedience. That is not the last word about Christian discipleship. It is at that very point that we discover the character of this change in relationship. 'I have called you friends'; and in a moment we are introduced into another realm of thought which we shall see does not negative the essential values of the first, but rather transfigures them and makes them glorious and beautiful. What are friends? When we begin to think seriously, we realize how we constantly abuse the great word *friend*, how casually and carelessly we make use of it. Sit down some time, and write a list of your *friends*. None of us have very many; many acquaintances — and thank God for the whole of them — but few friends. What is the basis of friendship? Reciprocal and self-emptying love; and consequently, mutual interest. Find me my friend, and I will say to you, This friend loves me to the forgetfulness of himself, and I love him to the forgetfulness of myself. He is forever seeking my interests, and I am always seeking his so far as our lives touch each other in this realm of human friendship. . . . Consequently, in friendship we have the fellowship of love as the inspiration and the atmosphere of fellowship in effort." — *Dr. G. Campbell Morgan.*

The late Dr. William Milligan comments on the words, "That whatsoever ye ask of the Father in my name, he may give it you": "Three times now have we met in this discourse the promise just given, and the attentive reader will easily perceive the interesting gradation in the circumstances in which those to whom it is successively given are supposed to be. In 14:12, 13, they are viewed simply as believers; in 15:7, they 'abide in Christ, and His sayings abide in them'; now they have 'gone away' and have borne abiding fruit. To each stage of Christian living and working the same promise in words belongs, but the fulness included in the words is dependent in each case on the amount of need to be supplied. . . . Jesus chooses out His disciples for work first, for correspondingly higher privilege afterwards; and those who faithfully bear fruit are here assured that in this sphere of fruit-bearing with all its difficulties, and temptations, and trials, they shall want nothing to impart courage, boldness, hope, to make them overcome the world, as He Himself overcame it."

III. **THE OPPOSITION OF THE WORLD TO CHRIST AND CHRIST'S FOLLOWERS,** 15:18–25. There can hardly be in all the Scriptures a more violent contrast than we have in the pre-eminence of love in the first half of this chapter, and the dominion of hatred that now immediately follows. 18. **If the world hateth you, ye know that it hath hated me before *it hated* you.** 19. **If ye**

111

19. If ye were of the world, the world would love its own: but because ye are not of the world, but I chose you out of the world, therefore the world hateth you.

---

were of the world, the world would love its own: but because ye are not of the world, but I chose you out of the world, therefore the world hateth you. This, I believe, is the first time in all of His teachings that our Lord refers to hatred of men toward Him, and toward His own. The hatred will be not simply an emotion of evil hearts, but will manifest itself in persecution, and often through the ages, in death itself. Though I have not seen this in a commentary, is it not true that perfect love will be seen in one dying for another, and perfect hatred will also be seen in dying, but it will be the wicked putting the followers of Christ to death. This is what they did to Christ, and what they have often done to believers, and are doing today. There is no more tragic sentence in the records of the New Testament than, "They hated me without a cause." "The quotation is in all probability from Psalm 69:4, with which Psalm 35:19 and 109:3 may be compared. The quotation is made for the purpose of bringing out the aggravated guilt of those who were rejecting Jesus. They had condemned their fathers because of the persecutions to which God's Righteous Servant of old had been exposed: yet they 'filled up the measure of their fathers.' Their pride and carnal dependence upon outward descent from Abraham blinded their eyes to the distinction between truth and falsehood, right and wrong, and made them do what they acknowledged in the light of Divine truth, of Scriptures which they honored, to be worthy of condemnation in their own fathers." — *William F. Moulton.* One would have thought that the sinless Christ, going about doing good, proclaiming the love of the Father, offering as a free gift eternal life, would have won the acclaim of all mankind; but such was not true. There is no greater proof of our Lord's divine foresight than His announcement that His followers, living righteous lives, conducting themselves as children of God, returning good for evil, would be hated by the world; and no greater proof of what John wrote, that the whole world lieth in the evil one, than the fact that Christ and His own are thus hated.

IV. **CHRIST'S SECOND PROMISE CONCERNING THE HOLY SPIRIT,** 15:26, 27. It is in these chapters, recording our Lord's final discourse with His disciples, that we find more teaching concerning the Person and work of the Holy Spirit than in all the Synoptics combined. In 14:16, 17, our Lord announces that He will send the Spirit of truth, who is called the Comforter, or the Advocate, the Greek word being *Perakletos*, meaning, *one called along side of,* that is, to help. The spirit of Antichrist and the spirit of the world is a spirit of falsehood, and thus we have false prophets, false christs, and false teachers concentrated at the end of the age. As Christians, we are indwelt by the Spirit of truth himself, who enables us to bear true testimony to Christ. "The emphasis on the 'I' of 'I will send' ought not to pass unnoticed. It is as if Jesus would say, 'You tremble at the prospect of my going away, you fear that you will be desolate, but it is not so. *I* will not forget you; *I* will be to you, through the Spirit, all that I have been; *I* will send the Advocate to be in you and by your side.' Could more be necessary to sustain them?" — *W. F. Moulton.*

V. **CHRIST WARNS THE DISCIPLES OF COMING PERSECUTION AND DISCUSSES HIS OWN IMMINENT DEATH AND RESURRECTION,** John 16.

In the week in which I am working on this lesson, the greatest dictator of all times, Joseph Stalin, passed away. What a contrast there is in his death and the death of Christ! One great difference may be pointed out from our lesson today. As far as we know, Stalin did not expect death at this time. The announcement of the stroke which brought about his death came upon the world as a shock. But our Lord, in perfect health, knew *when* He would die, and *how* He would die. Probably no words came from Stalin's lips the three days preceding his death, but

JOHN 16:1. These things have I spoken unto you, that ye should not be caused to stumble.

2. They shall put you out of the synagogues: yea, the hour cometh, that whosoever killeth you shall think that he offereth service unto God.

3. And these things will they do, because they have not known the Father, nor me.

4. But these things have I spoken unto you, that when their hour is come, ye may remember them, how that I told you. And these things I said not unto you from the beginning, because I was with you.

5. But now I go unto him that sent me; and none of you asketh me, Whither goest thou?

6. But because I have spoken these things unto you, sorrow hath filled your heart.

---

the most wonderful words that have ever passed the lips of any man came from our Lord Jesus during the three days immediately before His crucifixion. Normally, death is thought of as a very solemn and terrible experience — the Christian hope apart — but our Lord is not depressed, or even sad. He cannot speak of His approaching death without reference to His resurrection. He does not speak of leaving this earth except He talks about going home to be with His heavenly Father.

1. IN GENERAL, vs. 1-6. **1. These things have I spoken unto you, that ye should not be caused to stumble. 2. They shall put you out of the synagogues: yea, the hour cometh, that whosoever killeth you shall think that he offereth service unto God. 3. And these things will they do, because they have not known the Father, nor me. 4. But these things have I spoken unto you, that when their hour is come, ye may remember them, how that I told you. And these things I said not unto you from the beginning, because I was with you. 5. But now I go unto him that sent me; and none of you asketh me, Whither goest thou? 6. But because I have spoken these things unto you, sorrow hath filled your heart.** The little word *that*, which we find in verses 1 and 4 is significant. In chapters 13 through 16, our Lord gives five reasons for His various instructions and teachings to the disciples at this time: (1) that when His predictions come to pass, they might believe (13:19); (2) that His joy might remain in them (15:11); (3) that they should not stumble or be offended by anything that is now about to take place (16:1); (4) that they might remember in the days to come that these were the things Jesus had said (16:4); (5) that in Christ they might have peace (16:33). "Opposition on the part of the Jews is in these discourses the type of all opposition to the truth. Not merely excommunication, but death in every one of its varied forms shall be their portion. . . . Not in indifference only or in lightness of spirit shall they be slain, to make a Jewish or a Roman holiday, when perhaps their fate might be mourned over in soberer hours, but in such a manner that those who slay them shall return from the scene as men who have engaged in what they believe will gain for them the favour of heaven. It is impossible to imagine a darker picture of fanaticism. Yet the picture is heightened by the mention of 'an hour' an hour laden with the divine purpose, which must 'come' to them as it had come to Jesus Himself. . . . His 'going away' is an essential part of 'these things,' and with it all that he now says is so connected that it has its meaning only in the light of that departure. . . . General allusions to their coming suffering there might be and were. But that they would have to take His place, and in doing so, to find that His trials were their trials, He had never said. That solemn lesson was connected only with the present moment, when their training was completed, and they were to be sent forth to be as He had been." —*William Milligan.*

113

7. Nevertheless I tell you the truth: It is expedient for you that I go away; for if I go not away, the Comforter will not come unto you; but if I go, I will send him unto you.

8. And he, when he is come, will convict the world in respect of sin, and of righteousness and of judgment.

9. Of sin, because they believe not on me.

10. Of righteousness, because I go to the Father, and ye behold me no more.

11. Of judgment, because the prince of this world hath been judged.

---

2. CHRIST SPEAKS OF THE NECESSITY OF HIS GOING, vs. 7–11. We now approach one of the most profound passages in all the Gospels. Whole books have been written concerning these five verses: here we have space for only a few lines. **7. Nevertheless I tell you the truth: It is expedient for you that I go away; for if I go not away, the Comforter will not come unto you; but if I go, I will send him unto you. 8. And he, when he is come, will convict the world in respect of sin, and of righteousness and of judgment.** "The word *convict* signifies in the usage of the New Testament (a) to reprove, rebuke (Matt. 18:15; Luke 3:19; John 3:20; 1 Tim. 5:20; 2 Tim. 4:2; Titus 1:13; 2:15; Rev. 3:19). The rebuke is always just, though not always effective, because the offender may harden himself against it. (b) To chasten (Heb. 12:5). (c) To convict, i.e., make the truth so plain that he is guilty who refuses belief. Many *accused* Jesus but none *convicted* Him of sin (John 8:46; 1 Cor. 14:24; Eph. 5:11, 13; Titus 1:9; James 2:9; Jude 15). These with the present passage are all the instances of the use of the word in the New Testament. *Convict* is outward, objective; convince is inward, subjective. He is convicted who is shown to be in error, he is convinced who owns himself in error. *Convict* is therefore the better rendering here. It points to the nature, while *convince* would point to the *effect* of the Spirit's witness. He so presents the truth to men that they ought to believe; whether they *do* believe the word does not indicate." — *J. Ritchie Smith.* **9. Of sin, because they believe not on me.** "The Spirit convicts the world of sin through its unbelief. Since Jesus is the clearest revelation of God, not to believe in Him evinces the utmost blindness and hardness of heart. It is not said that the world is convicted of the sin of unbelief, but of sin through unbelief. The unbelief is the crowning evidence of the sin. The world is shown to be sinful by the fact of unbelief, which discloses that spirit of alienation from God which is the source whence all sin proceeds. . . . Does the world desire truth and righteousness and love? Let Calvary answer. Does the world love God? When He came to earth in the person of His Son, the world not only failed to recognize Him, but condemned and crucified Him as a malefactor. The Spirit makes plain to the world its sin by pressing upon it the fact of its unbelief." — *J. Ritchie Smith.* **10. Of righteousness, because I go to the Father, and ye behold me no more.** "Against the world's conception of righteousness the Spirit sets forth righteousness as it is found in Him. Crucified by the world as an evil-doer, He was declared righteous by His exaltation to the right hand of the Father (Acts 3:13–15; Rom. 1:4) and the power of His glorified estate was shown in the witness and work of His disciples. To the Jews He said, 'When ye have lifted up the Son of man, then shall ye know that I am he, and that I do nothing of myself, but as the Father taught me, I speak these things' (8:28). Upon His death and resurrection follows the manifestation of His righteousness in the outpouring of the Spirit and the ministry of the disciples." **11. Of judgment, because the prince of this world hath been judged.** "Jesus, condemned by the world, is exalted by God. Satan, the prince of the world, is condemned by God. The death of Jesus appeared to be the hour of Satan's triumph, yet in it he was condemned, his power broken (12:31). Through death he destroyed him that hath the power of death, even the devil (Heb. 2:14). This is made plain by the

12. I have yet many things to say unto you, but ye cannot bear them now.

13. Howbeit when he, the Spirit of truth, is come, he shall guide you into all the truth: for he shall not speak from himself; but what things soever he shall hear, *these* shall he speak: and he shall declare unto you the things that are to come.

---

results of the ministry of the apostles. When the seventy returned with joy, saying, 'Lord, even the demons are subject to us in thy name,' Jesus answered, 'I beheld Satan fall as lightning from heaven' (Luke 10:18). In the casting out of evil spirits was foreshadowed the overthrow of their chief. As the world lies in the wicked one (1 John 5:19) it is judged in him, but not finally condemned. The world is in sin, between the righteousness of Christ and the judgment of Satan, and must take its place on this side or on that." — *J. Ritchie Smith*. Notice particularly the phrase, "unto you," used twice in verse 7. I shall never forget the first time I ever heard the sainted missionary to the Jews in Germany, Pastor Dolman, many years ago. Speaking on the Holy Spirit working through us to the world, he drew with his finger the two sides of a right angle triangle. Pointing to heaven, from which the Holy Spirit proceeds, he drew an imaginary line down to our hearts, where the Holy Spirit dwells, and then another line, at right angles to that, out into the world. The point he was making was that the Holy Spirit can never reach the unbelieving world except through those in whom He dwells.

3. THE WORK OF THE HOLY SPIRIT IN BELIEVERS, vs. 12–15. **12. I have yet many things to say unto you, but ye cannot bear them now. 13. Howbeit when he, the Spirit of truth, is come, he shall guide you into all the truth: for he shall not speak from himself; but what things soever he shall hear, *these* shall he speak: and he shall declare unto you the things that are to come.** These verses are simply inexhaustible, and I regret having to pass them over so quickly. We have just considered the convicting work of the Holy Spirit, and now move on to His teaching ministry. For additional passages on this great truth see 1 John 1:5; 2:20, 21 and 27. "The Spirit guides men who follow His leading; He does not 'tell' his message without effort on their part. He also guides them 'into the Truth' which is the domain upon which they enter, and not something to be gazed upon from afar." — *B. F. Westcott*. By "all truth" our Lord of course did not mean that of mathematics, nuclear fission, relativity, etc., but truth concerning God, redemption, the forgiveness of sins, the love of God, judgment to come, eternal life, all the great teachings about which man really knows nothing except it is revealed through the Word and Christ. There is much dispute as to what the Lord meant in His reference to the Holy Spirit showing us "things to come." Westcott says that this refers mainly "to the constitution of the Christian Church, as representing hereafter the divine order in place of the Jewish economy." Professor Lenski believes that the reference is to the later writings of the New Testament, especially those that contain a great body of revelation on "future developments and events," and I think he is correct. The 14th verse, not in the printed text, is one of great beauty. My friend Mr. Kenneth S. Wuest has brought out the meaning of this verse more accurately than any other writer with whom I am acquainted. "There is a demonstrative pronoun in the Greek text which is not brought out in the English translation. 'That One shall glorify Me.' That is, our Lord says in effect: 'I will not glorify Myself. That One (the Holy Spirit) shall glorify Me.' The word 'receive' refers not to a passive acceptance, but to an active appropriation. The Holy Spirit's ministry is to take of the things of Christ and show them to the believer. In that way He expressed the Lord Jesus through the Christian. The Christian's life is a prism in which the Holy Spirit breaks up into its component graces, the beauty of our Lord. If the believer does not have an intelligent understanding of and subjection to the ministry of the Holy Spirit, there is little of the

Lord Jesus seen in his life. The Holy Spirit does the best He can under the limitations imposed upon Him by the believer, but He cannot do much under the circumstances."

4. THE SORROW OF THE DISCIPLES, vs. 16–22. Possibly no teacher will have time to consider the concluding verses of this chapter, but the words of Hoskyns in his recent work on John's Gospel are too important to overlook. "The paradox of sorrow and joy (Matt. 5:4) will be wrought out in the experience of the disciples and in the revised experience of the world through the events which are to occur in a little while. What is to cause the disciples acute pain (Luke 24:17; Mark 16:10) will become the ground of their fulfilled joy; what gives pleasure to the world will effect its grief-laden destruction. The reverse side of the paradox is, it is true, not at once fully expressed, and its expression is reserved until verse 33, 'I have overcome the world.' Since it is the sorrow and joy of the disciples that are here primarily emphasized, it seems illegitmate exegesis to press a further significance upon the woman who gives birth to the son, and, with Loisy, under the influence of Revelation 12, to allegorize her as the 'faithful synagogue' which gives painful birth to the Messiah, or as that faithful humanity which is the mother of the elect, though it must be owned that the Johannine expression 'born into the world' does suggest 1:9, 3:17, 16:28 etc."

5. THE PRIVILEGES OF PRAYER, vs. 23–33. In these last hours with His disciples, our Lord is far more concerned for their welfare, their peace of heart, their future service, their unshakable confidence in Him, and their unbroken fellowship with the three Persons of the Godhead, than He is with His own death. He is making every provision for a richness of life for each of them, which abides for all who are His, even down to this very hour. "In Christ's teaching on prayer there appear to be three stages in the prayer-life somewhat analogous. In the Sermon on the Mount we have the initial stage: His teaching is all comprised in one word, Father. Pray to your Father, your Father sees, hears, knows, and will reward: how much more than any earthly father! Only be childlike and trustful. Then comes later on something like the transition stage of conflict and conquest, in words like these: 'This sort goeth not out but by fasting and prayer'; 'Shall not God avenge His own elect who cry day and night unto Him?' And then we have in the parting words, a higher stage. The children have become men: they are now the Master's friends, from whom He has no secrets, to whom He says, 'All things that I heard from my Father I made known unto you'; and to whom, in the oft repeated 'whatsoever ye will,' He hands over the keys of the kingdom. Now the time has come for the power of prayer in His name to be proved. . . . What our prayer avails, depends upon what we are and what our life is. It is living in the Name of Christ that is the secret of praying in the Name of Christ; living in the Spirit that fits for praying in the Spirit. It is abiding in Christ that gives the right and power to ask what we will: the extent of the abiding is the exact measure of the power in prayer. It is the Spirit dwelling within us that prays, not in words and thoughts always, but in a breathing and a being deeper than utterance. Just so much as there is of Christ's Spirit in us, is there real prayer. Our lives, O let our lives be full of Christ and full of His Spirit, and the wonderfully unlimited promises to our prayer will no longer appear strange." — *Andrew Murray.*

Even though, as our Lord warns, the world will be against us, and persecution will arise, nevertheless, just as He, falsely accused, hated without cause, condemned and crucified, overcame the world every moment of His life, we may overcome the same world, whatever be the circumstances and conflicts of life, until that day comes when all the enemies of Christ will be put under His feet and we shall reign with Him who has already received from heaven His title, the Ruler of the kings of this earth.

THE LESSON IN LIFE, LITERATURE, AND ARCHAEOLOGY.

In the life of the great missionary, J. Hudson Taylor, there are some words of recollection by Mr. C. T. Fishe, who visited Mr. Taylor in Yang-chow in 1869, when Mr. Taylor was thirty-seven years of age.   Perhaps it will be helpful to include here the entire paragraph, relating how a man under heavy pressure, working long hours, continued to feed his soul on the Word of God.   "I was very young at the time and was much touched by Mr. Taylor's amiability.   He was very kind to me.   I helped him in his dispensary and medical work, and was with him a good deal whenever he was in Yang-chow.   He guided my studies, and was keen on the aspirates.   He was, of course, exceedingly busy, and appeared quite a young and lively man.   He loved playing with his children and did not seem burdened with care.   He was fond of music and singing, and used to play the harmonium for the Chinese on Sunday evenings for an hour at a time, and have them sing hymns. . . . His favourite theme in those days was the fifteenth chapter of John.   We had many helpful times of prayer and study.   He seemed to be growing much in spiritual things, and that passage was his special delight.   The noon prayer meeting was held daily."

A TRUTH FOR THE CLASS TO CARRY AWAY.

Here should be emphasized the great fact that the words just studied came from the heart and lips of the very Son of God, that He Himself once said, "Heaven and earth shall pass away, but my words shall never pass away."   Therefore, in a way not true of the words of any other person that ever taught on this earth, we can believe to the uttermost what Christ is here saying, and count day by day upon the fulfilment of these promises.   We should thus appropriate to ourselves the holy privilege of prayer and intercession, here offered to us so abundantly and emphatically.

Would you say that in the last twenty years opposition to Christianity and Christians has increased or decreased?   How many different reasons can you give for the world's antagonism to Christianity?   Recall some ways in which Christ's words in our lesson were fulfilled in the early Church.   Of Christ's promises in this chapter, which were particularly manifested on the Day of Pentecost.   In how many different ways is the pre-eminence and deity of Christ set forth for us in these two chapters?

117

B. PLOCKHORST. 1825—

RISEN LORD AND MARY MAGDALEN.

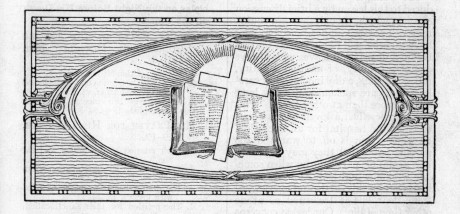

SECOND QUARTER.

APRIL 4 — JUNE 27, 1954.

JOHN—GOSPEL OF DIVINE LOVE (*Continued.*)
and
The NORTHERN KINGDOM AND ITS PROPHETS:

LESSON I. — April 4.

JESUS' INTERCESSORY PRAYER. — John 17.
PRINTED TEXT, John 17:1, 6–23.

Devotional Reading: 1 Timothy 2:1–8a.
Beginner Topic: THE WORLD GOD MADE.
    Lesson Material: Genesis 1:1–10, 14–16, 26–27.
    Memory Verse: He . . . hath made every thing beautiful in its time. Ecclesiastes 3:11.
Primary Topic: JESUS PRAYED FOR HIS FRIENDS.
    Lesson Material: John 17.
    Memory Verse: Pray one for another. James 5:16.
Junior Topic: JESUS PRAYED FOR HIS FRIENDS.
    Lesson Material: John 17.
    Memory Verse: Pray one for another. James 5:16.
Intermediate-Senior Topic: JESUS PRAYED FOR HIS FRIENDS.
    Lesson Material: John 17.
    Memory Verse: Whatsoever ye shall ask in my name, that will I do, that the Father may be glorified in the Son. John 14:13.
Topic for Young People and Adults: INTERCESSORY PRAYER.
    Lesson Material: John 17.
    Memory Verse: Whatsoever ye shall ask in my name, that will I do, that the Father may be glorified in the Son. John 14:13.

THE TEACHER AND HIS CLASS.

The Younger Classes may be introduced to this lesson by a brief discussion of a fact which, though they are young, they will not only understand, but may have experienced; namely, that the day before a dear friend leaves us is always one of solemnity, of unusual sanctity, full of meaning, a day in which few careless words are spoken, and every hour counts more than at other times. This is also true when a loved one is about to enter the hospital for an operation, or when a son is off to war and the parents know that they may never see him again, or, particularly, when someone we know and love has only a few hours left on this earth, and every word from their lips is treasured as at no other time of life. Our lesson concerns the prayer which Jesus offered for His disciples the night before he died on the cross.

The Older Classes will find here truths of such spiritual depth and height that in this day of rush and hurry, of weariness, of materialism, when our thoughts are on war, food, taxes, airplanes, automobiles, television and all the other distractions of our decaying civilization, many may almost feel that the lesson has no relation to them, that it is all very beautiful but not practical, that it belongs to the sinless Christ and not to us. This is an error indeed. This is not a prayer which Jesus offered primarily for Himself, an hour of exaltation in His holy life which is a whole world removed from us; rather, it is His prayer for us, His request of the Father for us, His desire for us, and there is no believer in Christ anywhere in this world for whom this prayer is not meant. It should be a magnet, lifting us out of the lower levels of life — and never have we more needed such a lift.

THE LESSON IN ITS SETTING.

Time. — Thursday evening, April 6, A.D. 30.

Place. — We do not know exactly where this prayer was offered, but it must have been in a quiet retreat.

THE PLAN OF THE LESSON.

SUBJECT: Christ's Prayer for His Disciples on the Night Before His Death on the Cross.

I. CHRIST PRAYS TO THE FATHER CONCERNING HIMSELF, John 17:1–8.
1. His one petition for Himself, v. 1.
2. He recalls the mission on which He was sent by the Father, vs. 2, 3.
3. He declares this mission has been accomplished, vs. 4–8.

II. HIS PRAYER FOR HIS DISCIPLES, 17:9–19.
1. Their relation to the Father and the Son, vs. 9, 10.
2. The petition for preservation from evil, vs. 11, 12, 15.
3. The desire that they might be filled with joy, vs. 13, 14.
4. The petition for their sanctification, vs. 16–19.

III. HIS PRAYER FOR ALL THOSE WHO WERE YET TO BELIEVE ON HIM, 17:20–23.

IV. THE TWO FINAL REQUESTS FOR HIS OWN, 17:24–26.
1. That they should be with Him in glory, vs. 24, 25.
2. That the love of Christ should indwell them, v. 26.

THE TEACHER'S LIBRARY.

The lives of Christ, even the more extensive ones, will not be found satisfactory here, and in this one lesson need not be consulted. Several commentaries are especially rich, such as those by Reith, Westcott, Lange, Lenski, Milligan and Moulton. There is an excellent chapter on this prayer in T. D. Bernard: *The Central Teaching of Jesus*, and in G. Campbell Morgan: *The Westminster Pulpit*, Vol. 8, pp. 217–224. One of the greatest devotional classics in the English language is devoted entirely to an exposition of this chapter, *The Lord's Prayer for Believers*, by Marcus Rainsford, which has appeared in many editions, and has been recently republished by Moody Press in the Wycliffe Series of Christian Classics, edited by my friend Dr. S. Maxwell Coder. I could wish that every teacher in America had a copy of this book. As far back as 1656, Anthony Burgess issued a large volume on this chapter. The following volumes are of value on these verses: verse 15, J. H. Jowett: *Apostolic Optimism*, 47–58; verse 17, Andrew Murray: *Holy in Christ*, 142–148; and J. Stuart Holden: *A Voice for God*, 257–275; on verse 19, H. B. Macartney: *For Their Sake I Sanctify Myself*, 82–114; Andrew Murray: *Holy in Christ*, 150–156; Alexander Whyte: *Lord Teach Us to Pray*, 116–129; and a magnificent sermon in a book now rarely come upon, Robert M. Edgar: *The Philosophy of the Cross*, 256–273; on verses 20, 21, G. Campbell Morgan in *The Westminster Pulpit*, Vol. 10, pp. 17–24; H. C. G. Moule: *Cathedral and University Sermons*, 245–262; and on verse 22, A. C. Gaebelein: *The Church in the House*, 77–88. On verses 16–19, may I refer to

a message of my own in *Keswick Week*, 1952, pp. 65–68.

_____

AUDIO-VISUAL AIDS.

No audio-visual aids discovered.

JOHN 17:1. These things spake Jesus; and lifting up his eyes to heaven, he said, Father, the hour is come: glorify thy Son, that the Son may glorify thee.

If there is any one verse, any one admonition in all the Bible that comes to mind as we contemplate a study of this chapter, it is the word of God to Moses at the burning bush, "Take thy shoes from off thy feet, for the ground whereon thou standest is holy ground" (Ex. 3:5). As another has said, "No attempt to describe this prayer can give a just idea of its sublimity, its pathos, its touching yet exalted character, its tone at once of tenderness and triumphant expectation. We are apt to read it as if it were full of sorrow, but that is only our own feeling reflected back upon what we suppose to have been the feelings of the Man of Sorrows. In the prayer itself sorrow has no place; and to think that it was uttered in a tone of sadness is entirely to mistake what must have been the spirit of Jesus at the time. It speaks throughout of work accomplished, of victory gained, of the immediate expectation of glorious reward." — *William Milligan.* Most commentators agree that the prayer divides into three parts: the Son and the Father, the Son and His immediate disciples, the Son and the Church. Many terminate the first division with verse 6, but it seems to me that verse 8 belongs in the first section. I have divided the last part into two major subjects. "In the earlier tradition the lonely prayers of Jesus are handled with great reserve (Mark 1:35; 6:46; 14:32–42, and parallels, Luke 3:21; 5:16; 9:18; 11:1, compare Matt. 11:25 sqq., Luke 10:21 sqq.), and the author of the Fourth Gospel has hitherto only on two occasions recorded anything which could be described as prayer (11:41, 42; 12:27, 28), and these are of the nature of ejaculations. Here, however, is set forth a collected, sustained address to the Father in the presence of the disciples." — *E. C. Hoskyns.*

I. **CHRIST PRAYS TO THE FATHER CONCERNING HIMSELF, 17:1–8.**
1. **These things spake Jesus;** and lifting up his eyes to heaven, he said, **Father, the hour is come: glorify thy Son, that the Son may glorify thee.** The opening verse of this chapter expresses three great truths: first, that of the relationship of God the Father to Christ His Son; secondly, that this was in the incarnate life of Christ *the* hour; and thirdly, that the Son asks to be glorified that in turn He might glorify the Father. Note that Christ does not address God as "Our Father," but simply as "Father," and elsewhere in the chapter, "righteous Father," or "holy Father" (vs. 5, 11, 21, 24, 25). "The hour" which had now come is the one referred to elsewhere, in 7:30; 8:20; 13:32. "The glory spoken of is that of Sonship, the glory belonging to the Son as the absolutely perfect expression of the Father, and especially of that love of the Father which is the essential element of the Father's being. "It is to be particularly observed that it is of the glorifying of the 'Son of man' that Jesus speaks in the words before us. His life on earth, not less than His previous life in heaven, had been the manifestation of the Father's love. But its 'glory' had not been seen. The world's idea of glory was altogether different; it had misunderstood and persecuted, and was about to crucify, Him whose life of lowly and self-denying service in love had been the highest and most glorious expression of the love of God to sinful men." — *Prof. William Milligan.*

In the same sentence, our Lord makes one of the most tremendous statements that ever issued from His lips, that the Father had given Him authority over all flesh, that upon all who were given Him, He should bestow eternal life. The word "give" is prominent in this chapter. A people is *given* to Christ; eternal life is *given* to His own; power over all flesh is *given* to Christ (v. 2); Christ was *given* a

6. I manifested thy name unto the men whom thou gavest me out of the world: thine they were, and thou gavest them to me; and they have kept thy word.

7. Now they know that all things whatsoever thou hast given me are from thee.

8. For the words which thou gavest me I have given unto them; and they received *them*, and knew of a truth that I came forth from thee, and they believed that thou didst send me.

---

work to do (v. 4); the Father's name was *given* to Christ (vs. 6, 12, 21); Christ affirms that the words God gave Him, he has *given* to His disciples (v. 8); and the glory which the Father had *given* Him He has in turn bestowed upon His own (v. 22). "Here, then are *seven* gifts to Christ; praise be to God they are given to *Christ*, given to One who can take care of them, One who can dispose of them, One who can make no mistake about the use of them: the people; the eternal life for the people; the power over all flesh; the work of salvation; Jehovah's name, that they may be kept in that name, united in that name, and filled with love divine in that name; the words — the means by which He manifests that name — and the glory to be yet revealed." — *Marcus Rainsford.* "The authority over all flesh is the rule and dominion over all men. When the Son came on his mission he received this authority. His mission was to the entire world of men, and hence, when he came on this mission he received this universal authority. . . . During his humiliation Jesus had this authority, but did not exercise it, save in a very limited degree. The humiliation was a brief, transient period, the prelude to the exaltation or glorification of the human nature, when Jesus exercises to the full, also in his human nature, the authority that came to it as the Father's gift in the assumption of the divine mission." — *R. C. H. Lenski.*

Inasmuch as the last full day of Christ's incarnate life on earth was now closing, it seems the perfect time for the Son to speak to the Father of the mission upon which He had been sent, and the fact that He had accomplished all that God sent Him to do. One cannot help but think of the words of the Apostle Paul as he came to the close of his life (2 Tim. 4:6–8) though of course his work was one altogether different from that of Christ. His was to preach the Gospel which Christ in His life and death provided. **6. I manifested thy name unto the men whom thou gavest me out of the world: thine they were, and thou gavest them to me; and they have kept thy word. 7. Now they know that all things whatsoever thou hast given me are from thee.** One of the ways in which our Lord sums up His work is in the phrase, "I manifested thy name unto the men whom thou gavest me out of the world." The word *name* is important. Here, as in many other places, especially in John's Gospel, it stands for the person, and particularly the character of the person to whom the name belongs. The significance of the name is revealed, for example, in the phrase, "Thou shalt call his name Immanuel," or, "God highly exalted him, and gave unto him the name which is above every name; that in the name of Jesus, every knee should bow . . . and every tongue confess that Jesus Christ is Lord, to the glory of God the Father" (Phil. 2:9–11), and the fact that we are to pray in the name of Christ, etc. Christ, by His life on this earth, had revealed the character of God in a way which no other person on earth ever has, or ever will, reveal it. **8. For the words which thou gavest me I have given unto them; and they received *them*, and knew of a truth that I came forth from thee, and they believed that thou didst send me.** The truth expressed here in this sentence is one that I have never seen fully expounded; nor have I ever fully satisfied myself as to its profound meaning. When did God give to Jesus these words? Was this in heaven, or was it day by day during His ministry on earth? It is, of course, a fulfillment of the prophecy of Deuteronomy 18:18, 19, and, pre-

9. I pray for them: I pray not for the world, but for those whom thou hast given me; for they are thine:

10. And all things that are mine are thine, and thine are mine: and I am glorified in them.

11. And I am no more in the world, and these are in the world, and I come to thee. Holy Father, keep them in thy name which thou hast given me, that they may be one, even as we *are*.

---

sumably, has something to do with Isaiah 61:1–3 (see also John 3:33, 34; 7:16). "Here we learn what is the surest, truest, and most unchangeable ground and resting place for our faith, the words Christ spake. . . . Oh! to examine them more carefully, and to live upon them more abidingly! Here, too, we have the ground of peace, and joy, and comfort, and hope, and blessing. May we hide *the words* in our hearts for His name's sake who gave them to us." — *Marcus Rainsford.*

II. **HIS PRAYER FOR HIS DISCIPLES,** 17:9–19. Christ has already mentioned His disciples to the Father, but He has not as yet uttered any petition for them. I find here three major longings in the heart of Jesus for the disciples — those who were already His, and I am sure those yet to come — that they should be preserved from evil, that they might be filled with joy, and that they might live a life of sanctification. Before making any request, Christ reaffirms the exalted, unique, God-given position into which His disciples had been brought: they belonged to God initially; they were given by the Father to the Son; all that He has belongs to the Father and the Son together; and in these disciples is Christ glorified. 9. **I pray for them: I pray not for the world, but for those whom thou hast given me; for they are thine: 10. and all things that are mine are thine, and thine are mine: and I am glorified in them.** "Wonderful language! But He meant it all; and He means it all. His words were the result and the expression of God's commended love! They are God's children, they are Christ's Church, they are the Holy Ghost's habitation — they are His beloved ones, they are His Bride, they are the Holy Ghost's charge, and He shall educate them for the positions that the Son's love and Father's love have appointed for them. They are Jehovah's portion, therefore they are Christ's purchase, and the Holy Ghost dwells in them 'the earnest of their inheritance until the redemption of the purchased possession.' They are the people of God 'formed for himself': 'created for his glory': and they are 'the glory of Christ.' . . . It was in order that our faith might be strengthened, our hope established, and our love deepened, that the Lord uttered these words to His Father — not in private, but in the hearing of His disciples, 'All mine are thine, and thine are mine.' We are mutually engaged in choosing, redeeming, sanctifying, saving, keeping, and glorifying them; and We are mutually interested in their persons, wants, troubles, difficulties, temptations, and welfare; in the formation of their characters and the consummation of their happiness." — *Marcus Rainsford.*

The first petition is that His own might be preserved from evil. 11. **And I am no more in the world, and these are in the world, and I come to thee. Holy Father, keep them in thy name which thou hast given me, that they may be one, even as we** *are*. "The train of thought evidently in the Lord's mind as He uttered these words is truly wonderful, beautiful, subduing, touching, 'I come to thee.' 'I come to thee,' — My rest, My portion, My home, — but 'these are in the world.' I come to Thy presence where there is fullness of joy, and to 'thy right hand where there are pleasures for evermore.' 'I come' — where no enemy can follow Me, where no temptation can assail Me, where no weariness can distress Me; but *these*, '*these* are in the world.' 'I come' — to reap the trophies of My great victory. 'I come' — to grasp the scepter, to wear the crown, and to ascend the Throne." —

12. While I was with them, I kept them in thy name, which thou hast given me: and I guarded them, and not one of them perished, but the son of perdition; that the scripture might be fulfilled.

15. I pray not that thou shouldest take them from the world, but that thou shouldest keep them from the evil *one*.

13. But now I come to thee; and these things I speak in the world, that they may have my joy made full in themselves.

14. I have given them thy word; and the world hated them, because they are not of the world, even as I am not of the world.

Marcus Rainsford. **12. While I was with them, I kept them in thy name, which thou hast given me: and I guarded them, and not one of them perished, but the son of perdition; that the scripture might be fulfilled.** What Christ asks the Father now to undertake, inasmuch as He is leaving this world and His disciples remain behind, is exactly what the Son had done for the disciples while He was with them these three and one-half years. We must use care in determining exactly what Christ meant in the words at the conclusion of this verse. A frequent misinterpretation is that He had kept eleven of the twelve whom the Father had given him, Judas being lost, in whom, some say, "all the guarding and protecting of Jesus failed." "But this is not correct — Judas is not an exception; he was never given by the Father to Jesus. . . . Likewise we must note the correspondence in terms: 'not one of them went to perdition, save the son of perdition.' . . .' Jesus indeed labored with Judas, as he did with the Jews, and persisted in his labors to the last; but, as in the cast of the Jews, Jesus knew that Judas was not his own. Not that Judas never believed — we may be quite sure that at first he did; but even then he was 'the son of perdition,' a son or product of eternal damnation; compare the similar designations in Matthew 23:15; 2 Thessalonians 2:2. For Judas is not given this awful title because he went to perdition and thus *ex eventu* became a son of perdition. The reverse is true, being a son of perdition, he went to perdition." — *R. C. H. Lenski.* **15. I pray not that thou shouldest take them from the world, but that thou shouldest keep them from the evil *one*.** If the last word of this sentence is taken as neuter, it should be translated "the evil," but if masculine, "the evil one." Lenski is right in saying that normally we would take this as neuter, but, because Christ had so often mentioned Satan, the devil, as the prince of this world during the last hours of His incarnate life (12:31; 14:30; 16:11) we are rather persuaded that He is referring to Satan here, who elsewhere in the teachings of Jesus, as in Luke 22:3, is called "the evil one"; see also 1 John 5:19, 20. It is most significant that our Lord should not pray that His disciples be kept from sorrow, or tribulation, or punishment, or even death. None of these things could stain their soul, none could interrupt their communion with God. The only thing that could weaken their testimony, pollute their hearts, render their prayers impotent, deprive them of divine power in testimony, rob them of abounding joy, keep them from bearing fruit which they were called to bear, would be that they should succumb to the wiles, the subtleties, and the allurements of Satan himself. Whatever be our temptations, whatever be our circumstances, whatever be our history up to this point, it is possible for every child of God to claim an affirmative answer to this prayer, for the Father and Son both long that we should be kept from the evil one, and they are able to keep us.

The second request is a strange one, for a night like this — that the disciples should have a continuous experience of joy, the very joy that was in the Lord Jesus. What an hour to speak of joy, and yet, Christ refers more frequently to His joy, and to the experience of rejoicing, in the last twenty-four hours of His life than in all the remainder of His ministry combined, as far as the record informs us. **13. But now I come to thee; and these things I speak in the world, that they may have my joy made full in themselves. 14. I have given them thy word; and the**

16. They are not of the world, even as I am not of the world.

17. Sanctify them in the truth: thy word is truth.

18. As thou didst send me into the world, even so sent I them into the world.

19. And for their sakes I sanctify myself, that they themselves also may be sanctified in truth.

world hated them, because they are not of the world, even as I am not of the world. See also 15:11 and 16:24. Even though Christ was to be betrayed this night, denied by Peter, brutally mistreated by the soldiers, falsely accused by the Sanhedrin, scourged in the morning and later crucified, nothing could take away the abounding joy of His life. " 'I come to thee — I' — My people's Representative; 'I' — the pledge of Thy love to them, the seal of Thy salvation to them; the earnest of Thy glory in them — I come to thee. I come, not invited as a matter of mercy, but in the right of My atoning finished work, and on the ground of justice and truth. 'I come to thee,' to Thy very throne, to Thy very heart, to Thy very glory, My Father and their Father, My God, and their God. What words of grace, what triumph! What love!" — *Marcus Rainsford.*

The final request of Christ for His disciples is that they might be *sanctified.* Let us have the entire passage before us, and then we can comment on it phrase by phrase, as space will permit. I trust I will be allowed to use here a message of mine on these verses given at the English Keswick Convention.

16. They are not of the world, even as I am not of the world. 17. Sanctify them in the truth: thy word is truth. 18. As thou didst send me into the world, even so sent I them into the world. 19. And for their sakes I sanctify myself, that they themselves also may be sanctified in truth. The great Dutch theologian, Bavinck, gives the following definition of sanctification: "Sanctification is setting apart, and something more. It means that by washing, by sacrifice, by sprinkling with blood, a thing loses its common character (a thing or a man loses its common character — which it possessed in common with other things or men) and has been given a new character, so that it now lives in this new condition." Not only are we separate, that is, positionally, but there is something experimental here. We have the basis for this word in this prayer of our Lord Jesus, "Sanctify them through Thy truth; Thy word is truth." The need for this sanctification is set forth in verse 11, "While I was with them, I kept them in Thy name . . . and I guarded them. . . ." Whether or not we recognize it, we need divine protection; and these two words, "keep" and "guard" mean a divine Father's watchful care. What do you guard? You guard your jewels, if you have any left after the income tax is paid. You guard your barns, your homes, your precious little children. You do not set a guard over the dirt in the backyard — you can get some more; that is common. You do not set a guard over a few bricks or a few flowers on the front lawn. You guard what is precious and what is in danger of being stolen or taken away. I am not speaking of salvation; God keeps guard of His own, and not one shall perish. . . . We are still here in the world, and consequently have two enemies of our souls — the world and the devil. Both of them would attack us and drag us into their environment, into their principles, into their way of living, into their sinfulness. We are in the world, and whether or not we are aware of it, the Lord said you and I need protection from the world and from the devil. He speaks of this to the Father more often than anything else, and then He says, "Sanctify them in the truth; Thy word is truth." What does it mean? Why not "Sanctify them *in holy living*" instead of *"in the truth"*? We must turn to another passage to better clarify this. In John 8:42–44 our Lord says, "If God were your Father, ye would love me: for I came forth and am come from God; neither came I of myself, but He sent me. Why do ye not understand my speech? Even because ye cannot hear my word. Ye are of your father, the devil . . ." — the evil one; put a "d" in the front of "evil" and you have "devil" — "and the lusts of your father

20. Neither for these only do I pray, but for them also that believe on me through their word.

21. That they may all be one; even as thou, Father, *art* in me, and I in thee, that they also may be in us: that the world may believe that thou didst send me.

it is your will to do. He was a murderer from the beginning, and he standeth not in the truth, because there is no truth in him. When he speaketh a lie, he speaketh of his own; he is a liar, and the father thereof." I cannot read these awful words without being reminded of something I heard over thirty years ago. I heard Dr. Griffith Thomas speak in Philadelphia on the work of Satan, and especially remember his prayer, before those two thousand people, that the devil himself might not paralyze his tongue as he came to expose the works of the evil one. "And because I say the truth, ye believe me not. If I say the truth, why do ye not believe me?" That is one of the greatest questions of all time. "He that is of God heareth the words of God: for this cause ye hear them not, because ye are not of God." "I pray that Thou shouldest keep them from the evil one." "He standeth not in the truth. . . . He is a liar, and the father of lies." How are we to be kept from the liar who is the father of lies? — by the truth. And faced with delusion and diabolical strategy, how are we to be delivered from the errors of the wicked one, except by the truth of God. We are marked off, we belong to the Lord Jesus; and He, aware of the allurement and fascination, the pressure and power of the world and of Satan, said to the Father, "Sanctify them in the truth: Thy word is truth."

III. HIS PRAYER FOR ALL THOSE WHO WERE YET TO BELIEVE ON HIM, 17:20–23. Our Lord's prayer looks in three directions: to the past, in the declaration that His mission is finished; to the present, in the requests for His disciples and for Himself; and into the future, especially emphasized in verses 20 and 24 — the former relating to what will occur on this earth, and the latter to the life of believers in glory. 20. **Neither for these only do I pray, but for them also that believe on me through their word.** In this prayer is revealed a three-fold movement, if we might say, of the Word of God: first, the Word is given by God to Christ (v. 8); then it is communicated through Christ to those who are His own, who received and believed His words (v. 8); and now, with Christ soon to ascend into glory, this same Word, proclaimed by the disciples will effectually fulfill its purpose as it enters the hearts of lost men, and, by revealing the truth of God's redeeming grace in Christ, will bring them to a place of faith and repentance. There can be no more solemn function or opportunity in all the world than that of being a channel of the eternal saving Word of God. 21. **That they may all be one; even as thou, Father, *art* in me, and I in thee, that they also may be in us: that the world may believe that thou didst send me.** "There are four unions revealed to us in the Word of God, and here we read how divine grace and love have connected them most marvelously and most closely with one another. First, the incomprehensible union, nowhere described or defined, but simply stated for the obedience of our faith, namely, the mutual union and indwelling of the three Persons in the Godhead; Father, Son and Holy Ghost. . . . The second, the mutual union and indwelling of the Man Christ Jesus with the second Person of the blessed Trinity, the Son of God, making one glorious Person, God-man, the Lord Jesus Christ, our Saviour, the Captain of our salvation, the Author and Finisher of our faith. The third is the mutual union and indwelling between Himself and His believing people; as the members of His mystical Body, He having taken our nature into heaven, we are one with Him *there*, and He with His Holy Spirit dwelleth within us evermore, He is one with us *here*. The fourth is the union and mutual membership and intercommunion of all of the believing people of God one with another; and this union obtains, whether we speak of those who have gone before, Abraham, Isaac, and Jacob, etc., or those who are at present upon

22. And the glory which thou hast given me I have given unto them; that they may be one, even as we *are* one.

23. I in them, and thou in me, that they may be perfected into one; that the world may know that thou didst send me, and lovedst them, even as thou lovedst me.

the earth, believing, or of the future ingathering of all who shall at any time believe on the Lord Jesus Christ; for He says, 'Neither pray I for these alone, but for them also which shall believe on me through their word; that they all may be one.' " — *Marcus Rainsford.* **22. And the glory which thou hast given me I have given unto them; that they may be one, even as we *are* one.** To me this is one of the richest (almost unbelievable) of all the statements that ever came from the lips of Christ. "It is impossible to dissociate the glory the Father has given to Jesus from the glory mentioned in verses 1 and 5. This is the eternal glory which the Logos had before the world was, the uncreated and essential glory of God, consisting of the sum of the divine attributes. This glory was given to Jesus in his human nature at the incarnation, when the Logos assumed that nature. This glory the apostles beheld in Jesus, shining through the veil of his flesh (1:14). . . . The perfect tense 'has given' is the proper form; the gift made in the instant of the Incarnation remains as such to this moment and on indefinitely. . . . This divine glory, which Jesus received in his human nature at the Incarnation, he says: 'I on my part have given to them' namely to all believers, for this part of the prayer deals with all of them. As the gift to Jesus was of necessity only in a way in which he could receive it, namely by way of his human nature, so again the giving of this gift to the believers was only in a way in which they could receive it. They received it by the indwelling of Jesus, by which they were made partakers of the divine nature (2 Pet. 1:4; 2 Cor. 3:18; Heb. 12:10; 1 John 3:2). This our glory, received from Jesus, is invisible now, while we are in what we may call our state of humiliation, the consummation at the Parousia will reveal it in all its excellence (Rev. 3:21)." — *R. C. H. Lenski.* **23. I in them, and thou in me, that they may be perfected into one; that the world may know that thou didst send me, and lovedst them, even as thou lovedst me.** There is nothing more amazing in the teachings of Jesus (and of the apostles to follow), than the comparisons set forth of that which passes between God the Father and God the Son, and that which passes between the Father and the Son and those who are his. Remember that it is not a disciple who is asking for this, but it is Christ the Son of God who is declaring it — that God loves us even as He loved the Lord Jesus. "The spiritual effect wrought in Christians, the visible manifestation of a power of love among them (compare 13:35) is declared to be a sufficient proof of the divine mission of Him from whom it comes, and of the continuance in them of the divine working. This working is not however such as might have been anticipated. The life of believers shews the same contrasts of joy and apparent failure as the life of Christ. But those contrasts are no disparagement of the perfectness of the love of God towards them." — *B. F. Westcott.*

IV. **THE TWO FINAL REQUESTS FOR HIS OWN,** 17:24–26. Though the remaining three verses of this inexhaustible chapter are not in the printed text, we must give them a brief consideration, for they form the conclusion to this prayer. Fundamentally, there are two final requests that pass the lips of our Lord here. They concern not Christ alone, or the disciples alone, but Christ in relation to the disciples, and the disciples in relation to Him. His first petition is that all who belong to Him may ultimately be with Him where He is, and behold His glory; and the second, as He once again directs His prayer to the subject of love, "that the love wherewith thou lovest me may be in them and I in them." "When we are painfully conscious of the hardness of our hearts, and the coldness of our love to Him who first loved us let us remember and not forget what is here taught us and promised to us. A day is coming when God's own love to Christ shall be in us, and we, too, shall love Christ with the love wherewith His Father loves Him: this shall be the reward of His travail, and there He will rest forever, inhabiting the praises of His people, and enshrined in their hearts, dwelling in the very love wherewith His Father loved Him.   Christ and perfect love must be evermore together; where He dwells, love dwells, the Father dwells; the Holy Ghost dwells, God dwells, and we shall dwell!" — *Marcus Rainsford.*

THE LESSON IN LIFE, LITERATURE, AND ARCHAEOLOGY.

Professor Emil Cailliet, of Princeton Theological Seminary, in his worthwhile volume, *The Clue to Pascal,* describes the crisis that faced this famous mathematician, and apologete, in 1654. "Alone in the darkness of his soul, Pascal turned to his Bible. He opened it at the beginning of the seventeenth chapter of The Gospel According to John, where Jesus is shown preparing himself for his sacrifice on the cross. Having given up all inclination to struggle or the slightest pretense to a power he might call his own, and at the same time infinitely weary, Blaise Pascal groped for Jesus in order to watch with him.   And all of a sudden, during the night of November 23, 1654, Blaise's room was flooded with the very Light of the flaming bush that burned and did not burn out. A divine message came to him, which he feverishly scribbled down on a slip of paper. He afterward copied, with a few variations, the text of this revelation on a parchment. Both documents were discovered only after his death, sewn into the lining of his coat. It testifies to the fact that the written Word of the Book and the living Word are one and the same Word. It shows that God speaks to his people in and through the Bible, often by illuminating such and such a verse for the seeker. It vindicates the ways of repentance and calls for nothing short of total surrender. Above all, it exalts Christ."

A TRUTH FOR THE CLASS TO CARRY AWAY.

It seems to me that the best way to close this lesson would be to stress a truth to which few Christians give any attention today; yet a holy and glorious truth it is — the intercessory work of our Lord Jesus.   In closing the study of this high priestly prayer, let us recall the truth set forth in Hebrews 7:25, "Wherefore also he is able to save to the uttermost them that draw near unto God through him, seeing he ever liveth to make intercession for them."

Why could such a prayer as this be uttered only by the Lord Jesus?   In what ways is the absolute pre-eminence of Christ revealed in these holy sentences? What characteristics of Christ are to be discovered in this prayer?   Of the many different subjects about which Christ prayed, what related only to that time, what petitions are still pregnant with meaning for us, and what ones relate to the future? In what ways would you say that Paul's prayer in Ephesians and Philippians embrace some of the truths of this prayer by our Lord?

LESSON II. — April 11.

BETRAYAL AND CRUCIFIXION. (Easter) John 18—19; 21:15.

PRINTED TEXT, John 18:1–8, 15–17; 19:17–30.

Devotional Reading: Psalm 16.
Beginner Topic: NAMES FOR THE ANIMALS.
    Lesson Material: Genesis 1:20–25; 2:19–20; Psalm 147:9.
    Memory Verse: Praise ye Jehovah: for Jehovah is good.   Psalm 135:3.
Primary Topic: HOW JESUS HELPED PETER.
    Lesson Material: John 18:1–27; 21:15.
    Memory Verse: The Father . . . having loved his own . . . loved them unto the end.   John 13:1.

Junior Topic: WHEN JESUS STOOD ALONE.
  Lesson Material: John 18:1—19:18, 38–42.
  Memory Verse: The Father . . . having loved his own . . . loved them unto the end.   John 13:1.
Intermediate-Senior Topic: THE CRUCIFIED KING.
  Lesson Material: John 18—19.
  Memory Verse: I, if I be lifted up from the earth, will draw all men unto myself.   John 12:32.
Topic for Young People and Adults: JESUS GIVES HIS LIFE.
  Lesson Material: John 18—19.
  Memory Verse: I, if I be lifted up from the earth, will draw all men unto myself.   John 12:32.

THE TEACHER AND HIS CLASS.

The Younger Classes may be introduced to this lesson concerning the death of our Lord by being reminded that in our land, transgression of the law is punished.   The teacher may begin by speaking of the courthouse, then of the county jail, a prison or penitentiary, and then in a quiet way lead into the subject of execution for a major crime.   The most tragic thing that can happen in such cases is for a man to be put to death for a crime, and later to be found innocent of that particular crime. In our lesson, no charge against Christ is ever proved, and yet He is put to death in a most terrible and shameful way.   The lesson today unveils the story of how this happened, while the remainder of the New Testament will tell us why it happened.

The Older Classes may be introduced to this lesson with the following anecdote, passed on to me by one of my colleagues: The distinguished writer on philosophy and civilization, Professor Will Durand, for many years at Columbia University, began a recent lecture with these words, "I have been asked what is the most important year in the history of the human race.   My answer is, any one of the three years in which Jesus walked on earth with His disciples."   Of those years, the last is the most significant, for it was the year of Christ's death and resurrection.

THE LESSON IN ITS SETTING.

Time. — The arrest of Jesus took place late Thursday night, April 7, A.D. 30; the trial before Pilate, from six to nine o'clock Friday morning; and the death of Christ, about three o'clock that afternoon.

Place. — The Garden of Gethsemane was on the lower western slope of the Mount of Olives, opposite Jerusalem. The trials took place in various buildings in that city.   The crucifixion occurred at a place called Golgotha, just outside the north wall of Jerusalem.

THE PLAN OF THE LESSON.

SUBJECT: How Christ, though Without Sin, was Condemned to Death, and the Part Played by Various Characters in the Execution of the Sentence.

I. THE BETRAYAL AND ARREST OF CHRIST, John 18:1–11.

II. THE DENIAL OF CHRIST BY SIMON PETER, John 18:15–18, 25–27.

III. THE TRIALS OF CHRIST, John 18:12–14, 19–24; 18:28—19:16.
  1. Before Annas, 18:12–14, 19–24.
  2. Before Pilate, 18:28—19:16.

IV. THE CRUCIFIXION OF CHRIST, John 19:17–37.

V. THE ENTOMBMENT OF CHRIST, John 19:38–42.

THE TEACHER'S LIBRARY.

In addition to the standard lives of Christ, and the more important commentaries on John's Gospel, all of the following works will be found devoted exclusively to the last hours of our Lord's life: James Stalker: *The Trial and Death of Jesus Christ;* F. W. Krummacher: *The Suffering Saviour;* W. M. Clow: *The Day of the Cross;* A. Tholuck: *Light From the Cross.*   The works by Tholuck and Krummacher, for years practically unobtainable, have been reprinted in the Wycliffe Series of Christian Classics, published by Moody Press.   See also A. F. W. Ingraham: *The Men Who Crucified Christ;* and two volumes that have excellent chapters on Judas, Pilate, Annas and the soldier who thrust a spear into Jesus' side — *The Son of God Among the Sons of Men*, by Everett F. Harrison, and *There They Crucified Him*, by John A. Hutton. In addition to these, all standard Bible Encyclopedias might be consulted for articles on Annas, Crucifixion, Death, Entombment, Gethsemane, Pilate, etc. The one by Moffatt on the "Trial of Christ" in Hastings: *Dictionary of Christ and the Gospels*, Vol. 2, extends to 20 columns.

AUDIO-VISUAL AIDS.

Gethsemane

FILMSTRIP: "Jesus in Gethsemane," Concordia No. C–2, 31 fr., col. Jesus and His disciples in the institution of the Lord's Supper; Jesus pointing out Judas as His betrayer. Text captions for each picture.

SLIDE SET: "Gethsemane," Move 49, Visserslides No. 328–340, 9 sl., col. The major events of this Garden experience in brilliant coloring.

Crucifixion

On the Crucifixion there are a number of films, most of which cover more than the actual event. Some care and counsel are required in selecting as important an aid as a film on this occasion.

FILM: "Barabbas the Robber," Religious Films, 38 min., sd., b&w. From the viewpoint of Barabbas the events of the death of Jesus are portrayed. Barabbas says in closing, "He died for me, now I must live for Him." Jesus does not actually appear on the screen.

FILM: "The Crucifixion," Living Word Films, 30 min., sd., col. Trial of Jesus before Herod and Pilate, crucifixion, conversion of the centurian.

FILMSTRIP: "The Crucifixion," (Life of Christ Visualized), Standard No. 7930 (SVE No. A700–10c), 50 fr., col. A rather lengthy presentation.

JOHN 18:1. When Jesus had spoken these words, he went forth with his disciples over the brook Kidron, where was a garden, into which he entered, himself and his disciples.

2. Now Judas also, who betrayed him, knew the place: for Jesus oft-times resorted thither with his disciples.

3. Judas then, having received the band *of soldiers*, and officers from the chief priests and the Pharisees, cometh thither with lanterns and torches and weapons.

The death of Christ is that to which the prophets pointed, that of which Christ Himself frequently spoke during His early ministry, that to which the Gospels give greater space than to any other event in the history of redemption, that which was continually foremost in the minds of those who wrote the Epistles and the Book of Revelation, and that which draws men magnetically to Christ, through which mankind has forgiveness of sins, and sinners are reconciled to God. More hymns, more great portraits, more epochal volumes have been born from a contemplation of this event than of any other in human history. We must be careful in this lesson to concentrate on only a few major themes, lest the half-hour assigned suddenly terminate, and we have not adequately emphasized the fundamental themes of these remarkable records.

I. **THE BETRAYAL AND ARREST OF CHRIST**, John 18:1–11. For parallel and supplementary accounts, see Matthew 26:30–56; Mark 14:26–52; Luke 22:39–53. All events recorded in the five preceding chapters took place in the afternoon and evening of this Thursday of Holy Week, when Christ has been in the most intimate fellowship with His closest disciples. He is now about to be taken from them. 1. **When Jesus had spoken these words, he went forth with his disciples over the brook Kidron, where was a garden, into which he entered, himself and his disciples.** It was across this brook Kidron that David fled from Absalom (2 Sam. 15:23). It is the same stream which flows in the valley separating Jerusalem from the Mount of Olives. The garden is still there, and it is thought by some that perhaps two or three of the olive trees now in the garden were there when Jesus entered that night. 2. **Now Judas also, who betrayed him, knew the place: for Jesus oft-times resorted thither with his disciples.** 3. **Judas then, having received the band *of soldiers*, and officers from the chief priests and the Pharisees,**

4. Jesus therefore, knowing all the things that were coming upon him, went forth, and saith unto them, Whom seek ye?

5. They answered him, Jesus of Nazareth. Jesus saith unto them, I am *he*. And Judas also, who betrayed him, was standing with them.

6. When therefore he said unto them, I am *he*, they went backward, and fell to the ground.

7. Again therefore he asked them, Whom seek ye? And they said, Jesus of Nazareth.

8. Jesus answered, I told you that I am *he;* if therefore ye seek me, let these go their way.

---

cometh thither with lanterns and torches and weapons. **4. Jesus therefore, knowing all the things that were coming upon him, went forth, and saith unto them, Whom seek ye?** We are now introduced to the first of those characters, and the most depraved of all of them, to participate in the injustices and cruelties of the trials, beatings and crucifixion of our Lord — Judas Iscariot, who was, for three years, in the company of the twelve disciples, having been called by Christ, and whose infamous deed has made his name to stand for the deepest kind of treason and betrayal. "The evil world which bore down upon the head of Jesus and crucified Him was a thing which could have had no power at all unless it had found its instruments, its human instruments. Judas, Pilate, Caiaphas, Herod, the chief priests, the crowd who represented the average public opinion at the moment — they had all their share in the guilt of Calvary: and what is of greater consequence to us to remember is that each of them was aware that he had his share. Before each of them the issue stood out quite clearly — either on the one hand to yield, or on the other to refuse. When all is said, there is no evil in the world except such as comes through human hands. It may be difficult for us to trace, as we look upon the victim of any evil thing, how precisely what is before our eyes took place; but we know that if we had the power to see, we should find that everything that is hard, malignant, cruel, has come directly and indirectly through the self-seeking of others." — *John A. Hutton.* The teacher should not be sidetracked here by a discussion as to whether or not Christ knew Judas would betray Him, and if so, why He took him into the apostolic company, etc. It is better to take the text as it is, and not devote time to questions which the Bible does not answer. **5. They answered him, Jesus of Nazareth. Jesus saith unto them, I am *he*. And Judas also, who betrayed him, was standing with them. 6. When therefore he said unto them, I am *he*, they went backward, and fell to the ground. 7. Again therefore he asked them, Whom seek ye? And they said, Jesus of Nazareth. 8. Jesus answered, I told you that I am *he;* if therefore ye seek me, let these go their way.** Milligan remarks on verse 6, "It is the divine majesty and innocence of Jesus that produced the effect. Like the buyers and sellers in the temple, the history of whose terror at the presence of the Redeemer is vouched for by the testimony of the earlier gospels, as much as by that of the fourth, they are overwhelmed with awe, and fall before Him. As soon as they recover, Jesus repeats His question." "Whether their falling was the natural effect of guilt meeting with absolute innocence, or a supernatural effect wrought by Christ's will, is a question which we have not the means of determining. . . . The result in this case proved both to the disciples and to His foes that His surrender was entirely voluntary (10:18)." — *Alfred Plummer.*

II. THE DENIAL OF CHRIST BY SIMON PETER, John 18:15–18, 25–27. Peter's denial is also recorded in Matthew 26:69–75; Mark 14:66–72; and Luke 22:56–62. In studying this particular incident, we will remember that our Lord had warned Peter this very day that before the cock would crow, Peter would deny

15. And Simon Peter followed Jesus, and *so did* another disciple. Now that disciple was known unto the high priest, and entered in with Jesus into the court of the high priest;

16. but Peter was standing at the door without. So the other disciple who was known unto the high priest, went out and spake unto her that kept the door, and brought in Peter.

17. The maid therefore that kept the door saith unto Peter, Art thou also *one* of this man's disciples?

Him thrice (13:36–38). **15. And Simon Peter followed Jesus, and *so did* another disciple. Now that disciple was known unto the high priest, and entered in with Jesus into the court of the high priest; 16. but Peter was standing at the door without. So the other disciple who was known unto the high priest, went out and spake unto her that kept the door, and brought in Peter. 17. The maid therefore that kept the door saith unto Peter, Art thou also *one* of this man's disciples?** The identity of this other disciple is not specifically revealed, but it is generally understood to be John the Apostle, the writer of this Gospel. "The friendship of the other disciple with the high priest enables Peter to enter the court, and the scene is set for his denial. The author thus explains the presence of Peter in the inner court (Mark 14:54). He is questioned first by the doorkeeper as he enters, not as in the synoptic narrative by a maid whilst he warms himself at the fire (Mark 14:66, 67 and parallels). The suggestion in Mark 14:68, 69 is, however, that she was the doorkeeper." — *E. C. Hoskyns.*

The narrative is now interrupted by an account of the earlier trials, but we ought here to consider verses 25–27, which complete the story of Peter's tragic fall this night. "The third accusation and denial was, as St. Luke tells us, about an hour after the second; so that our Lord must have 'turned and looked upon Peter' either from a room looking into the court, or as He was being led to receive the formal sentence of the Sanhedrin after the trial before Caiaphas, not as He was being taken from Annas to Caiaphas. . . . Just as the Evangelist implies (v. 11) without mentioning, the agony in the garden, so he implies (21:15) without mentioning, the repentance of St. Peter. . . . Christ's foreknowledge of the fall of His chief Apostle (13:38) illustrated both: it was evidence of His divinity (compare 2:24, 25) and it intensified His suffering." — *Alfred Plummer.*

III. **THE TRIALS OF CHRIST,** John 18:12–14, 19–24; 18:28—19:16. For parallel accounts of the trials of Christ, see Matthew 26:57—27:25; Mark 14:53—15:19; Luke 22:54—23:25. Christ is first led to Annas, then to Caiaphas, where He is first tried, then to the Sanhedrin, as recorded in Matthew 26:59–66, but not found in John's account, followed by another appearance before the Sanhedrin early in the morning (Matt. 27:1, 2) not mentioned in John's Gospel, the first trial before Pilate, the trial before Herod (only in Luke 23:6–12), and the last trial before Pilate — six trials in all, though some say seven. "John alone records this preliminary examination of Jesus by Annas preceding the appearance before the Sanhedrin. He says 'first' with an allusion to the examination before Caiaphas. Probably the reason was simply to keep Jesus in a secure place while the Sanhedrin were assembling for the trial. It was, besides, a mark of respect to this powerful ex-high priest, the head of the Sadducees. Annas had been high priest himself (A.D. 7–14) and he kept the office in the family till five successive sons held it besides his son-in-law Joseph Caiaphas who now has it (A.D. 18–36). . . . The question to Jesus about His disciples and His teaching was keenly resented by the Master who ignores the implied slur upon His disciples as the ignorant multitude (compare 7:49). As to the teaching of Jesus, that is public property (18:20 ff.), as Annas knows only too well by personal experience (compare Matt. 21:23—23:29)." — *A. T. Robertson.* Of the trial before Caiaphas, mentioned in verse 24, John gives no details.

We come now to the extended account of the trial before Pilate. Let us consider first the man himself. "If Pilate's life is somewhat obscure, his character is not. Of adventurous spirit, he spent his early days in frontier fighting, then took as his wife Claudia, daughter of Julia, the profligate daughter of Augustus. His father-in-law Tiberius made him procurator of Judea, whether from recognition of his administrative talents or as a marriage gift, or both. From the start, Pilate incurred the opposition and hatred of the Jews by ordering the standard of his cohorts taken into Jerusalem by night. These bore the image of the emperor and were bitterly resented by the Jews as a violation of their sacred law. . . . Pilate was obliged to relent and to withdraw the standards from Jerusalem. Another revelation of the man is given in Luke 13:1, where we read that he mingled the blood of certain Galileans with their sacrifices. . . . The Jewish writer Philo makes a sweeping indictment charging him with 'corruptibility, violence, robberies, ill-treatment of the people, grievances, continuous executions without even the form of a trial, endless and intolerable cruelties.' The remarkable thing is that the Evangelists, in recounting the darkest deed ever committed by Pilate, refrain altogether from any verbal attack on him. . . . Once more these sworn enemies faced each other — the scornful Gentile and the fanatical Jews. Between them stood the everlasting Man, not the cause but only the occasion for the guilt which both must bear for condemning the innocent. They could not know and did not care to know that He had come not merely to reconcile men unto God but to break down the enmity between Jew and Gentile, uniting both in Himself." — *E. F. Harrison.*

In a study of the four Gospel accounts of Christ's trials before Pontius Pilate — the one character, incidentally, in all this narrative mentioned in the Apostles' Creed — one will find that Pilate asks more questions of Jesus on this one morning than any other person in all the Gospels is recorded to have asked. So, we can rightly say that Pilate distinctly knew what he was doing, and who this person was whom he was about to condemn. He first asks the Jews what charge they bring against this man Jesus, which question they try to evade. Had the Jews the authority at this time to put to death those whom the Sanhedrin condemned, Jesus would have been stoned. The reason He was crucified is that this was the Roman method of putting to death those considered the worst criminals. Pilate now calls Jesus himself to him and asks, "Art thou the king of the Jews?" This discussion about Christ's kingship brings forth from our Lord's lips one of the greatest utterances of His entire ministry, "My kingdom is not of this world . . . to this end have I been born." "Jesus is indeed a King, but His Kingdom is not of this world. Had it been of this world, His servants would have organized themselves in self-defense. As it is, His Kingdom has its sanction and origin in the higher sphere. For this reason He can say to Pilate that He is a King, that He was born to be a King, and that He came into the world to be a King, but not in the material sense. Above this world is the world of the spirit which is the only true world, and Jesus came to bear witness of its truth. His Kingdom lies there, and everyone who is of 'the truth' everyone who has seen and embraced that world of divine realities, owns Him as Lord." — *William Manson.* All this is followed by one of Pilate's many clear pronouncements that concerning the person the Jews have brought to Him for condemnation, he can find nothing wrong. But the Jews stress their determination to have Christ put to death by telling Pilate that if according to a custom of mercy at that time of the year, one criminal is to be released, let it not be Jesus, but Barabbas. One terrible insult after another is now thrust at Jesus. One thing Pilate should now do; only one thing justice could lead him to do, to release this Person Jesus, or to proceed with a trial until he found something wrong. This latter he knew would never happen, for he had come to the conclusion that there was no fault at all in this Person. The countenance of Jesus, the tone in which Christ spoke, the spirituality of Christ's purposes, the evasiveness of the Jews — all these things united to confirm such a conviction in the heart of Pilate. There was only one *honest* thing to do — release this Person!

JOHN 19:17. They took Jesus therefore: and he went out, bearing the cross for himself, unto the place called The place of a skull, which is called in Hebrew Golgotha.

18. Where they crucified him, and with him two others, on either side one, and Jesus in the midst.

19. And Pilate wrote a title also, and put it on the cross. And there was written, JESUS OF NAZARETH, THE KING OF THE JEWS.

20. This title therefore read many of the Jews, for the place where Jesus was crucified was nigh to the city; and it was written in Hebrew, *and* in Latin, *and* in Greek.

He first suggested to the Jews that he would release Jesus, because it was the custom at the Passover to release one person at this season. At last they are forced to tell why they hate this Person. They first charged Him with claiming to be the King of the Jews; now they tell Pilate that He made Himself the Son of God! Ah! So that is it! When Pilate heard that, he was the more afraid. He went back to Jesus to ask Him whence He was. If he could only get a word from Christ that He was the Son of God, then perhaps he could continue the case until the Jews wearily departed. The time for decision had come, and there was no need for Jesus to speak again. "Jesus gave him no answer." Aware of the absolute innocence of Jesus, of the viciousness of the Jews who stood before him, and of the injustice that would be worked in the name of Rome, which prided itself on justice, should this man Jesus be condemned, Pilate is desperate. When Jesus refuses to talk to him further, he tries to reassert his own authority, telling Jesus that he has the power to do as he pleases with Him. To this Jesus replied that he had no power at all to put Him to death except it was given to him from above. Once more Pilate attempts to release Jesus; but it is too late. "His secret displeasure with himself would seek satisfaction in his indignation and disgust with them. He had shown his contempt for the Jews from the first, and now, with that contempt raised to its highest point, he says, 'Behold your King.' It is possible also that in these words the Evangelist sees one of those unconscious prophecies or Divine declarations concerning Jesus of which we have had repeated illustrations in this Gospel." — *William Milligan.*

IV. **THE CRUCIFIXION OF CHRIST,** John 19:17–37. While the narrative goes into great detail in reporting the conversations of Christ with His disciples, the agony in the garden, and the trials before the Sanhedrin and Pilate, of the crucifixion itself we have only the briefest account. None of the Gospel writers enter upon the gruesome minutia of this method of putting men to death. In later centuries, the agonies of the cross were drawn out in terrifying detail, but it is not according to the Spirit of God, who guided these writers in recording the death of the Son of God. 17. **They took Jesus therefore: and he went out, bearing the cross for himself, unto the place called The place of a skull, which is called in Hebrew Golgotha.** The word *Golgotha,* a Hebrew word, means "the hill of the skull," the Latin word *Calvaria,* from which comes our word *Calvary.* We do not know exactly where this place was, except that it was outside of the north wall, close to a garden and tombs of the old city. "As Isaac bore the wood for the burnt offering, so Jesus, the victim of God and the prisoner of men, was led forth from the city, bearing His cross, to a place elevated in the form of a skull, and named Golgotha." — *E. C. Hoskyns.* 18. **Where they crucified him, and with him two others, on either side one, and Jesus in the midst.** These two men crucified on either side of Jesus were robbers. Plummer has said that the whole of humanity is here represented — the sinless Saviour, the saved penitent, and the condemned impenitent. 19. **And Pilate wrote a title also, and put it on the cross. And there was written, JESUS OF NAZARETH, THE KING OF THE JEWS. 20. This title therefore read many of the Jews, for the place where Jesus was crucified was nigh to the city; and it was written in Hebrew, *and* in Latin, *and* in**

134

21. The chief priests of the Jews therefore said to Pilate, Write not, The King of the Jews; but, that he said, I am King of the Jews.

22. Pilate answered, What I have written, I have written.

23. The soldiers therefore, when they had crucified Jesus, took his garments and made four parts, to every soldier a part; and also the coat: now the coat was without seam, woven from the top throughout.

24. They said therefore one to another, Let us not rend it, but cast lots for it, whose it shall be: that the scripture might be fulfilled, which saith, They parted my garments among them, and upon my vesture did they cast lots.

25. These things therefore the soldiers did. But there were standing by the cross of Jesus his mother, and his mother's sister, Mary the *wife* of Clopas, and Mary Magdalene.

Greek. 21. The chief priests of the Jews therefore said to Pilate, Write not, The King of the Jews; but, that he said, I am King of the Jews. 22. Pilate answered, What I have written, I have written. A great deal has been made of this trilingual inscription, and rightly so. I recall hearing one of the most learned professors in a college speak on this text, reminding us that the Hebrew stood for religion, the Greek for literature and the arts, and the Roman for law and government. The request of the Jews to have this title changed to indicate that this was simply a claim of Christ instead of an announcement of fact, is rejected. "To the very last these high priests have hurled at Pilate the charge: 'King, king!' which he knew was false, and which he knew they knew was false. As a king they had forced Pilate to crucify Jesus. Very well then, they should have him on the cross, but only as a king, *their* King! Let all the world read: 'The King of the Jews'! In simply giving Jesus this title, without any added allegation, Pilate proclaims the innocence of Jesus of which he was completely certain." — *R. C. H. Lenski.*

The trials are over, our Lord is in the hands of soldiers. While it is true that Christ was despitefully used and brutally treated by the soldiers through the night, we should note that this is the only time in all the New Testament that soldiers act unjustly and cruelly toward Jesus. Every other centurion named in the Gospels, and in the Book of Acts, seemed to have great respect for the Lord; but of course on this day all moral law is cast to the winds. Satan is ruling. It is an hour of darkness. **23. The soldiers therefore, when they had crucified Jesus, took his garments and made four parts, to every soldier a part; and also the coat: now the coat was without seam, woven from the top throughout. 24. They said therefore one to another, Let us not rend it, but cast lots for it, whose it shall be: that the scripture might be fulfilled, which saith, They parted my garments among them, and upon my vesture did they cast lots.** The reference here is to Psalm 22:18. "The Greek word translated 'let us not rend' suggests not only the tearing of garments (Isa. 37:1) but also the division of the people of God into factions (7:43; 9:16; 10:19; compare 1 Kings 11:29 ff.; 1 Cor. 1:10; 11:18; 12:25). The indivisible robe, which is closely associated with the body of the Lord, may therefore symbolize the unity of the believers who are joined to the Lord and feed upon His Body, in contrast to the division of the Jews, who are torn into factions because of Him (10:16; 17:11, 20 ff.; contrasted with 7:43; 9:16; 10:19). The seamless robe of the High Priest (Josephus *Ant.* 3:161, based on Exod. 31:10; Lev. 21:10) which Philo interpreted as the cohesion of the world by the powers of the Logos may be suggested here." — *E. C. Hoskyns.*

The long series of tragedies, miscarriages of justice, acts of brutality, is now interrupted by the record of the women at the cross, including Mary the mother of our Lord. Words fail to interpret here the brief portrait John has given us. **25. These things therefore the soldiers did. But there were standing by the cross of Jesus his mother, and his mother's sister, Mary the *wife* of Clopas, and**

26. When Jesus therefore saw his mother, and the disciple standing by whom he loved, he saith unto his mother, Woman, behold thy son!

27. Then saith he to the disciple, Behold, thy mother! And from that hour the disciple took her unto his own *home.*

28. After this Jesus, knowing that all things are now finished, that the scripture might be accomplished, saith, I thirst.

29. There was set there a vessel full of vinegar; so they put a sponge full of vinegar upon hyssop, and brought it to his mouth.

30. When Jesus therefore had received the vinegar, he said, It is finished: and he bowed his head, and gave up his spirit.

Mary Magdalene. 26. When Jesus therefore saw his mother, and the disciple standing by whom he loved, he saith unto his mother, Woman, behold thy son! 27. Then saith he to the disciple, Behold, thy mother! And from that hour the disciple took her unto his own *home.* "The scene between Jesus and His mother is given only by John. He contrasts the soldiers with the group of women standing by the Cross of Christ. There seem to be four women in the group — Mary the mother of Jesus, Salome the mother of the sons of Zebedee (compare John 19:25; Mark 15:40; Matt. 27:56), Mary the wife of Clopas (mother of James the less and Joses, Matt. 27:56; Mark 15:40), and Mary Magdalene. The women are true, as one would expect, in an hour like this, whatever is the conduct of the men. The sword has pierced the soul of Mary, the mother of Jesus, as Simeon had said it would (Luke 2:35) but she did not flinch nor was she ashamed to own Jesus when the rulers have rejected Him. . . . It is a tender human touch in this Gospel when Jesus speaks from the Cross to His mother and to John and commends them as mother and son, titles of loving respect. John accepted the precious charge 'from that hour' and probably took Mary to his lodging at once, though it does not follow that he had a permanent home in Jerusalem at this time. . . . It was clearly impossible for Jesus to commend His mother to His own brothers, for they as yet disbelieved in Him." — *A. T. Robertson.*

If the words of all the four Gospels are put together, we discover, as the Church has always acknowledged, seven words from the cross. All of them are not given in any one of the Gospels. These two words recorded by John are the fifth and sixth cries from the cross; the word to Mary is the third. **28. After this Jesus, knowing that all things are now finished, that the scripture might be accomplished, saith, I thirst. 29. There was set there a vessel full of vinegar; so they put a sponge full of vinegar upon hyssop, and brought it to his mouth. 30. When Jesus therefore had received the vinegar, he said, It is finished: and he bowed his head, and gave up his spirit.** The word here translated *vinegar* "was either the *posca* or sour wine for the soldiers during their long watch, or something prepared for the sufferers. The sponge and the stalk of hyssop being ready at hand is in favour of the latter. Criminals sometimes lived a day or two on the cross. Vinegar is degenerate wine, and may symbolize the fallen nature of those who offered it. Hyssop cannot be identified with certainty. The caper-plant which is as likely as any, has stalks which run to two or three feet, and this would suffice. It is not probable that Christ's feet were on a level with the spectators' heads, as pictures represent: this would have involved needless trouble and expense. Moreover the mockery of the soldiers recorded by St. Luke is more intelligible if we suppose that they could almost put a vessel to His lips. St. John alone mentions the hyssop; another mark of exact knowledge. Did he see in it a coincidence with Exodus 12:22? — *Alfred Plummer.* This shout of victory, "It is finished!" has infinite depths in it. His redemptive work was now finished — He worked out none of our salvation in any underworld, as in hades or hell, for His spirit was now immediately to ascend to the presence of His Father. His sufferings were finished; no other indignity was ever inflicted upon Christ after this. The sacrifice of His precious, spotless self had now been completely presented to God. All temptations had been triumphantly overcome, and life, in the limitations of human flesh, was now at an end. Most of all, the pouring out of His soul unto death, the tasting of death for every man, the bearing of our sins in His own body on the tree — all this was now finished, and in His death there became available eternal life through the redemption He purchased for us.

Though our Lord has died — far more quickly than anyone expected He would, knowing the long time that most crucified men lingered on a cross — John continues to tell us what is happening around this most sacred spot When the soldiers came to Christ and found Him dead already, one of them, possibly as final evidence of the fact that He was put to death, pierced His side with a spear, with the result that there burst forth blood and water. Two passages of Scripture are here inserted by John as having been fulfilled — Exodus 12:46, linked with Numbers 9:12 and Zechariah 12:10. "John alone gives the story of the breaking of the legs of the two robbers by the soldiers at the request of the Jews so that the bodies could be taken down before the Sabbath began at sunset (six o'clock). The bodies were to come down by night anyway, but the approach of the Sabbath made the Jewish leaders very sensitive on the subject. The Gospels all (Matt. 27:62; Mark 15:42; Luke 23:54; John 19:31) explain that the day of the crucifixion is the 'Preparation,' that is the day before the Sabbath. This Sabbath was a 'high' day because it was also the passover week. But the legs of Jesus were not broken because it was not necessary. John takes pains to bear witness to the fact of seeing blood come out of the side of Jesus to show the reality of the human nature of Christ. The credibility of such an occurrence is vouched for by modern medical science on the theory of a rupture of the blood vessels of the heart as the cause of death. Literally, therefore, Jesus died of a broken heart, broken by the sin of the world (John 1:29; 2 Cor. 5:21) as He suffered alone in the darkness (Matt. 27:46)." — A. T. Robertson.

V. **THE ENTOMBMENT OF CHRIST,** John 19:38–42. For parallel passages see Matt. 27:57–66; Mark 15:42–47 and Luke 23:50–56. In the middle of the 17th century one of the greatest preachers of England was John Flavel. In his book, *The Fountain of Life*, in a sermon, "Christ's Funeral Illustrated," is the finest commentary on the burial of Jesus of which I know. "His body could not be buried till, by begging, his friends had obtained it as a favor from his judge. . . . But what need of spices to perfume that blessed body? His own love was enough to embalm it in the remembrance of his people to all generations; but hereby they manifest, as far as they are able, the dear affection they have for him." — *John Flavel.* Flavel then develops a series of reasons that Christ must be buried. "It was necessary Christ should be buried, (1) to ascertain his death; else it might have been looked upon as a cheat; for, as his enemies were ready to impose so gross a cheat upon the world at his resurrection, that 'the disciples came by night, and stole him away,' much more would they have denied at once the reality both of his death and resurrection, had he not been so perfumed and interred. (2) He must be buried to fulfil the types and prophecies. His abode in the grave was prefigured by Jonah's abode three days and nights in the belly of the whale. . . . (3) He must be buried to complete his humiliation, this being the lowest step he could possibly descend to in his abased state. 'They have brought me to the dust of death'; lower he could not be laid. (4) But the great end and reason of his interment was the conquering of death in its own dominion and territories; which victory over the grave furnished the saints with that triumphant song of deliverance, 'O death, where is thy sting? O grave, where is thy victory?' (1 Cor. 15:55). Our graves would not be so sweet and comfortable to us when we come to lie down in them, if Jesus had not lain there before us and for us." He concludes his sermon with these words: "Whenever you come to your grave, you shall find the enmity of the grave slain by Christ: it is no enemy; nay, you will find it a privileged place to you; it will be as sweet to you that are in Christ, as a soft bed in a still, quiet chamber to one that is weary. Therefore it is said, 'Death is yours,'

(1 Cor. 3:22); yours as a privilege, your friend: there you shall find sweet rest in Jesus; be hurried, pained, troubled no more." — *John Flavel.*

THE LESSON IN LIFE, LITERATURE, AND ARCHAEOLOGY.

Probably the most widely known and frequently recited poem relating to Christ written in the Middle Ages is "Stabat Mater" by Jacobus de Benedictis, who died in the early part of the 14th century. It has frequently been translated from the Latin. The following I take from the great volume by Philip Schaff and Arthur Gilman, *A Library of Religious Poetry:*

> Weeping stood his mother sighing
> By the cross where Jesus, dying,
>   Hung aloft on Calvary:
> Through her soul, in sorrow moaning,
> Bowed in grief, in spirit groaning,
>   Pierced the sword in misery.
>
> Filled with grief beyond all others,
> Mother — blessed among mothers
>   Of the God-begotten One!
> How she sorroweth and grieveth,
> Trembling as she thus perceiveth
>   Dying her unspotted One! . . .
>
> On the cross of Christ relying,
> Through his death redeemed from dying,
>   By his favor fortified
> When my mortal frame is perished,
> Let my spirit then be cherished,
>   And in heaven be glorified.

A TRUTH FOR THE CLASS TO CARRY AWAY.

Over and over again in the New Testament, the death of our Lord is directly related to the love of God, as in Romans 5:8 and many other passages all the way to Revelation 1:5. In drawing to a close this lesson in which our sinless Saviour is revealed as having suffered so much in mind, and body, and soul when every conceivable shame was heaped upon Him, let us remember that behind it all was the love of God, who, providing forgiveness through the shed blood of Christ, would have us to be with Him forever.

In this entire lesson, do you find anyone remaining true to Christ through these dark hours? What is the fundamental difference between the acts of Judas and those of Simon Peter on this occasion which led Judas to suicide, but made Peter's restoration possible? How many of the Ten Commandments were broken by men in relation to Christ in the last twenty-four hours of the Saviour's life? While John's Gospel is generally called "the Gospel of the deity of Christ," does he fill his narrative of Christ's death with supernatural events? (No.)

LESSON III. — April 18.

CHRIST THE LIVING LORD. — John 19:41–42; 20—21.

PRINTED TEXT, John 20:1, 11–16, 19; 20:24–29; 21:15–17.

Devotional Reading: 1 Peter 4:1–11.
Beginner Topic: Glad Sunday Morning.
    Lesson Material: Mark 16:1–7.
    Memory Verse: Thou art nigh, O Jehovah. Psalm 119:151.
Primary Topic: Jesus Lives.
    Lesson Material: John 19:41–42; 20:1–19.
    Memory Verse: The Lord is risen indeed. Luke 24:34.

138

Junior Topic: JESUS LIVES.
  Lesson Material: John 20:1-29.
  Memory Verse: The Lord is risen indeed.   Luke 24:34.
Intermediate-Senior Topic: OUR LIVING LORD.
  Lesson Material: John 20—21.
  Memory Verse: Blessed *are* they that have not seen, and *yet* have believed.
  John 20:29.
Topic for Young People and Adults: OUR LIVING LORD.
  Lesson Material: John 20—21.
  Memory Verse: Blessed *are* they that have not seen, and *yet* have believed.
  John 20:29.

THE TEACHER AND HIS CLASS.

The Younger Classes, and the Older Classes might be introduced to this lesson with the same illustration. Thomas Jefferson, one of our great founding fathers, definitely not a believer in Christ the Son of God, often entered into the field of religious discussion. One of the results of this was a work that acquired undeserved fame, *The Literary Bible of Thomas Jefferson.* An indication of his own repudiation of Christ's deity, and the supernatural factors which persuade us of such deity, is in his reprint of the Gospels. Here he deliberately eliminated those chapters which record the resurrection of Christ! But such passages were written by the same men who recorded Christ's birth, His life, His teachings, and to excide the narrative of the resurrection is to ignore the acknowledged unity of these Gospel writings. It is a deliberate refusal to recognize the facts which the narrative sets forth. We can never consider too often the evidence for the resurrection of Christ, and in these days of unbelief, the fact of that resurrection will become increasingly important.

THE LESSON IN ITS SETTING.

Time. — All the events of this lesson occurred in the year A.D. 30 — the resurrection of Christ on April 9, the interview with Thomas on April 16, and the episode recorded in John 21 some days later, though we do not know exactly when.

Place. — The events of the 20th chapter of John's Gospel took place in or near Jerusalem, in the garden where Christ was buried, and in the upper room within the city; while that recorded in chapter 21 occurred at the Sea of Galilee in the north.

THE PLAN OF THE LESSON.

SUBJECT: The Contemporary Evidences for the Resurrection of Jesus Christ From the Dead.

I. THE BURIAL OF JESUS, John 19:41, 42.

II. THE WITNESS OF THE EMPTY TOMB, John 20:1-10.

III. CHRIST APPEARS TO MARY MAGDALENE, John 20:11-18.

IV. THE TWO APPEARANCES TO THE DISCIPLES IN THE UPPER ROOM, John 20:19-29.
  1. On Easter night, vs. 19-24.
  2. One week later, vs. 25-29.

V. CHRIST APPEARS TO THE DISCIPLES AT THE SEA OF GALILEE, John 21.

THE TEACHER'S LIBRARY.

For the study of this lesson there is a vast amount of material available. All the major lives of Christ will devote considerable attention to the various aspects of Christ's resurrection. Commentaries on the Gospel of John are very helpful here; also Bible dictionaries, and books on Bible characters for chapters on Mary Magdalene, Thomas, and Simon Peter, who appear prominently in this lesson. The teacher will find the most help, however, in books dealing exclusively with the resurrection of our Lord. A rather extensive list of these will be found in an article of mine in *Moody Monthly*, March, 1952, pp. 471, 472.

Among the works that contain excellent chapters on all the post-resurrection appearances of Christ, I would mention the following, with definite approval: H. B. Swete: *The Appearances of Our Lord After the Passion;* Henry Latham: *The Risen Master;* J. M. Shaw: *The Resurrection of Christ;* Doremus A. Hayes: *The Resurrection Fact;* James Orr: *The Resurrection of Jesus;* Alexander Maclaren: *After the Resurrection;* R. McCheyne Edgar: *The Gospel of a*

Risen Saviour; W. J. Sparrow Simpson: *The Resurrection in Modern Thought.* (These last two books are, in my opinion, the most important volumes on the resurrection in our language.) See also the famous work by B. F. Westcott: *The Gospel of the Resurrection.*

On the last two chapters of John's Gospel there is nothing finer than the small volume by Bishop Moule: *Jesus and the Resurrection.* For the interview of Thomas with Jesus, see the excellent treatment by my friend and colleague, Everett F. Harrison, in his book, not as well known as it ought to be, *The Son of God Among the Sons of Men,* 223–235.

The best volume of *sermons* on the resurrection is H. P. Liddon: *Easter in St. Paul's.* I do not think it is necessary to give a list of other sermonic literature here, with the exception of the relevant material by Dr. G. Campbell Morgan in *The Westminster Pulpit* — on John 20:1–18, Vol. 4, pp. 161 168; on 20:27, Vol. 10, pp. 249–256; on 20:28, Vol. 5, pp. 129–136; and on 21:15–17, Vol. 4, pp. 169–176.

AUDIO-VISUAL AIDS.

There is now quite a lot of material available on the Easter theme, although a really satisfactory film is still lacking. Selection should be made carefully and well in advance. Rates are higher on these films during the Easter season.

FILMSTRIP: "The Resurrection" (The Life of Christ Visualized), Standard No. 7931 (SVE No. A700–11c), 50 fr., col. There are captions with each frame, and the color is good.

FILMSTRIP: "The First Easter," Concordia No. C–29, 31 fr., col. Paintings portray the main events of the resurrection.

FILMSTRIP: "He Is Risen," Concordia No. CP–301, 30 fr., col. A nicely done posed picture sequence.

SLIDE SET: "Garden Tomb," Move 53 (The Bible in Pictures), Visserslides No. 374–383, 11 sl., col.

SLIDE SET: "The Easter Story," Visserslides set No. 17, 17 sl., col. Includes death and burial.

FILM: "The First Easter," Harmon Foundation, sponsored by Religious Film Society of England, 35 min., sd, b&w. An old film, usable for presenting the facts of the Easter story, but the sound is somewhat difficult. Christ's face is not seen.

FILM: "The Light of the World," Foundation Films, 10 min., sd, b&w. A uniquely artistic presentation from painted pictures by Ted Henkel.

FILM: "The Resurrection — First Easter," United World, 30 min., sd, b&w. Christ and angels portrayed by shadow. Quality not the best.

The resurrection of Christ is the cornerstone of the Christian faith, and it was understood to be such from the very earliest days of the Christian Church. In a careful study of the sermons delivered in the Book of Acts, one finds that the resurrection is dominant in almost every one of them. It occupies one-half of the first sermon recorded after the formation of the Church, preached by Peter on the Day of Pentecost. In his famous defenses, Paul argued the resurrection more than anything else. At the beginning of the 15th chapter of First Corinthians, he says that the two great facts of the Gospel are that Christ died for our sins, and that He rose again from the dead according to the Scriptures. Then he goes on to say that if Christ be not risen, our faith is vain, and we are yet in our sins. My own opinion is — and I am sure that many would sustain me in this — that the evidence for the bodily resurrection of Christ presented in the four Gospels is so definite, so detailed (in Matthew and John the testimony is that of eyewitnesses), so coherent when put together, that in spite of all the attacks of those who would deny the supernatural aspects of the Christian faith, no crack has been made in this fortress. There are many theories to explain away the empty tomb, and the appearances of Jesus, and the faith of the disciples, but the unbelieving world has never been able to agree on any one of these speculations. They vary from age to age, and when carefully examined, they are found to be without any rational justification. Furthermore, where is our hope? As the Apostle Peter said, Christians are born again by a living hope, through the reality of the resurrection of Christ from the dead.

I. **THE BURIAL OF JESUS,** John 19:41, 42. The entombment of our Lord is recorded in all four Gospels — Matthew 27:57–60; Mark 15:43–47; Luke 23:50–56, and here. In a textbook widely used in this country in some of the more liberal theological seminaries, entitled *Jesus,* by Guignebert, for years Professor of the History of Christianity in the Sorbonne, a rationalist who rejects the virgin birth, the miracles, the resurrection and the deity of our Lord, it is said that the body of Jesus was thrown into a ditch along with those of two criminals who were crucified with Him that day. In this way, Guignebert, who admits that all the disciples believed in the resurrection of Christ and because of it were able to preach

JOHN 20:1. Now on the first *day* of the week cometh Mary Magdalene early, while it was yet dark, unto the tomb, and seeth the stone taken away from the tomb.

11. But Mary was standing without at the tomb weeping: so, as she wept, she stooped and looked into the tomb;

12. and she beholdeth two angels in white sitting, one at the head, and one at the feet, where the body of Jesus had lain.

with convincing power, is able to escape the problem of the empty tomb. But no man in the 20th century, in Europe, in the United States, or any other place in the world, can tell anything about what happened in the first century of our era unless he has some documentary evidence. Guignebert has no reference to any literature to support his theory. There are four records of the burial of Jesus — and no others — and these are in the four Gospels, which unite in saying that the body of Christ was placed in the tomb of Joseph of Arimathaea in his private garden just outside the walls of Jerusalem. Do not let any man, however learned he might be, persuade you that we know anything about the burial of Jesus outside of the New Testament.

II. THE WITNESS OF THE EMPTY TOMB, John 20:1–10. 1. Now on the first *day* of the week cometh Mary Magdalene early, while it was yet dark, unto the tomb, and seeth the stone taken away from the tomb.

That the tomb in which the body of Jesus had been placed and then sealed and then watched by soldiers, was empty on Easter morning everyone admits, Christian or non-Christian, believer or unbeliever. The tomb could only become empty in one of two ways. Either the body of Jesus was carried out of the tomb by someone else or Jesus came out of the tomb Himself, living from the dead. The first of these interpretations is impossible because on the one hand, no one had any reason for taking out the body. On the other hand, soldiers were there to make sure this did not happen. Moreover, such a removal of the body of Jesus cannot explain His appearances in His resurrection body to His followers.

III. CHRIST APPEARS TO MARY MAGDALENE, John 20:11–18. There were ten appearances of the Lord Jesus (to his disciples, exclusively), during the forty days between Easter Sunday and the day of His ascension (Acts 1:3). On the appearance to James (1 Cor. 15:7) we have no details. Five of these appearances were on Easter Sunday, in the vicinity of Jerusalem; a sixth was also in Jerusalem, the following Sunday; two were in Galilee; and the last, the ascension, was on the Mount of Olives. Jesus first appeared to Mary Magdalene, who, no doubt a woman of wealth, had been delivered from the terrible affliction of demon-possession, and from that time to the end of Christ's ministry had, with the other women of Galilee, ministered to the apostolic company of their substance in food, etc. "She seems to have been the leader in this company of ministering women, as prominent among them as Peter was in the company of the Twelve. In the New Testament she is named fourteen times. The Roman Catholic Church, and some Protestant writers, have done a gross injustice to Mary by identifying her with the unchaste woman who anointed the feet of Jesus, until the word Magdalene has come to mean a woman of the streets. Magdalene identifies Mary with the village of Magdala on the western shore of the Sea of Galilee." While Mary Magdalene's visit to the tomb is also recorded in Luke 23:55—24:9, and Mark 16:5, the appearance of our Lord to her alone is recorded only by John the Evangelist, though from Matthew 28:9, 10, we learn that all the women, including Mary, returning from the tomb with the commission given to them by the angel, met the Lord. 11. But Mary was standing without at the tomb weeping: so, as she wept, she stooped and looked into the tomb; 12. and she beholdeth two angels in white sitting, one at the head, and one at the feet, where the body of Jesus had lain. The word used for describing the whiteness in the manifestation of the

13. And they say unto her, Woman, why weepest thou? She saith unto them, Because they have taken away my Lord, and I know not where they have laid him.

14. When she had thus said, she turned herself back, and beholdeth Jesus standing, and knew not that it was Jesus.

15. Jesus saith unto her, Woman, why weepest thou? whom seekest thou? She, supposing him to be the gardener, saith unto him, Sir, if thou hast borne him hence, tell me where thou hast laid him, and I will take him away.

---

angels may be compared with that in the description of Christ's raiment at the Transfiguration (Mark 9:3). "Such a radiance, or something like it, shone in that garden sepulchre, touching with light its rocky roof, and walls, and floor, and 'the linen cloths' as they lay there. There, before this weeping disciple, this once possessed and miserable woman, sat revealed those two inhabitants of the heavenly home. To reassure her, to tell her that it is no delusion generated by her glancing tears, they speak to her, perhaps one by one, in human words, and with gentle, I might almost say respectful sympathy: 'Woman, why do you weep?' 'Woman,' as all know, is a word of perfect courtesy, a word of as much possible respectfulness as *lord* would be in an address to a man."—*H. C. G. Moule.* **13. And they say unto her, Woman, why weepest thou? She saith unto them, Because they have taken away my Lord, and I know not where they have laid him.** "Here grief had had time to deepen, and to fix itself on the absorbing fact of the absence of Jesus. And such was the bitterness of that absence of the Body which (to her mind at that time) was so soon to be dust — such was the grief of its absence, because He was her Lord, that the sight of two Angels, and their audible voices, were to her, wonderfully yet naturally, as nothing."—*H. C. G. Moule.* **14. When she had thus said, she turned herself back, and beholdeth Jesus standing, and knew not that it was Jesus.** The incident of Mary's turning back and beholding Jesus, though she knew Him not, has given rise to a natural question, to which (I think) it is not necessary to devote a great deal of space — What made her turn to look? Did she hear someone walking, or did she feel His presence? It may be fantastic, but I do believe that occasionally, when we are in a crowded room and a person of great fame, a genius, someone of great achievements, enters, we are mysteriously sensitive to his presence, even though we do not see him as he comes into the room. This would be superbly true with Jesus. "Though essentially the same, He was to her now different. Partly, no doubt, it was simply a case of imperfect sight. She did not see Him full; perhaps she did not look in His face at all; and she was in tears. But also we have here, surely, one of the many cases (Matt. 28:17; Mark 16:13; Luke 24:16, 37; John 21:4) where we trace a change in the aspect of the Risen Saviour, and also that it was His pleasure sometimes not to be recognized, checking the message of the eyes to the mind. In passing I see here again an evidence of truth. A fabricated narrative would hardly have gone out of its way to say that the Risen One, after forty hours' absence, was at first not recognized. . . . *All* the Gospels record this inability of the disciples to recognize their Lord at once, and then go on to show how fully the doubt was removed. And how *permanently* it was removed!"—*H. C. G. Moule.* **15. Jesus saith unto her, Woman, why weepest thou? whom seekest thou? She, supposing him to be the gardener, saith unto him, Sir, if thou hast borne him hence, tell me where thou hast laid him, and I will take him away.** Do we not treat this text irreverently when we dwell for some length of time on the fact that she took the Lord Jesus to be the gardener? Of course Mary's statement was a foolish one, but to be expected from someone under extreme tension, or possibly fright; namely, that if this person would tell her where the body of Jesus was resting, she would take it away. To begin with, she could not carry away the body of a grown man, and,

16. Jesus saith unto her, Mary. She turneth herself, and saith unto him in Hebrew, Rabboni; which is to say, Teacher.

19. When therefore it was evening, on that day, the first *day* of the week, and when the doors were shut where the disciples were, for fear of the Jews, Jesus came and stood in the midst, and saith unto them, Peace *be* unto you.

---

secondly, there would be no reason for such removal. **16. Jesus saith unto her, Mary. She turneth herself, and saith unto him in Hebrew, Rabboni; which is to say, Teacher.** "We cannot doubt that there would be more of the old tenderness of Jesus in the pronunciation of her name than in the words as yet spoken to her. The very mark, indeed, of the relation between Jesus and His people, when that relation is conceived of in its most tender form, is that 'He calleth His own sheep by name' (10:3). . . . By the name, by the tone in which the name is uttered, a whole flood of recollections is brought up. All the deepest and most solemn impressions that had been produced upon her by her former intercourse with Jesus are reawakened in power." — *William Milligan.*

The 17th verse of this chapter is not assigned to the printed text, but inasmuch as it has troubled many people, I think it should have some attention. "What was the touching? Why was it forbidden? What was the connection (observe the 'for') between the 'Touch me not' and the 'I have not yet gone up to My Father'? . . . We observe that the Greek verb is in the present, or continuing, imperative. Accordingly, by familiar laws of Greek usage, it conveys an order not to forbear touching Him at all, but to forbear a longer, a prolonged touching. She is not to linger over it: it is enough; let her remove the hand which feels the sacred limb. The verb *touch* occurs only here in St. John. But its general usage assures us that it indicates here nothing like clasping, or clinging, as when the women (Matt. 28:9) 'held him by the feet.' It means no more than simple touching. It occurs, for example, where the Lord (Mark 8:22) is asked to 'touch' a blind man's eyes; and where the suffering woman (Matt. 9:21) plans to 'touch' just the fringe of His garment. Here Mary Magdalene may have just laid her hand, in felt contact and no more, on His foot, or on His hand; not clinging, not embracing, only feeling, as if to make certain that no vision, but the living Lord was there."— *H. C. G. Moule.* Mary Magdalene now becomes the first witness to the medium through which the truth of the resurrection is communicated to the disciples. At this time she passes off the stage of New Testament history, never to be referred to again. She was not an apostle, but she brought the message of the resurrection of Christ to the disciples. Mother, you may never stand in a pulpit or speak before an audience, but you can be the messenger to the children, communicating the truth of the resurrection, by which someday they may become apostles of the Lord.

IV. **THE TWO APPEARANCES TO THE DISCIPLES IN THE UPPER ROOM,** John 20:19–29. Since His early appearance to Mary, Christ has also appeared to a group of women near the tomb, to Simon Peter alone, and to the two disciples on the road to Emmaus. The disciples have returned to Jerusalem from Emmaus, as Luke tells us, and ten of them — Judas being dead and Thomas being absent — are gathered together in an upper room. For a parallel account, see Luke 24:36–49. **19. When therefore it was evening, on that day, the first *day* of the week, and when the doors were shut where the disciples were, for fear of the Jews, Jesus came and stood in the midst, and saith unto them, Peace *be* unto you.** "The plural 'doors' does not occur often; we may think of the outer door to the building itself, and of the inner door to the room in which the company was gathered. Having these doors locked was a measure of precaution; but here it is mentioned with reference to the appearance of Jesus." — *R. C. H. Lenski.* The modern rationalistic mind will ask how Christ could have come through these doors. Lenski's extended explanation of this is worth quoting in its entirety.

24. But Thomas, one of the twelve, called Didymus, was not with them when Jesus came.

25. The other disciples therefore said unto him, We have seen the Lord. But he said unto them, Except I shall see in his hands the print of the nails, and put my finger into the print of the nails, and put my hand into his side, I will not believe.

"Among the ridiculous ideas connected with these words are these: Jesus climbed up a ladder and through a window; or descended from the roof down a stairway; or (the moderns generally take the prize) sneaked into the house before the doors were locked; or slipped in when the two from Emmaus were let in; or was allowed to come in through the connivance of the doorkeeper. These all agree in denying a miracle. Others make the doors open up of themselves to let Jesus walk in; or they leave them locked while Jesus walks through them as if they were not there; or they have him walk right through the walls of the house and of the room. This is miracle indeed, but conceived in the crudest fashion. Acts 12:10 is useless in this connection, for the body of Peter was not in the same state as that of the risen Saviour. In his risen and glorified state time, space, the rock of the tomb, the walls and doors of buildings no longer hamper the body of Jesus. He appears where he desires to appear, and his visible presence is gone when he desires to have it so. This is wholly supernatural, to our minds wholly incomprehensible. Nor may we ask or seek to comprehend where Jesus stayed in the intervals between his appearances during the forty days. When eventually our bodies shall enter the heavenly mode of existence, we may know something of these supreme mysteries, but we doubt if even then we shall really comprehend the profundities of the divine omnipresence of which the human nature of Jesus partakes, and which he exercised since his vivification in the tomb, as in these wondrous appearances." — *R. C. H. Lenski.*

We are not able to locate any of the other appearances of our Lord during the week between Easter Sunday and the Sunday that followed, in the evening of which all the eleven were present in the same upper room when Jesus appeared. This was probably the room in which the Lord's Supper was instituted. **24. But Thomas, one of the twelve, called Didymus, was not with them when Jesus came. 25. The other disciples therefore said unto him, We have seen the Lord. But he said unto them, Except I shall see in his hands the print of the nails, and put my finger into the print of the nails, and put my hand into his side, I will not believe.** This passage has strongly appealed to me through the years, as a pastor, for it is a perfect illustration of how faithful members of a church may, by prayer and personal witnessing, bring back into the fellowship of the church, and its accompanying blessings, someone who has, for one reason or another, long absented himself from the house of God. No doubt the other disciples had spoken to Thomas often, *that week*, of the blessing they had received, of the promise of the Holy Spirit, and the new commission given them. Thomas is stubbornly skeptical here. "The word 'believe' must be understood in a fuller and deeper sense at verse 8, and the same remark applies to its use in verse 29. It includes, therefore, belief in Jesus as the glorified Lord, as the Redeemer who has completely accomplished the purpose of His mission, and in whom the highest hopes of Israel are fulfilled. To Thomas the death upon the cross had appeared to crush these hopes for ever. Could he be convinced of the Resurrection, they would revive; and he would believe not merely in that miracle as an isolated fact, but in the whole redeeming work of which it was the culmination and the seal. . . . His mood has been one of disappointment and sorrow; and the sorrow is deepened in exact proportion to the height of his previous expectations, and to what he knows will be the joyful result if he be able to believe the tidings of the Resurrection." — *W. F. Moulton.*

26. And after eight days again his disciples were within, and Thomas with them. Jesus cometh, the doors being shut, and stood in the midst, and said, Peace *be* unto you.

27. Then saith he to Thomas, Reach hither thy finger, and see my hands; and reach *hither* thy hand, and put it into my side: and be not faithless, but believing.

28. Thomas answered and said unto him, My Lord and my God.

29. Jesus saith unto him, Because thou hast seen me, thou hast believed: blessed *are* they that have not seen, and *yet* have believed.

---

26. And after eight days again his disciples were within, and Thomas with them. Jesus cometh, the doors being shut, and stood in the midst, and said, Peace *be* unto you. "The resurrection of Jesus had the effect of reuniting the disciples again, after his crucifixion had scattered them. The bond of their living Lord drew them together once more. We are not averse to thinking that they had been together already on the previous days." — *R. C. H. Lenski.* **27. Then saith he to Thomas, Reach hither thy finger, and see my hands; and reach *hither* thy hand, and put it into my side: and be not faithless, but believing.** The command, or, if one wishes to call it, invitation of Jesus to Thomas seems abrupt. No preceding conversation is recorded. Of course the Lord knew what had been in Thomas' mind, and his emphatic insistence upon certain evidence as he spoke to the disciples on previous occasions. "Somehow Thomas is present. We are left to think that the old association drew him back into the circle. Where else should he go? The others surely invited him to be with them. . . . The reason for this action of Jesus is fully warranted. He is offering to all these disciples 'many infallible proofs' of his resurrection (Acts 1:3) by no means for their personal faith only, which might have been won with far less, but as the foundation for the faith of the church of all future ages. They are made 'witnesses' of his resurrection (Acts 2:32; 3:15) in the fullest possible sense of the word, 'witnesses' whose testimony was to stand as unassailable in all future ages." — *R. C. H. Lenski.* It is not said that Thomas even accepted the Lord's invitation; it is generally thought that he did not, though Moule says he probably did. **28. Thomas answered and said unto him, My Lord and my God.** " 'My God' — words impossible to explain away, for they were addressed obviously to Jesus direct, and they meant no less than proper Godhead, for they were uttered by an Israelite. So Thomas confessed Him, and received Him. Doubt was gone, reserve broken, the soul quite released from the sullen wish to keep its old isolated position in sorrowful pride. He is one with his brethren now, and they shall know it; for he has found in Jesus Risen all his desire, all his joy. It is no unique case. How often the most positive denials have been exchanged for the very simplest faith!"—*H. C. G. Moule.* No generation since the ascension of Jesus has had the opportunity that Thomas had this night, but on the testimony of the apostles every generation has rested its faith, and in the concluding verse of this scene, our Lord is thinking of all the millions that would come after, and bestows upon them a benediction. **29. Jesus saith unto him, Because thou hast seen me, thou hast believed: blessed *are* they that have not seen, and *yet* have believed.** "In the ages of the Church which were to follow the 'going away' of Jesus, it was needful that faith should rest first upon testimony; but it was not to pause there. It was to rest upon the spiritual apprehension of that to which testimony is borne — of that which the Lord is in Himself as the embodiment of the Divine, and the unchanging spring of the heavenly power and grace which are manifested in His people. Thus to us, who are separated by many centuries from the time when the Lord was personally present in the world, is the blessed assurance given that, though we have not seen Him, we may love Him; and that, though now we see Him not, we may rejoice in Him with a joy unspeakable and glorified (1 Pet. 1:8)." — *W. F. Moulton.*

JOHN 21:15. So when they had broken their fast, Jesus saith to Simon Peter, Simon, *son* of John, lovest thou me more than these? He saith unto him, Yea, Lord; thou knowest that I love thee. He saith unto him, Feed my lambs.

16. He saith to him again a second time, Simon, *son* of John, lovest thou me? He saith unto him, Yea, Lord; thou knowest that I love thee. He saith unto him, Tend my sheep.

17. He saith unto him the third time, Simon, *son* of John, lovest thou me? Peter was grieved because he said unto him the third time, Lovest thou me? And he said unto him, Lord, thou knowest all things; thou knowest that I love thee. Jesus saith unto him, Feed my sheep.

V. CHRIST APPEARS TO THE DISCIPLES AT THE SEA OF GALILEE,

John 21. In the account of Jesus' resurrection in Matthew's Gospel, we read that Jesus told the women who had come to the tomb on Easter morning, "Go tell my brethren that they go into Galilee and there shall they see me" (28:10). While the first appearances of Jesus did not take place in Galilee, He is now in that area and the disciples are likewise there, though probably not to meet Christ — at least there is no hint of it in this chapter. The entire chapter may be said to bear upon the subject of service, and nothing could be more timely than this, for our Lord is about to ascend into heaven, and the disciples will be left on earth for the great work of founding the Church. We have here an example of service without results, then, Christ being present, service with abundant results. The need for a love for Christ is emphasized, followed by specific directions from their Lord regarding the work of the apostles. Professor Swete aptly says, "One asks oneself with what purpose Peter and his party returned to their nets: whether it was merely to provide themselves with a meal, or whether with the intention of resuming their old life. Had they forgotten the great work opened before them by the commission received on Easter night? or had they never realized its meaning? No doubt it was a time of waiting, of uncertainty, even of suspense; nearly a fortnight had passed since the Resurrection, and no plans had yet been formed for the future. It may have been that a crisis was near; a little further delay, and Peter and the rest might have once more become mere fishermen. But this danger had not been overlooked; the Good Shepherd had gone before His sheep and interposed His guidance at the moment when it was needed."

15. So when they had broken their fast, Jesus saith to Simon Peter, Simon, *son* of John, lovest thou me more than these? He saith unto him, Yea, Lord; thou knowest that I love thee. He saith unto him, Feed my lambs. 16. He saith to him again a second time, Simon, *son* of John, lovest thou me? He saith unto him, Yea, Lord; thou knowest that I love thee. He saith unto him, Tend my sheep. 17. He saith unto him the third time, Simon, *son* of John, lovest thou me? Peter was grieved because he said unto him the third time, Lovest thou me? And he said unto him, Lord, thou knowest all things; thou knowest that I love thee. Jesus saith unto him, Feed my sheep. With the episode of the night's fishing, and of Jesus' preparing breakfast for the hungry men, we need not tarry. However, the command of Christ to feed His sheep needs consideration. "The three charges are progressive, and include the whole duty of the pastoral office: a duty which extends both to the young and immature, and to the older and riper members of the flock; which embraces both the feeding of all with food convenient for them, and the guidance and government of the entire Church. So the Chief Shepherd of the sheep commits to the care of the disciple who professed to love Him the pastoral work, which by his fall he had forfeited. Simon is readmitted to this apostolate, and at the same time provided with a vast field of labour in

which he must demonstrate his love till his life's end. For the sheep are not Peter's, but Christ's; and he must feed them because they are Christ's and for Christ's sake, because he loves Christ. What the end will be, he is warned; it will be no visible reward for his work, but on the contrary, a final and severest test of the sincerity of his devotion. . . . It was no concern of Peter to know how He would deal with another of His servants; if John were called to live to the end of the age, that would not touch the question of Peter's career or of his duty." —*H. B. Swete.*

THE LESSON IN LIFE, LITERATURE, AND ARCHAEOLOGY.

Dr. Clarence Edward Macartney in his superb chapter on that great blind preacher of Virginia, James Waddel, begins with the following paragraph:

"In a rude meeting-house in Southeastern Virginia, not far from the sea, the preacher had taken for his text the words of Christ to Peter, 'Simon, son of Jonas, lovest thou me?' In the midst of his sermon he put the inquiry, 'And what does Peter say?' With that, an old sailor, whose name was Peter, supposing the preacher had spoken to him, arose from his seat, and with tears running down his storm-beaten face, replied, 'Lord, thou knowest all things. Thou knowest that I love thee!' This is one of the many traditions still current about the marvellous eloquence of James Waddel."

A TRUTH FOR THE CLASS TO CARRY AWAY.

We may well call the resurrection of Christ the cornerstone of our faith. Paul said to the Athenians that by this resurrection God has assured us there will be a judgment to come. At the beginning of his Epistle to the Romans, he tells us that here is one of the great proofs of Christ's deity. Simon Peter at the beginning of his epistle tells us that by the resurrection of Christ we are begotten unto a living hope. Whatever be the mysteries of Christ's life and teaching, when we are convinced of His resurrection, we are assured of the truthfulness of all He ever said.

Why were the appearances of Christ after the resurrection only to His followers? How many different factors in this lesson assure us of the historical reality of Christ's resurrection? As a result of the resurrection, are the admonitions here those that lead to dreaming or to action? Do you find anything silly or ridiculous in this narrative? (Absolutely nothing.) What are the factors in this lesson which make impossible the theory that these disciples only saw a vision?

LESSON IV. — April 25.

AHIJAH FORESEES A DIVIDED KINGDOM. —
1 Kings 11:1—12:24.
PRINTED TEXT, 1 Kings 11:28-38.

Devotional Reading: Psalm 1.

Beginner Topic: GOD'S PLEASANT DARK.

    Lesson Material: Genesis 1:14–17; Job 9:1–10; Psalm 8; 19:1–4; Psalm 139:1–12; 147:4.

    Memory Verse: Jehovah . . . giveth the sun for a light by day. *He made* the stars also. Jer. 31:35; Gen. 1:16.

Primary Topic: TEN PIECES OF CLOTH.

    Lesson Material: 1 Kings 11:28–38.

    Memory Verse: If thou wilt hearken unto all that I command thee . . . I will be with thee. 1 Kings 11:38.

Junior Topic: TEN PIECES OF CLOTH.

    Lesson Material: 1 Kings 11:28–38.

    Memory Verse: If thou wilt hearken unto all that I command thee . . . I will be with thee. 1 Kings 11:38.

147

Intermediate-Senior Topic: A PROPHET ENCOURAGES REVOLT.
  Lesson Material: 1 Kings 11:28–38.
  Memory Verse: If thou wilt hearken unto all that I command thee, and wilt walk in my ways . . . I will be with thee, and will build thee a sure house. 1 Kings 11:38.
Topic for Young People and Adults: AHIJAH FORESEES A DIVIDED KINGDOM.
  Lesson Material: 1 Kings 11:1—12:24.
  Memory Verse: If thou wilt hearken unto all that I command thee, and wilt walk in my ways . . . I will be with thee, and will build thee a sure house. 1 Kings 11:38.

THE TEACHER AND HIS CLASS.

The Younger Classes may be asked, as an introduction to the lesson, to give the full title of our country. The pupils will no doubt immediately reply, The United States of America. It is interesting to note how many great groups of people today are collectively known by a title containing the word "United," or "Union." There is, for example, the Union of South Africa, which includes Transvaal, Cape Colony, Natal and the Orange Free State; and the Union of Soviet Socialist Republics, the United Nations, etc. Our lesson concerns the *united* nation of Israel, composed of the twelve tribes, each descending from one of the sons of Jacob, and records the tragedy of the breakup of this union, at which time ten nations formed one group, and two the other. The original union was never restored.

The Older Classes might be introduced to this lesson by an illustration of the tremendous influence of one outstanding character in an hour of great crisis, either for good or evil. An example would be that of Marshal Foch's effective leadership during the First World War, at a time when the Allies had almost lost hope of a real victory, and the revival of hope that came during the Second World War when Field Marshal Montgomery was sent to North Africa. The very night he arrived there swept through the weary, disheartened British troops a conviction that perhaps now the war could be won. Our lesson is an unfolding of the tragedies that came to a great people because of the weakness, the selfishness, and the sinfulness of two of the leaders. For the first time in decades, we have here the appearance of a true prophet from God.

THE LESSON IN ITS SETTING.

Time. — The reign of King Solomon is generally placed at 970 to 931 B.C.; of Rehoboam, from 931 to 914 B.C., and of Jeroboam, from 931 to 911 B.C.

Place. — The three principal locations of our lesson are Jerusalem, the capital of Israel when united, and of Judah when the kingdom was divided; Shechem, otherwise known as Nablus or Samaria; and Bethel, five miles northeast of Jerusalem.

THE PLAN OF THE LESSON.

SUBJECT: How the Prophecy of Coming Division in the Kingdom of Israel Was Fulfilled and Some of the Circumstances That Brought About This Fulfillment.

I. THE TRAGIC CLOSE OF SOLOMON'S REIGN AS KING, 1 Kings 11:1–25.
  1. His sensuality and compromise with idolatry, vs. 1–8.
  2. The divine announcement of the national consequences of Solomon's disobedience, vs. 9–13.
  3. Two disturbing episodes occurring at this time, vs. 14–25.
II. THE PROPHETIC MINISTRY OF AHIJAH, 11:26–38.
  1. The early labors of Jeroboam, vs. 26–28.
  2. Ahijah's prophetic act, vs. 29, 30.
  3. Ahijah's prophetic words, vs. 31–39.
III. THE DEATH OF SOLOMON, 11:40–43.
IV. THE PROPHECY REGARDING A DIVIDED KINGDOM IS FULFILLED, 12:1–24.

THE TEACHER'S LIBRARY.

For the study of this lesson the best commentaries are *The Pulpit Commentary;* Alfred Barry

148

in the *Bible Commentary for English Readers*, and F. W. Farrar in *The Expositor's Bible*. There are relevant chapters in the volume on the First Book of Kings in the *Devotional Commentary* series; all histories of Israel will have valuable pages on this lesson, a list of which may be found in the bibliographies in the introduction to this volume.

Though my library is fairly complete in Biblical biographies, I have not been able to find a single chapter devoted to the principal subject of our lesson today, Ahijah. Chapters on Jeroboam, however, will be helpful on parts of our lesson, especially that in Alexander Whyte: *Bible Characters, Ahithophel to Nehemiah*, 54–63, and by Alfred Rowland in *Men of the Bible, Some Lesser Known Characters*, 76–87. Of course all volumes on Solomon will have some material on the opening part of the lesson, particularly the work by F. W. Farrar

in the *Men of the Bible* series, and the seldom-seen volume by Thomas Kirk: *Solomon, His Life and Works*. There is a good chapter on "The Rending of the Kingdom" in F. D. Maurice: *The Prophets and Kings of the Old Testament*, pp. 90–107.

On the printed text itself, I have come upon only one sermon worthy of note here, and that is Alexander Maclaren: *Expositions of Holy Scripture, 2 Samuel and the Books of Kings*, 209–215. On some verses of our lesson there is an interesting sermon by John Hutton in his book, *The Fear of Things*, 124–138, entitled "The Love of God in the Embarrassments of Our Life."

AUDIO-VISUAL AIDS.

No audio-visual aids discovered.

We begin this new quarter of lessons as the greatness and glory of a united Israel is about to pass away. Three kings ruled over this united kingdom: Saul, whose life was terminated by suicide, at the time of the shameful victory of the Philistines on Mount Gilboa; David, who reigned forty years; and Solomon, whose wisdom and vast building enterprises made his name famous throughout the entire world of that day. Our study today has to do, first of all, with the tragic closing days of Solomon's reign. What a vast chasm separates this period from those opening days, when Solomon was often in prayer and in fellowship with God, and the whole nation was joyfully engaged in the erection of the Temple which bore the king's name.

I. **THE TRAGIC CLOSE OF SOLOMON'S REIGN AS KING,** 1 Kings 11:1–25. In the preceding chapter (vs. 23, 24) we read that "Solomon exceeded all the kings of the earth in riches, and in all wisdom, and all the earth sought the presence of Solomon to hear his wisdom which God had put in his heart." But the next verse tells us that Solomon had gathered together 1400 chariots and 12,000 horsemen, with horses for their use. Along with this extravagance and self-indulgence, Solomon brought into his harem 700 wives and 300 concubines. This in itself is a terrible indictment of Solomon, who, in his old age, had become exceedingly lascivious and sensuous. Moreover, many of these women were from the pagan, idolatrous nations round about, and brought with them their false gods, and the accompanying oriental immoralities, including no doubt scores, if not hundreds of priests of these abominable deities. As a result Solomon was even persuaded to erect high places and altars in the city of Jerusalem, that the filthy worship of these gods could be carried on. "There was not room for much morality in his huge harem. We cannot, of course, judge that incident by the standard of our own times; but it will not bear criticism in the light of his own times and immediate environment. There had never been anything approaching to it in Israel before. It had its origin, perhaps, in a desire to have everything on a huge and extravagant scale, proportioned to his greatness; but it was also not free from gross Eastern sensuality. . . . And so it came to pass that the man who had commenced with such noble resolves, shaping his future with the religious colors of an almost inspired dream, finished in the misery of a foolish dream, finished in the misery of a foolish and godless evening time. It is not an edifying story. The writer of the book of Ecclesiastes has apparently Solomon, the great king, in mind when he pictures a man who has tried all the good things of the world, and all the pleasurable things, and is utterly dissatisfied with them all, and with life itself — wisdom and knowledge, wealth and fame, music, women, and wine, and all the desires of the sons of men. He has tried to fill his life with these, and they have failed him. The cup has run dry, and life is empty and stale, and utterly wearying; and all is vanity and vexation of spirit, because in the main God has been left out." — *J. G. Greenhough.*

149

We remember that the historian's account of David's great sin with Bathsheba ends with this sentence, "David sent and took her home to his house and she became his wife and bear him a son, *but* the thing that David had done displeased Jehovah" (2 Samuel 11:27).   So here also we read that "Jehovah was angry with Solomon because his heart was turned away from Jehovah who had appeared unto him twice."   God was not intervening at this time in the lives of the kings of the pagan nations, such as Moab, Ammon, Edom, and the Hittites, for they were not God's children, and did not know Him.   They had not turned their backs on God, for they had never worshipped the true God.   But Solomon had been given this throne by God.   He had received wisdom, wealth, health, and forgiveness from God.   He had known God to answer his prayers, and had seen the smile of God upon his work.   He may turn his back on God, but God is not through dealing with him.   The Lord announces to him that because of these sins, and the breaking of the covenant, He would rend the kingdom from him upon his death, not during his lifetime, "for David my servant's sake, and for Jerusalem's sake which I have chosen."   I wonder what Solomon thought in his own heart when God finished speaking with him.   There is not the slightest hint here that he ever repented of his sins.   In one of his brilliant sermons, John Hutton says, "There is something very terrible in the way the Bible dismisses a man once he has had his chance and has failed.   Once God has given a man or a nation the chance of doing something, and the man or the nation has not done it, but has simply settled down to have a good time, I want you to notice how the Bible seems to give up that man or nation, as though it were saying, 'Come, let us hurry on, nothing more is to be looked for from that one. . . .'   It is one of the disastrous effects of time that it dries up this moisture of the soul, and brings us more and more under the bondage of law and custom.   Less and less are we masters of ourselves.   More and more do we become the victims of ourselves.   We have trained ourselves *not* to yield to the pure uprisings of the spirit, with the consequence that such uprisings do not easily take place within us." — *John Hutton*.   Before the division of the kingdom, the record tells us that two adversaries were raised up by God himself to plague Solomon in his last days.   One of these was Hadad the Edomite, who fled into Egypt and there found great favor with the ruling Pharaoh, marrying the king's own sister.   Just how this man troubled Solomon we are not told.   The other adversary was Rezon, who had earlier caused some uprising in the reign of Solomon (see 1 Kings 11:23) and now established an independent power in Damascus, which Solomon was too weak to prevent.

II. **THE PROPHETIC MINISTRY OF AHIJAH,** 1 Kings 11:26–38.   While the opposition of Hadad the Edomite, and Rezon, no doubt was a source of trouble, and also humiliation to the now weak and sin-chained Solomon, it was of minor importance compared to the activities of a man who now appears, Jeroboam, son of Nebat, who was to be the first ruler of the Northern Kingdom, when division takes place.   Of his parentage, we know only what verse 26 tells us, and of the rebellion here hinted at we know nothing further.   "That this attempt against Solomon should have been made shows how little Jeroboam was influenced by religious motives.   He stretched out a rash, self-willed hand to snatch the promised crown, and broke God's commandment even while he pretended to be keeping it. How different David's conduct in like circumstances!   David took no steps to bring about the fulfillment of Samuel's promise and his anointing, but patiently waited for God to do as he had said, in his own time, and meantime continued his lowly work.   God's time is the best time, and he who greedily grasps at a mature fulfillment of promised good will have to pay for it by defeat and exile from the modest good that he had." — *Alexander Maclaren*.   In spite of his previous rebellion against the king, he was given charge of a large group of laboring men. **28. And the man Jeroboam was a mighty man of valor; and Solomon saw the young man that he was industrious, and he gave him charge over all the labor of the house of Joseph.**   "The labor here spoken of is that compulsory work which the Israelites did by turns for parts of the year, and which the tributary subject-

1 Kings 11:28. And the man Jeroboam was a mighty man of valor; and Solomon saw the young man that he was industrious, and he gave him charge over all the labor of the house of Joseph.

29. And it came to pass at that time, when Jeroboam went out of Jerusalem, that the prophet Ahijah the Shilonite found him in the way; now *Ahijah* had clad himself with a new garment; and they two were alone in the field.

---

population were constantly employed upon. It is not difficult to conceive circumstances under which such duty might become very distasteful to the northern section of the kingdom. For between them and the people of Judah there was a pronounced opposition even in David's time. The compulsory labor on the walls of Jerusalem was just the sort of occupation to aggravate this old enmity. Jeroboam saw this, and took advantage of it." — *J. R. Lumby.* "Jeroboam's outstanding talents in public affairs, his skillful management of men, his great industry, and his great loyalty, as was thought, all combined to bring the son of Nebat under Solomon's royal eye, till there was no trust too important and no promotion too high for young Jeroboam. And then, to crown it all, as time went on, Satan more and more entered into Jeroboam's heart. And Jeroboam allowed Satan in his heart, and listened to Satan speaking in his heart. 'You are a greatly talented man. There is no other man in all the land fit to be your equal. Solomon is old, and his son is a fool. And who is to be king after Solomon dies? Thinkest thou ever who is fit to be king? Saul was but the son of Kish. David himself was but the son of Jesse. There has never been, and there never will be, respect of persons with the God of Israel. Jeroboam, you love your widowed mother. Play the man, then, but a little longer, and your mother will live to hear the cry of the people before she dies, this so sweet cry to her ears, "Long live King Jeroboam!"' And Jeroboam kept all these things and pondered them in his heart." — *Alexander Whyte.*

There now appears, for the first time in generations, a prophet in Israel. "The prophets had sunk to silence before the oracular autocrat who so frequently impressed on the people that there is 'a Divine sentence on the lips of kings.' No special inspiration seemed to be needed either to correct or to corroborate so infallible a wisdom. . . . What were the priests doing in the face of so fearful an apostasy? Apparently nothing. They seem to have sunk into comfortable acquiescence, satisfied with the augmentation of rank and revenue which the Temple and its offerings brought to them. . . . Nathan probably had died long before Solomon reached his zenith. Of Iddo we know almost nothing. Two prophets are mentioned, but only towards the close of the reign — Ahijah of Shiloh, and Shemaiah. . . . But the hour had now struck for a prophet to speak the word of the Lord. If the king, surrounded by formidable guards and a glittering court was too exalted to be reached by a humble son of the people, it was time for Ahijah to follow the precedent of Samuel. He obeyed a divine intimation in selecting the successor who should punish the great king's rebellion against God, and inaugurate a rule of purer obedience than now existed under the upas-shadow of the throne." — *F. W. Farrar.* There are three men in the Old Testament who bear the name of Ahijah. The first was the high priest in the reign of Saul, and generally identified with Ahimelech, who accompanied Saul's army as possessor of the ephod oracle (see 1 Samuel 14:3; 23:9; 30:7, etc.); the second, noted in 1 Kings 4:3, was a scribe, or secretary, of Solomon; and the third is the prophet appearing in this lesson, referred to in no other book of the Old Testament. **29. And it came to pass at that time, when Jeroboam went out of Jerusalem, that the prophet Ahijah the Shilonite found him in the way; now *Ahijah* had clad himself with a new garment; and they two were alone in the field.** "We find in Ahijah the first of the line of prophets who resumed a paramount influence like that of Samuel or Nathan, pro-

30. And Ahijah laid hold of the new garment that was on him, and rent it in twelve pieces.

31. And he said to Jeroboam, Take thee ten pieces; for thus saith Jehovah, the God of Israel, Behold, I will rend the kingdom out of the hand of Solomon, and will give ten tribes to thee.

32. (But he shall have one tribe, for my servant David's sake, and for Jerusalem's sake, the city which I have chosen out of all the tribes of Israel);

33. Because that they have forsaken me, and have worshipped Ashtoreth the goddess of the Sidonians, Chemosh the god of Moab, and Milcom the god of the children of Ammon; and they have not walked in my ways, to do that which is right in mine eyes, and *to keep* my statutes and mine ordinances, as did David his father.

tecting the spirituality of the land and the worship of God, and demanding both from king and people submission to the authority of the Lord Jehovah." — *Alfred Barry.* 30. And Ahijah laid hold of the new garment that was on him, and rent it in twelve pieces. 31. And he said to Jeroboam, Take thee ten pieces; for thus saith Jehovah, the God of Israel, Behold, I will rend the kingdom out of the hand of Solomon, and will give ten tribes to thee. "The use of symbolical acts is frequent in subsequent prophecy (especially see Jer. 13:1; 19:1; 27:2; Ezek. 4; 5; 12:1–7; 24:3, 15) often alternating with symbolical visions and symbolical parables or allegories. The object is, of course, to arrest attention, and call our inquiry (Ezek. 14:19): 'Wilt thou not tell us what these things are to us?' Ahijah's rending of his own new garment is used, like Saul's rending of Samuel's mantle (1 Sam. 15:27, 28) to symbolise the rending away of the kingdom. The message delivered by Ahijah first repeats exactly the former warning to Solomon (vs. 9–13) marking, by the two reserved pieces of the garment, the duality of the 'one tribe' reserved for the house of David; next, it conveys to Jeroboam a promise like that given to David (so far as it was a temporal promise) 'to build thee a sure house, as I built for David,' on condition of the obedience which David, with all his weakness and sin, had shown, and from which Solomon, in spite of all his wisdom, had fallen away; and lastly, declares in accordance with the famous declaration of 2 Samuel 7:14–16, that sin in the house of David should bring with it severe chastisement, but not final rejection. In estimating the 'sin of Jeroboam,' the existence of this promise of security and blessing to his kingdom must be always taken into consideration." — *Alfred Barry.* 32. (But he shall have one tribe, for my servant David's sake, and for Jerusalem's sake, the city which I have chosen out of all the tribes of Israel); 33. Because that they have forsaken me, and have worshipped Ashtoreth the goddess of the Sidonians, Chemosh the god of Moab, and Milcom the god of the children of Ammon; and they have not walked in my ways, to do that which is right in mine eyes, and *to keep* my statutes and mine ordinances, as did David his father. The idolatrous conditions prevailing in Jerusalem during the latter days of Solomon, as recorded in verses 5 and 7 of our chapter, are reiterated here in the prophet's pronouncement of judgment. "Ashtoreth was the goddess of the Zidonians, and possibly the Hittites, corresponding to Baal, the great Tyrian god, and representing the receptive and productive, as Baal the active and originative, power in Nature. As usual in all phases of Nature-worship, Ashtoreth is variously represented, sometimes by the moon, sometimes by the planet Venus. . . . Milcom is probably a variety of the word *Molech*, meaning king, or lord. The worship of 'Molech' with its horrible sacrifice of children, 'passing through the fire' is forbidden in Leviticus 18:21; 20:2, evidently as prevailing among the Canaanite races (compare Ps. 106:37, 38). . . . By comparison of Jeremiah 7:31; 19:5, 6, it is very evident that this human sacrifice to Molech is

34. Howbeit I will not take the whole kingdom out of his hand; but I will make him prince all the days of his life, for David my servant's sake whom I chose, who kept my commandments and my statutes:

35. But I will take the kingdom out of his son's hand, and will give it unto thee, even ten tribes.

36. And unto his son will I give one tribe, that David my servant may have a lamp alway before me in Jerusalem, the city which I have chosen me to put my name there.

37. And I will take thee, and thou shalt reign according to all that thy soul desireth, and shalt be king over Israel.

38. And it shall be, if thou wilt hearken unto all that I command thee, and wilt walk in my ways, and do that which is right in mine eyes, to keep my statutes and my commandments, as David my servant did; that I will be with thee, and will build thee a sure house, as I built for David, and will give Israel unto thee.

---

also called 'a burnt-offering to Baal'; and if Molech was the fire-god, and Baal the sun-god, the two deities might easily be regarded as cognate, if not identical. Chemosh, probably meaning *conqueror*, indicates a god of battles. He is again and again described as the god of the Moabites, who are called 'the people of Chemosh (see Num. 21:29; Jer. 48:7, 13, 46); and the Moabite Stone speaks of the slain in war as an offering to Chemosh, and even refers to a deity, 'Ashtar-Chemosh' which looks like a conjunction of Chemosh, like Baal with Ashtoreth." — *Alfred Barry*. 34. **Howbeit I will not take the whole kingdom out of his hand; but I will make him prince all the days of his life, for David my servant's sake whom I chose, who kept my commandments and my statutes; 35. but I will take the kingdom out of his son's hand, and will give it unto thee, even ten tribes. 36. And unto his son will I give one tribe, that David my servant may have a lamp alway before me in Jerusalem, the city which I have chosen me to put my name there.** "By the postponement of the chastisement, the blessing promised to his son personally would be still preserved; by the retaining of the kingdom, though shorn of its splendour, and limited to Judah, the larger and more important promise, the continuance of the family of David till the coming of the Messiah, would be fulfilled. The 'one tribe' is, of course, Judah, with which Benjamin was indissolubly united by the very position of the capital on its frontier." — *Alfred Barry*. The figure of speech, "that David my servant may have a lamp before me in Jerusalem," represents an oriental idea. "In the tent was hung the lamp, for constant lighting, and the permanency of the home is implied in the lamp which is not extinguished (compare Ps. 132:17). David's line was to last, though most of the kingdom was taken from his descendants." — *J. R. Lumby*. 37. **And I will take thee, and thou shalt reign according to all that thy soul desireth, and shalt be king over Israel.** 38. **And it shall be, if thou wilt hearken unto all that I command thee, and wilt walk in my ways, and do that which is right in mine eyes, to keep my statutes and my commandments, as David my servant did; that I will be with thee, and will build thee a sure house, as I built for David, and will give Israel unto thee.** The condescension, the grace, the longsuffering of God is here clearly set forth. God speaks more tenderly and hopefully to Jeroboam, who will be the king of Israel, than he does to Solomon who is now about to die. No doubt the reason is that Solomon had been the recipient of an infinite number of mercies, gifts, and honors from God, but in spite of all this, he turned his back on Jehovah and allowed to flourish in the holy city all this vice and idolatry; but Jeroboam, at the threshold of his reign, is still one of God's chosen people, and the Lord would have him to know that obedience on his part, walking in the will of God, would be

recognized not only by heaven, but would be rewarded in the permanent establishment of his seed upon the throne of the Northern Kingdom. But Jeroboam did
not meet the requirements of God, and with the reign of Nadab his dynasty was
terminated, and no other descendant of his ever sat upon the throne of Israel.
(See the conclusion of the lesson for May 2.)

III. **THE DEATH OF SOLOMON,** 1 Kings 11:40–43. In this passage is one
of the ever-fascinating statements regarding a literature of the people of Israel
that has been lost. The reference here is to "the books of the acts of Solomon."
We know nothing of its contents. "So Solomon passed away — the last king of
all Palestine till another king arose a thousand years later, like him in his fondness
for magnificence, like him in his tamperings with idolatry, like him in being builder
of the Temple, but in all other respects a far more grievous sinner and a far more
inexcusable tyrant — Herod, falsely called 'The Great.' " — *F. W. Farrar.*

IV. **THE PROPHECY REGARDING A DIVIDED KINGDOM FULFILLED,**
1 Kings 12:1–24. The opening verses of this chapter (paralleled in 2 Chron.
11:1–15), take us somewhat by surprise. Why should Rehoboam, Solomon's son,
go to *Shechem* to be crowned king? The text does not say. Shechem, referred
to previously as Sichem (in Genesis 12:6), located in the hill country of Ephraim,
was on the site of the modern Nablus. "It seems not improbable that the arrangement for this gathering at Shechem was a sort of protest by the men of the north
against the southern tribes, who, because Jerusalem, with the temple and the royal
dwellings was in their part of the land, may have claimed to be the ruling portion
of the nation." — *J. R. Lumby.*

The circumstances surrounding the division of the kingdom are familiar to all.
The words of Dr. Elmer W. Mould will be adequate in reviewing the narrative.
"The people of northern Israel tolerated Solomon with what grace they could so
long as he lived. With his death they felt the hour had come to seek redress
of their grievances. They meant to have at the very outset an understanding with
Rehoboam as to what rights they were to be allowed and how heavily they were
to be taxed. Therefore, when he came to Shechem to be made king by Israel,
they presented their petition. It was one of the truly great occasions of history,
when human liberties have been asserted in the face of tyranny. Rehoboam
prudently asked for time to consider the request. He took counsel first with the
old men. These were doubtless men who remembered the days before David had
assumed that autocratic attitude which developed to such an offensive degree under
Solomon. These older men knew that the king was the creature of the people,
for it had been a popular demand that led to the institution of the kingdom in
the first instance. . . . The elders, therefore, advised the king to grant the
people's demands. But from these experienced elders Rehoboam turned to the
young habituees of the court, who, like himself, had grown up amid the luxury of
Solomon's display, and had imbibed the autocratic spirit of the monarch. Their
idea of the kingship was that of an oriental despotism, which assumes that the
common people exist only to serve the monarch and have no inherent rights which
the monarch is bound to respect. What the young men advised the new king to do
was probably what he intended to do anyhow, and he therefore refused the people's
petition in words that can scarcely be surpassed for impudence and brutality. . . .
Undoubtedly the most active immediate cause of the disruption was the discontent
of the people over excessive taxation and forced labor. The heavy burden of
expense laid upon the people because of Solomon's enormous harem, his elaborate
and luxurious court, and his pretentious building enterprises was more than his
little kingdom could finance. He virtually reduced his fellow countrymen to the
status of serfs and they were forced to serve in the royal labor gangs in the Leba-
nons." When all Israel saw that the king refused to grant them their just request,
her representatives departed from the conference and left Rehoboam with an area
to rule over no larger than that with which David began upon the death of Saul.
The twelve tribes are here on the verge of a civil war, for Rehoboam, returning to
Jerusalem, gathered together an army of a hundred and eighty thousand men, to

go up against the Northern Kingdom. But God send word to him through Shemaiah that he was not to proceed with this plan, and that every man should return to his house. On this one occasion the king hearkened to the word of God.

A passage from the famous volume, *The Prophets and Kings of the Old Testament*, by Frederick Denison Maurice, may be used in closing this lesson.

"The schism of rival popes in the Western Church during the fifteenth century was as great a scandal to Christendom as can be conceived. Yet it was surely from the Lord. It led men to perceive that there was corruption in the head and in the members of the ecclesiastical polity; it led to those disputes respecting the relative powers of popes and councils, which showed that neither could heal the wounds of the Church or preserve its unity. It led to that movement in the sixteenth century, which we all, I trust, believe to have been from the Lord, and which was really a declaration of faith in a living God, against a system of idolatry, that was rapidly passing into a system of organized unbelief."

"O brethren! how intolerable would be these facts and recollections, which show every party in Church and State to have been the cause of shameful scandals, which forbid us to cast stones at others because we are in the same sin, if we might not recur again and again to the words which I have quoted so often. But if the thing is of the Lord, there must be an end of all those strifes by which He has ordained that our idolatries against Him and cruelties to our brethren should punish themselves. There must be a day when all things in heaven and earth which consist only by Christ shall be gathered manifestly together in Him, when it shall be known and confessed that there is one king, one priest, one sacrifice; that we have been at war with each other, because we have not done homage to that one king, drawn nigh to God through that one priest, omitted to present that one perfect sacrifice."

THE LESSON IN LIFE, LITERATURE, AND ARCHAEOLOGY.

It is strange how the deflection of Solomon even now has been used for the justification of polygamy. The great archaeologist, Professor Sayce visiting Egypt in 1891 tells the following story:

"Tewfik Pasha was the best ruler the Egyptians had ever had, and consequently, like Louis XVI in France, was called upon to suffer for the sins of his forefathers. He was the reverse of a genius, it is true, but he was that rare phenomenon among oriental princes, an unselfish man, and at the same time he was both devout and moral — two qualities which do not always coincide, more especially in Mohammedan countries. He set a good example to his subjects in the matter of family relations; there was no *harem*, much less a second wife. Keiley, the American judge in the Mixed Tribunal, who had fought on the Confederate side during the Civil War, but afterwards became the most loyal of Americans, introduced his wife, who was a Jewess, to the Khedive one evening when a ball was given at the palace. The Khedive asked her how she liked Egypt. 'Very much, your Highness,' she answered, 'except in one thing; I don't approve of your polygamy.' 'I do not approve of it either, Mrs. Keiley,' was the Khedive's reply, 'and, as you know, I have only one wife of my own; still, you must remember that Solomon was one of your great heroes, and he had more than a thousand wives.' "

A TRUTH FOR THE CLASS TO CARRY AWAY.

Just as in building there are laws that must be obeyed if the building does not collapse; in eating and drinking there are physiological laws that must be obeyed or we become ill; so in that great world of moral conduct, there remain the indestructible moral laws of God which, when obeyed, bring strength, peace of soul, the approval of God, and when disobeyed, as in this lesson, bring ruin upon one's self and others. What we sow that we reap.

Where do you think in life Solomon began to take the wrong road? Do you think that God sent the prophet to Solomon to warn him as He sent him to his successors? How does the close of Solomon's life differ deeply from the close of David's life? How many differences between Ahijah, the prophet, and Solomon, the king? What elements are here present that ultimately are going to result in the destruction of Israel and Judah both?

LESSON V. — May 2.

JUDGMENT ON JEROBOAM. — 1 Kings 12:25–33; 14:1–20.

PRINTED TEXT, 1 Kings 14:1–3, 5–10a, 12–16.

Devotional Reading: Psalm 9:1–8.
Beginner Topic: AFTER THE RAIN.
   Lesson Material: Gen. 9:12–17; Deut. 11:13–14; Job 5:8–10; 36:26–31; Psalm 68:9; 104:10–13; 147:7–8.
   Memory Verse: Jehovah sendeth rain upon the earth. He hath made everything beautiful in its time. 1 Kings 17:14; Ecclesiastes 3:11.
Primary Topic: BAD NEWS FOR THE KING.
   Lesson Material: 1 Kings 14:1–18.
   Memory Verse: Seek ye Jehovah and his strength. Psalm 105:4.
Junior Topic: A KING WHO FAILED.
   Lesson Material: 1 Kings 14:1–18.
   Memory Verse: Seek ye Jehovah and his strength;
                Seek his face evermore. Psalm 105:4.
Intermediate-Senior Topic: A POPULAR LEADER WHO FAILED.
   Lesson Material: 1 Kings 12:25–33; 14:1–20.
   Memory Verse: Beware lest thou forget Jehovah thy God, in not keeping his commandments. Deuteronomy 8:11.
Topic for Young People and Adults: JUDGMENT ON JEROBOAM.
   Lesson Material: 1 Kings 12:25–33; 14:1–20.
   Memory Verse: Beware lest thou forget Jehovah thy God, in not keeping his commandments. Deuteronomy 8:11.

THE TEACHER AND HIS CLASS.

The **Younger Classes** may find this a rather difficult lesson, or at least the teacher will be somewhat perplexed as to what truth can be drawn from it for the instruction or edification of children. An observation in the form of a question may be presented in opening the lesson period — Why is it that although thousands of men may be playing golf on the various courses of our country in any one day, the only golf game recorded on the front page of our newspapers, apart from international tournaments, is that of President Eisenhower. The reason is that he is the president of the United States, and as such, everything he does, every place he visits, all the people he meets, the way in which his wife dresses her hair, and the clothes she wears, are subjects of national interest. When his term of office is over, none of these things will be true for him, but will be true for his successor. Our lesson today centers around the death of a child. Hundreds of children die every day, and while the immediate family grieves, no extended record is made of the death, and there is no national mourning. The father of the child in this lesson, however, is the king of Israel, and in this particular death a prophecy is involved, a judgment of God, and the ultimate cessation of the king's line.

The **Older Classes** may be reminded at the beginning of this lesson that any one event may have two altogether different reactions in the hearts of two different people or groups of people. For example, when an expert forger of bank notes is apprehended and sent up to prison for twenty years, it is a disaster for the man, the end of his liberty; but for the United States government it is a great relief, for if not taken into custody, he could have ultimately flooded the country with false currency until our very economic system were imperiled. Many people are in prison today in all parts of the world. Some can sing songs, and pray, and still rejoice, for they have been walking in obedience to God; for others, the situation is disgraceful. So it is in the matter of death. I recently heard of a funeral of a dear friend of mine, a true saint and mighty servant of God, which, according to those in attendance, was really an hour of triumph and glory. To those who have no hope, the death of a loved one is indeed a terrible experience. Christians trusting God know that if their child is taken from them, there is a divine purpose in it, and that all things work together for good to those that love God, but in our lesson the death of a child of the king is an act of judgment on the part of God, and would bring nothing but grief to the family.

THE LESSON IN ITS SETTING.

Time. — The reign of Jeroboam extended from 931 to 911 B.C. The episodes of our lesson take place during the latter part of this period.

Place. — Dan was at the extreme northern end of Israel; Bethel, five miles northeast of Jerusalem; and Shiloh nine miles north of Bethel. The location of Tirzah is still a disputed subject, but on the latest Biblical maps it is placed, with a question mark, about eight miles east of the city of Samaria.

THE PLAN OF THE LESSON.

SUBJECT: How God Deals with a Man to Whom He has Given Author- ity Who Persists in Exercising that Authority Contrary to the Revealed Will of God.

I. JEROBOAM SINFULLY ESTABLISHES TWO NEW PLACES FOR WORSHIP, 1 Kings 12:25-33.

II. THE INTERVIEW OF JEROBOAM'S WIFE WITH THE PROPHET AHIJAH, 1 Kings 14:1-16.
1. The instructions from the king, vs. 1-4.
2. The foreannouncement from Jehovah, v. 5.
3. The message of doom, vs. 6-16.

III. TWO DEATHS IN THE ROYAL FAMILY, 1 Kings 14:17-20.
1. The death of the child, vs. 17, 18.
2. The death of the king, vs. 19, 20.

THE TEACHER'S LIBRARY.

The finest material for the study of this lesson will be found in the work by Farrar in *The Expositor's Bible*, and by Alfred Barry in *The Bible Commentary for English Readers*. One should also consult Alfred Edersheim: *History of Judah and Israel from the Birth of Solomon to the Reign of Ahab*, 136–156; and A. P. Stanley: *History of the Jewish Church*, Vol. 2, pp. 232–240. On Jeroboam, the following chapters will be found helpful: George Rawlinson: *The Kings of Israel and Judah*, 14–30; Alexander Whyte: *Bible Characters, Ahithophel to Nehemiah*, 54–63; F. D. Maurice: *The Prophets and Kings of the Old Testament*, 85–101; Clarence E. Macartney: *Bible Epitaphs*, 52–69; James Hastings: *Greater Men and Women of the Bible, Ruth to Naaman*, 306–317; James Burrell: *Wayfarers of the Bible*, 148–156; David Rowlands in *Men of the Old Testament, Solomon to Jonah*, 27–41; and articles in Bible dictionaries, especially the *International Standard Bible Encyclopedia*, Vol. 3, pp. 1593–1595.

Sermonic material on the printed text is almost non-existent. On verse 13, see W. L. Watkinson: *Lessons of Prosperity*, 71–83.

AUDIO-VISUAL AIDS.

No audio-visual aids discovered.

I. JEROBOAM SINFULLY ESTABLISHES TWO NEW PLACES FOR WORSHIP, 1 Kings 12:25-33. Our lesson today begins where last week's study terminated. The preceding paragraph reveals the activities of Rehoboam immediately after the disruption of the kingdom. The historian now turns to events occurring in the Northern Kingdom, Israel. We can hardly expect any major program on the part of Jeroboam to be wholly in accord with the will of God. A man who starts out on the wrong road cannot reach the right destination unless he gets back on the right road. Jeroboam had the wrong start, and he continued down that road to tragedy. Though the kingdom had been successfully divided, Jeroboam feared that his subjects would ultimately experience such a longing for the great annual celebrations taking place at the Temple of Jerusalem, and feel so keenly the necessity for participating in the sacrifices that had been ordained of

God, that they would often go down to Jerusalem for these sacred seasons. This would of course weaken Jeroboam's power over his northern subjects; their hearts would be divided. To be sure that such would not take place, he established two new places for worship, wholly contrary to the explicit will of God. One of these was far north at Dan, and the other near the southern extremity of his kingdom, at the ancient city of Bethel. "In choosing Dan and Bethel as the seats for his new altars, the king was not actuated by purely arbitrary considerations. They were ancient and venerated shrines of pilgrimage and worship (Judg. 18:30; 20:18, 26; 1 Sam. 10:3). He did not create any sacredness which was not already attached to them in the popular imagination. (For the sanctity of Bethel, 'House of God,' where God had twice appeared to Jacob, see Gen. 28:11-19; 35:9-15. The Ark had once rested there under Phinehas, Judg. 20:26-28, and it had been the home of Samuel. Dan, too, was 'a holy city' see Judg. 18:30, 31.) In point of fact he would have served the ends of a worldly policy much better if he had chosen Shechem; for Dan and Bethel were the two farthest parts of his kingdom. Dan was in constant danger from the Syrians, and Bethel, which is only twelve miles from Jerusalem, more than once fell into the hands of the kings of Judah, though they neither retained possession of it, nor disturbed the shrines, nor threw down the 'calf' of the new worship. Jeroboam could not have created the 'calf-worship' if he had not found everything prepared for its acceptance. Dan had been, since its earliest days, the seat of a chapelry and ephod served by the lineal descendants of Moses in unbroken succession; Bethel was associated with some of the nation's holiest memories since the days of their forefather Israel." — *F. W. Farrar.* One phrase needs explanation, that Jeroboam "made two calves of gold." "The choice of this symbol of the Divine Nature — turning, as the Psalmist says with indignant scorn, 'the glory of God into the similitude of a calf that eateth hay' (Ps. 106:20) — was probably due to a combination of causes. First, the very repetition of Aaron's words (Exod. 32:8) indicates that it was a revival of that ancient idolatry in the wilderness. Probably, like it, it was suggested by the animal worship of Egypt, with which Jeroboam had been recently familiar, and which (as is well known) varied from mere symbolism to gross creature worship. Next, the bull, as the emblem of Ephraim, would naturally become a religious cognisance of the new kingdom. It is, of course, to be understood that this idolatry, against which the prohibition of many sanctuaries was meant to guard, was a breach, not of the First Commandment, but of the Second — that making of 'a similitude' of the true God, so emphatically forbidden again and again in the Law. (See, for example, Deut. 4:15-18). Like all such veneration of images, it probably degenerated. From looking on the image as a mere symbol it would come to attach to it a local presence of the Deity and an intrinsic sacredness; and so would lead on, perhaps to a veiled polytheism, certainly to a superstitious and carnal conception of the Godhead." — *Alfred Barry.* Furthermore, the king made priests of the common order of the people, that is, from outside of the Levitical family. Dean Stanley has a profound comment here on this departure from the revealed law of God for Israel. " 'The sin of Jeroboam the son of Nebat, who made Israel to sin,' is the sin again and again repeated in the policy, half-worldly, half-religious, which has prevailed through large tracts of ecclesiastical history. Many are the forms of worship which, with high pretensions, have been nothing else but so many various and opposite ways of breaking the Second Commandment. Many a time has the end been held to justify the means, and the Divine character been degraded by the pretense, or even the sincere intention, of upholding His cause, for the sake of secular aggrandisement; for the sake of binding together good systems, which it was feared would otherwise fall to pieces; for the sake of supporting the faith of the multitude for the fear they should otherwise fall away to rival sects, or lest the enemy should come and take away their place and nation. False arguments have been used in support of religious truths, false miracles promulgated or tolerated, false readings in the sacred text defended. . . . And so the faith of mankind has been undermined by the

1 KINGS 14:1. At that time Abijah the son of Jeroboam fell sick.

2. And Jeroboam said to his wife, Arise, I pray thee, and disguise thyself, that thou be not known to be the wife of Jeroboam; and get thee to Shiloh: behold, there is Ahijah the prophet, who spake concerning me that I should be king over this people.

3. And take with thee ten loaves, and cakes, and a cruse of honey, and go to him: he will tell thee what shall become of the child.

5. And Jehovah said unto Ahijah, Behold, the wife of Jeroboam cometh to inquire of thee concerning her son; for he is sick: thus and thus shalt thou say unto her; for it will be, when she cometh in, that she will feign herself to be another woman.

6. And it was so, when Ahijah heard the sound of her feet, as she came in at the door, that he said, Come in, thou wife of Jeroboam; why feignest thou thyself to be another? for I am sent to thee with heavy tidings.

---

very means intended to preserve it. The whole subsequent history is a record of the mode by which, with the best intentions, a Church and nation may be corrupted." — *A. P. Stanley.*

II. **THE INTERVIEW OF JEROBOAM'S WIFE WITH THE PROPHET AHIJAH,** 1 Kings 14:1–16. Chapter 13 is passed by in the lesson material given here. The conclusion of it, however, reads that "Jeroboam turned not from his evil way . . . and this thing became sin unto the house of Jeroboam." All seems to be going well externally. New places of worship are established; a new priesthood has been appointed; much of the worship commanded by God in the days of Moses is being observed; the country is increasingly prosperous, and the king himself is being honored on every hand. At this very time, however, a most unexpected tragedy occurs in the royal household. The son, through whom Jeroboam expected his dynasty to continue, has fallen ill. The fact that the boy was called Abijah, which means "whose father is Jehovah," would seem to indicate some true faith in the Lord was in the heart of the king. What must the king do? Apparently he does not have access to God — how could he? He is daily disobeying God. Instead of repenting of his sins and reordering his life, Jeroboam gives instructions to his wife, that she should secretly go up to Shiloh, where lived the prophet who had first spoken to Jeroboam before the division of the kingdom, perchance the prophet would give her some helpful word concerning the recovery of the ailing child. **1. At that time Abijah the son of Jeroboam fell sick. 2. And Jeroboam said to his wife, Arise, I pray thee, and disguise thyself, that thou be not known to be the wife of Jeroboam; and get thee to Shiloh: behold, there is Ahijah the prophet, who spake concerning me that I should be king over this people. 3. And take with thee ten loaves, and cakes, and a cruse of honey, and go to him: he will tell thee what shall become of the child. 5. And Jehovah said unto Ahijah, Behold, the wife of Jeroboam cometh to inquire of thee concerning her son; for he is sick: thus and thus shalt thou say unto her; for it will be, when she cometh in, that she will feign herself to be another woman. 6. And it was so, when Ahijah heard the sound of her feet, as she came in at the door, that he said, Come in, thou wife of Jeroboam; why feignest thou thyself to be another? for I am sent to thee with heavy tidings.** "Jeroboam remembered that Ahijah's former prophecy had been fulfilled, and believed that he would again be able to reveal the future, and say whether the heir to the throne would recover. The queen obeyed; and if she were indeed the Egyptian princess Ano, it must have been for her a strange experience. Through the winding valley, she reached the home of the aged prophet unrecognised. But he had received a Divine intimation of her errand; and . . . at once addressed her by name when he heard the sound of her

7. Go, tell Jeroboam, Thus saith Jehovah, the God of Israel: Forasmuch as I exalted thee from among the people and made thee prince over my people Israel,

8. And rent the kingdom away from the house of David, and gave it thee; and yet thou hast not been as my servant David, who kept my commandments, and who followed me with all his heart, to do that only which was right in mine eyes.

9. But hast done evil above all that were before thee, and hast gone and made thee other gods, and molten images, to provoke me to anger, and hast cast me behind thy back.

10a. Therefore, behold, I will bring evil upon the house of Jeroboam, and will cut off from Jeroboam every man-child, him that is shut up and him that is left at large in Israel and will utterly sweep away the house of Jeroboam.

approaching footsteps. The message which he was bidden to pronounce was utterly terrible; it was unrelieved by a single gleam of mitigation or a single expression of pity. It reproached and denounced Jeroboam for faithless ingratitude in that he had cast God behind his back; it threatened hopeless and shameful extermination of all his house." — *F. W. Farrar.* A true prophet always communicates to those to whom he is sent the unadulterated, unexpurgated message received from God, even if it means his death — and Ahijah was such a prophet. **7. Go, tell Jeroboam, Thus saith Jehovah, the God of Israel: Forasmuch as I exalted thee from among the people and made thee prince over my people Israel, 8. and rent the kingdom away from the house of David, and gave it thee; and yet thou hast not been as my servant David, who kept my commandments, and who followed me with all his heart, to do that only which was right in mine eyes.** "There is throughout a close allusion to Ahijah's prophecy (11:31, 37, 38) which promised Jeroboam 'a sure house, like that of David,' on condition of the obedience of David. The sin of Jeroboam lay in this — that he had had a full probation, with unlimited opportunities, and had deliberately thrown it away, in the vain hope of making surer the kingdom which God's promise had already made sure. The lesson is, indeed, a general one. The resolution to succeed at all hazards, striking out new ways, with no respect for time-honoured laws and principles, is in all revolutions the secret of immediate success and ultimate disaster. But in the Scripture history, here as elsewhere, we are permitted to see the working of God's moral government of the world, unveiled in the inspired declarations of His prophetic messenger." — *Alfred Barry.* **9. But hast done evil above all that were before thee, and hast gone and made thee other gods, and molten images, to provoke me to anger, and hast cast me behind thy back.** "The language is strong, in the face of the many instances of the worship of false gods in the days of the Judges, and the recent apostasy of Solomon — to say nothing of the idolatry of the golden calf in the wilderness, and setting up of the idolatrous sanctuaries in olden times at Ophrah and at Dan (Judges 8:27; 18:30, 31). The guilt, indeed, of Jeroboam's act was enhanced by the presumptuous contempt of the special promise of God, given on the sole condition of obedience. In respect of this, perhaps he is said below — in an expression seldom used elsewhere — to have 'cast God Himself behind his back.' But probably the reference is mainly to the unprecedented effect of the sin, coming at a critical point in the history of Israel, and from that time onward poisoning the springs of national faith and worship. Other idolatries came and passed away; this continued, and at all times 'made Israel to sin.' " — *Alfred Barry.* **10a. Therefore, behold, I will bring evil upon the house of Jeroboam, and will cut off from Jeroboam every man-child, him that is shut up and him that is left at large in Israel and will utterly sweep away the house**

12. Arise thou therefore, get thee to thy house: *and* when thy feet enter into the city, the child shall die.

13. And all Israel shall mourn for him, and bury him; for he only of Jeroboam shall come to the grave, because in him there is found some good thing toward Jehovah, the God of Israel, in the house of Jeroboam.

14. Moreover Jehovah will raise him up a king over Israel, who shall cut off the house of Jeroboam that day: but what? even now.

15. For Jehovah will smite Israel, as a reed is shaken in the water; and he will root up Israel out of this good land which he gave to their fathers, and will scatter them beyond the River, because they have made their Ashserim provoking Jehovah to anger.

16. And he will give Israel up because of the sins of Jeroboam, which he hath sinned, and wherewith he hath made Israel to sin.

---

of Jeroboam. The terrible prophecy of verse 11, that he who would die of Jeroboam in the city the dogs would eat, and he that died in the field would the birds eat is repeated in 16:4 and 21:24; with this compare Jeremiah 36:30. "The 'dogs' are the half-wild dogs, the scavengers of every Eastern city; the 'fowls of the air' the vultures and other birds of prey. In ancient times the natural horror of insult to the remains of the dead was often intensified by the idea that in some way the denial of the rites of burial would inflict suffering or privation on the departed soul." — *Alfred Barry.*

The dreadful prophetic utterance is interrupted for a moment as the prophet tells the queen that in this child who is to die there has been found some good thing toward God in the house of Jeroboam. **12. Arise thou therefore, get thee to thy house:** *and* **when thy feet enter into the city, the child shall die. 13. And all Israel shall mourn for him, and bury him; for he only of Jeroboam shall come to the grave, because in him there is found some good thing toward Jehovah, the God of Israel, in the house of Jeroboam.** "Those are good in whom are good things towards the Lord God of Israel, good inclinations, good intentions, good desires, towards him. Where there is but *some* good thing of that kind it will be found: God, who seeks it, sees it be it ever so little and is pleased with it. A little grace goes a great way with great people. It is so rare to find princes well affected to religion that, when they are so, they are worthy of double honour. Pious dispositions are in a peculiar manner amiable and acceptable when they are found in those that are young. The divine image in miniature has a peculiar beauty and lustre in it. Those that are good in bad times and places shine very brightly in the eyes of God. A good child in the house of Jeroboam is a miracle of divine grace: to be there untainted is like being in the fiery furnace unhurt, unsinged. Observe the care taken of him: he only, of all Jeroboam's family, shall die in honour; shall be buried, and shall be lamented as one that lived desired. Those that are distinguished by divine grace shall be distinguished by divine providence. This hopeful child dies first of all the family, for God often takes those soonest whom he loves best. Heaven is the fittest place for them; this earth is not worthy of them." — *Matthew Henry.* **14. Moreoever Jehovah will raise him up a king over Israel, who shall cut off the house of Jeroboam that day: but what? even now. 15. For Jehovah will smite Israel, as a reed is shaken in the water; and he will root up Israel out of this good land which he gave to their fathers, and will scatter them beyond the River, because they have made their Ashserim provoking Jehovah to anger. 16. And he will give Israel up because of the sins of Jeroboam, which he hath sinned, and wherewith he hath made Israel to sin.** "The first prophecy of future captivity, and that 'beyond the river' (Euphrates) is here pronounced against the kingdom of Israel, on account of their share in the idolatry of Jeroboam, and in the worse abominations of the 'groves.' Of all such utterances we must remember the express declaration of Jeremiah 18:7, 8, 'At what instant I shall speak concerning a nation . . . to pluck up, and to pull down, and to destroy; if that nation . . . turn from their evil, I will repent of the evil that I thought to do unto them.' The prophecy uttered does not foreclose the probation of future ages. This is, after all, only one illustration of the great truth that — however impossible it is for us to comprehend the mystery — the foreknowledge of God does not preclude the freedom and responsibility of man. The metaphor is of the reed shaken to and fro in the river, till at last it is rooted up, swept down the stream, and cast up on some distant shore." — *Alfred Barry.* For the fulfillment of verse 14, see the concluding paragraph of this lesson.

III. TWO DEATHS IN THE ROYAL FAMILY, 1 Kings 14:17–20. Apparently there was no pleading with the prophet on the part of the queen, no request for leniency, for a cancellation of this utterance of doom, or an attempt to justify the character of her husband. She went to Ahijah because he was a man of God, and she well knew upon hearing these words that he was speaking for God. "As the hapless mother set foot on the threshold of her palace at beautiful Tirzah the young prince died, and she heard the wail of the mourners for him. He alone was buried in the grave of his fathers, and Israel mourned for him. He was evidently a prince of much hope and promise, and the deaths of such princes have always peculiarly affected the sympathy of nations. . . . When Louis le Bien-Aime lay ill of the fever at Metz which seemed likely to be fatal, all France wept and prayed for him. He recovered, and grew up to be that portent of selfish boredom and callous sensuality, Louis XV. It was better that Abijah should die than that he should live to be overwhelmed in the shameful ruin which soon overtook his house. It was better far that he should die than that he should grow up to frustrate the promise of his youth. He was beckoned by the hand of God 'because in him was found some good thing towards the Lord God of Israel.' We are not told wherein the goodness consisted, but Rabbinic tradition guessed that in opposition to his father he discountenanced the calf-worship and encouraged and helped the people to continue their visits to Jerusalem. Such a king might indeed have recovered the whole kingdom, and have dispossessed David's degenerate line. But it was not to be. The fiat against Israel had gone forth, though a long space was to intervene before it was fulfilled. And God's fiats are irrevocable, because with Him there is no changeableness neither shadow of turning.

> 'The moving finger writes, and having writ,
> Moves on; nor all thy piety nor wit
> Shall lure it back to cancel half a line
> Nor all thy tears wash out a word of it.'

But the passage about Abijah has a unique preciousness, because it stands alone in Scripture as an expression of the truth that early death is no sign at all of the Divine anger, and that the length or brevity of life are matters of little significance to God, seeing that, at the best, the longest life is but as one tick of the clock in the eternal silence." — *F. W. Farrar.*

The assigned text concludes with a brief notice of the king's death. His death, as recorded in 2 Chronicles 13:20, seems to be the result of some sudden visitation, for we read, "The Lord struck him and he died." Only two sons of Jeroboam are mentioned, but from 15:29 we might assume that there were others. Abijah has died, and there remains only Nadab to take the throne. Nadab reigned over Israel for the brief period of two years (15:25). While besieging the Philistine city of Gibbethon, he was assassinated by Baasha. Thus the whole Jeroboam dynasty is extinguished, and a new dynasty comes to rule Israel.

THE LESSON IN LIFE, LITERATURE, AND ARCHAEOLOGY.

"During the reign of Rehoboam, Sheshonk I (spelled 'Shishak' in the Bible) came from Egypt to Palestine and took the treasures of the temple at Jerusalem

(1 Kings 14:25ff.). Archaeological confirmation of this campaign of Shishak is found in his inscription on the wall of the great temple of Karnak in Egypt. The inscription shows Shishak grasping a group of cowering Semites by the hair and smiting them with a club. On the bodies of the people represented on the inscription are the names of many Palestinian towns, such as Taanach, Gibeon, Ajalon, Bethshan, and many others (BAB, 456). The archaeological material adds further light to what is revealed in the Bible, showing us that Shishak went to other towns in addition to Jerusalem (J. P. Free, op. cit.)."

A TRUTH FOR THE CLASS TO CARRY AWAY.

It seems to me that the great lesson for us in the life of Jeroboam is the terribleness of using the influence which belongs to the place and position God has given us in such a way that all who come within the circle of that influence are drawn down to a lower level, are drawn away from God and ultimately as a group, or, here, as a nation, suffer disaster. George Washington said he could not afford to live for himself when the destiny of the thirteen colonies depended upon him.

In how many ways does the history of Jeroboam's reign clearly reveal he is out of the will of God? How many attributes of God do we find revealed in this narrative? Do you think that God at any time today deals with nations as He dealt with Israel? How does our lesson offer evidence for the continued indictment of God at a later time that though He had sent prophets continually to Israel, the Israelites had not hearkened to them (see Jer. 7:24–27)? Why do you think Jeroboam sent his wife to the prophet and not some man in his royal court?

LESSON VI. — May 9.

ELIJAH CHALLENGES BAAL WORSHIP. — 1 Kings 17:1—19:18.

PRINTED TEXT, 1 Kings 17:1; 18:17–24, 36–39.

Devotional Reading: 1 Kings 18:30–36.
Beginner Topic: A POLITE MAN.
  Lesson Material: Luke 17:11–19.
  Memory Verse: Sang praises unto Jehovah . . . with gladness. 2 Chronicles 29:30.
Primary Topic: ELIJAH BUILDS AN ALTAR.
  Lesson Material: 1 Kings 18:30–39.
  Memory Verse: I will call on the name of Jehovah. 1 Kings 18:24.
Junior Topic: ONE AGAINST FOUR HUNDRED AND FIFTY.
  Lesson Material: 1 Kings 18:17–39.
  Memory Verse: I will call on the name of Jehovah. 1 Kings 18:24.
Intermediate-Senior Topic: ONE AGAINST THE CROWD.
  Lesson Material: 1 Kings 17:1—19:18.
  Memory Verse: How long go ye limping between the two sides? if Jehovah be God, follow him; but if Baal, then follow him. 1 Kings 18:21.
Topic for Young People and Adults: ELIJAH CHALLENGES BAAL WORSHIP.
  Lesson Material: 1 Kings 17:1—19:18.
  Memory Verse: How long go ye limping between the two sides? if Jehovah be God, follow him; but if Baal, then follow him. 1 Kings 18:21.

THE TEACHER AND HIS CLASS.

The Younger Classes could be introduced to this lesson in a very impressive way, if the teacher could borrow some images of Oriental idols, or at least show the class pictures of these idols. I have known missionaries to bring home a whole box full of them. How strange, and to us, how foolish to bow down and worship anything which a man has

163

made, which cannot walk, or talk, or see, or hear! Now the nations around Israel were worshippers of false gods and in this idolatry great wickedness prevailed. No one can truly worship two gods: when the Israelites turned to Baal they turned from God. Our lesson concerns a great hour in Israel's history, when the prophets and priests of this false god were challenged, defeated, and destroyed.

The Older Classes will find this lesson one of unusual significance, for today, much more so, I think, than, say, ten years ago, to the astonishment of us all, there is a very strange revival throughout the Orient of pagan religions, that everyone thought were in their last death-agonies. Japan is having a great revival of Buddhism, and Islam, though not idol-worshipping, has been greatly rejuvenated in the last few years. Pagan religions today are no more to be commended than in the days of Israel, and Elijah's bold challenge to the Baalism of old should be re-echoed today by every faithful ambassador of Christ in the pagan areas of our earth.

THE LESSON IN ITS SETTING.

Time. — The events of our lesson probably took place about 850 B.C.

Place. — Mount Carmel is that great range, rising from the plain of Esdraelon and sloping toward the Mediterranean, with the city of Haifa at its base, today a great harbor.

THE PLAN OF THE LESSON.

SUBJECT: How God Used One Prophet Wholly Yielded to Him to Deal to Contemporary Paganism a Mortal Blow and to Awaken a Nation to the Infinite Preëminence of Jehovah.

I. A NUMBER OF MIRACLES IN THE EARLIER MINISTRY OF ELIJAH, 1 Kings 17.

II. THE GREAT CONFLICT WITH THE PROPHETS OF BAAL ON MOUNT CARMEL, 1 Kings 18.
1. The bold challenge, vs. 1–19.
2. The stipulated rules, vs. 20–24.
3. The impotent prophets of Baal, vs. 25–29.
4. The omnipotent God of Elijah, vs. 30–39.
5. The destruction of the followers of Baal, v. 40.
6. Elijah and his servant, vs. 41–46.

III. THE PROPHET'S DEPRESSION AND THE TENDER CARE OF JEHOVAH, 1 Kings 19.

THE TEACHER'S LIBRARY.

Among the better commentaries on the First Book of Kings are those by J. R. Lumby in *The Cambridge Bible for Schools and Colleges;* Alfred Barry in *The Bible Commentary for English Readers;* and C. F. Keil in The Keil-Delitsch Series of *Commentaries on the Old Testament;* and H. J. Carpenter, in *The Devotional Commentary* Series. For good chapters on our lesson, see the lives of Elijah by William F. Taylor, F. B. Meyer, F. W. Krummacher, J. R. MacDuff, and Mark Guy Pearse. For historical background, A. P. Stanley: *Lectures on the History of the Jewish Church, Volume 2,* pp. 247–271; Alfred Edersheim: *The History of Israel and Judah from the Reign of Ahab to the Decline of the Two Kingdoms;* David Gregg: *New Epistles from Old Lands,* 237–255; John MacBeath: *The Hills of God,* 126–134; George Adam Smith: *The Historical Geography of the Holy Land,* 337–340.

For some strange reason, sermonic material on this dramatic episode is quite scarce. On the entire lesson, Joseph Parker: *The People's Bible,* Vol. 8, pp. 23–45; on verse 21, G. Campbell Morgan in *The Westminster Pulpit,* Vol. 7, pp. 225–232; on verse 24, John Henry Jowett, *Thirsting for the Springs,* 49–55. There are a number of good articles on Mount Carmel in our Bible dictionaries, the best of which is in one of the older ones, by George Grove in William Smith's *Dictionary of the Bible.*

AUDIO-VISUAL AIDS.

FILMSTRIP: "Elijah," (Picture Stories from the Bible Series), Filmfax Productions No. 22, 55 fr., col. Drawings.

SLIDE SET: "Elijah," Visserslides No. 697–708, 12 sl., col. Main events in Elijah's career.

I. A NUMBER OF MIRACLES IN THE EARLIER MINISTRY OF ELIJAH,
1 Kings 17. In the record of the lives of the two prophets, Elijah and Elisha, we have the greatest concentration of miracles to be found anywhere in the Old Testament, apart from the supernatural aspects of the Exodus from Egypt, and the wanderings in the wilderness. In this first chapter of our lesson we have three miracles, all of which have become famous in subsequent legend and story: the

1 KINGS 17:1. And Elijah the Tishbite, who was of the sojourners of Gilead, said unto Ahab, As Jehovah, the God of Israel, liveth, before whom I stand, there shall not be dew nor rain these years, but according to my word.

1 KINGS 18:17.   And it came to pass, when Ahab saw Elijah, that Ahab said unto him, Is it thou, thou troubler of Israel?

---

remarkable provision of food while the prophet was at the Brook cherith, brought to him by ravens; the miraculous multiplication of meal and oil at the widow's house at Zarepath; and the later raising of the same widow's son.   Inasmuch, however, as we have for our present study one of the most dramatic events in Old Testament history, we need add no comment to these preliminary manifestations of God's power, contenting ourselves with a striking passage from Joseph Parker, on the one verse of this chapter assigned to our lesson.   **17:1. And Elijah the Tishbite, who was of the sojourners of Gilead, said unto Ahab, As Jehovah, the God if Israel, liveth, before whom I stand, there shall not be dew nor rain these years, but according to my word.**   " 'As the Lord God of Israel liveth, before whom I stand.' — We must realise very clearly the circumstances of the case before we can set a proper value on these words.   To us they are but part of a general music. Our land is full of churches, and the wind of Christendom is charged with psalms. But in Ahab's wicked day — Ahab who did more to provoke the Lord God of Israel to anger than all the kings of Israel that were before him (16:33) — the words meant something which it is hardly possible for us to realise.

"Imagine the two men standing face to face: Ahab, the dissolute king, and Elijah the faithful prophet, and probably there is no finer picture in ancient history. Terrible indeed is the national crisis when king and prophet come into collision. There is not a combat between two men.   Mark that very closely.   It is Right against Wrong, Faithfulness against Treachery, Purity against Corruption.   Look at them, Ahab and Elijah, as they face one another! — Consider the boldness of the prophet.   Religion is never to be ashamed of its own testimony.   As we look at the scene, not wanting in the elements of the highest tragedy, we see (1) The value of one noble witness in the midst of public corruption and decay, and (2) The grandeur as well as necessity of a distinct personal profession of godliness. It is not enough to be godly, we must avow it in open conduct and articulate confession." — *Joseph Parker*.

II. **THE GREAT CONFLICT WITH THE PROPHETS OF BAAL ON MT. CARMEL,** 1 Kings 18.

1. THE BOLD CHALLENGE, 18:1–19.   Our chapter opens at about the end of the three terrible years of drouth, predicted by Elijah in the preceding chapter, a drouth that of course naturally was accompanied by a devastating famine.   In a desperate search for a few remaining patches of grass for the king's horses and mules, Ahab sent his God-fearing servant Obadiah up and down the land.   During his travels he suddenly was confronted by the bold and powerful prophet, who told the servant to at once report to Ahab that he, the prophet, would be waiting there to meet the king.   Obadiah asked immediately to be excused from this errand, "for," said he, "as it has happened before, so it will happen now.   When I tell the king where you now are and he comes to see you, the Spirit of God will have taken you away, and I will be slain."   To which the prophet replied, "I will surely show myself unto him today."   And with this promise the message was carried to the king.   **17. And it came to pass, when Ahab saw Elijah, that Ahab said unto him, Is it thou, thou troubler of Israel?**   "It does not seem to occur to the king that he himself was the 'troubler of Israel.'   He followed the course taken by the world in every age, when it lays the blame of all that unsettledness of mind which so often disturbs it in the midst of its sinful ease upon those who would awaken

165

18. And he answered, I have not troubled Israel; but thou, and thy father's house, in that ye have forsaken the commandments of Jehovah, and thou hast followed the Baalim.

19. Now therefore send, and gather to me all Israel unto mount Carmel, and the prophets of Baal four hundred and fifty, and the prophets of the Asherah four hundred, that eat at Jezebel's table.

---

it to a sense of responsibility." — *William Milligan.* **18. And he answered, I have not troubled Israel; but thou, and thy father's house, in that ye have forsaken the commandments of Jehovah, and thou hast followed the Baalim.** **19. Now therefore send, and gather to me all Israel unto mount Carmel, and the prophets of Baal four hundred and fifty, and the prophets of the Asherah four hundred, that eat at Jezebel's table.** Before proceeding any further we ought to have some account of Baal-worship. "Ashtoreth was the chief female divinity of the Phoenicians, as Baal was their chief male deity. As Baal has been identified with the sun, so Ashtoreth has by some been thought to be the moon. Recent investigations have however connected the name of Ashtoreth with the planet Venus, and by some it is thought that the name was applied in some parts of the Phoenician settlements to Venus, in others to the moon. Ashtoreth is identified with the Greek *Astarte*, and the name of an ancient city (Gen. 14:5) *Ashteroth-Karnaim*, i.e. Ashteroth of the two horns, seems to point to the crescent moon. This is accepted by Milton

> 'Ashtoreth, whom the Phoenicians called
> Astarte, queen of heaven, with crescent horns
> To whose bright image, nightly by the moon
> Sidonian virgins paid their vows and songs.'

The worship of Ashtoreth was very widespread, as might be expected from the wide commercial relations, and distant colonies, of the Phoenicians. Why Ashtoreth is here named 'goddess' while the other deities are called 'abominations' may be due to the greater intercourse between Sidon and the Holy Land than existed with other countries. The Phoenician workmen at the Temple had perhaps caused the Israelites to become more accustomed to the name and worship of Ashtoreth." — *J. R. Lumby.* What a terrible thing that the queen of Israel's ruler should be supporting, out of the royal treasury, eight hundred and fifty of these wicked prophets of a foul Syrian deity. The land must have been utterly saturated with their polluting influence. We should carefully note here that the challenge to the prophets of Baal was forced upon them by Elijah, and not spontaneously accepted by them. "Perhaps the common impression is that Elijah challenged the prophets directly, standing face to face with them, without any medium of communication. Nothing of the kind. Elijah first challenged king Ahab, and he snatched eagerly at the sensational chance, little knowing what he was snatching at! Having spoken first to the king, Elijah spoke next to the people, demanding why they hesitated between two opinions, and insisting that they should make a choice between Jehovah and Baal. Then Elijah made his grand appeal to the people of Israel, and they answered and said, 'It is well spoken'; then having secured the approval of the king and of the people, Elijah called upon the prophets to proceed to trial." — *Joseph Parker.*

2. THE STIPULATED RULES, 18:20–24. Before the actual trial on Mount Carmel is before us, let us try to picture in our mind the geographical features which so tremendously increase the vividness of this event. "No spot in Palestine is more beautiful, more bracing or healthful, than *Carmel*, "the Park-like." Up in the northwest, it juts as a promontory into the Mediterranean, rising to a height of five hundred feet. Thence it stretches about twelve miles to the S.S.E., rising into two other peaks. The first of these, about four miles from the promontory, is not less than 1740 feet high. Still farther to the south-east is a third peak, 1687 feet

20. So Ahab sent unto all the children of Israel, and gathered the prophets together unto mount Carmel.

21. And Elijah came near unto all the people, and said, How long go ye limping between the two sides? if Jehovah be God, follow him; but if Baal, then follow him. And the people answered him not a word.

22. Then said Elijah unto the people, I, even I only, am left a prophet of Jehovah; but Baal's prophets are four hundred and fifty men.

---

high, which to this day bears the name of *El-Mahrakah*, or 'place of burning' (sacrifice). This, there can scarcely be a doubt, was the place of Elijah's sacrifice. . . . On whichever side the mountain be ascended, the scene is one of unsurpassed beauty. . . . Not only flowering trees and delicious fragrant herbs, but all the flora of the North of Palestine seems gathered in this favoured spot. So early as November, the crocus, narcissus, pink cistus, and large daisy are in bloom, and the hawthorn in bud. . . . Numerous springs trickle along the foot of the mountain and fertilize the soil. Ascending to El-Mahrakah we catch glimpses of cliffs, which in some places descend sheer down to the plain. At last we reach a plateau, where at the edge of a steep slope there is a perennial well, filled with water even in the driest season. Yet a little higher rises another plateau of rich soil, shaded by olives; and finally we reach the topmost peak, a semi-isolated knoll. This was the place of the two altars. . . . Some 1400 feet beneath, where the rapid descent is close to steep precipices and by sharp crags, rolls that 'ancient river' Kishon, where the wild slaughter of the priests of Baal formed the closing scene in the drama of that day. But up on the topmost altar-height what an outlook! Westwards over Carmel and far to the sandhills around Caesarea; northwards, the Galilean hills, Lebanon and Hermon; eastwards, across the plain of Esdraelon, some six miles off, to Jezreel, — farther away, to Shunem, Endor, Nain, Tabor, Nazareth, and even distant Gilead. A theatre this, truly befitting what was to be enacted on it." — *Alfred Edersheim.* **20. So Ahab sent unto all the children of Israel, and gathered the prophets together unto mount Carmel. 21. And Elijah came near unto all the people, and said, How long go ye limping between the two sides? if Jehovah be God, follow him; but if Baal, then follow him. And the people answered him not a word.** Before Elijah confronts the prophets of Baal in the great challenge of the hour, he turns to the people of Israel, who will not be participants in this conflict, but eye-witnesses, and rebukes them for their vacillations. "The verb *limping* is an expressive word, and is used below for the irregular, stumbling sort of dance about the altar of Baal (verse 26). It indicates a lame uncertain gait. Hence it suits very well the conduct of Israel, now drawn toward Jehovah, but not earnest there, and then attracted to Baal, but not altogether satisfied with that worship." — *J. R. Lumby.* "These people wanted to combine the worship of Jehovah and Baal and not to assume a hostile attitude towards Jehovah by the worship of Baal." — *C. F. Kiel.* "The time had come for the nation to be arrested in its attempt to mingle the worship of Jehovah and of Baal and compelled to choose between the two issues that presented themselves." — *F. B. Meyer.* **22. Then said Elijah unto the people, I, even I only, am left a prophet of Jehovah; but Baal's prophets are four hundred and fifty men.** "Elijah means that he is the only one who now stands forward in Jehovah's name. No doubt there were others of those saved by Obadiah and in other ways, but in such dangerous days they kept out of sight. The scene on Carmel is full of sublimity. Elijah alone against the host of Baal-priests, and with the calm dignity befitting so solemn a time, in the midst of them all, proceeding to repair the broken altar of the Lord." — *J. R.*

23. Let them therefore give us two bullocks; and let them choose one bullock for themselves, and cut it in pieces, and lay it on the wood, and put no fire under; and I will dress the other bullock, and lay it on the wood, and put no fire under.

24. And call ye on the name of your god, and I will call on the name of Jehovah: and the God that answered by fire, let him be God. And all the people answered and said, It is well spoken.

Lumby. 23. **Let them therefore give us two bullocks; and let them choose one bullock for themselves, and cut it in pieces, and lay it on the wood, and put no fire under; and I will dress the other bullock, and lay it on the wood, and put no fire under. 24. And call ye on the name of your god, and I will call on the name of Jehovah: and the God that answered by fire, let him be God. And all the people answered and said, It is well spoken.** Note carefully that not only are all the rules for this day laid down by Elijah, but the prophets of Baal seem to be utterly cowed before this stern messenger of God. In courtesy Elijah asks the Baal prophets to perform their rites first.

3. THE IMPOTENT PROPHETS OF BAAL, vs. 25–29. The Baal prophets having placed their bullock on the altar, everyone convinced that no fire was anywhere about, they began to cry to their deity, "O Baal; hear us," to which no voice gave reply. So as Oriental dervishes have often been seen to perform in modern times, they cried the louder, and worked themselves up into a frenzy, cutting themselves with knives and lances for hour after hour, even until the evening oblation, and no answer to their prayers. "This repeated cry — the ever-recurring burden of the prayer, uttered probably first in measured chant, afterwards in a wild excited cry — stands in an instructive contrast (which has been splendidly emphasised in Mendelssohn's music) with the simple, earnest solemnity of the prayer of Elijah. It has been obvious to see in it an illustration of our Lord's condemnation of the worship of the heathen, who 'think that they shall be heard for their much speaking' (Matt. 6:7). There is a grave irony in the notice of the blank silence which followed this frenzied cry. 'There was no voice, nor any to answer, nor any that regarded.' " — *Alfred Barry.* The word translated "knives" is generally rendered "swords," and the word translated "lances" is constantly employed for spears. "*Heathenism has no true prayer.* Wild cries and passionate desires, flung upwards to an unloved god, are not prayer; and that solace and anchor of the troubled soul is wanting in all the dreary lands given up to idolatry.

"The melancholy persistence of the unanswered cries may stand as a symbol of the tragic obstinacy with which their devotees cling to their vain gods, — a rebuke to us with a more enlightened faith. The silence, which was the only answer, is put in strong contrast with the continuous roar of the four hundred and fifty, — so long and loud the hoarse cries here, so unmoved the stillness in the careless heaven. That, too, is typical of heathenism, which is sad with unavailing cries and ignorant of answers to any." — *Alexander MacLaren.*

4. THE OMNIPOTENT GOD OF ELIJAH, vs. 30–39. It is now Elijah's turn. I wonder if his heart beat with increased frequency, as the great hour of his own life and of this generation of Israelites had arrived. First of all, not wanting to be contaminated in any way with Baal-worship, or to even touch the altar fouled by their hands, he built a new altar. He repaired an altar which had been thrown down. "How mournfully would he bend over the stones of that altar, which was broken down! — broken down not by the wild weather, or the devastating hand of time; but by the wicked behest of Jezebel (1 Kings 18:32). How eagerly would he search out the original twelve stones, strewn recklessly afar, and covered by wild undergrowth. He would need them soon! How constantly would he stay himself upon his God, and pour out litanies of supplication for the people, and gird

36. And it came to pass at the time of the offering of the *evening* oblation, that Elijah the prophet came near, and said, O Jehovah, the God of Abraham, of Isaac, and of Israel, let it be known this day that thou art God in Israel, and that I am thy servant, and that I have done all these things at thy word.

37. Hear me, O Jehovah, hear me, that this people may know that thou, Jehovah, art God, and *that* thou hast turned their heart back again.

38. Then the fire of Jehovah fell, and consumed the burnt-offering, and the wood, and the stones, and the dust, and licked up the water that was in the trench.

---

himself for the coming conflict by effectual, fervent prayer." — *F. B. Meyer.* Then he made a trench around the altar for catching the water that was to be poured over the sacrifice — (the exact size of the trench is not quite clear from the text). Placing the wood on the altar and the bullock on the wood, he commanded his servants to pour four jars of water over the prepared sacrifice. Once, twice, and the third time. Now the moment has come for the God of Elijah to manifest Himself. **36. And it came to pass at the time of the offering of the** *evening* **oblation, that Elijah the prophet came near, and said, O Jehovah, the God of Abraham, of Isaac, and of Israel, let it be known this day that thou art God in Israel, and that I am thy servant, and that I have done all these things at thy word.** "In this solemn and earnest invocation of God (as in Exod. 3:15; 6:2, 3) the name JEHOVAH, describing God as He is in Himself — the One eternal self-existent Being — is united with the name which shows His special covenant with 'Abraham, and Isaac, and Israel.' In His own nature incomprehensible to finite being, He yet reveals Himself in moral and spiritual relations with His people, through which they 'know that which passeth knowledge.' The prominence of the name 'Jehovah,' thrice repeated in this short prayer of Elijah, is significant as of the special mission, symbolised in his very name, so also of his immediate purpose. He desires to efface himself. The God of Israel is to show Himself as the true worker, not only in the outer sphere by miracle, but in the inner sphere by that conversion of the hearts of the people, which to the prophet's eye is already effected." — *Alfred Barry.* **37. Hear me, O Jehovah, hear me, that this people may know that thou, Jehovah, art God, and** *that* **thou hast turned their heart back again.** "This is what Elijah desired, that it should be shown that to apply the name 'Elohim' to Baal, and idols like him, was a folly and a delusion. The heathen, and those who went after them, used this name for the objects of their worship, and Elijah in his mockery had employed their phrase (verse 27) and said of Baal 'He is Elohim.' " — *J. R. Lumby.* **38. Then the fire of Jehovah fell, and consumed the burnt-offering, and the wood, and the stones, and the dust, and licked up the water that was in the trench.** "Regarding this as an answer to prayer let us see what there is to account for it — (a) A great occasion; the false prophets had been challenged; they were present to witness the result; a king and a nation had been appealed to. (b) A Holy character; Elijah was not an experimentalist, not a speculator; he was a holy man tried and proved, and held in high esteem in heaven; it is constant holiness that flames out into exceptional and peculiar power. (c) A worthy object; it is for a distinct and indisputable revelation of God, and this revelation was required not so much for an intellectual as for a moral purpose, namely that the heart of the people might be turned back to God. Thus, however sensational (to use a word that is often misapplied) may have been the mere method of the answer, there are round about the whole incident reasons of the simplest and weightiest nature." — *Joseph Parker.* "The fire proceeding from Jehovah was not a natural flash of lightning, which could not produce any such

39. And when all the people saw it, they fell on their faces: and they said, Jehovah, he is God; Jehovah, he is God.

---

effect, but miraculous fire falling from heaven (as in 1 Chr. 21:26; 2 Chr. 7:1), the supernatural origin of which was manifested in the fact that it not only consumed the sacrifice with the pile of wood upon the altar, but also burned up the stones of the altar and the earth that was thrown up to form the trench and licked up the water in the trench." — *C. F. Keil.*   39. **And when all the people saw it, they fell on their faces: and they said, Jehovah, he is God; Jehovah, he is God.** No doubt the people were thoroughly persuaded of the truthfulness of what they now acclaimed, but that is not a synonym for repenting of their sins and of turning whole-heartedly to God to serve Him and Him only.

5. THE DESTRUCTION OF THE FOLLOWERS OF BAAL, v. 40. If in a barrel of good apples one rotten one is intermixed, there is only one thing to do — take out the rotten apple. In our national society law-breakers must be lifted out of the body politic and placed behind bars, where they will not be able to carry on their iniquitous schemes. What Elijah did to the prophets of Baal is not what the Christian church is called upon to do with heretics. Never! But it was the will of God then, at that hour.

6. ELIJAH AND HIS SERVANT, vs. 41–46. Turning to the king, Elijah made the announcement that the hour had come for the breaking of the drouth, and that clouds of rain, carrying water, were already arising from the horizon. "There was probably preparation made for the king's refreshment on the top of Carmel, where the offerings had been made, and the words of the prophet apply to Ahab's return from the Kishon, which was at a lower level. The expression 'eat and drink' has been taken by some to be spoken in mockery or uttered as if to one who was callous even after such a scene of butchery. It would rather seem as if Elijah had not yet despaired of Ahab, and was giving the king, who must have been paralysed by the scene, the best advice for his present need, after the long and tragic day. The words may also imply that now there was no longer any fear of want, for the rain was coming at once. Thus they would form a fit introduction for the announcement which follows." — *J. R. Lumby.*

III. **THE PROPHET'S DEPRESSION AND TENDER CARE OF JEHOVAH,** 1 Kings 19. Hardly has the curtain fallen upon this dramatic event than Ahab rushes down to Jezreel to pour out to the burning ears of his wicked wife what had happened to all of her prophets. And of course, bold in evil ways as this woman was, she at once determined to put the prophet to death. So, wisely no doubt, he fled to Beersheba in southern Palestine, and going into the wilderness sat down under a juniper tree and asked God if he might not die. With the events that follow we are not here concerned, and the famous statement that God was not in the wind and not in the earthquake and not in the fire, but revealed Himself in "a still small voice." "Strange as it may seem, these felt weaknesses of men like Elijah come upon us with almost a sense of relief. It is not only that we realise that these giants of faith are men of like passions with ourselves, but that the Divine in their work is thereby the more prominently brought out. It deserves special notice that Elijah proceeded on his hasty journey without any Divine direction to that effect. Attended only by his faithful servant, he passed without pausing to the farthest boundary of the neighbouring kingdom of Judah. But even that was not his final destination, nor could he in his mood at this time brook any companionship. Leaving his servant behind, he went into the wilderness of Paran. In its awful solitude he felt himself for the first time free to rest. Utterly broken down in body and spirit, he cast himself under one of those wide-spreading trees, which seemed as if they indicated that even in the vast, howling wilderness, the hand of the Great Creator had provided shelter for His poor, hardly bestead wanderers. There is something almost awful in the life-and-death conflicts of great souls. We witness them with a feeling akin to reverence. The deep despondency of Elijah's soul found utterance in the entreaty to be released from work and suffering. He toiled; like them he had failed; why should his painful mission be prolonged? But not so must he pass away. Like Moses of old, he must at least gain a distant view of the sweet land of beauty and rest. As so often, God in His tender mercy gave His beloved the precious relief of sleep. And more than that — he was to have evidence that even there he was not forsaken. An angel awakened him to minister to his wants. God careth for the body; and precious in His sight is not only the death, but also the felt need of His people. The same great Jehovah, Whose manifestation on Carmel had been so awful in its grandeur, condescended to His servant in the hour of his utmost need, and with unspeakable tenderness, like a mother, tended His weary child. Once more a season of sleep, and again the former heaven-given provision for the journey which he was to make — now in the guidance of God." — *Alfred Edersheim.*

THE LESSON IN LIFE, LITERATURE, AND ARCHAEOLOGY.

Milton has cast the story of the prophet at the brook Cherith into some of the finest lines of poetry he ever wrote:

> "Him thought he by the brook of Cherith
>   stood,
> And saw the ravens with their horny beaks
> Food to Elijah bringing even and morn;
> Though ravenous, taught to abstain from
>   what they brought.
> He saw the prophet also how he fled
> Into the desert, and how there he slept
> Under a juniper; then how awaked
> He found his supper on the coals prepared
> And by the angel was bid rise and eat,
> And ate the second time after repose,
> The strength whereof sufficed him forty days:
> Sometimes, that with Elijah he partook
> Or as a guest with Daniel at his pulse."

A TRUTH FOR THE CLASS TO CARRY AWAY.

This lesson is particularly appropriate at the present time because of the very dangerous insistence on the part of many professors and leaders of thought in our country that what the world now needs is one great religion, with each religious system contributing its best to a universal, non-supernatural religion. To advocate such a program means to give up every essential element of the Christian faith. The true and living God reveals himself only in the Scriptures and through Christ, not through Buddha or Karl Marx. Christ alone can save from sin, in Him alone is eternal life. We are not going to undertake a program that will harm the servants of world religions, but in love we must more and more insist upon the absolute uniqueness and finality of Christ.

Wherein was the power in the worship of these pagan gods that drew Israel away from loyalty to the true and living God? On what other occasions recorded in the Scriptures did fire come down from heaven? Was the depression of the prophet a normal or abnormal experience for one who had accomplished such a great work? Was the influence of Baalism stamped out by the victory of Jehovah on Mount Carmel? (I think the record indicates that it was not.) If God gave power for performing many miracles to these two prophets Elijah and Elisha, why do you think He does not bestow the same power upon men who are equally devoted to Him today?

171

LESSON VII. — May 16.

ELIJAH REBUKES AHAB. — 1 Kings 21.

PRINTED TEXT, 1 Kings 21:1–4, 15–20.

Devotional Reading: Psalm 32.
Beginner Topic: THE RULE DANIEL KEPT.
　Lesson Material: Daniel 1.
　Memory Verse: Praise ye Jehovah: for Jehovah is good.　Psalm 135:3.
Primary Topic: STORY OF A VINEYARD.
　Lesson Material: 1 Kings 21.
　Memory Verse: Thou shalt not covet.　Exodus 20:17.
Junior Topic: STORY OF NABOTH'S VINEYARD.
　Lesson Material: 1 Kings 21.
　Memory Verse: Thou shalt not covet.　Exodus 20:17.
Intermediate-Senior Topic: SPEAKING TRUTH TO A KING.
　Lesson Material: 1 Kings 21.
　Memory Verse: Thou shalt not covet.　Exodus 20:17.
Topic for Young People and Adults: ELIJAH REBUKES AHAB.
　Lesson Material: 1 Kings 21.
　Memory Verse: Thou shalt not covet.　Exodus 20:17.

THE TEACHER AND HIS CLASS.

The Younger Classes will find this lesson somewhat complex, but the introduction need not be too difficult. The teacher may want to lead the class into a discussion by a question: If a boy or girl has something that we would very much like to have, for instance, a scooter, what are four different ways in which we might obtain such a device? It might be given to us, either that very scooter by the one who owns it, or another, by someone who loves us. It could be purchased at a store, if we had the money to pay for it. One might be made for us. All these are innocent and honorable ways of getting a scooter. Another way would be by stealing it, and that would be a sin. In our lesson we are to learn of a king who, though having many possessions, wanted a certain small piece of land. The man who owned it did not want to sell it, and would not give this land to the king. This chapter tells us how the king finally got it.

The Older Classes will at once compare the events recorded in this lesson with those taking place in literally thousands of cases in Russia during the last thirty years. False charges were brought against innocent Naboth, so that he might be put to death, only because the king wanted his small vine-yard. In the very month in which I am writing this lesson, there has appeared in *Life* magazine a series of three articles, by a former Russian officer, now living in this country, giving an account, in elaborate detail, of the slaughter, on the orders of Stalin, of high officers who had served him well in the government. Without any guilt which would justify a trial and death, these men were compelled, by torture, and threat of death to members of their families, to confess to crimes they never committed. This is the tragic consequence of great power in the hands of cruel rulers.

THE LESSON IN ITS SETTING.

Time. — Ahab's reign extended from approximately 876 to 855 B.C. Just when in his reign the events of our lesson took place, we are not sure.

Place. — The entire narrative centers in a place called Jezreel, located on the eastern side of the great plain of Esdraelon, which, with Samaria, was made a place of royal residence in the days of Ahab.

THE PLAN OF THE LESSON.

SUBJECT: How a King and Queen Were Led into the Crime of Murder, which Brought Ultimate Doom on Their Nation by Selfishness in Relation to a Small Piece of Land.

I. KING AHAB IS THWARTED IN HIS DESIRE TO POSSESS NABOTH'S VINEYARD, 1 Kings 21:1–4.

II. THE PLOT OF JEZEBEL AND THE MURDER OF NABOTH, 1 Kings 21:5–16.

III. ELIJAH'S PROPHECY OF DOOM UPON AHAB'S HOUSE, 1 Kings 21:17–26.

IV. THE BRIEF POSTPONEMENT OF DOOM, 1 Kings 21:27–29.

THE TEACHER'S LIBRARY.

For the study of this lesson one should first consult the major commentaries on First Kings, a list of which is given in the lesson for April 25. Of course all volumes on Elijah will be found helpful, especially F. B. Meyer: *Elijah and the Secret of His Power;* F. W. Krummacher: *Elijah the Tishbite;* William Milligan: *Elijah, His Life and Times;* J. R. MacDuff: *The Prophet of Fire;* W. M. Taylor: *Elijah the Prophet;* Alexander Whyte: *Bible Characters, Ahithophel to Nehemiah,* 93–100; and James Hastings: *Greater Men and Women of the Bible, Ruth to Naaman,* 359–407. This same work by Hastings also has worthwhile chapters on Ahab, pp. 320–341, and Jezebel, pp. 344–357; also on Jezebel see Donald Davidson: *Mothers in the Bible,* 162–171. There is one biographical chapter devoted exclusively to the subject of Ahab and Naboth by J. J. Greenhough in *Men of the Old Testament, Solomon to Jonah,* 45–54.

Sermonic material on this chapter is amazingly scanty. On verse 20, see H. P. Liddon: *Sermons on Old Testament Subjects,* 209–223. On the entire episode there is a great sermon in Alexander Maclaren: *Expositions of Holy Scripture, 2 Samuel — Kings,* 286–296.

AUDIO-VISUAL AIDS.

The Elijah materials listed for the previous lesson could be shown here if not used there.

---

1 KINGS 21:1. And it came to pass after these things, that Naboth the Jezreelite had a vineyard which was in Jezreel, hard by the palace of Ahab king of Samaria.

2. And Ahab spake unto Naboth, saying, Give me thy vineyard, that I may have it for a garden of herbs, because it is near unto my house; and I will give thee for it a better vineyard than it: or, if it seem good to thee, I will give thee the worth of it in money.

Human nature has not changed since the Garden of Eden. Sin is still sin. Lies are still lies; murder is still murder — the law of God has not been altered. The great principles of life have not changed — "Whatsoever a man soweth, that shall he also reap." The Bible sets forth moral and ethical standards, as well as reveals to us those glorious truths concerning God, His Son, and the Holy Spirit which could never be known except by Divine revelation. But it also contains historical and biographical episodes to illustrate for us the laws of God, to serve as guide-posts in keeping us on the right road which leads to life everlasting, and warning us away from those allurements that can bring only sorrow and destruction. In these lessons from the kings and prophets of Israel, we see ourselves often, as in a mirror. Today we look into the life of one of Israel's most powerful kings, married to a woman known down through the centuries for her wickedness, Jezebel — a weak man dominated by his stronger wife, and led by her into many crimes and tragedies.

I. **KING AHAB IS THWARTED IN HIS DESIRE TO POSSESS NABOTH'S VINEYARD,** 1 Kings 21:1–4. The record of Ahab's reign begins with 1 Kings 16:29. In chapter 18 is recorded the famous meeting of Ahab with Elijah, and the destruction of the priests of Baal on Mount Carmel. In this lesson the king is to meet this prophet again. 1. **And it came to pass after these things, that Naboth the Jezreelite had a vineyard which was in Jezreel, hard by the palace of Ahab king of Samaria. 2. And Ahab spake unto Naboth, saying, Give me thy vineyard, that I may have it for a garden of herbs, because it is near unto my house; and I will give thee for it a better vineyard than it: or, if it seem good to**

3. And Naboth said to Ahab, Jehovah forbid it me, that I should give the inheritance of my fathers unto thee.

4. And Ahab came into his house heavy and displeased because of the word which Naboth the Jezreelite had spoken to him; for he had said, I will not give thee the inheritance of my fathers. And he laid him down upon his bed, and turned away his face, and would eat no bread.

---

thee, I will give thee the worth of it in money. 3. And Naboth said to Ahab, Jehovah forbid it me, that I should give the inheritance of my fathers unto thee. The king had vast areas of land in Israel, which he could call his own, but he was not satisfied. His heart desired not some palace of another king, nor a mountain in which precious stones could be mined, nor a great forest for hunting, but a simple vineyard belonging to an Israelite on the eastern slope of the hill of Jezreel looking toward the Jordan, close to his own residence. He sought first to secure this plot of land in an *honorable* way, by asking Naboth if he would either sell it, or exchange it for a better vineyard. However, this particular piece of land had been in the family of Naboth for some generations, and he had no desire to dispose of it, either by exchange or sale. "A plot of ground to us means so much money, and to get its worth in money is the same thing. To the peasant whose fathers have been there for generations, it is above all price, as precious as the nobleman's deer park, or the castle which tells of centuries of lofty deeds and heroic memories. All men, if they are worth calling men, have sentiments and affections, and pathetic clingings to this, that, and the other thing, which have little value in the market perhaps, but are worth more to them than all that the market can produce. If Naboth would have sold his vineyard, there are few things which he would not have sold. It would have been treachery to his father's memory, pawning not his land only, but his affections, for the king's favour and for gold." — *J. G. Greenhough.* In Leviticus 25:23 and Numbers 36:7, we have a law regarding the disposal of land, and no doubt many Israelites were grateful for the law. What should the king do with this refusal? He should have dismissed the matter from his mind, or reasoned, "Maybe when Naboth thinks over my proposal he will be glad to either exchange his land or accept the price I have offered; I will wait." But this is not the way the weakling Ahab reacted. **4. And Ahab came into his house heavy and displeased because of the word which Naboth the Jezreelite had spoken to him; for he had said, I will not give thee the inheritance of my fathers. And he laid him down upon his bed, and turned away his face, and would eat no bread.** "It is characteristic of the mean, feeble, thankless mind, to forget the abundance that is given and fret over the little that is withheld. Do we not all, in our baser moods, become like sulky children, oblivious of all life's joys, of all the wealth which is heaped up in our lot, and irritated in mind and heart because some toy is withheld on which we have set our heart, because our foolish will meets with some little obstacle and has to stoop or stop? Depend upon it, it is the one proof of the feeble mind that it cannot bear to be opposed in anything, that it looks upon every man who thwarts its inclinations in any way as an enemy, that it is determined to gratify its every whim, or failing that, to magnify every failure into a perpetual sore. You all know such men, and can take the measure of them from that simple fact. The strong man knows how to yield, and to do it gracefully. He is not everlastingly clamouring to have his own way, and worrying because his cup does not contain every little ingredient which his fancy would like to put into it. The Christian man especially learns to say concerning little things as well as in the greater trials of life, 'Not my will but Thine be done.' And unless there is this spirit, life must be to each one of us like a bundle of prickly thorns, and, alas, we shall always be pricking and irritating others." — *J. G. Greenhough.*

15. And it came to pass, when Jezebel heard that Naboth was stoned, and was dead, that Jezebel said to Ahab, Arise, take possession of the vineyard of Naboth the Jezreelite, which he refused to give thee for money; for Naboth is not alive, but dead.

16. And it came to pass, when Ahab heard that Naboth was dead, that Ahab rose up to go down to the vineyard of Naboth the Jezreelite, to take possession of it.

II. **THE PLOT OF JEZEBEL AND THE MURDER OF NABOTH**, 1 Kings 21:5-16. When Jezebel came into the room and found Ahab pouting and refusing to eat, she persuaded him to tell her what the trouble was, and then challenged him, "Dost thou now govern the kingdom of Israel?" and added that she would get the vineyard for him. In the excellent volume by Donald Davidson is a concise description of Jezebel which we should have before us. "She is first introduced to us as the daughter of Ethbaal, a heathen king of Sidon. As his name suggests he was probably both king and high-priest of his Baal-worshipping people. And therein, doubtless, was the origin of this evil character. For Baal-worship was a most demoralizing cult. All manner of immoralities and cruel superstitions were bound up in it. So, with a father who was high-priest of that idolatrous religion, it was not surprising that the princess brought up under such an influence should have been early corrupted by the poisonous atmosphere in which she lived. To this dangerous nest Ahab king of Israel turned for his bride. Politically it was no doubt an attractive alliance. But it was, of course, an open violation of God's law, for Israel had been expressly forbidden to contract marriages with the heathen nations round about them." On this goading question of Jezebel, Davidson says, "How often with these very words many a good wife — no Jezebel it is true — has stirred up her husband to a course of action that his own calm judgment would deprecate. The man comes home with the story of his little trouble in the workshop or the office. Some of his juniors have perhaps been overbearing. But his wife at once stings him into action that is inadvisable. 'Are you not master in your own house? Remember who you are!' The husband is probably a man of peace. But when he is reminded of his own importance, he puffs out his chest, and instead of overlooking what is perhaps after all a mere trifle, he determines to insist on his rights. And once we start to insist on our rights, what wrongs we commit to secure them!"

Let us observe that the queen is not going about this deed in some rash, crude way, that would bring down upon her the immediate hatred of the entire nation. Possibly she had some conscience left which, little though it was, had to be taken care of. So she sent letters to the elders and nobles living near Naboth, asking them to proclaim a fast, at which time Naboth was to receive unusual honors. At an appointed time in the schedule, two evil men, called sons of Belial, or, literally, "children of lawlessness," were to bear false witness against Naboth, declaring that they had heard him curse God and the king. The command of Jezebel was carried out to the letter. Apparently Naboth was given no opportunity to defend himself. They were determined to put him to death. This is exactly the way our blessed Lord was treated, falsely accused, and then crucified. The foul work completed, Jezebel went into the presence of the king to tell him that the man who refused to sell his vineyard was dead, so he could now possess the coveted garden! **15. And it came to pass, when Jezebel heard that Naboth was stoned, and was dead, that Jezebel said to Ahab, Arise, take possession of the vineyard of Naboth the Jezreelite, which he refused to give thee for money; for Naboth is not alive, but dead. 16. And it came to pass, when Ahab heard that Naboth was dead, that Ahab rose up to go down to the vineyard of| Naboth the Jezreelite, to take possession of it.** "It is characteristic of Ahab that he takes care to ask no question about Naboth's death, desirous 'to be innocent of the knowledge,' and yet tacitly

17. And the word of Jehovah came to Elijah the Tishbite, saying,

18. Arise, go down to meet Ahab king of Israel, who dwelleth in Samaria: behold, he is in the vineyard of Naboth, whither he is gone down to take possession of it.

19. And thou shalt speak unto him, saying, Thus saith Jehovah, Hast thou killed, and also taken possession? And thou shalt speak unto him, saying, Thus saith Jehovah, In the place where dogs licked the blood of Naboth shall dogs lick thy blood, even thine.

---

to 'applaud the deed.' The guilt is Jezebel; the fruit, his own." — *Alfred Barry.* Canon Liddon graphically portrays the king walking up and down in the garden. "There was Ahab, walking up and down the vineyard, and very well satisfied with his new acquisition. It had come to him by regular form of law, for its late owner had been convicted of treason, as well as of blasphemy: he and his sons had been executed (2 Kings 9:26); and the property had been forfeited to the Crown. This forfeiture was not prescribed by any rule laid down in the Mosaic Law: it resulted from the principle involved in the idea of high treason. Just as, according to the formal prescriptions of the law of Deuteronomy (13:16) the property of a blasphemer against God was consecrated to God, as a devoted thing; so in the case of a traitor to the king, the king succeeded to the property which the traitor had held. In the case of the double crime, a king like Ahab would be likely to plead the rights of the Crown. The vineyard therefore was legally King Ahab's, and he had determined to enjoy it. How admirable was the situation of the vineyard, especially for an occupant of the royal villa!" But the joy in the gratification of a deep desire is suddenly interrupted. There are some men in the land, prophets of God, who are bold to denounce such murderous acts, and are not afraid of either the king or his wife.

III. **ELIJAH'S PROPHECY OF DOOM UPON AHAB'S HOUSE**, 1 Kings 21:17–26. **17. And the word of Jehovah came to Elijah the Tishbite, saying, 18. Arise, go down to meet Ahab king of Israel, who dwelleth in Samaria: behold, he is in the vineyard of Naboth, whither he is gone down to take possession if it. 19. And thou shalt speak unto him, saying, Thus saith Jehovah, Hast thou killed, and also taken possession? And thou shalt speak unto him, saying, Thus saith Jehovah, In the place where dogs licked the blood of Naboth shall dogs lick thy blood, even thine.** One wonders where the prophet has been, in the years between the great defeat of the prophets of Baal and this hour, when God calls him back into service in a dangerous mission. "How many years had elapsed since last the word of the Lord had come to Elijah, we do not know; perhaps five or six. All this while he must have waited wistfully for the well-known accents of that voice, longing to hear it once again. And as the weary days, passing slowly by, prolonged his deferred hope into deep and yet deeper regret, he must have been driven to continued soul-questionings and searchings of heart; to bitter repentance for the past, and to renewed consecration for whatever service might be imposed upon him. . . . It may be that these words will be read by some, once prominent in the Christian service who have been lately cast aside. They have been removed from the sphere they once filled. They have found audiences slip away from them, and opportunities close up. They have seen younger men step in to fill the ranks from which they have fallen. This may be attributable to the sovereignty of the Great Master — who has a perfect right to do as He will with His own, and who takes up one and lays down another. . . . It is also quite possible that we are left unused for our own deeper teaching in the ways of God. . . . Our simple duty, then, is to keep clean, and filled, and ready; standing on the shelf, meet for the Master's use; sure that we serve if we only stand and wait; and knowing that He will accept and reward, the willingness for the deed. . . ." Note carefully that the prophet says nothing about Jezebel being responsible for the murder, but

176

20. And Ahab said to Elijah, Hast thou found me, O mine enemy? And he answered, I have found thee, because thou hast sold thyself to do that which is evil in the sight of Jehovah.

that the king himself is.   "The stern, indignant brevity of the accusation, at once shaming the subterfuge by which Ahab shifts his guilt to Jezebel, and unmasking the real object of the whole crime, leaves the king speechless as to defence, unable to stay the sentence which at once follows.   The marked particularity and emphasis of that sentence, 'In the place where the dogs licked the blood of Naboth shall dogs lick *thy blood, even thine*' preclude all explanations, which would seek its fulfilment in the fate of Jehoram (2 Kings 9:25); nor can such explanations be justified by reference to verse 29, for it is not this part of the sentence which is deferred by Ahab's repentance." — *Alfred Barry.*   Before Elijah has said a word, the king utters a question so contrary to reality that we can hardly believe that a man would speak in this way, except we know how blinded he can be because of sin, both to his own guilt and the worth of a noble man, with no fear of God.   20. **And Ahab said to Elijah, Hast thou found me, O mine enemy?   And he answered, I have found thee, because thou hast sold thyself to do that which is evil in the sight of Jehovah.**   "Ahab could not think of any truthful adviser as a friend.   Of Micaiah the son of Inlah, he said, at a later date, 'I hate him, for he doth not prophesy good concerning me, but evil.' (1 Kings 22:8).   Ahab tries to persuade himself that whatever Elijah might say would be dictated, not by a sense of truth, but by a personal hostility." — *H. P. Liddon.*   "Though the king knew it not, Elijah was his best friend; Jezebel his direst foe.   But sin distorts everything.   It is like the gray dawn which so obscures the most familiar objects that men mistake friends for foes, and foes for friends: as in the old story, the frenzied king of Wales slew the faithful hound that had saved his child from death.   Many a time have men repeated the error of the disciples, who mistook Jesus for an evil spirit, and cried out for fear.   When Christian friends remonstrate with evil-doers, and rebuke their sins, and warn them of their doom, they are scouted, hated, and denounced as enemies." — *F. B. Meyer.*   Without discussing Ahab's strange utterance, Elijah immediately proceeds to give the word of doom that he had from God.   "Distinct from that message of personal judgment is the doom of utter destruction pronounced on the dynasty of Omri — the same in substance, and almost in word, as that already pronounced in chapters 14:10, 11 and 16:3, 4.   It is, indeed, called forth by the last sin of Ahab, but the ground assigned for it (v. 22) extends to the whole course of idolatry and apostasy, 'making Israel to sin.'   It is only this more general sentence which is postponed by the repentance of Ahab (v. 29).   In all his address to Ahab, Elijah has, as yet, disdained to name the instigator on whom the coward king, no doubt, threw his guilt.   Ahab stands revealed as the true culprit before God, without a shred of subterfuge to veil his ultimate responsibility.   Now, briefly and sternly, the prophet notices the bolder criminal pronouncing against her a doom of shame and horror, seldom falling upon a woman, but rightly visiting one who had forsworn the pity and modesty of her sex.   In the 'ditch' (margin) outside the walls, where the refuse of the city gathers the half-wild dogs — the scavengers of Eastern cities — her dead body is to be thrown as offal, and to be torn and devoured." — *Alfred Barry.*

IV. **THE BRIEF POSTPONEMENT OF DOOM,** 1 Kings 21:27-29.   There is no doubt but that Ahab's repentance was, as far as his wicked heart was capable of such, an act of sincerity.   Perhaps he was now coming out of the stupor into which he had been thrown by his wife's passionate determination to carry out her evil plans, and satisfy her husband's desire for this land.   God gave him this extension of time as an encouragement to truly turn about and begin a new life for the years that remained to him as king, though apparently he did not take advantage of this divine act of mercy.   Dr. William Taylor concludes his chapter on this subject by this observation: "If God were so considerate of Ahab, the idolater, the murderer, the thief, will he not regard thee, O thou tearful one! who art bemoaning the number and aggravation of thy sins?   Go, then, to him; and let this be thine encouragement: 'Let the wicked forsake his way, and the unrighteous man his thoughts: and let him return unto the Lord, and he will have mercy upon him; and to our God, for he will abundantly pardon.'   But go at once; for if, after all this feeling on Ahab's part, his repentance was yet only temporary, and he perished at last, how knowest thou that it may not be so with thee if thou delay?   Felix trembled before Paul, as Ahab did here before Elijah; and yet he, too, went no further.   Agrippa was almost persuaded; but the 'almost' never became the 'altogether.'   Let these beacons on the roaring reef of procrastination warn thee of thy danger.   Let the feeling of this moment stiffen into the principle of thy life.   Let thy repentance be no mere regret for sin, but a loving and immediate acceptance of the Lord Jesus Christ as the Saviour of thy soul and the Lord of thy life.   'Today, if thou wilt hear his voice, harden not thy heart.' " — *Dr. William Taylor.*

THE LESSON IN LIFE, LITERATURE, AND ARCHAEOLOGY.

James Moffatt reminds us of the scene from *The Fortunes of Night*, where King James VI is hesitating to restore Lord Glenvarloch's estate, on the ground that his son and the Duke of Buckingham coveted it as the best hunting land in Scotland. Lord Huntinglen, who is pleading his countryman's cause, "listened with great composure and answered, 'An it please your Majesty, there was an answer yielded by Naboth when Ahab coveted his vineyard — The Lord forbid that I should give the inheritance of my fathers unto thee.' 'Ey, my lord — ey, my lord!' ejaculated James, while all the colour mounted both to his cheek and nose; 'I hope ye mean not to teach me divinity?   Ye need not fear, my lord, that I will shun to do justice to every man. . . .'   So saying, he hastily wrote an order on the Scottish Exchequer for the sum in question, and then added, '. . . and now you see, my Lord of Huntinglen, that I am neither an untrue man, to deny you the boon whilk I became bound for, nor an Ahab, to covet Naboth's vineyard.' "

A TRUTH FOR THE CLASS TO CARRY AWAY.

The last commandment in the Decalogue warns us of the sin of covetousness. It seems strange at first that such a sin should be listed with idolatry, disobedience to parents, murder, falsehood, and adultery.   The reason no doubt is that covetousness, while in itself strictly a condition of the heart, often leads to many crimes. Most of the embezzlement in our country, forgery, robbery, etc., can ultimately be traced to the desire on the part of those committing these crimes to possess something which their material resources cannot provide, and for which they are not willing to work.

What parallel can you find here with the narrative of Adam and Eve in the Garden of Eden?   Why did not Elijah the prophet go straight to Jezebel before she had carried out her evil scheme?   How many of the Ten Commandments are broken in this one episode?   How is the event recorded in this chapter similar to the sin of Ananias and Sapphira, recorded in Acts 5?   How do you account for the fact that Elijah, who undoubtedly was a poor man, coveted nothing, while the king who possessed so much was seized with this desire for a small piece of land?

LESSON VIII. — May 23.

MICAIAH WITHSTANDS FALSE PROPHETS. — 1 Kings 22:1-40.

PRINTED TEXT, 1 Kings 22:2-8, 13-18, 26-28.

Devotional Reading: Psalm 118:1-8.
Beginner Topic: TWO HAPPY FRIENDS.
  Lesson Material: Psalm 34:13-14; 19:14; Proverbs 16:24; 25:11; 1 Samuel 18:1-16; 20.
  Memory Verse: Be gentle towards all.   2 Timothy 2:24.
Primary Topic: STANDING FOR THE RIGHT.
  Lesson Material: 1 Kings 22:1-40.
  Memory Verse: What Jehovah saith unto me, that will I speak.   1 Kings 22:14.
Junior Topic: MICAIAH STANDS FOR THE RIGHT.
  Lesson Material: 1 Kings 22:1-40.
  Memory Verse: What Jehovah saith unto me, that will I speak.   1 Kings 22:14.
Intermediate-Senior Topic: A PROPHET WHO WOULD NOT COMPROMISE.
  Lesson Material: 1 Kings 22:1-40.
  Memory Verse: As Jehovah liveth, what Jehovah saith unto me, that will I speak.   1 Kings 22:14.
Topic for Young People and Adults: MICAIAH WITHSTANDS FALSE PROPHETS.
  Lesson Material: 1 Kings 22:1-40.
  Memory Verse: As Jehovah liveth, what Jehovah saith unto me, that will I speak.   1 Kings 22:14.

THE TEACHER AND HIS CLASS.

The Younger Classes may be introduced to this lesson by being asked a very simple question. If in a group of 401 people, a vote should be taken as to whether or not an action or deed was right, and all but one voted that it was right, what would you conclude? Normally we would conclude that the one person was stubborn, or ignorant, and certainly wrong in his view of the situation. Yet, in our lesson, that is exactly what happened, and the one person who stood alone was the only one who was right.

The Older Classes will be stimulated to thought at the beginning of the lesson period by a brief discussion of the title of Canon Farrar's chapter on this historical event, "One Against the World." It has often been true that the one who has stood against the world on an issue is the only one of a vast group who is remembered, and blessed. Think of Noah before the flood; John the Baptist standing before Herod; the Apostle Paul speaking before Agrippa; Martin Luther at the Diet of Worms, and John Knox. But one who takes such a position can rightly do so only if he knows that God is on his side. To do something just to be different from other people is not only foolish, but also often brings disaster. If we have direct leading from God, we can endure the ridicule of the world.

THE LESSON IN ITS SETTING.

Time. — The events of our lesson took place in the last year of Ahab's reign, which was from 876 to 855 B.C.
Place. — The location of Ramoth-gilead has been a matter of dispute. It probably refers to the city otherwise known as Mizpah, in the territory of Gad, one of the cities of refuge.

THE PLAN OF THE LESSON.

SUBJECT: How in a Group of Four Hundred and One Men Who Claimed to be Prophets, Only One Proved to have a Genuine Message from God.

179

I. AHAB, KING OF ISRAEL, SOLICITS THE HELP OF JEHOSHAPHAT, KING OF JUDAH, IN GOING TO BATTLE AGAINST THE KING OF SYRIA, 1 Kings 22:1-4.

II. THE FOUR HUNDRED PROPHETS OF ISRAEL UNANIMOUSLY APPROVE AHAB'S SCHEME, 1 Kings 22:5, 6.

III. THE PROPHECY OF MICAIAH, 1 Kings 22:7-28.
  1. Hated by Ahab, vs. 7, 8.
  2. Sent for by the king, vs. 9-14.
  3. His first prophecy, v. 15.
  4. His second prophecy, vs. 16, 17.
  5. Denounced by the king, v. 18.
  6. Condemns the false prophets, vs. 19-23.
  7. Smitten by Zedekiah, vs. 24, 25.
  8. Imprisoned by the king, vs. 26-28.

IV. AHAB SLAIN IN BATTLE AS MICAIAH PREDICTED, 1 Kings 22:29-40.

THE TEACHER'S LIBRARY.

The best material on this lesson in commentaries is in the *Bible Commentary for English Readers*, and, the chapters by Farrar in *The Expositor's Bible*. For historical background, one may still read with profit Alfred Edersheim· *The History of Israel and Judah· From the Reign of Ahab to the Decline of the Two Kingdoms*, 62-76, which I have here extensively used.

Sermonic material is not very abundant. I know of no separate character study of Micaiah There is a great sermon, however, in H. P Liddon: *Sermons on the Old Testament*, 224-239: also, Alexander Maclaren: *Expositions of Holy Scripture*, 2 *Samuel — Kings*, 305-314. On verse 14 see J. Gresham Machen in *Best Sermons*, 1928, pp. 117-131; and, on verse 16, John A. Hutton: *The Victory Over Victory*, 59-70.

AUDIO-VISUAL AIDS.

No audio-visual aids discovered.

---

1 KINGS 22:2. And it came to pass in the third year, that Jehoshaphat the king of Judah came down to the king of Israel.

3. And the king of Israel said unto his servants, Know ye that Ramoth-gilead is ours, and we are still, and take it not out of the hand of the king of Syria?

4. And he said unto Jehoshaphat, Wilt thou go with me to battle to Ramoth-gilead? And Jehoshaphat said to the king of Israel, I am as thou art, my people as thy people, my horses as thy horses.

I. AHAB, KING OF ISRAEL, SOLICITS THE HELP OF JEHOSHAPHAT, KING OF JUDAH, IN GOING TO BATTLE AGAINST THE KING OF SYRIA, 1 Kings 22:1-40. The events of our lesson take place over one hundred years after the division of the Kingdom of Israel, at which time ten tribes, in revolt, formed the Northern Kingdom, and Benjamin and Judah formed the Southern Kingdom, with the capital in Jerusalem. The reign of Ahab was a time of outer glory, and national prosperity, for Israel. At the same time, it was a period of inner corruption, of fearful increase in idolatrous practices, when over the land rested the ominous shadow of the wicked Queen Jezebel. At the time our lesson opens, the kingdom of Syria, immediately north of Israel, was threatening a large-scale invasion; in fact, some cities of the north had already been seized, including Ramoth-gilead. To prevent any further encroachments by this Gentile power, and with the hope that the city of Ramoth-gilead might be recovered, Ahab, the king of Israel, solicits the help of Jehoshaphat, the king of Judah, pleading that he co-operate with him in a strong military move against Syria. 2. **And it came to pass in the third year, that Jehoshaphat the king of Judah came down to the king of Israel. 3. And the king of Israel said unto his servants, Know ye that Ramoth-gilead is ours, and we are still, and take it not out of the hand of the king of Syria? 4. And he said unto Jehoshaphat, Wilt thou go with me to battle to Ramoth-gilead? And Jehoshaphat said to the king of Israel, I am as thou art, my people as thy people, my horses as thy horses.** "Ramoth-gilead was situated on the eastern bank of the Jordan — perhaps represented by the modern Es-Salt, and in that case pitched on a mountain-spur which far overlooks the country — and was, therefore, a threatening outpost for Syria to occupy, whence they might not only

5. And Jehoshaphat said unto the king of Israel, Inquire first, I pray thee, for the word of Jehovah.

6. Then the king of Israel gathered the prophets together, about four hundred men, and said unto them, Shall I go against Ramoth-gilead to battle, or shall I forbear? And they said, Go up; for the Lord will deliver it into the hand of the king.

---

watch Israel, but swoop across Jordan and up the valley to Jezreel, before even certain information of their advance could be brought to Israelitish headquarters. This city Ben-hadad had, under one or another pretext, not given up to Ahab, as by his treaty he had bound himself to do (1 Kings 20:34). We cannot wonder that Ahab should have desired to regain a place so important, and which, while in the possession of Syria, was a constant menace to him. But he should have remembered not only that the real blame rested with himself, but what the prophet had predicted as the punishment of his guilty folly in allowing Ben-hadad to escape (1 Kings 20:42). Accordingly he should not have taken such an expedition in hand without some express warrant from God. We are not told how the appeal to their patriotism was received by the officers of Ahab, but it was responded to by Jehoshaphat, to whom Ahab next addressed himself, in terms which sound terribly ominous, as we recall the word of the Lord in regard to the fate of any expedition of Ahab against Syria." — *Alfred Edersheim.* As far as we know, this is only the second time these kings ever met. "We remember that eight or nine years previously, Jehoram, the son of Jehoshaphat, then a youth of about fifteen or sixteen, had been married to Athaliah, the daughter of Ahab and Jezebel. The two monarchs had not personally met after that event, so far as we know. But when Israel, after the defeat of Ben-hadad, enjoyed a long period of peace, while Judah was in an equally prosperous condition (2 Chron. 18:1) it was both natural and easy for the two monarchs whose families and kingdoms were so closely connected to arrange a personal interview. We may conjecture that the proposal had come from Ahab, nor are we probably mistaken in supposing that in this the Israelitish king had the scheme of an alliance against Syria in his mind. At any rate this would accord with that systematic intriguing and desire to form alliances which we have repeatedly noticed as characteristic of Ahab." — *Alfred Edersheim.*

II. THE FOUR HUNDRED PROPHETS OF ISRAEL UNANIMOUSLY APPROVE AHAB'S SCHEME, 1 Kings 22:5, 6. While Jehoshaphat tentatively gave his consent to this united military effort, he at the same time desired a word from God as to whether or not such a venture met with divine approval; for this reason he asked Ahab to inquire of the Lord regarding it. **5. And Jehoshaphat said unto the king of Israel, Inquire first, I pray thee, for the word of Jehovah. 6. Then the king of Israel gathered the prophets together, about four hundred men, and said unto them, Shall I go against Ramoth-gilead to battle, or shall I forbear? And they said, Go up; for the Lord will deliver it into the hand of the king.** "These cannot have been the prophets of Baal, for their ringleader, Zedekiah, in verse 11, begins his speech, 'Thus saith Jehovah,' and in verse 24 speaks of 'the spirit of Jehovah' as being with him. But they were not true adherents of the Lord, otherwise Jehoshaphat would certainly have been content with their words. He went on with the project of the expedition even after Micaiah's prophetic warning; he never would have sought for more satisfaction, had he heard four hundred true prophets of Jehovah say, 'the Lord shall deliver it into the hand of the king.' These men were therefore the prophets who served in the worship of the calves. They would use Jehovah's name, just as constantly as the men who had not forsaken His commandment, and throughout the whole of Israel this number of them could no doubt be readily gathered, and these, though not his Baal-priests, Ahab would bring before Jehoshaphat." — *J. R. Lumby.* "Men of the world make up their minds as to what they mean to do on grounds independent of religion; but they are not sorry to be able to quote plausible moral and religious

7. But Jehoshaphat said, Is there not here a prophet of Jehovah besides, that we may inquire of him?

8. And the king of Israel said unto Jehoshaphat, There is yet one man by whom we may inquire of Jehovah, Micaiah, the son of Imlah: but I hate him; for he doth not prophesy good concerning me, but evil. And Jehoshaphat said, Let not the king say so.

---

reasons for their course of action.   For the true and adequate religious consideration of the question, Ahab had no heart or inclination. . . .   It does not follow
that when some public work has to be done for God and His Church, the man who
is by office the natural man to do it, is morally and religiously well fitted to do it.
The promised land had to be conquered; but the great leader who had brought
Israel through the wilderness to the banks of the Jordan was not permitted (and
that for religious reasons) to cross it.   The temple had to be built; but even David
might not build it, because he was a man who had shed much blood.   And if the
integrity of the kingdom of Israel was to be restored, it must perchance be restored
by other hands than those of a king whose weak character, not devoid of some
amiable characteristics, but entirely controlled by his unscrupulous and depraved
wife, had led him into so much violent wickedness.   Ahab was under the solemn
ban pronounced by Elijah after the murder of Naboth: and although this had not
prevented his succeeding in defensive warfare, it might forbid success when he was
taking the offensive, — when he was not fighting for freedom and life, but for
the restoration of its ancient glories to the kingdom of Israel, of its ancient limits
to the Land of Promise.   A religious view of the matter like this would have been
treated by Ahab, we may be sure, with great impatience.   Until a man has learned
to look at life from a higher point of view, he cannot understand why he should
be religiously disqualified for anything that he chooses to attempt." —*H. P.
Liddon.*

III. **THE PROPHECY OF MICAIAH,** 1 Kings 22:7–28.   Somehow this unanimous approval by the prophets of the Northern Kingdom sounded hollow and
insincere.   Coming from the Southern Kingdom, Jehoshaphat had a far greater
capacity for discerning spiritual truth than had Ahab.   These prophets probably
did not even look like they walked with God, and the way in which they shouted
their unanimous verdict probably persuaded Jehoshaphat that they had been
coached in this.   No time had been asked to allow for prayer, or meditation.
Insincerity in the pulpit can be detected immediately by those who are close to
the Lord.   There is nothing more tragic in Christendom than a man pretending
to speak for God who has no message from God.   **7. But Jehoshaphat said, Is
there not here a prophet of Jehovah besides, that we may inquire of him?   8. And
the king of Israel said unto Jehoshaphat, There is yet one man by whom we may
inquire of Jehovah, Micaiah, the son of Imlah: but I hate him; for he doth not
prophesy good concerning me, but evil.   And Jehoshaphat said, Let not the king
say so.**   But there was one prophet who was not in that group.   Ahab knew at
once that this man was not in the four hundred.   He did not even call to see if
Micaiah was with them, for he knew from previous experience that this prophet
would have nothing to do with these lying prophets.   Micaiah was of a different
prophetic order.   "But," said the king, "I hate him."   "Many an objector to
Christianity in our day, if he said what he really thinks, would say, 'I hate Christianity, because, if it is true, it does not prophesy good concerning me, but evil.
It makes such serious demands: it proposes so high a standard: it implies that so
much of what I think, say, and do is a great mistake, that I must away with it.
I cannot do and be what it enjoins without doing great violence to my inclinations,
my passions, my fixed habits of life and thought.'   This, before his conversion,
was the case with St. Augustine, that great servant of Christ.   Augustine tells us

13. And the messenger that went to call Micaiah spake unto him, saying, Behold now, the words of the prophets *declare* good unto the king with one mouth: let thy word, I pray thee, be like the word of one of them, and speak thou good.

14. And Micaiah said, As Jehovah liveth, what Jehovah saith unto me, that will I speak.

15. And when he was come to the king, the king said unto him, Micaiah, shall we go to Ramoth-gilead to battle, or shall we forbear? And he answered him, Go up and prosper; and Jehovah will deliver it into the hand of the king.

---

in his Confessions how completely he was enchained by his passions, and how, after he had become intellectually satisfied of the truth of the Creed of the Church of Christ, he was held back from conversion by the fear that he would have to give up so much to which he was attached. In the end we know he broke his chains, the chains which held Ahab captive. In such cases lasting self-deceit is easy. Men treat what is really a warp in the will as if it were a difficulty of the understanding; but the real agent — ought I not to say, the real culprit? — is the will. The will sees Revelation advancing to claim the allegiance of the soul; it sees that to admit this claim will oblige it to forego much and to do much that is unwelcome to flesh and blood, and so it makes an effort to clog or hinder the action of the understanding. Its public language is, 'I cannot accept this religion, because it makes this or that assertion which, to my mind, is open to historical, or philosophical, or moral objections of a decisive character.' But if it saw deeper into itself, it would say, 'I hate this Creed, for it doth not prophesy good concerning me, but evil, if I continue to live as I do.' " — *H. P. Liddon.* So the prophet was sent for. I am reminded here of another famous episode in the Old Testament when a prophet was summoned. The lords and ladies of the Babylonian empire were reeling in a drunken orgy, with the Medes surrounding the city, when Daniel was called in to interpret the handwriting on the wall (Daniel 5). There seems to be an atmosphere of fear enveloping this call to the prophet, for when the messenger arrived at the home of Micaiah, he pled with him to prophesy in agreement with the four hundred who had already spoken. **13. And the messenger that went to call Micaiah spake unto him, saying, Behold now, the words of the prophets *declare* good unto the king with one mouth: let thy word, I pray thee, be like the word of one of them, and speak thou good. 14. And Micaiah said, As Jehovah liveth, what Jehovah saith unto me, that will I speak. 15. And when he was come to the king, the king said unto him, Micaiah, shall we go to Ramoth-gilead to battle, or shall we forbear? And he answered him, Go up and prosper; and Jehovah will deliver it into the hand of the king.** Inasmuch as Micaiah's real prophecy was a warning to the king that he should not go up to Ramoth-gilead, what can he mean by first telling the king that he would be successful, and the Lord would deliver the city into his hands? "If the prophetic office was to fulfil its Divine object, or, indeed, to be continued in Israel, it was needful to state distinctly that the prophet would, without fear or favour, simply deliver the message of Jehovah. And this, rather than irony, seems to have been also the reason why, in answer to Ahab's inquiry, Micaiah at first spoke in the same terms as the false prophets. Such a mechanical outward conformity to them could not have been misunderstood. It meant that Ahab did not really wish to have a message from Jehovah; that he had chosen his own path and his own guides in it. Ahab evidently understood him so, and rendered bold by the scene which had been enacted, and by the apparent unwillingness, or, it might be, inability of Micaiah to interpose, he adjured him to speak only the truth in the name of Jehovah." — *Alfred Edersheim.* How strange that the king should know Micaiah had not yet

16. And the king said unto him, How many times shall I adjure thee that thou speak unto me nothing but the truth in the name of Jehovah?

17. And he said, I saw all Israel scattered upon the mountains, as sheep that have no shepherd: and Jehovah said, These have no master; let them return every man to his house in peace.

18. And the king of Israel said to Jehoshaphat, Did I not tell thee that he would not prophesy good concerning me, but evil?

26. And the king of Israel said, Take Micaiah, and carry him back unto Amon the governor of the city, and to Joash, the king's son;

27. And say, Thus saith the king, Put this fellow in the prison, and feed him with bread of affliction and with water of affliction, until I come in peace.

---

delivered the message that was on his heart. **16. And the king said unto him, How many times shall I adjure thee that thou speak unto me nothing but the truth in the name of Jehovah? 17. And he said, I saw all Israel scattered upon the mountains, as sheep that have no shepherd: and Jehovah said, These have no master; let them return every man to his house in peace. 18. And the king of Israel said to Jehoshaphat, Did I not tell thee that he would not prophesy good concerning me, but evil?** "Of course Ahab was desirous of representing to Jehoshaphat that it was out of ill will that Micaiah spake always evil; and he appears to have weakened the effect of the prophet's words in some way, or else, after such a solemn portending of disaster, Jehoshaphat would hardly have joined the expedition. It was perhaps with the consciousness of the effect which was being produced on the mind of the king of Judah, that Micaiah proceeds to unfold a further vision shewing how God was allowing Ahab to be led astray to his destruction." — *J. R. Lumby.*

To confirm the truthfulness of what he had said, Micaiah unfolds to the king a vision which he had seen, a vision of the Lord sitting on his throne and the host of heaven standing round about. Of this host, one spirit said that he would go down to the prophets who would be consulted by Ahab and put a lie in their mouth. This, he points out, is exactly what happened, the four hundred prophets had lied in their prophecy. "It was a real, external vision, God-directed, which the prophet describes; not a vision of what really occurred in heaven, but that which really occurred, the seduction of Ahab by his false prophets as the result of Divine judgment, was thus presented in a parable, as it were, from the heavenly point of view. The points to be kept in view are: that the final judgment which would come to Ahab in his self-chosen campaign against Syria was of the Lord; nay, that the seductive influence of the prophets was part of the Divine judgment, and therefore of the Divine appointment — at least in its permissive sense. Yet in all this Ahab's destruction would come through his own sin; being led to his ruin by those false prophets whom he had chosen, and by his unwillingness to hear the word of Jehovah which he regarded as the outcome of personal hostility. Thus his destruction would be really due to his deliberate choice of a course in direct opposition to the Will of God. For these two elements are always combined in a manner to us inexplicable, yet very really: the appointment of God and the free choice of man. And it was all the more necessary for Micaiah to state all this fully and fearlessly, since his first message had been interrupted by the peevish and false complaint of Ahab to Jehoshaphat that it had happened as he had expected, since Micaiah would never prophesy aught but evil of him." — *Alfred Edersheim.*

26. **And the king of Israel said, Take Micaiah, and carry him back unto Amon the governor of the city, and to Joash, the king's son; 27. and say, Thus saith the king, Put this fellow in the prison, and feed him with bread of affliction and with**

28. And Micaiah said, If thou return at all in peace, Jehovah hath not spoken by me. And he said, Hear, ye peoples, all of you.

---

water of affliction, until I come in peace. **28. And Micaiah said, If thou return at all in peace, Jehovah hath not spoken by me. And he said, Hear, ye peoples, all of you.** The moment Micaiah had finished speaking, one standing near, Zedekiah, smote him on the cheek and insultingly questioned him. Undisturbed, knowing that he had a word from God, the prophet simply declared that what he had predicted would surely come to pass. With this, the king ordered the prophet taken to prison until he should come back from battle — he had determined to go. In one last utterance, the prophet said that if Ahab did come back in peace, God had not spoken through him.

IV. **AHAB SLAIN IN BATTLE AS MICAIAH PREDICTED,** 1 Kings 22:29–40. Although determined to go up to battle, somehow Ahab felt that unless unusual precautions were taken, the conflict would go against him; thus, most unfortunately as it turned out, he went into battle disguised. How the Syrians ever recognized the king in this disguise, we do not know, "but so far from frustrating the judgment predicted, it only served the most clearly to show the Divine agency in his destruction. As the battle continued, a man 'drew a bow in his simplicity' — that is, without taking aim at any definite person — when the arrow struck the king of Israel 'between the joints and the breastplate,' that is, where the cuirass which covered the breast met the jointed armour that protected the lower part of the body. Such a wound would, of necessity, be mortal, and the king directed the driver of the chariot to take him away from the fight. But the Syrians were unaware that the king of Israel had received his fatal wound. Thicker and hotter grew the fight, and the command of Ahab could not be obeyed. It was a ghastly spectacle, the disguised king, mortally struck despite his disguise, now held up in his chariot, to continue against his will in the battle. Rarely has history so visibly and in every detail taught its Divine lessons. The sun was going down, and his slanting rays fell on the dying Ahab — more royal now than in his life. Presently the sound of battle was stilled, and the rest of darkness fell on the combatants. But as the tidings spread of the death of their king, the people must have recalled the prophecy of Micaiah. And the very remembrance of it led to its literal fulfilment. For through the host ran the proclamation which scattered them as sheep that have not a shepherd: 'Every man to his city, and every man to his own country.' While one prophecy was thus translated into fact, the knell of yet another was sounding in the hearing of the house of Ahab, had they but had ears to hear it. Through the darkness speeded the chariot that bore the dead body of Ahab, lying on its bloody bed. They reached Samaria, and there they buried their king. But the chariot full of his gore they took outside, to wash in the pool by the city. And, horrible to behold, in the pale moonlight, the wild masterless dogs, which in the East prowl at night about the city walls, lapped up the water mingled with gore which flowed out of the blood-dyed chariot as they washed it. And stranger and still more horrible, the red flood in large eddying circles mingled with the waters of the pool — that pool where 'the harlots washed,' — no doubt where Jezebel's priestesses of Astarte, the ministers of the worship of debauchery, nightly performed their semi-religious ablutions in that sacred fishpond, which here, as in all other places where the Syrian Astarte was worshipped, had been constructed and consecrated to the goddess. What a coincidence, and how full of deepest significance! But did Ahab's successor not think of the blood of Naboth and the curse which rested on Ahab, not only as the murderer of Naboth, but as he who had seduced Israel into idolatry and all sin? And did Jezebel not see in this red flood in which her priestesses of the worship of impurity performed their sacred ablutions, a warning token of that judgment which was gathering, like a dark cloud, over her own head?" — *Alfred Edersheim.*

Though I used this passage in a lesson of six years ago, I would like to insert here again the stirring words of that great defender of the faith and true prophet of God, for whose friendship I shall always be grateful, the late Dr. J. Gresham Machen. "My friends, if you be true prophets like Micaiah, you will be called upon to warn the Church. But you will also be called upon to warn individual men and women. And the thing about which you will be called upon to warn them is sin. In warning men of sin you will of course often have to cast popularity aside. Like some good physicians, you will be laughed at as alarmists and hated as those who take the pleasure out of life. Men love to be encouraged by false hopes; the world is full of quack remedies for sin. . . . In such a world of quackery and of false optimism you will have to come forward with your terrible diagnosis of sin. . . . Certainly if you preach this gospel of the cross, you will have to bear reproach. If you preach this gospel faithfully, you will see men whom you have called your friends, men whom you have served in the hour of need, turn against you and join the general hue and cry; you will be subjected to misrepresentation and slander of all kinds; you will bear both ridicule and abuse; you will be attacked behind and before. But there are some compensations in the prophet's life. Many will speak ill of you; but there is One who will say: 'Well done, good and faithful servant.' Men sometimes think that the day of Christian heroism is over. I do not believe it. There may come, sooner than we think, even physical persecutions. Even you will be called upon to endure hardness for the cross of Christ. You will face in subtle forms the age-long temptation to mitigate the exclusiveness of the gospel — to preach it as one way of salvation without denying that other ways may lead to the same end, to make your preaching, as Satan persuasively puts it, 'positive and not negative,' to be 'tolerant of opposing views,' to work contentedly in the Church with those who reject the cross of Christ, to preach Christ boldly in your pulpit (where preaching Him may cost you nothing) and then deny Him by your vote in Church councils and courts. But God grant that you may resist the Tempter's voice; God save you from the sin of paring down the gospel to suit the pride of men; God grant that you may deliver your message straight and full and plain. Only so, whatever else you may sacrifice, you will have one thing — the favor of the Lord Jesus Christ. And only so will you be the instrument in saving souls. . . . The churches are crowded where Zedekiah, the son of Chenaanah and his associates hold forth; one can sometimes in those churches scarcely obtain a seat; hundreds are turned away at the doors. But let us not be deceived by appearances. Among those crowds — contented though they may seem to a superficial observer to be — there are many hungry hearts. Despite all the apparent satisfaction of the world with this 'other gospel' of a non-doctrinal Christianity, this 'other gospel' that is dictated by human pride, there is deep down in the human heart a hunger for the Word of God. Despite all the efforts of modern prophets to promote confidence in human resources, despite all that Zedekiah and his far more than four hundred associates can do, despite all the hubbub of modern optimism, you will find, here and there at least, in this modern world, listening to these modern preachers, those who say, after listening to it all: 'Is there not here a prophet of the Lord besides, that we might enquire of him?' " — *J. Gresham Machen.*

THE LESSON IN LIFE, LITERATURE, AND ARCHAEOLOGY.

Verse 39 of our lesson has had a remarkable confirmation on the part of archaeologists. "Hitherto most people thought that ivory in this passage was only a figure of speech, referring perhaps to the dazzling whiteness of the masonry; but that the palace and its furnishings were really of ivory, or at least of ivory inlay, is proved by the discoveries of Professor Crowfoot in 1933, in this very city of Samaria. The city was destroyed with all its fragile beauty by the Assyrians in 722, but by amazing good fortune, some ivories had entirely escaped the fire and were found embedded in the clay floor, sufficiently well preserved to reveal the beauty of the carved work. Many of the ivory pieces bear marks showing they had been inlaid over other substances, decorated the panels, and laid into the wainscoting of the walls. There are figures of hawk-headed Horus, of Isis with her lotus flower, and a beautiful winged sphinx or cherub with the body of a lion, the crowned head of a man standing in a thicket of lotus flowers." — Stephen L. Caiger in *Bible and Spade.* (There is a picture of some of these beautiful ivories in the recently published volume, *Ancient Records and the Bible,* by Dr. J. McKee Adams, opposite p. 337).

A TRUTH FOR THE CLASS TO CARRY AWAY.

On the first page of the Bible Satan asks this question, "Yea, hath God spoken?" When we become convinced that God has spoken and that what He has said is in the Book we call the Bible, then we go through life living in the power of that truth, no matter how great a majority might be against us. The larger number of the people in the world today are not believers in Christ but that does not prove they are right.

How can you account for the fact that there were four hundred lying prophets in Israel in that time and apparently only one true prophet? Who can be truly called false prophets today? When Ahab went to battle, do you think he knew it was the hour of his doom? Do you think that any of these false prophets forsook their evil school after hearing a true prophet? What factors in this lesson remind us of some events in the trial of Christ before Pilate?

LESSON IX. — May 30.

ELISHA REVEALS SPIRITUAL RESOURCES. —

2 Kings 4:8–37; 6:8–23.

PRINTED TEXT, 2 Kings 4:8–10, 32, 33, 36, 37; 6:8–17.

Devotional Reading: Psalm 125.
Beginner Topic: A RULE JESUS KEPT.
　　Lesson Material: Exodus 20:12; Luke 2:39–52; Ephesians 6:1–4.
　　Memory Verse: Children, obey your parents. Colossians 3:20.
Primary Topic: THE ROOM ON THE ROOF.
　　Lesson Material: 2 Kings 4:8–15.
　　Memory Verse: Forget not to show love unto strangers. Hebrews 13:2.
Junior Topic: FRIENDLY ELISHA.
　　Lesson Material: 2 Kings 4:8–37; 6:8–23.
　　Memory Verse: Forget not to show love unto strangers. Hebrews 13:2.
Intermediate-Senior Topic: WHY ELISHA HAD COURAGE.
　　Lesson Material: 2 Kings 4:8–37; 6:8–23.
　　Memory Verse: If God *is* for us, who *is* against us? Romans 8:31.
Topic for Young People and Adults: DISCOVERING SPIRITUAL RESOURCES.
　　Lesson Material: 2 Kings 4:8–37; 6:8–23.
　　Memory Verse: If God *is* for us, who *is* against us? Romans 8:31.

THE TEACHER AND HIS CLASS.

The Younger Classes might be introduced to this lesson by a discussion of the different ways in which their mother would fix up a room in the house as a bedroom for an eight-year-old girl, for an uncle who is visiting, or for a school teacher who was to live in the home throughout the school year. This will lead them into the incident of the preparation of a room for the prophet Elisha for his use whenever he came to Shunam.

The Older Classes may be introduced to this lesson by the relating of an incident which the editor himself witnessed. Some years ago I was having tea with Dr. Howard A. Kelly in his library on Eutaw Place in Baltimore, when the maid introduced a sweet-faced elderly lady. She told the doctor that no doubt he would not remember her, but twenty years before he had performed an operation on her, most successfully, and when she left the hospital, he had put into her hands a copy of the Gospel of John. This was her first trip to Baltimore since that occasion, and she wanted to thank the doctor for what he had done, for the reading of the Gospel of John had brought her to a confession of Christ. Thus, even in this life do we often partake of the fruits of our labor for Christ. The Shunammite woman in our lesson, though she did not in any way plan or expect it, was abundantly repaid in an hour of sorrow for her kindness to the prophet Elisha.

THE LESSON IN ITS SETTING.

Time. — The events of our lesson are difficult to date with exactness, though we might mention 850 B.C.

Place. — The location of the city of Shunam has been a matter of some disagreement, but it is generally placed about three miles from Carmel. Dothan was in Samaria, not far from the city of Shechem.

THE PLAN OF THE LESSON.

SUBJECT: How a True Prophet of God, Ready for Any Emergency, Brought Blessing to Those Who Sheltered Him, and Was Used to Save His Nation From a Devastating War.

I. ELISHA IN THE HOME OF THE WEALTHY SHUNAMMITE WOMAN, 2 Kings 4:8–37.

1. The recipient of hospitality, vs. 8–11.
2. His prediction of the birth of a child, vs. 12–17.
3. Years later — he raises the boy from the dead, vs. 18–37.

II. ELISHA IS USED TO SAVE ISRAEL FROM A SYRIAN WAR, 2 Kings 6:8–23.

1. His foreknowledge of the location of the Syrian army, vs. 8–12.
2. The prophet's discernment of an encompassing heavenly host at Dothan, vs. 13–17.
3. The Syrian army, unknowingly led into Samaria, is sent back unmolested, vs. 18–23.

THE TEACHER'S LIBRARY.

From the abundance of material on these verses, see first of all the chapters by Canon Farrar in *The Expositor's Bible*, Canon Cook in *The Bible Commentary*, and J. R. Lumby in *The Cambridge Bible for Schools and Colleges*. There are excellent volumes devoted wholly to Elisha, especially the two classic works by Krummacher: *The Early Days of Elisha*, and, *The Last Days of Elisha;* one by the famous author of the life of Christ, Alfred Edersheim: *Elisha the Prophet;* a smaller work by W. W. Fereday with the same title; and above all, the fine study by Alexander Stewart: *A Prophet of Grace*. For separate studies, see Robert F. Horton: *Women of the Old Testament*, 217–231; W. M. Mackay: *The Woman of Tact*, 48–63; and various pages in Joseph Parker: *The People's Bible*, Vol. 8, pp. 120–131, 162–168.

For sermonic material, see Alexander Maclaren: *Expositions of Holy Scripture, 2 Samuel and the Books of Kings*, 352–359, 376–382. On 2 Kings 4, see Hugh Macmillan: *The Olive Leaf*, 136–151; on 6:17, H. P. Liddon: *Sermons on Old Testament Subjects*, 286–301; and Hugh Macmillan: *The Clock of Nature*, 31–42.

AUDIO-VISUAL AIDS.

SLIDE SET: "Elisha," Visserslides No. 709–715, 7 sl., col. Main events in Elisha's career.

FILMSTRIP: "Elisha," (Picture Stories from the Bible Series), Filmfax Productions No. 23, 46 fr., col. Drawings.

I. ELISHA IN THE HOME OF THE WEALTHY SHUNAMMITE WOMAN,

2 Kings 4:8–37. One whose beautiful and spiritually suggestive sermons are almost forgotten today, Dr. Hugh Macmillan, begins his sermon on the prophet in the home of this woman of Shunam with words that may well introduce our lesson. "The story of the Shunammite and her son is one of the most charming idyls in the Bible. It abounds in the most beautiful touches of nature; and though the mold in which it is cast is peculiarly eastern, its simple pathos appeals to the universal human heart. It is full of suggestive meanings and contains lessons upon which a whole volume might be written." — *Dr. Hugh Macmillan*. While our lesson does contain some miraculous occurrences, the opening scene is one of great

2 KINGS 4:8. And it fell on a day, that Elisha passed to Shumen, where was a great woman. And she constrained him to eat bread. And so it was, that as oft as he passed by, he turned in thither to eat bread.

9. And she said unto her husband, Behold now, I perceive that this is a holy man of God, that passeth by us continually.

10. Let us make, I pray thee, a little chamber on the wall; and let us set for him there a bed, and a table, and a seat, and a candlestick; and it shall be, when he cometh to us, that he shall turn in thither.

simplicity and naturalness. **8. And it fell on a day, that Elisha passed to Shumen, where was a great woman.** The word "great" here means wealthy. It is significant that though the woman's husband does appear in this narrative, it is she who is the prominent figure, and who is called "great." "Probably she had been an heiress, and had brought all the fields and the stock and the farmstead to her husband at his marriage; for we are told, not that he was a great man, but that she was a great woman. She was one of those woman — the richest possession of a countryside — who are never so happy as when they are amongst their own neighbors, visiting the sick, showing a kindly spirit in the simple lives of the cottagers, and abstaining from the ways of Society, because they are at once too busy and too happy for its distractions. And in this case the motherly concern for the poor, and the friendly interest in her neighbors, were the greater because her house was in a sense empty, and her heart was hungry; she had no son. That brightest joy of a Hebrew woman's heart was denied to her." — *Robert F. Horton.* **And she constrained him to eat bread. And so it was, that as oft as he passed by, he turned in thither to eat bread. 9. And she said unto her husband, Behold now, I perceive that this is a holy man of God, that passeth by us continually.** Two great truths spring out to us from these verses: First, a man's character will, sooner or later, be revealed to any individual or group of people with whom he has frequent contact, and whether or not a man is holy *will*, ultimately, be detected, for incidental expressions, spoken desires, comments and criticisms, together reveal one's inner life. Secondly, this woman must have had longings for a deeper spiritual life, or at least a hunger for spiritual fellowship with people who were walking with God. This is not true of everyone, for many prefer the world and its coarseness and materialism. Possibly for some time she had been looking for one who could bring a spiritual blessing, and at last she has found such in this man of God. **10. Let us make, I pray thee, a little chamber on the wall; and let us set for him there a bed, and a table, and a seat, and a candlestick; and it shall be, when he cometh to us, that he shall turn in thither.** The prophet himself had no home, but wandered here and there doing the work of God. Possibly there was not in this entire town a suitable place for the prophet to stay. Whether she and her husband built an additional room, or fixed up a part of the house already standing, we are not told, but she created a chamber in the home that was to be reserved exclusively for Elisha, from which comes the common expression, "the prophet's chamber." I cannot help recalling here the home to which Jesus himself so often retired. "And now, as often as the prophet lodged there, it seemed to the Shunammite, and her husband and all the house, as if the dwelling had suddenly been transformed into a temple, a sanctuary. They passed up and down the stairs with softer steps; the holy man, they thought, might be praying or meditating. Every countenance became more cheerful. They knew that this man stood in a wonderfully near and intimate relation to Jehovah, nay, they even felt, at times, as if Jehovah himself had taken up his abode with them." — *F. W. Krummacher.*

In gratitude for the continued warm hospitality of the home, the prophet sought, in some way, to repay the family. With him was his servant Gehazi, of whom we shall speak later, whom he sent to call the Shunammite to the prophet, when he asked if there was not something he could do for her, as, perhaps, speak to the king on her behalf, or the captain of the army. Her reply is a revelation of the quietness and depth of her own life — "I dwell among mine own people." Many a woman, especially in mid-life, would have seized such an opportunity as this to go up to court, to be introduced to the officials of the nation, and to move in the aristocratic circles of the land; but she was content to abide in the small town. Possibly while moving in and out among the servants in the home, Gehazi had heard that there was one shadow over the home — no child had been born to them. Upon hearing of this, the prophet called the woman to him the second time, and without further interrogation, he announced that she, in due season, would be blessed with a child, a prophecy she found hard to believe.

The child was born, as the prophet announced, and grew up in the home as a youth of whom they were proud — and then, the terrible enemy death came to the home. As a rule, I never bring into *Peloubet's Notes* a quotation of extreme pathos, but because it will make us understand this lesson more fully, I would like to use here the moving words of that great preacher of another day, F. W. Krummacher. "She carries the lifeless boy into Elisha's chamber; she lays the dear child softly and gently upon his bed, as if he were only sleeping. Then she gazes upon him once more, calls him once more by name. Ah! with that name she recalls a lost paradise, a life of a thousand joys now vanished! Once more she covers the pale face with her tears and kisses; then she tears herself violently from the beloved corpse, shuts the door upon him, hastens back to the servant who had brought the boy home, and strictly enjoins him to say nothing of this sad occurrence to her husband, who, at that time of harvest, was wont to remain until evening with the reapers. . . . Then she directs the servant to go out into the field to her husband and ask him to send her one of the young men and one of the asses, that she might go to the man of God and come again." In an hour like this, she knows of one to whom to turn, the prophet Elisha. How wonderful it is to have someone to count upon to pray for us in an hour of sorrow. Of the prophet, however, she no doubt expected the actual raising of her son. She must have known just where the prophet was. He may have given his itinerary to this family, so close to him. When the prophet saw her afar off, he sent his servant to ask if it was well with the husband and with the child, and she said it was. She could not pour out her sorrow to the servant. But the moment she came into the presence of Elisha, she fell at his feet, reminded him of his promise of a son and her earnest request that she be not deceived in this, as though now, in the death of the son, she had been. Elisha immediately commanded his servant, "Take my staff in thy hand, and go thy way," insisting that he stop to speak to no one until he reached the upper chamber, where he was to lay the prophet's staff upon the face of the child. It is most interesting that the mother did not accompany Gehazi, but let him go on, in a determination not to leave the prophet's side; as though here was safety, comfort, and hope, not to be found with the servant.

This man Gehazi should be considered for a moment. The description by Edersheim is not exaggerated. "Gehazi was a man keenly and quickly observant of all that passed around him. He could by a sort of instinct take in the whole situation without having gone through a process of elaborate reasoning. And his conclusions were, secularly viewed, generally correct. Where spirituality was not required, where secularity, 'the wisdom of the serpent' was requisite, Gehazi was invaluable. . . . He was weak and vain, boastful and intensely covetous and self-ish. Possibly all these things were unknown to himself; probably had he known them, he would have called them by other names, and thought that they could not interfere with his religion of secularities." — *A. Edersheim.* How often is it true that the power and unction of a great teacher does not fall upon any of his pupils, nor that of a prophet upon any of his successors, nor that of a father upon his son. Though the servant laid the prophet's staff upon the child's face, there was no movement of life. "Here is a remarkable thing in Bible history — nothing less

32. And when Elisha was come into the house, behold, the child was dead, and laid upon his bed.

33. He went in therefore, and shut the door upon them twain, and prayed unto Jehovah.

36. And he called Gehazi, and said, Call this Shunammite. So he called her. And when she was come in unto him, he said, Take up thy son.

---

than that a miracle should miscarry. Here is an attempt to work a miracle, which ends in failure. This is strange and most painful. Who knows what may fail next? . . . Does the staff ever come back without having done its work? We are bound to ask these sharp and serious questions. Do not let us hasten perfunctorily over the melancholy fact of our failure; let us face it and wisely consider it, and find out whether the blame be in Elisha, or Gehazi, or the staff, or whether God himself may be working out some mystery of wisdom in occasionally rebuking us in the use of means and instruments. . . . When the child is not awaked do not blame the staff; when the neighborhood is unaware of your spiritual presence do not blame the neighborhood or the word, but seriously say to yourself, 'Am I Gehazi? Am I the wrong man with the right staff? Have I got the right book, but am myself the wrong reader? . . .' When there is more of such self-inquisition, and self-searching and self-immolation, we shall awake to a nobler earnestness and give ourselves to a broader and deeper devotedness." — *Joseph Parker.*

By this time the prophet and the mother have arrived. **32. And when Elisha was come into the house, behold, the child was dead, and laid upon his bed. 33. He went in therefore, and shut the door upon them twain, and prayed unto Jehovah.** Going into the room and shutting the door, as our Lord did in the raising of the daughter of Jairus (Mark 5:40), Elisha stretched himself upon the son, "his mouth upon his mouth, his eyes upon his eyes, and his hands upon his hands." Life began to return. After walking up and down in the house, the prophet came back to the room and repeated what he had done before. I am not given to extreme or fanciful interpretations of the Scriptures, but I am sure that Maclaren (and Macmillan and many others), are right when they see here a picture of our Lord becoming man. "And how significant is all this of the Divine method of restoring the dead body of humanity through the life and death of Christ. Does not the stretching of the prophet upon the dead child — each member of his own body being applied to the corresponding member of the lifeless corpse, and by this sympathetic contact imparting his own vitality to it, and ultimately raising it to life — figure forth in the most beautiful and suggestive manner the incarnation of God, by which He brought His infinitude within the limitations of human nature and human existence, touching it at every sympathetic point, and so raised it from a death in sin to newness of life in Himself? . . . Is it not the wonderful fact that the Eternal God incarnated Himself in the body of a little child; was born in Bethlehem, lay as a helpless babe on a mother's breast, grew in wisdom as in stature, and lived in humble dependence upon and submission to earthly parents in a human home in Nazareth? Does it not tell us that God in Christ was united to us by blood-relationship; know all 'the things of a man'; filled all the moulds of our conduct, and passed along all the lines of our experience? Does it not powerfully proclaim to us the one only method of salvation, to which all other methods, by their weakness and failure, pointed, and for which all other methods prepared the way — the personal method of God, assuming the very nature that had sinned and suffered, and in that nature bringing back life and holiness and happiness and all that man had lost?" — *Hugh Macmillan.* **36. And he called Gehazi, and said, Call this Shunammite. So he called her. And when**

37. Then she went in, and fell at his feet, and bowed herself to the ground; and she took up her son, and went out.

2 KINGS 6:8. Now the king of Syria was warring against Israel; and he took counsel with his servants, saying, In such and such a place, shall be my camp.

9. And the man of God sent unto the king of Israel, saying, Beware that thou pass not such a place; for thither the Syrians are coming down.

10. And the king of Israel sent to the place which the man of God told him and warned him of; and he saved himself there, not once nor twice.

11. And the heart of the king of Syria was sore troubled for this thing; and he called his servants, and said unto them, Will ye not show me which of us is for the king of Israel?

12. And one of his servants said, Nay, my lord, O king; but Elisha, the prophet that is in Israel, telleth the king of Israel the words that thou speakest in thy bedchamber.

13. And he said, Go and see where he is, that I may send and fetch him. And it was told him, saying, Behold he is in Dothan.

---

she was come in unto him, he said, Take up thy son. 37. Then she went in, and fell at his feet, and bowed herself to the ground; and she took up her son, and went out. The text says she "went out." Krummacher asks "Whither?", and closes his great sermon with an answer. "Oh, we can guess indeed, yet we cannot follow her now. The narrative closes the door of the chamber behind her. With soft steps we walk by it. Within we hear sobs, half, as it seems from joy, and half from shame, and broken words interrupt them, words of contrition, adoration, and thanksgiving! Ah, let us leave her in her unspeakable emotion. She lies, with her child, at the feet of the Lord. She renews the surrender of her heart to the God of her salvation. She dedicates the boy to him as his everlasting possession. She lays down her all upon the steps of his throne. Hallowed, significant moment! But let us pass by, let us pass by, my dear hearers. At such moments we must not play the listener. But let us rejoice that the Lord has rendered his name so glorious among the sons of men, and that his goodness endures for ever, over those whose names he has once inscribed upon the Book of Life." — Dr. Krummacher.

II. ELISHA IS USED TO SAVE ISRAEL FROM A SYRIAN WAR, 2 Kings 6:8–23. In the fifth chapter of 2 Kings is the famous story of the healing of Naaman, captain of the Syrian host, a leper, which is passed by in this particular lesson. The king of Syria was threatening to invade the land of Israel, and the prophet Elisha himself now enters into this national thread — his ministry alternating between the quiet ministry in the home of the Shunammite and now a request of Jehovah that an entire army be blinded. 8. Now the king of Syria was warring against Israel; and he took counsel with his servants, saying, In such and such a place, shall be my camp. 9. And the man of God sent unto the king of Israel, saying, Beware that thou pass not such a place; for thither the Syrians are coming down. 10. And the king of Israel sent to the place which the man of God told him and warned him of; and he saved himself there, not once nor twice. 11. And the heart of the king of Syria was sore troubled for this thing; and he called his servants, and said unto them, Will ye not show me which of us is for the king of Israel? 12. And one of his servants said, Nay, my lord, O king; but Elisha, the prophet that is in Israel, telleth the king of Israel the words that thou speakest in thy bedchamber. 13. And he said, Go and see where he is, that I

14. Therefore sent he thither horses, and chariots, and a great host: and they came by night, and compassed the city about.

15. And when the servant of the man of God was risen early, and gone forth, behold, a host with horses and chariots was round about the city. And his servant said unto him, Alas, my master! how shall we do?

16. And he answered, Fear not; for they that are with us are more than they that are with them.

17. And Elisha prayed, and said, Jehovah, I pray thee, open his eyes that he may see. And Jehovah opened the eyes of the young man; and he saw; and behold, the mountain was full of horses and chariots of fire round about Elisha.

may send and fetch him. And it was told him, saying, Behold he is in Dothan. **14. Therefore sent he thither horses, and chariots, and a great host: and they came by night, and compassed the city about. 15. And when the servant of the the man of God was risen early, and gone forth, behold, a host with horses and chariots was round about the city. And his servant said unto him, Alas, my master! how shall we do?** The simple description of this incident by Hugh Macmillan well summarizes this incident. "We are told how the prophet Elisha knew the plans which the king of Syria formed in his own secret chamber for the invasion of the land of Israel, and revealed them to the king of Israel, who in consequence was prepared to defeat these plans at every point. Enraged at his purposes being thus always baffled, the king of Syria sent an army to Dothan to take the prophet alive and bring him into his presence. Dothan was a small village not far from Samaria, built upon the shoulder of a steep hill. The Syrians, knowing that they had a remarkable man to deal with, came to the foot of the hill under cover of the dark night, and there encamped with the utmost quietness, meaning on the morrow to surround the hill with a living wall of soldiers, so that the prophet could not escape. The servant of Elisha, a young man, happened to rise early, and on going out he saw the first rays of the rising sun glittering upon the spears and swords of a great army standing in battle array around the hill. In great alarm he ran to the bedside of the sleeping prophet, and aroused him, that he might come and see the extraordinary sight and tell what was to be done." — *Hugh Macmillan.* When a man walks with God, no emergency is too great. Though the servant was frightened, the prophet was not. He had seen divine resources that no one around him had even dreamed of. **16. And he answered, Fear not; for they that are with us are more than they that are with them. 17. And Elisha prayed, and said, Jehovah, I pray thee, open his eyes that he may see. And Jehovah opened the eyes of the young man; and he saw; and behold, the mountain was full of horses and chariots of fire round about Elisha.** "Were our eyes similarly opened, we too should see the reality of the Divine protection and providence, whether under the visible form of angelic ministrants or not. Scripture in general, and the Psalms in particular, are full of the serenity inspired by this conviction. The story of Elisha is a picture-commentary on the Psalmist's words: 'The angel of the Lord encampeth round them that fear Him, and delivereth them,' (Ps. 34:7). 'He shall give His angels charge over thee, to keep thee in all thy ways' (Ps. 91:11). 'And I will encamp about Mine house because of the army, because of him that passeth by, and because of him that returneth: and no oppressor shall pass through them any more: for now have I seen with Mine eyes' (Zech. 9:8). 'The angel of His presence saved them: in His love and in His pity He redeemed them; and He bare them, and carried them all the days of old' (Isa. 63:9). But what is the exact meaning of all these lovely promises? They do not mean that God's children and saints will always be shielded from anguish or defeat, from the triumph of their enemies, or even from apparently hopeless and final failure, or miserable death. The lesson is not that their persons shall be inviolable, or that the enemies who advance against them to eat up their flesh shall always stumble and fall. The experiences of tens of thousands of troubled lives and martyred ends instantly prove the futility of any such reading of these assurances. The saints of God, the prophets of God, have died in exile and in prison, have been tortured on the rack and broken on the wheel, and burnt to ashes at innumerable stakes; they have been destitute, afflicted, tormented, in their lives — stoned, beheaded, sawn asunder, in every form of hideous death; they have rotted in miry dungeons, have starved on desolate shores, have sighed out their souls into the agonising flame. . . . The presence of those horses and chariots of fire, unseen by the carnal eye — the promises which, if they be taken literally, all experience seems to frustrate — mean two things, which they who are the heirs of such promises, and who would without them be of all men most miserable, have clearly understood. They mean, first, that as long as a child of God is on the path of duty, and until that duty has been fulfilled, he is inviolable and invulnerable. God will not permit any mortal force, or any combination of forces, to hinder the accomplishment of the task entrusted to His servant. This is one lesson conveyed in the words of Christ when the Pharisees told Him that Herod desired to kill Him. He knew that Herod could not kill Him till He had done His Father's will and finished His work." — *F. W. Farrar.*

The closing incident of our lesson we may consider only with extreme brevity. Elisha offers another prayer, that the Syrian army might be smitten with blindness temporarily. When the prayer was answered, Elisha, somehow recognized by this stumbling military host as one who could guide them, brought the soldiers into Samaria, the territory of Israel. In response to a further prayer, their eyes were opened, and they saw themselves in the midst of the very enemy they had intended to destroy. The suggestion by the king of Israel that now they should fall upon this helpless host was immediately rejected; instead, food was provided for them and they were sent back to their master, with the result that "the bands of Syria came no more into the land of Israel." "Would that in our days the cry of Joram, 'Shall I smite them?' were less frequently heard in the streets of Samaria, and the same kind of zeal less urgently displayed. Would that the leaders of our spiritual Israel had more of the spirit of Elisha — the rather that, after all, those whom a Joram might propose to smite are not Syrians and enemies, but brethren, heirs of God, fellow-heirs with Christ, and of the household of faith." — *Alfred Edersheim.*

THE LESSON IN LIFE, LITERATURE, AND ARCHAEOLOGY.

The very week in which I am preparing this lesson, an article by Dr. Joseph P. Free of Wheaton, Illinois, appears in *The Sunday School Times* entitled, "Excavating Ancient Dothan." From this report we take the following paragraph: "The morning of the second day Mr. Kelsey, in D-1 at the top of the slope, found the lower stone of an ancient hand mill used for grinding wheat into flour. To visualize the size and shape of one of these millstones, imagine a long loaf of rye bread sliced in half horizontally. The lower half of the millstone resembles in shape the lower half of the loaf of rye bread. The actual material is black basalt stone, a semiporous volcanic material. In using one of these hand mills, a smaller upper stone was rubbed back and forth on the lower stone. In subsequent days we found some of the upper millstones, two more lower millstones, and many fragments of broken ones. With long usage the lower stone is worn into a slight concave curve, so that it resembles a saddle. Because of this shape, these hand mills, or 'querns,' are called 'saddle querns.' A quick checking of the published report of the University of Chicago on their archaeological expedition at ancient Megiddo (only a few miles from Dothan) showed that they found similar saddle querns dating from the Iron I period (1200–900 B.C.). This implication concerning the date was of interest to us, for the Bible shows that Elisha was at Dothan shortly after 900 B.C. (2 Kings 6:13)."

A TRUTH FOR THE CLASS TO CARRY AWAY.

Although we have not been given the privilege of performing actual miracles, there is a great truth here for every child of God, namely, that frequent communion with God, walking in the will of God, will prepare us for the emergencies of life; for, because the Lord is with us and His wisdom and strength are given to us, we will be able to bring a blessing to others in need, in sorrow, in bewilderment. This is why President Eisenhower, on the day of his inauguration, offered a prayer of his own to God for help and wisdom. The greater the emergency, the greater the opportunity, the greater is our need for wisdom from above.

From this lesson alone, what would you conclude were the primary elements of Elisha's character? In what homes in Israel would Elisha not be welcomed? How many different men appear in this one lesson, and what would be a characterizing phrase for each of them? What are some of the ways in which the Lord can use His followers as channels of blessing to others, and what is necessary on our part for such service?

LESSON X. — June 6.

AMOS CONDEMNS SOCIAL INJUSTICE. —
2 Kings 14:23–29; Amos 7—8.

PRINTED TEXT, Amos 7:10–17; 8:4–6, 8a.

Devotional Reading: Isaiah 58:1–8.
Beginner Topic: BY THE ROADSIDE.
  Lesson Material: Luke 10:25–37.
  Memory Verse: Be ye kind one to another. Ephesians 4:32.
Primary Topic: A SHEPHERD BECOMES A PREACHER.
  Lesson Material: 2 Kings 14:23–29; Amos 7:12–15.
  Memory Verse: Seek good, and not evil. Amos 5:14.
Junior Topic: A SHEPHERD BECOMES A PREACHER.
  Lesson Material: 2 Kings 14:23–29; Amos 7:10–17.
  Memory Verse: Seek good, and not evil. Amos 5:14.
Intermediate-Senior Topic: AMOS EXPOSES HYPOCRITES.
  Lesson Material: 2 Kings 14:23–29; Amos 7—8.
  Memory Verse: Seek good, and not evil, that ye may live; and so Jehovah, the God of hosts, will be with you. Amos 5:14.
Topic for Young People and Adults: AMOS CONDEMNS SOCIAL INJUSTICE.
  Lesson Material: 2 Kings 14:23–29; Amos 7—8.
  Memory Verse: Seek good, and not evil, that ye may live; and so Jehovah, the God of hosts, will be with you. Amos 5:14.

THE TEACHER AND HIS CLASS.

The Younger Classes may be introduced to this lesson (which in itself will be difficult for children) by the teacher describing an incident which could happen in any home of a pupil. The father, when he leaves home in the morning, asks his son to be sure to rake the backyard, and put all the trash together by the gate. Instead of that, the boy plays baseball, though he knows he is disobeying his father. Next door is another boy, about the same age, who was told by his father to clean the basement. Immediately after school he comes home, and performs that task. Now when the two fathers come home that evening, what will be the two dominant moods of these two boys? One will have some fear in his heart, knowing that he deserves punishment. The other will be filled with joy, because he is going to show his father what he has done. A man who obeys God can face the world, and be courageous, on every occasion. Our prophet in this lesson, faithful to God, is not afraid of the king, or the priest, or the nation.

The Older Classes might begin the lesson by being reminded of something that George Washington said during his presidency: "So much of the destiny of the United States seems to rest upon my shoulders that I cannot afford to engage in anything that is wrong or selfish." In our lesson we look upon a bold prophet, who seemed to stand alone as Israel was morally going to pieces, like Bishop Dibelius in East Germany today.

THE LESSON IN ITS SETTING.

Time. — Jeroboam II came to the throne of Israel 785 B.C. It was during his reign that Amos prophesied. He reigned forty-one years.

Place. — Tekoa, the residence of Amos, was six miles south of Bethlehem. Bethel was a short distance northeast of Jerusalem.

THE PLAN OF THE LESSON.

SUBJECT: The Courage That Possesses Any True Servant of God When He Is Obeying God, No Matter If His Message Is One of Judgment.

I. THE TRAGIC CONDITIONS PREVAILING IN ISRAEL WHEN JEROBOAM II BECAME KING, 2 Kings 14: 23–29.

II. THE PROPHET'S PRAYER FOR AN END OF A DEVASTATING INVASION OF LOCUSTS IS HEARD, Amos 7:1–6.

III. THE PROPHET IS INFORMED OF ISRAEL'S COMING JUDGMENT, Amos 7:7–9.

IV. THE PROPHET'S REPLY TO THE PRIEST'S DEMAND THAT HE DEPART, Amos 7:10–17.

V. ISRAEL'S SINS DEMAND DIVINE PUNISHMENT, Amos 8.
   1. The vision of summer fruit, vs. 1–3.
   2. Israel's sins enumerated, vs. 4–6.
   3. The inevitable judgment, vs. 7–14.

THE TEACHER'S LIBRARY.

For commentaries on the Book of Amos one will find excellent pages in the great volumes on the Minor Prophets by Franz Delitzsch, E. B. Pusey, and George Adam Smith, as well as E. R. Gandell in the *Anglican Bible Commentary*, and the work by E. A. Edgehill on Amos in the *Westminster Commentary* series. The two best expository works on Amos are those by H. G. Mitchell, published in 1893 (revised in 1900), and, *A Cry for Justice*, by J. E. McFadyen, New York, 1912. I am also using in this lesson, as I seldom do but should more often, the great work on the Minor Prophets by John Calvin. To my great surprise, though I have exhausted all bibliographical helps that I know of, I have not been able to find one single sermon worth referring to on any of the verses of the printed text.

AUDIO-VISUAL AIDS.

FILM: "Amos," Cathedral, 20 min., sd, b&w. Taking a specific incident of oppression, this film developes the social and religious message of the book. There is also a filmstrip version (35 fr., b&w.).

I. THE TRAGIC CONDITIONS PREVAILING IN ISRAEL WHEN JEROBOAM II BECAME KING, 2 Kings 14:23–29.

Professor G. G. Findlay, in his *Book of Prophets*, says that Amos may be considered as beginning the Assyrian period of prophecy in Israel. "For although this prophet never mentions Assyria by name, and though at the time of his appearance the two Israelite kingdoms enjoyed a rare degree of prosperity and power, and the Assyrian Empire was less threatening to its Western neighbours than it had been for eighty years past, the shadow of coming events had fallen deeply on the spirit of Amos; he foresees the certain and utter ruin of the kingdom of Samaria, and definitely predicts Israel's captivity (5:27; 6:14). . . .

"Israel was again mistress in her own land; the surrounding heathen who had harried and wasted her in the days of Obadiah and Joel, were under her feet. Assyria, which had defeated Benhadad of Damascus and Ahab at Karkar as far back as 854 B.C., and at the close of the ninth century seemed on the point of completing the conquest of Western Asia, just at this epoch fell into extreme weakness, while Egypt counted for little better than a cypher with the statesmen of Palestine. When Amos made his appearance at Bethel, about the year 770, the political horizon of Israel was unusually clear and favourable, and his gloomy vaticinations were received with the scornful indifference of men who were 'at ease in Zion, and secure in the mountains of Samaria' (6:1)." — *G. G. Findlay.*

"Samaria" in our passage refers to the city by that name, located in the middle of Palestine, the capital of the Northern Kingdom. Verse 25 describes for us its military successes, which did not prevent moral and religious decline in the life of these people. The conditions prevailing during Jeroboam's reign will be seen as we proceed to study the Book of Amos.

II. THE PROPHET'S PRAYER FOR AN END OF A DEVASTATING INVASION OF LOCUSTS IS HEARD, Amos 7:1–6. The seventh chapter of Amos with which our lesson begins, stands really at the beginning of what is generally called the third section of the Book of Amos. As the prophecy of Joel opens with a description of a terrible locust invasion, so here also we are confronted with a similar catastrophe in the nation's life. In the Syrian year there are practically two tides of verdure: one which starts after the early rains of October and continues through the winter, checked by the cold; and one which comes away with greater force under the influence of the latter rains and more genial airs of spring. Of these it was the later and richer which the locusts had attacked. . . . It was thus the very crisis of the year when the locusts appeared; the April crops devoured, there was no hope of further fodder till December. Still, the calamity had happened before, and had been survived; a nation so vigorous and wealthy as Israel was under Jeroboam II. need not have been frightened to death. But Amos felt it with a conscience. To him it was the beginning of that destruction of his people which the spirit within him knew that their sin had earned." — *George Adam Smith.* By the word "fire" in verse 4 it is thought that the prophet is simply referring, figuratively, to the drouth that had fallen upon the land. By the phrase "the great deep" he probably meant "the vast reservoirs whence the springs and streams of the earth were believed to be fed." Instead of standing helplessly by, simply bemoaning the terrible afflictions suffered by his people, the prophet cried unto God, beseeching Him that He would lift His hand of judgment from the nation, and give them relief from the scourging under which they were suffering. The prayer is answered. There is one phrase here in verse 6 that we ought to consider. It occurs frequently in the Old Testament, "Jehovah repented concerning this" (see 1 Sam, 15:29–35). The words of Calvin here are the finest, I think, to be found in any language: "Now as to the word *repent*, as applied to God, let us know, as it has been elsewhere stated, that God changes not His purpose so as to retract what He has once determined. He indeed knew what He would do before He showed the vision to His prophet Amos: but He accommodates Himself to the measure of men's understanding, when He mentions such changes. It was then the eternal purpose of God, to threaten the people, to show tokens of his displeasure, and yet to suspend for a time his vengeance, that their perverseness might be the more inexcusable. But in the meantime, as this was without advantage, he sets forth another thing — that he was already armed to execute His vengeance. God then does not relate what He had decreed, but what the Israelites deserved, and what punishment or reward was due to them. When, therefore, God begins to inflict punishment on sinners, it is as though he intended to execute fully His vengeance; He however forms a purpose in Himself, but that is hid from us. As soon then as He lifts up His finger, we ought to regard it as owing to His mercy, that we are not instantly reduced to nothing; when it so happens, it is as though He changed His purpose, or as though He withheld His hand. This then ought to be borne in mind, when the Prophet says, that God created locusts to devour all the grass, but that he suppliantly entreated God to put an end to this calamity." — *John Calvin.*

197

AMOS 7:10. Then Amaziah the priest of Beth-el sent to Jeroboam king of Israel, saying, Amos hath conspired against thee in the midst of the house of Israel: the land is not able to bear all his words.

11. For thus Amos saith, Jeroboam shall die by the sword, and Israel shall surely be led away captive out of his land.

III. **THE PROPHET IS INFORMED OF ISRAEL'S COMING JUDGMENT,** Amos 7:7–9. We have here the first of a number of visions which are given the prophet of revelations through acted parables. The Lord stands by him with a plumb-line, from which he will draw a lesson concerning the immanent judgment of God on the nation. "As the architect subjects a wall to the test of the plumb-line, so will I subject Israel to the test of justice, and just as the architect orders the destruction of a wall that cannot stand the test when applied, so will I command that my people be destroyed, because they are incurably wicked. See 2 Kings 21:13." — *H. G. Mitchell.* There is one phrase in this passage which, though it is not in the assigned printed text, has given a great deal of trouble to commentators, "the high places of Isaac." "*The high places* or *bamoth* were natural, or occasionally artificial, eminences, situated a little distance outside the towns to which they belonged. They were served by priests (cf. 1 K. 12:31, and 2 K. 23:8, 9, which gives a brief account of the position assigned by Josiah and the reformation party to the local priests), and throughout the monarchy sacrifice was regularly offered at these sanctuaries to Jehovah.

"Israel was by no means the only nation that had 'high places.' They were common in Moab (Is. 15:2; 16:12). . . . It needs no saying that there was every risk of the worship of Jehovah becoming contaminated with heathenish elements at these local sanctuaries with their Canaanite associations; and the dividing line between the religions of Israel and Canaan tended to become less and less distinct. . . .

"The royal house is condemned for the same cause as the high places with their priests. The king and his court were deeply involved in the system which gave rise to the social abuses against which the prophet cries. But above all, the king had forgotten his real prerogative — to set forth national justice and civic righteousness. Therefore he and his must be swept away." — *E. A. Edgehill.* Up to this point we have had nothing but judgment. The lesson opens with a preliminary judgment of locusts and drouth. This is followed by a prophecy of a great judgment to come. Before other visions of the same impending judgment are given to Amos, the record is interrupted with a graphic account of one of the most dramatic hours, recording the relationship of a righteous prophet confronted by a hypocritical priest, that we have in all literature.

IV. **THE PROPHET'S REPLY TO THE PRIEST'S DEMAND THAT HE DEPART,** Amos 7:10–17. Though we are not so informed, the text would seem clearly to imply that what Amos had seen in the vision just described, he has announced to the nation, which would soon come to the ears of the king, and of his leading priests. Gandell suggests that this man Amaziah was more than a mere priest, but actually the High Priest. **10. Then Amaziah the priest of Beth-el sent to Jeroboam king of Israel, saying, Amos hath conspired against thee in the midst of the house of Israel: the land is not able to bear all his words. 11. For thus Amos saith, Jeroboam shall die by the sword, and Israel shall surely be led away captive out of his land.** "We cannot be surprised at Amaziah's intervention. The last words of Amos were tantamount to a declaration of war. He had spoken against God and the king, the highest of high treason. Against God — for the local sanctuaries were not regarded as symbols of His universal presence, but as His actual dwelling-place; their overthrow and the overthrow of Israel involved, according to contemporary ideas, the overthrow of Jehovah Himself. And against the king — for had not the prophecy terminated with a threat against the reigning

198

12. Also Amaziah said unto Amos, O thou seer, go, flee thou away into the land of Judah, and there eat bread, and prophesy there.

13. But prophesy not again any more at Beth-el; for it is the king's sanctuary, and it is a royal house.

14. Then answered Amos, and said to Amaziah, I was no prophet, neither was I a prophet's son; but I was a herdsman, and a dresser of sycomore-trees.

---

dynasty?   Amos must have seemed to Amaziah guilty, as the first Christians were accounted guilty, of atheism and treason.

"So these two stood face to face, Amos and Amaziah, the prophet and the priest, the messenger of a living God and the mouthpiece of a doomed religion.   As the years roll on, places and people may change their language and ideas; but the two principles, for which on that feast day in Bethel these two men did battle, will ever wage unceasing war.   Of the end there can be no doubt. . . .

"Against the Lord Jesus were arrayed most of the men and all the institutions which stood for religion and morality and public order.   The ecclesiastical hierarchy combined with the civil government to send the Prophet to the scaffold. *He blasphemeth: He speaketh against Caesar.*   So, eight hundred years before, did the priest of Bethel, conscious of no spiritual power with which to oppose this preacher of unwelcome truths, fall back on the invariable resource of a barren and envious sacerdotalism.   *He speaketh against Caesar"* (John 19:12). — *E. A. Edgehill.*   Having charged the prophet, falsely, with conspiracy against the king, Amaziah proceeds to vehemently suggest to the prophet that he go down south into Judah, giving as one reason that he could find plenty to eat down there and probably that he might not be interfered with in his prophetic ministry.   12. **Also Amaziah said unto Amos, O thou seer, go, flee thou away into the land of Judah, and there eat bread, and prophesy there.**   "The religion which Amaziah represented had neither spiritual power nor spiritual discernment; the priest of Bethel, therefore, judged everybody by his own unspiritual standard.   Priesthood and prophecy were, in his eyes, means of making a living; honourable means, no doubt, though both priests and prophets (especially prophets such as Amos) sometimes fell short of the standard.   However, to make money was a prime necessity of life, whether for priest or prophet; and Amos had made a great mistake if he thought that his invective against the ruling classes and the established religion would bring him a livelihood in Israel.   But Judah would welcome the preacher of her rival's doom; there he would be assured of popular applause.   Amaziah affects a sort of sneering sympathy with what he imagines the prophet's aim to be: of course we know what all these visions and voices really mean; he is simply making a bold bid for popularity, or at least for notoriety, by passing as the public scourge for popular sins." — *E. A. Edgehill.*   13. **But prophesy not again any more at Beth-el; for it is the king's sanctuary, and it is a royal house.**   "To Amos the fact that Bethel was the religious center of the kingdom of Israel, was a reason why he should, rather than why he should not, prophesy there, since his object was not to please anybody, but to reach the heads of the nation with his warning." — *H. G. Mitchell.*

The reply of the bold prophet is one of the most famous utterances in the Old Testament.   14. **Then answered Amos, and said to Amaziah, I was no prophet, neither was I a prophet's son; but I was a herdsman, and a dresser of sycomore-trees.**   Amos says that he was not a prophet by profession as Isaiah and Jeremiah and Daniel were.   Neither was he a member of the prophetic guilds as Samuel was (1 Sam. 19:20), or Elijah (2 Kings 2:3).   He was a rural man who took care of sheep, and was a horticulturalist.   "The sycamore, once very common in Palestine, is still found in Philistia (1 Kings 10:27).   The wood, though durable, is not highly prized (Isa. 10:9).   The fruit, of which there are several crops during the

15. And Jehovah took me from following the flock, and Jehovah said unto me, Go, prophesy unto my people Israel.

16. Now therefore hear thou the word of Jehovah: Thou sayest, Prophesy not against Israel, and drop not *thy word* against the house of Isaac.

17. Therefore thus saith Jehovah: Thy wife shall be a harlot in the city, and thy sons and thy daughters shall fall by the sword, and thy land shall be divided by line; and thou thyself shalt die in a land that is unclean, and Israel shall surely be led away captive out of his land.

---

season, has to be pinched or scratched before it will ripen. It was a part of Amos' business thus to treat this fruit, when Jehovah called him to be a prophet. Whether he owned the trees that he tended or was employed by some wealthier person does not appear. Even in the former case he might have been far from rich, since the fruit of the sycamore was hardly worth the trouble of raising it." — *H. G. Mitchell.* **15. And Jehovah took me from following the flock, and Jehovah said unto me, Go, prophesy unto my people Israel. 16. Now therefore hear thou the word of Jehovah: Thou sayest, Prophesy not against Israel, and drop not *thy word* against the house of Isaac.** Though he was not a professional prophet, yet (and this is what gives him the courage which marks his entire ministry), he had a message from God, and he knew it was from God. For that reason he knew that what he had to say would come to pass, and that those who opposed him were servants of self, or of a corrupt nation. "In all his native simplicity he faces the greatest Churchman of his day, without flinching and without fear. God is for him, and he cares not though priests and princes and people be against him. He repudiates with dignity the insinuation that he is a professional prophet, preaching as he is paid and expected to preach. Of course he is a prophet, and he is not ashamed to call himself a prophet — in the deeper sense of the word. The voice of the Lord had spoken to his inmost soul, and said, 'Go and prophesy'; he is one of those who stand within the secret of the Lord, who does nothing in history without revealing that secret to His servants the prophets (13:7). . . . He preaches because he must. He is a prophet because he cannot help it. He is borne on by an irresistible impulse to utter the word which, for all he knows, may cost him his life. But when the lion roars, who can suppress his fear? and when the Lord speaks, who can help prophesying? He has received his commission from God Almighty, he has been 'licensed' by none other than the Lord Himself to preach his terrible gospel. . . . The Lord had said, Go, and he went, because he had heard Him and was possessed by Him, and could not help himself. . . . God was his friend, but he cannot have had many human friends after an utterance like that; and he left the festival at Bethel, at once vanquished and victor." — *J. E. McFadyen.* **17. Therefore thus saith Jehovah: Thy wife shall be a harlot in the city, and thy sons and thy daughters shall fall by the sword, and thy land shall be divided by line; and thou thyself shalt die in a land that is unclean, and Israel shall surely be led away captive out of his land.** The final predictions in his answer to this priest were the darkest of all; Israel would be invaded by her enemies, the priest's wife would play the harlot, the land would be divided, the soil would be polluted by a false religion (Hosea 9:3), and Israel was doomed to captivity. His words were fulfilled, in about twenty-five years. Tiglath-pileser III invaded Israel, and ten years later Samaria was destroyed.

V. ISRAEL'S SINS DEMAND DIVINE PUNISHMENT, Amos 8. One would think that the prophet's ministry could be concluded with these dire messages of impending doom, but that the people might be without excuse, unable ever to say that they were not warned, Jehovah gives additional visions of judgment to his prophet that his messages might come with double force.

AMOS 8:4. Hear this, O ye that would swallow up the needy, and cause the poor of the land to fail,

5. saying, When will the new moon be gone, that we may sell grain? and the sabbath, that we may set forth wheat, making the ephah small, and the shekel great, and dealing falsely with balances of deceit;

6. that we may buy the poor for silver, and the needy for a pair of shoes, and sell the refuse of the wheat?

---

1. THE VISION OF SUMMER FRUIT, vs. 1–3. The first thing seen in the eighth chapter is a basket of summer fruit, by which is meant, of course, that the summer season is over, because the fruit has been harvested. The Lord brings out of this the truth which He Himself utters, "The end is come upon My people Israel." It is interesting to note that the Hebrew words for "summer fruit" and "end" are quite similar in sound. Both derive from a root meaning "to cut off," the former being the word *kaitz* and the latter *ketz.* "Similarly in Jeremiah (1:11, 12) the almond tree is made the emblem of the prompt performance of God's words, since its blossoms shew that it is the earliest to *wake* from the sleep of winter. In Ezekiel (7:2, 6) there may be a reference to this place. There the word *end* is used with another of like form, which means to *awake* (v. 6, margin). . . .

"The general ruin fills them with recklessness and despair. The words *in every place* belong to what follows (according to the accents). And thus the meaning is, that the dead were buried, not in the sepulchres of their fathers, but everywhere, *anywhere.* Observe the wonderful brevity and force of the prophet's language." — *R. Gandell.*

2. ISRAEL'S SINS ENUMERATED, vs. 4–6. **4. Hear this, O ye that would swallow up the needy, and cause the poor of the land to fail, 5. saying, When will the new moon be gone, that we may sell grain? and the sabbath, that we may set forth wheat, making the ephah small, and the shekel great, and dealing falsely with balances of deceit; 6. that we may buy the poor for silver, and the needy for a pair of shoes, and sell the refuse of the wheat?** The Sabbath day is here mentioned for the first time in prophetic literature, and it is significant "that here as always where the idea of the Sabbath is bound up with the interests of the poorer classes." — *E. A. Edgehill.* While the Sabbath was observed, the Israelites chafed under such observances. The merchants wanted to be about the markets, squeezing the poor and making profit out of the helpless and exercising dishonest means in all their business transactions. No wonder they hated the Sabbath. The practice of shortweight is condemned in Deuteronomy 25:13 ff. "A shekel of gold or silver was, therefore, a certain quantity of one of these metals, weighed by the buyer to the seller in exchange for any commodity purchased (2 Kings 22:9). It is probable that by an enlarged shekel Amos here means an exorbitant price. The exact value of a shekel is not known, but it has been estimated that the gold shekel weighed about 16.37 grams, and was worth about $10.80, while the silver shekel weighed about 14.55 grams, and had a value of about $.60. . . . The balances are those used in weighing the price of the grain sold. Amos, therefore, charges these dealers in grain with selling scant measure for an exorbitant price, weighing in balances adjusted to their advantage, — a threefold crime. . . . The poorest soon had to buy the little that they needed on credit, and thus put themselves into the power of their creditors, who could at any time buy them of the judges before whom they were arraigned, for a trifling bribe. Moreover, and this is the climax of the indictment, dearly as they paid for it, those who had to buy grain got little satisfaction from it, for it was only — the refuse of the corn, that part, but little better than chaff, which consisted mostly of the lighter kernels, tailings." — *H. G. Mitchell.* The practices condemned in this passage are exceedingly common in the Orient, where everyone seems to expect to be cheated or to cheat. But these practices have been too widely indulged in in the western world as well.

201

8a. Shall not the land tremble for this, and every one mourn that dwelleth therein?

Every large city in America has a Department of Weights and Measures, and hardly a day passes in our metropolitan areas, but that some merchant is not discovered cheating his customers, in quantity or quality of merchandise, or both.
   3. The Inevitable Judgment, vs. 7–14.   Let us note here that the sins Amos is speaking of are *social* sins, more than what might be called violations of divinely established religious practices, and as we recall this, we should remember that our Lord Himself had much to say about social sins, especially at the beginning of His ministry, the Sermon on the Mount (see Matt. 5:17–37), and at the end of His ministry, in His terrible indictment of the Pharisees (Matt. 23, especially vs. 23–24).   8a. **Shall not the land tremble for this, and every one mourn that dwelleth therein?**   The remaining verses of our chapter need not be given extended consideration here.   By the phrase, "the sin of Samaria," the prophet "is clearly alluding to some concrete object, in fact to an idol, which was invoked by the people of Samaria.   Probably *'ashmath* (or better, *'ashimath*) is none other than *'Ashima*, the god of the Hamathites (2 Kings 17:30); and the fact that the Israelites worshipped a god of this name has lately come to light in the Aramaic papyri discovered at Elephantine in Upper Egypt." — *E. A. Edgehill*. There is one very strange theme here, however, on which I do want to say just a word.   The seventh chapter opens with the description of a famine of bread.   The eighth closes with a prophecy of a famine "of hearing the words of the Lord."   Note that it is not a famine of the Word, as though the world will be short of Bibles, but a famine of *hearing* the Word of the Lord, as though national perils, international conflicts, world-government, et cetera, will so crowd in upon the minds of men, that the clear unfolding of the Word of God will become increasingly scarce.   I am afraid that such a situation is becoming increasingly common in our land.   In the last two years I have actually become alarmed, in preaching in some of the outstanding conservative churches of our country, to discover that there is a deliberate omitting of the reading of the Word of God in public worship.   I find in so many places today, even where the Gospel is believed and proclaimed, that on Sunday nights, instead of having a message from the Word of God, churches are putting on movies.   Now the movies may be good — nature pointing to God, missionary activities, and other films, trying to impress one with the necessity of accepting Christ, but no film, no hour of dramatic interpretation, no concert, can ever be an adequate substitute for the Word of God!

THE LESSON IN LIFE, LITERATURE, AND ARCHAEOLOGY.

John Milton, in his great work, *The Christian Doctrine*, Chapter 14, on "The Second Class of Special Duties Towards Our Neighbor, Continued," uses two verses from our lesson in one paragraph.   'To justice in matters of sale and purchase, are opposed various frauds.   Proverbs 11:26 — 'he that withholdeth corn, the people shall curse him.'   Ezekiel 28:16 — 'by the multitude of thy merchandise they have filled the midst of thee with violence.'   So also when counterfeit or adulterated goods are sold for genuine.   Amos 8:6 — 'that we may well the refuse of the wheat.'   Or when false weights and measures are employed.   Leviticus 19:35 — 'ye shall do no unrighteousness in judgment, in meteyard, in weight, or in measure.'   Deuteronomy 25:13–15 — 'thou shalt not have in thy bag divers weights, a great and a small.'   Proverbs 11:1 — 'a false balance is abomination to Jehovah.'   Proverbs 20:10 — 'divers weights and divers measures, both of them are alike abomination to Jehovah.'   See also 5:23.   Hosea 12:7 — 'he is a merchant, the balances of deceit are in his hand.'   Amos 8:5 — 'maketh the ephah small.'   Micah 6:11 — 'shall I count them pure with the wicked balances?'   Or when the buyer, on his part, uses dishonest artifices in the conclusion of a bargain.   Proverbs 20:14 — 'It is naught, it is naught, saith the buyer.' " — *John Milton*.

A TRUTH FOR THE CLASS TO CARRY AWAY.

Here we have again, as in many of the lessons from the Old Testament, the great truth that God in His mercy warns a nation before sending judgment; just as our Lord warned the Jews of the coming destruction of Jerusalem, and practically all books of the New Testament speak of a day of the wrath of God to come, a final judgment. The God of the Old Testament is the God of the New. He sent prophets to ancient Israel: He has given the world His divine revelation, now translated into over a thousand languages. Mankind will be without excuse when that day dawns.

What made this priest, supposedly in the service of God, refuse to hearken to the message of Amos the prophet? In the Old Testament, why are the prophets much nearer to God than the priests? Do you think that calamities in nature, or military defeats, that fall upon modern nations are ever sent of God? Where in the Bible do we have predictions relating to the end of this age, when the natural calamities of the lesson just studied will fall upon the world in universal scope? (Matt. 24 and Rev. 6 ff.) Do you think that the world in its history moves away from God, as Israel did up to her day of judgment; or is the world increasingly obedient to the will of God?

LESSON XI. — June 13.

AMOS DENOUNCES INTEMPERANCE (TEMPERANCE). —
Amos 2:6–12; 4:1–2; 6.

PRINTED TEXT, Amos 2:11–12; 4:1–2; 6:1–7.

Devotional Reading: Romans 13:7–14.

⁂ Beginner Topic: TIMOTHY'S BIBLE VERSES.
   Lesson Material: Psalm 119:12–16; 2 Timothy 1:1–6; 2:15; 3:14–17.
   Memory Verse: Jehovah . . . giveth the sun for a light by day. He made the stars also, He hath made everything beautiful in its time. Jeremiah 31:35; Genesis 1:16; Ecclesiastes 3:11.

Primary Topic: AMOS IN THE MARKET PLACE.
   Lesson Material: Amos 6:1, 4–6.
   Memory Verse: Hate the evil, and love the good, and establish justice in the gate. Amos 5:15.

Junior Topic: AMOS IN THE MARKET PLACE.
   Lesson Material: Amos 2:10–12; 4:1; 6.
   Memory Verse: Hate the evil, and love the good, and establish justice in the gate. Amos 5:15.

Intermediate-Senior Topic: TO DRINK OR NOT TO DRINK.
   Lesson Material: Amos 2:6–12; 4:1–2; 6.
   Memory Verse: Let us walk becomingly, as in the day; not in revelling and drunkenness. Romans 13:13.

Topic for Young People and Adults: AMOS DENOUNCES INTEMPERANCE.
   Lesson Material: Amos 2:6–12; 4:1–2; 6.
   Memory Verse: Let us walk becomingly, as in the day; not in revelling and drunkenness. Romans 13:13.

THE TEACHER AND HIS CLASS.

The Younger Classes would normally find this a very difficult lesson, but I believe that we have come to a time in American life when young people, even in grammar school, need the solemn warnings of the Word of God regarding what we call social sins, sins toward others, or sinful practices engaged in with others. We are face to face in this country with a juvenile delinquency greater and more frightening than anything we have thus far known, and unless something of a radical nature takes place to turn this tide, it will grow worse. The teacher might ask the children, "Do some things happen occasionally at school about which you never tell your parents?" The answer will be yes.

The Older Classes greatly need the admonition found in our lesson today. Everywhere I go in this land just now I am finding not only gross imtemperance, but the matter of intoxicating liquors, cocktails, etc., seems to be the most common subject of conversation, on the trains, at restaurant tables, on the street. People no longer talk much about the war, or our great national problems, but rather, about the hours after work, when they can indulge themselves as they please in the desires of the flesh. One Christian publisher in this country told me that at a recent convention of secular publishers, which he attended by invitation, four cocktail parties were announced in a period of twenty-four hours. I do not think that scolding, or statistics, or a Sunday School lesson is going to change this nation, but the Spirit of God can, a revival can — perhaps it will take an act of judgment to awaken us out of our indifference.

THE LESSON IN ITS SETTING.

Time. — Amos prophesied during the reign of Jeroboam II, who came to the throne of Israel in 785 B.C.

Place. — Amos lived at Tekoa, six miles south of Bethlehem.

THE PLAN OF THE LESSON.

SUBJECT: The Sins of the Ruling Class, and the Rich, in Israel Toward Their Helpless Fellow-Israelites, Which God Could Not Ignore, and Because of Which He Must Bring His Own People Into Captivity.

I. THE SINS OF ISRAEL WHICH BROUGHT DOWN UPON HER THE JUDGMENT OF GOD, Amos 2:6–12; 6:4–6.
1. Oppression of the poor, 2:6.
2. Immorality, 2:7.
3. Drunkenness, 2:8.
4. Refusing to hear God's messengers, the prophets, 2:9–12.
5. Luxury, 6:4–6.

II. THEIR INDIFFERENCE TO COMING JUDGMENT, Amos 6:1–3.

III. THE COMING CAPTIVITY, Amos 4:1, 2; 6:7–14.

<hr/>

THE TEACHER'S LIBRARY.

The bibliography for the lesson of June 6 will be adequate for the study of this additional lesson from Amos. Sermonic material on verses assigned for the printed text is very scarce. However, on 2:11, 12, see S. R. Driver: *Sermons on Subjects Connected with the Old Testament*, 99–118; on 6:1–8, Charles H. Spurgeon: *Metropolitan Tabernacle Pulpit*, Vol. 8, #417 and Vol. 52, #2917; and Alexander Maclaren: *Expositions of Holy Scripture, Ezekiel to Minor Prophets*, 163–168.

<hr/>

AUDIO-VISUAL AIDS.

Same as for the previous lesson.

<hr/>

Though the prophet Amos lived 2700 years ago, the social sins of which he speaks here continually break forth in our so-called western culture with fearful force. There has probably never been a time in the history of our own nation when we were so truly guilty of what this prophet is here talking about as in this present hour.

I. THE SINS OF ISRAEL WHICH BROUGHT DOWN UPON HER THE JUDGMENT OF GOD, Amos 2:6–12; 6:4–6.

1. OPPRESSION OF THE POOR, 2:6. For this entire lesson, and especially for the opening verses, I find the commentary by Delitzsch still the very best. In verses 6–8, the prophet condemns four kinds of crimes. "The first is unjust treatment, or condemnation of the innocent in their administration of justice. Selling the righteous for silver, that is, for money, refers to the judges who were bribed to punish a man as guilty of the crime of which he was accused, when he was really righteous in a judicial, not in a moral sense, or innocent of any punishable crime. *Bakkeseph*, for money, that is, either to obtain money, or for the money which they had already received, viz. from the accuser, for condemning the innocent."

— *F. Delitzsch. Bakkeseph* is closely related to the most frequently heard word in the whole of the Near East — *Bakshesh.* No one ever travels in North Africa or the Near East but that the moment he leaves the boat, children and men who cannot speak a word of English crowd upon him with outstretched arms crying out this word. "The same expressions are repeated in another chapter (8:6): 'that we may buy the poor for silver, and the needy for a pair of shoes.' In each case a literal selling of the debtor by the creditor may be meant, not the perversion of justice by means of bribes. A poor Hebrew might sell himself, but his master must not treat him as a bondsman, but as a hired servant, through fear of God, Whose servants both alike were (see Lev. 25:39–43). But the law did not authorize the sale of a debtor by his creditor. The righteous represents one who was insolvent through no fault of his own. The 'shoes' are sandals, consisting of a sole of wood or leather fastened to the foot by straps. Those worn by women were sometimes made of finer materials (Song of Sol. 7:1; Ezek. 16:10). The poor man then was sold to get an article either of slight value or mere luxury." — *R. Gandell.*

2. IMMORALITY, 2:7. "To bend the way of the meek, that is, to bring them into a trap, or cast them headlong into destruction by impediments and stumbling blocks laid in their path. The way is the way of life, their outward course. The idea that the way refers to the judgment or legal process is too contracted. Another crime is their profanation of the name of God by shameless immorality. A man and his father, that is, both son and father, go to the girl, that is, to the prostitute. . . . This sin was tantamount to incest, which, according to the law, was to be punished with death (compare Lev. 18:7, 15 and 20:11). The profanation of the name of God by such conduct as this does not indicate prostitution in the temple itself, such as was required by the licentious worship of Baal and Asherah, but consisted in a daring contempt of the commandments of God, as the original passage (Lev. 22:32) from which Amos took the words clearly shows (compare Jer. 34:16)." — *F. Delitzsch.*

3. DRUNKENNESS, 2:8. "The garments were the outer garments that Orientals use not only during the day, but also during the night. Indeed, the poor have almost no other bedding. It was, therefore, but humane that, as the earliest code known to the Hebrews provided (Ex. 22:26) whenever a poor man had been obliged to pawn his cloak it should always be returned to him at night. Amos charges the usurers in Israel with disregarding this merciful provision and even spreading the garments of the poor on their couches at their religious feasts. At all of these altars, as often as there was a feast, anybody could see the dearest rights of the poor shamelessly disregarded, and this in the name of religion. 'The wine of such as have been fined they drink,' that is, wine purchased with the proceeds of fines. Amos does not say that these fines were unjustly imposed, but the character of the justice that was dispensed in Israel (v. 6) was such as to make it almost certain that they were excessive if not totally unmerited. The wine thus purchased was an essential of the meal that followed certain offerings (Ex. 32:6; Num. 25:2; 1 Sam. 10:3) and the 'drunkards of Ephraim' (Isa. 5:11; compare Amos 4:1) drank it." — *H. G. Mitchell.*

4. REFUSING TO HEAR GOD'S MESSENGERS, THE PROPHETS, 2:9–12. This passage opens with the contrasting conjunction *yet*, for in these verses the Lord, before enumerating other deep sins of Israel, would remind His chosen people upon whom judgment is soon to come, of two outstanding manifestations of divine grace, to which Israel owed its existence as an independent nation. "Amos mentions first of all the destruction of the former inhabitants of Canaan (Ex. 23:27, sqq.; 34:11); and secondly, what was earlier in point of time, namely, the deliverance out of Egypt and guidance through the Arabian desert; not because the former act of God was greater than the latter, but in order to place first what the Lord had done for the nation, and follow that up with what He had done to the nation, that He may be able to append to this what He still continues to do. The nations destroyed before Israel are called Amorites, from the most powerful of the Canaanit-

AMOS 2:11. And I raised up of your sons for prophets and of your young men for Nazirites. Is it not even thus, O ye children of Israel? saith Jehovah.

12. But ye gave the Nazirites wine to drink, and commanded the prophets, saying, Prophesy not.

AMOS 6:4. That lie upon beds of ivory, and stretch themselves upon their couches, and eat the lambs out of the flock, and the calves out of the midst of the stall;

5. That sing idle songs to the sound of the viol; that invent for themselves instruments of music, like David;

6. That drink wine in bowls, and anoint themselves with the chief oils; but they are not grieved for the affliction of Joseph.

---

ish tribes, as in Genesis 15:16; Joshua 24:15, etc. To show, however, that Israel was not able to destroy this people by its own strength, but that Jehovah the Almighty God alone could accomplish this, he proceeds to transfer to the whole nation what the Israelitish spies reported as to their size, more especially as to the size of particular giants (Num. 13:32, 33) and describes the Amorites as giants as lofty as trees and as strong as trees, and, continuing the same figure, depicts their utter destruction or extermination as the destruction of their fruit and of their roots. For this figure of speech in which the posterity of a nation is regarded as its fruit, and the kernel of the nation out of which it springs as the root, see Ezekiel 17:9; Hosea 9:16; Job 18:16. These two manifestations of divine mercy Moses impressed more than once upon the hearts of the people in his last addresses, to urge them in consequence to hold fast to the divine commandments and to the love of God (compare Deut. 8:2 ff.; 9:1–6; 29:1–8)." — *F. Delitzsch.* **11. And I raised up of your sons for prophets and of your young men for Nazirites. Is it not even thus, O ye children of Israel? saith Jehovah. 12. But ye gave the Nazirites wine to drink, and commanded the prophets, saying, Prophesy not.** The establishment of the Nazarite vow which included abstinency from wine etc. made by fermentation, found in Numbers 6. This was a sacred vow unto God and only the most ungodly would plan to persuade those who had taken this vow to break it. The refusal of Israel to hearken to the prophets sent by God is a theme referred to over and over again in the Old Testament, and with terrible sternness by our Lord in Matthew 23:29–34.

5. LUXURY, 6:4–6. **4. That lie upon beds of ivory, and stretch themselves upon their couches, and eat the lambs out of the flock, and the calves out of the midst of the stall; 5. That sing idle songs to the sound of the viol; that invent for themselves instruments of music, like David; 6. That drink wine in bowls, and anoint themselves with the chief oils; but they are not grieved for the affliction of Joseph.** The prosperity of the nation brought about a state of luxurious indulgence. This was the stage of Rome when she became mistress of the world, but was softened with the interpenetration of Oriental vices. "These gourmands, like their successors, prided themselves on having dainties out of season, because they were more costly then. And their feasts had the adornment of music, which the shepherd, who knew only the pastoral pipe that gathered his sheep, refers to with contempt. He uses a very rare word of uncertain meaning, which is probably best rendered in some such way as the Revised Version does: 'They sing idle songs.' To him their elaborate performances seemed like empty babble. Worse than that, they 'devise musical instruments like David.' But how unlike him in the use they make of art! What a descent from the praises of God to the 'idle songs' fit for the hot dining-halls and the guests there! Amos was indignant at the profanation of art, and thought it best used in the service of God. What

AMOS 6:1. Woe to them that are at ease in Zion, and to them that are secure in the mountain of Samaria, the notable men of the chief of the nations, to whom the house of Israel come!

2. Pass ye unto Calneh, and see; and from thence go ye to Hamath the great; then go down to Gath of the Philistines: are they better than these kingdoms? or is their border greater than your border?

3. Ye that put far away the evil day, and cause the seat of violence to come near.

AMOS 4:1. Hear this word, ye kine of Bashan, that are in the mountain of Samaria, that oppress the poor, that crush the needy, that say unto their lords, Bring, and let us drink.

---

would he have said if he had been 'fastened into a front-row box' and treated to a modern opera?" — *Alexander Maclaren.*

II. **THEIR INDIFFERENCE TO COMING JUDGMENT,** 6:1-3. 1. **Woe to them that are at ease in Zion, and to them that are secure in the mountain of Samaria, the notable men of the chief of the nations, to whom the house of Israel come!** The chapter opens with irony. Israel claimed to be the chief of the nations. "It is a people which speaks loud of its privileges and position, but thinks little of the responsibilities which that position involves. Jehovah loathes this proud boasting." — *E. A. Edgehill.* I am sure that this is a needed warning for our own land. 2. **Pass ye unto Calneh, and see; and from thence go ye to Hamath the great; then go down to Gath of the Philistines: are they better than these kingdoms? or is their border greater than your border?** Calneh here presents a problem in location, though it was probably a city in Babylonia. "Hamath the great" was originally a Canaanite settlement on the Orontes (Gen. 10:18) and was later under David's rule (2 Sam. 8:9). Gath was one of the five principal cities of Philistia. "The prophet thereby reminds Israel that Jehovah has given his people a fairer country, with wider borders, than either of the neighboring nations could boast. Having thus shown how Jehovah had favored the Hebrews as a people, Amos now describes how Israel in particular has requited his goodness." — *H. G. Mitchell.* 3. **Ye that put far away the evil day, and cause the seat of violence to come near.** This is one of the most tragic statements in the entire Book of Amos. "The farther off the day of evil was, the stronger the temptation to commit oppression. The word for *seat* means *dwelling* or *sitting*. The passage may be taken in more than one way. They gave a ready welcome to violence; made a home for it, sheltered and cherished it. Or, they countenanced and encouraged violence on the *seat* of the judge. With this may be compared the phrase, *the throne of iniquity* (Ps. 94:20) and the use of the verb *sit* frequently of kings and magistrates, as in Psalm 122:5." — *R. Gandell.* (See also Ezek. 12:27).

III. **THE COMING CAPTIVITY,** 4:1, 2; 6:7-14. With a heart torn with love for Israel, the prophet is compelled to use words of terrible violence, with the hope that Israel will thus be awakened from her slumber. 4:1. **Hear this word, ye kine of Bashan, that are in the mountain of Samaria, that oppress the poor, that crush the needy, that say unto their lords, Bring, and let us drink.** "In figurative language princes and the mighty are spoken of as 'fatlings of Bashan (Ezek. 39:18) and fierce, strong, unrelenting enemies are called 'strong bulls of Bashan' (Ps. 22:12). Here the prophet speaks of kine, and it might be supposed that in this phrase he pointed to women, who by their self-indulgent lives and extravagance occasioned the oppression of the weak and needy, because they required from their husbands whatever could gratify their wishes. But he has not used the feminine gender throughout, using the masculine several times." — *R. Gandell.* This is followed by a prediction of a coming captivity, a warning that fills the Book of Jeremiah, and is often found in the other prophets. Here, however, Amos uses a

2. The Lord Jehovah hath sworn by his holiness, that, lo, the days shall come upon you, that they shall take you away with hooks, and your residue with fish-hooks.

Amos 6:7. Therefore shall they now go captive with the first that go captive; and the revelry of them that stretched themselves shall pass away.

---

peculiar expression, that the Lord will take Israel away "with hooks." **2. The Lord Jehovah hath sworn by his holiness, that, lo, the days shall come upon you, that they shall take you away with hooks, and your residue with fish-hooks.** "The figure is not taken from animals, into whose noses hooks and rings are inserted to tame them, or from large fishes that are let down into the water again by nose-hooks; but from the catching of fishes that are drawn out of the fish-pond with hooks. Thus shall the voluptuous, wanton women be violently torn away or carried off from the midst of the superfluity and debauchery in which they lived as in their proper element." — *F. Delitzsch.* This same figure of speech is employed in relation to Sennacherib and his army (Isa. 37:29), Gog and Magog (Ezek. 38:4). The subject of captivity occupies the second half of the sixth chapter. **7. Therefore shall they now go captive with the first that go captive; and the revelry of them that stretched themselves shall pass away.** The terrible significance of this captivity of Israel can only be fully understood when we realize that while the prophecies of the later destruction of Jerusalem and the taking of the cities of Judah to Babylon embrace a promise of their return in seventy years (Jer. 25:10–14) no chronological prophecy of restoration is ever connected with judgments upon Israel.

In concluding this lesson, it is well to remind ourselves that in Amos we have a man extremely sensitive to Israel's wrong-doing. "Amos feels intensely the wrongs of the class to which he belongs. He is the champion of the landless poor. But for all this, and with the sense of social injustice rankling deeply in his breast, it is the rights of God for which he is supremely concerned. He is a religious reformer, not a socialistic agitator; a prophet, and not a politician. He is, above all things, a prophet of the majesty of Jehovah, — of that majesty alike in its natural and moral elements; and God's voice had called him from his village home and sent him on this errand, striking his soul with the same sudden and awful force with which the roar of the lion falls on the traveller's ear in the forest (3:7, 8). A solitary, untutored man, he must confront, in the name of that outraged Majesty, the pride of the court and the pomp of the sanctuary; he must bear Jehovah's fearful ultimatum to Israel, and bid her instantly 'prepare to meet her God.' This plain herdsman of the wilderness is chosen to be Jehovah's 'mouth' when he would speak with 'lips burning with indignation,' and with 'a tongue like devouring fire' against the shrines and palaces of Bethel and Samaria. It was a tremendous errand on which to send any man; but the instrument was well fitted for its task." — *G. G. Findlay.*

Every citizen of our country should carefully read and study the article "Crime Does Pay," by Virgil W. Peterson in the *Atlantic Monthly* for February, 1953.

THE LESSON IN LIFE, LITERATURE, AND ARCHAEOLOGY.

At the beginning of the third century, Clement of Alexandria wrote a notable work called "The Instructor," in which he has an entire chapter on the subject of drinking. In the middle of the chapter, he uses Amos 6:4–6 as follows: "Importations of wines from beyond seas are for an appetite enfeebled by excess, where the soul even before drunkenness is insane in its desires. For there are the fragrant Thasian wine, and the pleasant-breathing Lesbian, and a sweet Cretan wine, and sweet Syracusan wine, and Mendusian, an Egyptian wine, and the insular Naxian, the 'highly perfumed and flavoured,' another wine of the land of Italy. These are many names.   For the temperate drinker, one wine suffices, the product of the cultivation of the one God.   For why should not the wine of their own country satisfy men's desires, unless they were to import water also, like the foolish Persian kings?   The Choaspes, a river of India so-called, was that from which the best water for drinking — the Choaspian — was got.   As wine, when taken, makes people lovers of it, so does water too.   The Holy Spirit, uttering His voice by Amos, pronounces the rich to be wretched on account of their luxury: 'Those that drink strained wine, and recline on an ivory couch,' he says; and what else similar he adds by way of reproach." — *Clement of Alexandria.*

Something is taking place in our country which, if not soon remedied, will give us an even greater harvest of crime than we now have — already one of the worst records for crime of any civilized nation of the world.   I refer to the alarming increase in delinquency among children in our country.   More than one million children are picked up annually across our nation as juvenile delinquents; of this number, more than 300,000 reach the courts.   According to the Bureau of Census, within ten years the child population between 10 and 17 years of age — when delinquency most often occurs — will increase at least fifty per cent; and if nothing is done to prevent it, there will be 450,000 juvenile delinquents in the courts of our nation each year by 1960.   More than 500,000 children in this country are detained every year in adult jails, "because there is no other place to put them."   Juvenile delinquency has increased nineteen per cent in the last four years.   Though only in their teens, these boys and girls are already burglars, gangsters, drug addicts, and murderers.   In St. Louis, for example, the teen-age crime wave was so bad that an investigation was started, which reported that the police knew of at least fifteen juvenile gangs in that city.   Some house-breaking has been committed by children ten years of age.   Mr. J. Edgar Hoover reports that of every thousand murderers, 140 are under 21 years of age; and of every thousand robberies, 360 are committed by those under 21; and of every thousand accused of burglary, 510 are under 21 years of age.   Mr. Hoover adds, "I am not easily shocked or alarmed, but today, like thousands of others, I am both shocked and alarmed.   Some of the crimes youngsters are committing are almost unspeakable.   Prostitution, murder, rape — these are ugly words, but it is an ugly situation." — *J. Edgar Hoover.*

A TRUTH FOR THE CLASS TO CARRY AWAY.

The man of God who can be counted upon to be sensitive to the thing God approves, and to the sins that bring judgment and captivity, is the man who keeps close to the Word of God, yielded to the Spirit of God, seeking only the glory of God.   It is out of this type of godliness that true prophets come — and how we need them this day!

Which of the vices mentioned in our lesson are the most soul-deadening? Which do you think would stand first in a list of the iniquities of our nation today? Can you recall any statement of Christ Himself similar to these of the prophet? What has often resulted from the continued oppression of the poor in various nations of the world?   (Rebellion and revolution.)   What do you think of the argument that as there was a captivity for God's people followed by a restoration, so the final judgment will be followed by a final restoration of all mankind to God?

209

LESSON XII. — June 20.

HOSEA PLEADS WITH ISRAEL. — Hosea 4:6—7:16.

PRINTED TEXT, Hosea 6.

Devotional Reading: Hosea 11:1–4ab; 14:1–4.
Beginner Topic: An Outdoor Bible Reading.
    Lesson Material: Psalm 119:97–112; Nehemiah 8.
    Memory Verse: O give thanks unto Jehovah: for he is good.   Psalm 136:1.
Primary Topic: Hosea Tells of God's Love.
    Lesson Material: Hosea 4:6; 6:1–3, 6.
    Memory Verse: I desire goodness . . . and the knowledge of God.   Hosea 6:6.
Junior Topic: Hosea Tells of God's Love.
    Lesson Material: Hosea 4:6; 6:1–3, 6.
    Memory Verse: I desire goodness, and not sacrifice; and the knowledge of God more than burnt-offerings.   Hosea 6:6.
Intermediate-Senior Topic: Hosea Pleads with Israel.
    Lesson Material: Hosea 4:6—7:16.
    Memory Verse: I desire goodness, and not sacrifice; and the knowledge of God more than burnt-offerings.   Hosea 6:6.
Topic for Young People and Adults: Hosea Pleads with Israel.
    Lesson Material: Hosea 4:6—7:16.
    Memory Verse: I desire goodness, and not sacrifice; and the knowledge of God more than burnt-offerings.   Hosea 6:6.

THE TEACHER AND HIS CLASS.

The Younger Classes may be introduced to this lesson by an illustration from the editor's own recent experience. Some days ago I developed a very strange sort of pain in my left shoulder and arm, and then small clusters of red spots appeared on the arm. The doctor told me at once that it was serious, and must be checked immediately. He accurately diagnosed it as an infected nerve, the cause of which no one would know, and then instructed the nurse to give me a hypodermic injection of some medicine, every twenty-four hours. This brought relief, and within four days the pain had disappeared entirely. Had it continued, and spread, it could have become very serious. I did not know what the trouble was, but the doctor, an expert in the ailments and pains of the human body, knew at once. Now the prophets were men who walked with God, who were open to His messages, who lived holy lives, and they knew the diseases that were bringing on the disintegration and doom of the nation Israel. Through these prophets God pled with His people to forsake the sins that were destroying them. In our lesson we have one of the most moving passages in all the Old Testament setting forth the pleadings of God with his wayward people.

The Older Classes may also be introduced to the lesson with an illustration from the editor's experience. Recently a man called me on the phone from a city not far away, asking if I knew a Christian psychiatrist near-by. His tone was very solemn, and he said, "My family is in great need of some kind of help." I did not ask for specific details, but could gather from the conversation that some member of the family was behaving in an unnatural way, and the father knew that if this continued, it would lead to disaster, perhaps to crime. It was such a condition in Israel that Hosea is here diagnosing by the Spirit of God.

THE LESSON IN ITS SETTING.

Time. — The prophecies included in our lesson were uttered about 725 B.C.

Place. — There are no specific geographical terms in the lesson proper, with the exception of Ephraim, simply a synonym for Israel, the Northern Kingdom, to which Hosea prophesied.

THE PLAN OF THE LESSON.

SUBJECT: An Illustration from Israel's History of How an Entire Nation can Spurn the Pleadings and Love of a Holy God and Deliberately Continue to Pursue a Course of Evil and Rebellion Which She is Warned Will Lead Straight to Disaster.

I. THE INIQUITIES OF ISRAEL DEMAND DIVINE JUDGMENT, Hosea 4:6–19.
   1. Her iniquity in general, vs. 6–10.
   2. Her specific sins, vs. 11–14.
   3. A summary, vs. 15–19.

II. THE UNFAITHFULNESS OF EPHRAIM, Hosea 5.

III. JEHOVAH'S PLEADINGS WITH HIS PEOPLE ARE SPURNED, Hosea 6:1—7:16.
   1. The hope of repentance, 6:1–3.
   2. Israel refuses to hearken to the Word of God, 6:4–11.

   3. And stubbornly continues to abandon herself to sin, 7:1–7.
   4. In which she proves herself foolish, 7:8–16.

THE TEACHER'S LIBRARY.

For chapters on Hosea, one might consult A. F. Kirkpatrick: *The Doctrine of the Prophets,* 109–142; G. G. Findlay: *The Books of the Prophets,* Vol. 1, pp. 155–187; Adam C. Welch: *The Kings and Prophets of Israel* (London, 1952) 130–184; and George L. Robinson: *The Twelve Minor Prophets.*

On the Book of Hosea itself, for a strict commentary, I have found the best volume to be the one by S. L. Brown in The *Westminster Commentary* Series (London, 1932); but the great classic in exposition of this book is G. Campbell Morgan's volume, *Hosea: the Heart and Holiness of God,* published in 1934. Inasmuch as many of the readers of these pages will not have access to either of these two volumes, I shall lean heavily upon them for the interpretation of our lesson.

I know of no great sermons on any portion of the printed text, though, on 6:3, see W. M. Clow: *The Secret of the Lord,* 337 ff.

AUDIO-VISUAL AIDS.

No audio-visual aids discovered.

It is understood by all students of this book that it divides into two parts: the first three chapters concern Hosea's own tragic experience, in being married to a woman who was deliberately and continually unfaithful to him, and the remaining eleven chapters take up this same theme of unfaithfulness as it was manifested in the nation Israel. Our lesson falls entirely within this second division. Before considering the specific passages assigned to us, we ought briefly to review the life and ministry of this great prophet. "Unlike his austere predecessor, Hosea was of a gentle, sensitive nature, pensive perhaps and inclined to melancholy, but frank, affectionate, and full of domestic and patriotic feeling. His piety is of the most inward type — fervent, heart-felt, trustful and clingingly submissive. Hosea is predominantly the man of sentiment, as Amos is the man of principle. He excels in pathos, in description, in power of appeal and expostulation, in acute observation and rich and various fancy. Hosea's address is the transparent expression of the man and his message. His style is emotional in a high degree, quick and sometimes violent in movement — elliptical, exclamatory, crowded with allusion and metaphor, saying twenty things at once. His sentences are not built into regular periods, but thrown out in brief, glancing spear-thrusts; while Amos plants his blows with the measured crushing swing of the hammer-stroke. . . . Hosea has been called the Jeremiah of the Northern Kingdom. Both were ardent patriots, and men of finely sensitive, religious nature; the ministry of each was a martyrdom. . . . Jeremiah has more of the theologian's wisdom, Hosea of the poet's heart. . . . Hosea is the first and tenderest of the prophets of Israel's sorrow, — the servants of the Lord whose experience is summed up and idealised, and again projected onto the canvas of the future, in the grand picture of the Suffering Servant drawn in Isaiah 53. These men drank in bitter draughts from 'the wine of the wrath of God'; they tasted by anticipation the anguish of God's judgments on a guilty people. They felt for their nation when the nation had no heart to feel for itself. 'Stricken for the transgression of their people,' these martyr-prophets showed beforehand the sufferings of the Christ and came as near as sinful men might do to the sacrifice of the cross. None of his predecessors had entered into the compassions of God or touched so intimately the secret of the Divine Fatherhood, as Hosea does." — *G. G. Findlay.*

I. **THE INIQUITIES OF ISRAEL DEMAND DIVINE JUDGMENT**, Hosea 4:6–19. In studying the Book of Hosea we should carefully observe from whom the words of any one paragraph proceed. Some of the words here are those of the prophet, some of the nation, but most of them from Jehovah himself, as are these three paragraphs of the fourth chapter. Notice the repetition of the phrase, "my people." The fundamental theme here is the ignorance of the people of Israel concerning the law of God, and their determination to continue in sin. The accusation here is directed against the priests. "The word rendered 'law' (*torah*) comes from a root meaning 'to direct,' and is used in the Old Testament of the 'direction' given by the priests to the laity on matters of moral and ceremonial duty. . . . Jehovah's *Torah* is regarded by Hosea as the foundation of morality, and he attributes the crimes which are rampant in Israel to the priests' forgetfulness of its true character, and to their disregard of that 'knowledge' of God, which the possession of such a revelation of His will implies. Compare Malachi 2:6, 7 (based perhaps on Deut. 33:8–11) for the Old Testament ideal of what the priesthood should be. Hosea's teaching, like that of Malachi, has a strangely modern ring about it; for the Gospel no less than the Law has its message to the intellect, the laity still seek direction at the mouths of its priests, and when they cannot obtain it, they 'take hurt and hindrance by our negligence." — *S. L. Brown.* Secondly, "The priests' incomes have been increased by pandering to a lower type of religion; they have turned from their primary duty of declaring Jehovah's *Torah* to the easier and more gainful business of conducting a debased worship." — *S. L. Brown.* Thirdly, they have become drunkards so that their very understanding has left them; and fourthly, they are guilty of offering sacrifices to Canaanitish gods. One of the most famous axiomatic phrases in the Old Testament is to be found in this passage — "Like people, like priest." Of course, what a priest, supposedly a servant of God, does, the people may well think they can do also. There is an excellent illustration of this truth in the life of the sons of Eli the high priest (1 Sam. 2:22–24).

II. **THE UNFAITHFULNESS OF EPHRAIM**, Hosea 5. The first half of this chapter pursues further the accusations of the preceding chapter, declaring that both the priesthood and the court, because of the sensuality of their worship, have led the people into the snare of sin; and the last half of the chapter turns to Judah, who is as guilty in these things as the Northern Kingdom. Two passages here need extended study: the 5th verse because of the problem it raises, and the last verse because of the great principle it sets forth. The opening phrase of verse 5, "the pride of Israel," contains a word that sometimes means *majesty*, in a good sense, as the majesty of God in Hosea 2:10, 19, 21, etc., but here no doubt it refers to Israel's confidence in an external, ceremonial religion, her pride in the fact that she has a revelation from God. It is the last verse, however, that we want to especially consider here — "I will go and return to my place, till they acknowledge their offence, and seek my face: in their affliction they will seek me earnestly." The commentary of Dr. G. Campbell Morgan on Hosea cannot be surpassed here. "That is the ultimate judgment of God upon a sinning people, the withdrawal of Himself, the withdrawal of His presence, that is in the sense of guiding or governing; the abandonment of the people to their own elections, and their own choices, and their own perversities. But we saw that the solemn word of warning ended with the leaving open of the door. . . . Certainly one of the most tender and beautiful appeals of all the Biblical literature, is contained in the first three verses of chapter 6. The prophet said to the people, in view of the illuminative word of imminent judgment, and of the fact that in uttering it God had indicated His willingness to return, 'Come, and let us return unto Jehovah; for He hath torn, and He will heal us.' It was a great appeal, thrilling with Messianic promise, the final meaning of which was never found until in the fullness of time the Messiah

212

HOSEA 6:1. Come, and let us return unto Jehovah; for he hath torn, and he will heal us; he hath smitten, and he will bind us up.

2. After two days will he revive us: on the third day he will raise us up, and we shall live before him.

3. And let us know, let us follow on to know Jehovah: his going forth is sure as the morning; and he will come unto us as the rain, as the latter rain that watereth the earth.

4. O Ephraim, what shall I do unto thee? O Judah, what shall I do unto thee? for your goodness is as a morning cloud, and as the dew that goeth early away.

---

came, while yet it had an immediate value for those who heard it." — *Dr. G. Campbell Morgan.*

III. JEHOVAH'S PLEADINGS WITH HIS PEOPLE ARE SPURNED, Hosea 6:1—7:16.

1. THE HOPE OF REPENTANCE, 6:1–3. The opening paragraph of the printed text is framed as an exhortation of the people of Israel, one to another, to return to God, with the confidence that He would quicken and renew them. 1. **Come, and let us return unto Jehovah; for he hath torn, and he will heal us; he hath smitten, and he will bind us up. 2. After two days will he revive us: on the third day he will raise us up, and we shall live before him. 3. And let us know, let us follow on to know Jehovah: his going forth is sure as the morning; and he will come unto us as the rain, as the latter rain that watereth the earth.** The question arises as to whether or not this repentance is sincere. George Adam Smith thinks not, but rather that "it offers but one more symptom of the optimism of this light-hearted people, whom no discipline and no judgment can impress with the reality of their incurable decay." Professor Brown agrees, and says that this confessional prayer is so superficial that God must reject it, for He can accept nothing short of an actual change of heart. The second verse is one of great significance, for it is here that we have a specific reference to resurrection occurring on the third day. This is one of those passages in the Old Testament to which the Apostle Paul must have been referring in 1 Corinthians 15:4, when he said not only did Christ die for our sins according to the Scriptures, but that He was raised again from the dead on the third day, "according to the Scriptures." I have always thought that even the third day of creation has in it resurrection truth (Gen. 1:9–13), when the earth came up out of the darkness of the deep, and when life first appeared in the history of our earth, as far as we know. Another great passage, of course, would be the one to which Jesus referred, to Jonah's being three days and three nights in the belly of the great fish (Matt. 12:38–41). With this compare Isaiah 26:19. The figure of rain in verse 3 indicates moral and spiritual refreshment. "As the rains of winter and spring revive the land, so Jehovah will revive His people." The rain here corresponds in function to the wind of Ezekiel 37:9, and to the dew of Isaiah 26:19 (compare Hosea 14:5). Israel relies on the return of Jehovah's favour as the husbandman relies on the former and latter rains." — *S. L. Brown.*

2. ISRAEL REFUSES TO HEARKEN TO THE WORD OF GOD, 6:4–11. The cries of Jehovah in this chapter, if one may say it reverently, are pitiful indeed. He seems to be baffled — though of course God is never really baffled — for the question arises as to what He is to do with His people, because He loves them and they continue in sin, which means that they must be judged more terribly than they know. 4. **O Ephraim, what shall I do unto thee? O Judah, what shall I do unto thee? for your goodness is as a morning cloud, and as the dew that goeth early away.** "The morning cloud, as the sun is rising, is smitten with beauty; and dew in the beauty of the morning, when every blade of grass is glistening in rainbow loveliness, is equally glorious. The morning cloud is a thing of exquisite

213

5. Therefore have I hewed them by the prophets; I have slain them by the words of my mouth: and thy judgments are *as* the light that goeth forth.

6. For I desire goodness, and not sacrifice; and the knowledge of God more than burnt-offerings.

7. But they like Adam have transgressed the covenant: there have they dealt treacherously against me.

---

beauty, and the dew a thing of infinite tenderness. But read on, and we have the revealing expression, 'which goeth early away.' A morning cloud, the dew; both excellent, but evanescent; too feeble to produce a harvest, dissipated by the heat of the sun, ere any permanent result can be gained. Goodness evanescent, that is what creates God's difficulty. I am quite willing to put this superlatively. God's difficulty is not created by vulgar sins; God's difficulty is not created in the human soul by reason of pollution and whoredom and beastliness. With these things God can deal; but God is in great difficulty when goodness is only like the morning cloud, is only like the dew that goeth early away." — *G. Campbell Morgan.* **5. Therefore have I hewed them by the prophets; I have slain them by the words of my mouth: and thy judgments are *as* the light that goeth forth.** "Israel is not likened to wood or stone which is being shaped, but to wood or stone which is being hewn to pieces through the agency of the prophets. (Compare Jer. 23:29.) For 'by the words of My mouth,' compare Psalm 45:3, 5; Isaiah 11:4; Hebrews 4:12; Revelation 1:16. Hosea may have prophets like Samuel, Elijah, and Elisha in mind (1 Sam. 15:33; 1 Kings 18:40) when he uses these metaphors." — *S. L. Brown.* **6. For I desire goodness, and not sacrifice; and the knowledge of God more than burnt-offerings.** "The message of the prophets in the past and the judgments they announced were intended to teach Israel that Jehovah demands reality in religion, and that message is now repeated. What He delights in is that love and knowledge of Himself which they alone have who do His will, rather than ceremonial and the outward observances of religion. . . . The first part of this verse is twice quoted by our Lord (Matt. 9:13; 12:7). In the former passage, He shows how the Pharisaic attitude of mind which shrinks from consorting with publicans and sinners is incompatible with the prophet's message of charity towards one's fellows. In the latter, He ascribes the condemnation of His disciples for a technical offence on the Sabbath to a perverted sentiment, which looks upon ceremonial observances as the whole of religion." — *S. L. Brown.* The word here translated "goodness" is the Hebrew word *'hesedh*, which appears also in 2:19; 4:1; 10:12; 12:6, etc. When Hosea uses this word, "he always means love for God, but he knows no love for God which does not show itself in love for one's fellow-men; nor, on the other hand, does he know any love for man which is not inspired by love for God. If Hosea were pressed to distinguish between the various shades of meaning which belong to *'hesedh* as he uses it, he would say that on the side of Jehovah it is the free, unmerited generosity to which Israel owes everything and which we should call grace; that on the side of Israel as a community it is a grateful recognition of the debt which the nation owes to Jehovah together with the loyalty inspired by that grateful recognition; and that, since all the members of the community are members of Jehovah's family, *'hesedh* should govern their relations to one another as well as their relation to Him. But he does not, as a matter of fact, make any such distinction, because to him the three are essentially one, and all are comprised in the same convenant. It is therefore unnecessary and unprofitable to ask in every instance whether loyal affection to Jehovah or kindness to one's fellow-Israelites is intended. The two belong together: there can be no true love for Jehovah which does not carry with it love for those who belong to Jehovah's family." — *S. L. Brown.* **7. But they like Adam have transgressed the covenant: there have they dealt treacherously against**

8. Gilead is a city of them that work iniquity; it is stained with blood.

9. And as troops of robbers wait for a man, so the company of priests murder in the way toward Shechem; yea, they have committed lewdness.

10. In the house of Israel I have seen a horrible thing: there whoredom is *found* in Ephraim, Israel is defiled.

11. Also, O Judah, there is a harvest appointed for thee, when I bring back the captivity of my people.

me. Here we have one of the few references to Adam after the Book of Genesis. **8. Gilead is a city of them that work iniquity; it is stained with blood.   9. And as troops of robbers wait for a man, so the company of priests murder in the way toward Shechem; yea, they have committed lewdness.** "The general sense of the verse is that even the priests form into bands to waylay and murder travellers, but translation is difficult owing to the state of the text. As the text stands, a literal rendering would be: 'as the lying in wait for a man of marauding-bands' (or, treating 'man' and 'marauding-bands' as in apposition, 'as the lying in wait of marauding-bands') is the gang of priests; they murder on the way to Shechem, yea, they do enormity. Shechem (the modern Nablus) was both a city of priests and a city of refuge (Josh. 20:7; 21:21) and therefore a place of pilgrimage. It lay on the road from Samaria and the North to Bethel. It was also 'of all the centres on the Western Range most open to approach from Eastern Palestine, by the fords of Jordan only eighteen miles away, and thus 'the way to Shechem' comes in here naturally after 'Gilead' in the preceding verse.' In the days of Abimelech Shechem was destroyed as a punishment for the highway robberies of its inhabitants (Judges 9:25, 45)."— *S. L. Brown.* **10. In the house of Israel I have seen a horrible thing: there whoredom is *found* in Ephraim, Israel is defiled. 11. Also, O Judah, there is a harvest appointed for thee, when I bring back the captivity of my people.** This chapter concludes, as many of the prophetic books of the Old Testament conclude — with a promise that although His people are going into captivity (for Israel this will occur within fifty years of Hosea's prophecy) the time is coming when God will bring them back into the land which He promised to Abraham and his children as their possession forever (Ezek. 34:23–30; 37; Isa. 11:10, and many other passages).

3. AND STUBBORNLY CONTINUES TO ABANDON HERSELF TO SIN, 7:1–7. Note here the many figures of speech, particularly that referring to the baker's oven. "The thought seems to be that as the baker only leaves the fire to smoulder while the dough is being kneaded and leavened, so the rulers and people only rest from inflaming their passions till they regain their strength for the next piece of wickedness."— *S. L. Brown.* Delitzsch, with his usual genius and insight has said, "As the dangerous nature of a wound is often first brought out by the attempt to heal it, so was the corruption of Israel only brought truly to light by the effort to stem it. Here again Ephraim is not the particular tribe, but is synonymous with Israel, the people or kingdom of the ten tribes; and Samaria is especially mentioned in connection with it, as the capital and principal seat of the corruption of morals, just as Judah and Jerusalem are frequently classed together by the prophets. They do not consider that God will remember their evil deeds, and punish them; they are surrounded by them on all sides, and perform them without shame or fear before the face of God himself. To such a depth have even the rulers of the nation fallen that they not only fail to punish the sins, but take pleasure in their being committed."— *F. Delitzsch.*

4. IN WHICH SHE PROVES HERSELF FOOLISH, 7:8–16. Israel's continued stubborn persistence in sin, in spite of the warnings and callings of God, is likened to a foolish person whose hair is turning gray but he does not know it; to a silly dove

215

without understanding. They are wholly occupied with eating and drinking, and have no sense of the shame of their sins and their rebelliousness toward God. The well-known phrase in verse 8, "Ephraim is a cake not turned," seems to express the idea that, "when political and commercial relations were opened with the outside world, Israel accepted foreign customs, fashions, and ideas, with the result that her moral strength was undermined. Ephraim has become like a cake that is full of heathen ingredients and *unturned*, that is, scorched on one side and so unfit to be eaten. The cake referred to is the flat, round cake of the East which is baked on hot stones (compare 1 Kings 19:6). The point of the simile is either that the country is half ruined by its association with heathen nations or (more probably) that the weakness of the national character, with its fickleness, inconsistencies, and lack of direction is such that it can only be likened to a half-baked scone." — S. L. Brown.

Let us close with Dr. G. Campbell Morgan's classic comment on the last half of verse 9, "Gray hairs are here and there upon him, and he knoweth it not." "The first thing I would like to say in considering the figure employed is that the suggestion it makes is entirely contrary to Nature. Now I ask you, if any of you were unconscious when the gray hairs began to appear! I do not think any one would claim such ignorance. It is never so in actual experience. We discover the gray hairs, some of us sooner than others, but we discover them! So here is something employed as a figure of speech which is contrary to Nature, and therefore is the most arresting. . . . And yet, this thing entirely unnatural in the physical, is constantly true in the moral and spiritual realms, and so the figure of the prophet is warranted and indeed most graphic. Signs of decadence, which are patent to others, are undiscovered by ourselves; and we go on, and on, and on, the victims of ebbing strength, spiritually and morally becoming degenerate, without knowing it! We are blind to the signs which are self-evident to onlookers. There is no condition more perilous to our highest well-being than this of unconscious decadence. The skilful physician knows how often the cessation of suffering means that mortification has set in, and that in the moral realm may be the meaning of ignorance of gray hairs. There is one text in the Bible that, as God is my witness, I never read without trembling. It is a text that tells the story of Samson: 'He wist not that the Spirit of God had departed from him.' . . . The signs of moral and spiritual degeneracy are abounding, and they are seen by others, but not by ourselves. I repeat, there is no condition into which a man or a nation can pass more full of peril, more calamitous than that. Moral degeneracy and spiritual failure are cursing them, and all the while they are unconscious of it, going through the same motions, but without vital significance." — *Dr. G. Campbell Morgan.*

THE LESSON IN LIFE, LITERATURE, AND ARCHAEOLOGY.

There is a remarkable use of one of the passages in our lesson at the close of the famous treatise against Marcion, by the African theologian, Tertullian, written at the beginning of the third century. "It was very meet that the man who buried the Lord should thus be noticed in prophecy, and thenceforth be 'blessed'; since prophecy does not omit the office of the women who resorted before day-break to the sepulchre with the spices which they had prepared (Luke 24:1). For of this incident it is said by Hosea: 'To seek my face they will watch till day-light, saying unto me, Come and let us return to the Lord; for He hath taken away, and He will heal us; He hath smitten, and He will bind us up; after two days will He revive us: in the third day He will raise us up' (Hos. 5:15; 6:1, 2). For who can refuse to believe that these words often revolved in the thought of those women between the sorrow of that desertion with which at present they seemed to themselves to have been smitten by the Lord, and the hope of the resurrection itself, by which they rightly supposed that all would be restored to them?" — *Tertullian.*

A TRUTH FOR THE CLASS TO CARRY AWAY.

There is a danger in studying a lesson such as this, the events of which occurred hundreds of years before the advent of our Lord, in a far-distant land, that we should fail to apply the stern principles of holy living to our own lives. We must ask ourselves the question, Are we practicing any of the sins condemned here by the Spirit of God through the prophet? The New Testament speaks just as frequently of a judgment to come as the Old Testament ever did; in fact, the judgments of the Old Testament were, for the most part, pronounced against Israel, but those in the New Testament are of universal scope. Furthermore, we today have more evidence of the love of God than Israel had, for between this lesson and the present time, Christ was crucified for us.

In what ways was the prophetic ministry of Jesus like that of Hosea? How does continued indulgence in sin close ears to the Word of God? How can you account for the fact that the priests here are identified with Israel's darkest sins, while the prophet stands aloof from them? Why do men so boldly and continually refuse to harken to the warnings of a loving God?

LESSON XIII. — June 27.

JUDGMENT COMES TO ISRAEL. — 2 Kings 17.

PRINTED TEXT, 2 Kings 17:5–14, 22, 23.

Devotional Reading: Psalm 85:1–7.
Beginner Topic: A CHARIOT RIDE.
　　Lesson Material: John 5:17, 39; 20:30–31; Acts 8:3–8, 26–40.
　　Memory Verse: God . . . loved us, and sent his Son, 1 John 4:10.
Primary Topic: LOVING AND SERVING GOD.
　　Lesson Material: 2 Kings 17:7–13, 22–23.
　　Memory Verse: The ways of Jehovah are right, and the just shall walk in them. Hosea 14:9.
Junior Topic: THE END OF A KINGDOM.
　　Lesson Material: 2 Kings 17:7–13, 22–23.
　　Memory Verse: The ways of Jehovah are right, and the just shall walk in them. Hosea 14:9.
Intermediate-Senior Topic: A NATION LOST.
　　Lesson Material: 2 Kings 17.
　　Memory Verse: The ways of Jehovah are right, and the just shall walk in them; but transgressors shall fall therein. Hosea 14:9.
Topic for Young People and Adults: JUDGMENT COMES TO ISRAEL.
　　Lesson Material: 2 Kings 17.
　　Memory Verse: The ways of Jehovah are right, and the just shall walk in them; but transgressors shall fall therein. Hosea 14:9.

THE TEACHER AND HIS CLASS.

The Younger Classes may be introduced to this lesson by an illustration which I am sure they will understand. In an institution in which I had the privilege of teaching, a certain individual had been found guilty of an indiscretion which could not be tolerated in Christian work. He was warned that a repetition of this would necessitate his dismissal. On the second occasion, though the offense was not of such a serious nature, it was again found necessary to discipline this person, and another warning was given. Several years later the transgression was repeated, and he was asked to leave at once. Several warnings had been given, and the matter *had* to be judged for the welfare of the institution. In the same way, Israel, the Northern Kingdom, had been warned,

217

over and over again, that if she did not turn from her sins to God and righteous living, God would punish her. She refused to hearken to the prophets, and the time for judgment had now come.

The Older Classes may be reminded at the beginning of this lesson of the great principle, sometimes forgotten, that God does use worldly forces or pagan agencies for the chastisement of His own children. Examples of this may be found in modern history. In our lesson, a pagan people, Assyria, is allowed to capture a kingdom whose people were supposedly servants of God, who worshipped the omnipotent God of Abraham, Isaac, and Jacob, but who were hypocrites in their worship and had become idolatrous, immoral, and proud. God does not give a pagan nation the place that his own chosen people have in His program of redemption. He will continue to discipline His own until they turn to Him, but He often uses unbelieving nations to carry out this judgment.

THE LESSON IN ITS SETTING.

Time. — The fall of Samaria took place in 721 or 722 B.C., and inasmuch as the seige lasted for some three years, this lesson may be dated 724–721 B.C.

Place. — The nation taken into captivity in this lesson is Israel, embracing the ten tribes, with its capital at Samaria.

THE PLAN OF THE LESSON.

SUBJECT: How, by the Overthrow of a Proud and Beautiful City, According to the Program of God, Sin is Punished, Prophecies are Fulfilled, and the Holiness of God is Displayed.

I. ISRAEL CARRIED INTO CAPTIVITY, 2 Kings 17:1–6.

II. THE SINS WHICH BROUGHT UPON THEM THIS DIVINE JUDGMENT, 2 Kings 17:7–23.

III. THE BEGINNING OF THE SAMARITAN NATION, 2 Kings 17:24–41.

THE TEACHER'S LIBRARY.

Before consulting commentaries, it would be wise for the teacher to read a few chapters on the history of Israel in the latter days. May I suggest an older work, but still good, Alfred Edersheim: *The History of Israel and Judah,* Vol. 7, 110–121; Ira Morris Price: *The Monuments and the Old Testament,* 282–306 (with superb illustrations); A. P. Stanley: *Lectures on the History of the Jewish Church,* Vol. 2, 307–324. Then, of course all of the characters appearing in our lesson have up-to-date articles in the new *Harper's Bible Dictionary.*

Archaeological material here will be found exceedingly interesting; e.g., Sir Frederick Kenyon: *The Bible and Archaeology,* 181–186; Joseph P. Free: *Archaeology and Bible History,* 192–209; Jack Finegan: *Light from the Ancient East,* 154–157.

Turning to commentaries, Canon Farrar is still good, in the *Expositor's Bible;* C. J. Ball in *The Bible Commentary for English Readers;* George Rawlinson in *The Bible Commentary;* William E. Barnes in *The Cambridge Bible for Schools and Colleges;* H. J. Carpenter in the *Devotional Commentary* series; and the monumental, very technical, and scholarly volume by James Montgomery, posthumously published recently in *The International Critical Commentary.*

Sermonic material is amazingly scarce. See Joseph Parker: *The People's Bible,* Vol. 8, 267–278; Alexander Maclaren: *Expositions of Holy Scripture, 2 Kings 8 — Nehemiah,* 34–40; and Charles H. Spurgeon: *Metropolitan Tabernacle Pulpit,* Vol. 51.

AUDIO-VISUAL AIDS.

No audio-visual aids discovered.

All students of the Bible will recall that after the death of Solomon, the nation of Israel, made up of twelve tribes (taking their names from the twelve sons of Jacob), divided into two parts. Solomon's son, Rehoboam, legitimate heir to the throne of David, insisted upon increasing the already too heavy taxes of his subjects, and the ten northern tribes, for some time inflamed with jealousy against the pre-eminence of the house of David, the greatness of Jerusalem, and the primacy of Judah, took this occasion to revolt against the king. Thus it was that the greater part of the nation, and the richer part, set up a kingdom of its own. This schism was never healed. While Judah in her subsequent history experienced some truly great religious revivals, the Northern Kingdom was *never* to know one. On the throne of Judah, in the south, sat only descendants of David, but in the

2 KINGS 17:5. Then the king of Assyria came up throughout all the
land, and went up to Samaria, and besieged it three years.

6. In the ninth year of Hoshea, the king of Assyria took Samaria,
and carried Israel away unto Assyria, and placed them in Halah, and
on the Habor, the river of Gozan, and in the cities of the Medes.

Northern Kingdom, many different dynasties appeared and then were extinguished. While Jerusalem did not fall until 586, Samaria and the Northern Kingdom were overwhelmingly destroyed nearly 140 years before this. The end of the
Northern Kingdom, recorded only in the Second Book of Kings, is before us for
study today. The latter part of chapter 15 might be called a prelude to chapter
17. Pekah was the eighteenth king of Israel and next to the last, reigning from
740 to 732 B.C. Even now we read that Tiglath-pileser, who was Tiglath-pileser
III, king of Assyria from 746 to 728 B.C., probably a military leader who put himself upon the throne, reorganized the armies of Assyria and set out to enlarge its
boundaries. He took a number of cities, seemingly without any great effort, and
carried the inhabitants to Assyria. Pekah was followed by Hoshea, who reigned
from 732 to the fall of the city of Samaria.

I. ISRAEL CARRIED INTO CAPTIVITY, 2 Kings 17:1–6. One would have
thought that the terrible devastation wrought in Israel by Tiglath-pileser would
send the remaining part of the kingdom to its knees, crying to God for deliverance.
Such experiences often led to true repentance during the days of the Judges; but
by now the nation as a whole had so far departed from God that they seem to be
in a stupefied state. Sin had numbed them, and possibly the very idea of a redeeming God had been abandoned. "When Tiglath-pileser died, about 728 B.C.,
Hoshea apparently became tired of paying his annual tribute of about $300,000
in gold and about $2,000,000 in silver to Assyria, and looked to Egypt for help in
resisting Assyria. The new king of Assyria, Shalmaneser V (728–722 B.C.) swept
into Canaan and besieged the city of Samaria. After a three years' assault, the
city fell. The principal inhabitants of the Northern Kingdom were carried off
into captivity by the Assyrians, bringing to an end the Northern Kingdom and
beginning the captivity of Israel, about 722 B.C." — Joseph Free. 5. Then the
king of Assyria came up throughout all the land, and went up to Samaria, and besieged it three years. 6. In the ninth year of Hoshea, the king of Assyria took
Samaria, and carried Israel away unto Assyria, and placed them in Halah, and on
the Habor, the river of Gozan, and in the cities of the Medes. There has been a
great deal of discussion as to the identity of the king who captured Samaria.
The words of my friend Dr. Free of Wheaton, Illinois, will be of help here. "Sargon, in some of his extant documents, indicates that he captured Samaria. Most
recent writers have accepted this indication, and have held that, while Shalmaneser
initiated and carried on the siege of Samaria, it was Sargon who completed the
capture of the city. According to this view, Sargon is to be identified with the
'king of Assyria' in 2 Kings 17:6, who took the inhabitants of Samaria to Assyria.
Olmstead had pointed out, however, that Sargon is silent concerning the capture
of Samaria in his own earlier accounts, and that the Babylonian account seems to
justify the ascribing of the capture to Shalmaneser V just at the end of his reign,
in 723–722, rather than to Sargon during his first year of rule, 722–721 B.C. Thus
it is possible that it was Shalmaneser V, and not Sargon III who captured Samaria,
and that, with the passing of the years, Sargon's 'press bureau' ascribed the siege
to this latter king. It is only in the royal chronicles recorded in the later part of
his reign that Sargon is credited with the taking of Samaria. Most writers have
overlooked the implication of this evidence, and consequently almost all books on
archaeology and related fields name Sargon, without qualification, as the one who
captured Samaria, after it had been besieged three years by Shalmaneser V." —
Dr. Free.

We will get a far clearer picture of the events described in this chapter if we have

7. And it was so, because the children of Israel had sinned against Jehovah their God, who brought them up out of the land of Egypt from under the hand of Pharaoh king of Egypt, and had feared other gods,

8. And walked in the statutes of the nations, whom Jehovah cast out from before the children of Israel, and of the kings of Israel, which they made.

---

before us some concept of the greatness of this captured city, Samaria. "Next in importance to Jerusalem, capital of the kingdom of Judah, comes Samaria, capital of the kingdom of Israel; but its history is shorter and of less significance. It begins with the selection of the site of Omri, about 880 B.C. to be the capital of his kingdom in place of Shechem and Tirzah, where the court had previously been placed since the revolt of Jeroboam. Shechem lay in the pass between the mountains of Ebal and Gerizim, in the neighborhood of Nablus, and was badly placed for defence; and Tirzah, the site of which has not been certainly determined, was evidently never of much importance. Samaria, on the other hand, occupied one of the finest sites in Palestine, on a low hill set in the middle of a wide cup, bordered on all sides by mountains at a considerable distance, though with a distant view of the sea to the west. On this hill Omri set his town and guarded it with strong walls. It does not seem ever to have been taken by storm. Benhadad blockaded it, and nearly took it by starvation (2 Kings 6:24—7:20), and Shalmaneser and Sargon besieged it for three years before the latter took it, presumably in the same way (2 Kings 17:5, 6)." — *Frederic Kenyon.* "Omri and Ahab evidently levelled the top of the hill, banked its sides, and built inner and outer walls with geometrical precision around the summit. Later walls were built on the middle terraces and also on the lower slopes of the hill, thus rendering the city exceedingly well fortified. These walls constitute a graphic commentary on the two sieges which Samaria underwent, the first when the city held out against the Syrians to the terrible lengths described in 2 Kings 6:24–30, and the second when Samaria withstood the mighty Assyrians for so long before succumbing (2 Kings 17:5). The city has also been found to have been provided with a number of large cisterns which were very important in time of siege since there is no natural water supply. The Hebrew kings built their palaces within the walls on the western brow of the hill. The first palace was relatively simple but served as a core for later and more splendid structures. The palace which hitherto has been ascribed to Ahab, but perhaps belonged to Jeroboam II instead, was built from large blocks of limestone, and boasted a strong rectangular tower and an extensive outer court. At the north end of the palace courtyard was a cemented water pool, which may even have been the 'pool of Samaria' in which the blood-stained chariot of Ahab was washed (1 Kings 22:38)." — *Jack Finegan.*

II. **THE SINS WHICH BROUGHT UPON THEM THIS DIVINE JUDGMENT,** 2 Kings 17:7–23. **7. And it was so, because.** There is one thing that we should always remember about every executed judgment of God recorded in the Old Testament — God always gives a warning of the judgment to come, and an opportunity for those involved in this warning to turn to Him and thereby escape such judgment. Far back, at the end of the second chapter of Genesis, man is warned of the consequences of disobeying God. The pre-Noahic world was warned of a coming flood, and God forewarned Lot, and through him, the cities of Sodom and Gomorrah, of His intention to destroy the cities of the plain by fire. So here, not only did God send prophets warning the children of Israel of inevitable judgment upon their sins, but now the historian, under divine guidance, gives the reasons that Samaria is to be destroyed. **The children of Israel had sinned against Jehovah their God, who brought them up out of the land of Egypt from under the hand of Pharaoh king of Egypt, and had feared other gods, 8. and walked in the**

9. And the children of Israel did secretly things that were not right against Jehovah their God: and they built them high places in all their cities, from the tower of the watchmen to the fortified city.

10. And they set them up pillars and Asherim upon every high hill, and under every green tree.

11. And there they burnt incense in all the high places, as did the nations whom Jehovah carried away before them; and they wrought wicked things to provoke Jehovah to anger;

12. and they served idols, whereof Jehovah had said unto them, Ye shall not do this thing.

13. Yet Jehovah testified unto Israel, and unto Judah, by every prophet, and every seer, saying, Turn ye from your evil ways, and keep my commandments and my statutes, according to all the law which I commanded your fathers, and which I sent to you by my servants the prophets.

statutes of the nations, whom Jehovah cast out from before the children of Israel, and of the kings of Israel, which they made. On the idolatrous practices of Israel, see Amos 5:25, 26; Ezek. 8:14, 16; Jer. 7:9; 9:14; 11:13; 23:27). **9. And the children of Israel did secretly things that were not right against Jehovah their God; and they built them high places in all their cities, from the tower of the watchmen to the fortified city.** The literal meaning of the word translated "secretly" is *covered*. Hebrew verbs expressing the idea of covering and hiding are often used in a sense of acting deceitfully. The verse is a testimony to a law of God implanted in the human heart which, while not preventing men from sinning in this gross way, gives them nevertheless a sense of shame in doing these things. We cannot but think here of the Psalmist's words, "Thou hast set our iniquities before thee, our secret sins in the light of thy countenance" (90:8); of the words of Paul to the Ephesians, "For the things which are done by them in secret it is a shame even to speak of" (5:12); and of course, the New Testament teaching that the secret things of men will be brought to light for judgment in that last day (Rom. 2:16; 1 Cor. 14:25). The towers here referred to are mentioned in 2 Chronicles 26:10 as occupied by herdsmen. **10. And they set them up pillars and Asherim upon every high hill, and under every green tree.** "The green trees became *obumbratrices scelerum*, the secret bowers of their iniquities. They burnt incense on the *bamoth*, and served idols, and wrought wickedness. Useless had been the voices of all the prophets and the seers. They went after vain things, and became vain. Beginning with the two 'calves' they proceeded to lewd and orgiastic idolatries. Ahab and Jezebel seduced them into Tyrian Baal-worship. From the Assyrians they learnt and practised the adoration of the host of heaven. From Moab and Ammon they borrowed the abominable rites of Moloch, and used divination and enchantments by means of belomancy (Ezek. 21:21, 22) and necromancy, and sold themselves to do wickedness." — *F. W. Farrar*. **11. And there they burnt incense in all the high places, as did the nations whom Jehovah carried away before them; and they wrought wicked things to provoke Jehovah to anger; 12. and they served idols, whereof Jehovah had said unto them, Ye shall not do this thing.** For the first exhortation to Israel regarding the abomination of idolatry in the sight of Jehovah, see Exodus 20:4. **13. Yet Jehovah testified unto Israel, and unto Judah, by every prophet, and every seer, saying, Turn ye from your evil ways, and keep my commandments and my statutes, according to all the law which I commanded your fathers, and which I sent to you by my servants the prophets.** By "seers" here the writer means, "such persons as, without belonging to the prophetic order, came forward in times of emergency upon a sudden divine impulse." — *C. J. Ball*. This phrase, "my servants the prophets" sets out the

14. Notwithstanding, they would not hear, but hardened their neck, like to the neck of their fathers, who believed not in Jehovah their God.

---

prophetic order as one of unusual privilege in communicating with God and doing His will. Moses himself was such a prophet in the prophetic warnings which he gave to Israel, recorded at the end of the Book of Deuteronomy. Samuel was another, especially toward the close of his faithful ministry (1 Samuel 12). Isaiah, Jeremiah, Joel, and Amos are filled with these warnings. "The mission of the prophets was God's reply to Israel's rebellion, and was equally the sign of His anger and of His love. The more sin abounds, the more does God multiply means to draw back to Himself. The deafer the ears, the louder the beseeching voice of His grieved and yet pitying love. His anger clothes itself in more stringent appeals and clearer revelations of Himself before it takes its slaughtering weapons in hand. The darker the background of sin, the brighter the beams of His light show against it. Man's sin is made the occasion for a more glorious display of God's character and heart. It is on the storm-cloud that the sun paints the rainbow. Each successive stage in man's departure from God evoked a corresponding increase in the divine effort to attract him back, till 'last of all He sent unto them His Son.' In nature, attraction diminishes as distance increases; in the realms of grace, it grows with distance. The one desire of God's heart is that sinners would return from their evil ways, and He presses on them the solemn thought of the abundant intimations of His will which have been given from of old, and are pealed again into all ears by living voices. His law for us is not merely an old story spoken centuries ago, but is vocal in our consciences today, and fresh as when Sinai flamed and thundered above the camp, and the trumpet thrilled each heart." — *Alexander Maclaren.* 14. **Notwithstanding, they would not hear, but hardened their neck, like to the neck of their fathers, who believed not in Jehovah their God.** Such hardening of the heart we find as far back as Exodus 32:9; 33:3, commented upon by St. Stephen in Acts 7:51 (see also Jeremiah 17:23). This indictment of Israel as failing to heed the messages of the divinely-sent prophets is referred to again and again in the New Testament; for instance, by our Lord (Matt. 23:31–37); St. Stephen (Acts 7:52); St. Paul (Acts 28:25–28). Though it is not in the printed text, verse 16 should have some consideration here. The word translated *Asherah* means "a grove," and was used "as the designation of the commonest material representation of the goddess. It consisted of a block of wood, of considerable size (Judges 6:26) and resembling a tree, as is shown by the expressions used in connection with it, such as 'setting up,' 'planting,' and 'cutting down' (2 Kings 17:10; Deut. 16:21; Judges 6:28; 2 Kings 18:4, etc.). In Isaiah 27:9 the LXX actually renders 'tree'; and so the Peshito in Deuteronomy 6:21; Micah 5:13. Hence we must not think of pillars like the Greek Hermae, but of a real trunk planted in the ground, rootless, but not branchless; for which purpose pines and evergreens were preferred. The tree signifies, according to an ancient and wide-spread conception, nature, or the world, which in this case stands as goddess at the side of the Baal — the lord of the world." — *C. J. Ball.* By the "host of heaven" (also in 21:3 and 23:4) is meant, of course, the stars. This is exactly what the Apostle Paul said in the first chapter of Romans, though referring to the pagan world — Israel took the same steps — that after knowing God they turned from him, and their senseless heart being darkened, they turned to the worship of creatures, of material things, of heavenly bodies. One is reminded here of the words of Joseph Parker: "What is the wonderful charm of evil? Surely the philosophers have not answered that inquiry completely. There must be some peculiar inexpressible charm in evil, or men would not do it, and do it with both hands earnestly, and live in the doing of it, and reap in its execution some kind of harvest of contentment and gladness. What is this charm? Men repeat the evil even whilst denominating it iniquity and marking it as vile. In this matter we are curiously and wondrously made. We go back to the evil. The devil seems to be more attractive than God. One would have thought that one vision of truth, beauty, heaven's own light, would have

22. And the children of Israel walked in all the sins of Jeroboam which he did; they departed not from them;

23. Until Jehovah removed Israel out of his sight, as he spake by all his servants the prophets. So Israel was carried away out of their own land to Assyria unto this day.

forever fascinated us, and made us incapable of meanness, wrong-doing, untruthfulness, or any form or colour of iniquity. But it is not so. The devil is most charmful! We know he tells lies, but he tells them eloquently. We are aware that he cannot keep any promise that he ever made, yet when he puts out his black hand to us we grope for it in the dark, and think the fellowship not without advantage! Who can explain this?" — *Joseph Parker.*

In the word *Judah* is included Benjamin, though the Southern Kingdom was now called Judah exclusively. Even she becomes increasingly guilty of those sins which brought ruin upon the northern nation, and will ultimately bring disaster to her. We now have a historical résumé of Israel's sins, going back to the revolt of Jeroboam, the founder of the Northern Kingdom. 22. **And the children of Israel walked in all the sins of Jeroboam which he did; they departed not from them; 23. Until Jehovah removed Israel out of his sight, as he spake by all his servants the prophets. So Israel was carried away out of their own land to Assyria unto this day.** Though Jeroboam had been dead for 250 years, the influence of his evil life was still cursing the people. "Jeroboam's sins were not the sins of a common man. It is only kings, and kings' counsellors, and popes, and bishops, and ministers, and elders, and such like, who can sin and make nations and churches and congregations to sin. But they can do it. And they are doing it every day. All who divide, and keep divided, nations, and churches, and families, and friends, in order to make a name, or a living, or a party, or just a despite for themselves out of such divisions, they are the true seed of Jeroboam. All who inflame and perpetuate such divisions lest they should lose their stake of money, or of influence, or of occupation, or of pure ill-will; all able men who prostitute their talents to write or speak about men on the other side, as they would not like themselves to be spoken or written about — let them lay it to heart in whose lot they shall surely stand when every man shall give an account of himself to God. But common and mean men are not incapacitated and shut out by their commonness and meanness from sharing in Jeroboam's royal sin. The commonest and meanest man among us has more than enough of this terrible power of both sinning himself and making other men to sin. Every man among us has, in countless ways, and on countless occasions, first sinned himself and then made other men to sin." — *Alexander Whyte.*

III. **THE BEGINNING OF THE SAMARITAN NATION,** 2 Kings 17:24-41. In the Gospels, we often come upon the statement that there was hatred between the Jews and the Samaritans, a hatred, incidentally, that is still there to this very day (John 4:9; 8:48). The origin of this strange people, of whom less than two hundred exist today, all living in the city of Nablus, not far from the site of the ancient capital of Samaria itself, is an interesting study. I believe the words of Dr. Jack Finegan in his superb work, *Light from the Ancient East,* will be adequate for the interpretation of this final paragraph. "When the city of Samaria fell to Sargon II, 27,290 of its people were carried off captive. Doubtless these constituted the flower of the population, and those who remained behind were the poorest people. Then 'the king of Assyria brought men from Babylon, and from Cuthah, and from Avva, and from Hamath and Sepharvaim, and placed them in the cities of Samaria' (2 Kings 17:24) to take the place of those who had been deported. The descendants of the remnant of Israelites and the newly introduced foreigners constituted a mixed race which was looked upon with suspicion by the exiles who returned to Jerusalem. Any participation by the Samaritans in the rebuilding of the temple was spurned by the Jews (Ezra 4:3; Nehemiah 2:20), and Nehemiah expelled from Jerusalem the grandson of Eliashib, the high priest, because he was married to the daughter of Sanballat the Samaritan leader (Nehemiah 13:28). Eliashib's grandson was probably the Manasseh under whom the Samaritans set up their own rival priesthood and built their own temple on Mount Gerizim. The breach between the two groups was never healed. During the weak rule of the high priest Onias II (d. c. 198 B.C.) the Samaritans carried off Jews into slavery, and later John Hyrcanus made an expedition into Samaria and destroyed the Gerizim temple (c. 128 B.C.). In the time of unrest after the deposition of Archelaus (A.D. 6) the Samaritans defiled the Jerusalem temple by throwing in dead men's bodies at night. Later a number of Galilean pilgrims were killed at Ginea (Jenin) as they started to cross Samaria on their way to Jerusalem. Thereupon a virtual civil war broke out which had to be appealed to Claudius Caesar (A.D. 51). The metropolis and chief center of the Samaritans was at Shechem, near Mounts Gerizim and Ebal and on the most direct route from Galilee to Jerusalem. It was rebuilt as Flavia Neapolis in A.D. 72, and is today the village of Nablus, still inhabited by the remnant of the Samaritans. The village of Sychar which figures in John 4:5 has sometimes been identified with Shechem itself, but is more probably to be found in the present-day village of Askar at the southeastern foot of Mount Ebal." — *Jack Finegan.*

THE LESSON IN LIFE, LITERATURE, AND ARCHAEOLOGY.

It is this chapter, recording the taking of Israel to Babylon, that has given rise to the entire subject of the so-called Ten Lost Tribes, out of which has come a vast and fantastic literature. Joseph Gaer in his recent book, *The Lore of the Old Testament,* summarizes this in the following paragraph: "The literature on the fate of the Ten Lost Tribes is extensive. Practically every distant race or nation has been accounted for, at one time or another, by the claim that they were the descendants of the Ten Lost Tribes. In his *Epitome of the Ancient History of Japan,* N. McLeod advances the theory that the Japanese Shindai are descended from the Ten Lost Tribes. J. Adair, in his *History of the American Indians,* published in London in 1775, expresses the belief that the Indians were of Israelite origin. And until recently, large numbers of people held tenaciously to the conviction that the British are direct descendants of the Lost Tribes, and such claimed to offer proof, scripturally, historically and philologically. One book on the topic, the *Identification of the British Nation with Lost Israel,* by Edward Hines, published as late as 1871, sold over a quarter of a million copies, mostly to people who held his views. In the Book of Mormon, the First Book of Nephi, we find the statement, which the author bases on revelation, that the inhabitants of America were, in part, descendants of the Lost Tribes."

A TRUTH FOR THE CLASS TO CARRY AWAY.

Israel was carried into captivity. Sin brings men into bondage. We begin by sinning because we will; we end by sinning because we must. It is the height of folly to think that God can be outwitted and His warnings evaded, for while judgment may seem slow its coming is sure. "Whatsoever a man soweth, **that** shall he also reap." Israel followed rebellion unto ruin when she might have found repentance unto life.

Along life's highway God has posted this warning sign: "He that being often reproved hardeneth his neck, shall suddenly be destroyed, and that without remedy."

How many forces drew the Israelites away from loyalty to God to the worship of idols? How does this lesson illustrate the truth set forth by St. Paul in Romans 2:4, that the goodness and forbearance of God should lead us to repentance? Why was the sin of idolatry in Israel a more grievous thing in the sight of God than the idolatrous practices, for example, of Babylon? What greater rejection of God's messenger are His people to be guilty of in a future century? (The rejection of the Messiah.) Do you think that the sin of idolatry is one of which modern man is guilty?

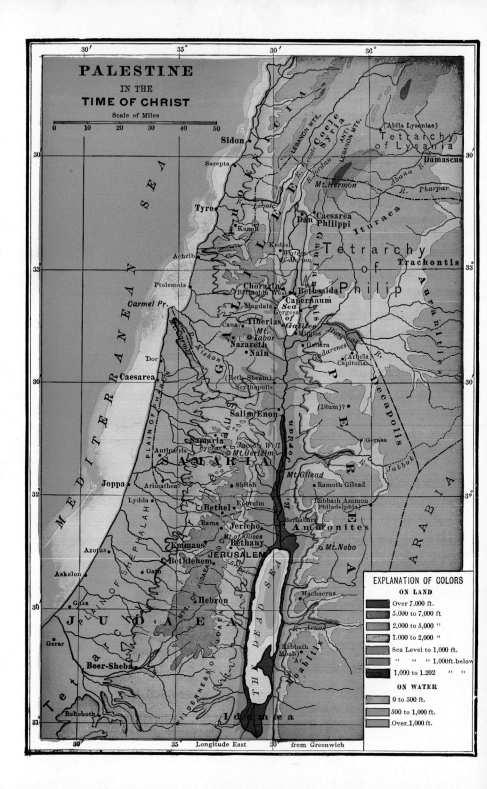

PALESTINE
IN THE
TIME OF CHRIST

Scale of Miles

0   10   20   30   40   50

EXPLANATION OF COLORS

ON LAND

Over 7,000 ft.
5,000 to 7,000 ft
2,000 to 5,000 "
1,000 to 2,000 "
Sea Level to 1,000 ft.
" " " 1,000ft.below
1,000 to 1.202 " "

ON WATER

0 to 500 ft.
500 to 1,000 ft.
Over 1,000 ft.

Sidon

Sarepta

Tyre

Achzib

Ptolemais

Carmel Pr.

Dor

Caesarea

Joppa

Antipatris

Lydda

Arimathea?

Rama

Azotus

Askelon

Bethlehem

Gath

Gaza

Gerar

Hebron

Beer-Sheba

Rehoboth

MEDITERRANEAN SEA

PHOENICIA

LEBANON MTS.

Leontes R.

R. Leone

Coele Syria

ANTI LEBANON MTS.

R. Jordan

Abila Lysaniae)

Tetrarchy of Lysania

Damascus

Abana R.

Mt. Hermon

R. Pharpar

Caesarea Philippi

Dan

Kedesh

Waters of Merom

Ituraea

Gaulanitis

Tetrarchy of Philip

Trachontis

Auranitis

Chorazin

Bethsaida West

Capernaum

Bethsaida

Magdala

Gergesa

Sea of Galilee

Cana?

Tiberias

Mt. Tabor

Nazareth

Nain

GALILEE

Hippos

Gadara

Gadarenes

Arbela

Capitolias

R. Hieromax

Decapolis

(Beth-Sheam)

Scythopolis

(Dium)?

Salim/Enon

Samaria

Sychar

Jacob's Well

Mt. Gerizim

SAMARIA

Gerasa

PEREA

R. Jordan

R. Jabbok

Shiloh

Bethel

Ephraim

Mt. Gilead

Ramoth Gilead

Jericho

Mt. of Olives

Bethany

Rabbath Ammon (Philadelphia)

Bethabara

Ammonites

JERUSALEM

Emmaus?

Mt. Nebo

ARABIA

Machaerus

JUDAEA

PLAIN OF SHEPHALAH

WILDERNESS OF JUDAEA

THE DEAD SEA

R. Arnon

Rabbath Moab?

Ar.

Moabitis

Tetrarchy

Idumaea

THIRD QUARTER.

JULY 4 — SEPTEMBER 26, 1954.

GROWTH IN CHRISTIAN LIVING.

LESSON I. — July 4.

JESUS, OUR EXAMPLE AND LORD. — Luke 2:40–52.

PRINTED TEXT, Luke 2:40–52.

Devotional Reading: Isaiah 55:3–7.
Beginner Topic: HELPER SAMUEL.
    Lesson Material: 1 Samuel 1:22 to 3:1, 18–21; Proverbs 20:11; Ecclesiastes 9:10; 1 Thessalonians 4:11–12.
    Memory Verse: We . . . are helpers. 2 Corinthians 1:24.
Primary Topic: HOW JESUS GREW.
    Lesson Material: Luke 2:40–52.
    Memory Verse: The child grew, and waxed strong. Luke 2:40.
Junior Topic: HOW JESUS GREW.
    Lesson Material: Luke 2:40–52.
    Memory Verse: The child grew, and waxed strong, filled with wisdom: and the grace of God was upon him. Luke 2:40.
Intermediate-Senior Topic: JESUS, OUR EXAMPLE.
    Lesson Material: Luke 2:40–52.
    Memory Verse: Jesus advanced in wisdom and stature, and in favor with God and men. Luke 2:52.
Topic for Young People and Adults: JESUS, OUR EXAMPLE.
    Lesson Material: Luke 2:40–52.
    Memory Verse: Jesus advanced in wisdom and stature, and in favor with God and men. Luke 2:52.

THE TEACHER AND HIS CLASS.

The **Younger Classes** may be introduced to this lesson by being asked a question which should arouse immediate interest: Is it possible to see a little child walking ahead of us, and to know, without ever looking into his face, whether he is approximately two years old, five years old, or ten years old? Can we tell the difference between a person ten years of age and twenty years of age? Of course the answer is yes. How do we tell? By their size. Could you tell the difference between a person twenty-five years old and one forty years old, without seeing their faces? Probably not. In other words, it is normal for children to *grow*, but there comes a time when physical growth ceases. Our lesson today is concerned with the *growth* of the boy Jesus.

The Older Classes may be reminded at the beginning of the lesson that we are living in an age when children have become pronouncedly independent, and, consequently, flagrantly disobedient to their parents, as the Apostle Paul said they would in the last days (2 Timothy 3). There is a cure for this, and that is conversion, the indwelling of the spirit of Christ. I have seen young people in grammar school, and high school, giving their parents trouble and anxiety in their spirit of anarchy, but upon genuine conversion, changing their whole attitude. The spirit of Christ will inculcate in us, among other things, the spirit of obedience.

THE LESSON IN ITS SETTING.

Time. — The visit of Christ to Jerusalem occurred in April, A.D. 8.

Place. — The principal event of this lesson took place in Jerusalem, but the residence of the holy family was in Nazareth, about ninety miles north.

THE PLAN OF THE LESSON.

SUBJECT: How the Life of Jesus Christ, Even As a Boy, is Shown to be Wholly Pleasing to God, and the Perfect Example for Any Young Life.

I. THE THREEFOLD GROWTH OF THE CHILD JESUS, Luke 2:40.

II. CHRIST IN THE TEMPLE WITH THE DOCTORS, 2:41–51.

  1. Lost to his parents, vs. 41–45.
  2. Amazing the doctors, vs. 46, 47.
  3. Rebuked by his parents, v. 49.

  4. His higher relationship, v. 49.
  5. Misunderstood by his parents, v. 50.
  6. Obedient to his parents, v. 51.

III. THE THREEFOLD GROWTH OF JESUS AS A YOUNG MAN, 2:52.

THE TEACHER'S LIBRARY.

Apart from that by Lenski, I find commentaries on Luke's Gospel not adequate for this chapter. The finest single exposition in any volume dealing with the Gospel of Luke is in that by G. Campbell Morgan, pp. 43–47, a masterpiece indeed. The material there is worked out in greater detail in his *Westminster Pulpit*, Vol. 10, pp. 129–144, in my opinion the best fifteen pages on the passage we are about to study that has ever been written. Next to that — and, for minute details on various Greek words, even better — is the marvelous article, "Boyhood of Jesus," by George Farmer in James Hastings: *Dictionary of Christ and the Gospels*, Vol. 1, pp. 224–230. Then, done with great beauty and insight, is Alexander Whyte: *The Walk, Conversation and Character of Jesus Christ Our Lord*, 40–75.

For an exhaustive study of the religious life in Jerusalem at the time of Christ, see Alfred Edersheim: *The Temple, Its Ministry and Service As They Were at the Time of Christ*, though in these four hundred pages, for some reason, he gives no attention to this passage. For geographical and archaeological background material for this lesson, see the volume by Edmond Stapfer: *Jesus Christ Before His Ministry* (1896).

There are a number of volumes on the boyhood of Jesus, such as the profound work by P. J. Temple: *The Boyhood Consciousness of Jesus* (1922), a Roman Catholic work; William Ramsay: *The Education of Christ* (1911), beautifully written, but in parts fanciful; and, best of all, Dean Edward Goulburn: *The Gospel of the Childhood* (1873), 240 pages on the text. The volume by Hugh Chapman, *The Beautiful Childhood* (1926) I have not seen.

Sermonic literature I am not recording. If one wishes a collection of material there is James Hastings: *Great Texts of the Bible;* on verse 40, pp. 82–101, 104–42. I must refer to a notable sermon, however, by the great Dean Stanley, on verse 40, in his volume, *The Child Jesus*, pp. 5–14. There are interesting things relating to our lesson in Canon Farrar's work, *Christ in Art*, 271–291. Finally, on verse 52, there are some profound things in Abraham Kuyper: *The Work of the Holy Spirit*, 94–96.

AUDIO-VISUAL AIDS.

Slide set: "Move 2," Visserslides No. 40–46, 5 sl., col. The flight into Egypt and return and the little home in Nazareth with "the little helper."

LUKE 2:40. And the child grew, and waxed strong, filled with wisdom: and the grace of God was upon him.

Many details of our Lord's birth are given by both Matthew and Luke, and some account, in each of the Gospels, of the preliminary ministry of John the Baptist, but only in Luke's Gospel do we find anything about the life of Jesus from the time He was approximately three years of age, when the holy family returned to Nazareth from Egypt, until His thirtieth year, and the beginning of His public ministry — twenty-seven years of silence, of which we know nothing, apart from these thirteen verses of our study today, and one brief later statement, "Is not this the carpenter?" (Mark 6:3). Though this passage has often come up for consideration in the International Lessons, we somehow never grow tired of it, and there are always new truths to bring forth from these verses. Here I shall try to introduce material never before used, for the most part, but I cannot avoid again quoting from the pages of Dr. G. Campbell Morgan.

I. **THE THREEFOLD GROWTH OF THE CHILD JESUS**, Luke 2:40. **40. And the child grew, and waxed strong, filled with wisdom: and the grace of God was upon him.** We might, first of all, fasten our attention upon the word *grew*, for this will attract the attention of the pupils. "He grew in stature, and he grew in character and goodness. He did not stand still. Although it was God himself who was revealed to us in the life of Jesus Christ, yet this did not prevent him from being made like unto us in all things, sin only excepted. It has been reverently and truly said: —

> Was not our Lord a little child,
>   Taught by degrees to pray;
> By father dear and mother mild
>   Instructed day by day?

Yes, he was: we need not fear to say so; and in this lies the example for us. Each one of us, whether old or young, must remember that progress, improvement, going on, advance, change into something better and better, wiser and wiser, year by year — that this is the only condition, the only way of our becoming like Christ, and, therefore, like God. Do not think that you will always be, that you must always be, as you are now. No: you will grow up gradually to be something very different; you must increase and grow in mind as well as in body, in wisdom as well as in stature. The world moves, and you and all of us must move with it. God calls us, one and all, ever to something higher and higher, and that higher state you and I and the whole word must reach by steadily advancing towards it." — *A. P. Stanley.*

The deep insight of Dr. Campbell Morgan into this passage ever astonishes me. "The word 'child' here is a diminutive; the Childing, that is, the little Child. In the understanding of that there is something of value, for it is a word that suggests two inclusive facts about the Child during the whole period from babyhood to boyhood; the facts of Immaturity and Potentiality. Of the Child — the little Child, from babyhood up through those sweet and wonderful years until that mystic and tremendous age of about twelve to thirteen is reached — these are the essential facts. It is immature, not having come to maturity in any department of its life. The proportion in which in those years a child is mature is the proportion of the tragedy of that child's life. If there be maturity, spiritual, mental, or physical, it will be the ruin of the child when the child becomes a man. But it is also a period of potentiality. . . . 'Grew' is a word that speaks of enlargement and development potentially and naturally. It is the period when the life-forces are operating naturally for the growth of the child. 'Waxed strong' is *increased in vigour*. This is the necessary result of natural growth; not merely the enlargement of the child, but the life forces within — physical, mental, spiritual, all increasing in strength. 'Becoming filled with wisdom.' Here I take the last word first. Wisdom. It is a wonderful thing that that word should be used here.

227

41. And his parents went every year to Jerusalem at the feast of the passover.

It is at once the simplest and the greatest word. It stands for essential truth. It represents clear knowledge. It represents that finality of truth which the philosophers of this period were seeking, after which they are still seeking. . . . The word 'filled' suggests furnishing, making replete. It suggests development, no longer merely by the forces that are within, but by the observation of things that are without, and by the instruction which is being given to the child concerning these things that are without. This, then, is a picture of Jesus from babyhood to boyhood, becoming filled with wisdom, seeing things and asking questions and being answered. . . . Now let us read a little further. Grace! I sometimes think that is the most wonderful word in the Bible; a word even more wonderful than love, notwithstanding the fact that grace is but an expression of love, that love is its inspiration, its cause, its reason. . . . It describes that which can only be predicated perfectly of God; 'the Grace of God,' that is, love in its outworking. Grace includes all that is strong and beautiful, in the highest, brightest, deepest, richest, tenderest senses of those words. The phrase here suggests rather the results produced in the Lord than the producing cause, manifesting itself to others in His tone, and in His temper. . . . I observe in the next place that in the orderly arrangement of my text, I have a revelation of the true lines of development during those years, the things that are important, and the order in which they are important. The statement is that 'He grew and waxed strong' — the physical is first; 'becoming filled with wisdom' — the mental is second; and the third is not necessarily third in order, and yet its statement is third because it is so largely a matter that lies within the realm of the grace of God that it is put last — 'the Grace of God was upon Him.' " — *G. Campbell Morgan.*

II. **CHRIST IN THE TEMPLE WITH THE DOCTORS,** Luke 2:41–51. Before entering upon the interpretation of these verses, it might be helpful to have before us a summarizing account of childhood among the Jewish people at the time of Jesus. "Jesus belonged to a people unsurpassed for the care bestowed upon the education of children. His earliest teacher would be His mother; and we cannot doubt that of all Jewish mothers, none could excel Mary ('blessed among women') in all such work. Among other things He would probably learn from her the *Shema* (Deut. 6:4) — that sacred formula which attends the devout Jew from his earliest years to his latest moment. This is quite consistent with the fact that education was one of the things for which the father was held responsible as regards his son. At an early age Jesus would be sent to school at the synagogue, there to be taught by the *hazzan*, or schoolmaster, to read and recite the Jewish Scriptures. The instruction given did not go beyond this, with writing and possibly a little arithmetic as additional and subordinate subjects. It was in a supreme degree a religious education, designed to fit children for the practical duties of life. The education of Jesus was just that of the great mass of the people: unlike Saul of Tarsus, no *beth ha Midrash*, or college of Scribes, received Him as a student ('*Whence* hath this man these things?' Mark 6:2; compare John 7:15)." — *J. S. Clemens.*

41. **And his parents went every year to Jerusalem at the feast of the passover.** "From our Lord's own presence at other feasts, both of Divine and human appointment, and from the large crowds at them, we are led to reject the idea that pious Jews at this time went to Jerusalem only for the Passover. No doubt the greatest attendance was at that feast, and those who could attend only one probably chose it. Jews resident outside the Holy Land seem, probably on account of the more favourable season for travelling, to have preferred Pentecost (Acts 2:1, 11; 18:21; 20:16; 21:27; 24:18; 1 Cor. 16:8). Women were not *bound* to attend any feast (Deut. 16:16, 'all thy males'). If women went to any one feast, it would be, if possible, to the Passover, partly because it was the most esteemed, partly because the Supper (both sacrificial and social) was an essential element in it, and partly

42. And when he was twelve years old, they went up after the custom of the feast.

43. And when they had fulfilled the days, as they were returning, the boy Jesus tarried behind in Jerusalem; and his parents knew it not.

44. But supposing him to be in the company, they went a day's journey; and they sought for him among their kinsfolk and acquaintance:

45. And when they found him not, they returned to Jerusalem seeking for him.

46. And it came to pass, after three days they found him in the temple, sitting in the midst of the teachers, both hearing them, and asking them questions:

---

because of the examples of Peninnah and Hannah (1 Sam. 1:3, 7, 21)." 42. **And when he was twelve years old, they went up after the custom of the feast.** "Does this imply that He had never been with them before? We doubt it. The mention of His age may be made only in order to mark at what period of His life the incident which follows occurred. The commentators, etc., lay great stress on His having become a 'son of the Law' or a 'son of the Precept,' and represent this Passover visit to Jerusalem as a sort of 'First Communion' after a sort of 'Confirmation.' The whole of the legislation about the *bar-mizvah* dates *after* the destruction of the Jewish polity in A.D. 70. . . . But if it was our Lord's *first* Passover (which St. Luke does *not* say) we can find another reason than the age He had reached for the previous omission. Herod the Great had tried to kill the Child, Archelaus was considered by Joseph to be as dangerous, and therefore Jesus was kept out of his dominions." — *George Farmer.* 43. **And when they had fulfilled the days, as they were returning, the boy Jesus tarried behind in Jerusalem; and his parents knew it not.** "Among the countless throngs of Jews who flocked to the Passover — nearly three millions according to Josephus — nothing could be easier than to lose sight of one young boy in the thronged streets, or among the thousands of booths outside the city walls. Indeed it is an incident which to this day often occurs at Jerusalem in similar cases. It should be also remembered that at the age of 12 an Eastern boy is far more mature than is the case in Northern nations, and that at that age a wider liberty was allowed him." — *F. W. Farrar.* "All the pilgrims used to go to the Temple on the day of their departure, by a rule possibly based on 1 Samuel 1:19. There would be a great crowd, and the temporary separation of a family in the colonades and on the steps would be (as in great public gatherings now) a natural occurrence, causing little alarm. Possibly Joseph and Mary joined their fellow-travellers from Galilee, in the belief that the Child, who would know the time and point of departure, was among the younger pilgrims. The little fear they felt on the first day rather supports the view mentioned earlier, that it was not Jesus' first Passover." — *George Farmer.* 44. **But supposing him to be in the company, they went a day's journey; and they sought for him among their kinsfolk and acquaintance: 45. and when they found him not, they returned to Jerusalem seeking for him.** The words of Dr. Alexander Whyte are well taken here. "There was one thing in Joseph and in Mary that passover-week that always greatly amazes me. Why did they not proceed to the temple at once when they returned back to the city to seek for their child? . . . Had any of you who are fathers, been in Joseph's place that week, and had any of you who are mothers, been in Mary's place that week, what would you have done? . . . You would have gone straight to the temple, would you not? You would have said to one another as you hastened back to the city — 'Let us go first of all to the temple and look for our child. He is sure to be still tarrying there. For He was absolutely possessed with the temple, and with all that He saw and heard in the temple.' " — *Alexander Whyte.* 46. **And it came to pass, after three days they**

47. and all that heard him were amazed at his understanding and his answers.

48. And when they saw him, they were astonished; and his mother said unto him, Son, why hast thou thus dealt with us? behold, thy father and I sought thee sorrowing.

49. And he said unto them, How is it that ye sought me? knew ye not that I must be in my Father's house?

---

found him in the temple, sitting in the midst of the teachers, both hearing them, and asking them questions: 47. and all that heard him were amazed at his understanding and his answers. "It is said that members of the Sanhedrin did sometimes, on extraordinary occasions, admit an inquirer to the same seat as themselves. It would be a probable thing to do, where the youth of the person made him, as in this case, liable to partial concealment among older and taller bystanders. There is no ground for supposing that Christ *disputed* with the Rabbis. It is clear that He in nowise offended their prejudices on this occasion. All that he said, although remarkable for His age, was suitable to it. The mode of higher religious teaching among the Jews seems to have been by mutual interrogation between the teacher and the scholar. Hence the freedom used by the disciples and others in questioning *their* Teacher. Christ answered some questions and put others, no doubt with all marks of respect to those who 'sat in Moses' seat' (Matt. 23:2). What led to Christ's desire to interview the Rabbis at all, and what was the subject of His questions? We can understand His intense interest in the recently celebrated Feast, its history and its meaning. . . . Questions such as those discussed in Matthew 2:4, 6; Mark 9:11; John 7:42 would be raised and would interest Him. Luke 20:22, 28–33 and Mark 10:2 give us other authentic instances of the points discussed by the Jewish teachers of that age." — *George Farmer.*

48. **And when they saw him, they were astonished; and his mother said unto him, Son, why hast thou thus dealt with us? behold, thy father and I sought thee sorrowing.** " 'Unto him his mother said.' Such is the order of the words in the original, though in our English translation it is, 'and his mother said unto him.' There must be some reason for 'unto him' being put first in the original. Probably by adopting this order of words, St. Luke meant to convey to his readers that what the Virgin said was addressed to our Lord alone, said in a low voice, when He came up close to her, and not meant to be heard by others — 'unto him' (apart from all others) 'his mother said.' His mother! and why not Joseph, His supposed father? The words of the mother convey a gentle reproof, or, at all events, a gentle expostulation; they are at least a remonstrance, and insinuate that He had behaved thoughtlessly, and without due consideration of them. Now, this would come more naturally from the father than from the mother of a child; the father would be the more likely parent of the two to speak in accents of censure, and to find fault. But Joseph must have known that he was not the real father of the Holy Child. . . . 'Son, why hast thou thus dealt with us?' The words may usefully remind us that the dealings of the Lord Jesus with those who sincerely love and serve Him are often very strange. Not only does He try them by ordinary troubles, such as loss of health and loss of friends, but sometimes He takes away from them all spiritual comfort, and leaves their souls dark and disconsolate." — *E. M. Goulburn.* 49. **And he said unto them, How is it that ye sought me? knew ye not that I must be in my Father's house?** Dr. J. Gresham Machen has said of this verse, "There are depths in this utterance which have never been fathomed even by the framers of the Nicene and Chalcedonian creeds. It will be a sad day, indeed, if the Church comes to suppose that *nothing* in this word of the boy Jesus can be understood; but it will also be a sad day if it supposes that *all* can be understood. Mary can surely be pardoned for her wonder, and for her failure to understand." — *Dr. J. Gresham Machen.* There is actually no word here in the Greek to be translated "house." It is simply, "I must be in my Father's," so that

50. And they understood not the saying which he spake unto them.

51. And he went down with them, and came to Nazareth; and he was subject unto them: and his mother kept all *these* sayings in her heart.

52. And Jesus advanced in wisdom and stature, and in favor with God and man.

---

some add the word "business" or "things." "These words are very memorable as being the first recorded words of Jesus. They bear upon them the stamp of authenticity in their half-vexed astonishment, and perfect mixture of dignity and humility." — *F. W. Farrar*. With this compare John 4:34. **50. And they understood not the saying which he spake unto them.** Farrar says that these words "might stand as the epitome of much of Christ's ministry (9:45; 18:34; Mark 9:32; John 10:6). The meaning, however, is not that they had any doubt as to what the grammatical construction of His words implied; but only as to their bearing and appropriateness to the circumstances of so young a child." — *F. W. Farrar*. **51. And he went down with them, and came to Nazareth; and he was subject unto them: and his mother kept all *these* sayings in her heart.** "Our Lord's subjection and submission were made perfect, and were thus made the pattern of our subjection and submission, just by His living day after day, day after day, for thirty years in the small house with His mother and His brothers and His sisters. Like ourselves in our homes also, His mother and His brothers and His sisters would all insist that their way was the only right way in this and in that, and that His way was the wrong way. . . . He never disputed or fell out with any of His brothers or sisters, because He every day read it on the tables of His own humble heart, not to look every man on his own things, but every man also on the things of others. Follow peace with all men, was His daily meditation every day both at home and abroad. And when His mother's house became divided, as the best houses will sometimes become divided, He would only go away the oftener to secret prayer till He came back saying to Himself, As much as lieth in you, live peaceably with all men, especially with those of your own mother's household. No. He did not need to enter the Essene monasteries of the Dead Sea in order to practise a meek and a quiet heart, and in order to subject Himself to His superiors." — *Alexander Whyte*. In Luke 4:16, Nazareth is referred to as the place "where he had been brought up." "Its general aspect was dull and mean. Nazareth was a cluster of cubical houses without character or elegance, built in terraces in the hollow of an amphitheatre of rocky hills. Irregularly disposed, they formed a confused medley of small white flat-roofed dwellings, threshing-floors and wine-presses. Here were pits hollowed out of the ground; there tombs hewn out of the rock. The fig-tree, the olive, the cactus grew everywhere, and now and then, between the houses, a tiny field of wheat. We are told that Nazareth contained three or four thousand inhabitants. This estimate is certainly excessive. Judging by the small area which it covered, Nazareth was a mere village. It is true that in the Orient men and beasts can huddle themselves into a very small space; but we cannot credit more than fifteen hundred or two thousand inhabitants to a village which had only one synagogue, one fountain, and one public square." — *Edmond Stapfer*. Our Lord is here perfectly obeying the fourth commandment, regarding obedience to parents on the part of children (Ex. 20:12). Jesus quotes this very commandment in Matthew 15:4 and 19:19, as St. Paul also does in Ephesians 6:2. III. **THE THREEFOLD GROWTH OF JESUS AS A YOUNG MAN**, Luke 2:52. **And Jesus advanced in wisdom and stature, and in favor with God and man.** Verse 40 is a summary of the growth of Jesus to the age of twelve. It is generally understood that the concluding verses of this chapter summarize the nature of His growth up to the time of full manhood, approaching the first year of His public ministry. Believing that most of my readers do not have access to

Dr. Morgan's great sermon in The *Westminster Pulpit*, I am quoting from it rather extensively. "We have here exactly the same facts as in the growth of the child: 'The child grew and waxed strong; becoming filled with wisdom; and the grace of God was upon Him'; but here is a different order and relation. In those earlier years from babyhood to boyhood the physical is supreme, necessarily so; and we violate the life of a child between babyhood and boyhood if we attempt to make the mental supreme. But now things are altered: the mental is supreme; He advanced in wisdom, and this development in wisdom accompanied and governed the development in stature. The supreme thing in these years is wisdom, subservient to it, not degraded by it, but ennobled by it, yet nevertheless subservient to it, is development in stature. Here again we observe another difference; the spiritual has now passed from the subjective to the objective, from privilege merely to grave responsibility. The whole beautiful spiritual fact of childhood was declared in the words, 'The grace of God was upon Him.' . . . The grace of God had to do with the child; but it was ever 'upon' the child. Now note the difference. Here let me say what I have omitted to say earlier; the word *favour* is exactly the same as the word *grace*. He grew in grace with God and men. . . . Now the youth is seen having reached the age of responsibility, not merely about the mind and about the body, but about grace. This advancement in grace is dependent entirely upon advancement in wisdom and in stature. . . . The word 'wisdom' here covers the whole vast area of knowledge; the realm of ideas, reason, truth. . . . Grace, as the term is used in the text, refers to a double relation; with God and men. . . . On the one hand is described the poise of His soul God-ward. His soul was so poised toward God, so adjusted toward God, that He received from God the things of God, and became like the God to Whom He yielded Himself; growing, advancing, developing, in all those characteristics resulting from the right relationship of His soul to God. . . . The grace of God which was upon Him in childhood without volition, remained with Him, permeated Him, manifested itself through Him in youth, because volitionally He yielded Himself to its gracious light and its insistent claim. Consequently He advanced in grace with men. That describes the attitude of His soul man-ward."

A passage from Abraham Kuyper's monumental work on the Holy Spirit must conclude our study today. "Although His heart contained the germ of all wisdom, yet as a child of one year, e.g., He could not know the Scripture by means of His human understanding. As the Eternal Son He knew it, for He Himself had given it to His Church. But His human knowledge had no free access to His divine knowledge. On the contrary, while the latter never increased, knowing all things from eternity, the former was to learn everything; it had nothing of itself. This is the increase in wisdom of which St. Luke speaks — an increase not of the faculty, but of its exercise. And this affords us a glimpse into the extent of His humiliation. He that knew all things by virtue of His divine nature began as man with knowing nothing; and that which He knew as a man He acquired by learning it under the influence of the Holy Spirit." — *Abraham Kuyper*.

THE LESSON IN LIFE, LITERATURE, AND ARCHAEOLOGY.

Here we can most appropriately use one of the concluding stanzas of the tender poem by Oliver Wendell Holmes, "The Mother's Secret."

> The tale was told to Nazareth's sober men,
> And Nazareth's matrons told it oft again;
> The maids retold it at the fountain's side,
> The youthful shepherds doubted or denied;
> It passed around among the listening friends,
> With all that fancy adds and fiction lends,
> Till newer marvels dimmed the young renown
> Of Joseph's son, who talked the Rabbis down.
> But Mary, faithful to its lightest word,
> Kept in her heart the sayings she had heard,
> Till the dread morning rent the Temple's veil,
> And shuddering earth confirmed the wondrous tale.

A TRUTH FOR THE CLASS TO CARRY AWAY.

The description given here of growth at two different periods in the life of Jesus is the ideal for youth in the mind of God, and ought to be the normal experience of every young person, at least in an elementary way. Should we not then be zealous in creating, as far as we can, that kind of an atmosphere for boys and girls, young men and women, that will nurture and encourage such growth as we have here — physical, mental, and spiritual? The first two seem to be almost inevitable in the life of a normal boy or girl, but the third must be watched, cultivated, encouraged, day by day, year by year.

What do you think it was in the questions and answers of Jesus that actually astonished the learned men with whom he was conversing in the Temple? Can you recall another occasion in our Lord's life when men were astonished at His knowledge, knowing that He had not attended rabbinical schools? (See John 7:15). Was our Lord in a position to ask questions of these doctors of the law that He was not able to ask of anyone in His own village of Nazareth? Do you see here any factors that bespeak the supernaturalness of Christ? With all of His amazing knowledge of holy things and His own self-consciousness of His divine calling, even as a boy, do you think that Jesus was easy to get along with?

LESSON II. — July 11.

ARE WE GROWING AS CHRISTIANS? — 1 Corinthians 3:1–3; Ephesians 4:11–16; 2 Peter 1:5–7; 3:18.

PRINTED TEXT, 1 Corinthians 3:1–3; Ephesians 4:11–16; 2 Peter 1:5–7; 3:18.

Devotional Reading: Ephesians 4:25—5:2.

Beginner Topic: A KIND SHEPHERD.
　　Lesson Material: Exodus 23:12. Deuteronomy 22:6–7. Proverbs 12:10. Matthew 18:12–14. Luke 14:5; 15:1–7.
　　Memory Verse: Be gentle towards all. 2 Timothy 2:24.

Primary Topic: HOW WE GROW LIKE JESUS.
　　Lesson Material: Ephesians 4:11–16.
　　Memory Verse: Speaking truth in love, may grow up in all things into him. Ephesians 4:15.

Junior Topic: HOW WE GROW LIKE JESUS.
　　Lesson Material: Ephesians 4:11–16.
　　Memory Verse: Speaking truth in love, may grow up in all things into him. Ephesians 4:15.

Intermediate-Senior Topic: A LOOK AT OURSELVES.
　　Lesson Material: 1 Corinthians 3:1–3; Ephesians 4:11–16; 2 Peter 1:5–8; 3:18.
　　Memory Verse: Grow in the grace and knowledge of our Lord and Saviour Jesus Christ. 2 Peter 3:18.

Topic for Young People and Adults: ARE WE GROWING AS CHRISTIANS?
　　Lesson Material: 1 Corinthians 3:1–3; Ephesians 4:11–16; 2 Peter 1:5–8; 3:18.
　　Memory Verse: Grow in the grace and knowledge of our Lord and Saviour Jesus Christ. 2 Peter 3:18.

233

THE TEACHER AND HIS CLASS.

The **Younger Classes** might be introduced to this lesson with an illustration from rural life, inasmuch as many of the pupils probably live on farms, or at least in rural communities. On any farm, the growth of plants, vegetables, or fruit trees will at once indicate whether or not the farm or orchard is going to be profitable. I remember when as a boy spending summers in Michigan, every week passing by a farm midway between Walkerville and Hart in Oceana County where the corn was only a foot high, when it should have been waist high, but was thin, and sickly looking. The soil was not rich enough to grow a crop of corn that would prove profitable. A fruit tree that does not grow will not bear fruit and thus does not fulfill its function. We are to grow as Christians, so that we may bear fruit in our lives.

The **Older Classes** might be introduced to this lesson by a simple statement of fact: A young man desiring to achieve something worthwhile in the field of engineering, or science will try to secure as many degrees as he can by years of study, continually adding subjects to his knowledge. Through the years, we all desire to add something to our bank account. This is normal. I am afraid, however, that in our spiritual lives instead of continually adding year by year, we sometimes lose what we have, and often when a man reaches fifty, he has less spiritual wealth than he had at twenty-five years of age. Our lesson today is an encouragement to begin this whole process of spiritual development.

THE LESSON IN ITS SETTING.

Time. — The First Epistle of Paul to the Corinthians was written about A.D. 57 or 58; that to the Ephesians, perhaps A.D. 63 or 64; and the Second Epistle of Peter, about A.D. 67.

Place. — Corinth was a great city in Greece, the capital of the province of Achaia. Ephesus, one of the most famous cities in the world, was near the seacoast of Asia Minor.

THE PLAN OF THE LESSON.

SUBJECT: The Naturalness of Growth to a Healthy Christian Life, and Some Rules to Assist in this Experience.

I. The Tragedy of Undeveloped Christian Life, 1 Corinthians 3:1-3.

II. The Ideal of a Growing Church, Ephesians 4:11-16.

III. Peter's Dual Exhortation to Grow, 2 Peter 1:5-7; 3:18.
  1. In relation to the elements of Christian character, 1:5-7.
  2. In relation to the knowledge of Christ, 3:18.

THE TEACHER'S LIBRARY.

On the matter of growth, there is an excellent sermon in a volume now too seldom seen, James M. Gray: *Salvation from Start to Finish.* On the First Epistle to the Corinthians, the volume by Godet will be found helpful in the study of this lesson, but hardly any other commentary for these particular verses, apart from that by Charles Hodge. There is a superb discussion of Christian carnality in L. S. Chafer: *Systematic Theology,* Vol. 7, pp. 68-70. The only good sermon with which I am acquainted on this particular passage is in Andrew Murray: *Absolute Surrender,* 24-40.

For the verses from the Ephesian Epistle, one should first read the classic chapter, "The Growth of the Church," in the volume on Ephesians in the *Expositor's Bible,* by G. G. Findlay. For rich analysis and interpretation of every word, one should look at the great work published in 1854, *A Commentary on the Epistle to the Ephesians,* by John Eadie, 281-310; one might also read with profit L. S. Chafer: *Systematic Theology,* Vol. 4, pp. 68-71.

On the passage from the Second Epistle of Peter, there is an excellent chapter in the volume in the *Expositor's Bible* by J. R. Lumby, 245-253; see also John Henry Jowett: *The Redeemed Family of God,* 227-236, and some helpful sermonic material: on 1:5-7, see W. Y. Fullerton: *The Christly Life,* 79-89; Alexander Maclaren: *Expositions of Holy Scripture, First and Second Peter and First John,* 198-206; and seven sermons in Henry Howard: *The Summits of the Soul,* 3-79. For a collection of material, see James Hastings: *Great Texts of the Bible, James to Jude,* 152-192; a volume devoted entirely to this passage, which I do not possess, is John N. Gibson: *The Gamut of Graces* (London, 1926). On 2 Peter 3:18, see J. H. Jowett, as above, 334-345, and Hastings, as above, 194-214.

AUDIO-VISUAL AIDS.

No audio-visual aids discovered.

1 Corinthians 3:1. And I, brethren, could not speak unto you as unto spiritual, but as unto carnal, as unto babes in Christ.

2. I fed you with milk, not with meat; for ye were not yet able *to bear it:* nay, not even now are ye able;

3. For ye are yet carnal: for whereas there. is among you jealousy and strife, are ye not carnal, and do ye not walk after the manner of men?

This lesson is closely connected with the one immediately preceding, in that both have to do with the matter of growth. Last week we studied the growth of the child Jesus: today we are to consider that kind of growth which should be normal and natural in the life of any healthy Christian, and then the transfer of this idea to the growth of the Church, in which all of us are expected to participate. There are, we might say, three kinds of growth, namely, biological growth of plants, animals, tissues, etc.; mathematical growth, as a crowd grows, a bank account grows, or a library grows; and, structural growth, as seen in the erection of a building. The last two types are to be seen in our lesson.

I. THE TRAGEDY OF UNDEVELOPED CHRISTIAN LIFE, 1 Corinthians 3:1–3. The First Epistle of Paul to the Church at Corinth tells us that the church there was honeycombed with jealousy, strife, and immorality. Men were suing each other in the courts; there was drunkenness at the Lord's table; there was immorality among the members of the grossest kind; there was a bitter quarrel regarding meat offered to idols; and there were schismatic groups gathered around various prominent names in the apostolic church. In the brief passage from this Epistle assigned to our lesson, Paul puts his finger upon the major cause for this shameful state of the Corinthian Christians. 1. And I, brethren, could not speak unto you as unto spiritual, but as unto carnal, as unto babes in Christ. Paul uses three words in classifying mankind — the *natural* man, the *spiritual* man, who is ruled by the Holy Spirit, and the *carnal* man. The word *carnal* is a translation of the Greek word meaning *flesh.* "Carnality is caused not by the unspiritual things which one may do, but fundamentally by a lack of yieldedness to the mind and will of God. The carnal Christian does unspiritual things because he is carnal or fleshly. . . . The carnal person is a true believer and therefore saved. Such are addressed as 'brethren' — a salutation which never includes unregenerate persons, and they are said to be 'babes in Christ.' While, because of carnality, they are termed 'babes in Christ,' nothing could give greater assurance of their security for time and eternity than the fact that they are 'in Christ.' This revealing passage not only indicates the limitations of the carnal believer but reveals the state of affairs which, in the case of the Corinthians, came about because of their carnality. Being unyielded to God, they could not receive the 'strong meat' of the Word of God; they could only receive the 'milk.' By so much their spiritual limitations are revealed. Their carnality was manifest in the divisions among them, with a tendency to follow human leaders. Such conduct signified a violent disregard for the unity of the Spirit — the one Body of believers — which unity the Apostle declares must be kept (Eph. 4:3). Since this sin of sectarian divisions is first on the list of evils for which the Apostle condemns the Corinthian believers — there is even mention of it before he points out their immoralities — its exceeding sinfulness in the sight of God becomes plain; yet like divisions are evident whenever sectarianism and denominational loyalty are stressed above the doctrine of the one Body of believers." — *L. S. Chafer.* 2. I fed you with milk, not with meat; for ye were not yet able *to bear it:* nay, not even now are ye able; 3. For ye are yet carnal: for whereas there is among you jealousy and strife, are ye not carnal, and do ye not walk after the manner of men? "Milk, according to 2:2, denotes the preaching of Jesus crucified, with its simplest contents and its most immediate consequences, expiation, justification by faith, the sanctification of the justified believer by the Holy Spirit what saves by converting and regenerating.

235

EPHESIANS 4:11. And he gave some *to be* apostles; and some, prophets; and some, evangelists, and some, pastors, and teachers.

Meat represents what Paul has just called wisdom, the contemplation of the Divine plan in its entirety from its eternal predestination to its final consummation. The same figure occurs in Hebrews 5:12 and 6:2, but with this difference, that there the persons in question are former Hebrews, and that the rudiments of religious knowledge (milk) are not exactly the same for those who were formerly Jews as for those who were formerly heathen." — *F. Godet.*

II. **THE IDEAL OF A GROWING CHURCH**, Ephesians 4:11–16. Paul's Epistle to the Ephesians is without doubt the loftiest single writing in the entire New Testament, as one will see before he finishes reading the first chapter. It is here that the noblest aspects of truth regarding the *Church* are set forth, with the divine ideal for the body of Christ here on earth. In our passage the Apostle, by use of an appropriate figure of speech, compares the Church to a human body, showing how Christ, the head of the Church, has so ordained that each member, and especially the officers, of the church should contribute some vital part to the growth of this body. Verse 11 sets forth the titles of the officers; verse 12, the ultimate end for which they are to work; and verses 13–16, the consummation of the growth they are to strive for. I would like to begin this discussion with an introductory passage from Dr. Lewis Sperry Chafer. "The writer declares that the ministry of these gifted men, especially the pastor and teacher, is for the perfecting of the saints unto *their* work of the ministry. In this age, as in no other, there is a specific message to be preached to every creature, and while there are leadership men who are God's gift to the Church, the obligation to witness rests upon every Christian alike. Too much recognition cannot be given to the uncounted multitudes of faithful witnesses who are discharging their commissions as Sunday School teachers, mission workers, personal soul-winners, and living exponents of divine grace. This is the God-appointed New Testament evangelism. The latent evangelizing forces of a congregation of believers are beyond all human calculation; but they need to be trained for their task, and God has prescribed definitely that they should be trained. How else would they be accurate and skillful even in their limited sphere of service? That they are to be trained is indicated in Ephesians 4:11–12. The revelation here is not only of the fact that the saints have a witnessing service to perform, but also of the fact that they are to be *equipped* for this service by the gifted men whom God has placed over them as their leaders. The word here translated *perfecting* is a noun which is but once used in the New Testament and means *equipment*, and so refers to that preparation which all saints should have that they may be effective witnesses for Christ. . . . According to this passage, the pastor and teacher is responsible for the equipment of those given into his care. Although this equipment does involve methods of work, it includes much more, namely, an accurate knowledge of the truth. But the pastor and teacher must be trained for his leadership task. Under existing conditions this preparation is committed to the professors in the theological seminary. Their responsibility is greater than that of other men inasmuch as the heavenly things transcend the things of earth. . . . Whatever truth and ideals the professor imparts to students in training, they, in turn, will later impart to the larger groups over which they are given spiritual care. If a congregation is not actively engaged in soul-winning and missionary work, it is usually because of the fact that they have been deprived of the God-intended leadership to that end. If the pastor has no soul-winning passion, no missionary vision, is limited in his proficiency, and inaccurate as an exponent of the Word of God, his lack in these respects may generally be traced to the fact that he has been deprived of the God-intended spiritual and vital training in the seminary." — *Dr. Lewis S. Chafer.*

Verse 11 deserves very careful attention, and I trust my readers will be helped by the extensive use here made of material from the great Scotch commentator, John Eadie. **11. And he gave some *to be* apostles.** "The apostles were the first

12. For the perfecting of the saints, unto the work of ministering, unto the building up of the body of Christ.

13. Till we all attain unto the unity of the faith, and of the knowledge of the Son of God, unto a fullgrown man, unto the measure of the stature of the fulness of Christ.

and highest order of office-bearers. The essential elements of their office were (1) that they should receive their commission immediately from the living lips of Christ (Matt. 10:5, etc.); (2) that having seen the Saviour after he rose again, they should be qualified to attest the truth of his resurrection (Acts 1:21, 22); (3) they enjoyed a special inspiration (John 14:26, etc.) and infallible exposition of Divine truth was their work; (4) their authority was supreme — the church was under their unrestricted administration (1 Cor. 5:3–6); (5) they enjoyed the power of working miracles; (6) their commission was universal and not limited to any section of the church (2 Cor. 11:28)." — *John Eadie.* **And some, prophets.** "The prophets ranked next in order to the apostles, but wanted some of their peculiar qualifications. They spake under the influence of the Spirit; and as their instructions were infallible, so the church was built on their foundation as well as that of the apostles (2:20). Prophecy is marked out as one of the special endowments of the Holy Ghost (1 Cor. 12:28) where it stands after the apostolic prerogative of working miracles. The revelation enjoyed by apostles was communicated also to prophets (3:5). . . . The prophets of the New Testament were men who were peculiarly susceptible of Divine influence, and on whom that afflatus powerfully rested. . . . Apostles planted and prophets watered, the germs engrafted by the one were nurtured and matured by the other. What the churches gain now by the spiritual study of Scripture, they obtained in those days by such *prophetical* expositions of apostolical truth." — *John Eadie.* **And some, evangelists.** "While the prophets spoke only as occasion required, and their language was an excited outpouring of brilliant and piercing thoughts, the evangelists might be more continuous, and tamer, too, in their work. They passed from place to place with the wondrous story of salvation and the cross, for their characteristic function was didactic in its nature. Entering into the society of such as frequented not the places of Christian worship, they pressed Christ on their acceptance, and their hands were freed all the while from matters of detail in reference to organization, ritual, and discipline. Were not the seventy sent forth by our Lord a species of evangelists, and might not Mark, Luke, Silas, Apollos, Tychichus and Trophimus, merit such a designation? The evangelist Timothy was commended by Paul to the church in Corinth." — *John Eadie.* **And some, pastors.** Literally, the word might be translated *shepherd.* "The image of a shepherd with his flock, picturing out the relation of a spiritual ruler, and those committed to his charge, often occurs (Ps. 23:1; 80:1; Jer. 2:8; 3:15, and in many other places). Such pastors and guides rule as well as feed the flock, for the keeping or tending is essential to the successful feeding." **And teachers.** "The peculiar work of these people was to expound the truths of Christianity; see 1 Timothy 3:2." — *John Eadie.* **12. For the perfecting of the saints, unto the work of ministering, unto the building up of the body of Christ.** "The work of the ministry is directed to the preparation of the saints — the whole body of the faithful — for the twofold work which in due measure belongs to all Christians, a personal work and a social work. Every believer is charged with the duty of personal service to his fellow-believers, and to his fellow-men (2 Peter 1:7) and has some part in building up the fabric of the Christian society. . . . The body of Christ, like our own frames, is built up by the addition of each element which is required for its completion; compare verse 16; 1 Peter 2:5 ff." — *B. F. Westcott.* **13. Till we all attain unto the unity of the faith, and of the knowledge of the Son of God, unto a fullgrown man, unto the measure of the stature of the fulness of Christ.** Personally, I have always felt that this was one of the greatest single passages in the New Testament. "The mark at which the Church has to arrive is set forth, in harmony with the tenor of the epistle, in a

14. That we may be no longer children, tossed to and fro and carried about with every wind of doctrine, by the sleight of men, in craftiness, after the wiles of error.

15. But speaking truth in love, may grow up in all things into him, who is the head, *even* Christ.

16. From whom all the body fitly framed and knit together through that which every joint supplieth, according to the working in *due* measure of each several part, maketh the increase of the body unto the building up of itself in love.

twofold way — in its *collective* and its *individual* aspects. We must all 'unitedly attain the oneness of the faith and the knowledge of the Son of God'; and we must attain, each of us, 'a perfect manhood, the measure of the stature of the fulness of Christ.' . . . When 'we all' believe heartily and understandingly in 'the word of truth, the gospel of our salvation,' the goal will be in sight. All our defects are, at the bottom, deficiencies of faith. We fail to apprehend and appropriate the fulness of God in Christ. Faith is the essence of the heart's life: it forms the common consciousness of the body of Christ. While faith is the central organ of the Church's life, the Son of God is its central object. The dangers assailing the Church and the divisions threatening its unity, touched His Person; and whatever touches the Head, vitally affects the health of the body and the well-being of every member in it. Many had believed in Jesus as the Christ and received blessing from Him, whose knowledge of Him as the Son of God was defective." — *G. G. Findlay.* 14. **That we may be no longer children, tossed to and fro and carried about with every wind of doctrine, by the sleight of men, in craftiness, after the wiles of error.** "Some men have just enough of Christian intelligence to unsettle them, and make them the prey of every idle suggestion, and the sport of every religious novelty. How many go the round of all sects, parties, and creeds, and never receive satisfaction? If in the pride of reason they fall into rationalism, then if they recover they rebound into mysticism. From the one extreme of legalism, they recoil to the farthest verge of Antinomianism, having travelled at easy stages all the intermediate distances. Decision and firmness are indispensable to spiritual improvement. Only one form of teaching is beneficial, and all deviations are pernicious." — *John Eadie.* There is hardly any verse in the New Testament more needful today than this, when we have so many false cults on the horizon drawing thousands away from the evangelical Church. These groups do not seek to win the lost for Christ, but to draw Christian believers out of the Church of Christ. They are parasites and deceivers, and many fall under their spell. The word translated *sleight* means "a cube, or one of the dice, signifying gambling, and then by an easy and well-known process, it means the common accompaniment and result of gambling — fraud and imposition." 15. **But speaking truth in love, may grow up in all things into him, who is the head, *even* Christ.** Actually, there is no word in this verse to be translated *speak*. If one should translate literally, it would be "truthing in love." In Galatians 5:22, we have another exhortation to love, beginning with the word "but" — "But the fruit of the Spirit is love." In his epistles, Paul constantly beseeches Christians to love one another, even as Christ has loved us. The First Epistle of John is filled with this theme. We are the children of God and fellow-members in the family of God. Here it would seem as though healthy life in the body of Christ depended upon this love life. And is it not true that when a Christian, by deed or word, is living or speaking falsely, that is, contrary to the will of God, the example of Christ and the leading of the Holy Spirit, he cannot grow spiritually and cannot contribute anything vital to the growth of the body of Christ. Here again the Apostle makes central the fact that Christ is the head of the Church; see, e.g., Ephesians 1:22; Colossians 1:18 and 2:19. 16. **From whom all the body fitly framed and knit together through that**

2 PETER 1:5. Yea, and for this very cause adding on your part all diligence, in your faith supply virtue; and in *your* virtue knowledge;

---

which every joint supplieth, according to the working in *due* measure of each several part, maketh the increase of the body unto the building up of itself in love. "Each local *ecclesia*, or assembly of saints, will have its stated officers, its regulated and seemly order in worship and in work. And within this fit frame, there must be the warm union of hearts, the frank exchange of thought and feeling, the brotherly counsel in all things touching the kingdom of God, by which Christian men in each place of their assembling are 'knit together.' From these local and congregational centres, the Christian fellowship spreads out its arms to embrace all that love our Lord Jesus Christ." — *G. G. Findlay.*

III. PETER'S DUAL EXHORTATION TO GROW, 2 Peter 1:5–7; 3:18. The man who wrote this Epistle was in great need of spiritual growth himself when Jesus found him, and probably of all the twelve apostles, he is the one who underwent the greatest change, and manifested the most remarkable growth. Peter knows from experience that of which he speaks. The statement immediately preceding the printed text is truly amazing — "that ye may become partakers of the divine nature." With all these precious promises, through which we may become partakers of the divine nature, Peter now exhorts believers to grow by the appropriation of this wealth which is theirs. 5. **Yea, and for this very cause adding on your part all diligence.** The *diligence* here referred to could be a word covering all that follows. "It is a demand for business vigilance in the realm of the spirit. We are not to close our eyes and allow our limbs to hang limp, in the expectancy that the Lord will carry us like blind logs. He made us of clay, but he formed us men, and as men He purposes that we shall live and move and have our being. And so He calls for 'diligence.' It is a word which elsewhere is translated haste, carefulness, business. It is very wonderful how commonly the New Testament takes its similes from the commercial world." — *J. H. Jowett.* **In your faith supply virtue.** "Virtue means the best development of such power as a man possesses. It may be little or great, but in its kind, it is to be made excellent. And here it is that the Christian workers in every sphere must surpass others. They work from a higher motive. What they do is a constant attestation of their faith, is done as in God's sight, and in the confidence that in every act it is possible to give Him glory. There can be no carelessness in such lives, for they are filled with a sense of responsibility, which is the first-fruit of a living faith." — *J. R. Lumby.* Virtue was one of the great ethical ideals of the ancient world. From an article of many years ago by a classical scholar, I would like to quote the following: "Virtue was applied by the Romans to every quality that belongs to an efficient and vigorous character, or to such a character as composed of such qualities. But *virtus*, or *virtutes*, the *vir* was distinguished from the mere *homo*. A *vir* was a man considered so endowed with *vires*, or powers. Strength of mind, practical wisdom, resolution, courage, perseverance, energy, entirely apart from any thought of morality, were called virtues. Along with this general signification the word was also used in the sense commonly given to it at the present day; and so designated moral principle, the habitual disposition to do right, or any specific development of such principle. Influenced by the broad conception of virtue, the ancients frequently failed to emphasize the distinction between the moral and the non-moral elements of character; to remedy which defect the Schoolmen divided virtues into the intellectual and the moral. . . . They taught that mundane life should be regulated by four principal or 'cardinal' virtues, namely, prudence, temperance, fortitude, and justice." **And in *your* virtue knowledge.** "That is the first time we have come across the idea of knowledge as a Christian virtue, a bit of the Christly life. This stop in the organ I will call the *Clarion.* You are not only to believe, but to 'give a reason for the hope that is in you.' You are to be able to answer the adversary. You cannot actually believe a thing

6. And in *your* knowledge self-control; and in *your* self-control patience; and in *your* patience godliness.

7. And in *your* godliness brotherly kindness; and in *your* brotherly kindness love.

2 PETER 3:18. But grow in the grace and knowledge of our Lord and Saviour Jesus Christ. To him *be* the glory both now and for ever. Amen.

---

that you cannot to your own mind give a reason for. You cannot really and permanently believe anything that is not reasonable. Supply knowledge. Here comes the office of a much derided thing called theology. You need theology of some kind. We are to have knowledge; we are to have an intellectual apprehension of faith, not only a sentimental apprehension of it." *—W. Y. Fullerton.*
6. **And in *your* knowledge self-control.** "The word for 'temperance' has a wider range than the modern sense of the English term. 'Self-government' or 'self-control' would be better equivalents." *— E. H. Plumptre.* **And in *your* self-control patience.** "This is the true sequence of spiritual self-control. Life is sure to supply for the godly man trials in abundance. But he is daily striving to die unto the world. The effort fixes his mind firmly on the Divine purposes, and lifts him above the circumstances of time. He is a pilgrim and sojourner amidst them, but is in no bondage to them, nor will he be moved, even by great afflictions, to waver in his trust. He can look on, as seeing Him that is invisible, and can persevere without being unduly cast down." *— J. R. Lumby.* **And in *your* patience godliness.** "A man may be as much a man of God as another man may be a man of the world; a man may be as much a man of the Kingdom as another man may be a man of affairs. 'God hath set apart him that is godly for himself.' Let us covet this virtue in our Christly life — that we shall be godly, that wherever we go people will be reminded of God, will say, 'That man is like Jesus.'" *—W. Y. Fullerton.* 7. **And in *your* godliness brotherly kindness.** This is the same idea as we find expressed in 1 Peter 1:22. The very word 'brother' implies a family relationship. It was almost never used in any way outside of a family bound together by cords of direct relationship among the Greeks, but became a common word among Christians who are together in the family of God. **And in *your* brotherly kindness love.** "And so we come to 'love,' the thing that harmonizes all the chorus, and fills it out, and makes it beautiful and glorious. We cannot get away from love if we speak about the Christly life. We began it with the first day, and the second day, and we end with it today. Faith, hope, love, the first day; faith and love today; with the other six virtues in between, and the whole man called into play with these six virtues. If virtue is added to faith, the will is exercised; if knowledge comes in, there is intellect; if self-control comes in, there is passion; if patience or endurance comes in, there is imagination; if godliness comes in, there is conscience; if brotherly kindness comes in, there is affection. When you have put on all the armour of Christ, you have to put on as the bond of perfectness, love — the girdle that binds all together." *— W. Y. Fullerton.*
3:18. **But grow in the grace and knowledge of our Lord and Saviour Jesus Christ. To him *be* the glory both now and for ever. Amen.** At the conclusion of his Epistle, the Apostle comes back to the concept of growth. The word here translated *grow* is the word *auxano*, from which comes our word *auxiliary*. It is used in reference to the growth of plants (as in Matt. 6:28; 13:32, etc.), and then in relation to infants, even of our Lord (Luke 2:40). There are two spheres of growth mentioned in this verse: first, the grace of the Lord Jesus, and secondly, the knowledge of the Lord Jesus. Grace is defined by the Apostle Paul in Titus 3:4, 5 as "the kindness and love of God our Saviour toward man." Spurgeon well says, "There is a vast difference in grace: God's grace never grows; it is always infinite, it cannot be more; it is always everlasting." To grow in grace is to grow

in those things which spring from the grace of God, and which should make us grace-filled, or gracious, people. The idea of growing in a knowledge of Christ might well be traced back to the opening of our Lord's high priestly prayer, where He defines life eternal as "knowing God and Jesus Christ whom God has sent," (John 17:3). At the end of his life, Paul prays that he might know Christ, the power of His resurrection, and the fellowship of His sufferings (Phil. 3:10). In the Ephesian Epistle, he prays that God may give unto us, "a spirit of wisdom and revelation in the knowledge of Him" (1:17). How may we grow in a knowledge of Christ? The only account of Christ that we have in all of literature is in the New Testament. We begin to grow in a knowledge of Christ as we read, study, meditate upon the revelation of Christ in the Holy Scriptures — His titles, His pre-eminence, His marvelous birth, His deeds, His character, His teachings, so inexhaustible, His death, His Resurrection, His ascension, His coming again, His ultimate rule in the universe. As we come to know Christ better, we will love Him the more deeply, and obey Him the more consistently. And by growing in this way in a knowledge of Him from the Scriptures, and a loving obedience to Him, we shall not only increase in the knowledge of Christ, but shall become like him — growing up into the image of the Son of God.

THE LESSON IN LIFE, LITERATURE, AND ARCHAEOLOGY.

Dr. John Stuart Blackie (1809–1895) one of the most learned men of Scotland in the 19th century, was appointed Professor of Humanities at Aberdeen University when thirty years of age, and in 1852, was appointed Professor of Greek in Edinburgh University, a chair he kept for thirty years, during which time he became "the most prominent feature of the patriotic and literary life of Edinburgh." This scholarly and gracious man took for the motto of his life the words from Ephesians 4:15, "Speaking the truth in love," and would write it in the Greek form on every envelope he addressed. "It became," said another, "the key-note of his character."

A TRUTH FOR THE CLASS TO CARRY AWAY.

There are two major factors in any normal healthy growth. On the one hand, that which grows must have the right kind of food, nourishment — our spiritual nourishment is in Christ; but, on the other hand, normal growth can be expected only when there is no serious obstruction or weakening poison in the system. We would think it abnormal if our son at fifteen years of age was not any larger than a normal boy at the age of four. But how many of us allow our souls to remain in a state of infancy?

In how many ways did Simon Peter himself grow from the time Christ called him at the Seat of Galilee to the time he wrote this Epistle? How many of these elements of growth do you find listed in the "fruit of the Spirit" in Galatians 5:22, 23? If these characteristics are the fruit of the Spirit, why are we told to add one to the other? Do you think that a church once vigorous and powerful can lose its strength, and ultimately fade away? (Yes, the church at Ephesus is an example of this.) What do you think are the major signs of true growth in the church of which you are a member?

LESSON III. — July 18.

GROWING THROUGH BIBLE STUDY. — Acts 17:10–11; 1 Timothy 4:13–16; 2 Timothy 1:5; 2:15; 3:14–17; Hebrews 4:12.

PRINTED TEXT, Acts 17:10–11; 1 Timothy 4:13–16; 2 Timothy 1:5; 2:15; 3:14–17; Hebrews 4:12.

Devotional Reading: Psalm 119:9–16.
Beginner Topic: A WALL TO BUILD.
　　Lesson Material: Nehemiah 2:11 to 6:16.
　　Memory Verse: Be ye kind one to another. Ephesians 4:32.
Primary Topic: THE BIBLE HELPS US TO GROW.
　　Lesson Material: 2 Timothy 1:5; 3:14–17.
　　Memory Verse: Teach me thy way, O Jehovah. Psalm 86:11.
Junior Topic: THE BIBLE HELPS US TO GROW.
　　Lesson Material: 2 Timothy 1:5; 3:14–17.
　　Memory Verse: Teach me thy way, O Jehovah; I will walk in thy truth. Psalm 86:11.
Intermediate-Senior Topic: GROWING THROUGH BIBLE STUDY.
　　Lesson Material: Acts 17:10–11; 1 Timothy 4:13–16; 2 Timothy 2:15; 3:14–17; Hebrews 4:12.
　　Memory Verse: Thy word have I laid up in my heart, That I might not sin against thee. Psalm 119:11.
Topic for Young People and Adults: GROWING THROUGH BIBLE STUDY.
　　Lesson Material: Acts 17:10–11; 1 Timothy 4:13–16; 2 Timothy 2:15; 3:14–17; Hebrews 4:12.
　　Memory Verse: Every scripture inspired of God *is* also profitable for teaching, for reproof, for correction, for instruction which is in righteousness: that the man of God may be complete, furnished completely unto every good work. 2 Timothy 3:16, 17.

THE TEACHER AND HIS CLASS.

The Younger Classes may be introduced to this lesson with the simple illustration that because in the work and play of daily life our bodies need fuel, which consists of food and liquid, without which we soon become weak, then anemic, and if food is not taken, we become liable to all the diseases that are floating about. Now in a similar way our souls, contending for purity and righteousness in a wicked world, and against our own lower natures, need spiritual food. This is found in the Word of God, as even our Lord said at the time of His temptation, quoting from the Book of Deuteronomy, that man does not live by bread only, but by every word that proceeds out of the mouth of God, which is the Word of God.

The Older Classes should have this lesson presented to them in a very earnest way, the teacher seeking for the definite practice of what is here being emphasized. We hear so many messages in respect to the necessity for prayer, and yet we do so little praying. We stress the need for personal work, and we speak to so few. We emphasize the vital importance of Bible study, setting forth the blessed results of such an exercise, and yet in the Church today there is less real meditation of the Word of God than there was years ago; nevertheless, the need today is greater than ever.

THE LESSON IN ITS SETTING.

Time. — Paul's visit to the Bereans occurred on his second missionary journey, A.D. 51–54. His letters to Timothy were written at the very close of his life, probably A.D. 67 or 68.

Place. — Berea is fifty miles west of Thessalonica, in Northern Greece.

THE PLAN OF THE LESSON.

SUBJECT: St. Paul's Conception of the Place of Bible Study in the Life of a Growing and Useful Christian.

I. THE ZEAL FOR BIBLE STUDY AMONG THE BEREANS, Acts 17:10, 11.

II. PAUL'S EXHORTATIONS TO TIMOTHY REGARDING THE STUDY OF THE SCRIPTURES, 1 Timothy 4:13-16; 2 Timothy 1:5; 3:14–17.
  1. In relation to his life as a minister, 1 Timothy 4:13–16.
  2. His advantage in being instructed in the Scriptures as a boy, 2 Timothy 1:5; 3:14, 15.

III. THE CLASSIC PASSAGE ON THE STUDY OF THE SCRIPTURES, 2 Timothy 2:15.

IV. THE DIVINE ORIGIN AND PROFITABLENESS OF THE SCRIPTURES, 2 Timothy 3:16, 17.

V. THE WORD OF GOD, THE DIAGNOSTICIAN OF THE SOUL, Hebrews 4:12.

THE TEACHER'S LIBRARY.

The more important volumes on the Pastoral Epistles will be found helpful here, particularly the great work by Alfred Plummer in the *Expositor's Bible*, the older work by Patrick Fairbairn, and the newer work by Lenski. In the *Devotional Commentary Series*, Gurney is good on the First Epistle, and Bishop Moule is superb on the Second Epistle. The greatest treatment of 2 Timothy 3:16, 17 is to be found in the volume by B. B. Warfield, *The Inspiration and Authority of the Bible*. On Timothy, his mother and grandmother, see the glorious pages in Alexander Whyte, *Bible Characters, Stephen to Timothy*, 285–303. On the verses from 1 Timothy, Andrew Murray, *The Children For Christ*, 373–401. There is a good deal of material on some of the verses in this lesson in my brochure, *The Minister and the Word of God*, the Fourth Annual Campbell Morgan Lecture, delivered in London, July, 1952. On Bible study as a whole, I trust I may be allowed to refer to my own volume, *Profitable Bible Study*. W. H. Griffith Thomas wrote a good book some years ago, *Methods of Bible Study*.

On 2 Timothy 1:5, see also Andrew Murray: *The Children for Christ*, 393–401.

AUDIO-VISUAL AIDS.

No audio-visual aids discovered.

We are living in a day when, probably more than at any time in this modern age, we are witnessing stronger currents pulling people away from the consistent, serious study of the Word of God. While I have nothing against television as such, I am afraid that being chained to television programs every night in the week, from seven to ten, in millions of homes in our country, is going to have a disastrous effect upon reading great books, and so, a disastrous effect upon Bible study. I am not the man to say that moving pictures are wrong in the church on the Lord's day (I am speaking about Christian movies), but this I know that no motion picture, however noble, however Christian, can be a substitute for the Word of God! I am finding straight across our land an amazing phenomenon, which I cannot account for as yet, that even the reading aloud of the Word of God in our conservative churches, in the Sunday morning service, is being gradually eliminated. Two weeks before writing this very lesson, in preaching in one of the greatest strongholds of conservatism in America, I found no place for the reading of the Word of God. God's Word is far more important than any word of man! With all the crazy cults now growing so phenomenally in our country, drawing thousands of immortal souls into their deceiving teachings, we need to throw ourselves back upon this Word, which is settled in heaven forever. Our lesson today gives us an illustration of an entire church in the Greek world devoted to the study of the Word of God, and then we have some of the finest passages Paul ever wrote on the nature and the value and the study of the Holy Scriptures.

I. THE ZEAL FOR BIBLE STUDY AMONG THE BEREANS, Acts 17:10, 11. This 17th chapter of Acts is one of the greatest in all the Bible, because it is here that we have the record of Paul's epochal visit to the Athenians and a summary of his famous sermon preached there. The chapter opens with an account of Paul's visit to Thessalonica, to which later he wrote his First Epistle, which contained, by the way, many references to the Word of God. Ultimately driven from this city by the Jews, he went on to Berea fifty miles west, where he found the Jews of the synagogue not simply ready to receive his message, but determined to test it from the Scriptures. Of course the only Scriptures they had at this time

ACTS 17:10. And the brethren immediately sent away Paul and Silas by night unto Beroea: who when they were come thither went into the synagogue of the Jews.

11. Now these were more noble than those in Thessalonica, in that they received the word with all readiness of mind, examining the scriptures daily, whether these things were so.

were the Old Testament books, filled, however, with Messianic promises. **10. And the brethren immediately sent away Paul and Silas by night unto Beroea: who when they were come thither went into the synagogue of the Jews. 11. Now these were more noble than those in Thessalonica, in that they received the word with all readiness of mind, examining the scriptures daily, whether these things were so.** The word here translated "noble" comes from the Greek word, *eugenes,* from which comes our word, *eugenics.* Originally the word meant nobility of birth, and then, those qualities of character which one would expect to be manifested by people noble-born. Dr. Campbell Morgan in his epochal work on Acts, has a great page on these Bereans: "In what did their nobility consist? We generally say in reading the story, that they were more noble in that they manifested greater readiness to receive. That is so, but in what did that readiness consist? In that they were determined to find out. It was not quick belief that made them noble, for they were sceptical; but their scepticism was accompanied by determined anxiety to find out. The noble hearer is not the man who immediately says Yes, to the interpretation of the preacher. The noble hearer is the man who appeals again and again to the Scriptures themselves, to find out if these things be true. I sometimes think that the great advantage that the Bereans had was that they lived on the byway, and not on the highway. We who live in cities come to strange conceits, that all the intelligence is in the cities. By no means. . . . Among the mountains of Wales, and in the highlands of Scotland, are men and women who will make the preacher preach as it is by no means necessary that he should always do in London; men who will get their Bibles down, and say, Is this man right? That is nobility. It is not the nobility of readiness to believe anything. It is the nobility of being determined to find out if human interpretation is in accord with the actual Scripture. Paul interpreted the Scripture before the Bereans, and they listened with a sceptical and honest enquiry, a determination to seek and know and examine, and they made the Scriptures the test of the interpretation. It is an interesting fact that the word used for the belief of those in Thessalonica is not the word used for the belief of those in Berea. . . . The word used of those in Thessalonica means persuaded by argument. The word used of those in Berea means that fullness of belief which is not only persuasion by argument, but full spiritual apprehension. The men who were not so noble, needed persuasion, and came into belief on the ground of persuasion; but the men who sifted for themselves, and were sceptical, came to find a larger faith their own." — *Dr. G. Campbell Morgan.*

II. **PAUL'S EXHORTATION TO TIMOTHY REGARDING THE STUDY OF THE SCRIPTURES,** 1 Timothy 4:13–16; 2 Timothy 1:5; 3:14–17. We have often had Timothy as a subject for study in our lessons, but still I think we need just a word at the beginning of this lesson to refresh our minds concerning this young man: "Paul was on the constant lookout for young preachers. He saw the tremendous demand for them if Christianity was to grow and extend over the world. Jesus had sorrowed as he saw the harvest ripe and the labourers so few (Matt. 9:37 f.). Timothy was converted during the first mission and was one of Paul's converts because he called him 'my true child in faith' (1 Tim. 1:2); 'my child Timothy' (1:18); 'my beloved child' (2 Tim. 1:2); 'my beloved and faithful child in the Lord' (1 Cor. 4:17). When Paul came to Lystra on the second mission tour, 'him would Paul have to go forth with him' (Acts 16:3). This was after the break between Paul and Barnabas over John Mark when Paul and Silas

244

1 TIMOTHY 4:13. Till I come, give heed to reading, to exhortation, to teaching.

14. Neglect not the gift that is in thee, which was given thee by prophecy, with the laying on of the hands of the presbytery.

15. Be diligent in these things; give thyself wholly to them; that thy progress may be manifest unto all.

16. Take heed to thyself, and to thy teaching. Continue in these things; for in doing this thou shalt save both thyself and them that hear thee.

---

started out together (15:36–40). At Lystra, Timothy was picked up and was with Paul for most of his ministry while Mark had varying fortunes and final success with Barnabas and Peter and again with Paul. Few things in Paul's life gave him more comfort than the finding of Timothy. . . . From the ordination service on through the years Paul had Timothy on his heart and tried to steer his course aright. But there was no patronising of Timothy by Paul. He spoke of him to others in the noblest way as, 'our brother and God's minister in the Gospel of Christ' (1 Thess. 3:2); 'for he worketh the work of the Lord as I also do' (1 Cor. 16:10); 'Timothy our brother' (2 Cor. 1:1; Col. 1:1; Philemon 1), 'Paul and Timothy, slaves of Jesus Christ' (Phil. 1:1), 'Timothy my fellow-worker' (Rom. 16:21). Paul's protégé became his co-worker on the level of high service for Christ." — *A. T. Robertson.* Before even beginning the exposition of these lessons it is important to note, that it is in these Epistles where Paul refers to the deceptions of the times, and is forced to use five different verbs in thirteen passages to set forth the idea of turning from or departing from the truth, and at the same time, he had but one proposal to make for unswerving adherance to the truth. Here he uses the words: Scripture, truth, doctrine, the Word of God, et cetera, more frequently than in any other of his writings that have come down to us. The first passage we take is of a rather personal nature, — Paul's specific command to Timothy, who at this time was laboring, probably, in Ephesus. 1 Timothy 4:13–15. **13. Till I come, give heed to reading, to exhortation, to teaching. 14. Neglect not the gift that is in thee, which was given thee by prophecy, with the laying on of the hands of the presbytery. 15. Be diligent in these things; give thyself wholly to them; that thy progress may be manifest unto all.** There is no doubt that Paul's reference here to *reading* refers to the public reading of the Scriptures. "The Church found it in the Synagogue (Acts 15:21; 2 Cor. 3:15); and our Lord (St. Luke 4:16) and His Apostles (Acts 13:15, 27) availed themselves of it in the work of propagating Christianity." — *H. P. Liddon.* The three words, reading, exhortation, and teaching, are well defined by Gurney as follows: "The first describes that feature in the services of the primitive Christian Church which was directly derived from the services of the synagogue. The second and third describe the preaching and teaching which are so essential a part of the Pastoral office, the 'sermon' and the 'lecture'; — the appeal to the Will and the appeal to the Intellect; the emphasis of Christian practice, and the setting forth of Christian doctrine. They are found together again in 1 Timothy 6:2, and previously in Romans 12:7, 8." — *T. A. Gurney.* One would find it very interesting to make a careful study of what Paul says all ministers should do with the Word of God. One is found in verse 16, **Take heed to thyself, and to thy teaching. Continue in these things; for in doing this thou shalt save both thyself and them that hear thee.** The word translated, *continue,* is the Greek word, *maneo,* from which comes our word *remain,* and our word *mansion.* Now I sometimes visit San Francisco, Chicago, New York, or Boston, but I *abide* in San Marino, California; that is my home. We may *visit* the great literatures of the world, reading in the Greek classics, philosophy, history, et cetera, but a minister is to *live* in the Word of God, and when he does not, his own soul, his preaching, and then the

245

2 TIMOTHY 1:5. Having been reminded of the unfeigned faith that is in thee; which dwelt first in thy grandmother Lois, and thy mother Eunice; and, I am persuaded, in thee also.

souls of his people will dry up. Alexander Whyte's page on this matter of reading I have used before, but I must use it again: "Now if these words were addressed by an experienced minister to a new beginner in our day, something like this would be universally understood. 'Attend to your studies. Be always at your studies. Grudge every moment that is stolen from your studies. Never sit down without a book and a pen in your hand. And let it never be an ephemeral, or an impertinent, or an unproductive, book. You have not the time. You have not the money. Read nothing that is not the very best of its kind. Neither in religion, nor in letters, nor in anything else. Be like John Milton in his noble youth, be both select and industrious in your reading.'

"But there is another interpretation of these words, and that on high authority too. 'Reading,' in Timothy's day, — so the text is sometimes interpreted, — would mean to him very much what is nowadays called expository preaching or 'lecturing,' as we say in Scotland. Timothy is here exhorted to read Nehemiah's autobiography and then to imitate that great reformer and his great colleagues in their exegetic and homiletic way of dealing with the law of God. . . . Nehemiah's method was our Lord's method also as often as the Book was delivered to Him by the minister in the synagogue on the Sabbath day. And from the Acts we learn that this was the universal method of the Apostles also. Both the Greek and the Latin fathers followed this same Scriptural method; the expository lectures of Chrysostom and Augustine are extant to us to this day. Calvin also stood upon his pulpit of wood, and read the Word of God distinctly, and caused the people of Geneva to understand the reading. Just as he still causes us to understand the reading as often as we consult his incomparable commentaries." — *Alexander Whyte.*

We now turn a page to look at the last letter Paul ever wrote, the second one to Timothy, in which he becomes even more personal. First of all, he desires to encourage Timothy in his work as a minister, by reminding him of the wonderful upbringing he had enjoyed on the part of a godly mother and a godly grandmother. 2 Timothy 1:5. **Having been reminded of the unfeigned faith that is in thee; which dwelt first in thy grandmother Lois, and thy mother Eunice; and, I am persuaded, in thee also.** This family is referred to, in general terms, in Acts 16:1. I must here also lean heavily upon Alexander Whyte, for no one has written as vividly as he upon this boy Timothy. "With such an unfeigned faith as that the two lonely women set themselves to bring up their little fatherless son in the nurture and admonition of the Lord. And they succeeded, if ever unfeigned women succeeded. And such unfeigned women as they were have always succeeded, and will always succeed, till the last of such women shall be called up to get her full wages from God. Such women, such mothers in Israel, as Hannah, and Elisabeth, and Mary, and Monica, and Halyburton's mother, and Wesley's mother, and the mother of Jonathan Edward's children, and the mother of Thomas Boston's children, and many more. And in all those mothers it was their unfeigned faith that did it. Their unfeigned faith laid hold, first on God, and then on their children. For, not to speak of God, this kind of faith, and this kind of faith alone, takes hold of a child's heart. You cannot feign faith before your children. Even while they are still children they will find you out to their great pain and shame on account of their feigning mother. You may go on feigning faith with some success before everyone else, but not before your children. You must walk with an unfeigned faith, and with a perfect heart at home, if you have such a child's eyes set on you as were set on both Lois and Eunice. Whatever the husbands and the fathers in our households may do, let all wives and mothers live a life like the lives of Lois and Eunice, and they will have their reward. . . .

246

2 TIMOTHY 3:14. But abide thou in the things which thou hast learned and hast been assured of, knowing of whom thou hast learned them;

15. and that from a babe thou hast known the sacred writings which are able to make thee wise unto salvation through faith which is in Christ Jesus.

2 TIMOTHY 2:15. Give diligence to present thyself approved unto God, a workman that needeth not to be ashamed, handling aright the word of truth.

Speaking for myself, I would value above all else that God can give me in this world to see all my children truly converted like Timothy. And I would rejoice to receive their conversion through any instrumentality that it pleases God to employ. A new minister; a passing-by evangelist; a good book; a dispensation of family or personal providence; or what not. But O! if it pleases God let me have all my children's souls myself! Let them all say in after days — 'it was my father that did it.' That would make my cup to run over indeed." — *Alexander Whyte.*

The third chapter of 2 Timothy contains the second most terrible picture of mankind to be found anywhere in the New Testament. It is a picture of the character of men to be manifested universally in the last days. The very word of Paul as it is in the King James version, "In the last days perilous times shall come," is exactly the idea referred to by President Eisenhower in the Fireside Chat which he gave this very week that I am writing this lesson, when he said, "We are living in times of peril." Paul gives about eighteen characteristics of evil men in the last days and then he writes a sentence of contrast for Timothy, beginning *"But you,"* by which he means Timothy is not going to go the way of these Satanically ruled men. 2 Tim. 3:14, 15. **14. But abide thou in the things which thou hast learned and hast been assured of, knowing of whom thou hast learned them; 15. and that from a babe thou hast known the sacred writings which are able to make thee wise unto salvation through faith which is in Christ Jesus.** Here once again St. Paul refers "in the first instance to Timothy's home of old, in that turbulent Lystra where Lois and Eunice found it yet possible to live the calm life of faith, and where they taught the child of their hearts the lore of salvation; opening to him the blessed Book, Law, Prophets, Psalms, and telling him of the Lord in whom now all had been fulfilled. We seem safe in this assumption when we read, almost in one sentence, of 'the persons from whom he had learnt' and of the *early childhood* in which he had already begun to know his Bible. Taking these notices in connection with the words of 1:5 above and with our study of that passage, we are bold to say that the main reference here is to the dear voices which, in that long vanished home, as now most probably it was, had gently trained him into faith.

"We need not exclude a reference to other helpers of his soul. St. Paul may have also in mind here his own instructions, given long ago to the young man he loved so well and used so much. But the reference, we cannot mistake it, is mainly to the earliest days and to the faces and voices of the dear remembered home." — *H. C. G. Moule.*

III. **THE CLASSIC PASSAGE ON THE STUDY OF THE SCRIPTURES,** 2 Timothy 2:15. The verse we are now about to consider has indeed a universal application. **15. Give diligence to present thyself approved unto God, a workman that needeth not to be ashamed, handling aright the word of truth.** Here is another verb indicating what we ought to do with the Word of God. We are to rightly divide it. The margin translates, "holding a straight course in the Word of God." It is the only place in the New Testament where this Greek word occurs. Calvin has a penetrating remark on this. "Instead of rightly dividing

2 TIMOTHY 3:16. Every scripture inspired of God *is* also profitable for teaching, for reproof, for correction, for instruction which is in righteousness:

17. that the man of God may be complete, furnished completely unto every good work.

---

the Word, some mutilate it, others tear it, others torture it, others break it in pieces, others keeping by the outside never come to the soul of doctrine." We wrongly divide the Word when we live only in the New Testament, and ignore the Old. We wrongly divide the Word when we preach nothing but grace, and never refer to God's great commands. Let us remember that though we are saved by grace alone, apart from work, yet Paul refers favorably to good works in the life of the believer nineteen times in his epistles. How many of us have ever heard a sermon on good works? It is wrong to preach parables, ethical ideals, the saving work of Christ, the hope of His resurrection, and never to mention the great prophecies of the Bible. I recall once a wealthy member of a church I had the honour to serve who at the same time was a deep student of the Scriptures, and who was asked by a distinguished and conservative Old Testament professor, now in glory, if he would be inclined to help finance a book on Old Testament Introduction he had just finished writing. My friend said he would be inclined, but first he wanted to ask him a question: What had he done with Old Testament predictive prophecy? And this servant of God and deep student of His Word wrote back and said that though he had been teaching for nearly forty years he regretted that he had never investigated the subject of predictive prophecy, and hence my friend declined to give assistance. It is strange how in almost all of our theologies we develop the attributes of God, with long Latin words and arguments for God, but when you go to look for a treatment on the fatherhood of God, in a systematic theology, you can hardly even find the idea in an index, yet our blessed Lord Jesus referred to God as our Father over forty times. I would like myself to confess here that though I have been studying the Bible now for thirty years and more I feel that I am just beginning to acquire an understanding of it, and there is nothing I would like more than to devote the next twenty years, day and night, to nothing but the study of this inexhaustible Book.

IV. **THE DIVINE ORIGIN AND PROFITABLENESS OF THE SCRIPTURES.** 2 Timothy 3:16, 17. We have often looked at this famous passage in the last few years. (There is a long discussion of it, for example, in *Peloubet's Notes*, 1953, in the lesson of October 30.) And so I shall be, comparatively speaking, brief at this point. 16. **Every scripture inspired of God *is* also profitable for teaching, for reproof, for correction, for instruction which is in righteousness: 17. that the man of God may be complete, furnished completely unto every good work.** Incidentally, the Revised Standard Version returns to the order of words in the King James Version at this point, which reads, "All Scripture is inspired of God," et cetera. Only one Greek word stands behind the phrase, "inspired of God," which means "God-breathed," "deriving from God," "given by God," and therefore absolutely dependable, the truth settled in heaven forever. The first word that Satan ever said to man was one which attempted to instill in the heart of our first parents a doubt of this great fact, "Yea, hath God said?" (Gen. 3:1). That is why the Bible is called the Word of God, even in this Epistle. This is the same idea set forth by the Apostle Peter (2 Peter 1:21). Now because the Bible is given by God, it is *profitable*. Paul mentions four ways in which it is profitable: first, for *teaching*, that is, teaching the truth as against the deceptions of Satan and evil men, breaking through darkness and ignorance with the light of His Word. The Bible teaches us those things which man himself has never been able to discover, the origin of the world, the character of God, forgiveness of sins through the atoning work of Christ, the glories of the life to come, the final destiny of this world. It is then good for *reproof*, that is, for conviction of sin, which is

HEBREWS 4:12. For the word of God is living, and active, and sharper than any two-edged sword, and piercing even to the dividing of soul and spirit, of both joints and marrow, and quick to discern the thoughts and intents of the heart.

never brought about by Shakespeare, by anything from Beethoven, by a movie, or by mere legislation. Then the Bible *corrects* us, the word here translated correction meaning "to restore," "to guide back again into the right channel," because so many forces in the world are drawing us out of the holy will of God. And then finally the Bible instructs us in a life of righteousness. We are to bear the fruits of righteousness. Righteousness is simply that which is right. It is honest living, publicly and privately, in the home, in business, in social circles, in every transaction. Three-fourths of our newspapers today are taken up with the unrighteous acts of men, and you will note how few of them are loyal members of the Church. The man of God of whom Paul is speaking here is not a clergyman, or a priest, or a Christian of unusual piety. It is any child of God who is living consistently to his high calling in Christ. It means a man set apart by God, indwelt by the Spirit of God, living for God. How wonderful it would be if each one of us were so living that people would say of us, not to our face, but to one another, "There is a true man of God." The Scriptures, then, when studied, embraced, obeyed, give us equipment for the good works which should mark our lives. Good works are never referred to in the New Testament except commendably. (See Matt. 5:16, 2 Cor. 9:8, Col. 1:10, Eph. 2:10, 2 Tim. 2:21, and 1 Pet. 2:12.)

V. **THE WORD OF GOD THE DIAGNOSTICIAN OF THE SOUL,** Hebrews 4:12. **For the word of God is living, and active, and sharper than any two-edged sword, and piercing even to the dividing of soul and spirit, of both joints and marrow, and quick to discern the thoughts and intents of the heart.** The reason I have entitled this section of our lesson, "The Word of God the Diagnostician of the Soul," is that the Greek word here translated *discern* is *kritikos*, from which of course is derived our word *critic*. "The word" has probably here a double meaning. First of all it is the Scriptures, and thus the Old Testament Scriptures, and then, "the Christian gospel declared authoritatively by men like the writer, an inspired message which carries on the Old Testament revelation of God's promises and threats and which is vitally effective." — *James Moffatt.* The idea of the Word of God as something living is also to be found in Acts 7:38 and 1 Peter 1:23, and also in our Lord's own teachings (John 6:63). The idea of the Word as a sword is also to be found in Ephesians 6:17, and, symbolically, Revelation 1:16. My friend G. H. Lang in his recent excellent commentary on Hebrews has well interpreted this passage. "The Word of God enables us to distinguish between what in our thoughts and intentions is merely natural, of the soul, and what is spiritual, of the Spirit of life working in us. It is all too easy to be actuated mainly, or even only, by the instincts and notions of the natural man. It was very natural that Israel feared to face giants and attack walls fortified up to heaven. Only faith in God gave Caleb and Joshua victory over natural fear and inspired them with conquering courage. The joints connect the limbs together, the marrow is the vehicle of life; without the latter, joints and limbs were dead, powerless. Similarly, the soul contains and combines our various faculties; but these are dead Godward unless vitalized by the life of God acting through the regenerated spirit of man. This distinction is peculiar to the Word of God, and it is vital to a right conception of the perils and the possibilities of the believer." — *G. H. Lang.*

THE LESSON IN LIFE, LITERATURE, AND ARCHAEOLOGY.

While not a member of the Episcopal Church, I am the first to acknowledge that its service for the ordination of clergymen, called by them, priests, is the most solemn and moving of any such service in Protestantism. Few realize how great an emphasis is placed upon the necessity for the minister being a continual student of the Scriptures. The following is only a part of the service which refers to this pre-eminently important matter:

The Bishop asks, "Are you persuaded that the Holy Scriptures contain all doctrine required as necessary for eternal salvation through faith in Jesus Christ? and are you determined out of the said Scriptures to instruct the people committed to your church, and to teach nothing as necessary to eternal salvation but that which you shall be persuaded may be concluded and proved by the Scriptures?" When the candidate has answered that he is so persuaded, the Bishop asks, "Will you be ready with all faithful diligence to banish and drive away from the Church all erroneous and strange doctrines contrary to God's Word?" To this the reply is made, "I will, the Lord being my helper."

A TRUTH FOR THE CLASS TO CARRY AWAY.

It seems to me that the ideal way for a teacher to conclude this lesson is to take the final five minutes for suggesting to the class some simple but definite program of Bible study, so that the members of the class will not go away with only a determination to make a new beginning here, but will have presented to them one method, at least, for the systematic study of the Word of God.

How are Paul's exhortations to Timothy in our lesson illustrated from his own life? Can you think of any significant event in the New Testament in which the Scriptures were wrongly divided? (In the trial of our Lord.) Do you think that all ministers who are faithful preachers of the Word of God will necessarily draw large audiences? (I think not, though some say otherwise; note the first four verses of the last chapter of 2 Timothy.) How do you account for the fact that although everything else in our world is changing, no book has ever appeared since the closing of the New Testament Scriptures that could ever be called a substitute for the Word of God in preaching and teaching?

LESSON IV. — July 25.

GROWING THROUGH PRAYER. — Psalm 46:10; Isaiah 40:30, 31; Luke 11:1–13; Philippians 4:6–7; Hebrews 4:14–16.

PRINTED TEXT, Psalm 46:10; Isaiah 40:30, 31; Luke 11:1–13; Philippians 4:6, 7.

Devotional Reading: Psalm 4.
Beginner Topic: READY FOR COMPANY.
    Lesson Material: 2 Kings 4:8–17.
    Memory Verse: We . . . are helpers. 2 Corinthians 1:24.
Primary Topic: WHEN WE PRAY.
    Lesson Material: Luke 11:1–4; Philippians 4:6–7.
    Memory Verse: Be still, and know that I am God. Psalm 46:10.
Junior Topic: WHEN WE PRAY.
    Lesson Material: Luke 11:1–4; Philippians 4:6–7.
    Memory Verse: Be still, and know that I am God. Psalm 46:10.
Intermediate-Senior Topic: LEARNING TO PRAY.
    Lesson Material: Psalm 46:10; Luke 11:1–13; Philippians 4:6, 7; Hebrews 4:14–16.
    Memory Verse: Rejoice always; pray without ceasing; in everything give thanks: for this is the will of God in Christ Jesus to you-ward. 1 Thessalonians 5:16–18.

Topic for Young People and Adults: GROWING THROUGH PRAYER AND MEDITA-
TION.

Lesson Material: Psalm 46:10; Isaiah 40:30–31; Luke 11:1–13; Philippians
4:6–7; Hebrews 4:14–16.

Memory Verse: Rejoice always; pray without ceasing; in everything give
thanks: for this is the will of God in Christ Jesus to you-ward. 1 Thessalonians 5:16–18.

THE TEACHER AND HIS CLASS.

The Younger Classes may be introduced to this lesson on prayer by being
asked to whom they go when they want
a schoolbag, a new pair of shoes, permission to visit a friend's home, money
for a gift for another member of the
family. Even if there are two hundred
families living in their community,
there is only one place they would go
with this request — *home*, to father and
mother. It would be considered utterly foolish for us to go to any other
place, but perfectly natural to present
these needs and desires to our parents.
We who know Christ are in the family
of God. We are His children, and He
has encouraged us, from the beginning
of the Bible to the end, to come to Him
with all of our needs, our problems, our
troubles, our plans, our hopes, for He is
our Father who is in heaven.

The Older Classes may be reminded,
in beginning this lesson, that from the
beginning of a separated people of God,
Abraham and the Hebrew nation, down
to the last verse of the Bible, the saints
and servants of God, and the Son of
God, have all been found praying. In
the Old and New Testament alike, God
exhorts us to pray, and throughout the
Bible are scores of promises for those
who faithfully pray. Why is it true
then that our prayer life is so barren?
May it begin to be less so after the
study of this lesson.

THE LESSON IN ITS SETTING.

Time. — The prophecy of Isaiah
from which these verses were taken
may have been uttered about 670 B.C.
The words of our Lord were spoken in
December, A.D. 29. Paul wrote his
letter to the Philippians about A.D.
64, and the Epistle to the Hebrews was
written about that time also.

Place. — The words of our Lord were
uttered in Perea. Paul wrote to

Philippi, a city in Greece, from his
Roman imprisonment.

THE PLAN OF THE LESSON.

**SUBJECT: Divine Assurances, Invita-
tions and Promises to the Children
of God Regarding the Privilege and
Power of Prayer.**

I. STILLNESS OF SOUL THE PROPER
   PREPARATION FOR PRAYER,
   Psalm 46:10.

II. STRENGTH FROM PRAYER, Isaiah
    40:30, 31.

III. CHRIST'S TEACHINGS ABOUT
     PRAYER, Luke 11:1–13.
   1. The disciples yearn to know how to
      pray, v. 1.
   2. The model prayer, vs. 2–4.
   3. The illustrating parable, vs. 5–8.
   4. Encouragements to pray, vs. 9–13.

IV. THE SENTINEL OF THE HEART,
    Philippians 4:6, 7.

V. CHRIST OUR GREAT HIGH PRIEST,
   Hebrews 4:14–16.

THE TEACHER'S LIBRARY.

On the subject of prayer itself, the following
volumes will be of help: W. Graham Scroggie:
Method in Prayer (1916); Andrew Murray: *The
Prayer-Life;* James Little: *In Touch with the
Throne;* Samuel Zwemer: *Taking Hold of God;*
Norman B. Harrison: *His in a Life of Prayer;*
James Hastings: *The Christian Doctrine of
Prayer;* and the following too-little known, but
wonderfully rich books, by the late E. M.
Bounds: *The Possibilities of Prayer* (1923); *The
Reality of Prayer* (1924); *The Essentials of
Prayer* (1925); *The Necessity of Prayer* (1929).
On the prayer life of our Lord, see E. L. Pell:
What Did Jesus Really Teach About Prayer?
(1923); A. C. Wieand: *The Prayer-Life and
Teachings of Jesus* (1932).
Among the best books on the Lord's Prayer
are G. Campbell Morgan: *The Practice of
Prayer;* Marcus Dods: *The Prayer that Teaches
Us to Pray;* James W. Thirtle: *The Lord's
Prayer;* G. D. Boardman: *Studies in the Model
Prayer;* John Cumming: *Teach Us to Pray;*
Adolph Saphir: *The Lord's Prayer* (exception-
ally rich).
On the verses taken from Luke's Gospel, see
especially Andrew Murray: *With Christ in the*

School of Prayer, 48–62; G. Campbell Morgan: The Parables and Metaphors of Our Lord, 181–186; and above all, one of the most moving chapters in the whole literature of prayer with which I am acquainted, Alexander Whyte on "The Friend Who Knocked at Midnight," in his book, Lord Teach Us to Pray, 169–182.

On Philippians 4:6–7, see an excellent condensed interpretation in Norman B. Harrison: His in a Life of Prayer, 60–61; and J. Stuart Holden: The Pre-Eminent Lord, 131–141.

On the words from the Epistle to the Hebrews, see the superb commentaries on this Epistle by Andrew Murray, Aldolph Saphir, R. C. H. Lenski, and Franz Delitzsch.

AUDIO-VISUAL AIDS.

FILMSTRIP: "Christian Prayer," ChurchCraft No. FCP, 52 fr., b&w.

PSALM 46:10. Be still, and know that I am God: I will be exalted among the nations, I will be exalted in the earth.

ISAIAH 40:30. Even the youths shall faint and be weary, and the young men shall utterly fall:

31. but they that wait for Jehovah shall renew their strength; they shall mount up with wings as eagles; they shall run and not be weary; they shall walk, and not faint.

I. STILLNESS OF SOUL THE PROPER PREPARATION FOR PRAYER, Psalm 46:10. The late Dean Perowne reminds us that this Psalm, and the two following, are hymns of triumph, composed on the occasion of some great deliverance, and he is inclined to think "that they all celebrate the same event, the sudden and miraculous destruction of the army of Sennacherib under the walls of Jerusalem." The Psalm begins with that famous confession, "God is our refuge and strength, a very present help in trouble." 10. **Be still, and know that I am God: I will be exalted among the nations, I will be exalted in the earth.** The verb translated "be still" found also in 1 Samuel 15:16, means literally, "let your hand sink down," that is, cease your efforts; and thus Spurgeon interprets the sentence, "Holy off your hands, ye enemies! Sit down and wait in patience, ye believers! Acknowledge that Jehovah is God, ye who feel the terrors of his wrath! Adore him, and him only, ye who partake in the protections of his grace. Since none can worthily proclaim his nature, let 'expressive silence muse his praise.' The boasts of the ungodly and the timorous forebodings of the saints should certainly be hushed by a sight of what the Lord has done in past ages. 'I will be exalted among the heathen.' They forget God, they worship idols, but Jehovah will yet be honoured by them. Reader, the prospects of missions are bright, bright as the promises of God. Let no man's heart fail him; the solemn declarations of this verse must be fulfilled." — Charles H. Spurgeon.

II. STRENGTH FROM PRAYER, Isaiah 40:30, 31. 30. **Even the youths shall faint and be weary, and the young men shall utterly fall: 31. but they that wait for Jehovah shall renew their strength; they shall mount up with wings as eagles; they shall run and not be weary; they shall walk, and not faint.** Dr. C. I. Scofield begins his sermon on these verses by asking a question, and then answering it. "What does that mean? Why as eagles? Why not with wings as doves? I think it is because the eagle is the only bird that goes so high that he is lost to sight in the upper heights. Think of some of the peculiarities of the eagle. He is the most solitary of birds. Did you ever see or hear of a flock of eagles? You may sometimes see two together, but very rarely. His eyrie is on some beetling, inaccessible crag. The eagle has to do with great things, mountains and heights and depths. An eagle can also be very still. No creature holds such reserves of quietness; there is no restlessness in him. There is the repose of perfect power. He can be quiet when it is time to be quiet. But when the sun rises and his eye catches the first ray, you may see him stretch his mighty wings, launch out over the abyss and begin that tremendous spiral flight up, up, up, higher and higher, until he is lost to sight; and all day, on balanced wing, he is there in the vast upper realm of light, above all storms, in the great tranquillity of the upper spaces.

252

LUKE 11:1. And it came to pass, as he was praying in a certain place, that when he ceased, one of his disciples said unto him, Lord, teach us to pray, even as John also taught his disciples.

That is mounting up with wings as eagles. To be up there, as we might say, with God. No Christian ever comes into God's best things who does not learn to walk alone with God. . . . 'They shall run and not be weary; they shall walk and not faint.' What! must we come down and run and walk here on this stupid, prosaic earth after these eagle flights? Yes, precisely. The eagle flight is unto that. We go up there that we may serve down here, and we never can serve down here according to God's thought of service, until we trace the spirals of the upper air and have learned to be alone in the silent spaces with God. It is only the man who comes down from interviews with God who can touch human lives with the power of God. . . . We live a common life, a life of everyday duty, plain prosaic, and unbeautiful, but we may 'walk, and not faint' under the wear and petty vexations and frictions of everyday life, only on condition that we have been 'waiting upon God.' The man who does that will be a reservoir of sweetness, quietness, and power." — C. I. Scofield. George Adam Smith adds a marvelous statement to the last clause of this passage. "When the prophet says last, and most impressively, of his people's fortunes, that they shall *walk* and not faint, he has perhaps just those long centuries in view, when, instead of a nation of enthusiasts taking humanity by storm, we see small bands of pioneers pushing their way from city to city by the slow methods of ancient travel — Damascus, Antioch, Tarsus, Iconium, Ephesus, Thessalonica, Athens, Corinth, and Rome — everywhere that Paul and the missionaries of the Cross found a pulpit and a congregation ready for the gospel; toiling from day to day at their trades, serving the alien for wages, here and there founding a synagogue, now and then completing a version of their Scriptures, oftentimes achieving martyrdom, but ever living a pure and a testifying life in face of the heathen, with the passion of these prophecies at their hearts. It was certainly for such centuries and such men that the word was written, 'they shall walk and not faint.' " — George Adam Smith.

III. **CHRIST'S TEACHINGS ABOUT PRAYER,** Luke 11:1-13. The verses which we call "the Lord's Prayer" appear at two different times in our Lord's ministry, as recorded in the Synoptic accounts: first, in the Sermon on the Mount (Matt. 6:5-13), and, in briefer form, in the record of His ministry in Perea. Here Christ's teaching on prayer is prompted by the request of the disciples, who, overhearing Him pray — and this must have happened often — asked if He would teach them to pray, even as John the Baptist taught his disciples. 1. **And it came to pass, as he was praying in a certain place, that when he ceased, one of his disciples said unto him, Lord, teach us to pray, even as John also taught his disciples.** Maclaren points out the fact that although this is called the "Lord's Prayer," it is not truly such, but rather, "His teaching of the servants' prayer. It is not a formula, but a pattern. We may repeat it or not, but we use it aright when it teaches us to shape our desires after its spirit. All the essentials are preserved in Luke's shorter version. There is first the child's cry to the Father. All Christian prayer begins with that, and Christ makes it possible so to begin, by giving to those who believe on His name power to become sons of God. Consciousness of sonship, confidence in the Father's love, the child's yearning towards Him, and the assurance that He hears, are all expressed in that one word, and, without these, our prayers are of small account. Note the order of petitions. Those bearing on God's glory must be first; and those touching on ourselves second. True filial love will subordinate self to God, and our heart's desires are not what they should be, unless they set with stronger current towards His glory than towards our own good. How little of our prayers is 'after this manner'!" — *Alexander Maclaren.*

2. And he said unto them, When ye pray, say, Father, Hallowed be thy name, thy kingdom come.

3. Give us day by day our daily bread.

4. And forgive us our sins; for we ourselves also forgive every one that is indebted to us, and bring us not into temptation.

---

2. And he said unto them, When ye pray, say, Father, Hallowed be thy name. What do we mean by God being our Father? First, there is a definite relationship implied here, a relationship of love. The relationship between teacher and pupil is one of knowledge; between an employer and employee it is one of business and money; between landlord and tenant it is one of property; between a storekeeper and a customer, the relationship is one based on merchandise. The relationship between a father and a son is one of love. Furthermore, there is a likeness between the father and the son. Then, the father loving the son, there is a provision for the son's needs, a watchful care over him, a desire always on the father's part to so guide and provide for the son as to give him every possible chance to be the finest man, the happiest, most successful man, possible. All these things we find here in our passage: the Father knows, the Father cares, the Father provides. In calling God our Father we imply that we are His children. Therefore, we have a relationship to Him. In this relationship we are to be ever sanctifying His name (Isa. 29:23). We do so by ever remembering God is holy, and then by so living that He Himself is revealed as a Holy God in our life. **Thy kingdom come.** A kingdom implies at least two factors, an area over which the king rules, and a king who is sovereign. "The kingdom of God on earth is the domain in which God's holy will is done in and among men." — *George Stevens*. We enter this kingdom by repentance, by faith, by new birth. The Kingdom of God is coming. It is already in the hearts of those who have yielded to His sovereign will. Some day the whole earth will be a part of the Kingdom of God, and every living person on it. How we need the coming of that kingdom today! "If we pray 'thy kingdom come,' that is a monstrous hypocrisy if we are, every day of our lives, hindering and thwarting the advance of that kingdom; it is an hypocrisy if we are indifferent to all its laws and all its interests. It is only a reality if, with however many imperfections, however feebly, however unworthy, we are yet endeavoring sincerely to the clearest of our lights, to the best of our powers, to prepare the throne of that kingdom, to make straight paths for its advancing chariot in our hearts and in the world." — *F. W. Farrar*. **3. Give us day by day our daily bread.** Bread is an absolute necessity of life. We are not here asking for delicacies, but for that very elemental material by which we may live, in the simplest but most vital way. Before there is bread, there must be a living kernel of seed, then there must be the planting of that seed in the ground, then its proper nourishment in a mysterious way; while it rests in the soil, coming to maturity in growth, there must be rain, and heat, which science itself can never manufacture, with any adequacy. There must be protection from mildew, from fungus and frost. The harvested wheat must be kept from the wheat-moth and from fire. "If the farmer's crop fails, all the money in the world cannot make a loaf of bread." Notice especially the pronoun *our*, which implies that we are not only to pray for ourselves but for others that they, too, might be fed. **4. And forgive us our sins; for we ourselves also forgive every one that is indebted to us.** "All transgressions of duty are debts to Him, and we need His forgiveness for them, not in order to escape the penalties of our wrong-doing, but in order that the loving relation between Father and child may be restored. The sense of sin is perhaps as general as the sense of bodily need, but it is not as frequently felt. The one cannot long be forgotten or ignored, but the other may be; and the constant use of this petition helps to keep alive in our hearts the sense of sin and consequent need of forgiveness. 'As we also have forgiven our debtors.' The 'as' must not be pressed to mean that the fulness of the Father's forgiveness is to be

5. And he said unto them, Which of you shall have a friend, and shall go unto him at midnight, and say to him, Friend, lend me three loaves;

6. For a friend of mine is come to me from a journey, and I have nothing to set before him.

7. And he from within shall answer and say, Trouble me not: the door is now shut, and my children are with me in bed; I cannot rise and give thee?

8. I say unto you, Though he will not rise and give him because he is his friend, yet because of his importunity he will arise and give him as many as he needeth.

---

measured by the extent to which we forgive our fellow-men. No such hard bargaining is to be understood. What is meant is, that we ourselves must cultivate a spirit of forgiveness towards those who seem to have wronged us, before we venture to claim forgiveness for ourselves. God has more to forgive to each individual than any human being can have; and He is more ready to forgive; it is impossible for men to equal Him in this. But men can try to imitate Him (Eph. 5:1) and only so far as they imitate Him have they the right to use this petition." — *Alfred Plummer.* **And bring us not into temptation.** "This is the language of a cautious heart, of the man who recognizes how terrible an experience temptation is. . . . We are to be afraid of temptation. We are not to be foolhardy, treating it as of no account. We are to shrink in its presence with that cautiousness which makes for courage. But the most important thing is that we should be delivered perfectly from evil. This is to be my prayer every day to God who governs in hell as well as in heaven. Recognition of the force of temptation and its subtlety will make me pray, 'Bring me not into temptation,' but the deepest passion of my whole life will be — 'deliver me from evil.' " — *G. Campbell Morgan.*

Christ follows His teaching with a simple parable. No one has commented on this passage with such vividness, penetration, and moving power as Alexander Whyte, and I shall confine myself entirely to his interpretation. **5. And he said unto them, Which of you shall have a friend, and shall go unto him at midnight, and say to him, Friend, lend me three loaves; 6. for a friend of mine is come to me from a journey, and I have nothing to set before him. 7. And he from within shall answer and say, Trouble me not: the door is now shut, and my children are with me in bed; I cannot rise and give thee? 8. I say unto you, Though he will not rise and give him because he is his friend, yet because of his importunity he will arise and give him as many as he needeth.** "It is midnight. It is midnight. The night is dark. All the lights are out, and everybody is in bed. 'Friend! lend me three loaves!' . . . He knocks again. 'Friend! lend me three loaves!' He waits awhile and then he knocks again. 'Friend, friend! I must have three loaves!' 'Trouble me not: the door is now shut; I cannot rise and give thee!' He is dumb, for a time. He stands still. He turns to go home. But he cannot go home. He dare not go home. He comes back. He knocks again. 'Friend!' he cries, till the dogs bark at him. He puts his ear to the door. There is a sound inside, and then the light of a candle shines through the hole of the door. The bars of the door are drawn back, and he gets not three loaves only but as many as he needs. . . . 'Importunity,' — 'because of his importunity,' — does not do justice to our Lord's style — to call it style. What our Lord said was far more to the purpose than 'importunity,' excellent as that is. What He said was 'shamelessness.' . . . 'Think shame!' the man cried out, who was in bed, with his door shut. 'Think shame!' the disturbed neighbours cried out. 'Think shame!' the late passer-by said. 'Hold your peace,' they said, 'and let honest men's doors alone at this time of night.' 'Never mind,' says our Lord on the other hand. 'Never

9. And I say unto you, Ask, and it shall be given you; seek, and ye shall find; knock, and it shall be opened unto you.

10. For every one that asketh receiveth; and he that seeketh findeth; and to him that knocketh it shall be opened.

11. And of which of you that is a father shall his son ask a loaf, and he give him a stone? or a fish, and he for a fish give him a serpent?

you mind them: they have bread enough at home: and easy for them to cry shame to a starving man. Never you mind, knock you on. I have been in your place Myself, till they said that I was beside Myself. Knock you on: and I will stand beside you till I see the door open. He must rise if you go on knocking. Give him no rest. Well done! Knock again!' Yes, — shamelessness! . . . How many nights have I had no time to give to God! And, now, to expect that when I lift up my finger, and go down five minutes on my carpeted knees, God Almighty is to hasten and set everything aside to hear me!' . . . Yes — it is this that so increases and so aggravates the shamelessness of your case. The shameful things you have to ask for. The disgraceful — the incredible things you have to admit and confess. The life you have lived. The way you have spent your days and nights. And what all that has brought you to. . . . What an indescribable feeling is that in our hearts, when, after years of prayer, followed with midnight after midnight of importunity and agony, light begins to break through: and God's hand is reached out, and our souls taste the strength and the sweetness of the Bread from heaven. Jacob does not feel his thigh any more. David's couch, wet with his tears, is all answered now. The bloody sweat of Gethsemane itself is all forgotten now." — *Alexander Whyte.*

After giving the disciples an example of a true prayer, and a parable illustrating importunity in prayer, Christ proceeds to burn these words into their hearts in inviting, and urging them to engage in prayer. **9. And I say unto you, Ask, and it shall be given you; seek, and ye shall find; knock, and it shall be opened unto you. 10. For every one that asketh receiveth; and he that seeketh findeth; and to him that knocketh it shall be opened.** "In the three words the Lord uses, *ask, seek, knock,* a difference in meaning has been sought. If such was indeed His purpose, then, the first, *ask,* refers to the gifts we pray for. But I may ask and receive the gift without the Giver. *Seek* is the word Scripture uses of God Himself; Christ assures me that I can find Himself. But it is not enough to find God in time of need, without coming to abiding fellowship: *knock* speaks of admission to dwell with Him and in Him. Asking and receiving the gift would thus lead to seeking and finding the Giver, and this again to the knocking and opening of the door of the Father's home and love. One thing is sure: the Lord does want us to count most certainly on it that asking, seeking, knocking, cannot be in vain: receiving an answer, finding God, the opened heart and home of God, are the certain fruit of prayer. . . . If you ask and receive not, it must be because there is something amiss or wanting in the prayer. Hold on; let the Word and Spirit teach you to pray aright, but do not let go the confidence He seeks to awaken: Every one that asketh, receiveth. . . . Beloved fellow-disciples in the school of Jesus! let us set ourselves to learn this lesson well. Let us take these words just as they were spoken. Let us not suffer human reason to weaken their force. Let us take them as Jesus gives them, and believe them. He will teach us in due time how to understand them fully: let us begin by implicitly believing them. Let us take time, as often as we pray, to listen to His voice: Every one that asketh, receiveth. Let us not make the feeble experiences of our unbelief the measure of what our faith may expect. Let us seek, not only just in our seasons of prayer, but at all times, to hold fast the joyful assurance: man's prayer on earth and God's answer in heaven are meant for each other. Let us trust Jesus to teach us so to pray that the answer can come. He will do it, if we hold fast the word He gives today: 'Ask, and ye shall receive.'" — *Andrew Murray.* **11. And of**

12. Or *if* he shall ask an egg, will he give him a scorpion?

13. If ye then, being evil, know how to give good gifts unto your children, how much more shall *your* heavenly Father give the Holy Spirit to them that ask him?

PHILIPPIANS 4:6. In nothing be anxious; but in everything by prayer and supplication with thanksgiving let your requests be made known unto God.

7. And the peace of God, which passeth all understanding, shall guard your hearts and your thoughts in Christ Jesus.

---

which of you that is a father shall his son ask a loaf, and he give him a stone? or a fish, and he for a fish give him a serpent? 12. Or *if* he shall ask an egg, will he give him a scorpion? 13. If ye then, being evil, know how to give good gifts unto your children, how much more shall *your* heavenly Father give the Holy Spirit to them that ask him? "*Me* is the question word that involves a no as the only answer in the speaker's mind, and is always hard to render because we have no such question word. From friend to friend Jesus advances to son and father. For the English reader much is lost when *ortos* is made 'loaf.' This was a small flat cake of bread, and thus resembled a stone; compare 4:3. A son who is hungry does not ask his parent for a whole loaf in our sense of loaf — he could not eat it all — but for such a cake, which he could easily consume. . . . A snake may resemble a fish, but is unfit to eat. The idea of harmfulness is imported, for certainly the snake would not be alive (as little as the fish) and if it were it would strike the father's hand before it struck the son's. The point is in the deceptions attempted by such a father, reducing his fatherhood, and thus the sonship of his innocent and trusting child, to an illusion. . . . The argument from the less to the greater is unanswerable. It clinches all that precedes on the assurance that our prayers to our Father will be heard. As earthly fathers prove themselves fathers by giving 'good gifts,' to their children, so your Father proves to you that he is indeed your Father, and you are indeed his children, by giving to you in answer to your asking in your need, as Matthew has it, things beneficial to you, or as Luke has it 'the Holy Spirit' at once meaning the highest and greatest spiritual gift, involving every other spiritual gift, and certainly thus also every necessary temporal gift, for these lie on the lowest plane." — *R. C. H. Lenski.*

IV. **THE SENTINEL OF THE HEART**, Philippians 4:6, 7. I have taken the title for this section of our lesson directly from the chapter heading for verse 7 in F. B. Meyer's excellent volume on Philippians in the Devotional Commentary Series, and I think we can do no better than to confine ourselves to his comments on these two verses. 6. **In nothing be anxious; but in everything by prayer and supplication with thanksgiving let your requests be made known unto God.** "*Anxiety* comes from the same root as anger, and refers to the physical act of choking. Worry chokes the life of faith; it does not help us to meet our difficulties; so far from this it unfits us, for our mind is too flurried to think clearly and carefully, our hand trembles too much to perform the delicate operation. Therefore, the perpetual injunction of the New Testament to the children of God is, as Jesus puts it, 'Take no anxious thought.' . . . Whenever the least shadow of care threatens our life we should go at once to our knees, and in the silence of private prayer hand over the burden and responsibility to our Infinite and Allwise Father. We have to make our requests known. Not that He will always give us what we ask, but will read into our prayers the meaning that we would put in them, were we as well informed as He is of what is best." — *F. B. Meyer.*
7. **And the peace of God, which passeth all understanding, shall guard your hearts and your thoughts in Christ Jesus.** "It is not enough for us to have the peace which arises from earthly conditions, and the possession of good things. There is a deeper, sweeter peace, which the Apostle describes as passing all under-

standing; and our Lord refers to it when He says, 'My peace I give, not as the world giveth.' This was the peace of Christ and His Apostles. There was nothing to account for it. . . . The word *keep* is the term used for sentry duty. It is as though the peace of God, like some sentinel angel, went to and fro before the portal of our inner life, keeping back all intruders who would break in upon the purity of our affections, or the integrity of our thoughts. How often we have been flurried and agitated! How suddenly things have broken in upon us which have rocked the waters of the inner lake to storm! How frequently the fever of the world has entered, for want of a disinfecting barrier, to raise the pulses of our souls to fever heat! But all this may be prevented when the peace that passeth understanding keeps us." — *F. B. Meyer.*

V. **CHRIST OUR GREAT HIGH PRIEST,** Hebrews 4:14–16. One can hardly mention any great subject concerning the Lord Jesus in the New Testament that is so consistently ignored by the majority of Christians as the priestly work of our Lord. Christ has three principal offices: He came as prophet; His priestly work began with the sacrifice of Himself, and will continue until the entire church is gathered together unto Him; His kingly work will then begin in reality. A prophet is one who comes from the presence of God with a message for men; a priest is one who goes to God with the needs of men. Probably most of my readers have not as yet seen the new, helpful commentary on Hebrews by G. H. Lang, published by the Paternoster Press in London (1951). Here I find an excellent, concise unfolding of these two verses. The author first sets forth seven aspects of Christ our priest as revealed in these verses. "(1) The priest exists. We have Him. The present participle 'having' indicates that He exists and acts as priest continuously, without intermission. At all times He is available. (2) He is no *insignificant* person. Jeroboam was ready to appoint as priest any nobody that came along (1 Kings 13:33); but God's Priest is 'great' in person and standing and power. (3) He is *high* priest, not a subordinate. He has access to the throne, He has authority over all God's affairs, He dispenses all God's bounties, He can introduce unto God all whom He will (Matt. 11:27; John 6:37–40). (4) He has passed *through* the heavens, as the high priest in Israel passed through the courts and the veils into the audience chamber of the Most High. None can debar Him access; He is already there and there permanently. (5) He is *Jesus,* the man of human nature, experience, sympathy. . . . (6) He is *the Son of God,* personally acceptable to the Father, the Son He loves pre-eminently; able to understand God and His rights and able to meet them fully; even as He understands man and his needs and is able to meet them fully. . . . (7) He is *without sin.* In Him there was nothing carnal to respond to temptation. He felt it, indeed, the more keenly that His susceptibilities were not dulled by sinful indulgence; but in Him there was no response to its overtures, but perfect revulsion and complete rejection. . . .

"Because of this full provision to meet our need we are required: (1) To *hold fast* our confession. . . . (2) We must *draw near* unto God. — *G. H. Lang.*

THE LESSON IN LIFE, LITERATURE, AND ARCHAEOLOGY.

Canon Liddon, preaching in St. Paul's, London, tells an exquisite story from the life of E. B. Pusey, who, though the moving power in the revival of high-churchmanship, was nevertheless a true saint. "Five years before he left us, one who has since his death been much in men's minds, especially within these walls, had an illness which was of a very critical character. For some days he said nothing and was supposed to be quite unconscious. After his recovery, he referred one day to this, the presumably unconscious, part of his illness. 'People thought,' he said, 'that I was unconscious, but the fact was, that although I could not speak I heard all that went on in the room and I was well occupied.' To the question, 'What were you doing?' he answered, 'By God's mercy, I could remember the Epistle for the fourth Sunday in Advent, out of the Philippians, which begins, 'Rejoice in the Lord alway.' This I made a framework for prayer; saying the

Lord's Prayer two or three times between each clause, and so dwelling on the several relations of each clause to each petition in the Lord's Prayer.' How he did this he explained at some length, and then added, 'It lasted me, I should think, four or five hours.' To the question, 'What did you do after that?' he answered, 'I began it over again. I was very happy: and had it been God's will, did not wish to get better.' " — *Canon Liddon.*

A TRUTH FOR THE CLASS TO CARRY AWAY.

Though it is not in the assigned text, I believe that the teacher should close this lesson with words which our Lord uttered just before He gave the Lord's Prayer to His disciples in the Sermon on the Mount, "When thou prayest, enter into thine inner chamber, and having shut thy door, pray to thy Father who is in secret, and thy Father who seeth in secret shall recompense thee." Unless my experience is one wholly out of the ordinary — and I do not think it is — I believe we are living in a time marked by increasing noise — of traffic, of planes overhead, of radios turned on loud, of men and women, intoxicated or semi-intoxicated keeping a neighborhood awake through the night, or slamming doors and shouting through the halls of a hotel. This all bears upon our inner spiritual life, and we must be more determined than ever that we are going to have some time every day, or every night, for a period of quiet, even though it be ten minutes, for prayer and communion with God. And let us beware of many modern shibboleths about this time of quiet. The Psalmist did not say, "My soul wait," but rather, "My soul wait *before God.*" So many advertisements today give as a cure for our tensions and fevers — "relax." Just to relax is not to pray. Let us shut this door.

Do you think that in our public prayers we should think out what we are going to say before uttering them? What is there in the very title of God our Father that encourages us to believe our prayers will be heard and answered? What people do you think have a right to pray to God as their heavenly Father? Can you think of an outstanding illustration of the priestly work of Christ recorded in the Gospels? (See Luke 22:32). How far do you think we should let this phrase, "in everything" extend? (By this I mean, it seems that we are not to ask God when we sit down at the table what we should eat, for He gives us common sense for that; nor need we ask Him if we should go to work, for we ought to go to work every morning. Nevertheless, we can ask Him to give us safety as we travel to work, and give us skill for the work, and ask that strength be given us from the food, to be used to His glory. I believe that more and more our prayers need to embrace matters other than the trivialities of life.)

LESSON V. — August 1.

CHRISTIAN WORSHIP AND FELLOWSHIP. — Acts 2:46–47;
Colossians 3:12–17; Hebrews 10:23–25.

PRINTED TEXT, Acts 2:46–47; Colossians 3:12–17; Hebrews 10:23–25.

Devotional Reading: Psalm 122.
Beginner Topic: IN A TINY HOUSE.
    Lesson Material: Exodus 2:1–10; Psalm 68:6a; James 1:16–17.
    Memory Verse: Thou, Jehovah, hast made me glad. Psalm 92:4.
Primary Topic: CHURCH FRIENDS HELP ONE ANOTHER.
    Lesson Material: Acts 2:46–47; Hebrews 10:23–25.
    Memory Verse: And let us consider one another to provoke unto love and good words. Hebrews 10:24.

Junior Topic: CHURCH FRIENDS HELP ONE ANOTHER.
    Lesson Material: Acts 2:46–47; Hebrews 10:23–25.
    Memory Verse: And let us consider one another to provoke unto love and good works. Hebrews 10:24.
Intermediate-Senior Topic: WE WORSHIP TOGETHER.
    Lesson Material: Acts 2:46–47; Colossians 3:12–17; Hebrews 10:23–25.
    Memory Verse: And let us consider one another to provoke unto love and good works, not forsaking our own assembling together. Hebrews 10:24, 25.
Topic for Young People and Adults: CHRISTIAN WORSHIP AND FELLOWSHIP.
    Lesson Material: Acts 2:46–47; Colossians 3:12–17; Hebrews 10:23–25.
    Memory Verse: And let us consider one another to provoke unto love and good works, not forsaking our own assembling together. Hebrews 10:24, 25.

THE TEACHER AND HIS CLASS.

The Younger Classes may begin this lesson, which concerns the coming together of Christian people for fellowship and worship, by being asked, What are some of the things in our country that draw multitudes of people together? Well, there would be baseball, or football, or basketball; then, there would be the visit of the President of the United States, or General MacArthur, to one of our cities, especially if this involved a parade. There are family gatherings, annually, or otherwise; and there are alumni meetings of our schools when old friends come together. But apart from the home, there are no ties so deep, born of love, as those which unite Christians in the family of God, and, once a member of that family, if their life is normal, they will long to have fellowship with other Christian people.

The Older Classes might be introduced to this lesson by the teacher bringing up the matter of the members of the church in which this lesson is being taught, especially those who are "on the books," but are never seen in church services. What do we say of these people? We say, "There must be something wrong with Mr. So-and-so or Mrs. So-and-so. They never come to church." This means that church attendance is the *normal and natural* regular experience of believers. If they do not come, and are really members of the church, there *is* something wrong, either in the church or in their own hearts.

THE LESSON IN ITS SETTING.

Time. — Events of the second chapter of Acts took place in the same year in which our Lord was crucified, A.D. 30. The Epistle to the Colossians was written from Rome, possibly A.D. 65, which may be also the time when the Epistle to the Hebrews was written.

Place. — The events of the second chapter of Acts occurred in Jerusalem. Colosse was a city in Asia Minor, inward from Miletus. We have no idea where the Epistle of the Hebrews was written.

THE PLAN OF THE LESSON.

SUBJECT: The Facts and Forces That From the Beginning of the Christian Church Have Brought Believers Together for Christian Fellowship and Worship.

I. THE CHARACTERISTICS OF THE FELLOWSHIP OF THE EARLIEST CHRISTIANS, Acts 2:46, 47.

II. SOME CHARACTERISTICS OF THE OUTER AND INNER LIFE OF ALL THOSE TRULY UNITED TO CHRIST, Colossians 3:12–17.
   1. Our conduct toward others, vs. 12–14.
   2. Two marks of the inner life, vs. 15–16.
   3. The all-inclusive Name, v. 17.

III. THE OBLIGATION FOR CHRISTIANS TO ASSEMBLE IN PUBLIC WORSHIP, Hebrews 10:23–25.

THE TEACHER'S LIBRARY.

All of the larger volumes on the Book of Acts will have some worthwhile comments on the two verses in our lesson, especially the volume by Dr. G. Campbell Morgan. On the Epistle to the Colossians there are rich volumes: Maclaren's work in *The Expositor's Bible* is a classic; see also a volume by Bishop Moule in *The Cambridge Bible for Schools and Colleges;* T. K. Abbott in *The International Critical Commentary;* for those who can handle Greek, the monumental work by J. B. Lightfoot; and, one of the great pieces of expository preaching of fifty years ago, Bishop William R. Nicholson's *Oneness With Christ.* On the Epistle to the Hebrews, I have found most helpful for this lesson the second volume of Adolph Saphir's *Exposition of the Epistle to the Hebrews.* For some reason, sermonic material that actually interprets the lesson is scarce, but on the phrase,

"and be ye thankful," Colossians 3:15, there is a superb sermon in Dinsdale T. Young, *The Enthusiasm of God*, 161-173; on Colossians 3:16, see G. Campbell Morgan, *The Life of the Christian*, 25-44. On the entire subject of our lesson one might consult A. B. MacDonald, *Christian Worship in the Primitive Church*, Edinborough, 1934.

AUDIO-VISUAL AIDS.

FILMSTRIP: "God of the Hills," Church Screen, 30 fr., b&w. A worship service featuring hymns, Scripture, prayers and related material with beautiful photographs of America's hills and mountains.

ACTS 2:46. And day by day, continuing stedfastly with one accord in the temple, and breaking bread at home, they took their food with gladness and singleness of heart.

Unless the editor of this volume is greatly mistaken, the matter of regular church attendance is certain to become a subject of increasing importance, more and more a real problem in our country, in the next few years. One reason for this is the pull of television, which is already severely cutting into Sunday evening audiences in many churches throughout our land. Even outstanding ministers of large congregations are admitting the seriousness of this situation. A second reason is the breaking up of concentrated masses, living within the city limits of our larger metropolitan areas, and the vast development of suburban life in America, made possible by rapid transportation, especially the automobile. This means that many churches, where once great audiences gathered, are finding themselves in the midst of factories and office buildings, or in a neighborhood that is rapidly changing. For example, I know one of the great Protestant churches of this country to which the carfare is twenty cents for each individual. If a father and mother and two children come to church on Sunday morning, by streetcar, they have paid out $1.60 before anything is put in the offering. They live fifteen miles from the church, which is surrounded by an undesirable element. They are not coming back at night. Another factor entering into this matter is the radio. Some of the best preachers of America can be heard every Sunday over the air, with the result that many are asking why they should travel a long distance to hear a mediocre sermon when they can hear one of the highest quality in their own home. Finally, an increasing lukewarmness toward the great Christian verities will inevitably lesson one's longing for the house of God. For this reason, true believers on the one hand will have to be more determined than ever that they are going to be faithful in these things, and, on the other hand, the minister will, more than ever, have to seek the help of God in making his services infinitely worthwhile.

I. THE CHARACTERISTICS OF THE FELLOWSHIP OF THE EARLIEST CHRISTIANS, Acts 2:46-47. While this chapter is a record of a manifestation of supernatural power in the coming of the Holy Spirit upon the apostles and in the marvelous results of this first Christian sermon (that of St. Peter on Pentecost, with 3,000 conversions), what follows is just the natural consequence of conversion to Christ, of a recognition that we are all one in Him. What we have here regarding the meeting together of Christians you will note is not the result of a commandment or of an apostolic decree or of anything sensational drawing them together. 46. And day by day, continuing stedfastly with one accord in the temple, and breaking bread at home, they took their food with gladness and singleness of heart. The word here translated "accord" is a prominent one in the Book of Acts. (See, e.g., 1:14, 2:1, 4:24, 5:12, 8:6, 12:20, and 15:25. It is

47. Praising God, and having favor with all the people. And the Lord added to them day by day those that were saved.

COLOSSIANS 3:12. Put on therefore as God's elect, holy and beloved, a heart of compassion, kindness, lowliness, meekness, longsuffering;

---

also used of mobs coming together, 7:57; 18:12; 19:29). The word means "of one mind." The word translated "gladness" means literally "abounding in joy," and is used twice in the opening chapter of Luke's Gospel (vs. 14 and 44). "The word is full of significance — it is connected with the birth of the forerunner, by an angel's message to Zacharias; the verb denotes the exultant joy with which the church, age after age, has rejoiced in the song of the incarnation." — *R. J. Knowling.* Wherever you have a revival in the Old Testament, or New Testament, or in subsequent history, you have a people singing with joy. 47. **Praising God, and having favor with all the people. And the Lord added to them day by day those that were saved.** "It is God's will for His ideal of a Christian church that continuously it should be gathering into its fellowship those that are being saved." Dr. Alexander Maclaren, preaching on this text to his own people, in Manchester, asked: "Why does not the Lord add daily to us? I beseech you, make your communion such that it will repel as well as attract, and that people will find nothing here to draw them to an easy religion of words and formalism, beneath which all vermin of worldliness and selfishness may lurk, but will recognize in us a church of men and women who are bent upon holiness and longing for more and more conformity to the Divine Master." — *Alexander Maclaren.*

II. **SOME CHARACTERISTICS OF THE OUTER AND INNER LIFE OF ALL THOSE TRULY UNITED TO CHRIST,** Colossians 3:12–17. We could here give some account of the history of Colosse, and the reason for Paul's writing this Epistle, but it seems that this one paragraph does not need such facts for its understanding, for it could have been written to any Christian assembly in the world at that time. In verses 9 and 10 Paul uses a figure of speech taken from our daily habit of putting on garments and putting them off, a metaphor he now repeats at the beginning of our printed text. In the preceding paragraph he has described the garment that a believer should put off, the old man. He now describes the garment of a new man in Christ. 12. **Put on therefore as God's elect . . .** This word is a favorite one with St. Paul (see for example Romans 8:33, Titus 1:1, et cetera), and means, "those called out." It is closely related, in the Greek, to the word for *church*, a church being an assembly of those who have been called out of death into life, out of worldliness and selfishness into holiness. **holy and beloved, a heart of compassion . . .** "That is, deep, earnest, yearning, genuine compassion, a heart of compassion, of interest, deep fellow-feeling." — *W. R. Nicholson.* **kindness . . .** "The character which offers sympathy and invites confidence." — *Bishop Moule.* "It does not require us to be blind to facts or to live in fancies, but it does require us to cherish a habit of goodwill." — *A. Maclaren.* **lowliness . . .** "That is, the moral habit from which the two preceding graces spring, since self-conceit, pride, or arrogance can never produce them. Nor can mere natural temperament sufficiently supply and sustain them. Only a true sense of our own ill-desert before God is the fountain of hearty compassion and sustained kindness toward the miserable. It is as we think and feel in a lowly manner of ourselves that we think and feel according to what is the truth." **meekness . . .** "which is one of the effects of humility and has reference primarily to our relations with God. (See James 1:21.) But this submissiveness toward God immediately operates in all our relations towards men, for it means that submission to God in the trials which come to us in His providence from men. (See 2 Sam. 16:11.) It is opposed to rudeness and harshness." **longsuffering . . .** "The temper indicated is the opposite to that *haste* of spirit which gives the man no time, under pressure of pain or wrong,

13. Forbearing one another, and forgiving each other, if any man
have a complaint against any; even as the Lord forgave you, so also
do ye;

14. And above all these things *put on* love, which is the bond of
perfectness.

15. And let the peace of Christ rule in your hearts, to the which also
ye were called in one body; and be ye thankful.

---

to remember what is due to others, and to the Lord." — *Bishop Moule.*   13. **Forbearing one another, and forgiving each other, if any man have a complaint against
any; even as the Lord forgave you, so also do ye.** "Forbearing and forgiving,
two words which explain the operation of meekness and long-suffering.   Forbearing
to be impatient and to avenge one's self, and, on the contrary, to be forgiving.
And this whenever we have a complaint.   The formal act of forgiveness, indeed,
cannot be performed without repentance and confession on the part of the offender;
but in the absence of such repentance and confession the spirit of forgiveness
should be within our hearts in the fulness of its power.   We should essentially
forgive even though the formal forgiveness cannot be pronounced.   And the powerful motive for this is that the Lord forgave us.

"*Love.*   This grace is to put on over all the others as a kind of outer garment,
or, more properly, to use the figure of the apostle, as 'the bond of perfectness,'
that is, the bond which holds together all the graces of perfection, which embraces
them as is seen in 1 Corinthians 13:4–7.   Without it they are all delusive; compassion is only sentiment, humility is debasement, and meekness is cajolery and
deceit without love.

"*Peace;* and notice that this is the peace of Christ (John 14:27; Eph. 2:14).   It
is indeed the same as the peace of God (Phil. 4:7), only there it is opposed to
anxious worldliness, while here to the hard and unloving spirit.   The peace
of Christ is not merely a judicial fact such as that peace with God referred to in
Romans 5:1, but a kind of feeling which we are to possess and exhibit towards
others.   And this peace is inseparable from love, for our love is the result of our
sense of God's love.   The peace, in other words, that fills us with serenity and
tranquillity in all our relations with men." — *W. R. Nicholson.*

"In Ephesians 4:2, which is parallel, there is added 'in love.'   This is a more
difficult part of the dress to assume than what succeeds it, but it is also more
Divine.   It is the same word which our Lord used in His saying, 'how long shall
I *suffer* you?'   It is literally 'up-bear.'   The same word was used of Divine forgiveness in 2:13 — the meaning being 'graced.'   It beautifully expresses the character of genuine Christ-like forgiveness — a gracious act graciously performed.
Peace-keeping and peace-making are the two graces here enjoined. . . .   The
principle of forgiveness here enunciated is that of our Lord's teaching and of the
prayer He taught His disciples." — *S. R. Macphail.*   14. **and above all these
things** *put on* **love, which is the bond of perfectness.**   "Again the figure of clothing
is used and reference is made to the girdle by which the robes of an Eastern man
were held together.   It is interesting that there are three passages which speak
of the girdle: the girdle of truth (Eph. 6:14); the girdle of peace (Eph. 4:3); and
here the girdle of love.   Love is regarded as that which holds together the various
Christian graces already mentioned." — *W. H. Griffith Thomas.*   15. **And let the
peace of Christ rule in your hearts, to the which also ye were called in one body;
and be ye thankful.**   The phrase pointing to unity here is "one body."   This
means the body of Christ, of which all believers are members, a figure of speech
often used by the Apostle Paul, especially in the Epistle to the Ephesians (as in
2:16, 4:4; etc.).   This union is brought about by the Holy Spirit.   It is that which
is bestowed upon us.   On the last phrase, as I noticed in the bibliography, "be ye
thankful," Dinsdale Young has a great sermon, from which the following may be

16. Let the word of Christ dwell in you richly; in all wisdom teaching and admonishing one another with psalms *and* hymns *and* spiritual songs, singing with grace in your hearts unto God.

---

taken: "Note that this grace of thankfulness is a *climacteric grace:* "*And* be ye thankful.*" That "and" is very significant. There is a lesson in practical divinity in that homely copulative term. Such a succession of graces has greeted our gladdened eyes as we have read! Already these Colossians are 'holy and beloved.' They are urged to such qualities as 'kindness,' 'humility,' 'longsuffering.' They are entreated to be 'forbearing' and 'forgiving.' 'Love, which is the bond of perfectness,' is to safeguard and adorn them like a strong and exquisite girdle. 'The peace of Christ' is to reign as a king in the palace of their regenerated hearts. '*And* be ye thankful' adds this wise master-builder of souls. Thankfulness is the crown of the graces. Your conquering brow lacks its garland if you are wanting this celestial quality. Do we realise that gratitude to God is a completion of character? Devoid of this we are woefully inadequate. Oh to carry this gem on our forehead! Give it its Biblical place in your life. Do not be content till this vaster music rolls through your days. No soul is complete in Christ that is not thankful. Add this to your store. There is no characteristic so essential to 'perfect love' as thankfulness." — *Dinsdale T. Young.* 16. **Let the word of Christ dwell in you richly.** This is the only time in the New Testament where we have this exact phrase. But we often hear of the word of the cross, the word of God, the word of truth, et cetera. This word is, first of all, the body of teaching coming from the lips of Christ, and, secondly, that great body of truth which relates to Christ, His incarnation, His life, His death, His deity, resurrection, et cetera. This is the very sustenance of our soul. As Dr. Campbell Morgan has said, "My life in Christ is not self-sufficient. It is only as it receives from the outside that it can continue and develop. As in the physical life of man, so in the spiritual, there are two elements of necessary sustenance, proper food and proper atmosphere. Both the food of the Christian and the atmosphere in which he is to live are indicated in the passages at the commencement of this chapter. Christ says, 'He that believeth hath eternal life. I am the bread of life.' That is to say, that He is the sustenance of the life we have received from Him. The Christ life can only be fed by Christ. Not by something He gives me as apart from Himself, not by blessings He bestows upon me, but by the fact that the values and the virtues and the victory of His life are mine in Him, and are all available for the sustenance of His life in me.

"Christ, then, is the bread of life, and the soul having received the life of the Christ, is now to be fed and sustained by Christ. The atmosphere of the life is the Holy Spirit in all His powers. Neither of these means of sustenance can be neglected without peril to Christian life. In the full use of both there will be constant development and growth without effort or undue consciousness." — *Dr. G. Campbell Morgan.*

. . . **in all wisdom teaching and admonishing one another with psalms *and* hymns *and* spiritual songs, singing with grace in your hearts unto God.** "While the leading idea of *Psalms* is a musical accompaniment and that of *hymns*, praise to God, the last word Paul uses is the general word for a song, whether accompanied or unaccompanied, whether of praise or any other subject. Thus it was quite possible for the same song to be at once all of the three mentioned in this clause. The reference to *psalms* is especially, though not exclusively, to the psalms of David, which would early form part of the religious worship of the Christian brotherhood. On the other hand, *hymns* would more appropriately designate those hymns of praise which were composed by the Christians themselves on distinctly Christian themes." — *J. B. Lightfoot.* For instances of singing hymns or psalms in the apostolic age, see Acts 4:24; 16:25; 1 Corinthians 14:15 and 26.

17. And whatsoever ye do, in word or in deed, *do* all in the name of the Lord Jesus, giving thanks to God the Father through him.

Hebrews 10:23. Let us hold fast the confession of our hope that it waver not; for he is faithful that promised.

24. And let us consider one another to provoke unto love and good works.

25. Not forsaking our own assembling together, as the custom of some is, but exhorting *one another;* and so much the more, as ye see the day drawing nigh.

---

17. And whatsoever ye do, in word or in deed, *do* all in the name of the Lord Jesus, giving thanks to God the Father through him.   Once more we have this matter of thanksgiving, and a general all-embracing statement covering every act and word of life, one of the most perfect mottos for Christian living to be found in any single sentence in the New Testament.   "It is confidence in His name, not in my praying, nor in myself who pray, nor in anything about me, which makes me thank God for the answer before it comes.   When of old Jehoshaphat went to meet his enemies, the singers went praising before the army.   So still if we pray as we ought." — *S. R. Macphail.*

III. THE OBLIGATION FOR CHRISTIANS TO ASSEMBLE IN PUBLIC WORSHIP, Hebrews 10:23–25.   This Epistle, as the title indicates, was written to *Hebrew* people, children of Abraham, who had received Christ as their Savior, in the generation immediately following our Lord's ascension.   They were being severely persecuted (see e.g., in this very chapter, vs. 32–39), and as a result some were being tempted and some looking back with affection upon their Jewish rites and comparing the simplicity and plainness of the worship of believers with the gorgeous ceremonies of the Temple were in danger of leaving Christ.   Constantly in this Epistle then, we have exhortations as in verse 22, "Let us draw near"; and in this verse, "Let us hold fast." 23. **Let us hold fast the confession of our hope that it waver not; for he is faithful that promised.**   "Faith rests on the past, the accomplished work of Jesus; hope looks to the future, the return of our Saviour.   And the more we realize Jesus as the living Lord, the more shall we look forward, waiting for His coming, and going forth to meet Him.   If we believe that He has come, we also hope that He will come.   If we know the salvation-bringing grace of God which hath appeared, we shall with confiding hope look for the coming of our great God and Saviour.   Thus 'the hope' is the most comprehensive view of Christ's relation to a believer.   Hence, when Paul said that 'he stood and was judged for the hope of the promise made of God unto our fathers,' he spoke out of his inmost heart.   A dead faith is without hope; it does not behold Christ living; it does not desire Christ's return; it has never known Christ crucified. . . .

"The profession of our hope is most practical and testing.   Hereby we profess that we are strangers and pilgrims upon earth, that we are seeking heavenly things, labouring for heavenly rewards, laying up for ourselves heavenly treasures. We must forsake the sins, pleasures, and honours of Egypt; we must purify ourselves, as Christ is pure.   If we profess *hope*, we must also rejoice, though we be in tribulation; we must view the sufferings and trials of this present life as not worthy to be compared with the coming glory." — *Adolph Saphir.*   24. **And let us consider one another to provoke unto love and good works.**   Westcott has a wonderfully suggestive paragraph here, in which he says, "It is our duty to declare what we are and what we look for; it is our duty also to consider what others are. The well-being of each believer is bound up with the well-being of the whole body. He is therefore constrained to give careful heed to others in the hope that he may rouse them to nobler action; and again that he may himself draw encouragement and inspiration from nobler examples." — *B. F. Westcott.*   25. **Not forsaking our own assembling together, as the custom of some is, but exhorting *one another;***

and so much the more, as ye see the day drawing nigh. That superb expositor of a former generation, Dr. Adolph Saphir, has in my opinion the finest interpretation of this verse to be found in any volume of exposition on Hebrews: "Christianity is eminently an individual heart-affair; but it is also eminently social. . . . As a congregation we are to show the death of the Lord. The voice of melody is heard in the assembly of saints. . . .

"In times of persecution or of lukewarmness, Christian fellowship is specially important; it is likewise a test of our faithfulness. Are we ashamed of the Lord, of His truth, of His followers, of His reproach? The Hebrews, it seems, needed this word of exhortation, and the apostle confirms it by the solemn addition, 'Forasmuch as ye see the day approaching.' The apostle refers, doubtless, to the approaching judgment on Jerusalem, connecting it, according to the law of prophetic vista, with the final crisis. Because the Lord is at hand, we are to be patient, loving, gentle, exercising forbearance towards our brother, while examining with strict care our own work.

"The second advent of our Lord is the most powerful, as well as the most constraining motive. Do we hope to be with Christ and all the saints in glory, and shall we not love the brethren, and minister unto them, while we are waiting together for His coming? Do we expect Christ to acknowledge us as His brethren, and shall we be ashamed of Christ's members, or treat them with cold neglect and indifference? Have we all to appear before the tribunal of Christ and to account for our stewardship, and shall we not be faithful and diligent in exercising whatever ministry is entrusted to us, as God hath bestowed unto each one of us his own measure and gift? Called to eternal fellowship of love in joy and glory, let us fulfill the ministry of love in suffering and service, and let every day see some help and consolation given to our fellow-pilgrim." — *Dr. Adolph Saphir.*

THE LESSON IN LIFE, LITERATURE, AND ARCHAEOLOGY.

While it does not incorporate the exact words of our assigned text, the following is a magnificent illustration, and I am sure will be appreciated by many. This is taken from the first volume of Spurgeon's Autobiography, the chapter that speaks of his youth. "The first lessons I ever had in theology were from an old cook in the school at Newmarket where I was an usher. She was a good old soul, and used to read *The Gospel Standard.* Many a time we went over the covenant of grace together, and talked of the personal election of the saints, their union to Christ, their final perseverance, and what vital godliness meant; and I do believe that I learned more from her than I should have learned from any six doctors of divinity of the sort we have nowadays. There are some Christian people who taste, and see, and enjoy religion in their own souls, and who get at a deeper knowledge of it than books can ever give them, though they should search all their days. The cook at Newmarket was a godly experienced woman, from whom I learned far more than I did from the minister of the chapel we attended. I asked her once, 'Why do you go to such a place?' She replied, 'Well, there is no other place of worship to which I can go.' I said, 'But it must be better to stay at home than to hear such stuff.' 'Perhaps so,' she answered; 'but I like to go out to worship even if I get nothing by going. You see a hen sometimes scratching all over a heap of rubbish to try to find some corn; she does not get any, but it shows that she is looking for it, and using the means to get it, and then, too, the exercise warms her.' So the old lady said that scratching over the poor sermons she heard was a blessing to her because it exercised her spiritual faculties and warmed her spirit. On another occasion I told her that I had not found a crumb in the whole sermon, and asked how she had fared. 'Oh!' she answered, 'I got on better tonight, for to all the preacher said, I just put in a *not,* and that turned his talk into real gospel.' " — *C. H. Spurgeon.*

A TRUTH FOR THE CLASS TO CARRY AWAY.

On this one occasion, I trust that my readers will allow me to direct this final paragraph to ministers, for I was a pastor myself for twenty years. Often in looking out of my study window on Sunday morning, and watching people wend their way to divine services, I have been compelled to ask myself over and over, "Is what you have to say this morning worth people traveling across the city to hear?" As the matter of church attendance becomes an increasingly difficult problem, all who are ministers of the Gospel will find it necessary to seek an increased enduement of power, to make their services more and more of such a nature that people will be compelled to come to the house of God — and by this I do not mean through something sensational, but the offering of food for the weary souls of men and women.

What are some of the points of contrast between the weekly meetings of our service clubs and the gathering of Christians in the House of God? How did Christ show His own obedience to the truths of this lesson? Do you think that Christians in a church audience on Sunday should be given more or less opportunity to participate in the service than is normal today? What is the primary difference between the service that the Roman Catholic attends on Sunday and that which the Protestant attends? (The Catholic goes to mass and sees a rite performed in a language he does not understand, while the Protestant hears a sermon from the Word of God.) What are some of the primary reasons that individual members of a Christian church remain away from divine service for a prolonged length of time? How can we remedy a situation everywhere prevalent in our land, in which our churches are filled to capacity twice on Easter Sunday morning, but most of them not again until the next year?

LESSON VI. — August 8.

CHOOSING THE BEST. — Matthew 6:19–34; Galatians 5:16–23; Philippians 1:9–11; 4:8; 1 Thessalonians 5:21–22.

PRINTED TEXT, Matthew 6:24–33; Philippians 1:9–11; 4:8.

Devotional Reading: Deuteronomy 30:15–20.
Beginner Topic: IN THE FRIENDLY DARK.
　　Lesson Material: Matthew 2:1–2, 12–23; (see also Job 9:1–10; Psalm 8:19; Psalm 139:1–12; 147:4).
　　Memory Verse: God . . . made the stars. Thou Jehovah hast made me glad. Genesis 1:16; Psalm 92:4.
Primary Topic: CHOOSING THE BEST.
　　Lesson Material: Matthew 6:24–29; Philippians 4:8.
　　Memory Verse: Hold fast that which is good. 1 Thessalonians 5:21.
Junior Topic: CHOOSING THE BEST.
　　Lesson Material: Matthew 6:24–29; Philippians 4:8.
　　Memory Verse: Prove all things; hold fast that which is good. 1 Thessalonians 5:21.
Intermediate-Senior Topic: CHOOSING THE BEST.
　　Lesson Material: Matthew 6:19–34; Galatians 5:16–23; Philippians 1:9–11; 4:8; 1 Thessalonians 5:21–22.
　　Memory Verse: And this I pray, that your love may abound yet more and more in knowledge and all discernment; so that ye may approve the things that are excellent. Philippians 1:9–10a.
Topic for Young People and Adults: CHOOSING THE BEST.
　　Lesson Material: Matthew 6:19–34; Galatians 5:16–23; Philippians 1:9–11; 4:8; 1 Thessalonians 5:21–22.
　　Memory Verse: And this I pray, that your love may abound yet more and more in knowledge and all discernment; so that ye may approve the things that are excellent. Philippians 1:9–10a.

THE TEACHER AND HIS CLASS.

The Younger Classes might be introduced to this lesson with an illustration I came upon recently, in visiting the home of some friends. I asked what their son was going to do this summer (he is a junior in high school), and they said that it would be necessary for him to remain in town for some weeks to take a summer school course in geometry. Upon further inquiry, I learned that he had become so intensely interested in his appointment as official photographer for the high school annual, that he had neglected his studies. He was putting second things first — maybe even third things first.

The Older Classes might have their interest in this lesson awakened by the teacher's putting on the blackboard, in capital letters, the word *first*, and then asking the class for a definition of it. As with many of our fundamental words, this comes from an old English word meaning *highest*, and sometimes, as in Danish, meaning *prince*. Of the many definitions of this word in the *Oxford English Dictionary*, the first is, "That which is before all others; earliest in time; foremost in position or importance." A later definition which applies aptly to our lesson is, "Preceding all others in dignity, rank, importance or excellence."

THE LESSON IN ITS SETTING.

Time. — The Sermon on the Mount was delivered in the spring of A.D. 27. First Thessalonians was written about A.D. 56; Galatians about A.D. 58; and Philippians approximately A.D. 65.

Place. — The Sermon on the Mount was delivered on an unidentified mountain in Galilee. Galatia was a province of Asia Minor. Philippi and Thessalonica were cities in Greece.

THE PLAN OF THE LESSON.

SUBJECT: The Importance of Giving Definite Values to Various Experiences, Tasks, and Objectives in Life, and How to Determine These Values.

I. TREASURES IN HEAVEN TO BE PREFERRED TO TREASURES ON EARTH, Matthew 6:19–24.

II. SEEKING THE KINGDOM OF GOD — NOT ANXIOUS FOR OUR DAILY NEEDS, Matthew 6:25–34.

III. THE MARKS OF A SPIRIT-CONTROLLED LIFE, Galatians 5:16–23.

IV. THE ROOT AND FRUIT OF CONSTANTLY CHOOSING THE BEST, Philippians 1:9–11.

   1. The root — love, v. 9.
   2. The choice — the "excellent," v. 10.
   3. The fruit of righteousness, v. 11.

V. A CLUSTER OF BETTER THINGS, Philippians 4:8.

VI. A FINAL EXHORTATION, 1 Thessalonians 5:21, 22.

THE TEACHER'S LIBRARY.

On the verses taken from the Sermon on the Mount, we have often given bibliographies, but I would mention here again the volumes by J. Oswald Dykes, R. Govet, Cleland B. Macafee, and, the three volumes by various writers, entitled, *The Sermon on the Mount: a Practical Exposition*. All of the major commentaries on Matthew's Gospel will be found helpful here, especially those by G. Campbell Morgan, John Broadus, and R. C. H. Lenski.

For the verses assigned from the Epistle to the Philippians, see the commentaries on this volume by Robert Rainy, in *The Expositor's Bible;* F. B. Meyer in the *Devotional Commentary* series; the small volume by Charles R. Erdman; *Philippians in the Greek New Testament for English Readers*, by my friend Kenneth S. Wuest; and, for those who can handle the Greek, the monumental work by J. B. Lightfoot.

For sermonic material, on Matthrew 6:24, see G. Campbell Morgan in *The Westminster Pulpit*, Vol. 2, pp. 49–56; G. H. Knight: *The Master's Questions to His Disciples*, 2–7; and on the entire passage, Marcus Dods: *The Prayer That Teaches to Pray*, 177–211. On verse 30, see H. P. Liddon: *Sermons on Some Words of Christ*, 33–48; and on verse 33, A. M. Fairbairn: *The City of God*, 317–344; Henry Howard: *The Summits of the Soul*, 57–88.

AUDIO-VISUAL AIDS.

No audio-visual aids directly pertinent to this lesson.

The matter of choosing between that which is best and that which is merely good, arises almost every day, sometimes in minor matters, and then again, in events of great importance.   If there are oranges in a grocery store at four different prices, the housekeeper must determine which she is going to buy.   When a young man decides that he is going to college, he must make a decision as to which college is the best.   It may be that he cannot get into the one he wants, and then will have to choose one of a lower standing.   Sometimes we are circumscribed in what we can choose: we may want the best and not be able to get it.   But in our lesson, what is designated best, is available for all who wish it.   One does not have to be a genius, or rich, or possess great influence — the choices of this lesson are those set before all who know God and would serve Him.

I. TREASURES IN HEAVEN TO BE PREFERRED TO TREASURES ON EARTH, Matthew 6:19-24.   We shall never understand the deeper teaching of our Lord in this passage, and indeed may have a distorted view of what our Lord is here saying, unless we get a proper idea of what he means by "laying up treasures."   "Literally, the idea in this word *treasure* is to place something *horizontally*.   It means to lay something aside, that is, to store something up, to keep it; not to place something perpendicularly, ready for activity, and work, but to hoard it.   It is the laying of things up, one thing upon another, piece upon piece, horizontally, that we may possess them, take care of them, and accumulate them.   Now the King does not say that it is wrong to lay up. . . .   The principle revealed is not that it is wrong to lay up treasures for *ourselves;* for when the Master comes to the positive statement, he distinctly says, 'Lay up for yourselves.'   The secret is discovered in the treasures: treasures upon earth, treasures in heaven.   What Christ says is that we are to remember that we are not the child of today, not of the earth; we are of the eternities.   Make your fortune, but store it where it will greet you in the dawning of the new morning when the whole earth passes from you.   Possess not the things of the now, but the things of the new and the forever." — *G. Campbell Morgan.*   "The garments of the Jews, as of other Oriental nations, seldom changed their fashion; and hence great stores of garments, perhaps in part inherited, would often form an important item in one's possessions (Gen. 45:22; 2 Kings 5:5; Job 27:16).   These were liable to be destroyed by moths.   The term rendered 'rust' signifies 'eat,' and so consumption in whatever way.   It might be understood here in the general sense of that which consumes or destroys property; or in the special sense of rust, just as we say that rust 'eats.' " — *John A. Broadus.*

Have you ever noticed how often Jesus speaks about the *heart?*   By this, of course, He means not so much the organ of our physical bodies which pumps blood, but the very center and citadel of our being; as we think of it in such an expression as we love a person "with all our heart."   (Matt. 5:8, 28; 9:4; 12:34; 13:19; 15:8, 18, 19; 22:37; John 14:1, 27; 16:6, 22.)   All the teaching of Jesus goes straight to the center of life, where character is formed, and where eternal destinies are determined.   Let us thank God before we read another line that the Teacher who came down from heaven was one who concerned Himself primarily and continually with the deepest things that concern human life.

The editor does not seem to be able to find in any commentary a real explanation of *how* we may lay up treasure in heaven.   To begin with, it certainly has to do with spiritual things.   We are not sending bags of gold and silver, or chests of precious stones, up to heaven; heaven does not need them, and there is no one to take such treasures of ours up there, nor would they be of any value to us when we arrived in glory.   If, then, these treasures are in the realm of spiritual things, they must belong to us; that is, they must have some definite relationship to each of us.   Just as your earthly treasure is yours because you have inherited it, or have accumulated it by hard work, and that treasure does not belong to any one else, so the treasures which each one of us should have in heaven have a definite relationship to our own lives here on earth.   To go a step farther, it would hardly seem that these treasures are the gifts of God's grace through Jesus Christ, which

MATTHEW 6:24. No man can serve two masters: for either he will hate the one, and love the other; or else he will hold to one, and despise the other. Ye cannot serve God and mammon.

25. Therefore I say unto you, Be not anxious for your life, what ye shall eat, or what ye shall drink; nor yet for your body, what ye shall put on. Is not the life more than food, and the body than the raiment.

---

we do not "lay up" but receive and appropriate. They are the consequences of the things that we do, the things we say, the prayers we offer. . . . We lay up such treasures when our lives are bearing fruit, when blessing goes forth from our hearts to hearts of others to the glory of God, when by the Holy Spirit we have led others into a saving knowledge of Jesus Christ, when we have manifested the love of God shed abroad in our hearts to others, when we have edified one another in the Lord, when we have participated in missionary ventures at home or abroad, when we have opened the word of God to others individually or in a class. In other words, when we labor in the things which God would have us do, even if it is offering a cup of cold water in the name of Christ, we shall lay up treasures in heaven. . . . Some very poor people on earth will be exceedingly rich in glory, and some very rich people on earth will be almost paupers in glory; likewise, some poor people on earth will be just as poor in heaven, and some rich Christians on earth will be just as rich in a different way in heaven.

Matthew 6:24. 24. **No man can serve two masters: for either he will hate the one, and love the other; or else he will hold to one, and despise the other. Ye cannot serve God and mammon.** "Mammon is the transliteration of the Greek equivalent for a late Aramaic term denoting wealth or riches or treasure. In the Gospels it means worldliness in the form of wealth, and occurs twice — once here, and the parallel passage in Luke 16:9, 11." — *James Moffatt.* Mammon is not to be taken as the name of a Syrian god. This verse has to do with the sin that is commonly called avarice, which is "the most exacting of all vices. It is never off its guard, and it never relaxes its hold. Sights which make even the hardest sinner compassionate for a brief space make the miser draw his purse-strings the tighter. The claims, not only of relations, friends, and country, but even of honor, comfort, and health — all are disregarded when money is at stake. Mammon is here personified as the rival of God and all experience shows that he who has allowed himself to become its slave can serve no one else; least of all can he devote himself to the service of God, who claims exclusive service. Devotion to money is the covetousness which is idolatry (Col. 3:5). But neither here nor elsewhere is the possession of wealth condemned: it is being enslaved to riches that is fatal, and to possess great riches without being enslaved is not easy." — *Alfred Plummer.*

II. SEEKING THE KINGDOM OF GOD — NOT ANXIOUS FOR OUR DAILY NEEDS, Matthew 6:25–34. 25. **Therefore I say unto you, Be not anxious for your life, what ye shall eat, or what ye shall drink; nor yet for your body, what ye shall put on. Is not the life more than food, and the body than the raiment.** What our Lord here wishes men to realize is that if they spend all their energy and thought in providing for things to eat, and things to wear, in a mood of anxiety, after they have enough to eat and to wear, they are still in that mood regarding the same things for the next day, and, after hard labor and intense effort, all they have is food and clothes, but nothing of the inner, precious things that make life really worth living — peace, joy, contentment, gratitude, leisure for prayer, and time for spiritual growth. This warning of Christ can apply to the rich as well as to the poor. We have actually seen people who, no matter what happened, though assured of comfort the remainder of the days of their life, worrying themselves into an early grave because of a flighty stock market, etc. There is probably no more general cause for families going "on the rocks," and husbands

26. Behold, the birds of the heaven, that they sow not, neither do they reap, nor gather into barns; and your heavenly Father feedeth them. Are not ye of much more value than they?

27. And which of you by being anxious can add one cubit unto the measure of his life?

28. And why are ye anxious concerning raiment? Consider the lilies of the field, how they grow; they toil not, neither do they spin:

29. Yet I say unto you, that even Solomon in all his glory was not arrayed like one of these.

30. But if God doth so clothe the grass of the field, which today is, and tomorrow is cast into the oven, *shall he* not much more *clothe* you, O ye of little faith?

and wives parting, than constant wrangling over money, and the things that money buys. **26. Behold, the birds of the heaven, that they sow not, neither do they reap, nor gather into barns; and your heavenly Father feedeth them. Are not ye of much more value than they?** Dr. Alexander Maclaren in his own inimitable way illuminates this verse with the following words: "It is part of the characteristics that mark the birds as lower than we that they have not to work for the future. Partly in this, amongst other things that God has given us, is the privilege of influencing the future by our faithful toil, by the sweat of our brow and the labor of our hands. These creatures labor not, and yet they are fed, and the lesson for us is, much more may we, whom God has blessed with the power of work, and with forces to mold the future, be sure he will bless the exercise of the prerogative by which he exalts us above these inferior creatures. Then there comes another inferiority. They cannot say, 'Father,' and yet they are fed. You are above them by the necessary relation which you sustain to your Father in heaven. He is their Maker, and showers his goodness upon them; he is your Father, and he will not forget his child. They cannot trust; you can." — *Dr. Alexander Maclaren.* **27. And which of you by being anxious can add one cubit unto the measure of his life?** "Here our Lord's question is, 'Which of you by taking anxious thought can add a single cubit to the length of his days?' It is another argument against 'taking anxious thought for one's life.' How foolish, in Hazlitt's phrase, to 'fret one's self to death with trying to be what one is not, and to do what one cannot'! And how faithless, since it is all at our heavenly Father's disposal." — *David Smith.* **28. And why are ye anxious concerning raiment? Consider the lilies of the field, how they grow; they toil not, neither do they spin: 29. Yet I say unto you, that even Solomon in all his glory was not arrayed like one of these.** We are not quite sure to what flower the Lord here refers. "From the expression 'lilies of the field' we gather that they were wild flowers, while the comparison of them with the regal robe of Solomon implies that they were not white, but colored. The plant that best accords with these is the anemone, with which in the spring of the year the Galilean hillsides are clothed. The nature of the reference might, however, favor the opinion that our Lord used the term 'lilies' in a very general way, and that it should be taken as comprising a variety of flowers, anemones, poppies, and tulips." — *Hugh Duncan.* "Take the finest fabric that monarch ever wore, and submit it to microscopic examination, and it is sack-cloth. Take the lily, and submit its garment of delicate velvet to microscopic examination and investigation, and the more perfect your lens, the more exquisite the weaving of the robe of the lily will be seen to be. Christ is not indulging in hyperbole. He is stating cold fact." — *G. Campbell Morgan.* **30. But if God doth so clothe the grass of the field, which today is, and tomorrow is cast into the oven, *shall he* not much more *clothe* you, O ye of little faith?** If God lavishes even upon a blade of grass, which within a few weeks after it appears above the ground

31. Be not therefore anxious, saying, What shall we eat? or, What shall we drink? or, Wherewithal shall we be clothed?

32. For after all these things do the Gentiles seek; for your heavenly Father knoweth that ye have need of all these things.

33. But seek ye first his kingdom and his righteousness; and all these things shall be added unto you.

---

is consigned to the flames of an oven, and is to be consumed to ashes from which it will never reappear, the wonderful wisdom which we see in the laws which govern its growing, its coloring, its absorption of the minerals of the ground and the sunlight from the air, how easy it should be to trust him to care for us with that same wisdom and omnipotence, extended in many more wonderful ways, when we are his children forever, and will some day stand in his very presence, in the likeness of his own Son, the Lord Jesus Christ. 31. **Be not therefore anxious, saying, What shall we eat? or, What shall we drink? or, Wherewithal shall we be clothed?** The emphasis in this verse should be on the conjunction "therefore," which is always a word following a series of statements which cannot be contradicted, and which introduces an inevitable conclusion. It is a word of argument, a word of logic. (1) We must not attach ourselves as servants to the material things of this earth; (2) there is something in life higher and more to be desired than mere food and drink and clothing; (3) there is a Father in heaven who cares for the birds and the grass, which have been brought into existence by his creation, and he is our Father, and we are his children — *therefore* while we must eat and drink and be clothed, and, indeed, we must work for these things, and get tired working for them, we must not, we ought not to be fretting, worrying, anxious about them. 32. **For after all these things do the Gentiles seek; for your heavenly Father knoweth that ye have need of all these things.** Another reason now comes from our Lord's lips to supplement all that he has previously given, and to support his second command that we are not to be anxious. The people who know not God, the pagan people, those who are given utterly to the things of this world, are the ones who seek food, and drink, and things to wear, as the primary objectives of life, but we, who know God as our Father, have made these things secondary.

33. **But seek ye first his kingdom and his righteousness; and all these things shall be added unto you.** Our Lord began this particular section of the Sermon on the Mount relating to the danger of covetousness, and of being a slave to the material things of this life, with a negative statement, placed in contrast with a positive statement — Lay not up on earth, but lay up in heaven. He ends this part of the discourse with a great positive. When the Holy Spirit, through the Apostle Paul, commands us to put off the old man with his deeds, he always at the same time commands us to put on the new man with his deeds (Eph. 4:22–32). A mere negative life, one "do not" after another, is an empty existence, and is in the greatest danger of becoming a very wicked life. If some things are to go out of our life permanently, then other things, with God's approval, are to come into our life. Thus, for instance, most normal men and women must have some goal in life, something to seek after, some aspiration, some consuming desire and ambition. What do we mean by seeking God's kingdom and righteousness? Certainly it means longing to do only those things which are in harmony with God's righteous character, which would meet His fullest approval. The kingdom of God includes all over which and over whom God rules. We are not seeking the kingdom of God . . . if any part of our life is in rebellion against God, if in our thoughts or deeds, our home, our business, our public or private life, in the letters we write, in the places we go, in the words we speak, we live unholy, sensual, earthly, unclean, intemperate, untruthful, insincere lives. What we all need is not so much to enter into a long, heated discussion concerning the meaning of

these words, which are quite simple, but a true yielding to God, asking Him to make these things real and deep and abiding in us.

III. THE MARKS OF A SPIRIT-CONTROLLED LIFE, Galatians 5:16–23.

This brief passage contrasts the life of one identified with Christ, and one without Christ. It opens with a pronouncement regarding the conflict between our fleshly life and the leading of the Holy Spirit. The late Professor J. Agar Beet summarizes this conflict excellently. "The flesh is the visible side of man, animated matter. Mysteriously pervading it, preserving it from corruption and giving to it growth and well-being, is the invisible spirit. Thus in man meet, and at every point interpenetrate the seen and unseen worlds; the one destined to crumble soon into its original dust, the other created for endless life. We have thus the unseen world within us, actually present to our inmost consciousness. Now each of these elements claims to rule our entire action and to mould our inner life. And they are in absolute opposition. The flesh, acting upon us through desires aroused by material objects around, tends to beget various kinds of actions, many of them indisputably bad. . . . But in absolute opposition to the flesh is the one Spirit of God, whom God has given to dwell in the hearts of His people, that thus their spirit may have (Rom. 8:10) immortal life, and be in them an all-wise guide. . . . The evil influences of the flesh are still a power against which the Christian must needs be ever on his guard. But his warfare is shared by the Spirit of God, against whom even the flesh is powerless. Consequently, the presence of the Spirit in our hearts has already in us put an end, as we abide in faith, to the rule of the flesh." — *Prof. J. Agar Beet.*

This statement is followed by two lists — the works of the flesh (vs. 19–21), and the fruit of the Spirit (vs. 22, 23). "The list of fleshly vices is not complete, but it is comprehensive. Those selected were prevalent in all parts of the Roman Empire and were probably those most common in Galatia. They are pitifully prevalent in all parts of the world today. It is possible to divide the list as follows: (1) Sins of impurity; (2) idolatry; (3) infractions of the law of love; (4) intemperance. The first includes 'fornication,' 'uncleanness,' and 'lasciviousness,' the last of which denotes open and shameless indulgence in impurity. In the second group are 'idolatry' and 'sorcery.' The former was commonly united in its practices with the vices which precede; while its usual attendant was 'sorcery.' The latter denotes those forms of magic which ascribe to natural objects supernatural powers and are the result of false views of God and his world. The third group contains eight of the fifteen 'works of the flesh' here enumerated. All have their common origin in a heart devoid of love. The last group of vices includes sins of excess: 'drunkenness' and 'revellings,' which latter term may denote the more open and riotous orgies from which 'drunkenness' may result." — *C. R. Erdman.*

We cannot go into detail regarding this beautiful cluster of the fruits of the Spirit, but let us continue briefly from the very rich pages of my friend Dr. Charles Erdman. "By way of striking contrast there is now arrayed against these fleshly vices a list of Christian virtues, under the term 'the fruit of the Spirit.' This fruit is one, yet manifold. All these graces spring from a common root. All are the products of a soul which is controlled by the Spirit of Christ. It is common to divide these graces into three groups, although such a division may be unnecessary and somewhat arbitrary. First of all stands 'love,' the queen of the graces. This, with 'joy' and 'peace' turns the thought toward God. . . . The second group of graces directs the attention toward our fellow men. 'Longsuffering' denotes that patient endurance under continual provocation which Paul praises in his hymn of love (1 Cor. 13). It bears all things and endures all things; it never fails. 'Kindness' . . . indicates a desire for the welfare even of those who are continually taxing our patience. 'Goodness' is love in action. It not only desires the welfare of others; it secures that welfare. . . . The last three graces refer more particularly to oneself. 'Faithfulness' or fidelity, denotes the quality of a heart which is ever conscious of its own integrity and honesty and sincerity. 'Meekness' denotes

273

PHILIPPIANS 1:9. And this I pray, that your love may abound yet more and more in knowledge and all discernment.

10. So that we may approve the things that are excellent. That ye may be sincere and void of offence unto the day of Christ.

11. Being filled with the fruits of righteousness, which are through Jesus Christ, unto the glory and praise of God.

---

a patient endurance of wrongs, contentedness, quietness, self-effacement. 'Self-control' implies the rational restraint of all the natural impulses. It may, therefore, well crown the list of virtues which are mentioned in connection with the conflict between 'the flesh' and 'the Spirit'; for it is exactly this matter of self-control which is especially in mind." — *Dr. Charles Erdman.*

IV. **THE ROOT AND FRUIT OF CONSTANTLY CHOOSING THE BEST,** Philippians 1:9–11. This has been for years one of my favorite chapters. Here Paul tells believers four things which they should do with the Gospel that has saved them. In the midst of the chapter is one of Paul's prayers, and it is this prayer that is assigned to our lesson. 9. **And this I pray, that your love may abound yet more and more in knowledge and all discernment.** "The Greek word is — That your love shall pour over — as the bucket which stands under a streamlet issuing from a fissure in the rocks pours over on all sides; I pray, he says, that your love may pour over towards each other, and specially towards God. Oh, that we might know this and be perfected in love, that there might be room for nothing more, that this might effect our whole being; for, depend upon it, when the love of God really fills the heart, the accent of the voice, the movements of our body, the look on the face, the demeanour, everything is affected. . . . If your love abounds more and more, you will not only know, but you will discern, you will be able to detect the traces of the footsteps of your Lord where other men fail to detect them, and hear His voice amid the jangling mart and the hubbub of the city." — *F. B. Meyer.* The word here translated *discernment* is that from which we derive our word *aesthetics*, occurring here only in the New Testament, although a closely related word is found in Hebrews 5:14, where it is used "to denote the organs of moral sense." 10. **So that we may approve the things that are excellent.** The word translated "approve" is the verb *dokimazo*, and inasmuch as it occurs also in 1 Thessalonians 5:21, assigned to our lesson, and seems to be the key word, I would like to place before my readers the rich study by my friend Mr. Kenneth S. Wuest. "The word has in it the idea of proving a thing whether it be worthy to be received or not. In classical Greek, it is the technical word for putting money to the test. In the New Testament almost always it implies that the proof is victoriously surmounted. The word further implies that the trial was itself made in the expectation and hope that the issue would be such. In all events, there was no contrary hope or expectation. *Dokimazo* is used generally of God, but never of Satan, for Satan never puts to the test in order that he may approve." — *Kenneth S. Wuest.* **That ye may be sincere and void of offence unto the day of Christ.** "*Sincere* signifies simplicity of purpose, and singleness of heart in following out that purpose. Sincere Christians cherish in their hearts no views, no principles, adverse to the Christian calling. . . . *Without offence* is the character of the man who walks without stumbling. For there are obstacles in the way, and they are often unexpected. Grant a man to be in a measure sincere — the call of the gospel has really won his heart. Yet as he goes, there fall in trials, temptations, difficulties, that seem to come upon him from without, as it were, and he stumbles: he fails to preserve the uprightness of his life, and to keep his eye fixed with due steadiness on the end of his faith." — *Robert Rainy.* 11. **Being filled with the fruits of righteousness, which are through Jesus Christ, unto the glory and praise of God.** " 'Righteousness' indicates a true relation to God made possible by faith, and then denotes, as in this verse, that moral uprightness and

PHILIPPIANS 4:8. Finally, brethren, whatsoever things are true, whatsoever things are honorable, whatsoever things are just, whatsoever things are pure, whatsoever things are lovely, whatsoever things are of good report; if there be any virtue, and if there be any praise, think on these things.

---

that holy activity which result in a harvest of good works. Fruitful lives should be the visible outcome of wise and discerning love. This is the very purpose of the apostle's prayer. However, fruitfulness is possible only by union with Christ. Just as it is understood that the sensitive moral judgments and discriminations for which Paul prays are possible only by the power of the indwelling Spirit, so, as here expressed, fruitfulness in life and service is dependent upon the power of Christ and upon a continual abiding in him. . . . When Christians show toward one another a love which, while fervent, is at the same time wise and discriminating, when their choices develop into characters which are transparent and free from offense, when their lives are rich in the 'fruits of righteousness,' then God is glorified, for such transformed human lives are a demonstration of divine power." — *Charles R. Erdman*.

V. **A CLUSTER OF BETTER THINGS,** Philippians 4:8. **Finally, brethren, whatsoever things are true, whatsoever things are honorable, whatsoever things are just, whatsoever things are pure, whatsoever things are lovely, whatsoever things are of good report; if there be any virtue, and if there be any praise, think on these things.** The Apostle seems to have wanted to conclude at 3:1, and now seeks to conclude again, using the same word, "finally." "Speaking roughly, the words here may be said to be arranged in a descending scale. The first four describe the character of the actions themselves; the fifth and sixth point to the moral approbation which they conciliate, while the seventh and eighth are thrown in as an after-thought that no motive may be omitted." — *J. B. Lightfoot*. *Virtue* "is the *virile* element of the common humanity that comes out in virtue. It is virtue when the will, against a thousand pleas of expediency and of ease, decides for duty against gain, against selfish pleasure, against a comfortable drift down the stream of unworthy popular opinion or popular practice. It is virtue which says, perhaps with the whole world of man's society on the other side, that this must be my choice, for the solitary reason that it is right." — *H. C. G. Moule*.

VI. **A FINAL EXHORTATION,** 1 Thessalonians 5:21, 22. Though this passage is not assigned for the printed text, we ought to have it before us: "Prove all things; hold fast that which is good; abstain from every form of evil." The word here translated *prove* is the same as *approve* in Philippians 1:10, which we have already discussed. There is a double exhortation here, positive and negative. Normally Paul places the negative first, followed by the positive, but here he reverses the order. If we have put to the test all things that come before us for decision, and have differentiated the good from the evil, we are admonished here to cling to the one, whatever happens, and to shun the other. (The verb, *hold fast* is found also in Luke 8:15; 1 Corinthians 11:2; Hebrews 3:6.)

THE LESSON IN LIFE, LITERATURE, AND ARCHAEOLOGY.

The famous English poetess, Dora Greenwell, wrote from the beautiful Keswick lake district in 1864, "Nature is very fair, but to me she can never be but the background to some affection which puts a soul into her; then she smiles and speaks. One feels very near to God, I think, among these hills, and near to all whom one best loves; near, too, to one's youth and childhood, and to all that might have been in one's life, and was not, and to all the unspeakable felicity that God will yet work within us through Him whom He has chosen. How often, during these past days, have I thought of the words — 'If God so clothe the grass of the field.' Every stone seems here instinct with beauty, something lovely thrusting itself out of every chink. . . . Mountains I have a respect for, as things having life in themselves; they are companions, full of steadfastness, yet of change and mystery." — *Dora Greenwell.*

A TRUTH FOR THE CLASS TO CARRY AWAY.

Our lesson begins with an exhortation concerning the kingdom of God. A kingdom means a king, and the exercise of authority. We have recently seen the great love of a people for a newly crowned queen in the coronation at London. But Britain is poor today. She has lost her place as the great empire of the earth, and spiritually she is at a low ebb. When the kingdom of God is finally established, it will be one of absolute righteousness, when all the enemies of God and man will forever be defeated (see 1 Cor. 15:25). That kingdom has not yet been established, and you and I are not kings, but we can live as members of that kingdom now, and those who belong to Christ will be the only eternal and blessed subjects of that beneficent reign.

Is the kingdom of God actually established by men or by God? Do you think that the nations of the earth today are nearer the New Testament ideal of the kingdom of God than they were at the beginning of this century, or further away? Can a person's faculty for discerning the best be cultivated? How did Christ himself illustrate throughout His life this principle of choosing the best? Where would you say was just about the ideal example in human relationships of one choosing the best for another? (I would think it would be in the desires of a Christian father and mother for any one of their children, with plans that make for the realization of these ideals.)

LESSON VII. — August 15.

SELF-DISCIPLINE FOR GROWTH (TEMPERANCE). —
Matthew 16:24–25; 1 Corinthians 9:24–27; 2 Timothy 2:3–5; Hebrews 12:1–4.

PRINTED TEXT, Matthew 16:24, 25; 1 Corinthians 9:24–27; 2 Timothy 2:4, 5; Hebrews 12:1–4.

Devotional Reading: Exodus 20:1–17.

Beginner Topic: GLAD IN GOD'S HOUSE.
> Lesson Material: 2 Chronicles 34; Psalm 84.
> Memory Verse: I was glad when they said unto me, Let us go unto the house of Jehovah. Psalm 122:1.

Primary Topic: LEARNING TO DO RIGHT.
> Lesson Material: 1 Corinthians 9:24–25.
> Memory Verse: And thou shalt do that which is right and good in the sight of Jehovah. Deuteronomy 6:18.

Junior Topic: LEARNING TO DO RIGHT.
> Lesson Material: 1 Corinthians 9:24–25; 2 Timothy 2:4–5.
> Memory Verse: And thou shalt do that which is right and good in the sight of Jehovah. Deuteronomy 6:18.

Intermediate-Senior Topic: MASTERING OURSELVES.
> Lesson Material: Matthew 16:24–25; 1 Corinthians 9:24–27; 2 Timothy 2:3–5; Hebrews 12:1–4.
> Memory Verse: If any man would come after me, let him deny himself, and take up his cross, and follow me. Matthew 16:24.

Topic for Young People and Adults: SELF-DISCIPLINE FOR GROWTH.
> Lesson Material: Matthew 16:24–25; 1 Corinthians 9:24–27; 2 Timothy 2:3–5; Hebrews 12:1–4.
> Memory Verse: If any man would come after me, let him deny himself, and take up his cross, and follow me. Matthew 16:24.

THE TEACHER AND HIS CLASS.

The Younger Classes may begin this lesson on self-discipline and self-control with an illustration from the editor's own experience. Every year while a pastor in Coatesville, Pa., it was my privilege to have as a speaker for the men's group of the church Dr. Howard A. Kelly, one of the greatest surgeons of his generation, and a devout Christian. About ten o'clock one evening, when the meeting was over, ice cream with strawberries, cake and coffee were passed. Dr. Kelly touched none of it, and I dared to ask him why this was so. He replied that he was to perform a major operation the next morning and could not afford to stay awake that night. In other words, he deprived himself of something he would have greatly enjoyed for the sake of his patient. This is a lesson in self-denial for Jesus' sake.

The Older Classes may be introduced to this lesson by an incident from the life of the editor, taking place this very month. Contemplating a trip to Boston, I wrote to a friend, one of the most brilliant young college men in the country today, now on a teaching fellowship at Harvard University, asking if we could have dinner together some evening. He replied in the affirmative. When the time came, however, the young man called to say that he was studying for oral examinations, preparatory to being accepted as a candidate for a doctorate degree, and was sleeping only three or four hours a night, so would like to be excused. He had a great goal before him and was allowing nothing to interfere with his progress toward that goal.

THE LESSON IN ITS SETTING.

Time. — The words taken from Matthew's Gospel were uttered in April, A.D. 29. The First Epistle to the Corinthians was written A.D. 57–59; the Second Epistle to Timothy about A.D. 65, and the Epistle to the Hebrews approximately the same time.

Place. — The words from our Lord were given near Caesarea Philippi. Corinth was a great city in Greece.

Paul was in Rome when he wrote the letters to Timothy.

THE PLAN OF THE LESSON.

SUBJECT: The Principles of Self-Repudiation and Self-Control for Any Man Desiring to Follow Christ as Set Forth by Our Lord and the Early Church.

I. The Surrender of Self, the Prerequisite for Christian Discipleship, Matthew 16:24, 25.

II. The Principle Requirement in Running the Christian Race, 1 Corinthians 9:24–27.

III. The Christian as a Soldier, 2 Timothy 2:3–5.

IV. The Example of Christ, Hebrews 12:1–4.

THE TEACHER'S LIBRARY.

On Matthew 16:24, 25, see especially a great series of sermons in W. M. Clow: *The Secret of the Lord*, 96–109; H. P. Liddon: *Sermons on Some Words of Christ*, 79–99; R. F. Horton: *The Commandments of Jesus*, 31–46; G. Campbell Morgan: *The Westminster Pulpit*, Vol. 2, pp. 105–112; W. M. Clow: *The Cross in Christian Experience*, 231–242; James Hastings: *Great Texts of the Bible*, St. Mark, 318–333; H. T. Trumbull: *Our Misunderstood Bible*, 130–144; and J. M. Gibbon in the *Contemporary Pulpit*, 2nd series, Vol. 8, pp. 84–102.

On 1 Corinthians 9:24–27, in addition to commentaries on this Epistle, see Alexander Maclaren: *Expositions of Holy Scripture, Corinthians*, 146–153; on verse 25, a magnificent sermon which few will be able to consult, by J. A. Beet, in The *Contemporary Pulpit*, 2nd series, Vol. 7, pp. 85–110; James Hastings: *Great Texts of the Bible, First Corinthians*, 264–270, and Alexander Maclaren, as above, 153–163. On verse 27, see J. S. Holden: *The Gospel of the Second Chance*, 39–54. On the historical aspects of the entire passage there is a fine chapter in J. S. Howson: *The Metaphors of St. Paul*, 125–176.

On 2 Timothy 2:3, see John Henry Jowett: *The Whole Armour of God*, 163–178. On Hebrews 12:1, 2, the following will be found helpful: G. Campbell Morgan: *The Westminster Pulpit*, Vol. 4, pp. 81–88; Vol. 3, pp. 185–192; John Hutton: *There They Crucified Him*, 1–11; and on 3 and 4, Robert M. Edgar: *The Philosophy of the Cross*, 238–255.

AUDIO-VISUAL AIDS.

FILMSTRIP: "Chance of a Lifetime," National W.C.T.U., 53 fr., b&w. "Gives simple scientific explanation of relation of alcohol to traffic accidents."

| FILMSTRIP: "Dollars and Sense," National W.C.T.U., 52 fr., b&w. Deals with gambling, drinking and smoking. Shows common sense attitudes toward these evils. | FILMSTRIP: "Tower of Strength," National W.C.T.U., 55 fr., b&w. A highly picturized story of the rules of good health. Brings in total abstinence from alcohol at end. |

MATTHEW 16:24. Then said Jesus unto his disciples, If any man would come after me, let him deny himself, and take up his cross, and follow me.

Probably no lesson on self-discipline and self-control can be called a pleasant study, but it does present a great Biblical truth too often neglected, though emphasized both in the teachings of our Lord and the life of His apostles. Unless there is something of this in our lives as Christians we are not manifesting to the world our relationship to Christ as we should.

I. THE SURRENDER OF SELF — THE PREREQUISITE FOR CHRISTIAN DISCIPLESHIP, Matthew 16:24, 25. In the verses immediately preceding those assigned here, we read that it has been necessary for the Lord to rebuke Peter, who was attempting to persuade Jesus that He need not go up to Jerusalem to suffer and die, as He had just announced. The words spoken here are also to be found in Mark 8:34, 35 and Luke 9:23, 24. These words were often repeated by the Lord Jesus. Matthew gives them elsewhere in 10:37–39; Luke, in 14:25–27 and 17:33; and John, in 12:25. 24. Then said Jesus unto his disciples, If any man would come after me, let him deny himself, and take up his cross, and follow me. The word *disciple* means a *learner*, a *pupil*, and then, a *follower*. This is the idea expressed in the Lord's great commission found at the end of this Gospel (Matt. 28:19). There has been a great deal written on this matter of taking up one's cross. We may first look at the general interpretation as expressed by W. M. Clow. "Your cross is something you can take or you can refuse. It may be some special burden of the cares of others, or of the service of man which you can decline. It may be some limitation or poverty which you can leave behind you by accepting some lower ideal of life. It may be some mode of life, humbling and difficult which you might avoid. It may be some refusal of place, or power, or ease, or home, or love, which in conscience you are compelled to make. It may be some sacrifice of a high aim, an alluring ambition, a heart-satisfying purpose, and a meek acceptance of obscurity and toil. It is surely to live chastely in an impure world, to be just and true, and loving to those who scorn you, to care for the glory of God above everything else, to lay your powers on the altar of sacrifice to Christ, and to follow Him, cost what it may." — *W. M. Clow.*

I believe, however, that the deeper idea in the mind of Christ has been properly set forth by that fine scholar, Dr. Henry Clay Trumbull, when he says, " 'Cross-bearing' is ordinarily considered the bearing of burdens, or the enduring of trials in Christ's service, or for Christ's sake. 'Taking up the cross,' or 'bearing the cross,' as the phrase is employed in the New Testament text, or as it was understood at the opening of our Christian era, was the surrender or devotion of one's life to Christ's service. The 'cross,' or, more literally, the 'stake' was the instrument of execution for criminals, as that word was employed in classic and in Jewish literature. It being customary for a condemned criminal, on his way to the place of execution, to carry upon his shoulder the stake to which he was to be fastened, or by which he was to be transfixed, the term 'taking up the cross,' or 'bearing the cross,' came to be equivalent to our modern term, 'halter-wearing,' or 'going to the gallows.' He who bore a cross on his shoulder was recognized as one who was appointed to die, and he must stand or move with that grim fact staring him in the face." — *H. C. Trumbull.* "As men redeemed by Jesus Crucified, you cannot be like your Lord if you go softly through life, crowned not with thorns but with roses, bearing in your hands all that makes life a pleasant dream, such as Pagan poets loved to picture it, and knowing nothing of the moral illumination which they share who freely choose to carry the Cross of Christ. When life

25. For whosoever would save his life shall lose it: and whosoever shall lose his life for my sake shall find it.

1 CORINTHIANS 9:24. Know ye not that they that run in a race run all, but one receiveth the prize? Even so run; that ye may attain.

---

is cushioned and carpeted with the refinements of civilization, it is not possible to follow Christ without some determined effort, some plan and method of action, which confronts self in the details of action, and takes up the cross in the midst of ordinary social duties." — *H. P. Liddon.* 25. **For whosoever would save his life shall lose it: and whosoever shall lose his life for my sake shall find it.** "Now what is man's own self? Is it his body? is it his mind? is it his spirit? or is it all three harmoniously combined, and in co-operation? No. Body, mind, and spirit are rather the God-given materials, they are the agents and the instruments, by which and out of which a man's true self is to be built and raised up. Body, mind, and spirit, as they are given us by God in birth, constitute the gamut. What is bad, then, or good, is man's own self; the body and character that he makes for himself out of the materials which God has given him. And that character, the man's own self, may become so good that at death God will judge it worthy of having new material entrusted to its charge. . . . A man's own self is a man's character, that which a man elects to become, that which he wants to become, that which it is his aim and intention to be. Character is self, character is life. A man's own self is that which he chooses to become in the sight of God. Well, now then the question is, 'What shall it profit a man if he gain the whole world, and lose or damage his own self? or what shall a man give in exchange for his character?' The loss of the soul is a great mystery. . . . Souls are not simply lost at death. The losing of a soul is a process. When you lose a piece of money from your pocket it is quite instantaneous. But losing of a soul cannot be done in that way. A man cannot jump down from goodness to badness. A man cannot become a devil by merely willing to become one. There is a process, and you can watch a soul deteriorate, fluttering down, down, lower, lower." — *J. M. Gibbon.* Of course ultimate loss of the soul is eternal death — from which there is only one deliverance — salvation in Christ. "Think for a moment what a splendid procession of men and women pass before our eyes whose lives give assent to that truth. Spenser, refusing to be patronized, and living in neglect and penury, but leaving his 'Faerie Queene' as an immortal flower of his spirit. Milton, disdaining the joys which courted him and the honours he might have worn, choosing to suffer affliction with those whom he held to be the people of God, and leaving behind him that record of a life lived out as in the great Taskmaster's eye, and that poem whose visions are shining with heavenly light. Joan of Arc, relinquishing all that is sweet and tender to youth, and refusing to be seduced by the glittering rewards that were laid at her feet, neither quailing nor uttering querulous complaint when she faced scorn and calumny and death, and yet finding a life which was larger and nobler than she dreamed, and a praise which was sweeter than she coveted. Mazzini, giving up all that men commonly think makes life worth living, spending his years in privation and in peril, and yet entering into a life of such scope and power, that Italy knows no dearer name and no loftier inspiration. Florence Nightingale twice turning her back on the sweet and joy of life, once to lift up the mean lives of helpless girls in a London street, and again to walk in Scutari, 'through miles of pallets thickly laid, with sickness in its foulest guise,' and finding a life which every good woman would count it a supreme joy to live." — *W. M. Clow.*

II. THE PRINCIPLE REQUIREMENT IN RUNNING THE CHRISTIAN RACE, 1 Corinthians 9:24-27. We turn now from the theme of cross-bearing to another which presents self-discipline and self-control under a different figure of speech — the running of a race. Many of St. Paul's illustrations are taken from the great athletic games, so popular and famous in Greek civilization. 24. **Know**

25. And every man that striveth in the games exerciseth self-control in all things. Now they *do it* to receive a corruptible crown; but we an incorruptible.

26. I therefore so run, as not uncertainly; so fight I, as not beating the air.

---

ye not that they that run in a race run all, but one receiveth the prize? **Even so run; that ye may attain.** The words of Dr. Charles R. Erdman, in his valuable little book on this Epistle, may serve as a perfect introduction to the study of this passage. "His reference is probably to the Isthmian games, named from the isthmus on which Corinth stood. These contests, like the Olympian, Pythian, and Nemean, constituted a great national and religious festival, and every second year drew eager throngs to the city of Corinth. Only freemen could contend in these games, and the contestants must give satisfactory proof that for ten months they had undergone the necessary preliminary training. For thirty days before the contests, all candidates were required to attend exercises at the gymnasium, and only when they had properly fulfilled all such conditions were they allowed to contend in the sight of the assembled throngs. The herald proclaimed the name and the country of each contestant, and also announced the name of the victor, who was crowned with a garland of pine leaves or parsley or ivy. The family of the victor was regarded with honor, and when he returned to his native city a breach was made in the walls to allow him to enter, the purpose of this being to indicate that a town to which such a citizen belonged had no need of walls for its defense. The victorious hero was immortalized in verse; he was assigned a foremost seat when attending all future contests." — *Dr. Charles R. Erdman.* (For other passages in Paul's writings, referring to life as a race, see especially Philippians 3:12–14; 2 Timothy 4:7, 8, and Hebrews 12:1.) **25. And every man that striveth in the games exerciseth self-control in all things. Now they *do it* to receive a corruptible crown; but we an incorruptible.** The words of Professor J. Agar Beet on this passage are especially rich, and are rarely seen today. "Now mark this — no young Greek ever woke up in the morning and found his brow encircled with a wreath. No young Greek ever obtained the prize because he was somebody's son. No one ever obtained it by money. The only way in which it could possibly be obtained was by a personal victory — by a mighty personal effort, and by a personal victory. What a lesson that is for you and me. If you and I are to wear a crown, we must get it as the Greek athletes got it. We must get it by a conflict which requires our uttermost effort. We can get it only by a victory over a personal antagonist. St. Paul's idea was that if he was ever to be crowned, he must do it by a victory that required all his effort."

The same metaphor of training occurs in 2 Timothy 2:5. "It is a crown of 'glory' and that means a lustrousness of character imparted by radiation and reflection from the central light of the glory of God. 'Then shall the righteous blaze out like the sun in the Kingdom of My Father.' Our eyes are dim, but we can at least divine the far-off flashing of that great light, and may ponder upon what hidden depths and miracles of transformed perfectness and unimagined lustre wait for us, dark and limited as we are here, in the assurance that we all shall be changed into the 'likeness of the body of His glory.' It is a crown of 'righteousness.' Though that phrase may mean the wreath that rewards righteousness, it seems more in accordance with the other similar expressions to regard it as the material of which the crown is composed. It is not enough that there should be festal gladness, but enough that there should be fulness of life. To accord with the intense moral earnestness of the Christian system there must be, emphatically, in the Christian hope, cessation of all sin and investiture with all purity." — *Alexander Maclaren.*

26. **I therefore so run, as not uncertainly; so fight I, as not beating the air.** To run uncertainly is to run without a definite object, and to beat the air means

27. But I buffet my body, and bring it into bondage. Lest by any means, after that I have preached to others, I myself should be rejected.

to go through all the motions of battle without defeating anyone. Paul says he is determined to run with an object before him, and whenever he strikes, to really strike an enemy. **27. But I buffet my body, and bring it into bondage.** "Literally, the first part of this phrase means, 'I strike under the eye, I beat black and blue.' The body was to be the absolute property of the spirit, to obey its directions implicitly, as a slave those of its master. By a series of violent blows on the face, as it were, it was to be taught to submit itself to the dictation of its superior." — *J. J. Lias.* "Boxers generally strike someone else's body, but here this boxer strikes his own body. Now that is very characteristic of St. Paul. Every man has an antagonist in his own flesh and blood. That is the teaching of it. Let your flesh and blood rule, and you are ruined. It will be a fetter that will fasten you down into sloth. Your flesh and blood will prompt all kinds of evil, directly and indirectly. Every man has a foe in his own flesh and blood. Now mark, every time you force your flesh and blood, for God's sake, go to and do what otherwise it would not do, a blow is struck against your antagonist; it is a blow struck against the dominion of flesh and blood." — *J. A. Beet.* **Lest by any means, after that I have preached to others, I myself should be rejected.** "There is no greater danger attaching to the life of Christian service than the danger of presumptuous pride. I mean the pride which manifests itself in an independence of the ordinary means of grace, or prayer, and of the Word of God. I am convinced that that is the cause of much of the failure in many lives here. There is a pride which says, 'I can dispense with the Word of God,' which persists in living on a minimum of prayer and communion with God, and in yet going about the work of God as of old; a pride, which, like Uzziah's, seeks carnal prominence in spiritual things. For that was his sin. He sought a carnal prominence in service which God had ordained was to be of an entirely spiritual order. How many men likewise have taken carnal methods to secure positions in the Church of God. How many have proudly taken the government of life into their own hands, priding themselves on what they call 'pulling wires'? How many of us are there who have done despite to the Spirit of God in usurping His office in our own lives? . . . Is it possible to avoid the peril of unheeded self-discovery, the peril of presumptuous pride, the peril of the uncounted cost? Yes, blessed be God, it is! How? By prayerful, careful, honest and humble union with Jesus Christ. We have all heard of the captain who was taking his vessel through a rocky channel when a nervous passenger said to him, in order to assure herself of her safety, 'Captain, I suppose you know all the rocks round about here?' 'No, madam, not one of them. But I know where the deep water is.' These are only some of the rocks — there are many more and they are all charted — but, praise be to God, here is the deep water — fellowship, close and clear with the Son of God." — *J. Stuart Holden.*

III. **THE CHRISTIAN AS A SOLDIER,** 2 Timothy 2:3–5. The Second Epistle of Paul to Timothy was the last letter Paul ever wrote that is included in the Canonical Scriptures of the New Testament. He wrote this from the deep dungeons of the Mamertine prison in Rome shortly before he was executed under Nero, perhaps within a very few days of his death. Calvin, metaphorically, says that the Epistle was written with Paul's own blood. This, with the First Epistle to Timothy and the Epistle to Titus are called the Pastoral Epistles, Paul's final word to Timothy and other ministers of the Gospel regarding their conduct, their life, their work, and frequent passages of a prophetic nature concerning the dark days that were ahead for the Church. In the three verses preceding this second chapter, Paul speaks of some of the sufferings he was undergoing at this very time, in addition to being a prisoner of Rome, chained day and night to a soldier. Knowing that Timothy also might some day suffer in a similar way, he thus writes

281

2 TIMOTHY 2:4. No soldier on service entangleth himself in the affairs of *this* life; that he may please him who enrolled him as a soldier.

5. And if also a man contend in the games, he is not crowned, except he have contended lawfully.

HEBREWS 12:1. Therefore let us also, seeing we are compassed about with so great a cloud of witnesses, lay aside every weight, and the sin which doth so easily beset us, and let us run with patience the race that is set before us.

---

to him. **4. No soldier on service entangleth himself in the affairs of *this* life; that he may please him who enrolled him as a soldier. 5. And if also a man contend in the games, he is not crowned, except he have contended lawfully.** "The Roman army was the one great organization of which it was still possible, in that age of boundless social corruption, to think and speak with right-minded admiration and respect. . . . Even during active warfare it checked individual license; and when the conquest was over it was the representative and mainstay of order and justice against high-handed anarchy and wrong. Its officers several times appear in the narrative portions of the New Testament, and they make a favourable impression upon us. If they are fair specimens of the military men in the Roman Empire at that period, then the Roman army must have been indeed a fine service. . . . But military service implies, what athletic contests do not, vigilant, unwearying and organized foe. In many athletic contests one's opponent is a rival rather than an enemy. . . . Military service is either perpetual warfare or perpetual preparation for it. And just such is the Christian life: it is either a conflict, or a preparation for one. The soldier, so long as he remains in the service, can never say, 'I may lay aside my arms and my drill: all enemies are conquered: there will never be another war.' And the Christian, so long as he remains in this world, can never think that he may cease to watch and to pray, because the victory is won, and he will never be tempted any more." — *Alfred Plummer.*

IV. **THE EXAMPLE OF CHRIST,** Hebrews 12:1–4. This passage opens with the word *therefore,* which means the exhortation here logically follows what preceded it, namely, the remarkable chapter on the persevering heroes of faith. **1. Therefore let us also, seeing we are compassed about with so great a cloud of witnesses.** Only last week I received a letter asking what I thought this "cloud of witnesses" might be, if it could mean loved ones gone before looking down from heaven. Lenski is right, I believe, when he says, "The souls of the saints are at rest, no longer concerned with the trials occurring on earth; the Scriptures teach that they behold the heavenly glories, and say nothing about their beholding and watching earthly events. These saints are not 'witnesses' that see our faith and testify about us; God does not ask them to testify about us. They are witnesses, whose life, works, sufferings, death attest their own faith, testify to us through the pages of Holy Writ and in other history that they were true men of faith indeed (the faith defined in 11:1)." — *R. C. H. Lenski.* **Lay aside every weight, and the sin which doth so easily beset us, and let us run with patience the race that is set before us.** "Anything that hinders running toward that goal. Love may be a weight, learning may be a weight. I am mentioning the highest things of set purpose, feeling that it is not necessary to discuss the lower. Anything that dims the vision of the ultimate, that kills the passion, is a weight. 'Ye did run well. What did hinder you?' Well, that which hindered you is the weight, and in view of this large purpose, in view of this ultimate victory, in view of this stupendous intention of God, beneficent, and glorious, and beautiful, the writer charges the men who name the name of Christ to lay aside the weights. Yet, brethren, I think he touches something that lies nearer to the centre of the whole necessity, when he says, 'and the sin that doth so easily beset.' What is the sin that doth so easily beset? I recognize the difficulty of answering the question. I take that

2. Looking unto Jesus the author and perfecter of *our* faith, who for the joy that was set before him endured the cross, despising shame, and hath sat down at the right hand of the throne of God.

3. For consider him that hath endured such gainsaying of sinners against himself, that ye wax not weary, fainting in your souls.

4. Ye have not yet resisted unto blood, striving against sin.

---

word and bluntly translate, 'the sin in good standing around.' I suggest to you that the word means just exactly that — that the plain translation touches its deepest meaning. Sin in good standing around, sin that is not looked upon as vulgar. The word *sin* here must be interpreted by its use throughout this letter, and the sin against which he warns those who would run the race is the sin of unbelief." — *G. Campbell Morgan.* **2. Looking unto Jesus the author and perfecter of *our* faith, who for the joy that was set before him endured the cross, despising shame, and hath sat down at the right hand of the throne of God. 3. For consider him that hath endured such gainsaying of sinners against himself, that ye wax not weary, fainting in your souls. 4. Ye have not yet resisted unto blood, striving against sin.** "But such an one must have an Object before him as well, in order to keep up his courage unto the end; and so the believer is bidden to look stedfastly upon Jesus, who Himself is the Leader and Completer of faith; not exactly our faith, as we have it in the Authorized Version, but of faith as such. His was the life of faith in all its perfection. In view of the joy set before Him, the joy of having His own redeemed ones with Him in the glory, He went through the bitter anguish of the cross, despising its shame, and now, in answer to all that, God the Father has seated Him as Man at His own right hand on the eternal throne. His victory is ours as we recognize our union with Him. He then is to be the Object before the souls of His people. And so we read, 'Consider him that endureth such contradiction of sinners against Himself, lest ye be wearied and faint in your minds.' In the hour of discouragement when one feels inclined to cry with Jacob, 'All these things are against me,' lift up your eyes, tempted one, and look upon Him who knew such grief as you shall never know, and yet who sits as Victor now in highest glory. Let Him be your heart's Object. Let Him be your soul's delight, and lifted above the cares and griefs of the present moment, you will be enabled to run unweariedly and without fainting, your appointed race. And if at times you are tempted to think that no one else has ever been called upon to endure such trials as those to which you have been exposed, learn to think soberly in regard to this, for the fact of the matter is, many another has suffered unspeakable tortures, such as you have not known. It is not of Christ he speaks in verse 4, but of those who for Christ's sake loved not their lives unto death, but chose death rather than any compromise with iniquity. To this great and final test manifestly no living saint has yet been called." — *H. A. Ironside.*

THE LESSON IN LIFE, LITERATURE, AND ARCHAEOLOGY.

Origen, in his great discourse, *Against Celsus*, in speaking about eating, drinking and fasting, said, "And therefore, so far as we are concerned, the followers of Pythagoras, who abstain from all things that contain life, may do as they please; only observe the different reason for abstaining from things that have life on the part of the Pythagoreans and our ascetics. For the former abstain on account of the fable about the transmigration of souls. We, however, when we do abstain, do so because 'we keep under our body, and bring it into subjection,' and desire 'to mortify our members that are upon the earth, fornication, uncleanness, inordinate affection, evil concupiscence'; and we use every effort to 'mortify the deeds of the flesh.'"

A TRUTH FOR THE CLASS TO CARRY AWAY.

At the conclusion of the lesson the fact should be emphasized that those who wrote these words — that is, those who wrote the major part of our lesson text — Paul, and the writer to the Hebrews, were real men who endured suffering, who met the realities of life, who practiced what they preached, and who finished the course set before them. We are not here reading philosophy or ethics, but the teaching of the Holy Spirit given through the lives of men living out what they wrote.

How did the Apostle Paul in his life fulfill the words of Christ in our lesson? How did Christ in His earthly life set forth the principles of 2 Corinthians 2:3–5? What phrase in the passage from the Epistle to the Hebrews could never apply to Christ? ("The sin that doth so easily beset us.") What happens if Christians prefer not to live this life of self-control? Where in the Gospels do we have a good illustration of one who in his early days did not practice what is set forth here? (Peter.)

LESSON VIII. — August 22.

CHRISTIAN GIVING. — Acts 20:35; 1 Corinthians 16:1–2; 2 Corinthians 8:1–9.

PRINTED TEXT, 1 Corinthians 16:1–2; 2 Corinthians 8:1–9.

Devotional Reading: Philippians 4:15–20.
Beginner Topic: THE CHILDREN'S GLAD DAY.
  Lesson Material: Matthew 19:13–15; Mark 10:13–16; Luke 18:15–17.
  Memory Verse: Sing praises unto Jehovah . . . with gladness. 2 Chronicles 29:30.
Primary Topic: GIVING OUR BEST.
  Lesson Material: 2 Corinthians 8:1–5.
  Memory Verse: It is more blessed to give than to receive. Acts 20:35.
Junior Topic: GIVING OUR BEST.
  Lesson Material: 2 Corinthians 8:1–5.
  Memory Verse: In all things I gave you an example, that so laboring ye ought to help the weak, and to remember the words of the Lord Jesus, that he himself said, It is more blessed to give than to receive. Acts 20:35.
Intermediate-Senior Topic: JOY IN GIVING.
  Lesson Material: Acts 20:35; 1 Corinthians 16:1–2; 2 Corinthians 8:1–9.
  Memory Verse: It is more blessed to give than to receive. Acts 20:35.
Topic for Young People and Adults: GROWTH THROUGH CHRISTIAN GIVING.
  Lesson Material: Acts 20:35; 1 Corinthians 16:1–2; 2 Corinthians 8:1–9.
  Memory Verse: It is more blessed to give than to receive. Acts 20:35.

THE TEACHER AND HIS CLASS.

The Younger Classes may be introduced to this lesson on giving by the teacher asking a very simple question: At what season of the year do people in all Christian lands give gifts? Of course, Christmas. Now *why* do we give gifts, that is, what is the deep reason? Well, it is because we want to show our love for other people. It is not the size of the gift, nor the cost of it, but the idea of remembering others. Now the giving in our lesson comes from love, love for God and love for other fellow-Christians, but it is lifted up above the ordinary plane that marks our giving, because it is unto the Lord, for the glory of the Lord, and for bringing others close to the Lord.

The Older Classes may be introduced

to this lesson by being reminded of a great fundamental principle of life, that most of the grosser sins of life are only the perversion of things that are right. Gluttony is simply overeating, but eating in itself is necessary; sensuality is simply natural desires gone wild, and made first; a miser is one who not only makes money, but holds it and refuses to share or help others so that this matter of money can become a curse or a blessing. Wealth is never denounced in the Bible, but because we have to live, transact business, handle money, buy and sell, the Bible, and especially the New Testament, has innumerable passages regarding its proper use. Frankly, there is more about money in the teaching of Christ than there is about His atonement, though His atonement is far more important. There is more about money in Paul's two letters to Timothy than there is about the resurrection of Christ, though the resurrection is far more important.

THE LESSON IN ITS SETTING.

Time. — Paul's farewell to the Ephesian elders, which took place at the close of his third missionary journey, may be placed about A.D. 57. His two letters to the Corinthians were written about A.D. 59 and 60.

Place. — The passage taken from Acts was uttered by Paul at Miletus, on the seacoast of Asia Minor. The city of Corinth, to which the Corinthian letters were written, was a great metropolis in Greece.

THE PLAN OF THE LESSON.

SUBJECT: The Cardinal Place of Giving in the Normal Life of a Child of God.

I. A Word of Christ About the Blessedness of Giving, Acts 20:35.

II. Two Fundamental Principles in Christian Giving, 1 Corinthians 16:1, 2.

III. The Example of the Churches of Macedonia in the Matter of Giving, 2 Corinthians 8:1-6.

IV. Some Characteristics and Consequences of Christian Giving, 2 Corinthians 8:7-9.

THE TEACHER'S LIBRARY.

There is a vast literature on the subject of giving and Christian stewardship, among which the following can be recommended: James McConkey: *Money, the Acid Test;* John M. Versteeg: *The Deeper Meaning of Stewardship,* Abingdon Press, 1923; Charles A. Cook: *The Larger Stewardship,* Judson Press, 1923; Ina C. Brown: *Jesus' Teaching on the Use of Money;* P. E. Burroughs: *Our Lord's and Ours,* Sunday School Board of the Southern Baptist Convention; and an excellent tract by Robert E. Speer: "Proportionate Giving."

On the Corinthian Epistles I am using in this lesson, principally, the volume by Charles R. Erdman, the two massive commentaries on 1st and 2nd Corinthians by Charles Hodge, and that remarkable piece of concise exegesis in *The Interpreter's Commentary* on these two epistles, by J. A. McFadyen. On 2 Corinthians 8:1-9 see Alexander Maclaren: *Expositions of Holy Scripture, 2 Corinthians 7 — Philippians,* 20-35; on verse 7, G. Campbell Morgan in *The Westminster Pulpit,* Vol. 4, pp. 17-24; John Henry Jowett: *God Our Contemporary,* 142-154; on verse 5, a great sermon by Charles H. Spurgeon in *The Metropolitan Tabernacle Pulpit* for 1891, Vol. 38, pp. 625-636. On the whole passage one of the richest treatments is in a little volume by Andrew Murray: *Money,* 42-96. On 1 Corinthians 16:1 a great sermon by John Henry Jowett: *Apostolic Optimism,* 156-170. See also a superb article by J. R. Willis, "Collection," in James Hasting's *Dictionary of the Apostolic Church,* Vol. 1, pp. 223-225. Finally, one may find some good things in W. E. Chadwick: *The Pastoral Teaching of St. Paul,* especially pages 139 ff.

Just after completing this lesson, I received from the Zondervan Publishing Company a very interesting volume, *Christian Stewardship and Church Finance,* by H. W. Ellis, with a Foreword by J. D. Grey, president of the Southern Baptist Convention.

An excellent "Stewardship Bibliography and Audio-Visual Aids" may be purchased from the Joint Department of Stewardship and Benevolence of the National Council of the Churches of Christ, 297 Fourth Avenue, New York 10, for five cents.

AUDIO-VISUAL AIDS.

SOUND SLIDEFILM: "I Give Myself," Evangelical and Reformed Church, 77 fr., b&w. Manual. Two 12" 78 rpm records. Designed to produce deeper consecration in all areas of life, with the dedication of time, talent and possessions.

FILMSTRIP: "Why do we Live?" Church-Craft, 39 fr., b&w. This is part of the Living for Christ series, and shows stewardship of time, talent and talents.

There are a number of motion pictures on the general theme of stewardship, most of which would be suitable for the whole congregation.

They should probably be used as a whole church project in connection with a stewardship Sunday. One of the best is "All That I Have" (Concordia, 60 min., sd., b&w.). Others are "And Now I See" (Cathedral, 36 min., sd., b&w.), "Dedicated Men" (Family Films, 30 min., sd., b&w.), "For Good or Evil" (Wartburg, 45 min., sd., b&w.) and "No Greater Power" (Cathedral, 20 min., sd., b&w.).

---

1 CORINTHIANS 16:1. Now concerning the collection for the saints, as I gave order to the churches of Galatia, so also do ye.

Before we begin our study of this one aspect of the Christian life, giving, the teacher ought to make it clear that the practice of giving for a Christian is not something which he may ignore, if he chooses, and be just as good a Christian as those who live out the New Testament ideal of giving. There are certain things in life which we can ignore, and get along without, but which ignoring impoverishes us and dwarfs our very nature. A man can get along without friends, but it narrows his life, it greatly reduces the joy of living, it results in increasing selfishness, and it means an ever deepening loneliness, with which no man can be happy. So also in these Christian virtues, praying, Bible study, social work for the Lord Jesus, fruit bearing — we can get along without them; they do not save us. But in ignoring any one of them we greatly reduce the usefulness of our lives; our spiritual life shrivels instead of enlarging and becoming abundant, and we are displeasing to God. So as we begin this lesson let us take this with deadly seriousness. It is not something merely to talk about; it is something to practice and to rejoice in.

I. A WORD OF CHRIST ABOUT THE BLESSEDNESS OF GIVING, Acts 20:35. At the end of Paul's third missionary journey he had a strong intuition that he would never be in Asia Minor again, where some of his greatest work was done and where he had probably more friends than in any other one area in the world. Here were the Provinces of Galatia, Capadocia, Asia, Pamphilia, et cetera, the cities of Philadelphia, Colosse, Ephesus, Pergamus, Lystra and Derbe, et cetera. Travelling back to Jerusalem, he sent word ahead that he would like to see the elders of the great church at Ephesus, who came down to the shore at Miletus to meet him. His farewell is one of the most pathetic scenes in the Scripture. The verse for our lesson today is taken from the profound words, warnings and exhortations of the apostle, delivered at this time. Though it is not assigned to our printed text, I think we should quote it: "In all things I gave you an example, that so laboring ye ought to help the weak, and to remember the words of the Lord Jesus, that he himself said, It is more blessed to give than to receive" (Acts 20:35). The first thing about this verse is that though it quotes a statement of Christ's, actually one of His beatitudes, the words are not to be found in the Gospels. "We do not know on what particular occasion the words were spoken by the Lord, but we cannot read the Gospels and find a day on which He was not saying them in His life. It was the one thing which He who came not to be ministered unto but to minister was ever saying and which Calvary finally illustrated." — W. M. Furneaux. In all the church fathers of the first two centuries we will not find ten sentences from the lips of Jesus not recorded in the Gospels. This is the only one given in the New Testament not found in the Gospels.

II. TWO FUNDAMENTAL PRINCIPLES IN CHRISTIAN GIVING, 1 Corinthians 16:1, 2. Any serious Christian knows that the greatest single chapter on the resurrection in the Bible, and one of the greatest chapters in all the Scriptures, is Paul's magnificent unfolding of this truth in the 15th chapter of 1 Corinthians. We may well doubt, however, if one out of twenty-five of these would know how the *next* chapter begins (and when he finds out he will be greatly surprised!) It starts with the words, "Now concerning the collection." We should remember that the Apostle did not mark off chapters, so that his inspired chapter on the resurrection was not interrupted by the number sixteen as he begins to talk about the collection. 1. Now concerning the collection for the saints, as I gave order to the churches of Galatia, so also do ye. Dr. Jowett has well brought out the

2. Upon the first day of the week let each one of you lay by him in store, as he may prosper, that no collections be made when I come.

significance of this: "Are you conscious of a sudden and painful descent in the plane of the thought? Do you perceive a chilling change in the temperature? 'O death, where is thy sting? O grave, where is thy victory? . . . Now concerning the collection.' Is the association unworthy? Is the transition harsh and jarring? No such feeling of the incongruous possessed the consciousness of the Apostle Paul. He passed from one to the other without any perception of unwelcome change. The intrusion of a duty did not mar the heavenly music, but rather completed it. The apostle bore the sublime about in him, and so everything he touched was sublimed. . . . What was the occasion of this collection? There was a large body of poor Jews in Jerusalem who had eagerly received the Christ of God. Their hearts were as dry as a blasted heath, and they panted for the water of life. They found the refreshment they sought in Jesus the Christ. They turned to Him, and offered Him the homage of their minds and hearts. For this they were excommunicated, outlawed, banned. Because of their life they were denied a living, and they began to be in want. I don't think we are able to form any adequate conception of the intense hatred and repulsion with which the Jews regard those whom they consider renegade members of their race. During my ministry in Newcastle it was my privilege to baptize a young Jew, who had been wooed by the beauty of the Christ into the warmer light of the Christian faith. At once the parental instinct seemed to be benumbed. His father and mother forsook him. He was turned adrift. He was regarded as a dog. He was denied his daily bread. These were precisely the conditions which prevailed in Jerusalem, only in Jerusalem the ban of excommunication almost annihilated the chances of earning one's bread, and inevitably drove the outlaw into poverty and want. But Christianity fostered humanity; faith evoked philanthropy; and from their fellow-believers in wider fields there flowed a steady stream of beneficence to alleviate their distress." — *J. H. Jowett*. Paul has no more than introduced the idea of the collection than he pens probably the greatest single statement on giving to be found in any one sentence in all his epistles: 2. **Upon the first day of the week let each one of you lay by him in store, as he may prosper, that no collections be made when I come.** "The collection was to be made every Lord's day; every one was to contribute; and the contributions were to be in proportion to the means of the giver. These are the three principles which the apostle had established among the churches of Galatia, and which he urged the Corinthians to adopt. . . . The Hebrew word, sabbath (*rest*), is used not only in the singular, but also in the plural form, both for the seventh day, and for the whole week, Luke 18:12. The first day of the week was, by divine appointment, made the sacred day for Christians. . . . It was an important feature of these apostolic arrangements, that the contributions were not to be confined to any one class of the people. The same amount might perhaps have been raised from the rich few. But this would not have answered one important end which the apostle had in view. It was the religious effect which these gifts were to produce in promoting Christian fellowship, in evincing the truth and power of the gospel, and in calling forth gratitude and praise to God, even more than the relief of the temporal necessities of the poor, that Paul desired to see accomplished, 2 Corinthians 9:12–14." . . . "The words do not mean *to lay by at home*, but *to lay by himself*. The direction is nothing more definite than, *let him place by himself*, i.e. let him take to himself what he means to give. What he was to do with it, or where he was to deposit it, is not expressed. The Greek means *putting into the treasury*, or *hoarding up*, and is perfectly consistent with the assumption that the place of deposit was some common treasury, and not every man's own house. . . . The only reason that can be assigned for requiring the thing to be done on the first day of the week, is, that on that day the Christians were accustomed to meet, and what each one had laid aside from his

2 CORINTHIANS 8:1. Moreover, brethren, we make known to you the grace of God which hath been given in the churches of Macedonia;

2. How that in much proof of affliction the abundance of their joy and their deep poverty abounded unto the riches of their liberality.

3. For according to their power, I bear witness, yea and beyond their power, *they gave* of their own accord,

4. Beseeching us with much entreaty in regard of this grace and the fellowship in the ministering to the saints.

---

weekly gains could be treasured up, i.e. put into the common treasury of the church. The end which the apostle desired to accomplish could not otherwise have been effected. He wished that *there might be no collections when he came.* But if every man had his money laid by at home, the collection would be still to be made. The probability is, therefore, Paul intended to direct the Corinthians to make a collection every Lord's day for the poor, when they met for worship." — *Charles Hodge.*

III. **THE EXAMPLE OF THE CHURCHES OF MACEDONIA IN THE MATTER OF GIVING,** 2 Corinthians 8:1–6. It is amazing how much space the Apostle Paul assigns to this matter of giving in the Corinthian epistles. In addition to other passages, all of chapters eight and nine of this second Epistle are exclusively devoted to this matter, thirty-nine verses, almost one-sixth of the Epistle. Before we begin the actual interpretation of these words, we should again remind ourselves of the situation which led to Paul's taking this collection. "In order to appreciate rightly the necessity for this work of good will it will be useful to recall the wretched condition of the poor in Jerusalem at the time. The plundering and bloodshed accompanying the successive administrations of contemporary procurators brought about a state of anarchy, chronic rebellion, and famine. Murderous bands infested the provinces and the streets of Jerusalem witnessed innumerable deeds of cruelty and bloodshed. Famine, bitter and chronic, was the inevitable outcome and none suffered so severely as the humble disciples of the despised Nazarene. The relief fund in the Jerusalem church was not only a failure in itself, but must soon have disappeared in these social upheavals. Appeal to outside sources became necessary. The character of the dispute which raged so long and so fiercely between St. Paul and the church in Corinth was to a large extent developed and molded by the niggardliness and suspicious meanness of its members (2 Cor. 11:8 and 12:13). Their response to the appeal of Titus who was the original deputed organizer of the Corinthian collection was prompt and willing and yet they seem to have repented soon of their promised support and to have accused St. Paul of having hurried them deceitfully unto an unwelcome undertaking (2 Cor. 7:2 and 12:16)." — *J. R. Willis.* Money matters are always delicate and especially when we are asking for gifts. The apostle lifts this whole matter up on to the loftiest plane. In these Corinthian letters he uses seven different words for the collection: first, the word *collection* (1 Cor. 16:1); *this grace* (2 Cor. 8:6); *communion* (2 Cor. 8:4); *bounty* (2 Cor. 8:20); *blessing* (2 Cor. 9:5) (here translated bounty, later blessing); *ministration* (2 Cor. 9:12); the word from which we derive our word, liturgy; and ministry (2 Cor. 9:1, etc.), the word meaning service from which comes our word, deacon. 1. **Moreover, brethren, we make known to you the grace of God which hath been given in the churches of Macedonia; 2. how that in much proof of affliction the abundance of their joy and their deep poverty abounded unto the riches of their liberality. 3. For according to their power, I bear witness, yea and beyond their power, *they gave* of their own accord, 4. beseeching us with much entreaty in regard of this grace and the fellowship in the ministering to the saints.** "By their 'affliction' the apostle meant some particular persecution or distress which he was witnessing while among them. Its particular character is uncertain. Such sufferings were all too

5. And *this*, not as we had hoped, but first they gave their own selves to the Lord, and to us through the will of God.

6. Insomuch that we exhorted Titus, that as he had made a beginning before, so he would also complete in you this grace also.

---

common among the Christians of the Early Church. Suffering and joy were usually united. It is of peculiar interest to note that Paul was at this time in Macedonia, probably in Philippi. . . .

"In addition to their 'affliction,' Paul makes mention of 'their deep poverty.' This also was an experience with which the members of the Early Church were only too well acquainted. It is true, however, that Macedonia felt in a peculiar measure the oppression of Roman rule, and that as a colony it was continually complaining of its commercial difficulties and its financial straits. What Paul tells his Corinthian readers is that the test of affliction and the pitiful povery issued in a rich stream of liberality. This last word originally meant simplicity or simplemindedness. It seems to have meant that singleness of purpose which is directed toward the relief of others, with no selfish thought and no ulterior motive in mind; hence the word came to denote, as it does here, generosity or liberality. . . .

"Paul declares of these Macedonian believers that 'according to their power . . . and beyond their power, they gave of their own accord.' That is, their giving was not only in accordance with their means, but it went far beyond the limits of their slender resources, and, furthermore, it was purely voluntary and spontaneous; it was 'of their own accord.'

"These Christians had shown their liberality still further in that, without waiting for any suggestion from the apostle, they had begged him as a special favor to allow them the privilege of having a part in the offering which was to be devoted to the relief of their fellow Christians in Jerusalem." — *Charles Erdman.* **5. And *this*, not as we had hoped, but first they gave their own selves to the Lord, and to us through the will of God.** "In this sentence we have one of the most beautiful expressions for what is needed to salvation, and what it is in which full salvation consists. A man who has given himself to the Lord: that comprises all our Lord asks of us; all the rest He will do. The expression is nowhere else found in Scripture; we owe it to this dealing with the matter of the collection. It tells us that giving money will have no value, except we first give ourselves; that all our giving must just be the renewal and carrying out of the first great act of self-surrender; that each new gift of money may be a renewal of the blessedness of entire consecration.

"It is only this thought that can lift our giving out of the ordinary level of Christian duty, and make it truly the manifestation and the strengthening of the grace of God in us. We are not under the law, but under grace. And yet so much of our giving, whether in the church plate, or on the subscription list, or on special occasions, is done as a matter of course, without aught of the direct relation to our Lord. A truly consecrated life is a life moment by moment in His love; it is this that will bring us to what appears so difficult, ever to give in the right spirit and as an act of worship. It is this will make 'the abundance of our joy abound to the riches of our liberality.'" — *Andrew Murray.* **6. Insomuch that we exhorted Titus, that as he had made a beginning before, so he would also complete in you this grace also.** "When Paul came to Macedonia and found how liberally the churches there had contributed, he urged Titus to return to Corinth and complete what he had so successfully begun. The exhortation therefore addressed to Titus, of which the apostle here speaks, was not the exhortation given him before the visit from which he had just returned, but that which he gave him in reference to a renewed visit yet to be made. . . . It was a disposition of the mind that Titus was exhorted to bring into full exercise among the Corinthians. The grace spoken

7. But as ye abound in everything, *in* faith, and utterance, and knowledge, and *in* all earnestness, and *in* your love to us, *see* that ye abound in this grace also.

8. I speak not by way of commandment, but as proving through the earnestness of others the sincerity also of your love.

9. For ye know the grace of our Lord Jesus Christ, that, though he was rich, yet for your sakes he became poor, that ye through his poverty might become rich.

---

of was something which belongs to the same category with faith, knowledge, and love." — *Charles Hodge.*

IV. **SOME CHARACTERISTICS AND CONSEQUENCES OF CHRISTIAN GIVING**, 2 Corinthians 8:7–9. Instead of scolding the Corinthians, Paul lets them know that he is absolutely counting upon their doing what he seeks in a very abundant way, as abundant as their faith and utterance and knowledge. Actually from here to the end of the chapter Paul gives five arguments for the duty of liberality. The Corinthian church boasted of its ability to speak in tongues and of other gifts of the Holy Spirit. Paul urges them to have the same fullness of experience in the matter of giving. 7. **But as ye abound in everything, *in* faith, and utterance, and knowledge, and *in* all earnestness, and *in* your love to us, *see* that ye abound in this grace also.** 8. **I speak not by way of commandment, but as proving through the earnestness of others the sincerity also of your love.** 9. **For ye know the grace of our Lord Jesus Christ, that, though he was rich, yet for your sakes he became poor, that ye through his povery might become rich.** The Apostle soars to the very height of Christian truth, in the midst of this chapter on the collection, making a statement quite unique in his Christology. "Every branch and leaf and blossom of the mightiest oak derives its life from the same strong root that bears the stem. The life in the tiniest bud is the same as in the strongest branch. We are branches in Christ the Living Vine; the very life that lived and worked in Him. Of what consequence that we should know well what His life is, that we may intelligently and willingly yield to it. Here we have one of its deepest roots laid open; 'Though he was rich, yet for your sakes he became poor, that ye through his poverty might become rich.' To enrich and bless us, He impoverished Himself. . . . How little did the Macedonian Christians know that they were, in their deep poverty, and in the riches of their liberality, giving beyond their power, just acting out what the Spirit and grace of Jesus was working in them. How little we would have expected that the simple gift of these poor people would become the text of such high and holy and heart-searching teaching. . . . And how we need to bring our giving to the cross, and to seek Christ's death to the world and its possessions as the power for ours. So will we make others rich through our poverty, and our life be somewhat like St. Paul's: 'poor, yet making many rich.' " — *Andrew Murray.* Maclaren closes his sermon on this verse, "Rich, Yet Poor," with these words: "My text was spoken originally as presenting the motive and the example for a little piece of pecuniary liability. Do you take the cradle and the Cross as the law of your lives? For depend upon it, the same necessity which obliged Jesus to come down to our level, if He would lift us to His; to live our life and die our death, if He would make us partakers of His immortal life, and deliver us from death; makes it absolutely necessary that if we are to live for anything nobler than our own poor, transitory self-aggrandisement, we too must learn to stoop to forgive, to impart ourselves, and must die by self-surrender and sacrifice, if we are ever to communicate any life, or good of life, to others." — *Alexander Maclaren.* While this has nothing directly to do with the matter of giving we should not pass this verse by without noticing that it is one of the cardinal passages proving the pre-existence of our Lord. He was poor from the time He was born in a manger in Bethlehem; then when was He rich?

He was rich when He dwelt with the Father and possessed that glory of which He spoke in His High Priestly prayer. "There are signs of wasteful and even prodigal squandering on every side. We have the example of Governments which are not taking the lead in wise economy. We have Governments steadily and obstinately proposing that we spend millions in decking up militarism in glaring and alluring attire. This is the kind of evil leadership which acts contagiously upon the whole country. Think of what is being spent in pleasure. Look at the crowded theatres and the cinemas with their long waiting queues. I do not object to these things, and I appreciate the reasonable reaction after all the strain and the fear and terror of the war. But it is unhealthy when we spend a large proportion of our income on amusement and have no reserves to meet the demands of noble necessity. Millions of professedly Christian people give more money to see one performance in a cinema than they give to the cause of God's kingdom in a whole year. I do not attribute this lack of beneficence to meanness, or to a stinginess which locks up its resources; it is explained by want of thoughtfulness, and by lack of method, and conscience, and piloted devotion." — *J. H. Jowett.*

THE LESSON IN LIFE, LITERATURE, AND ARCHAEOLOGY.

Canon H. P. Liddon in his famous Bampton Lectures on the Divinity of our Lord and Saviour Jesus Christ, uses a verse from our text in his chapter on Christ's pre-existence. After quoting 2 Corinthians 8:9, he says, "Here Christ's eternal wealth is in contrast with His temporal impoverishment. For His poverty began with the manger of Bethlehem; He became poor by the act of His incarnation; being rich according to the unbegun, unending Life of His higher nature, He became poor in Time." — *Canon H. B. Liddon.*

A TRUTH FOR THE CLASS TO CARRY AWAY.

A good way to clinch this lesson, I believe, would be for the teacher to ascertain the per capita giving of the church of which he is a member and in which he is teaching. This will probably surprise the class. Then he might compare this with the amount of money spent by each family on gasoline for pleasure driving during one week, or with the price of a single good dinner in a near-by restaurant. I leave the results with the teacher.

In what way or ways does the life of St. Paul illustrate the pages we have in this lesson from his pen? What does the lesson say regarding the definite relationship of the Lord Jesus Christ to the matter of giving? What characteristic of giving found in the lesson are we least likely to manifest? Was the giving which Paul urged upon the Corinthian church directed toward a specific object, or was it in general only?

LESSON IX. — August 29.

GROWTH THROUGH CHRISTIAN SERVICE. — Acts 10:38;
Galatians 6:1–2; James 1:22, 26–27; 2:14–17; 1 John 3:16–18.

PRINTED TEXT, Galatians 6:1, 2; James 1:22, 26, 27; 2:14–17; 1 John 3:16–18.

Devotional Reading: Matthew 10:40–42.
Beginner Topic: A FRIENDLY HELPER.
    Lesson Material: Psalm 117; 33:3–5; Luke 10:25–37.
    Memory Verse: I will praise the name of God with a song.   Psalm 69:30.
Primary Topic: HELPING IN TIMES OF NEED.
    Lesson Material: James 2:14–17; 1 John 3:17–18.
    Memory Verse: Through love be servants one to another.   Galatians 5:13.

Junior Topic: GROWING BY HELPING.
> **Lesson Material:** James 2:14–17; 1 John 3:17–18.
> **Memory Verse:** Through love be servants one to another. Galatians 5:13.

Intermediate-Senior Topic: CHRISTIANITY IN ACTION.
> **Lesson Material:** Acts 10:38; Galatians 6:1–2; James 1:22, 26, 27; 2:14–17; 1 John 3:16–18.
> **Memory Verse:** Bear ye one another's burdens, and so fulfil the law of Christ. Galatians 6:2.

Topic for Young People and Adults: GROWTH THROUGH CHRISTIAN SERVICE.
> **Lesson Material:** Acts 10:38; Galatians 6:1–2; James 1:22, 26, 27; 2:14–17; 1 John 3:16–18.
> **Memory Verse:** Bear ye one another's burdens, and so fulfil the law of Christ. Galatians 6:2.

THE TEACHER AND HIS CLASS.

The Younger Classes may be introduced to this lesson with a simple illustration from nature. A fruit grower orders some Northern Spy shoots to plant in the ground, that part of his orchard might bear Northern Spy apples. After eight or ten years, when the fruit should appear, not an apple has been borne by any of these trees. What would you think if the orchardist should go to the nurseryman from whom he bought these plantings and complain that he was not getting any fruit, and the nurseryman should reply, "Are not the trees vigorous and beautiful, and the blossoms abundant and fragrant?" All this might be true, *but* the tree was planted to bear fruit, and how is the orchardist to have a profitable Northern Spy apple tree unless the fruit makes it to be so. We as Christians have divine life in us, and this life is to produce certain fruits, which are called elsewhere "good works," and if none of these appear, how will anyone know that we really have this new life in us? The Epistle of James was written to emphasize this necessity of an outward manifestation of an inward spiritual experience.

The Older Classes may be introduced to this lesson by the teacher's quoting a verse from our Lord's high priestly prayer: "As thou didst send me into the world, even so sent I them into the world" (John 17:18). Thus we begin the lesson with a marvelous, concise statement about Christ's life of service on earth, and then turn to the Epistles to learn of the characteristics of our own life of service. Incidentally, in the high priestly prayer that Jesus offered, there is a great deal said about separation from the world, a theme we shall find repeated in this lesson.

THE LESSON IN ITS SETTING.

Time. — The sermon by Peter in the house of Cornelius may be placed between A.D. 36 and 38. The Epistle of Paul to the Galatians and the Epistle of James may both be placed somewhere between A.D. 50 and 54.

Place. — The sermon of the Apostle Peter was preached in Caesarea Philippi. Galatia was a province in Asia Minor.

THE PLAN OF THE LESSON.

SUBJECT: A Man's Inner Faith in God and Christ is Found to be Genuine When it Produces the Fruit that is Pleasing to God.

I. A SUMMARY OF CHRIST'S MINISTRY ON EARTH, Acts 10:38.

II. TWO BEAUTIFUL RULES FOR A CHRISTIAN IN HIS RELATION TO OTHERS, Galatians 6:1, 2.
   1. Toward those who have transgressed the law, v. 1.
   2. Toward the heavy-burdened, v. 2.

III. THE OBLIGATION DEVOLVING UPON ALL WHO KNOW THE WORD OF GOD, James 1:22.

IV. MARKS OF A TRULY RELIGIOUS MAN, James 1:26, 27.

V. TRUE FAITH ALWAYS IS ACCOMPANIED BY GOOD WORKS, James 2:14–17.

VI. A Word from John Revealing a True Test of Genuine Love, 1 John 3:16–18.

THE TEACHER'S LIBRARY.

On the two verses taken from the Epistle to the Galatians, I have used only two books in this lesson, and they will be found adequate — one by my friend Kenneth S. Wuest, *Galatians in the Greek New Testament*, and the other, the very rich commentary on this Epistle, now seldom seen, by John Eadie.

There is much material on the Epistle of James. See especially the commentary by Alfred Plummer in *The Expositor's Bible*; R. W. Dale: *The Epistle of James*; the commentaries by John Adam (Edinburgh, 1867) and W. Maynard Smith (Oxford, 1914); the massive work on the Greek text by J. P. Mayer (London, 1913) and the volume by E. H. Plumptre in the *Cambridge Bible for Schools*

and Colleges. On what are called the Catholic Epistles, among which is James, one should consult the older work by P. J. Gloag, pp. 23–108, and a more recent volume by Doremus Hayes: *The Catholic Epistles*.

Sermonic material is abundant, but not too important. On James 1:27, see J. Stuart Holden: *Redeeming Vision*, 94–100; A. C. Dixon: *Milk and Meat*, 196–207; A. M. Fairbairn: *Christ in the Centuries*, 165–186; and a great deal of material in *The Speaker's Bible*, *the Epistle of St. James*, 85–100. On James 2:14–26, I do not know anything better than the discussion in W. G. Moorehead: *Outline Studies in the New Testament: the Catholic Epistles*, 27–29. Spurgeon has good sermons on James 1:22–25, e.g., Vol. 25 (1879) 197–204 and Vol. 31 (1885) 361–372, in the *Metropolitan Tabernacle Pulpit*.

AUDIO-VISUAL AIDS.

No audio-visual aids discovered.

I. A SUMMARY OF CHRIST'S MINISTRY ON EARTH, Acts 10:38. This sentence is the most compressed summary of the ministry of Christ, from the time of His baptism to the week of His passion, to be found anywhere, outside of the Gospels, in the New Testament, and even the Gospel records do not contain such a summary as this. The anointing of the Holy Spirit of course refers to the time of His baptism. The second phrase, "went about doing good," is a general review of the three and one-half years of His public ministry, whereas the subsequent phrase, "healing all that were oppressed of the devil," describes one specific area in which He labored. It is very strange that commentators seem to almost totally ignore this verse. It was used by Canon Liddon as the text of his last sermon in St. Paul's, in 1890, and because it appears in a very rare work, I am quoting it in part. "Cornelius knew that in his own Italy the poor, and especially the sick and the hungry poor, were not simply of no account, they were looked upon as incumbrances of national life. As they could be of no service to the state, either in the army or in the public works, there appeared to be no object in keeping them alive, and no effort was made to do so. This very class, it would have struck Cornelius, was the object of our Lord's particular attention. . . . The highest and greatest good which He did was done for the souls of men. To have done everything for man's bodily frame and leave his spiritual being untouched would have been a poor and worthless kind of doing good in the estimation of Jesus Christ. It would have been such a good as man would have needed, and would have been satisfied with, had he been only an animal with no assured destiny beyond the tomb, with no conscience within him, with no judgment awaiting him. . . . But besides this He . . . relieved the pain of hunger. He enabled the poor and the suffering to fight the battle of life, as they could not have fought it without Him. . . . If our Lord was not, in the restricted modern sense, the first social reformer, He was undoubtedly, in the true and ample sense of the word, the first philanthropist. He loved man as man; He loved not one part but the whole of man; He loved man as none had ever loved him before or since; He died for the being whom He loved so well. And when our Lord had left the earth the spirit of His work became that of the Christian Church. It, too, after its measure, went about the world doing good. The New Testament guides us through the first stage of the subject." — *Canon Liddon.*

II. TWO BEAUTIFUL RULES FOR A CHRISTIAN IN HIS RELATION TO OTHERS, Galatians 6:1, 2. At the conclusion of the preceding chapter, the Apostle Paul has set forth the seven-fold fruit that should appear in the conduct

GALATIONS 6:1. Brethren, even if a man be overtaken in any trespass, ye who are spiritual, restore such a one in a spirit of gentleness; looking to thyself, lest thou also be tempted.

2. Bear ye one another's burdens, and so fulfil the law of Christ.

and character of every true believer. He is now going to illustrate the principles therein referred to by giving some practical applications.

1. TOWARD THOSE WHO HAVE TRANSGRESSED THE LAW, 6:1. **Brethren, even if a man be overtaken in any trespass, ye who are spiritual, restore such a one in a spirit of gentleness; looking to thyself, lest thou also be tempted.** The Apostle is here addressing those who are spiritual. "These are not the presbyters, nor those who thought themselves spiritual, but those in possession of that spirit on which stress has been laid in the previous paragraph. Those ruled by the flesh cannot do the duty here set forth." — *John Eadie.* My friend Mr. Kenneth Wuest has one of the finest interpretations of this passage with which I am acquainted, and I do not hesitate to use it, possibly for the second time, in this series of *Peloubet's Notes.* "Two of our Greek authorities, Lightfoot and Alford, think that the reference here is to the act of a Christian detecting a fellow-Christian in the commission of a sin, thus catching him unawares in it, and establishing by that means the fact of the sin. Four — Burton, Vincent, Expositor's, and Meyer — think that it refers to the Christian himself being overtaken by the sin before he is aware that he has done wrong. Robertson merely defines the word without interpreting it. The context rules in favor of the opinion of the four. . . . The word *restore* is from *katartizo.* This word has the following meanings: 'to repair, to restore to a former good condition, to prepare, to fit out, to equip.' It is used of reconciling factions, of setting bones, of putting a dislocated limb into place, of mending nets, of manning a fleet, of supplying an army with provisions. It is used by Paul usually in a metaphorical sense of setting a person to rights, of bringing him into line. Those Galatians who had not abandoned their dependence upon the Holy Spirit, now are asked by Paul to set those Galatians right who had been seized unawares by sin because they had deprived themselves of the ministry of the Spirit. The primary thing that they needed to be set right about was not the act of sin which they committed, but that they had wandered off the right road of grace and were stumbling in the quagmire of self-dependence and legalism." — *Mr. Kenneth Wuest.* "The restoration of a fallen brother is not to be undertaken in a distant or haughty spirit, or in a hard, dictatorial, or censorious style, which dwells bitterly on the sin, or brings its aggravations into undue relief, or condemns in self-complacent severity the weakness which led to the fall. The spirit of meekness conpassionates which it must blame, soothes while it may expostulate; its fidelity is full of sympathy — itself the image of that gentleness which in the benign Exemplar did not 'break the bruised reed, nor quench the smoking flax.' " — *John Eadie.*

2. TOWARD THE HEAVY-BURDENED, 6:2. **Bear ye one another's burdens, and so fulfil the law of Christ.** Here, also, I would like to use the helpful interpretation of Mr. Wuest. "The word *burdens* has the following meaning: either 'a burden that is desirable' as in 2 Corinthians 4:17 (weight) or 'one which is hard to bear' (Acts 15:28; Rev. 2:24). The context indicates the specific meaning. The burdens in this context refer to the responsibility each saint should feel for the spiritual welfare of his fellow-saints, especially when they have sinned. In this particular instance, the Spirit-dominated saints should feel the responsibility of rescuing their brethren who have put themselves under legalism, from an abject slavery to law, and of transferring their dependence again upon the Spirit; and in the case of the sin which has taken him by surprise, of helping the sinning brother to go to the Lord Jesus with a confession of that sin. The word *bear* is from *bastazo*, which means 'to bear what is burdensome.' By bearing another's burdens, Paul does not mean simply the enduring of these burdens in an enforced, reluctant manner

JAMES 1:22. But be ye doers of the word, and not hearers only, deluding your own selves.

26. If any man thinketh himself to be religious, while he bridleth not his tongue, but deceiveth his heart, this man's religion is vain.

as in 5:10 where the same word is used, but the assuming of those burdens in a willing, helpful, sympathetic way, despite the fact that the bearing of them may involve unpleasantness and heartache. The word *fulfil* is from *pleroo* which here means 'to satisfy the requirements of.' It is found in the papyri where it is used with reference to the fulfilling of the requirements of a contract. The definite article appears before the word *Christ* in the Greek text. The use of the term 'the Christ' gives the law here an official character. It is the law which Christ gave. Paul thought of that law as expressed in one word, *love*, the divine love produced in the heart of the yielded believer by the Holy Spirit, which exercises a restraint over the individual that takes the place of the restraint which the Mosaic law had imposed." — *Mr. Kenneth Wuest.*

III. **THE OBLIGATION DEVOLVING UPON ALL WHO KNOW THE WORD OF GOD,** James 1:22. **But be ye doers of the word, and not hearers only, deluding your own selves.** Before interpreting the few verses taken from this Epistle, we should be reminded of the three outstanding characteristics of these chapters: (1) a great many references to the Old Testament; (2) more passages similar to our Lord's teaching (Sermon on the Mount) than in any other part of the New Testament; and (3) a great number of illustrations taken from nature. We might call the Epistle of James the Wisdom Literature of the New Testament, as Job, Proverbs, and Ecclesiastes are in the Old Testament. It is a book of exhortations, not setting forth primarily great Christian doctrines, but the characteristics that should mark the lives of those who embrace the Christian truth. In verses 22–25, James is emphasizing the absolute necessity for putting into practice the things one has heard from the Word of God. This is exactly the truth solemnly set forth by our Lord at the conclusion of the Sermon on the Mount (Matt. 7:24–27); elsewhere our Lord had insisted on the truth that men would be known by their fruits (Matt. 7:16–20). "The Word here intended is, of course, the Divine word, that word which is all given by inspiration of God, and has the grand distinction of being able to save sinful, ruined souls. The doers of it are those who are ruled by it, who really and practically comply with its requirements, who not only read, hear, understand, and believe it, but submit to its authority, regulate their tempers and lives by its precepts, walk not in their own ways, not according to the course of the world, but in the path of its holy commandments and ordinances. The term, too, is expressive of continuance, permanence. . . . An habitual, systematic service, a sustained and enduring obedience. We must live and move in this element, we must find our occupation here the chief employment and delight of our existence. It is only such doing that constitutes a doer of the word." — *John Adam.*

IV. **MARKS OF A TRULY RELIGIOUS MAN,** James 1:26, 27. **26. If any man thinketh himself to be religious, while he bridleth not his tongue, but deceiveth his heart, this man's religion is vain.** The man of this verse who thinks he is religious, and wants to be known as such, deceives himself in this very matter if he has no control over his tongue. The subject of the control of the tongue is given great emphasis in this short Epistle; in fact, a discussion of a man's uttered words occupies almost the entire third chapter. Before proceeding to comment on this verse and the subsequent one, we must come to an understanding of the use of the word here translated *religious*, and in the next verse, *religion*. "Since the sixteenth century, we have come to use these words in a wider meaning, and they no longer represent the Greek. The passage refers to the external practice of the Faith; and perhaps the nearest words we can suggest are *devout* and *devotion*, but even they have a too extended significance." — *H. Maynard Smith.* Professor

295

27. Pure religion and undefiled before our God and Father is this, to visit the fatherless and widows in their affliction, *and* to keep oneself unspotted from the world.

Hatch says that the words refer to "religion in its external aspect as worship, or as one mode of worship contrasted with another." "As we are afterwards told in this Epistle the tongue is an unruly evil, full of deadly poison. It is a fire, a world of iniquity. It resembles a wild beast that needs to be tamed. It is like a horse which requires the bit, must be held in with the bridle. The man does not thus command and restrain it who indulges in profane or impure conversation. The blasphemer, the swearer, he who takes God's great name in vain, or who lets filthy communications of any kind proceed out of his mouth, is exposed to this charge in the most obvious manner and the most heinous form. But this case is not precisely that which is here intended, for such an one can scarcely persuade himself that he is a Christian; it is hardly possible that he who does that can seem either to others or himself to be religious. He openly casts off all fear of God and is an avowed, daring rebel against the Majesty of heaven. . . . The person who speaks uncharitably, maliciously, slanderously, who gives ready utterance, free circulation to calumnies, suspicions, insinuations — who propagates false charges, or true ones in a bitter, envious, or malignant spirit — he assuredly bridles not his tongue. The reviler, the backbiter, the whisperer, the reckless, abusive partisan, the inventor and publisher of bad names and injurious rumours — all such are clearly involved in this condemnation." — *John Adam.* Paul says elsewhere that no corrupt communication is to proceed out of our mouth; see, e.g., Ephesians 4:29; 5:4; Colossians 3:8; and also 1 Peter 3:9, 10. This is the principal theme of our Lord's discourse concerning a tree bearing good fruit — words.

27. Pure religion and undefiled before our God and Father is this, to visit the fatherless and widows in their affliction, *and* to keep oneself unspotted from the world. This verse has often been understood, though wrongly, to represent all that God requires of any of His children. That is not correct. James is not here giving the essence of the Christian faith, nor a summary of Christian doctrine, nor even telling men what they are to believe. He is speaking of the external life of a religious man and some of the characteristics that are to mark it. Notice that this is not a mere humanitarian action. This kind of a life is lived "before our God and Father." "The life of sonship is thus in the very nature of the case absolutely independent of the world, and this is one of the secrets of unspottedness. The man who lives 'before God,' passing all his choices and actions under His review, has learned the secret of integrity, and is thus empowered to make right response to the holiness of God, both in its standards and demands." — *J. Stuart Holden.* There are two manifestations of this form of life mentioned here — one in relation to others, in visiting those who are suffering and in trouble, and the other in relation to ourselves, keeping unspotted from the world. "It is the clean vessel to whom the treasure is entrusted, and through whom the Water of Life flows to others. Hence the definition of true religion includes not only sanctity but service, and it is necessary that he who is himself unspotted is the one also who visits the fatherless and the widow. This, of course, is but an example, and not the only form of Christian service, though a very blessed one, and sometimes more so for the visitor than the visited. But it is expressive of the whole essence of pure religion that the man who has it should serve. 'Pure religion and undefiled' has in it no element of selfishness, no mere seeking after happiness in this world or the next, for pure religion is pure love. . . . It is said of the Lord Himself that He was 'a Lamb without spot,' and thus pure religion is a daily approximation to His likeness and character, and a daily increasing correspondence of the servants to their Master. Indeed I may paraphrase the text thus: 'Pure religion is to be like Jesus, and to be more like Jesus, and to be more like Jesus still.' The practical consideration is as to whether your religion is of this sort, and, if not, as to whether you will have it, cost what it may." — *J. Stuart Holden.*

James 2:14. What doth it profit, my brethren, if a man say he hath faith, but have not works? can that faith save him?

15. If a brother or sister be naked and in lack of daily food,

16. And one of you say unto them, Go in peace, be ye warmed and filled; and yet ye give them not the things needful to the body; what doth it profit?

17. Even so faith, if it have not works, is dead in itself.

V. TRUE FAITH IS ALWAYS ACCOMPANIED BY GOOD WORKS, James 2:14–17. 14. What doth it profit, my brethren, if a man say he hath faith, but have not works? can that faith save him? 15. If a brother or sister be naked and in lack of daily food, 16. and one of you say unto them, Go in peace, be ye warmed and filled; and yet ye give them not the things needful to the body; what doth it profit? 17. Even so faith, if it have not works, is dead in itself. This passage has been discussed, debated, perverted and misinterpreted by commentators and exegetes of every age. Some say that here St. James is contradicting St. Paul, while others claim that works are as important in the Christian life as faith, and a man can never be saved unless he produces works — this would have been difficult to apply to the thief on the cross. St. James is not here setting forth a doctrine contrary to the great fundamental truth of Paul's Epistles — justification by faith alone. Over and over again the New Testament insists that we are saved not by our works, but by the grace of God and faith in Christ. James is examining this faith: In chapter 1, he speaks of "the proving of your faith" (v. 3), and asking in faith (v. 6); he assumes that his hearers have faith (2:1), and that they profess to have faith (vs. 14–19). But he does insist (vs. 17, 20, 26) that faith apart from the Christian practice is dead. Faith brings Divine life into our entire being. "In the matter of justification Paul knows no other kind of faith than that which is genuine and active; an inactive faith is with him not faith but faithlessness. His writings abound with precepts addressed to those who believe, thus connecting the faith which justifies with obedience to the law of God (Titus 3:8). It is by this faith, productive of works, that Paul says we are justified; and in this he is perfectly at one with James, who lays great stress on good works as a necessary accompaniment of saving faith. James uses the term *faith* in a somewhat different sense. Whilst with Paul the term is limited to genuine and active faith, James uses it in a more general acceptation, so as to include theoretical as well as active faith. He speaks not only of genuine faith — a firm confidence in God as the hearer of prayer (James 1:6) — but also of a faith which is dead and unproductive, and consequently incapable of justifying. He compares such a faith to an inactive love which expends itself in good words and kind wishes, but never proceeds to works of benevolence (James 2:14–17). As this love is of no value, so neither is the faith of him who professes to believe the gospel, and yet does not walk up to his profession. James compares such a faith to that which the devils possess: 'Thou believest that there is one God; thou doest well: the devils also believe and tremble. But wilt thou know, O vain man, that faith without works is dead' (2:19, 20). It is to this dead, inactive faith that James denies justification; it is wholly unproductive; it cannot profit. And indeed, on one occasion, Paul uses faith in the same sense, and in as strong language as James denies to it any saving or justifying efficacy: 'Though I have all faith, so that I could remove mountains, and have not charity, I am nothing' (1 Cor. 13:2). The faith which justifies is a faith which worketh by love — this is the doctrine of Paul; not a faith which is destitute of love — this is the doctrine of James. . . . There are two distinct parts in the doctrine of justification: the one, that a man is justified by faith in the merits of Christ, and the other, that the faith which justifies must be active. Paul dwells chiefly on the first part, and James on the second; so that, instead of a contradiction in their views, there is a development of the truth. 'The relation between these two apostles, as well their difference as their agreement,' observes

1 JOHN 3:16. Hereby know we love, because he laid down his life for us: and we ought to lay down our lives for the brethren.

17. But whoso hath the world's goods, and beholdeth his brother in need, and shutteth up his compassion from him, how doth the love of God abide in him?

18. *My* little children, let us not love in word, neither with the tongue; but in deed and truth.

Schaff, 'may be thus stated: James proceeds from without inward, from phenomenon to principle, from periphery to centre, from the fruit to the tree. Paul, on the contrary proceeds from within outward, from principle to phenomenon, from centre to circumference, from the root to the blossom and the fruit.' " — *P. J. Gloag.*

VI. **A WORD FROM JOHN REVEALING A TRUE TEST OF GENUINE LOVE,** 1 John 3:16–18. In verse 11 of this chapter, the Apostle John lays down the great truth that Christians should love one another, and to illustrate this, he uses Cain as a negative example, in that instead of loving his brother, he slew him. He then proceeds at once to the cross, as a perfect illustration of a love that gives everything for the sake of others. **16. Hereby know we love, because he laid down his life for us: and we ought to lay down our lives for the brethren.** This great principle is immediately applied in a most practical and humble way. **17. But whoso hath the world's goods, and beholdeth his brother in need, and shutteth up his compassion from him, how doth the love of God abide in him? 18. *My* little children, let us not love in word, neither with the tongue; but in deed and truth.** "In the first days the duty stated in this passage was no ideal requirement, no stretch of an heroic fancy. Every Christian held himself at the disposal of the community. At any time martyrdom might be called for; already many a dear life had been laid down for the brethren's sake. When we excuse ourselves from demands that involve the surrender of cherished earthly good, or when Christ's service in dangerous lands calls for reinforcements that are not sent, the Church is holding back what belongs to Him and shows herself unworthy of the Lord that bought her, and untrue to her own history. We are condemned by the love to which we owe ourselves, if we are not such as can hazard their lives for the name of the Lord Jesus, if we have not the heart to die for those whom Christ purchased by His blood. . . . Christian charity was then new in the world; and habits of neglect and callousness, especially when they have become engrained and traditional, are slowly overcome. The beneficence so renowned in the early Church was the outcome of any acquired disposition, that did not spring into activity at once as the immediate consequence of the new love to God felt by Christian men. Like all practical virtues, the grace of charity required inculcation, discipline, habituation, to bring it to proper exercise; the spirit of brotherly love grew by use into the temper of brotherly love and the aptitude for its expression. To this end much of the ethical teaching of the New Testament is devoted. St. John must perforce reiterate and insist upon it, though it be a thing so plain. The Apostle's last word here warns his readers against making philanthropic talk and social theory a substitute for personal deeds of compassion." — *G. G. Findlay.*

THE LESSON IN LIFE, LITERATURE, AND ARCHAEOLOGY.

Toward the close of the life of J. Hudson Taylor, and his vast labors in China, his son, Dr. Howard Taylor and his young bride arrived in Shanghai only to find that his father and mother had gone on into the interior, and this was just the beginning of the hot season. He overtook them at Hankow. There were no railways in the inland provinces and much exposure ahead for those who traveled through the burning sun and tropical rains. The son pleaded with him, saying at last, "It may cost your life, father." "Yes," was the reply so gently made that it seemed no reproof, "and let us not forget, 'we ought to lay down our lives for the brethren.'" There was nothing more to be said.

A TRUTH FOR THE CLASS TO CARRY AWAY.

In this matter of personal kindness to others, of bearing the burdens of others, helping the poor, etc., we in this country find ourselves in a generation which witnesses three factors that seem to deprive believers somewhat of the privilege of this unique kind of work. First of all, we have vast charitable institutions under the auspices of national, state, and local governments; secondly, those who live in cities of any size annually participate in the raising of funds for the Community Chest, which cares for the needy in many areas of life; and thirdly, our country is so amazingly prosperous that many people, simply driving to and from work each day, may not actually encounter a poor family. And yet, poor there are. If we cannot find those who are poor in our own community, we must remember that never before in history have there been so many impoverished people in other parts of the world, separated from their families and living in constant heartache. Also, I fear that the visiting of one another among Christians is a lost art. Let us begin here and live out the life set forth in this lesson.

What are some of the incidents in the life of Christ which illustrate Acts 10:38? What did Christianity bring into the Roman world at this time of a humanitarian nature that had scarcely been seen before? What happens to a man when over and over again he hears the Word of God, and even says he believes it, but does not practice what he hears? Are most of the exhortations in this lesson directed to Christians in their attitude toward other believers, or to strangers and the unconverted? What is the difference between the charitable acts of an unbeliever and the good works of a Christian?

LESSON X. — September 5.

GROWTH THROUGH USEFUL WORK. — Colossians 3:23–24; 1 Thessalonians 4:10b–11; 2 Thessalonians 3:6–13.

PRINTED TEXT, Colossians 3:23–24; 1 Thessalonians 4:10b–11; 2 Thessalonians 3:6–13.

Devotional Reading: Psalm 19:14–17.
Beginner Topic: BIG BOY DANIEL.
  Lesson Material: Proverbs 3:1–4; Daniel 1.
  Memory Verse: Children, obey your parents. Colossians 3: 20.
Primary Topic: EVERYONE HAS WORK TO DO.
  Lesson Material: 2 Thessalonians 3:6–13.
  Memory Verse: Whatsoever ye do, work heartily, as unto the Lord. Colossians 3:23.
Junior Topic: EVERYONE HAS WORK TO DO.
  Lesson Material: 2 Thessalonians 3:6–13.
  Memory Verse: Whatsoever ye do, work heartily, as unto the Lord. Colossians 3:23.
Intermediate-Senior Topic: YOU AND YOUR JOB.
  Lesson Material: Colossians 3:23–24; 1 Thessalonians 4:10b–11; 2 Thessalonians 3:6–13.
  Memory Verse: Whatsoever ye do, work heartily, as unto the Lord, and not unto men. Colossians 3:23.
Topic for Young People and Adults: GROWTH THROUGH USEFUL WORK.
  Lesson Material: Colossians 3:23–24; 1 Thessalonians 4:10b–11; 2 Thessalonians 3:6–13.
  Memory Verse: Whatsoever ye do, work heartily, as unto the Lord, and not unto men. Colossians 3:23.

THE TEACHER AND HIS CLASS.

The Younger Classes may be introduced to this lesson on *work* by being reminded of how common this word is in their own home. Over and over again the mother will have to say to the daughter, or son, "You cannot go out to play until you have done your *homework*." The duties of a mother around the house are called *housework*, and every morning the father goes off to *work*. The Bible has a great deal to say about work, how honorable it is, and the sins from which it helps to keep us.

The Older Classes will find this lesson one of great importance, for we are living in a time when work is looked upon as something to be got rid of as quickly as possible, each day, and for our lifetime. Our pension systems — and we can be grateful for them — seem to create in many a longing to see the day when they will not have to work any more. The amount of travel involved in so many occupations, time-killing as it is, is often extended unnecessarily, and the actual hours of work often become very few indeed. Some late policies in our government have persuaded millions of people that two hours of solid work in an eight-hour day is about all that is expected. Unions have done a great deal for the working man, but some of them do forbid their men to work at peak capacity.

THE LESSON IN ITS SETTING.

Time. — The Epistles of Paul to the Thessalonians were the first written in his ministry, about A.D. 54, and that to the Colossians was written toward the end of his ministry, while in prison about eleven years later.

Place. — Thessalonica was a great city on the eastern seacoast of northern Greece, and Colosse, a famous city in what we now call Asia Minor.

THE PLAN OF THE LESSON.

SUBJECT: Some of the Wholesome Consequences of Devotion to Work, and Paul's Illustration of the Place of Work in His Own Life.

I. The Secret of Fervor in Work, Colossians 3:23, 24.

II. How Work Gives Balance to Life, 1 Thessalonians 4:10b, 11.

III. The Example of Paul in the Matter of Work, 2 Thessalonians 3:6–13.

   1. Paul recalls his own labor in their midst, vs. 6–10.

   2. The need for this exhortation, vs. 11–13.

THE TEACHER'S LIBRARY.

On the subject of work as a whole, see an excellent chapter in Edwin A. Hughes: *The Bible and Life*, 125–150. A volume entitled, *Work, What It Has Meant to Men Through the Ages*, by Adriana Tilgher, published in 1931, I have not seen.

On the Epistles to the Thessalonians, there is nothing better than the two superb volumes by Alfred Plummer, which will be of more value if one can handle the Greek text; see also the volumes by R. C. H. Lenski, James Denny in the *Expositor's Bible*, and all books that contain chapters on Paul's Epistles, e.g., D. A. Hayes: *Paul and His Epistles*, 139–186.

Sermonic material on the assigned text is very meagre. On 1 Thessalonians 4:10, 11, see W. L. Watkinson: *The Moral Paradoxes*, 1–25, and on verse 11, George H. Morrison: *The Wings of the Morning*, 310–318. On Paul's work in Thessalonica, and the subsequent epistles to that city, see the great work by Conybeare and Howson: *The Life and Epistles of St. Paul*, Vol. 1, pp. 345–362.

AUDIO-VISUAL AIDS.

No audio-visual aids discovered.

My readers may be interested in a very important bit of evidence indicating the great part that work plays in human life, which I came upon in preparing for this lesson. Of course there are many synonyms for this word *work*, such as toil, labor, etc., but this one word *work*, alone, in the final volume of the great *Oxford English Dictionary*, is assigned 27 columns, embracing 39 different definitions. Work is actually mentioned in the Ten Commandments (Ex. 20:9, etc.); the Book of Proverbs frequently speaks of it (10:16; 14:23). Our Lord refers to His own work, and the work of the Father (John 5:17; 17:4). In fact, on the very first page of the Bible (Gen. 2:2) is the phrase, "And on the seventh day God finished his work." Justice Oliver Wendell Holmes, who lived to the age of ninety-four, once said,

COLOSSIANS 3:23. Whatsoever ye do, work heartily, as unto the Lord, and not unto men;

24. Knowing that from the Lord ye shall receive the recompense of the inheritance: ye serve the Lord Christ.

"Work keeps me young; if I should quit, I would die." Years ago Dr. W. J. Dawson truly said, "It is a matter of observation on which the world is agreed, that where Nature is most bountiful, man is morally at his weakest. The perfect climate means the most imperfect men. It is where man has to battle most strenuously with Nature that manhood is most noble. In the languorous air of the tropics the moral forces seem to drain themselves away, and where the earth gives everything without labour, man is most vile, most impotent for good, most thoroughly the slave of his animal desires." — *Dr. W. J. Dawson.*

I. **THE SECRET OF FERVOR IN WORK**, Colossians 3:23, 24. The Apostle has just been writing about various human relationships, and God's ideal for these — for wives, husbands, children, fathers, servants. The two verses assigned to our text are a part of the sentence beginning at verse 22, and while these words relate first of all to servants, they carry truth for us all; for every man who works for someone else is, after all, serving that person. 23. **Whatsoever ye do, work heartily, as unto the Lord, and not unto men; 24. knowing that from the Lord ye shall receive the recompense of the inheritance: ye serve the Lord Christ.** The phrase, "do it heartily," may be translated literally, "work from the soul." What a beautiful concept of labor! How much of our work is just external, mechanical, compulsory, as it were. Many men and women are dissatisfied with the work in which they are engaged, and, in many cases, justly so. The ideal for work, however, is that it be of such a nature that we can rejoice in it, that we can put all we have into it, so that we may be pleased with its result, and not be ashamed before those who employ us. As he does so often, the Apostle Paul now brings in a heavenly truth, to illuminate and lift this whole subject. When discussing marriage, Paul admonishes husbands to love their wives, and adds the lofty truth, "even as Christ loved the Church and gave Himself for it." The words here are somewhat of an interpretation of 1 Corinthians 15:58. I cannot help but feel that the work to which Paul refers here is not necessarily what we call work for the Lord, but the daily work in which we are employed, seen by God, and when faithfully done, receiving its reward (see 1 Peter 1:4; Ephesians 1:14).

II. **HOW WORK GIVES BALANCE TO LIFE**, 1 Thessalonians 4:10b, 11. Inasmuch as the major part of our lesson is taken from the two epistles which Paul addressed to the church at Thessalonica, I think perhaps we ought to have before us a brief word concerning the city itself. "In the first Christian century Thessalonica was the chief city of Macedonia. It was a seaport city with about two hundred thousand inhabitants. It lay at the northeast corner of the Thermaic Gulf, the most magnificent of the many bays on the eastern shores of Greece. . . . Back of it stood Mount Olympus, the fabled home of the gods of Greece, snow-capped and resplendent as a royal palace high in air. When Cicero was exiled from Rome he lived here in Thessalonica for seven months with Plancius the quaester, and he tells us that he looked for the gods on Mount Olympus, but found there only ice and snow. Through the city of Thessalonica from east to west ran the great Egnatian highway which connected the imperial city of Rome with the Orient. . . . Thessalonica was thus a center of commerce by land and by sea. It was called 'the mother of all Macedonia.' It was at the height of its prosperity at the beginning of the Christian era, but it had been a city of importance for more than four hundred years. . . . It was the most populous city in all Macedonia, and, like all other large and prosperous cities in the empire at this time, it had a proportion of Jewish citizens and they had a synagogue." From the same author is this statement regarding this first letter. "It is the first epistle which has been preserved, written by a Christian to Christians, if we ex-

1 Thessalonians 4:10b. But we exhort you, brethren, that ye abound more and more;

11. And that ye study to be quiet, and to do your own business, and to work with your hands, even as we charged you.

---

cept the brief official document sent after the Jerusalem council to the church at Antioch (Acts 15:23–29). Chronologically, it is the first of the New Testament books to be written. It marks the beginning of Christian literature. It is the earliest important document of the Christian faith. Jesus had written nothing. The twelve apostles had written nothing. Paul is the pioneer in the field of Christian authorship. In all the multitude of those who have followed him in all the centuries since Paul has had no superior. It is to be questioned whether he has had even a single peer. The First Epistle to the Thessalonians is noteworthy by its position, leading the van of the mighty host of tracts, sermons, epistles, treatises, and books with which Christianity has enriched the world; and its intrinsic value makes it worthy of that leadership." Paul had visited this city on his second missionary journey, and was intimately acquainted with the characteristics, the needs, and the perils of this early Christian community. 10b. But we exhort you, brethren, that ye abound more and more; 11. and that ye study to be quiet, and to do your own business, and to work with your hands, even as we charged you. Though I did not expect to find it there, the volume by the late Professor Doremus Hayes contains one of the finest interpretations of this passage that I have seen anywhere. I shall use it in its entirety. "Here we find three things for which Paul thought the Thessalonians might safely be ambitious. Ambition is in bad repute in some quarters. We venture to say that it depends altogether upon the nature of an ambition, upon the end at which it aims, as to whether it is bad or good. There may be a holy ambition as well as an evil one. Paul was an ambitious man. He says so himself, and he tells us what his ambitions were. In Romans 15:20, he says that he was ambitious to evangelize where Christ had not yet been named. That, surely, was a worthy ambition. . . . To the realization of that ambition Paul sacrificed his life. In 2 Corinthians 5:9, Paul tells us of another of his ambitions. We are ambitious, he says, to be well-pleasing unto God. Paul loved honor, but it was the honor of God which he coveted. He sought for glory, but, as he told the Thessalonians, he did not seek the glory of men. He was ambitious, but his only ambition was to please God. That, surely, was a worthy ambition. To the realization of that ambition Paul dedicated his life. . . . In this passage Paul exhorts the Thessalonians to be ambitious in three respects, in order that two results may follow. On the supposition that Paul would not exhort others to do anything which he was not doing himself, we may add these three ambitions to Paul's list. What are they? First, an ambition to be quiet! This is another oxymoron. . . . Strive, wrestle, agonize, work hard at it, and so — enter into rest! Trying to rest, and working hard at it — that seems like a contradiction of terms. Being ambitious and being quiet — that seems to be utterly inconsistent again. The ambitious man is up and doing. He is keeping himself in the public eye. He is restless and unquiet and always eager for greater prominence and power. . . . Paul says that the Thessalonians ought to be ambitious 'to mind their own business,' to attend to their own affairs, to see that these were managed well and that all the things for which they were responsible were taken care of and brought to a successful consummation! How much more rapidly the work of the world would be done if everybody would follow this ambition! The third ambition mentioned in this list is the ambition to have employment in manual labor, 'to work with the hands.' Satan still has some work for idle hands to do. Paul was ambitious to keep his fingers so busy with legitimate and necessary occupation that the devil would not find them fit for his purpose at any time. He would rather weave the coarse goats' hair into coarse tent cloth than to weave the devil's web. He was a workingman, and this letter to the Thessalonians is a

2 Thessalonians 3:6. Now we command you, brethren, in the name of our Lord Jesus Christ, that ye withdraw yourselves from every brother that walketh disorderly, and not after the tradition which they received of us.

---

letter from a workingman to workingmen. He knew that steady employment was a help to the moral life. He knew that manual labor kept body and mind in good condition, and so was conducive to the best spiritual state." — *Prof. Doremus Hayes.*

The word translated "study" means literally, "be anxious of distinction"; Plummer translates it, "make a vigorous endeavor." "No matter how humble a man's task may be, no matter how ordinary and uninteresting, he cannot set himself to do it faithfully without imprinting his very being on it; and if within the man there be no peace, but a surging of excitement or unrest, that inward tumult will tell on all his toil and subtly influence everything he does. It is one of the legends of our Saviour's childhood that in Joseph's workshop He was a perfect worker. If He made a plough, it was a faultless plough. If He made a toy, there was not a flaw in it. It is only a legend, and yet, like every legend, it leans for its secret of beauty on a truth, and the truth is that here was perfect peace, and perfect peace produced the perfect work. Study to be quiet, and to do thy business. Make it thine ambition to have a heart at leisure. Without that there is no perfecting of fellowship and without it no perfecting of toil." — *George Morrison.* But Paul is not finished with this matter of work. It is just introduced here, as it were, but in his next letter to the same church, written soon after, he elaborates on the importance of labor among these Christians.

III. **THE EXAMPLE OF PAUL IN THE MATTER OF WORK,** 2 Thessalonians 3:6–13. Professor Plummer recalls to mind that this second letter was written in the light of reports that had come to Paul concerning some Christians in the Thessalonian church, which information was "of a mixed character. On the one hand, the converts were enduring bitter persecution and affliction with great fortitude, and were growing in brotherly love towards one another (1:3, 4). On the other hand, there had been serious misapprehension, if not deliberate misrepresentation, of the Apostle's teaching respecting the Second Advent (2:2, 3) and it was necessary to correct this. Moreover the brief warning against disorderly conduct (1 Thes. 5:14) had had little or no effect; the evil had seriously increased, and it was necessary to give strict injunctions with a view to putting a stop to it." — *Prof. Alfred Plummer.* To this problem the Apostle now directs the concluding portion of his letter. I shall lean heavily here upon the classic work on this Epistle by Dr. Alfred Plummer, for there is nothing to compare with it in the interpretation of Paul's words. 6. **Now we command you, brethren, in the name of our Lord Jesus Christ.** "The writers have sufficient authority of their own, but it is not claimed on personal grounds; and they can appeal to something much higher. This statement, placed in advance of the commands, prepares us for a matter of grave import; compare 1 Thessalonians 4:2. Like 'Brethren,' it may serve to remind the recipients of what is required of those who have Christ as their Lord. Again we have an expression which in the Old Testament is used of Jehovah (Exod. 5:23; Lev. 19:12; Deut. 18:22; Jer. 11:21, etc.) transferred readily to Christ (1 Cor. 6:11; Eph. 5:20; Col. 3:17, etc.). The injunctions which follow are more definite and stringent than those in 1 Thessalonians. The need for them has become more urgent. All this is natural and in favor of genuineness." — *Dr. Alfred Plummer.* **That ye withdraw yourselves from every brother that walketh disorderly, and not after the tradition which they received of us.** "There are to be no exceptions even in the case of those who in other respects seem to be living correctly. The case is similar to the one in 1 Corinthians 5:11; but there 'who bears the name of a brother' implies that such grave offenders have forfeited the name of Christian. Here the condemnation is less stern. The disorderly

7. For yourselves know how ye ought to imitate us: for we behaved not ourselves disorderly among you.

8. Neither did we eat bread for nought at any man's hand, but in labor and travail, working night and day, that we might not burden any of you:

9. not because we have not the right, but to make ourselves an ensample unto you, that ye should imitate us.

10. For even when we were with you, this we commanded you, If any will not work, neither let him eat.

11. For we hear of some that walk among you disorderly, that work not at all, but are busybodies.

12. Now them that are such we command and exhort in the Lord Jesus Christ, that with quietness they work, and eat their own bread.

---

people are to be left severely alone, partly that they may realize how serious their misbehaviour is, and partly to prevent other Christians from being corrupted. The common view that this disorderly idleness was the result of the belief that the end of the world had begun is probable enough, as experience in later ages has shown. But the connection is neither stated nor clearly implied in the letter." **7. For yourselves know how ye ought to imitate us: for we behaved not ourselves disorderly among you.** "They know, because they saw the way in which the missionaries lived, for they lived in their midst. We have here another understatement, not mournful, as in verse 2, but modest." **8. Neither did we eat bread for nought at any man's hand, but in labor and travail, working night and day, that we might not burden any of you: 9. not because we have not the right, but to make ourselves an ensample unto you, that ye should imitate us.** "So far from living on others, the preachers worked hard to maintain themselves. Acts 18:3 leaves us in doubt about St. Paul's handicraft. Did he weave material for tent making? or only cut it out and stitch it together? And what was the material? Cloth (*cilicium*) or leather? About the way in which Silvanus and Timothy maintained themselves we know nothing. His enemies said that like other impostors, the Apostle preached to fill his pockets. It was important to give no handle for this, but be independent of his converts. He was not afraid of being tempted to shape his preaching with a view to profit. While in Thessalonica he accepted help from the Philippians (Phil. 4:16). That did not endanger his independence at Thessalonica." **10. For even when we were with you, this we commanded you, If any will not work, neither let him eat.** The phrase, "will not work," should be translated literally, "does not choose to work." "The Jews recognized this principle, deducing it from Genesis 3:19, 'In the sweat of thy face shalt thou eat bread.' 'Let not him who would not labour before the Sabbath eat on the Sabbath. . . . This apostolic principle (which is often quoted by Jerome and by Cassian) indicates that inherited wealth does not absolve a man from the duty of work. Wealth is a trust, and to administer it rightly involves much thought and labour. Calvin uses the charge as a stone to throw at monks." — *Alfred Plummer.*

11. For we hear of some that walk among you disorderly, that work not at all, but are busybodies. 12. Now them that are such we command and exhort in the Lord Jesus Christ, that with quietness they work, and eat their own bread. "In their excited restlessness they were failing to recognize the truth that in this world of sin work is a blessing, because it is a safeguard. They were in danger of giving illustration of the Eastern adage, that 'the devil tempts other men, but idle men tempt the devil.' Hence the words of mingled severity and mildness. In tranquillity, sedateness of heart and life, they are severally not only to work, but to do their own work, and so 'have need of no man.' Thus the bread which is their own will be doubly sweet to them. If we revert to the military metaphor which under-

13. But ye, brethren, be not weary in well-doing.

---

lies the word 'disorderly,' and may also underlie, as we have seen, the word 'withdraw' we may place another saying of the apostle's into connection with these injunctions — 'Every man shall bear his own burden' (Gal. 6:5) — his own personal and proper load. The word is used to signify a soldier's kit or knapsack. In Christian warfare, then, each faithful soldier must see that he has his own weight, and that he does not encumber another with it, or take up another's instead of his own. All acts of this kind are a walking disorderly. Believers, then, have daily work to do — not only Christian work, but all work done in a Christian spirit. The record of their days must never be like that said to have been found in the diary of Louis XVI, after the first French Revolution — the simple word occurring almost on every page, 'nothing, nothing.' Time rather must be redeemed, not wasted. Thus, in the ceaseless devotion of the whole life, the faithful Christian 'through enduring pain, links month to month, with long drawn chain of knitted purport.' The Master's midnight call will be heard with gladness by those only who are 'diligent in business, fervent in spirit, serving the Lord.' " — *J. Hutchison.* **13. But ye, brethren, be not weary in well-doing.** The idea of doing well in itself covers every aspect of life, not only our labor or work. There can be many reasons, some more active at one time than another, for our proneness to be weary in well-doing. One is that we get weary in work. Most members of the adult human race can say when the sun sets, "I am tired." And there is nothing wrong in being tired; in fact, the sin is in spending our lives in such a way that we never do enough to get tired. Even Christ at times was weary. Then, often we see people prospering while pursuing evil practices in business, whereas we have difficulty making ends meet financially, and we thus get weary in doing things honestly. Also, it is human nature to want recognition of a task well done, and yet, many people work faithfully for years and never hear a word of appreciation. How many thousands of missionaries have worked alone for years in the lonesome places of heathenism, and instead of being commended, have been persecuted, insulted, and asked to leave! All this Paul, too, endured, but we never hear him planning to give up his work. He does not intend to quit, for he knows that the day is coming when, whatever happens on earth, he will hear his Lord's commendation.

This lesson may well be concluded with a paragraph from the excellent volume by the late Bishop Hughes, *The Bible and Life,* in which he says that in the Bible we find "a procession of workers, and from this procession God selects many of his chosen leaders. Moses was tending his flock on the hillside when the voice of the Lord summoned him to his manifold leadership. Saul was seeking his father's cattle when he found the kingdom of which he was to be king. David was busy in the sheepfold when the prophet called him to his work as warrior and monarch. Ruth was gleaning in the fields, in her pathetic effort to care for her widowed mother-in-law and herself, when she found her way into happiness and into the ancestry of our Lord. Gideon was beating out wheat in the wine press when he was drafted for the campaign that was to break the power of the Midianites. Elisha was plowing with twelve yoke of oxen when the mantle of Elijah was cast over his shoulders. Nehemiah was serving as cupbearer to the king when he evoked from Artaxerxes the permission to return and rebuild the walls of his beloved city. Amos was among the herdsmen of Takoa when the word of God took him captive and sent him to his prophetic career. The New Testament is less specific in its descriptions, but it often gives us the like hint. Matthew was at the seat of custom when he was invited into the fellowship of the disciples that he might tell men of the eternal exchange. James and John were engaged in their occupation as fishermen when they heard the voice on the shore and pulled their boat over the blue waves that they might become fishers of men. The shepherds were in faithful watch over their flocks by night when they heard the evangel of song and were startled by the message of peace. The illustrations make us feel that the favorite meeting place of God with man is the meeting place of man with his work." — *Bishop Hughes.*

THE LESSON IN LIFE, LITERATURE, AND ARCHAEOLOGY.

The famous African Church Father, Tertullian, in his famous treatment, "Idolatry," points out the fact that some enemies of the church used Paul's statement, "Let each one work with his own hands," in justifying various sins: "If this precept is maintained in respect to *all* hands, I believe even the bath-thieves live by their hands, and robbers themselves gain the means to live by their hands; forgers, again, execute their evil hand-writings, not of course with their feet, but hands; actors, however, achieve a livelihood not with hands alone, but with their entire limbs. Let the Church, therefore, stand open to all who are supported by their hands and by their own work; if there is no exception of arts which the Discipline of God receives not." — *Tertullian.*

A TRUTH FOR THE CLASS TO CARRY AWAY.

Inasmuch as in our own country there is a great deal of bustle, keen competition, and millions who really work hard, some more than they ought, I believe that the main message of this lesson should not be so much an encouragement to work, which possibly most of those who listen to us do not need, but rather, a new conception of work, as ordained of God, and something in which we should find joy and satisfaction. I am sure that the Apostle Paul would have rather preached than make tents, but we can be sure that while he was making tents, his face was radiant, his thoughts were high and noble, and those who conversed with him during his hours of labor were edified and encouraged.

Do you think that, normally speaking, work is more pleasant in a Christian land than in the areas ruled by paganism? What are some of the consequences in the life of a man, who, though in normal health, refuses to work? Can unpleasant work be done joyfully? What type of work brings the greatest joy? From your knowledge of men in general, would you say that God has distributed gifts for various types of work, and also put in the hearts of some men a love for one type of work, and in the hearts of others, a desire for another type? (I would most emphatically say yes; e.g., millions of people do not want to go to sea and work on ships, while thousands of sailors who must be on the water constantly enjoy that work, and many men shrink from the particular labor involved in farming, while others find that the one passion of life.)

LESSON XI. — September 12.

CHRISTIAN CITIZENSHIP AND CO-OPERATION. — Acts 6:1–6; Romans 12:9–16; 13:1–10; 1 Corinthians 3:4–9; Galatians 5:13–15.

PRINTED TEXT, Romans 12:9–16; 13:1–10; 1 Corinthians 3:4–9.

Devotional Reading: Isaiah 41:6–10.

Beginner Topic: New Friends.
> Lesson Material: Proverbs 18:24; Ecclesiastes 4:9–10; John 1:35–42; Hebrews 13:1–2; 1 Peter 3:8–11.
> Memory Verse: Thou, Jehovah hast made me glad. Psalm 92:4.

Primary Topic: Neighbors Everywhere.
> Lesson Material: Acts 6:1–6; Romans 12:9–16; Galatians 5:13–15.
> Memory Verse: Thou shalt love thy neighbor as thyself. Galatians 5:14.

Junior Topic: Neighbors Everywhere.
> Lesson Material: Acts 6:1–6; Romans 12:9–16; Galatians 5:13–15.
> Memory Verse: Thou shalt love thy neighbor as thyself. Galatians 5:14.

Intermediate-Senior Topic: DOING OUR PART.
    Lesson Material: Romans 13:1-10; 1 Corinthians 3:4-9; Galatians 5:13-15.
    Memory Verse: We are God's fellow-workers.   1 Corinthians 3:9.
Topic for Young People and Adults: CHRISTIAN CITIZENSHIP AND CO-OPERATION.
    Lesson Material: Romans 13:1-10; 1 Corinthians 3:4-9; Galatians 5:13-15.
    Memory Verse: Love worketh no ill to his neighbor: love therefore is the fulfilment of the law.   Romans 13:10.

THE TEACHER AND HIS CLASS.

The Younger Classes will recognize the subject of this lesson as one that confronts us almost from the time we can walk — right relationships with other people. It is interesting to watch very young children, two or three years old, when meeting each other for the first time.   One may push the other down, or they may walk off holding hands.   Soon children begin to play together in the neighborhood; then they have to live together in school every day; thousands now have to live with others in the army for a year or two; all of us have to live with people in our work; and everyone has some relationship to the government under which he lives.

The Older Classes may be introduced to this lesson in a way similar to that suggested for the younger classes. Man is a social creature. For this reason, homes are established, clubs are formed, partnerships are entered into; and people of like mind in the things of God are to be found together in a church, as God has ordained.   The family, the state, and the church are divinely-established institutions, and the right way to live in each of them is something to which the Scriptures frequently make reference.   The tragedy of our world today is that millions are out of the will of God in these matters.

THE LESSON IN ITS SETTING.

Time. — The scene from the early Church recorded in Acts 6 occurred about A.D. 35.   The Epistles to the Romans, Corinthians, and Galatians were written between A.D. 57 and 60.
Place. — The events of Acts 6 took place in Jerusalem. Rome, of course, was the eternal city, the capital of the world.   Corinth was a great city in Greece.

THE PLAN OF THE LESSON.

SUBJECT: The Privileges, Responsibilities, and Fundamental Characteristics that Should Prevail in the Corporate Relationships of Men and Women.

  I. THE SENSE OF MUTUAL OBLIGATION TOWARD THE NEEDFUL IN THE EARLY CHURCH, Acts 6:1-6.

 II. SOME CHARACTERISTICS OF LIFE WITHIN THE CHURCH WHEN LOVE RULES, Romans 12:9-16; 13:8-10; Galatians 5:13-15.
    1. In general, Romans 12:9-12.
    2. Toward those in need, Romans 12:13.
    3. Toward our persecutors, Romans 12:14.
    4. The bond of sympathy, Romans 12:15, 16.
    5. The sovereignty of love, Romans 13:8-10; Galatians 5:13-15.

III. THE APOSTLE PAUL'S CLASSIC STATEMENT REGARDING THE CHRISTIAN AND THE STATE, Romans 13:1-7.

IV. THE SIN OF DIVISIONS IN THE CHURCH AND THE TRUTH THAT ACKNOWLEDGED WILL PREVENT SUCH, 1 Corinthians 3:4-9.

THE TEACHER'S LIBRARY.

Holding to the passages assigned for the printed text, the teacher will find the great commentaries on Romans by Godet, Moule, Hodge, Lenski and W. H. Griffith Thomas more than adequate. On the Corinthian passage, I am using only the volume by McFadyen.
  There is an extensive literature on the Christian concept of the state. Among the volumes to which no reference has been made in these pages, I think, are the following: W. Edward Chadwick: *The Social Teaching of St. Paul* (1906) 125–128; Archibald B. D. Alexander: *Christianity and Ethics* (1938) 229–244; Sydney Cave: *The Christian Way* (1949) 233–262; L. H. Marshall: *The Challenge of New Testament Ethics,* 343–348.
  On the fundamental factor of love underlying our relationships with one another are some excellent pages in C. J. Barker: *The Way of Life* (1946), 151–170; and Paul Ramsey: *Basic Christian Ethics* (1950) 92–132, 234–248, 326–366.

I am purposely omitting all sermonic material, because it is not the type of help we most need for the study of this lesson. However, I must refer to some pages in Alexander Maclaren: *Expositions of Holy Scripture, Romans;* on the verses from chapter 12, 261–269; and from chapter 13, 304–317. On Romans 13:12, F. B. Meyer: *The Dedicated Life.*

AUDIO-VISUAL AIDS.

FILMSTRIP: "The Christian Citizen,"

Church Screen, 44 fr., b&w. Some phases of good citizenship are pointed up in a helpful way, but does not cover all phases.

FILM: "Joe Turner, American," National Association of Manufacturers, Produced by Apex Film Corporation, 27 min., sd., b&w. This is a free loan film, and not religious in viewpoint, but shows how one man came to take an interest in his community when his grandson dies of an illness contracted from poor city water.

In the opening pages of the Bible we have the divine statement, "It is not good that the man should be alone" (Gen. 2:18). The very fact that God made us in His image testifies to the reality of man being a social creature, even as God is. The fact that God loves us, and we can love God, together with the great emphasis on love for our fellow-men throughout the Scriptures, all testify to the inescapable truth that man was made to live with his fellow man. A person who shuns others is called a misanthrope. The greatest joys of life arise from the right relationships of mankind, and the greatest tragedies from the miscarriage of these relationships.

I. THE SENSE OF MUTUAL OBLIGATION TOWARD THE NEEDFUL IN THE EARLY CHURCH, Acts 6:1–6. As soon as men, whether Jew or Gentile, experienced regeneration, their hearts flooded with love by the indwelling of the Holy Spirit, they naturally, yea, they inevitably sought out one another knowing that they were all children together in the family of God, and thus was the Church established. Apart from the family, no cords of love bind people so closely as those of redemption in Christ. These Christians at once felt an obligation, one to the other, economically as well as religiously. The poor, the widows, and the orphans were provided for immediately, as never before in any other human institution. The 6th chapter of Acts gives us a brief picture of the situation arising in the Jerusalem church when it seemed that the widows of the native Palestinian Jews, especially those of Jerusalem, were receiving more charitable attention than the widows from outside the dispersion. For the rectification of this, the Spirit of God led the Church to appoint men who would care for the material, economic, monetary side of the corporate life of the Church. These men were later known as Deacons. Dr. G. Campbell Morgan has a magnificent discussion, which I wish did not have to be quoted as a fragment. "The sense of relation existing is manifest first in the complaint. These people complained because they recognized the unity, the inter-relationship, the mutual responsibility, and felt that it was not being realized. I leave out of count the question as to whether the complaint was warranted or not, as something which cannot be decided, because the story is silent concerning it. The fact of the complaint is demonstration of an underlying consciousness of unity. Those Hellenists who imagined that the Hellenist widows were being neglected, felt the neglect was a violation of that great fellowship, of which we have already spoken; and so the complaint was the manifestation of the underlying sense of unity. That unity has most clear manifestation in the organization of the Church, which resulted from this particular schism. . . . The organization of the Christian Church is its unified variety at work; all the variety unified in order to work; the whole Church obedient to one life-principle, which is service; the whole Church working without friction, which is strength; then the accomplishment of results, which is success. 'The Word of God increased.' This is a most remarkable expression, showing that true growth of organization is a growth of capacity for revealing Jesus. 'The number of the disciples multiplied,' and that in the heart of opposition — Jerusalem. By fulfilment of function there was growth of the organism, and by growth of the organism there was increase of power and increase of work. Luke put the final touch upon the story when he wrote a most astonishing thing, 'A great company of priests were obedient to the faith.'" — *Dr. G. Campbell Morgan.*

ROMANS 12:9. Let love be without hypocrisy. Abhor that which is evil; cleave to that which is good.

10. In love of the brethren be tenderly affectioned one to another; in honor preferring one another.

II. SOME CHARACTERISTICS OF LIFE WITHIN THE CHURCH WHEN LOVE RULES, Romans 12:9–16; 13:8–10; Galatians 5:13–15. Inasmuch as we shall be observing the factor of love prevailing in the subjects now to be discussed, we might begin with some words on the general theme of Christian love, taken from a comparatively new work, *The Way of Life*, by C. J. Barker, formerly of Christ Church, Oxford. "The Christian idea of Love was so distinctive that the early writers did not use either of the commoner Greek words for love; but adopted one that was more rarely used, and somewhat shadowy in its content — *Agape*. Into that word the New Testament writers have poured a new wealth of meaning. . . . For a Christian doctrine of Agape, the New Testament furnishes three facts as a starting-point: (1) God is 'love.' (2) We 'love' because He first 'loved' us. (3) The 'love' of God and the 'love' of neighbour are indissolubly joined together. . . . Any exposition of the Christian's love of God and man must start with an understanding of the nature of God's love for man. Closely allied with the idea of Agape was that of Charis — Grace. Both stress one fact, that God's action towards us originates from His own character, and not as response to the attractiveness of man. . . . Love of man and love of God go closely together in this also: that God and man are both, as persons, the carriers of value; God of the ultimate, man of the penultimate, value, deriving his value from God's. . . . Under no circumstances may we regard or treat man or God as means to our own gratification or advancement: both are to us ends, not means. Judged by this touchstone, little of human conduct is seen to be wholly clear from the taint of self-centredness. The theocentric life means that in our ideals we set ourselves alongside of God at the centre as we look out upon the world of men, and look at all men from His viewpoint, as they come within the orbit of His love." — *C. J. Barker*.

1. IN GENERAL, Romans 12:9–12. 9. **Let love be without hypocrisy.** In other words, let our love be sincere, not just words. Occasionally in an emotional urge, people speak of their love for us, when we know that the day before they had been speaking evil of us. **Abhor that which is evil; cleave to that which is good.** "The words rendered 'to abhor' and 'to cleave to' are peculiarly forcible, and express the highest degree of hatred on the one hand, and of persevering devotion on the other. The latter word, in the active form, properly means 'to glue,' and in the middle, 'to attach' one's self to any person or thing. The words 'evil' and 'good' in this passage, may be understood of moral good and evil; and the exhortation be considered as a general direction to hate the one and love the other." 10. **In love of the brethren be tenderly affectioned one to another.** "The word translated 'tenderly affectioned' expresses properly the strong natural affection between parents and children, but is applied also to tender affection of any kind. Here it implies that Christians should love each other with the same sincerity and tenderness as if they were the nearest relatives." — *Charles Hodge*. **In honor preferring one another.** Hodge says this admonition means that "instead of waiting for others to honor us, we should be beforehand with them in the manifestation of respect." I would like to here inject a personal word. One of the greatest sins among conservative, believing Christians today, especially those in public life, leaders in the Church, is self-adulation, thinking more of themselves than they ought, and trying to make a deep impression upon others. This is manifested in many ways. I have known ministers in this country to tell friends that they had been invited to certain outstanding pulpits or conferences, when my accurate knowledge of the situation led me to know that such invitations had not been extended. I grieve to see ministers drawing up their own advertisements and calling themselves "internationally famous Bible teachers," when they are not known

11. In diligence not slothful; fervent in spirit; serving the Lord;

12. Rejoicing in hope; patient in tribulation; continuing stedfastly in prayer;

13. Communicating to the necessities of the saints; given to hospitality.

14. Bless them that persecute you; bless, and curse not.

15. Rejoice with them that rejoice; weep with them that weep.

---

outside of the state in which they live.   **11. In diligence not slothful; fervent in spirit; serving the Lord.**   "No man will work long at a task that his heart is not in; or if he does, because he is obliged, the work will be slavery.   In order, then, that diligence may neither languish and become slothfulness, nor be felt to be a heavy weight and an unwelcome necessity, Paul here bids us see to it that our hearts are moved because there is a fire below which makes 'the soul's depths boil in earnest.' . . .   The reason for our diligence: 'Thou Christ hast died for me, and livest for me; truly I am Thy slave.'   You can carry that motive — as we all know, and as we all forget when the pinch comes — into your shop, your study, your office, your mill, your kitchen, or wherever you go." — *A. Maclaren.*   **12. Rejoicing in hope; patient in tribulation; continuing stedfastly in prayer.**   "These exhortations refer to nearly related duties: Christians are to be joyful, patient, and prayerful.   However adverse their circumstances, hope, patience and prayer are not only duties, but the richest sources of consolation and support. . . .   This hope of salvation is the most effectual means of producing patience under present afflictions; for if we feel 'that the sufferings of this present time are not worthy to be compared with the glory which shall be revealed in us,' it will not be difficult to bear them patiently. Intercourse with God, however, is necessary to the exercise of this and all other virtues, and therefore the apostle immediately adds, 'continuing instant in prayer.' There are no attributes of acceptable prayer more frequently presented in the Scriptures than those here referred to, that is, perseverance and fervour, which, from their nature, imply faith in the ability and willingness of God to grant us needed good (Acts 1:14; 6:4; Eph. 6:18, etc.)." — *Charles Hodge.*

2. TOWARD THOSE IN NEED, Romans 12:13.   **Communicating to the necessities of the saints; given to hospitality.**   This matter of hospitality had a larger place in the early Church than it does now, for as Christians, especially teachers, preachers, and evangelists, went from city to city in the pagan world where hotels were hardly known — and the few that were in existence, centers of gross immorality — it was in the homes of other believers that they found rest, shelter, food and comfort.   Paul emphasizes this matter of hospitality throughout most of his epistles. The ideal was that kind of hospitality offered to Jesus in the home of Mary and Martha at Bethany.   And what wonderful spiritual blessings have many left in such homes during their stay — this can be true in the 20th century as well as in the first.   The word "communicating" relates to our word "communion," and it means to share one with another.

3. TOWARD OUR PERSECUTORS, Romans 12:14.   **Bless them that persecute you; bless, and curse not.**   "This was a solemnly appropriate precept, for the community over which, eight years later, the first great persecution was to break in 'blood, and fire, and vapour of smoke.'   And no doubt there was abundant present occasion for it, even while the scene was comparatively tranquil.   Every modern mission-field can illustrate the possibilities of a 'persecution' which may be altogether private, or which at most may touch only a narrow neighborhood; which may never reach the point of technical outrage, yet may apply a truly 'fiery trial' to the faithful convert.'" — *H. C. G. Moule.*

4. THE BOND OF SYMPATHY, Romans 12:15, 16.   **15. Rejoice with them that rejoice; weep with them that weep.**   "Alas, there is such a phenomenon, not altogether rare, as a life whose self-surrender, in some main aspects cannot be doubted,

16. Be of the same mind one toward another. Set not your mind on high things, but condescend to things that are lowly. Be not wise in your own conceits.

Romans 13:8. Owe no man anything, save to love one another: for he that loveth his neighbor hath fulfilled the law.

but which utterly fails in sympathy. A certain spiritual exaltation is allowed actually to harden, or at least to seem to harden, the consecrated heart; and the man who perhaps witnesses for God with a prophet's ardor is yet not one to whom the mourner would go for tears and prayer in his bereavement, or the child for a perfectly human smile in its play. But this is not as the Lord would have it be. If indeed the Christian has 'given his body over,' it is that his eyes, and lips, and hands, may be ready to give loving tokens of fellowship in sorrow, and (what is less obvious) in gladness too, to the human hearts around him." — *H. C. G. Moule.*
16. **Be of the same mind one toward another. Set not your mind on high things, but condescend to things that are lowly. Be not wise in your own conceits.** The idea of concord or unanimity of opinion and affection is found elsewhere in 2 Corinthians 13:11; Philippians 2:2; Romans 15:5. The initial admonition of the verse is elaborated upon in the remaining clauses. We are to allow ourselves "to be carried along together by lowly things; that is, instead of being concerned about high things, let lowly things occupy and control you. The last precept is ultimately connected with the preceding, since ambition and contempt for lowly persons and pursuits generally arise from overweening self-estimation. No species of pride is more insidious or more injurious than the pride of intellect, or a fancied superiority to those around us, which leads to a contempt of their opinions, and a confident reliance upon ourselves. The temper which the gospel requires is that of a little child, docile, diffident, and humble (see 11:25; Prov. 3:7; Jer. 1:6)." — *Charles Hodge.*

Before proceeding to other verses assigned for our lesson, we should be reminded again of the truth set forth by Bishop Moule. "Let us not forget that the Apostle lays his main emphasis here rather on being than on doing. Nothing is said of great spiritual enterprises; everything has to do with the personal conduct of the men who, if such enterprises are done, must do them. This too is characteristic of the New Testament. Very rarely do the Apostles say anything about their converts' duty, for instance, to carry the message of Christ around them in evangelistic aggression. . . . What the Christian does is even more important than what he says. What he is is the all-important antecedent to what he does. He is 'nothing yet as he ought to be' if, amidst, even innumerable efforts and aggressions, he has not 'presented his body a living sacrifice' for his Lord's purposes, not his own; if he has not learned, in his Lord, an unaffected love, a holy family affection, a sympathy with griefs and joys around him, a humble esteem of himself, and the blessed art of giving way to wrath, and of overcoming evil in 'the good' of the presence of the Lord." — *Bishop Moule.*

5. The Sovereignty of Love, Romans 13:8–10; Galatians 5:13–15. Romans 13:8. **Owe no man anything, save to love one another: for he that loveth his neighbor hath fulfilled the law.** The late W. E. Chadwick, one of England's distinguished scholars at the beginning of our century, in his volume, *The Social Teaching of St. Paul,* has an excellent statement on this verse. "Translated into the language of modern thought, the teaching of these verses runs: — God has ordained for man's welfare a great, universal social law — a part of the one Divine law which governs the universe. The 'Ten Words' were at least a partial revelation of that law. The Sermon on the Mount was a much fuller revelation. The life of Christ was a perfect expression (or revelation) of a life — lived socially, that is, among men — fully understanding, and perfectly obeying, that law. (To realise this ideal in all the varying circumstances of human experience must be the ideal of every member of the Christ-society.) . . . Christ practically recognised

9. For this, Thou shalt not commit adultery, Thou shalt not kill, Thou shalt not steal, Thou shalt not covet, and if there be any other commandment, it is summed up in this word, namely, Thou shalt love thy neighbor as thyself.

10. Love worketh no ill to his neighbor: love therefore is the fulfilment of the law.

ROMANS 13:1. Let every soul be in subjection to the higher powers: for there is no power but of God; and the *powers* that be are ordained of God.

2. Therefore he that resisteth the power, withstandeth the ordinance of God: and they that withstand shall receive to themselves judgment.

---

the debt and paid it to the uttermost. Christ is the end of the Law for righteousness. The purpose of the Law was righteousness, that purpose was fulfilled in Christ. 'I came to fulfil the Law.' The Law was fulfilled only through the infinite and incarnate Love. Thus love has been, and is, the only possible fulfilment of Law. The infinite righteousness is the expression of the infinite love. The breaches of law contemplated by the commandments quoted by St. Paul are all issues of selfishness — the antithesis of love. They are social sins issuing in social crimes." — *W. E. Chadwick.* 9. **For this, Thou shalt not commit adultery, Thou shalt not kill, Thou shalt not steal, Thou shalt not covet, and if there be any other commandment, it is summed up in this word, namely, Thou shalt love thy neighbor as thyself.** All of this verse is, of course, from the Ten Commandments, found in Exodus 20, with the exception of the last clause, which is taken from Leviticus 19:18, and quoted by our Lord in Matthew 19:19. 10. **Love worketh no ill to his neighbor: love therefore is the fulfilment of the law.** "The man who 'loves his neighbor as himself' will be as considerate of his neighbour's feelings as of his own, in respect of abstinence from injury and annoyance. But he will be more; he will be actively desirous of his neighbour's good. He will reckon it as much 'evil' to be indifferent to his positive true interests as he would reckon it unnatural to be apathetic about his own. The true divine commentary on this brief paragraph is the nearly contemporary passage written by the same author, 1 Corinthians 13. It has been said that 'love is holiness, spelt short.' . . . The holy man in human life is the man who, with the Scriptures open before him as his informant and his guide, while the Lord Christ dwells in his heart by faith as his Reason and his Power, forgets himself in a work for others, which is kept at once gentle, wise, and persistent to the end, by the love which, whatever else it does, knows how to sympathize and to serve." — *H. C. G. Moule.*

III. **THE APOSTLE PAUL'S CLASSIC STATEMENT REGARDING THE CHRISTIAN AND THE STATE,** Romans 13:1–7. Every event taking place in the New Testament was in the environment of the Roman empire, which was not altogether evil. There was some justice in the Roman government. Its citizens were protected, as Paul often discovered. And yet, of course, the empire itself was pagan, many of its emperors demanding the worship to which only deity is entitled. Rome ultimately turned against the Christians and destroyed hundreds and thousands of them in an attempt to suppress Christianity. The very name of Nero, emperor during the last years of Paul's life, is a synonym for almost everything barbaric and evil; and yet, nowhere does the New Testament even suggest that Christians should revolt against Rome. The state is emphatically an institution ordained of God, ultimately deriving its power from God's divine institution of government. Let us have before us the opening statement of this paragraph, and then a recent commentary upon the entire subject. 1. **Let every soul be in subjection to the higher powers: for there is no power but of God; and the** *powers* **that be are ordained of God.** 2. **Therefore he that resisteth the power, with-**

3. For rulers are not a terror to the good work, but to the evil. And wouldest thou have no fear of the power? do that which is good, and thou shalt have praise from the same:

4. For he is a minister of God to thee for good. But if thou do that which is evil, be afraid; for he beareth not the sword in vain: for he is a minister of God, an avenger for wrath to him that doeth evil.

5. Wherefore *ye* must needs be in subjection, not only because of the wrath, but also for conscience' sake.

6. For for this cause ye pay tribute also; for they are ministers of God's service, attending continually upon this very thing.

7. Render to all their dues: tribute to whom tribute *is due;* custom to whom custom; fear to whom fear; honor to whom honor.

---

standeth the ordinance of God: and they that withstand shall receive to themselves judgment. 3. For rulers are not a terror to the good work, but to the evil. And wouldest thou have no fear of the power? do that which is good, and thou shalt have praise from the same: 4. for he is a minister of God to thee for good. But if thou do that which is evil, be afraid; for he beareth not the sword in vain: for he is a minister of God, an avenger for wrath to him that doeth evil. 5. Wherefore *ye* must needs be in subjection, not only because of the wrath, but also for conscience' sake. Our comment here is taken from a recently published notable work, *The Christian Way*, by Sydney Cave, Principal of New College, London. He begins his chapter, "The Community of the State," with the following words: "'Suffered under Pontius Pilate': these words of the Apostles' Creed may serve to remind us of the enigma of the State. God is 'the Father Almighty, Maker of heaven and earth.' Yet on earth the State has power; the Christian faith in 'Jesus Christ His only Son our Lord' includes the recognition that He suffered at the orders of the Roman State, and goes on to affirm that He who thus suffered will be the final judge of all. 'God the Father Almighty,' and yet His Son suffered under Pontius Pilate. Those who secured the crucifixion of Jesus have their counterpart in the modern world and should be remembered by them. . . . These words, 'Suffered under Pontius Pilate,' epitomize the gravest problem of Christian ethics. Christians are called to live a life of love in the fellowship of the Church, and yet they have to recognize the authority of the State. A State should be the sphere of justice; yet it is constituted not by justice but by power, and power, which in itself is morally neutral, may be used, as Pilate used it, not justly but unjustly. . . . We who live in an age in which totalitarian governments have demanded the unconditional obedience of their subjects, note at once the limits which our Lord's words impose on the authority of the State. . . . The ruler is 'a minister of God,' the embodiment of the 'Wrath,' that principle of retribution by which the world is governed. Christians must therefore be in subjection to the ruler, not only because of the 'Wrath,' the retribution which would befall the disobedient, but for conscience' sake." 6. For for this cause ye pay tribute also; for they are ministers of God's service, attending continually upon this very thing. 7. Render to all their dues: tribute to whom tribute *is due;* custom to whom custom; fear to whom fear; honor to whom honor. "Magistrates are not only appointed for the public good, but they are the ministers of God, and consequently it is his will that we should contribute whatever is necessary to enable them to discharge their duty. The word rendered *ministers* means public servants, men appointed for any public work, civil or religious. Among the Greek democratical states, especially at Athens, those persons were particularly so called, who were required to perform some public service at their own expense. It is used in Scripture in a general sense, for servants or ministers (Rom. 15:16; Heb. 1:7; 8:2). The magistrates are divinely commissioned, or authorized to collect tribute. This

1 CORINTHIANS 3:4. For when one saith, I am of Paul; and another, I am of Apollos; are ye not men?

5. What then is Apollos? and what is Paul? Ministers through whom ye believed; and each as the Lord gave to him.

6. I planted, Apollos watered; but God gave the increase.

7. So then neither is he that planteth anything, neither he that watereth; but God that giveth the increase.

8. Now he that planteth and he that watereth are one: but each shall receive his own reward according to his own labor.

9. For we are God's fellow-workers: ye are God's husbandry, God's building.

---

is necessary to the support of government; and government being a divine institution, God, in ordaining the end, has thereby ordained the means." — *Charles Hodge*. Of course we cannot read Paul's admonition to pay tribute to Caesar without remembering at once similar words of our blessed Lord in Matthew 22:21; Luke 20:22 and 23:2.

IV. THE SIN OF DIVISIONS IN THE CHURCH AND THE TRUTH THAT ACKNOWLEDGED WILL PREVENT SUCH, 1 Corinthians 3:4-9. Teachers may want to omit this final division, not only for lack of time, but because it may seem a little out of place here. Probably it was assigned to this lesson because it shows how the lack of Christian love brought about some very serious divisions in the Corinthian church, and perhaps in others, and also sets forth the truth which, if recognized, will heal these divisions — that Christian leaders in themselves are not responsible for the flourishing condition of a church, for while some plant and others water, it is God Himself who gives the increase. **4. For when one saith, I am of Paul; and another, I am of Apollos; are ye not men? 5. What then is Apollos? and what is Paul? Ministers through whom ye believed; and each as the Lord gave to him. 6. I planted, Apollos watered; but God gave the increase. 7. So then neither is he that planteth anything, neither he that watereth; but God that giveth the increase. 8. Now he that planteth and he that watereth are one: but each shall receive his own reward according to his own labor. 9. For we are God's fellow-workers: ye are God's husbandry, God's building.** The one who plants and the one who waters are not rivals, as the Corinthians had been representing them. We are all laborers together with God, His field and His building. "In all three clauses, the first word is very emphatic. This is the real shame of the party spirit, that they are all God's: as God's, they must be one. There must be no factions: planter and waterer are 'fellow-workers' — not rivals; and they were *God's* workers — therefore, in any case, one in Him. The meaning is not 'fellow-workers *with* God,' but belonging to God. The church has already been described by implication as a field (vs. 6-8), in the next section (vs. 10-16) it is described as a building; the last clauses of verse 9 summarize the one section and introduce the other." — *J. E. McFadyen*. I have known outstanding Christian men, in the midst of a mighty work for God, confess gladly and frankly that they were not able, by any standards they knew, any virtue they possessed, or by any particular merit of their messages, to account for the great blessing and unusual presence of God being experienced; so they would simply conclude, "This is all of the Lord."

THE LESSON IN LIFE, LITERATURE, AND ARCHAEOLOGY.

The first paragraph of the 13th chapter of the Roman Epistle was used over and over again in the days of the Commonwealth, and among the Puritans as they revolted against the immoralities of kings, and the yoke of some monarchs. Milton, in his "Treatise of Civil Power," remarked on the phrase, "Let every soul be subject to the higher powers: "First, how prove they that the apostle means other powers than such as they to whom he writes were then under; who medld not at all in ecclesiastical causes, unless as tyrants and persecuters; and from them, I hope, they will not derive either the right of magistrates to judge in spiritual things, or the dutie of such our obedience.   How prove they next, that he entitles them here to spiritual causes, from whom he witheld, as much as in him lay, the judging of civil (1 Cor. 6:1, etc.).   If he himself appealed to Cesar, it was to judge his innocence, not his religion."   On the phrase, "He is the minister of God to thee for good," he added, "But in that office and to that end and by those means which in this place must be clearly found, if from this place they intend to argue.   And how for thy good by forcing, oppressing and insnaring thy conscience?   Many are the ministers of God, and their offices no less different then many; none more different than state and church government.   Who seeks to govern both must needs be worse than lord prelate or church-pluralist: for he in his own facultie and profession, the other not in his own and for the most part not thoroughly understood makes himself supreme lord or pope of the church as far as his civil jurisdiction stretches, and all the ministers of God therein, his ministers, or his curates rather in the function only, not in the government: while he himself assumes to rule by civil power things to be ruled only by spiritual."

A TRUTH FOR THE CLASS TO CARRY AWAY.

Among conservative believers, it seems there has never been a time, at least in this century, of so much quarreling, division, bitter words, unjustified accusations, etc., in the Church as today.   Too many Christian leaders are walking around with chips on their shoulders just waiting for someone to do something or say something with which they can disagree.   As children of God, indwelt by the Holy Spirit, with the command of love for one another upon us, we should vow before God that everything we say and do, and every word we write concerning other Christians will be done in love.

What are the differences between the relation of a Christian to the Church and his relation to the State?   What should a Christian do if the State commands him to bow down in adoration to a human being?   Where in the Old Testament do we find an illustration of a man who, though holding a high office in the State, nevertheless put God first?   (See Daniel 6.)   Was the Roman state fair to the Apostle Paul?   What can you recall in Christ's teachings that would almost parallel those of Paul on the State?

LESSON XII. — September 19.

GROWING IN CHRISTIAN LOVE. — Matthew 5:43–48; 18:21–35; Ephesians 4:25—5:2; 1 John 4:7–21.

PRINTED TEXT, Matthew 5:43–48; 1 John 4:11–19.

Devotional Reading: 1 John 3:18–24.
Beginner Topic: AT ZACCHEUS' HOUSE.
 Lesson Material: Luke 19:1–10; 1 John 3:16–18.
 Memory Verse: Be ye kind one to another.   Ephesians 4:32.
Primary Topic: LOVING AND FORGIVING.
 Lesson Material: Matthew 5:43–48; 18:21–35; 1 John 4:16–21.
 Memory Verse: Let us love one another; for love is of God.   1 John 4:7.
Junior Topic: LOVING AND FORGIVING.
 Lesson Material: Matthew 5:43–48; 18:21–35; 1 John 4:16–21.
 Memory Verse: Let us love one another; for love is of God.   1 John 4:7.

315

Intermediate-Senior Topic: GROWING IN CHRISTIAN LOVE.
  Lesson Material: Matthew 5:43–48; Ephesians 4:25—5:2; 1 John 4:7–21.
  Memory Verse: Above all these things *put on* love, which is the bond of perfectness. Colossians 3:14.
Topic for Young People and Adults: GROWING IN CHRISTIAN LOVE.
  Lesson Material: Matthew 5:43–48; Ephesians 4:25—5:2; 1 John 4:7–21.
  Memory Verse: Above all these things *put on* love, which is the bond of perfectness. Colossians 3:14.

THE TEACHER AND HIS CLASS.

The Younger Classes might be asked if they have had any wrong done to them during the week, that is, if someone slapped them, pushed them over on their bicycles, broke one of their toys, stole a pencil, or told an untruth about them. No doubt each one will have something to say, even if it is not quite according to fact. Then we should ask, what do we do? Well, we get angry; maybe we fight; maybe we try to do the same thing to them as they have done to us. Now in the New Testament there is another way of solving such a situation as this, and that is the way of *forgiveness*, which means not only not taking revenge, or doing to others what they have done to us, but, if the heart of the wrong-doer is repentant, to forgive him, to blot it out, to go on as though it had never happened, to be the same friends again, if the forgiveness is genuine.

The Older Classes will find the truth of this lesson more needed today, probably, than ever in history, for a totalitarian government (and two-thirds of the world is under the dominion of such) inculcates hatred. Hitler and those who were with him said that the Christian virtues of mercy and forgiveness led to softness. They should be abandoned and hate and hardness should take their place. In the schools of Russia hymns of hate are sung and young people are taught to hate the democracies. Out of this comes war, treachery, and brutality. The Archbishop of York, Dr. Cyril Garbett, recently said, "Demons of hate and suspicion are at large." All Soviet propaganda is now occupied with one major theme — hate America.

THE LESSON IN ITS SETTING.

Time. — The Sermon on the Mount was delivered in the summer of A.D. 28.

The words taken from Matthew 18 were spoken in the Autumn of A.D. 29. Paul wrote his letter to the Ephesians in prison, perhaps between A.D. 65 and 67. The First Epistle of John may have been written as late as A.D. 95.

Place. — We do not know on what mount the Sermon on the Mount was delivered. The discourse from Matthew 18 was delivered in Capernaum. Ephesus was a great city in Asia Minor. It may have been that John was living there when he wrote the First Epistle.

THE PLAN OF THE LESSON.

SUBJECT: The Inevitable Consequences in the Life of Any Man or Woman Where the Root of All Action and Thought Is the Indwelling Love of God.

I. "LOVE YOUR ENEMIES" — SO CHRIST SAID, Matthew 5:43–48.

II. THE LAW OF FORGIVENESS, Matthew 18:21–35.
  1. The principle, vs. 21–22.
  2. The illustrating parable, vs. 23–35.

III. THE LIFE OF THE NEW MAN IN CHRIST, Ephesians 4:25—5:2.

IV. THE LIFE OF LOVE IN THE FAMILY OF GOD, 1 John 4:7–21.

THE TEACHER'S LIBRARY.

On the verses taken from the Sermon on the Mount one of the finest chapters will be found in J. O. Dykes' *The Manifesto of the King*, 311–329. There are some good things on forgiveness in a new book by Paul Ramsay, *Basic Christian Ethics*. For sermonic material on this paragraph, see J. H. Jowett, *Brooks by the Traveller's Way*, 129–140, and J. S. Holden, *Your Reasonable Service*, 69–80. On the First Epistle of John there are three great volumes, in addition to others of lesser importance: Robert Law, *The Tests of Life*; Robert Candlish, *Lectures on the First Epistle of John*, which has recently been reprinted, a book every Christian should possess; and, George G. Findlay, *Fellowship in the Life Eternal*. It is not necessary to give here sermonic material, so I am giving only the following: James Hastings', *Great Texts of the Bible, James — Jude,* 367–386; Charles H. Spurgeon, *The Metropolitan Tabernacle Pulpit,* Vol. 17, *1871,* 481–492; and Vol. 22, *1876,* 337–348.

AUDIO-VISUAL AIDS.

FILM: "Love Thy Neighbor," Family Films,

30 min., sd., b&w. Lem, the postman contrives to teach a lesson of neighborly helpfulness in a situation which turns to real love between a widow and a young neighbor, while a grouchy landlord is ministered to while he is sick and comes to be a happy, helpful citizen. Not a real development of Christian love, but an application of neighborly concern.

MATTHEW 5:43. Ye have heard that it was said, Thou shalt love thy neighbor, and hate thine enemy:

44. But I say unto you, Love your enemies, andpray for them that persecute you;

45. That ye may be sons of your Father who is in heaven: for he maketh his sun to rise on the evil and the good, and sendeth rain on the just and the unjust.

46. For if ye love them that love you, what reward have ye? do not even the publicans the same?

47. And if ye salute your brethren only, what do ye more *than others?* do not even the Gentiles the same?

48. Ye therefore shall be perfect, as your heavenly Father is perfect.

I. "LOVE YOUR ENEMIES" — SO CHRIST SAID, Matthew 5:43–48. The paragraph assigned for the beginning of our lesson is found in the midst of the Sermon on the Mount. Let us have the verses before us, and then try to understand the meaning. 43. Ye have heard that it was said, Thou shalt love thy neighbor, and hate thine enemy: 44. but I say unto you, Love your enemies, and pray for them that persecute you; 45. that ye may be sons of your Father who is in heaven: for he maketh his sun to rise on the evil and the good, and sendeth rain on the just and the unjust. 46. For if ye love them that love you, what reward have ye? do not even the publicans the same? 47. And if ye salute your brethren only, what do ye more *than others?* do not even the Gentiles the same? 48. Ye therefore shall be perfect, as your heavenly Father is perfect. To begin with, let us recognize that love for our enemies is not something unheard of until New Testament times. While it is true that in Leviticus 19:18 it does say, "Thou shalt love thy neighbor as thyself," still in such a passage as Exodus 23:4 and 5 we have a principle of honesty and mercy toward our enemy. And in Proverbs 24:17–18 we read: "Rejoice not when thine enemy falleth, and let not thine heart be glad when he is overthrown." Still our Lord's words lift this whole matter onto a higher plane. Oswald Dykes, in the volume mentioned above, has well said: "It is the son's mark and glory to be like his father. Now the chief characteristic of the divine goodness is, that it is over all, wide as His works, embracing evil as well as good. So wide, so unconfined, so free from selfishness and passion, ought your love to be, if you would carry on your soul the family features of the 'sons of God.' . . . Those barriers which are raised by ancestry, climate, education, or society, to sunder brother-men, and make them no true neighbours to each other, oppose no obstacle to His equal bounty." — *Oswald Dykes.* "The brilliance of the ideal almost consumes me. The vastness of the height tends to make me faint and despondent even before I leave the base. Let us hold the commandment squarely before us. 'Love your enemies.' The man who makes your misery his policy, who dogs your steps, who sets snares for your feet, who twists your words, who is always pointing out the fly in the ointment, and who is never happier than when he is slowly dropping bitterness into your cup; *your enemy, love him.* There must be no fiery retaliation, no mere chilling toleration, no proud and lofty contempt. I must remain well-disposed toward him, watching my opportunity to save him from himself." — *J. H. Jowett.* Let me close our discussion of this passage with some more recent words by Professor Ramsay, in the work referred to above: "If a person has love for his enemy-neighbor from whom he can expect no good in return but only hostility and persecution, then alone does it become certain that he does not simply love himself in loving his neighbor.   If you wish to assure yourself that love is disinterested, you must remove every possibility of requital.   Among relationships with living men this is exactly what happens with respect to the enemy.   If love persists notwithstanding hostility, then it is in truth disinterested. If, therefore, you wish to prove whether you love disinterestedly, then sometimes pay attention to how you behave toward your enemy.   Much love, unquestionably the most, if subjected to such sharp testing, would appear to be selfishness. . . . A Christian does not love his enemy for being his enemy any more than he loves his friend merely for being his friend: in either case he loves his neighbor, in spite of his hostility or, what may be just as much a hindrance, *in spite of* his friendship. Love for enemy simply provides a crucial test for the presence or absence of regard for the neighbor for his own sake." — *Paul Ramsay.*

II. **THE LAW OF FORGIVENESS,** Matthew 18:21–35.   The Jewish rabbis of the time of Christ said that forgiveness should be offered three times and no more, basing their declaration on Amos 1:3 and 2:6 and Job 33:29–30.   Simon Peter, however, already imbibing some of the spirit of Christ, asked if forgiveness offered seven times would be adequate in the new Christian dispensation.   The immediate answer of our Lord is, "No, not seven times, but seventy times seven."   That is, the number of times we forgive should be unlimited.   He illustrates this with the famous parable of the unmerciful forgiven servant.   A certain servant owed a king 10,000 talents, or about $12,000,000.00, which was about five times the total annual tax for Galilee and Perea.   "But Oriental kings were free in the use of money and in making debts like the native kings of India today."   When it was clear that the servant could never clear this debt, the king commanded that his wife and children and all his property be sold, Roman law asserting that a debtor's wife and children were part of his property.   Overwhelmed with grief, the servant fell down before his lord, beseeching him to have mercy, and making a promise he could never keep, that if he had time he would pay the entire debt. Though the lord knew that such a debt could never be cleared in the lifetime of a servant, moved with compassion he forgave him, that is, he cancelled the debt. Now it so happened that this servant was the creditor of a fellow-servant who owed him a hundred shillings, here in our money something less than $20.00.   When he demanded the debt be paid and the fellow-servant likewise fell down, beseeching him for mercy and time, the forgiven servant, hard of heart, cast him into prison. When other servants, knowing how the king had forgiven the unforgiving one, went to the lord and told him, the cruel though forgiven servant was brought before him, rebuked for his unmerciful attitude, and now cast into prison.   And thus our Lord said, "So also shall my heavenly Father do unto you if ye forgive not every one his brother from your hearts."   Now we must ask what this means.   I like the words of the late Dr. Robert C. McQuilkin: "What can this mean?   That Christians will be delivered to the tormentors?   Will Peter and others ever sin in this way and lose their salvation?   Let us ask the parable only one question, What is its central message?   Is it not a message concerning the attitude of the Christian's heart toward those who have sinned against them?   As God has forgiven me a debt of sin against Him, which is beyond all reckoning, I must from my heart forgive my brother who has sinned against me.   These wrongs are as nothing compared with what I have been forgiven.   I do not forgive men in order to be forgiven, but because I have been forgiven.   One who persists in his unforgiving spirit may by that indicate that he has never been born of the Spirit.   A true Christian who holds an unforgiving spirit will be chastened by the Lord, even to the extent of losing his physical life.   (See 1 Cor. 11:30–32.)   The withdrawal of the remission of the debt by the king in the parable does not mean that the Lord withdraws His salvation from the saved man, or that He has ever granted His salvation to the professing Christian who is not saved.   The parabolic teaching is a warning to all professing Christians: the real Christian evidences the fact that he is saved by heeding the warning." — *Dr. Robert C. McQuilkin.*

III. **THE LIFE OF THE NEW MAN IN CHRIST,** Ephesians 4:25—5:2.   In the first three chapters of this Epistle our great privileges in Christ, and the work of the Holy Spirit in a believer, is set forth in some of the most exalted sentences that ever came from Paul's pen.   The second half of the Epistle is occupied with a discussion of the outworking of this Divine life, imparted to us through Christ. In the preceding paragraph, verses 17–24, the old life, which a Christian leaves behind, is summarized, while in the paragraph before us the new life which he is to live is unfolded.   Professor Findlay entitles his chapter discussing this paragraph: "Discarded Vices."   Bishop Moule entitles his chapter on the same verses, "Total Abstinence from Sinning in the Forgiven Life."   "Let us observe at the outset that St. Paul deals with the actual and pressing temptations of his readers.   He recalls what they had been, and forbids them to be such again.   The associations and habits of former life, the hereditary force of evil, the atmosphere of Gentile society, and added to all this, as we discover from chapter 5:6, the persuasions of the sophistical teachers now beginning to infest the Church, tended to draw the Asian Christians back to Gentile ways and to break down the moral distinctions that separated them from the pagan world.

"Amongst the discarded vices of the forsaken Gentile life, the following are here distinguished: *lying, theft, anger, idle speech, malice, impurity, greed.*   These may be reduced to sins of temper, of word, and of act." — *G. G. Findlay.*

It is impossible to discuss each of these words minutely, inasmuch as this paragraph is not in the printed text, but the words of verse 31 are excellently interpreted in the following lines of Professor Findlay: "The last of these terms is the most typical.   *Malice* is badness of disposition, the aptness to envy and hatred, which apart from any special occasion is always ready to break out in bitterness and wrath.   *Bitterness* is malice sharpened to a point and directed against the exasperating object.   *Wrath* and *anger* are synonymous, the former being the passionate outburst of resentment in rage, the latter the settled indignation of the aggrieved soul: this passion was put under restraint already in verses 26, 27.   *Clamour* and *railing* give audible expression to these and their kindred tempers.   Clamour is the loud self-assertion of the angry man, who will make every one hear his grievance; while the railer carries the war of the tongue into his enemy's camp, and vents his displeasure in abuse and insult." — *G. G. Findlay.*

The root of this kind of a life, where these vices are discarded, is nothing less than the love of God in Christ, and I know of no one who has concisely set this forth with finer understanding than the one from whom we have already quoted: "God is love; but love is not everything in God.   Justice is also Divine, and absolute in its own realm.   Law can no more forgo its rights than love forget its compassions.   Love must fulfil all righteousness; it must suffer law to mark out its path of obedience, or it remains an effusive, ineffectual sentiment, helpless to bless and save.   Christ's feet followed the stern and strait path of self-devotion; 'He humbled Himself and became obedient,' He was 'born under law.'   And the law of God imposing death as the penalty for sin, which shaped Christ's sacrifice, made it acceptable to God.   Thus it was 'an odour of a sweet smell.' " — *G. G. Findlay.*

IV. **THE LIFE OF LOVE IN THE FAMILY OF GOD,** 1 John 4:7–21.   The First Epistle of John is a love-letter.   Nine times God is set forth here as our Father.   Over and over again we are called the children of God and brothers one of another.   The word *love* is a noun and a verb, is found nearly 40 times in this Epistle.   The great passage we are now to study deserves a whole book, and I regret we can give it so little space.   In the first four verses of our lesson we have God's love emphasized: first, that God is love, second, that love is of God, third, that God first loved us, proving it by sending His Son to be the propitiation for our sins, and then the great consequent statement that "Every one that loveth is begotten of God and knoweth God."   I shall frequently use here the most remarkable interpretation of this Epistle, in my opinion, ever written, that by Robert

1 John 4:11. Beloved, if God so loved us, we also ought to love one another.

Candlish, many years ago principal of New College, Edinburgh. Let us begin with his interpretation of the phrase, "God is love." "It is a necessity of his nature, it is his very nature, to love. He cannot exist without loving. He cannot but love. He is, he has ever been, love. From all eternity, from before all worlds, God is love. Love never is or can be, never was or could be, absent from his being. He never is or can be, he never was or could be, God, without being also love; without loving. I say without loving; actually loving.

"For this love, which is thus identified with His very being, is not dormant or quiescent; potential merely; *in posse*, and not *in esse*. It never is or can be so, — it never has been or could have been so. . . . It is, it has ever been, active, forth-going, self-manifesting, self-communicating. It is, it has ever been, in exercise. Before creation, it is so. In the bosom of the everlasting Father is his own eternal, only begotten Son. And with the Father and the Son is the Holy Ghost. So God is love, before all creation; love in exercise; love not possible merely but actual; love forthgoing and communicative of itself; from the Father, the fountain of deity, to the Son; from the Father and the Son to the Holy Ghost. . . .

"None but one born of God can thus love, with the love which, in this sense, is of God; therefore one who so loves must needs be one who is born of God. This is almost self-evident. . . . It is something different from the love enjoined in the 'royal law,' — 'Thou shalt love thy neighbour as thyself.' It is the very love with which the Father loves, the love manifested in his not sparing his beloved Son. It is the very love with which the Son loves, the love proved by his laying down his life for us. That is the love, the love of the 'new commandment,' which is here in question. Of that love I think it may be said that God alone originally is capable of it; others are capable of it, only in so far as God communicates himself to them; not by a process of mere creative power; but by begetting them into participation with himself in his own very life." — *Robert Candlish.*

A paragraph on the death of Christ, the proof of God's love, belongs here: " 'God commendeth *His own love* to us,' says St. Paul, 'in that Christ died for us' (Rom. 5:8). The proof lies in the cost of the sacrifice to Him who 'spared not His own Son.' Granting Jesus Christ to be the very Son of God, here on the Father's business and under His direction, no other explanation of the event of His death is possible. From love to men and with the purpose of redeeming them from sin, God sent His Son to suffer and die, and contemplated the sacrifice from eternity. Indeed, our Lord seems to say that God loved *Him* for this very reason — not for His own sake merely, but for His devotion to us: 'Therefore doth the Father love me, because I lay down my life' (John 10:17). St. John, with St. Paul, glories in nothing so much as in the cross of his Lord, because the propitiation that it makes for sin displays the love of God in its uttermost reach, and reveals a grace that overmatches man's abounding guilt. When one knows this love, he knows God. The universe has no greater secret to tell him; heaven and eternity will be but the unfolding of 'the love of God which is in Christ Jesus our Lord.' " — *George G. Findlay.* **11. Beloved, if God so loved us, we also ought to love one another.** "When the Apostle writes, 'If God so loved us, we ought also to love one another,' what is his argument? where does the obligation lie? Does he mean, 'We must pay the great Lover back in kind; we must love the children for the Father's sake'? It is a loftier and directer appeal that he really makes; the logic is that of imitation, not of bare gratitude: . . . the Father's own love to men beats in our breast; for He is in us, He has given us of His Spirit' (vers. 13, 16). . . . Since He has called these aliens into His household and bestowed on them His Spirit, 'giving them the like gift as to us,' His love to them may not be gainsaid; we must give it free course. This man or that may be antipathetic to myself, his temper averse from mine, his style and habits of mind uncongenial, — naturally, I should dislike and avoid him;

320

12. No man hath beheld God at any time: if we love one another, God abideth in us, and his love is perfected in us:

13. Hereby we know that we abide in him and he in us, because he hath given us of his Spirit.

14. And we have beheld and bear witness that the Father hath sent the Son *to be* the Saviour of the world.

15. Whosoever shall confess that Jesus is the Son of God, God abideth in him, and he in God.

---

but God loves and owns the man — how can I oppose His gracious will or despise what God esteems? This is the argument that beats down pride, and makes coldness of heart amongst Christians a mean and miserable thing." — *George G. Findlay*.

12. No man hath beheld God at any time: if we love one another, God abideth in us, and his love is perfected in us: 13. hereby we know that we abide in him and he in us, because he hath given us of his Spirit. "As the human parent once for all imparts his own nature to his offspring, so, in virtue of the Divine Begetting, the Divine nature is permanently imparted to the children of God (3:9 'His' *i.e.* God's, 'seed abideth in him'). But, whereas in the human relationship the life-germ thus communicated is developed in a separate and independent existence, in the higher relationship it is not so. The life imparted is dependent for its sustenance and growth upon a continuous inflex of life from the parent-source. Thus the analogy followed is taken from the facts of vegetable rather than of animal life; originally, as has been said, from the similitudes of the Vine and the branches. The branches of a tree are actually children of the tree. . . . It is the sap of the parent vine that vitalizes all the branches, 'weaves all the green and golden lacework of their foliage, unfolds all their blossoms, mellows all their clusters, and is perfected in their fruitfulness.' So does the Life of God vitalize him in whom He abides, sustaining and fostering in him those energies — Righteousness, Love, and Truth, — which are the Divine nature itself. . . . Though the manner of it is inexplicable, as all vital processes are, this actual communication of the actual Life of God is the core of the Johannine theology. . . .

It may be useful to exhibit this in tabular form.

I. That God abides in us is certified —
    (a) by our keeping His commandments (3:24a);
    (b) by our loving one another (4:12);
    (c) by our confessing that Jesus is the Son of God (4:15), or by (the exact equivalent of this) the Spirit God hath given us (3:24b; 4:13).

II. That we abide in God is certified —
    (a) if we walk as Christ walked (2:6), if we sin not (3:6), if we keep His commandments (3:24a);
    (b) if we abide in Love (4:16);
    (c) if we have the Spirit that confesses Jesus as the Son of God (4:13).

III. The full reciprocal relation, that God abides in us and we in Him, is certified —
    (a) if we keep His commandments (3:24b);
    (b) if we abide in Love (4:16);
    (c) if we have the Spirit of God (4:13), the Spirit, namely, that confesses that Jesus is the Son of God (4:15). . . .

"Although the Epistle does not directly represent the Holy Spirit as the agent of this Divine Immanence, Christian Theology in doing so has only taken the next step in an inevitable process of thought. Eternal Life is the Divine nature reproducing itself in human nature; is the energy of the Spirit of God, of the Father and of the Son, in the spiritual nature of man." — *Robert Law*. **14. And we have beheld and bear witness that the Father hath sent the Son *to be* the Saviour of the world. 15. Whosoever shall confess that Jesus is the Son of God, God abideth**

16. And we know and have believed the love which God hath in us. God is love: and he that abideth in love abideth in God, and God abideth in him.

17. Herein is love made perfect with us, that we may have boldness in the day of judgment; because as he is, even so are we in this world.

18. There is no fear in love: but perfect love casteth out fear, because fear hath punishment; and he that feareth is not made perfect in love.

in him, and he in God. "How should the confession of a mere matter of fact be so certain a token of God's 'giving us of his Spirit,' and of his 'dwelling in us'? For it is a plain historical matter of fact, such as may be known and ascertained like other ordinary facts in history. It is to be received on the very same ground and warrant of historical evidence and testimony. (See 1:1–3.)

"The answer must be found in the nature and character of the fact believed, the truth confessed; or in the aspect in which it is presented, or presents itself to me. What is it in itself? What is it to me? If it is a fact or truth of a merely historical sort, and is so apprehended by me, my admission and avowal of it will be no proof or presumption of God's having 'given me of his Spirit, and dwelling in me,' — any more than my admission and avowal of any well-attested event that ever happened in the world. That may be my case; if so, it is a sad one. It may be to me a mere fact or truth of history; not only in its original form, naked and bald, 'Jesus Christ is come in the flesh'; but even in the more warm and living substance which it takes, when it is, as it were, clothed upon with the love which is from heaven. . . . It is God's Spirit dealing with my spirit, and that too upon a special theme; a specific subject; Jesus Christ come in the flesh, as the very Son of God, sent by the Father to be the Saviour of the world. . . . There, in the gospel, it is his love manifested to us. Here, in our hearts, it is his love felt in us; — not merely felt by us as the conscious objects of it, but felt by us as his love in us; — in us, so as to make us the conscious depositories of it, as it were, and the dispensers of it to others who are as much its objects as we are ourselves. The love of God, having us for its objects, passes from God's outer record into our inner life." — *Robert Candlish.*

16. **And we know and have believed the love which God hath in us. God is love: and he that abideth in love abideth in God, and God abideth in him.** 17. **Herein is love made perfect with us, that we may have boldness in the day of judgment; because as he is, even so are we in this world.** "Clearly, then, it is in the exercise of brotherly love that Love is here said to be perfected. Further, if we inquire why this is so, — what specific idea the Apostle intends to convey by the 'perfecting' of Love, — this also becomes clear when we compare the two passages in which this 'perfecting' is described: 'Whosoever keepeth His word, in him verily is the love of God perfected' (2:5); and 'If we love one another, God abideth in us, and His love is perfected in us' (4:12). Manifestly, the conception common to 'keeping His word' and 'loving one another' is the embodiment of Love in actual conduct. The assertion of perfectness refers, not to the strength or purity of Love as a sentiment, but solely to its bearing fruit in deeds which prove its reality and fulfil its purpose. The idea is that, not of qualitative, but of effective perfection. . . . It is only when we love one another with the love of God — the love which is His own, and which He begets in us — that His love is *fulfilled* in us. Then Love's circuit is complete, from God to us, from us to our brother, and through our brother back to God. (Cf. Matt. 25:40.) . . .

"All that life most profoundly signifies is contained in the thought of our final responsibility to God (2 Cor. 5:9, 10). This confidence is a present possession, not only because the Apostle thinks of the Day of Judgment as at hand, but because the thought of that Day and of its issue for us is, or ought to be, present to our minds." — *Robert Law.* 18. **There is no fear in love: but perfect love casteth out fear, because fear hath punishment; and he that feareth is not made perfect in**

19. We love, because he first loved us.

love. "In the preceding verse it has been asserted that Love 'fulfilled' establishes the Christian in confidence toward God, as being the fruit and the test of his fellowship with Christ. . . . . Fear towards God is the product of the self-accusing heart. But 'there is no Fear in Love.' In loving one another there is no matter of self-accusation, there is nothing to give occasion to fear. Fear is the sentinel of life; the self-protective instinct that gives warning of danger, and calls to arms against it; and Fear towards God is the sign that not all is well in our relation to Him, and that we instinctively know it. But Love gives no such warning signal. When we are living in Love we are doing those things which are 'well-pleasing in His sight' (3:22); we are 'abiding in the Light' (2:10); we have 'fellowship one with another, and the blood of Jesus, His Son, cleanseth us from all sin' (1:7)." — *Robert Law.*

19. **We love, because he first loved us.** Spurgeon often preached on this verse and each time he had a different title for the sermon. One was, "Love's Logic"; another, "Love's Birth and Parentage." We have only space to quote less than a page from the more than sixty pages that can be found in the great *Metropolitan Tabernacle Pulpit* on this short sentence. "The love of God is before our seeking; he draws us before we run after him. We do not seek that love; that love seeks us. We wander further and further from it, resist it, and prove ourselves unworthy of it: such are our nature and our practice, that they offer nothing congenial to divine love, but the love of God arises in its freeness and stays our mad career by its power over the conscience and the will. 'Ye have not chosen me, but I have chosen you,' is the voice of sovereign grace; let our response be, 'By the grace of God we are what we are.'

"The Lord's love is before any repentance on our part. Impenitent sinners never would repent if God did not love them first. The Lord hates sin, but yet he loves sinners; he compassionately loved us when sin was pleasant to us, when we rolled it under our tongue as a sweet morsel, when neither the thunders of his law nor the wooings of his gospel could persuade us to turn from it. When in our bosoms there were no convictions of sin, when there were no evangelical lamentations because of offences against a gracious God, he loved us then. Today, brethren, we are possessors of faith in Jesus Christ, but our faith in Jesus Christ did not come before his love; on the contrary, our faith rests in what that love has done for us of old. When we were unbelieving and hard of heart, and resisted the testimony of the Holy Spirit, and put from us the word of eternal life, even then the Lord pitied us, and had mercy upon us; and continued still to invite, still to entreat, still to persuade, till at last the happy hour came when we believed and entered into a sense of his love. There are many things about you now, beloved of the Lord, which are the objects of divine approbation, but they were not there at first; they did not precede divine love, but are the fruits of it. To use an old English word which has somewhat lost its meaning, the love of God is *preventing* love — it goes before any right motions of the soul, and in order of time it is *first*, before any desires, wishes, aspirations, or prayers on our part. Are you this day devout? Yet he loved you not at the first because you were devout, for originally you were not so: his love was first before your devotion." — *Charles H. Spurgeon.*

THE LESSON IN LIFE, LITERATURE, AND ARCHAEOLOGY.

My beloved friend, the late Dr. Harry Ironside, in his precious little volume, *Addresses on the Epistles of John*, speaks in a personal way of the 17th verse of our lesson. "I confess to you that there were years in my Christian life when I had the most confused ideas as to what these words really meant, and yet today I know of no passage of Scripture that gives me greater joy or seems clearer, than this verse which puzzled me for so long. Shortly after I was converted, I pored over it and said, 'I can't understand it.' Of course I was misled by the authorized reading, and did not notice how beautifully it is corrected in the margin. I pored over the words, 'Herein is our love made perfect, that we may have boldness in the day of judgment: because as He is, so are we in this world,' and I said to myself, 'If boldness in the day of judgment depends upon my love being perfect, how can I ever be sure that everything will be right with me?' I was looking at myself and within my own heart for perfect love, and as I searched that poor heart, I was always finding something there that was contrary to perfect love, and I would say to myself, 'Am I ever going to be perfect in love? I cannot have boldness in the day of judgment until my love is perfect.' . . . It was like a second and even more glorious conversion than when I was first saved, when God showed me that perfect love is in another Man altogether. I had been looking for it in this man for six and one-half years after my conversion, and God one day turned me away from myself and said to me, 'Look up there!' And by faith I saw another Man, the Man Christ Jesus, seated in highest glory at the Father's right hand, and God said to me, as it were, 'There it is; perfect love is displayed in Christ.' 'Herein' — wherein? Why, 'In this was manifested the love of God toward us, because that God sent His only begotten Son into the world, that we might live through Him.' " — *Dr. Harry Ironsides.*

A TRUTH FOR THE CLASS TO CARRY AWAY.

There is a danger that a lesson on such a mystical, delicate, indefinable subject as love for one another and love for God though taught accurately and earnestly, may come to an end without any definite resolution on the part of the class to carry out these great principles. Thus, it seems to me that the teacher would do well to conclude this lesson by urging the class to begin that day a positive practice of the truths just considered; e.g., are we not neglecting a letter to a loved one, a father or mother, telling them that we love them? I recall one of the greatest preachers of America saying in a circle of friends one night that though he had invitations from all over the world to teach and speak, he would like one experience to be his before he died — to have a member of his church come to the front door of his home and say, "Doctor, I have not come with any request or any criticism, but have just come to tell you that I love you and am praying for you."

How are the truths of this lesson illustrated in the life of Christ recorded in the Gospels? Where would you say was the greatest single illustration of the truths of this lesson in the life and writings of the Apostle Paul? (Is it not in the first five verses of Romans 9?) What is the appropriateness of this letter of love, the First Epistle of John, being written by the "disciple whom Jesus loved"? Do you think it is possible for the Christian Church, by definite effort, to grow in the manifestation of the Christian virtues set forth in this lesson? What forces in the world today are inculcating hate rather than love?

LESSON XIII. — September 26.

LIVING WITNESSES. — Matthew 5:13–16; John 1:40–42a; Acts 4:13–20; 8:4–8, 26–40; 2 Corinthians 5:11–20; 1 Peter 3:13–16.

PRINTED TEXT, Matthew 5:13–16; Acts 8:4–8; 2 Corinthians 5:14–20.

Devotional Reading: Romans 10:4–15.

Beginner Topic: AS TIMOTHY GREW.

    Lesson Material: Acts 16:1–5; 2 Timothy 1:1–6; 2:15; 3:14–17.

    Memory Verse: Thou art nigh, O Jehovah. Psalm 119:151.

Primary Topic: FRIENDS OF JESUS.

    Lesson Material: Acts 8:4–8.

    Memory Verse: Ye are my friends, if ye do the things which I command you. John 15:14.

Junior Topic: BRAVE FRIENDS OF JESUS.
> **Lesson Material:** Acts 4:13–20; 8:4–8.
> **Memory Verse:** By this shall all men know that ye are my disciples, if ye have love one to another.   John 13:35.

Intermediate-Senior Topic: LIVING WITNESSES.
> **Lesson Material:** Matthew 5:13–16; Acts 4:13–16; 8:4–8, 26–40; 2 Corinthians 5:11–20; 1 Peter 3:13–16.
> **Memory Verse:** Let your light shine before men; that they may see your good works, and glorify your Father who is in heaven.   Matthew 5:16.

Topic for Young People and Adults: LIVING WITNESSES.
> **Lesson Material:** Matthew 5:13–16; Acts 4:13–16; 8:4–8, 26–40; 2 Corinthians 5:11–20; 1 Peter 3:13–16.
> **Memory Verse:** Let your light shine before men; that they may see your good works, and glorify your Father who is in heaven.   Matthew 5:16.

THE TEACHER AND HIS CLASS.

The Younger Classes may be introduced to this lesson by having their attention directed to a word appearing toward the end of the text, which represents one aspect of Christian witnessing, the principal subject of our lesson — the word *ambassador*. An ambassador to our land from a foreign country, or *vice versa*, must first be fully acquainted with the will and interests of the people he represents. He must unselfishly seek to forward the interest of his own country. He must be loyal to those whom he represents, and should have those characteristics and qualities which will win for his country the respect of the people to whom he is sent. An ambassador in any country has the highest rating of any foreign citizen residing in that land.

The Older Classes may well have emphasized, in an hour like this, the word here translated *witness, martyr,* and the teacher may want to begin the lesson with a discussion of this word *martyr*, which he will find in subsequent notes.

THE LESSON IN ITS SETTING.

Time. — The Sermon on the Mount was delivered in the spring of A.D. 27. The event recorded in the first chapter of John's Gospel occurred in February, A.D. 27. The experience of the apostles in Acts 4 may be placed at A.D. 30–31; the ministry of Philip, A.D. 35; and the writing of the Second Epistle to the Corinthians and possibly the First Epistle of Peter, A.D. 60.

Place. — We are not sure where the Sermon on the Mount was delivered, but it was probably in Galilee. The incident involving the early disciples took place near Capernaum. The events of Acts 4 occurred in Jerusalem, and the ministry of Philip was carried on principally in Samaria, the great area between Judea and Galilee.

THE PLAN OF THE LESSON.

SUBJECT: The World's Need for Faithful Witnesses to Christ, and Some Illustrations of How This was Met in the Early Church, Together with Some of the Great Truths that Should Create an Urgency for Witnessing on Our Part.

I. TWO ILLUSTRATIONS OF THE MEANING OF WITNESSING, Matthew 5:13–16.
   1. We are as salt, v. 13.
   2. We are to shine as lights, vs. 14–16.

II. EARLY ATTEMPTS TO SUPPRESS WITNESSING FOR CHRIST, Acts 4:13–20.

III. TWO EXAMPLES OF EFFECTIVE WITNESSING.
   1. Among Christ's earliest disciples, John 1:40–42a.
   2. Philip the evangelist, Acts 8:4–8, 26–40.

IV. ALL CHRISTIANS ARE AMBASSADORS OF CHRIST, 2 Corinthians 5:14–20.

V. THE PREREQUISITE OF RIGHTEOUS LIVING, 1 Peter 3:13–16.

THE TEACHER'S LIBRARY.

From among all the volumes devoted to the subject of the Sermon on the Mount, I would suggest the following for the verses of our lesson: J. Oswald Dykes: *The Manifesto of the King;* W. Boyd Carpenter: *The Great Charter of Christ,* 133–147; and G. D. Boardman: *Studies in the Mountain Instruction,* 61–83.

The finest comment on the verses from the first chapter of John is in the commentary by R. C. H. Lenski. On the Book of Acts, see the great volumes by G. Campbell Morgan, R. C. H. Lenski, W. M. Furneaux, R. B. Rackham, G. T. Stokes in the *Expositor's Bible.* On the ministry of Philip, see James Hastings: *The Greater Men and Women of the Bible,* Vol. 6, *St. Luke — Titus,* 114–134, and many pages in Alexander Maclaren: *Expositions of Holy Scripture, Acts — Romans 1–12.* On the verses from First Corinthians, the most magnificent treatment I know of will be found in the rich pages of James Denney in *The Expositor's Bible;* also, one might consult with profit the work on the two Corinthian Epistles by J. E. McFadyen.

For sermonic material, see John A. Hutton: *There They Crucified Him,* 197–208; J. H. Jowett: *Apostolic Optimism,* 171–188; H. P. Liddon: *University Sermons,* 183–202. On the entire subject of witnessing, see an article in James Hastings: *Dictionary of Christ and the Gospels,* Vol. 2, pp. 830–832; and a sermon in Canon Liddon: Easter in St. Paul's; also a study of the Greek word *martur,* by R. P. Casey, in *The Beginnings of Christianity,* Vol. 5, pp. 32–37.

AUDIO-VISUAL AIDS.

FILM: "Tammy," Lutheran Church — Missouri Synod, 40 min., sd., b&w. A little nine year old girl witnesses in her own home and wins finally her stubborn and embittered father to the Lord and the church. The way of salvation is faithfully presented.

MATTHEW 5:13. Ye are the salt of the earth: but if the salt have lost its savor, wherewith shall it be salted? it is thenceforth good for nothing, but to be cast out and trodden under foot of men.

14. Ye are the light of the world. A city set on a hill cannot be hid.

15. Neither do *men* light a lamp, and put it under the bushel, but on the stand; and it shineth unto all that are in the house.

16. Even so let your light shine before men; that they may see your good works, and glorify your Father who is in heaven.

I. TWO ILLUSTRATIONS OF THE MEANING OF WITNESSING, Matthew 5:13–16. These verses, so pregnant with meaning, are taken from the early part of the Sermon on the Mount, immediately following the Beatitudes. They are not addressed to an ordinary multitude of men and women, but to Christ's own followers and disciples, as the first verse of the chapter indicates: for no one can be salt and light, in the meaning that Jesus here assigns, unless he is united with Him. 13. **Ye are the salt of the earth: but if the salt have lost its savor, wherewith shall it be salted? it is thenceforth good for nothing, but to be cast out and trodden under foot of men.** The definite implication of this verse is that the world itself is corrupt and corrupting, that Christians (Gal. 6:8, 2 Pet. 1:4; 2:12, 19) as they live here among men, are to exert an influence retarding this corruption, as salt by its distinctive chemical nature retards and often prevents corruption taking place in meats, and other forms of food to which salt is applied. "Believers are as salt in society because their moral life is under the control of the Holy Spirit, their ideals are derived from the Word of God, and they live to please the Son of God. Again and again we find the word *wholesome* in the New Testament, which is the Greek word *hygiaino,* from which comes our English word 'hygiene.' (As in Matt. 12:13; John 5:4, 6, 9, 11; 1 Tim. 1:10; 2 Tim. 1:13; 4:3; Titus 1:9, 13). Thus each believer's life is, as it were, a stream of purifying, preserving power, poured into the social body of each age, maintaining in the midst of corruption a testimony to and a manifestation of those things that speak of abounding life, of soundness of character, of purity of conduct, of wholesomeness of speech, of justice, and love, and honor, and godliness. The foulness of the Roman world in the day of Christ, and the normal life of a *truly* Christian nation in modern times, reveals a contrast so striking as to illustrate vividly the salt work of the Church."

14. **Ye are the light of the world. A city set on a hill cannot be hid. 15. Neither do *men* light a lamp, and put it under the bushel, but on the stand; and it shineth unto all that are in the house. 16. Even so let your light shine before men; that they may see your good works, and glorify your Father who is in heaven.** "Jesus

elsewhere declares that he himself is the Light of the world (John 8:12; 9:5; 12:35; 1 John 1:7 ff). We of course understand that the light which his people emit is really derived from him (Eph. 5:8). In Philippians 2:15, they are compared to the heavenly luminaries; in John 5:35, the Baptist is called literally, 'the burning and shining lamp' — which Jesus had probably said before he spoke the Sermon on the Mount. . . . Christians are the light by means of which the world, the mass of mankind, may see the things of religion, may see the truth about God and his service. Anything that gives light will be observed, and Christians, as being the light of the world, cannot escape observation if they would. He does not say 'may glorify you,' for the good words of God's children are all due to him, and hence the beholders ought not to praise them, but to glorify their Father." — *J. R. Broadus.* "It is an awful thing to think that the world always — *always* — takes its conception of Christianity from the Church, and neither from the Bible nor from Christ; and that it is you and your like, you inconsistent Christians, you people that say your sins are forgiven and yet are doing the old sins day by day which you say are pardoned, you low-toned, unpraying, worldly Christian men, who have no elevation of character and no self-restraint of life and no purity of conduct above the men in your own profession and in your own circumstances all round you — it is you that are hindering the coming of Christ's Kingdom, it is you that are the standing disgrace of the Church, and the weaknesses and diseases of Christendom." — *Alexander Maclaren.* "Light clear, distinct and encouraging, may shine from every human life, and may make the pathway of a brother-man clearer and easier. It is true that it is not given to every man to make fresh discoveries, but every man may be a witness to the moral order of the universe, to the true grounds of happiness, to the responsibility of life." — *W. Boyd Carpenter.*

II. **EARLY ATTEMPTS TO SUPPRESS WITNESSING FOR CHRIST,** Acts 4:13–20. All students of the New Testament know that the Church was born at Pentecost at which time we have the preaching of the first great sermon by Simon Peter when many souls were saved as he set forth Jesus as Saviour and Lord under the anointing of the Holy Spirit, as recorded in the second chapter of the Book of Acts. The third chapter gives us a record of the first healing miracle performed by the apostles after the ascension of our Lord, and, the second sermon from Simon Peter. So great now was the movement from Judaism toward the recognition of Christ as the Messiah, whom, a year before, the Sanhedrin had condemned to death, that the Sadducees, and other officials of Judaism in Jerusalem, arrested these apostles, put them in prison, and then brought them up for trial, asking by what power, or in what name they were performing these miracles. The interesting point here is that they did not deny the miracles. The Apostle Peter, filled with the Holy Ghost, told them immediately, boldly, and clearly, that it was through the name of Jesus Christ, the very one they had crucified, now raised from the dead, that men were being healed, that salvation was being offered to mankind. The stone which they had set at nought had become the head of the corner. At this time these opponents had not yet prepared an answer to these statements. After consultation, they determined that, for the time being, all they would do would be to threaten them and command them to speak no longer or teach in the name of Jesus. To all this Peter and John replied with words that have been on the lips of many witnesses and martyrs since, "Whether it is right in the sight of God to hearken unto you rather than unto God, judge ye: for we cannot but speak the things which we saw and heard" (4:19, 20). In this incident, the Church begins to know the truthfulness, and witness the fulfilment of the prophetic words of Christ, uttered on Tuesday of Holy Week: "But take ye heed to yourselves: for they shall deliver you up to councils; and in synagogues shall ye be beaten; and before governors and kings shall ye stand for my sake, for a testimony unto them" (Mark 13:9). The unflinching faithfulness of the apostles at this hour has been matched by the servants of Christ in every generation. Only the day of resurrection will reveal how many millions have suffered death for Christ's sake.

ACTS 8:4. They therefore that were scattered abroad went about preaching the word.

III. **TWO EXAMPLES OF EFFECTIVE WITNESSING,** John 1:40–42a; Acts 8:4–8, 26–40. Those arranging our lesson-material have done well to give us two outstanding examples of effective witnessing for Christ in the early days of Christianity — one, recorded in John's Gospel, occurring in the first year of our Lord's public ministry, and the other, recorded in Acts 8, taking place in the early days of the Christian Church. Following the great Prologue which opens the Gospel of John, we have an account of the witness of John the Baptist to the coming Messiah. The hour having arrived for Jesus himself to appear, the forerunner cries out, "Behold, the Lamb of God." Two of the disciples of John the Baptist immediately turned, and followed Jesus, one of them being Andrew, and the other, no doubt, the writer of the Fourth Gospel, John the Evangelist. Andrew, a minor character in the Gospels, had not been in the presence of Jesus many hours before he became profoundly convinced that this person Jesus of Nazareth was none other than the Messiah, of whom Moses and the prophets did speak, and at once he went to find his brother, Simon Peter, who would for years be the head of the apostolic company. The Greek word translated *find* in this passage occurs three times in the chapter: here, again of Christ's finding Philip in verse 43, and then of Philip's finding Nathanael in verse 45. "From the verb 'finds' we cannot determine whether Andrew, and also John, sought his brother or only happened upon him when leaving Jesus. But the situation itself as here portrayed, especially the deep impression made by Jesus on the hearts of the two visitors inclines us to think that both forthwith sought, and so found, their brothers. They could not refrain from imparting what they had found in Jesus. . . . At best our seeking is only like a blind groping, which would be useless if God in his mercy did not lay the great treasure so near us, direct our groping hands, and blind eyes right to it, until touching it at last, lo, we find it! Andrew's finding his own brother, John's finding his, is an excellent example of home mission zeal. Also right from the start we see a communion of saints in the following of Jesus: first two, whose faith is so blended together in the moment of its origin that we cannot tell which was first, that of John or that of Andrew. And at once, the number doubles, and the two are increased to four, with two more immediately to join the four. This is how the church has grown and still grows to the present day." — *R. C. H. Lenski.* "The Hebrew *Mashiah*, Aramaic *Meshiha*, is the Greek *Christos*, a verbal adjective turned into a noun, signifying 'the Anointed One.' The Greek is from the ceremonial verb 'to anoint,' as contrasted with any smearing with oil. The term is appellative, like a descriptive title, and designates the high office of the Promised One, whoever he may be in his person. When this person was known as Jesus, the title 'Christ' was used directly to name him, yet always retained the original reference to the office involved. So also Andrew declares that he and John have found the person who is the Messiah." — *R. C. H. Lenski.*

In the 6th chapter of Acts we have an account of the appointment of a number of men, out of the company of believers in Jesus, to take care of the *business* matters of the church, the distribution of funds to the poor, etc., so that the apostles might give themselves more completely to prayer and the ministry of the Word. These men were not only full of the Holy Ghost, but they must have been men with a capacity for business and, of course, of transparent character. Among them was Philip. He was not one of the apostles, and was not called, originally, to preach. Nevertheless this business man does carry on a mighty ministry in witnessing, to which much more space is given than to many of the apostles in the New Testament. It would seem that it was the great persecution by Saul of Tarsus which, scattering the disciples, drove Philip north into Samaria. Acts 8:4–8. **4. They therefore that were scattered abroad went about preaching the**

328

5. And Philip went down to the city of Samaria, and proclaimed unto them the Christ.

6. And the multitudes gave heed with one accord unto the things that were spoken by Philip, when they heard, and saw the signs which he did.

7. For *from* many of those that had unclean spirits, they came out, crying with a loud voice: and many that were palsied, and that were lame, were healed.

8. And there was much joy in that city.

---

word. **5. And Philip went down to the city of Samaria, and proclaimed unto them the Christ. 6. And the multitudes gave heed with one accord unto the things that were spoken by Philip, when they heard, and saw the signs which he did. 7. For *from* many of those that had unclean spirits, they came out, crying with a loud voice: and many that were palsied, and that were lame, were healed. 8. And there was much joy in that city.** "The Samaritans were not entirely an alien race; there was Israelitish blood in their veins. But when they advanced pretensions to possession of the true law and temple, a violent quarrel with the Jews was the result. The Samaritans were worse than aliens. They were heretics, schismatics. In the Old Testament the bitterest enemy of Israel had been his brother Edom; so now the Jews had no dealings with the Samaritans. . . . The Lord himself had preached to the Samaritans at Sychar (about 7 miles from Samaria) for two days, and the conversation of the Samaritan woman shewed their strong Messianic convictions (John 4:4–42). Now Philip goes down to their capital, the old Samaria, which had been rebuilt by Herod the Great on a magnificent scale and called after Augustus — in Greek Sebastos — Sebaste. Here like a herald he proclaimed the Messiah, that is, the establishment of the kingdom of God (v. 12). This kingdom was neither the Jewish ecclesia nor the rival Samaritan ecclesia, but a new ecclesia which bore the name of Jesus, who had been anointed as its Messianic king or *Christ.* Philip confirmed his words by working many signs of healing. The superstition of the Samaritans made them specially liable to amazement (vs. 9, 11, 13) or, as the Authorized Version implies, to 'being bewitched' by a power they could not understand. Accordingly, the miracles were necessary in order to overthrow the power and influence which Simon had acquired over them by his false miracles. Those of Philip were real, and the result was corresponding. The attention of the whole population was won; the healings caused great joy; the people at once believed that Philip's words must likewise be true, and many began to carry their belief into action by being baptized. It is surprising that no opposition was offered by Simon." — *R. B. Rackham.*

The story of Philip's being divinely sent to intercept the Ethiopian eunuch returning from Jerusalem is too well-known to require detail here, for we have some very important verses yet to cover in this lesson. However, the following lessons can be quickly drawn from this passage: (1) The Holy Spirit does send specific men, on specific missions, and it behooves all of us to be sensitive to, and available for, the guidance of the Holy Spirit in these matters. (2) The Holy Spirit knows the need and condition of the heart of the one to whom he is sending a messenger, and He never makes a mistake in the messenger He sends. (3) If the Holy Spirit is already at work in the heart of one, and He has chosen a messenger to deal with this person's need, we can be sure that the result will be definite, a divine work of grace. (4) It behooves the disciples of Christ to be sufficiently acquainted with the Word of God, so as to be able to answer the questions of seekers regarding the great fundamental passages of Holy Writ.

IV. **ALL CHRISTIANS ARE AMBASSADORS OF CHRIST, 2** Corinthians 5:11–20. For some years, in teaching English Bible, I assumed — and I am afraid wrongly taught — that we might look upon this Second letter of Paul to the

2 CORINTHIANS 5:14. For the love of Christ constraineth us; because we thus judge, that one died for all, therefore all died.

15. And he died for all, that they that live should no longer live unto themselves, but unto him who for their sakes died and rose again.

Corinthian Church as something of a rather secondary nature, inferior in importance to the First Epistle, which contains the great chapter on church problems, the beautiful hymn of love, and the magnificent chapter on the resurrection. Recently, however, I have come to recognize that the 5th chapter of this Second Epistle, alone, makes it one of the great writings of the New Testament; for here we have unfolded some marvelous things concerning the resurrection body, judgment to come, and then two of the greatest statements concerning the person and work of Christ that are to be found in all of Scripture: "God was in Christ reconciling the world unto himself" (v. 19), and, "He hath made him to be sin for us who knew no sin" (v. 21). The significant thing about this chapter, however, is that though compounded of great doctrines, it carries, at the same time, one of the most urgent appeals for Christian activity and witnessing in all the New Testament. On the phrase, "we persuade men" (verse 11), Dr. J. E. McFadyen says, "It is not clear whether, in this somewhat general phrase, Paul means that he persuades men to embrace the gospel, or that he persuades them of his own sincerity; both are perhaps involved. But whether he is preaching or defending his motives, he always speaks with the solemn consciousness of his final accountability. Indeed, without waiting till he stands before the judgment-seat of Christ, he knows that his life is already searched, open, and transparent; in his efforts to persuade *men*, he knows that he has to reckon with a present *God* — hence he adds, 'and to God we are manifest' (compare v. 10). The future judgment, and the present consciousness of God, would be an effective deterrent to insincerity, did such exist." — *Dr. J. E. McFadyen.* 14. **For the love of Christ constraineth us; because we thus judge, that one died for all, therefore all died.** Dr. John Hutton entitles his sermon on vs. 14–17, "Our Response to the Cross." " 'Constraineth' is one of the most expressive words in the New Testament; the love of Christ has hold of the Apostle on both sides, as it were, and urges him on in a course which he cannot avoid. It has him in its grasp, and he has no choice, under its irresistible constraint, but to be what he is, and to do what he does, whether men think him in his mind or out of his mind. That the love of Christ means Christ's love to us, and not our love to Him, is shown by the fact that Paul goes on at once to describe in what it consists. 'It constrains us,' he says, 'because we have come to this mind about it: One died for all; so then all died.' Here, we may say, is the content of Christ's love, the essence of it, that which gives it its soul-subduing and constraining power: He loved us, and gave Himself for us; He died for all, and in that death of His all died. . . . But the intelligence must get hold somehow even of things inconceivably great, and the New Testament writers, with all their diversity of spiritual gifts, are at one as to what is essential here. They all find Christ's love concentrated and focussed in His death. They all find it there inasmuch as that death was a death for us." — *James Denney.* 15. **And he died for all, that they that live should no longer live unto themselves, but unto him who for their sakes died and rose again.** Here is one of the great statements concerning the substitutionary, vicarious death of our Lord. "His death is not only the supreme rebuke of selfishness, but its annihilation. This life is for Him, and not for themselves: they live for Him who died for them. . . . It says very little for human nature that such a man as Paul should have had to defend himself against the imputations of a selfish policy. If ever a man forgot and denied himself in the effort to serve and assert his Master, that man was Paul. Here he urges two motives, either of which would render any other conduct on his part altogether inconceivable. One is the thought of the judgment-seat of Christ, at the end, and the ever-present scrutiny of God here and now, before whom all his

16. Wherefore we henceforth know no man after the flesh: even though we have known Christ after the flesh, yet now we know *him so* no more.

17. Wherefore if any man is in Christ, *he is* a new creature: the old things are passed away; behold, they are become new.

18. But all things are of God, who reconciled us to himself through Christ, and gave unto us the ministry of reconciliation.

19. To wit, that God was in Christ reconciling the world unto himself, not reckoning unto them their trespasses, and having committed unto us the word of reconciliation.

---

inner life is bare; the other is the thought of the infinite love of Christ, supremely manifested in His death. That love left him no alternative but to live for Him who had died for him; and he lived for Him when he lived for those others for whom He had also died. This love was the destruction of every seed of selfishness; it grasped his life round and round, it constrained him." — *J. E. McFadyen*. 16. **Wherefore we henceforth know no man after the flesh: even though we have known Christ after the flesh, yet now we know *him so* no more.** One phrase in this verse is difficult, namely, that Paul no longer knows Christ "after the flesh." "He no longer regards Christ merely as a man in his human character and relationships. He is concerned with the divine, risen, glorified Christ. Upon such a Christ his thought now centers. Such a Christ forms the very sphere in which he lives. The change in his own experience has been radical and vital, and this will be true of all those who are so related to Christ and are resolved to live for him 'who for their sakes died and rose again.' " — *C. R. Erdman*. 17. **Wherefore if any man is in Christ, *he is* a new creature: the old things are passed away; behold, they are become new.** . . . "Every reader knows the things which bulked most largely in his life before he knew Christ, and it is easy for him to tell the difference due to being in the Lord. In a sense the new creation is in process as long as we live; it is ideally that faith in Christ means death in His death; ideally that with faith the old passes and the new is there; the actual putting away of the old, the actual production of the new, are the daily task of faith as it unites the soul to Christ." — *James Denney*. 18. **But all things are of God, who reconciled us to himself through Christ, and gave unto us the ministry of reconciliation.** Here is introduced another word relating to our witnessing, "the ministry of reconciliation." "According to Paul, the obstacle to be overcome consists not only in the enmity of man; there is also something to be overcome on the side of God. When he says that, in Christ, God was reconciling the world to Himself, he does not only mean that the goodness of God, as manifested in Christ, disarmed men's hostility, and inspired them with trust and confidence in Himself, but that in Christ, who 'for us was made sin' (v. 21) and who, as such 'died for us all' (v. 14), God's condemnation of sin was put away. The reconciliation is not one which we offer or which we work out for ourselves; it is one which we 'receive.' It is interesting to note the blend of general and particular expressions throughout this paragraph: God was reconciling '*the world*,' He reconciled '*us*'; He does not reckon unto '*them*' their trespasses, He gave '*us*' the ministry of reconciliation. Paul has an overwhelming consciousness of personally sharing in the reconciliation accomplished by God through Christ, but he has an equally glad consciousness of the special honour that is his, in having entrusted to him the ministry of reconciliation." — *J. E. McFadyen*. We should not pass by this verse without recalling that as reconciliation here is definitely related to the death of Christ, so in the other great passage on reconciliation, in Colossians 1:20–29, it is likewise identified with the death of Christ. 19. **To wit, that God was in Christ reconciling the world unto himself, not reckoning unto them their trespasses, and having committed unto us the word of reconciliation.** Whole

20. We are ambassadors therefore on behalf of Christ, as though God were entreating by us: we beseech *you* on behalf of Christ, be ye reconciled to God.

volumes have been written on this one verse. The words of Campbell Morgan are especially helpful, and must suffice. "So there came into human history two thousand years ago, a Man through Whose personality, whether of mind, or of will, or of force, I fling the lines out into immensity, and the result is God. A new revelation of man has resulted in a new revelation of God. At the back of all the activity of this Man love was the motive. The expression of His activity was service rendered to others, and all the way I see Him flaming in white hot anger against everything that bruises and hurts; and whether I watch Him taking children in His arms and blessing them, or watch Him when in quiet dignity He pronounces the eight Woes upon a guilty city, it is ever the vision of God that is breaking on my life. 'God was in Christ,' and what is the result? We have found God, and He is a God of joy and a God of sorrow, a God intimately interested in all the details of human life, a God for ever active; and all these things I have come to know through the Child, and Boy, and Youth, and Man of Nazareth. — *Dr. G. Campbell Morgan.* 20. **We are ambassadors therefore on behalf of Christ, as though God were entreating by us: we beseech *you* on behalf of Christ, be ye reconciled to God.** McFadyen says of this, "The reconciliation of the world to God is wrought through and in Christ, so that it is Christ and His cause that Paul, in his apostolic capacity, represents; but as it is God who has entrusted him with the word of reconciliation, in a sense it is God who is speaking through him. There is here the same consciousness as that of the old Hebrew prophets, when they prefaced their messages with 'Thus saith the Lord.' The burden of Paul's message as Christ's ambassador is, 'Be reconciled to God.' This does not mean: As you look at the reconciling love of God as manifested in Christ, cleanse your hearts of all hostility and distrust. The reconciliation is one effected by God Himself, one which we receive (Rom. 5:11). The phrase therefore means, Accept the reconciliation provided by God: those who accept it are reconciled to God, and their hostility and distrust are disarmed as a consequence." — *Dr. J. E. McFadyen.*

V. **THE PREREQUISITE OF RIGHTEOUS LIVING,** 1 Peter 3:13–16. In this lesson on witnessing, we could possibly do without this passage, and the teacher may not have time to expound it. I presume it is included here to emphasize the truth that only those who are leading righteous lives and who have a conscience void of offense before God and before men, can expect to have an effective witness for Christ; so that if we do suffer for our testimony, it is nothing of which to be ashamed. We might dwell on only one clause here — "Being ready always to give answer to every man that asketh you a reason concerning the hope that is in you, yet with meekness and fear. "Every cultivated, sensible man was expected by the Greeks to be prepared to discuss questions or opinions of conduct intelligently and temperately, to give and receive a reason. It is surely not fanciful to see here an allusion to St. Peter's own experience. When a critical moment came upon him, he was not ready with his answer, and so denied his Lord (Matt. 26:69–75)."

THE LESSON IN LIFE, LITERATURE, AND ARCHAEOLOGY.

The great Bishop Westcott, whose name will always be identified with the Westcott of the text of the Greek New Testament, and one of the true adornments of the Christian Church of the 19th century, wrote, while he was an undergraduate at Cambridge University, to the one who was in the days ahead to be his wife, "If I were to recommend any one text for your particular study, as containing the whole summary of a Christian's life, it would be the first of those beautiful sentences read in our Communion Service — 'Let your light so shine before men, that they may see your good works, and glorify your Father which is in heaven.' What can be so great an honour to poor, frail, sinful mortals as to add to the extent of God's glory? What human distinction can compare with this? What title, what reward shall be found equal to that of being permitted to see our Father's kingdom advanced by our means?" — *Bishop Westcott.*

A TRUTH FOR THE CLASS TO CARRY AWAY.

The urgency of witnessing for Christ in this hour may be vividly recognized as we recall the simple fact that there are more people living now in the United States without Christ than the entire population of the Roman Empire when Christ came to this earth. With this in mind, the teacher should close this lesson with some definite, specific, simple program for witnessing — to our neighbors, to a newly settled community, to a trailer court, in a letter to an unsaved loved one, through a column in the local paper, etc. The consequences and the rewards for such faithfulness are eternal.

To what kind of people does God commit this sacred privilege and obligation of witnessing? Can an unsaved man bear witness to the saving work of Christ? What is there in the Gospel, which originates from the love of God and consummates in eternal life, that raises so much opposition, and sometimes persecution? Do you think that there is any difference between the opposition of men to the Gospel now, and the opposition we find in this lesson to the same Gospel? What do you think is the principal aspect of the Gospel of Christ which needs the most emphasis in our witnessing in this generation?

The Louvre.   DOMENICHINO.   1581-1641
KING DAVID.

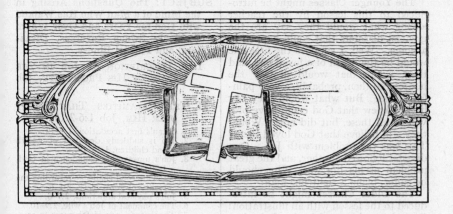

FOURTH QUARTER.

OCTOBER 3 — DECEMBER 26, 1954.

WISDOM AND WORSHIP IN OLD TESTAMENT LITERATURE—JOB, PSALMS, PROVERBS, ECCLESIASTES.

LESSON I. — October 3.

JOB'S STRUGGLE TO UNDERSTAND LIFE. — Job 1—2; 19—23.

PRINTED TEXT, Job 1:1-3, 13-15, 17, 20, 22; 19:7-10; 23:3-10.

Devotional Reading: Romans 8:33–39.
Beginner Topic: SAMUEL'S GOOD FRIEND.
  Lesson Material: 1 Samuel 1:19–28.
  Memory Verse: I was glad when they said unto me, Let us go unto the house of Jehovah. Psalm 122:1.
Primary Topic: WHEN JOB WAS SAD.
  Lesson Material: Job 1.
  Memory Verse: Blessed be the name of the Jehovah. Job 1:21.
Junior Topic: HOW JOB FACED TROUBLE.
  Lesson Material: Job 1.
  Memory Verse: Blessed be the name of the Jehovah. Job 1:21.
Intermediate-Senior Topic: IF I COULD ONLY UNDERSTAND!
  Lesson Material: Job 1—2; 19—23.
  Memory Verse: Ye shall seek me, and find me, when ye shall search for me with all your heart. Jeremiah 29:13.
Topic for Young People and Adults: MAN'S STRUGGLE TO UNDERSTAND LIFE.
  Lesson Material: Job 1—2; 19—23.
  Memory Verse: Ye shall seek me, and find me, when ye shall search for me with all your heart. Jeremiah 29:13.

335

THE TEACHER AND HIS CLASS.

The Younger Classes might be introduced to this lesson by the teacher asking what would they say are the greatest disasters that could happen in a home. Well, I suppose the first one would be the death of a loved one, and then, a fire that would destroy the house; and then, probably, a very painful illness. But what would they say if they knew that God could have prevented all these, but did not? Would they still believe that God loved them? This was the problem with Job. One disaster followed another, and the great problem of his life was, Why should he suffer, being a righteous man?

The Older Classes might be introduced to the lesson with an illustration: One of my dearest friends of the last six years was Mr. Fred Mitchell, of London, Home Director for the China Inland Mission, a man of God, widely read in the choicest spiritual literature of the Christian church, a man of prayer, who had left blessings in the hearts of thousands. In the recent crash of the Comet over India, he was among the passengers killed. The question came at once to my mind, What do we mean by the providence of God? Why should this servant of God be allowed to perish in this disaster? Job is the classical treatment in the Scriptures of the great problem of disasters in human life, of suffering on the part of a child of God.

THE LESSON IN ITS SETTING.

Time. — We do not know when Job lived. Josephus says it was in the time of the patriarchs, which most commentators have echoed until modern times. Today few place the book that early. We must remember, however, that there is not a single reference here to any Mosaic Law, nor to Jerusalem, nor the Temple, nor any character in Hebrew history. The date cannot be ascertained.

Place. — The land of Uz was in the northern part of the Arabian peninsula between Palestine and the Euphrates.

THE PLAN OF THE LESSON.

SUBJECT: The Questions Arising in the Mind of a Man Who Has Walked with God for Years and Over Whom Suddenly Sweep Reverses, Disasters, and Painful Illness.

I. A DESCRIPTION OF JOB IN THE DAYS OF HIS PROSPERITY, Job 1:1–5.

II. THE CALAMITIES THAT SWEPT OVER HIM, Job 1:6–2:13.
  1. Satan's first accusation, 1:6–12.
  2. Job is suddenly deprived of wealth and children, 1:13–19.
  3. Job's unwavering confidence in God, 1:20–22.
  4. Satan's second challenge regarding the reality of Job's piety, 2:1–6.
  5. Job's physical afflictions, 2:7–8.
  6. The comment of Job's wife, 2:9–10.
  7. The three friends of Job come to comfort him, 2:11–13.

III. JOB REHEARSES THE AFFLICTIONS GOD HAS SENT UPON HIM, Job 19.

IV. LATER DISCOURSES OF ZOPHAR, JOB, AND ELIPHAZ, Job 20–22.

V. JOB'S ANGUISH OF SOUL IN FAILING TO FIND GOD, Job 23.

THE TEACHER'S LIBRARY.

There is a vast literature connected with the Book of Job. All Bible dictionaries will have some interesting articles, of course, and all volumes dealing with the Wisdom Literature of the Old Testament, e.g., the one by W. T. Davison, 20–105. There is a good chapter in C. Alphonso Smith: *Keynote Studies in Keynote Books of the Bible*, 82–110. One of the most widely used commentaries on Job is the notable one in the *Cambridge Bible for Schools and Colleges*, by A. B. Davidson. My own opinion is that the most helpful of all exegetical works is Samuel Cox: *A Commentary on the Book of Job*, London, 1880. F. C. Cook in *The Bible Commentary* is exceedingly helpful, and also the beautifully written passage in the work by James Strahan, *The Book of Job*, Edinburgh, 1914. The pages by Fausset in the famous *Jamieson, Fausset, and Brown Commentary* are exceedingly good. A beautiful volume is the epic one of James F. Gensing. A smaller volume is *Baffled to Fight Better*, by Oswald Chambers. For some strange reason sermonic material is almost nil; on 23:10 see J. S. Holden, *The Confidence of Faith*, 9–16. A volume filled with the richest material, not too well known, is one by David Thomas, published in 1878, *Problemata Mundi, The Book of Job*.

AUDIO-VISUAL AIDS.

No audio-visual aids discovered.

JOB 1:1. There was a man in the land of Uz, whose name was Job; and that man was perfect and upright, and one that feared God, and turned away from evil.

2. And there were born unto him seven sons and three daughters.

3. His substance also was seven thousand sheep, and three thousand camels, and five hundred yoke of oxen, and five hundred she asses, and a very great household; so that this man was the greatest of all the children of the east.

I think the first question we ought to face in the discussion of this lesson is whether Job was an historical character or not. Many modern writers say that this is only a drama, as Goethe's "Faust" or Shakespeare's "MacBeth," setting forth in dramatic form the great problem of why God-fearing men are allowed to suffer. That it is in dramatic form no one would doubt, but it would seem that from Ezekiel 14:14 and James 5:11, where Job is linked with other characters indisputably historic that we should consider Job also to be an actual character in ancient times, who experienced the sufferings here recorded. Moreover, as Fausset says: "The names of persons and places are specified with a particularity not to be looked for in an allegory. Probably the debate itself occupied several sittings and the number of speeches assigned to each was arranged by pre-concerted agreement, which will account for no one's speaking out of turn." — *Fausset.*

The first two chapters of the book form the prologue. The next twenty-nine chapters are taken up with dialogues in three cycles, chapters 3-14, 15-21, 22-31. In the first two cycles the three friends of Job speak in the same order, Eliphaz, Bildad, Zophar. In the third series Zophar does not speak. Chapters 32-37 are taken up with the monologue by Elihu. The next four chapters are devoted to the marvelous discourse of Jehovah Himself. The first six verses of the last chapter record Job's vision of God, the remaining verses being devoted to the epilogue.

Tennyson said that the Book of Job was "the greatest poem of ancient or modern times." Carlyle once wrote, "I call it apart from all theories about it one of the greatest things ever written with pen, a noble book; all men's books. There is nothing written, I think, in the Bible or out of it, of equal merit."

I. A DESCRIPTION OF JOB IN THE DAYS OF HIS PROSPERITY, 1:1-3.
1. **There was a man in the land of Uz, whose name was Job; and that man was perfect and upright, and one that feared God, and turned away from evil.** The location of Uz is given above. The name Job was also borne by a son of Issachar (Gen. 46:13). The high tributes paid to Job in this verse are ratified later by God Himself (see 1:8 and 2:3). The word translated "perfect" means "single-hearted," undefiled, while the word "upright" describes Job in his relationships to his fellowmen, both of which derive from "an inward, abiding sense of God's holiness, attested by abhorrence of evil" (see Matt. 8:10-11; Acts 10:2-4). 2. **And there were born unto him seven sons and three daughters.** 3. **His substance also was seven thousand sheep, and three thousand camels, and five hundred yoke of oxen, and five hundred she asses, and a very great household; so that this man was the greatest of all the children of the east.** Canon Cook says that "the numbers in this part of the narrative are significant, representing the completeness of God's providential gifts — striking coincidences between outward facts and ideal numbers are not uncommon in the purely historical portions of Scripture." — *Canon Cook.* We cannot read the phrase "the men of the east" without thinking of the wisemen who centuries later came from the East (Matt. 2:1).

The events of the book begin by a series of feasts, one each day given by the seven sons of Job. "Upon their completion Job sent for his sons and caused them

337

whence comest thou? From going too fro in the earth + fm wauhing up + dmur in it-

JOB 1:13–15.   LESSON I.   FOURTH QUARTER.

13. And it fell on a day when his sons and his daughters were eating and drinking wine in their eldest brother's house,

14. that there came a messenger unto Job, and said, The oxen were plowing, and the asses feeding beside them;

15. and the Sabeans fell *upon them*, and took them away: yea, they have slain the servants with the edge of the sword; and I only am escaped alone to tell thee.

---

to perform the ceremonial ablutions which were customary before offering any sacrifice. The whole family thus assembled weekly at their father's house to take part in the religious service. Job was his own priest. The burnt offering was the only form of sacrifice known to the patriarchs (see Gen. 8:20)." — *E. C. Cook.* This day of sacrifice must have fallen on the eighth day, and thus as Delitzsch so significantly says: "Here we have a remarkable prelude to the New Testament celebration of Sunday in the age before the giving of the Law, which is a type of the New Testament time after the Law." — *F. Delitzsch.*

II. **THE CALAMITIES THAT SWEPT OVER HIM,** Job 1:6–2:13.

1. SATAN'S FIRST ACCUSATION, 1:6–12. We are here confronted with an event which has proved, we think needlessly, a stumbling block to many. The scene is in heaven. The occasion is a time when the sons of God, no doubt angelic beings, presented themselves before the Lord (see Ps. 109:6), and among them was Satan. The word Satan means "adversary." "Though malignant and evil this spirit is evidently counted among the angels by origin and nature. He comes among them as one of their order. His presence is evidently expected and recognized. Like them he has to give an account of what he has observed. This representation is in accordance with other notices in the Bible; see e.g. 1 Kings 22:19–22; Zech. 3:1, 2. The existence of a malignant spirit, permitted to range the earth, tempting and calumniating God's rational creatures, is implied or asserted in all Scripture from Genesis to Revelation. There is no ground for the assumption that the notion was derived from foreign sources. . . . Satan is altogether subject to God, acts only permissively, and by his acts brings the cause of truth into stronger relief. It is to be observed that the final expulsion of this spirit from the higher region is represented in the New Testament as a result of the Saviour's coming. The mystery which hangs over such representations is common to all questions which concern the origin or continuance of moral evil." — *F. C. Cook.* Satan, who was always looked upon as an enemy of God and man both, is asked by Jehovah if he had considered the noble character of this man, Job, to which Satan replied that the reason Job feared God was because God had prospered him, or, because he knew that prosperity would follow such obedience, and, he added, if these material possessions were taken away from Job he would curse God to His face. He does not deny the righteous character of Job. With this God gave him permission to take away these earthly possessions to discover whether Job's fear of God derived from such wealth. Permission is granted, but remember, it is permission. "Great as Satan is, mighty as is his influence in the world, he is not an independent existence, he is in the hands of the Everlasting Father, Who sustains him every hour, and Who uses him as His instrument. Infinite Goodness makes this foul fiend an engine for good in His government. He links him to His triumphant chariot. No rider has such command over his steed as God has over him. He may bound and prance, fired with all the passions of hell, but he can never break away." — *David Thomas.*

2. JOB IS SUDDENLY DEPRIVED OF WEALTH AND CHILDREN, 1:13–15. **13. And it fell on a day when his sons and his daughters were eating and drinking wine in their eldest brother's house, 14. that there came a messenger unto Job, and said, The oxen were plowing, and the asses feeding beside them; 15. and the Sabeans fell *upon them*, and took them away: yea, they have slain the servants with the**

17. While he was yet speaking, there came also another, and said, The Chaldeans made three bands, and fell upon the camels, and have taken them away, yea, and slain the servants with the edge of the sword; and I only am escaped alone to tell thee.

20. Then Job arose, and rent his robe, and shaved his head, and fell down upon the ground, and worshipped.

22. In all this Job sinned not, nor charged God foolishly.

---

edge of the sword; and I only am escaped alone to tell thee. Plowing in this area of the world takes place in January. "It is to be remarked that all the oxen were at the same time in one district; this too is curiously confirmed by the present custom of the Hauran: in order to protect themselves from marauders the inhabitants plough the lands in succession, bringing all their oxen, with their guards, into the same district." — *Canon Cook.* The Sabeans came from Sheba in southern Arabia. Another messenger now reports fire from heaven having destroyed domestic animals and their servants. This fire was either brimstone and fire, as in Genesis 19:24, or lightning (Ps. 78:48). "A storm extending over the vast tracts occupied by seven thousand sheep and destroying them together with their guards would scarcely be attributed to merely natural causes." — *E. C. Cook.*
17. While he was yet speaking, there came also another, and said, The Chaldeans made three bands, and fell upon the camels, and have taken them away, yea, and slain the servants with the edge of the sword; and I only am escaped alone to tell thee. Each disaster as reported seems to be greater than the one before. The camels now are taken by the Chaldeans, a powerful race living at the head of the Persian Gulf, and at the same time all his servants but one were slain. The greatest disaster is yet to be reported. A fearful wind, probably a tornado, rips the house apart in which his children were feasting, and but one servant lived to report what had happened. "In one day Job is now bereft of everything which he accounted the gift of Jehovah. Satan has summoned the elements and men for the destruction of Job's possessions by repeated strokes."

3. JOB'S UNWAVERING CONFIDENCE IN GOD, 1:20–22. **20. Then Job arose, and rent his robe, and shaved his head, and fell down upon the ground, and worshipped.** "The first three messengers Job has heard, sitting, and in silence; but at the news of the death of his children, brought by the fourth, he can no longer overcome his grief. The intensity of his feeling is indicated by rising up (cf. Jonah 3:6); his torn heart, by the rending of his mantle; the conscious loss of his dearest ones, by cutting off the hair of his head. He does not, however, act like one in despair, but, humbling himself under the mighty hand of God, falls to the ground and prostrates himself, *i.e.* worshipping God, so that his face touches the earth." — *F. Delitzsch.* In verse 21 by the phrase "return thither" is meant of course "return to dust" or Mother Earth. **22. In all this Job sinned not, nor charged God foolishly.** Thus far all the trials and testings which Job has endured have failed to justify the false charge of Satan. Now without possessions he has the same faith in and fear of God as in the days of his wealth.

4. SATAN'S CHALLENGE REGARDING THE REALITY OF JOB'S PIETY, 2:1–6. Having failed in his first attempt to prove Job's piety a superficial affair, Satan now asks permission to afflict Job with bodily pain, a permission that is granted, with the accompanying command that he is not allowed to take Job's life.

5. JOB'S PHYSICAL AFFLICTIONS, 2:7–8. "The meaning of the words of Satan is this: One gives up one's skin to preserve skin; one endures pain on a sickly part of the skin for the sake of saving the whole skin. But man for his life, his highest good, willingly gives up everything without exception that can be given up and life itself still be retained." The description of Job's disease recalls to our mind Deuteronomy 28:27 and 35. Probably what we now know as elephantiasis, so-called because the limbs become jointless lumps like elephant's legs. The disease

begins with the rising of tubercular boils, and at length resembles a cancer spreading itself over the whole body, by which the body is so affected, that some of the limbs fall completely away.   Scraping with a potsherd will not only relieve the intolerable itching of the skin, but also remove the matter.   Incidentally, Satan does not appear again throughout the whole book." — *F. Delitzsch.*

6. The Comment of Job's Wife, 2:9, 10.   About as unsympathetic expression as could ever pass the lips of a wife are those that Job's wife spoke to him, "Curse God and die."   Job, fully retaining his confidence in God, rightly rebukes her for this, and thus his answer "was a real victory over the last and most grievous temptation."

7. The Three Friends of Job Come to Comfort Him, 2:11–13.   The three friends of Job who are to take such a prominent part throughout the remaining chapters now approach him.   Eliphaz, probably a descendant of Esau (Gen. 36:4), lived in Teman, a district located in Edom whose inhabitants were noted for wisdom (Jer. 49:7–10).   Bildad was from a district named after a son of Abraham (Gen. 25:2), to the east of the Hauran.   Zophar came from an area the location of which is not definitely known.   For seven days and seven nights they said nothing, though they displayed every Oriental token of grief over their friend's physical distress.   "Job's third and severest trial consists, not in any new bereavement or loss, but in the interpretation put on his former losses and sorrows by the Friends, and, if by his friends, then by all his world.   He had now to taste the bitter anguish of finding himself abandoned and condemned by men as well as forsaken by God, of standing alone, with absolutely nothing to back him save his conscience, against the whole world, against the whole universe.   Those who have known what it is to enter into conflict with the very forms of thought and faith which they themselves once held, and which are still so firmly held by the men of their generation as that they are at once cut off from all fellowship and sympathy the moment they call them in question, are in some measure able to enter into the anguish which now pierced Job's spirit to the quick. . . .

"But in doing justice to Job, let us not do injustice to the Friends.   They were good men.   That Job accounted them his friends says much for them.   And, indeed, as they disclose themselves to us in their speeches, they say much for themselves.   Pious they were, and devout, and even wise in the wisdom of their time.   Their grave fault was — and it is a common fault with 'the religious' — that they were not looking for more light; that they thought the whole truth was included in the simple and portable creed which they had adopted; that they put dogma above fact." — *Samuel Cox.*

III. **JOB REHEARSES THE AFFLICTIONS GOD HAS SENT UPON HIM,** Job. 19.   Our lesson passes over the first cycle of the speeches of Job's three friends, and Job's three replies, and also passes over the second speech of Eliphaz, Job's reply (chapters 16 and 17), and the second speech of Bildad (chapter 18), bringing us now to what is really the fifth speech made by Job in reply to the accusations of his friends.   Bildad, in chapter 18, simply repeats what he had said on a previous occasion (chapter 8), that such calamities as had fallen upon Job could only be accounted for by Job's own wickedness.   In fact, he says that Job is one who knows not God (vs. 21).   The chapter is wholly without any suggestion of hope or without a hint of the possibility of Job finally becoming reconciled to God.   "Bildad had threatened him that his name would be forgotten, or that posterity would remember only to execrate him.   And, now, Job replies with a formal and deliberate appeal to posterity.   He has that to say which the generations that come after him must never forget, since a great truth once revealed is the everlasting heritage of the race.   And the great truth he would fain have cut deep on a rock for ever is, *that God is his Redeemer;* or, rather, the great fact he would have recorded for the comfort of after ages is that, even out of the depths of his despair, he can look up and see a great star of hope shining above his head; that even 'through the hollow eyes of death' he 'spies life peering,' and is assured that on some distant happy day all the wrongs of time will be redressed. . . .

JOB 19:7. Behold, I cry out of wrong, but I am not heard: I cry for help, but there is no justice.

8. He hath walled up my way that I cannot pass, And hath set darkness in my paths.

9. He hath stripped me of my glory, And taken the crown from my head.

10. He hath broken me down on every side, and I am gone; And my hope hath he plucked up like a tree.

He knows that the God in whom he has already found an Umpire, an Advocate, a Witness, a Surety, will at last reveal Himself as his Redeemer, to clear him of every charge, and to save him from all evil. God will publicly declare his innocence, and he, even though he die, shall live, and hear that declaration for himself." — *Samuel Cox.* **7. Behold, I cry out of wrong, but I am not heard: I cry for help, but there is no justice. 8. He hath walled up my way that I cannot pass, And hath set darkness in my paths. 9. He hath stripped me of my glory, And taken the crown from my head. 10. He hath broken me down on every side, and I am gone; And my hope hath he plucked up like a tree.** Job in the opening paragraph of this chapter complains about his friends; in the second part he complains of the conduct of God, that God had overthrown and confounded him and that "his cries to Heaven awake no response, and his endeavours to march on to a better and happier life were like that of a traveller whose way was blocked up with obstructions and black with night. He complains that he was utterly deprived of his honours and his hope. '*He hath stripped me of my glory.*' Once he was held in honour by society, prospered on every side of his life, and abounded in hope; but now all was gone, glory, crown, prosperity: on every side all gone. His hope was like an uprooted tree, never to sprout again." — *David Thomas.*

However, at the end of this chapter we find one of the greatest statements regarding the hope of life to come on the part of a God-fearing man to be discovered anywhere in the Old Testament. In verse 25, Job cries out that he knows that his Redeemer lives and that the Redeemer in the latter days will appear on earth and that though worms destroy his body, yet in his own flesh the day will come when he will see God. "*Goel* is a name for the next of kin, who, among the Hebrews and Arabs, was bound to redeem a kinsman who had fallen into debt or bondage, and to avenge his blood if he had been slain in a *vendetta*, in a family or clan quarrel. . . . Though he now lies crushed and abandoned on the earth, Job is sure that his Goel will interpose both to rescue him from his bondage to loss and pain, calumny and death, and to avenge him on those who, while professing to be his friends, are nevertheless his 'adversaries without cause.' And assuredly, Job had no mere man, or kinsman, in his thoughts. Men, even the best and most beloved, had utterly failed him, and revolted from him, deeming him to be accursed. . . . His Goel could only be the God whom he had already besought to decide for a man against Himself, of whose eternal justice he was so fully persuaded as to believe that He would raise and vindicate the very man whom He Himself had smitten to the earth. This point — an important one — is put beyond all doubt by the first clause of the next verse, from which we learn both that Job expected to *see* this Goel, and *to find God* in Him — 'from my flesh shall I see *God*.' " — *Samuel Cox.*

IV. **LATER DISCOURSES OF ZOPHAR, JOB, AND ELIPHAZ,** Job. 20–22. In chapter 20 "Zophar repeats with more vehemence, and even coarseness, the old and well-nigh exhausted argument to prove that wickedness and hypocrisy inevitably bring with them such misery as that which has befallen Job. Like the other speakers he takes Job as the representative of guilty sufferers; each separate affliction is a witness, all his griefs tell one tale, the hatred of God and the certainty of Job's complete destruction. The whole speech is singularly character-

JOB 23:3. Oh that I knew where I might find him! That I might come even to his seat!

4. I would set my cause in order before him, and fill my mouth with arguments.

5. I would know the words which he would answer me, and understand what he would say unto me.

6. Would he contend with me in the greatness of his power? Nay; but he would give heed unto me.

---

istic of the speaker, who appears no more in the dialogue. He has reached the limit beyond which nothing can be said, and is dismissed, so to speak, with contempt." — *Canon Cook*.

In chapter 21 we have the last reply of Job in the second series of speeches. "As in the first cycle of the debate, so in the second, Job does not reply to the arguments and assertions of his friends until each of them has spoken. They have appealed to the course of the world from the beginning of time, as proving the law that the good and ill fortunes of men are determined by their characters; they have revelled in lurid descriptions of the fate of the wicked, and Zophar, in particular, has just declared that, while the ungodly man may prosper for a little while, his ruin is sudden, swift, and overwhelming. . . . It is with no light heart that Job points out grave anomalies in the government of the world, for all that is highest in him rises up in protest against injustice in God; but he has to face the truth that the godless attain power, live on the fat of the land, have large and happy families, attain a good old age, and die in peace. At the same time, he scornfully rebukes the presumption that would impose petty theories upon God, and prescribe the laws by which the world *ought* to be governed. His friends have emphasized the difference between the fates of the righteous and the wicked, making virtue and happiness, vice and misery, correlative terms; but to him it is the equality of the righteous and the wicked that is inexplicable. He appeals to the reports of men who have travelled with open eyes in other lands, where they have seen how the ungodly are prosperous in life, honoured in death, remembered and imitated in after days. With such facts staring him in the face, he refuses to accept the bittersweet doctrine of his friends." — *James Strahan*.

In chapter 22 we have the beginning of the third and concluding series of discourses. Eliphaz actually charges Job with specific sins, especially verses 5–14. These are social sins and not one of these charges rests upon facts. What he probably thinks he is doing is reading Job's mind and finding in it the crimes he enumerates. He then pleads with Job to return to God and to put away his iniquity. But Job has no such iniquities to put away as Eliphaz here charges him with.

V. JOB'S ANGUISH OF SOUL IN FAILING TO FIND GOD, Job 23. Job's reply to Eliphaz occupies chapters 23 and 24. He declares in chapter 23, verses 3–7 that if he were tried before God's tribunal he would be justified by God, but he says (vs. 6–9) that God hides Himself so that Job cannot find Him, and in verses 10–12 that God knows Job is innocent. And because of all the mysteries mounting up in Job's mind as the result of God's continued scourging of him, he becomes afraid of God Himself. **3. Oh that I knew where I might find him! That I might come even to his seat! 4. I would set my cause in order before him, and fill my mouth with arguments. 5. I would know the words which he would answer me, And understand what he would say unto me.** "It is the chief distinction between Job and his friends that he desires to meet God and they do not. Satisfied with a distant acquaintance with God (22:21), they have the old-world idea that no man can see God and live." — *James Strahan*. **6. Would he contend with me in the greatness of his power? Nay; but he would give heed unto me.** "These words measure the progress of Job's thoughts of God. On two

7. There the upright might reason with him; So should I be delivered for ever from my judge.

8. Behold, I go forward, but he is not *there;* And backward, but I cannot perceive him;

9. On the left hand, when he doth work, but I cannot behold him; He hideth himself on the right hand, that I cannot see him.

10. But he knoweth the way that I take; When he hath tried me, I shall come forth as gold.

---

former occasions (9:34; 13:21), when he expressed his desire to meet with God, he almost regretted his audacity; for he had the secret dread, born of all the calamities which had come crashing upon him, that, when the hour of meeting came, God would strike him dumb, either dazzling him with the glory of His majesty or overwhelming him with the terrors of His might. As he recalls his earlier fears, he cannot help asking still, 'Would He contend with me in the greatness of His power?' but he now answers his own question with an emphatic 'Nay.' " — *James Strahan.* **7. There the upright might reason with him; So should I be delivered for ever from my judge.** Job asks for a trial, not in order that he may be delivered for ever from his Judge, but that he may hear his Judge vindicate his innocence and give him back his good name as an everlasting possession. From such a Judge he can have no desire to flee. To such a God he wishes to flee, as to a pavilion from the strife of tongues." — *James Strahan.* **8. Behold, I go forward, but he is not *there;* And backward, but I cannot perceive him; 9. on the left hand, when he doth work, but I cannot behold him; He hideth himself on the right hand, that I cannot see him.** "He goes *east* and *west, north* and *south* (so the words should probably be translated, cf. 18:20), and finds that while He is everywhere operative He is always elusive. . . . It is not the non-existence of God that is dreaded, but the possibility that He is non-moral; not atheism, but Manicheism; not the empty Eye-socket of Richter's apologue, but an awful Evil Eye. . . . The most pathetic thing in the world is the search of man for a God after his own heart. A quest so sincere and so unwearied is the best evidence that man is naturally and eternally religious." — *James Strahan.* **10. But he knoweth the way that I take; When he hath tried me, I shall come forth as gold.** " 'Tribulation worketh patience.' How does affliction benefit? It serves — (1) to develop the powers of the mind — (2) to quicken the spiritual life — (3) to impress with the sense of personal responsibility — (4) to detach from the world. It gradually breaks down the materialism in which the soul is caged, and lets it free into the open air and light of the spiritual domains where God is seen and enjoyed." — *David Thomas.* (See Ps. 66:10 and James 1:12.) We have not yet come to the solution of Job's problem. The end of our lesson leaves us with Job baffled, tortured in mind and body, but with all of this he has not cursed God. His piety, his fear of God remains. Mysteries there are, but he has not cursed God, as Satan predicted he would.

THE LESSON IN LIFE, LITERATURE, AND ARCHAEOLOGY.

Christopher Columbus, on his fourth voyage, felt that he was suffering even as Job, and in a letter which he wrote in 1502 are found these words, "The tempest was terrible throughout the night, all the ships were separated, and each one driven to the last extremity, without hope of anything but death; each of them also looked upon the loss of the rest as a matter of certainty. What man was ever born, not even excepting Job, who would not have been ready to die of despair at finding himself as I then was, in anxious fear for my own safety, and that of my son, my brother, and my friends, and yet refused permission either to land or to put into harbor on the shores which by God's mercy I had gained for Spain sweating blood?" — *Christopher Columbus.*

A TRUTH FOR THE CLASS TO CARRY AWAY.

While none of us has ever suffered as Job, all of us have suffered some, and a few greatly. Moreover, every true child of God knows something of the antagonism of Satan. It seems to me that the great lesson here for us today is that God is sovereign, all-powerful. Satan is powerful, world rulers are powerful; but God is all-powerful, and this means that there is a limit to what Satan can do, that righteousness and love will ultimately conquer, and that whatever be the tribulations of this life, there is for all who put their trust in God the assurance of an eternity without shadow or pain.

In what ways do the sufferings of Job differ from those of Christ and St. Paul? How did Satan reveal himself as the accuser in the life of the Lord Jesus? Do all the experiences of suffering and the loss of home or loved ones come from Satanic opposition? (I would say most emphatically not.) What fundamental questions come from Job's heart in this lesson that are not answered until the advent of Christ in the New Testament?

LESSON II. — October 10.

GOD'S ANSWER TO JOB'S PERPLEXITY. — Job 38—42.

PRINTED TEXT, Job 38:1–7; 42:1–6, 10a.

Devotional Reading: John 14:1–11.
Beginner Topic: A SONG TO JESUS.
    Lesson Material: Matthew 21:1–17.
    Memory Verse: I will sing unto Jehovah. Exodus 15:1.
Primary Topic: JOB AND HIS FRIENDS.
    Lesson Material: Job 42.
    Memory Verse: Pray one for another. James 5:16.
Junior Topic: WHEN JOB PRAYED FOR HIS FRIENDS.
    Lesson Material: Job 42.
    Memory Verse: Pray one for another. . . . The supplication of a righteous man availeth much. James 5:16.
Intermediate-Senior Topic: THERE *is* AN ANSWER.
    Lesson Material: Job 38—42.
    Memory Verse: Be still, and know that I am God. Psalm 46:10.
Topic for Young People and Adults: GOD'S ANSWER TO MAN'S PERPLEXITY.
    Lesson Material: Job 38—42.
    Memory Verse: Be still, and know that I am God. Psalm 46:10.

THE TEACHER AND HIS CLASS.

The Younger Classes, inasmuch as this lesson is taken up almost entirely with vivid descriptions of phenomena in nature, probably should be introduced to it by some simple statement concerning the wonders of nature. I wonder if it would be out of order if I repeated something here that I heard William Jennings Bryan say many years ago? If this is too trivial for my readers, please forgive it. Bryan once asked: "How can we explain how a brown cow, eating green grass, gives white milk, which, when it is churned,

makes yellow butter?" This is a simple fact in nature, but even this, I think, cannot be wholly explained by any *laws* we now know.

The Older Classes might be introduced to this lesson on nature by being reminded of only one truth about our universe which to our forefathers would have seemed utterly fantastic. By the great 200-inch telescope on Mt. Palomar astronomers have been able to see celestial bodies as far away as 1,600,000,000 light-years. Now a light-year is 5,880,000,000,000 miles away. Therefore, we now know that the diameter of our universe is *at least* 5,308,-000,000,000,000,000,000 miles away. One could only wish that our growing knowledge of nature was accompanied by an ever deeper reverence for God the Creator.

THE LESSON IN ITS SETTING.

Time. — We do not know when the book was written.

Place. — Job lived in the land of Uz, located in the north of the Arabian Penisula.

THE PLAN OF THE LESSON.

SUBJECT: How an Overwhelming Revelation of the Power, Wisdom, and Eternity of God, Brought Job to a Realization of His Own Sinfulness and Unworthiness.

I. THE DISCOURSE OF JEHOVAH, Job 38–41.

1. Prefatory admonition, 38:1-3.
2. Concerning the origin of given phenomena in nature, 38:4-15.

3. Concerning some of the mysteries of natural phenomena, 38:16-38.
4. Concerning certain animals, 38:39-41:34.
   a. Various species, 38:39-40:14.
   b. Behemoth, 40:15-24.
   c. Leviathan, 41:1-34.

II. JOB'S SPIRIT OF SELF-VINDICATION IS BROKEN, Job 42:1-6.

III. THE PROSPERITY AND BLESSEDNESS OF THE CLOSING YEARS OF JOB'S LIFE, Job 42:7-17.

THE TEACHER'S LIBRARY.

The principal volumes for the study of Job were given in the bibliography of the preceding lesson. For some strange reason sermonic material on any of the verses of the printed text are exceedingly scarce. The only one I have seen of any value is a sermon on Job 42:10, by Charles H. Spurgeon in the *Metropolitan Tabernacle Pulpit, 1875*, Vol. 21, pp. 613-624.

AUDIO-VISUAL AIDS.

No audio-visual aids discovered.

If my indexes are correct, chapters 38 to 41 of the Book of Job were never assigned in the Internationsl Sunday School Lesson series until the lesson for July 13th and July 20, 1947, so that this is only the second time in eighty years that we have had the opportunity for teaching this portion of the Word of God. The longest discourse in the book, that by Elihu, chapters 32–37, has just been concluded. Before Elihu speaks, Job expresses a great desire to plead his cause before God, and a longing for God to reveal Himself. His prayer is granted, for the revelation is now given, though not as Job expected. "The almighty Creator, clad in the glory and the terror of the universe, more majestic and awful than Job had ever anticipated, speaks out of the thunderstorm. Clouds and darkness are still round about Him, and His speech seems at first as remarkable for what it leaves unsaid as for what it contains. . . . He does not shed a single ray of light upon the mystery of his sufferings, neither praising him for his supreme patience under the shocks of calamity, nor confiding to him how he has convinced the sons of the Elohim that men can serve God unselfishly, nor assuring him that the heaviest blows have been dealt by the hand of love, nor revealing to him the disciplinary and remedial value of pain. . . . He does not lift the veil which hangs over the gates of death, nor promise that the enigmas of the present will be solved, and its wrongs redressed, in an after-life. In truth, He scarcely touches the problem which Job and his friends have been so passionately debating." — *James Strahan.* While the Bible is filled from beginning to end with passages that concern the varied phenomena of nature, yet only in this discourse of Jehovah, as Professor C. Alphonso Smith once said, "Will one find so detailed a panorama of natural ways or so eloquent a portrayal of her mystery for men. It is an inspired commentary on the first chapter of Genesis." — *Prof. C. A. Smith.* This glorious passage opens with a series of questions.

JOB 38:1. Then Jehovah answered Job out of the whirlwind, and said,

2. Who is this that darkeneth counsel By words without knowledge?

3. Gird up now thy loins like a man; For I will demand of thee, and declare thou unto me.

4. Where wast thou when I laid the foundations of the earth? Declare, if thou hast understanding.

5. Who determined the measures thereof, if thou knowest? Or who stretched the line upon it?

6. Whereupon were the foundations thereof fastened? Or who laid the cornerstone thereof,

7. When the morning stars sang together, And all the sons of God shouted for joy?

I. **THE DISCOURSE OF JEHOVAH,** Job 38:1–7. 1. PREFATORY ADMONITION, 38:1–3. 1. **Then Jehovah answered Job out of the whirlwind, and said,** "From this expression it may be inferred that the voice of the Lord was heard, though no form was seen. . . . As the storm was passing away with a vehement wind, clearing the heavens and presenting a lively symbol of the terrible majesty of God, Job feels the near presence of his Maker (cf. 1 Kings 19:11, 12); the Word rings through his heart, it brings back all that he had ever learned of His works, creation arises before him to witness for its Maker, the Spirit of God moulds his thoughts and completes his knowledge, and leads him to the one conclusion, which, once accepted, leaves no place for doubts, for murmurs, for struggles, for aught but implicit submission to infinite wisdom and love." — *Canon Cook.* 2. **Who is this that darkeneth counsel By words without knowledge?** "The word 'counsel' indicates that God does not leave things to chance; He has a well-considered purpose, though it may be beyond the comprehension of man. Whereas Job's personal afflictions, and the moral condition of the world around him, have tempted him to question the goodness of God, he must be convicted of speaking 'without knowledge.' His perplexity arises from his own limitations. Given a fuller acquaintance with the facts of the case, he would see that the sum of things is 'a mighty maze, but not without a plan.' " — *James Strahan.* 3. **Gird up now thy loins like a man; For I will demand of thee, and declare thou unto me.** God accepts the challenge which Job has so often given Him, as in 9:34; 10:2–4; 13:3, 13–19; 23:3–13.

2. CONCERNING THE ORIGIN OF GIVEN PHENOMENA IN NATURE, 38:4–15. Jehovah now takes Job back to the time of creation to reveal to him how insignificant man is in time, in strength, and in wisdom, as compared with the Almighty Who created the entire universe. 4. **Where wast thou when I laid the foundations of the earth? Declare, if thou hast understanding.** 5. **Who determined the measures thereof, if thou knowest? Or who stretched the line upon it?** We have expressed here one of the great fundamental truths concerning which scientists become more and more convinced with every new discovery, that is, the absolute orderliness prevailing in the natural world. Man has a life of briefest span: the world is now estimated to be at least five billion years old. 6. **Whereupon were the foundations thereof fastened? Or who laid the cornerstone thereof,** "The expressions here are metaphorical; the earth is compared to a building, the word 'foundations' here is quite distinct from that in verse 4. It means properly the bases of a column, here we are to understand the lower strata on which the earth's surface rests: the expression represents with singular accuracy facts but lately disclosed by science." — *Canon Cook.* See Psalm 18:22, Zechariah 4:5. 7. **When the morning stars sang together, And all the sons of God shouted for joy?** "When shall we learn that to treat a Sacred Poem as if it were a scien-

tific treatise, and to extract an accurate cosmogony from the very metaphors of the Bible, is a perilous and fatal course, if we do not learn it when studying a Poem which probably contains as many metaphors at variance with the scientific conceptions of the present age as of those which are in harmony with it?

"What the Poet is thinking of in verse 7 is not scientific facts but the mystic connection everywhere assumed in Holy Writ between 'stars' and 'angels,' and of that strange sympathy between heaven and earth in virtue of which we are affected by all the motions of the celestial sphere, while they in heaven are tremulously sensitive to all that passes on earth. . . .   The mystical conceptions it embalms are not peculiar to any race or time; as, for example, the familiar passage from Shakespeare which no repetition can stale:

> 'Look how the floor of heaven
> Is thick laid with patines of bright gold:
> There's not the smallest orb which thou
>   behold'st
> But in his motion like an angel sings,
> Still quiring to the young-eyed cherubim.'

and in which, not only the connection of stars with angels is reproduced, and the music which heaven pipes to the dancing earth, but even that metaphor of a building which dominates verses 5 and 6.   Nor should we fail to note the exquisite propriety of the epithet which sets 'the stars of the *morning*' to sing in the morning of the new-made world. . . .   The angelic hosts, the armies of the skies, rushing forth from heaven so soon as its cornerstone was laid, to gaze, admire, and hymn *his* praise with songs and choral symphonies and shouts of joy." — *Samuel Cox.* In the remaining verses of our section one primary truth is set forth, the fact that God has set bounds to the movements of the oceans.   "Breaking forth from the chaotic earth, like some gigantic and portentous birth, swaddled in mists and with clouds for its garments, the mighty ocean, which no man hath tamed or can tame, was shut in and confined within its rocky barriers by the hand of God.   Lawless as it seems, it is under law to Him.   In its wildest and most furious moods it does but execute His decree; nor in its maddest rage can it overstep the bounds He has appointed for it." — *Samuel Cox.*

3. Concerning Some of the Mysteries of Natural Phenomena, 38:16–38. From a discussion of light and of the sea, the Lord now turns to those mysteries "which encompass all our knowledge, and which we sometimes foolishly permit to poison all our knowledge, still engage the Poet's mind.   His thoughts still circle round 'the cosmical phenomena' — round sea and land, light and darkness; and still he maintains the tone of ironical challenge which he has taken throughout. 'Hast thou' — it is demanded of Job, the implication being of course that he has *not* — 'descended to the springs of the sea, or traversed the recesses of the deep?' And, again (verse 17); 'Hast thou entered into the gates of death, or so much as seen the very portals of Hades?'   And here, doubtless, Job would be reminded of his own confession (chap. 26:5, 6) that the Shades tremble so often as the Divine glance penetrates the waters that roll above their gloomy habitation, and that to Jehovah Hades itself lies bare, and there is no covering to Abaddon; while *we* cannot fail to be reminded of the immense labour and straining effort by which Job had risen to and grasped the hope that, beyond the sea of death, there might be a land of light in which he would find a vindication and a home (Cf. chap. 17). . . . The secrets of snow and hail, of the distribution of light and wind, of rain and lightning, dew and ice, are demanded of the man who had assumed to judge and censure the ways of God mainly because he could not comprehend them, and demanded with an overwhelming rapidity and force which leave but little scope for touches whether of graphic description or of moral reflection.

" 'The Cluster' of verse 31 is, of course, the constellation known to us as the Pleiades, and 'the Giant,' Orion.   The first meaning of the question is: 'Canst thou bind together the several jewels of the celestian Cluster, so that the Pleiades shall be grouped or strung together as in a girdle or a brooch; or canst thou unbind and displace the stars which compose the belt or chain or Orion, so that the Giant shall be freed from his bands?' . . .

"In verses 34–38 the Lord recurs to the agencies of rain and storm in order still more deeply to impress upon us the feebleness of man and the inscrutable mysteries involved even in the forces with which he is most familiar. The verses are full of graphic and picturesque touches which, while they shew the most careful and imaginative observation of the facts of Nature, owe much of their power to the naive and childlike spirit with which he regarded them." — *Samuel Cox*.

4. CONCERNING CERTAIN ANIMALS, 38:39–41:34. It might be interesting here to note that the great British botanist of the 19th century, J. D. Hooker, once said, "The deeper I go, the more convinced I am that there are now 50,000 species of flowering plants known," while in 1909 Professor Shipley estimated that there are 790,000 species of living animals that have been described, including 9,955 mammals and nearly half a million insects. After this brief consideration of the original creation of the boundaries set by God upon the vast seas of the earth, and a brief but beautiful consideration of the phenomena of light, we have, for the next ninety-one verses, remarkably vivid, accurate, even though poetical descriptions of various animals of the natural world. Let me first list the animals as they come before us, and then consider briefly three of them: the lion and raven, 38:39–41; the rock-goat, 39:1–4; the wild ass, 39:5–8; the rum, an ox-like animal similar to bison, 39:9–12; the ostrich, 39:13–18; the horse, 39:19–25; the hawk, eagle, and other birds, 39:26–30. Of the two great beasts last mentioned we will speak more in detail shortly.

The only description in this group that we ought to dwell on for a moment is that of a horse. The late Professor Samuel Cox has well said: "As might have been expected in an Arabian poem, the description of the Horse, with its heroic beauty and its impetuous lust of battle, is by far the grandest of all these animal 'pieces.' Probably there is no finer description of this noble creature in the whole range of literature, nor even any worthy to be compared with it as a whole, although in other ancient authors we meet with occasional touches resembling those employed here." — *Samuel Cox*. The word here translated "thunder" "denotes convulsive trembling, not of fear, but rage: or, as a secondary meaning, thunder. The point which struck those who saw for the first time the mighty war-horse in battle must have been the terror of the neck with its quivering muscles and tossing mane, and the word here used denotes most probably that impression. . . . Carlyle, with the instinct of genius, selects this as a special instance of the truthfulness of the description in Job. 'So *true* every way; true eyesight and vision for all things; material things not less than spiritual; the Horse — 'hast thou clothed his neck with thunder?' " — *Canon Cook*.

We are now ready to briefly consider the animal named "behemoth," in the last ten verses of chapter forty. I here return to the excellent lines of Samuel Cox: "The Hebrew word *Behemoth* means simply 'the beast,' i.e., the beast *par excellence*. Many of the elder Commentators supposed that in these verses we had an ideal description of 'the typical great beast,' an abstract and brief chronicle which combined the more notable features of several species, such as the elephant, the aueroch, and even the mammoth, with other extinct pachyderms. But since the time of Bochart most of the Commentators are agreed that, though the Poet may be describing a type or ideal, he has the Hippopotamus alone in his eye; that, if we have an ideal here, it is the ideal *Pihemont*, as the Egyptians call this 'ox of the water.' And, beyond a doubt, this large beast answers sufficiently to every detail of his description. For the hippopotamus does 'feed on grass like the ox'; he is strictly herbivorous, 'and makes sad havoc among the rice fields and cultivated grounds when at night he issues forth from the reedy fens.' His mouth is enormously large and shovel-shaped, so that it can grasp a vast quantity of food in a single bite. His appetite is immense, and his formidable tusks are so modified in shape that he 'can eat the grass as neatly *as if it were mown by a scythe*' (verse 19). Though a denizen of the water, the hippopotamus feeds on land, climbing

JOB 42:1. Then Job answered Jehovah, and said,

2. I know that thou canst do all things, And that no purpose of thine can be restrained.

---

the high grounds adjoining the river in which he has his haunt; 'the mountains also yield him pasture.' " — *Samuel Cox.*

The entire forty-first chapter is taken up with a description of another great and terrible beast, *leviathan.* Beyond a doubt this refers to the crocodile. . . . "Herodotus (Book 2, chap. 69) says: 'The crocodile is esteemed sacred by some of the Egyptians, by others he is treated as an enemy. Those who live near Thebes, and those who dwell around Lake Moeris, regard them with especial veneration. . . .'

"The impenetrable hide of the Crocodile, referred to or described in verses 7, 15–17, 26–29, is one of his most remarkable features. His whole head, back, and tail are covered with horny quadrangular plates, or scales, set so closely together that the sharpest spear can seldom find its way through them, and even a rifle ball glances off them if it strike obliquely.

"Another characteristic feature is noted in verses 13 and 14. 'The Crocodile has a single row of teeth in each jaw, implanted in sockets, from which they are reproduced when lost or broken.' The teeth are all made for snatching and tearing, but not for masticating, the Crocodile swallowing its prey entire when possible; and when the animal is too large to be eaten entire, the reptile tears it to pieces, and swallows the fragments without attempting to masticate them. It has no lips to hide its formidable jaws. . . .

"The 'threshing-sledge' of verse 30 is of course *the tail* of the Crocodile. And this is his most formidable weapon, at least on shore. It is 'one mass of muscle and sinew.' Sweeping it from side to side, this heavy unwieldy-looking reptile *sculls* himself through the water at a rate well-nigh incredible. Modern Egyptians affirm that with a single blow of its tail it can break all four legs of an ox or a horse." — *Samuel Cox.*

We must ask, as we come to the conclusion of Jehovah's speech, what impression this amazing revelation of the mysteries and various phenomena of nature would make upon Job. Canon Cook summarizes all of this, I believe, better than anyone else: "We must remember the profoundly religious and serious character of the eastern patriarch. When images were presented to his mind, which spoke of tremendous power, and purposes utterly beyond his conception, he could have no thought but of his own nothingness. It never entered into his spirit to doubt of God's wisdom; but when he reflected upon the marvellous care which God bestowed upon every part of an animal so utterly useless to man, he must have felt that the goodness which was to him but another word for perfect wisdom, must be something far different from that which in his narrowness and presumption man is wont to assume . . . a mind, in which the facts furnished by careful and lively observation are interpreted by a spiritual process, by God's words addressed to the inward sense, learns at once the truths on which the deepest religious convictions, and the soundest judgment of the relations between God and man, are based. Every minute detail becomes interesting and affecting, viewed thus as a matter of human consciousness, quickened by God's Spirit, and issuing in the highest practical results." — *Canon Cook.*

II. JOB'S SPIRIT OF SELF-VINDICATION IS BROKEN, 42:1–6. In these few verses Job confesses a change in five areas of his thinking: first, that God is all powerful and of infinite wisdom, even to the understanding of the innermost thoughts of men. 1. **Then Job answered Jehovah, and said, 2. I know that thou canst do all things, and that no purpose of thine can be restrained.** "His confession corresponds to the Almighty's address to him. That address did not insist on any one Divine attribute, but rather presented God in the whole circle of His attributes, power and wisdom but also goodness. . . . The Divine nature is not

3. Who is this that hideth counsel without knowledge? Therefore have I uttered that which I understood not, Things too wonderful for me, which I knew not.

4. Hear, I beseech thee, and I will speak; I will demand of thee, and declare thou unto me.

5. I had heard of thee by the hearing of the ear; But now mine eye seeth thee:

---

a segment but a circle. Any one Divine attribute implies all others. Omnipotence cannot exist apart from righteousness. Similarly Job's reply reflects the great, general impression of God now made on him. The exhibition of the Divine wisdom as it operates in nature has led him to feel that within his own history also there is a divine 'thought' or 'counsel,' though he is unable to understand it. . . . He is not teaching general principles here, but shewing the position which just thoughts of God will induce a man to take, even when God's dealings may be beyond his understanding." — *A. B. Davidson.* Secondly, Job confesses that many of the things he has been saying were based on ignorance, that he had been trying to fathom things that were really too wonderful for him. **3. Who is this that hideth counsel without knowledge? Therefore have I uttered that which I understood not, Things too wonderful for me, which I knew not.** "Job has discovered that there are questions in reference to which agnosticism is a virtue and dogmatism a sin. In his eagerness to solve the enigmas of his life, he has put forward hypotheses as if they were ascertained truths; he has charged God with injustice when he should have charged himself with ignorance; he has confidently pronounced judgment on things beyond his comprehension. But the vision of God has made him intellectually humble. He now acknowledges that things are far more wonderful than he has ever realised. Henceforth, instead of trying to explain all mysteries, he will recognise that it may be an act of piety towards God and of charity towards men to leave not a few of them unexplained." — *James Strahan.* Thirdly, he acknowledges that the knowledge he now has of God is infinitely more intimate and accurate than any he had known before. **4. Hear, I beseech thee, and I will speak; I will demand of thee, and declare thou unto me. 5. I had heard of thee by the hearing of the ear; But now mine eye seeth thee:** God "is often the subject of general conversation and frequently of special discourse. All in Christendom, — most, perhaps, throughout the world, who have come to years of thought, — have heard something about the Supreme in some form or other. . . . In how many counsels from parents, conversations with friends, and sermons from ministers have we heard of Him by the *hearing of the ear.* Something about Him every day falls on the ear. Very *common*, indeed, is this *second-hand* knowledge. But the other method by which man obtains knowledge is *rare*. Abraham, Moses, Elijah, Isaiah, Paul, in fact all the patriarchs, prophets, and apostles, were brought into *conscious* contact with God. God came personally and directly to them, so now he came to Job. '*Now mine eye seeth Thee.*' Why is this direct knowledge so rare? Not because He is not everywhere manifest and ever prepared to reveal Himself to every human soul, but because souls are involved in such a dark atmosphere of depravity that it shuts Him out. . . . No man can really know God, only as God reveals Himself. If the solar orb is to be seen, he must show himself. All the stars that blaze in the midnight heavens cannot reveal Him. No theologies can reveal God." — *David Thomas.* Fourthly, Job now, instead of insisting upon his own self-righteousness, *abhors* himself. In the Hebrew text the object of abhorring "himself" is unexpressed. The margin translates it, "I loathe my words." Literally it means to retract or repudiate what he has been saying. "Job is not ashamed to change his opinions, but he is profoundly ashamed of the opinions which he

350

6. Wherefore I abhor *myself*, and repent in dust and ashes.

10a. And Jehovah turned the captivity of Job, when he prayed for his friends.

changes." — *James Strahan*.   6. **Wherefore I abhor** *myself,* **and repent in dust and ashes.** Finally, Job prostrates himself to the ground and repents of his boastfulness, his self-righteousness, his sins. For a similar phrase, see Isaiah 58:5, Jonah 3:6, et cetera.

III. **THE PROSPERITY AND BLESSEDNESS OF THE CLOSING YEARS OF JOB'S LIFE,** 42:7–17. The conclusion of the book is not necessarily to be taken as a type of the conclusion of all experiences of the children of God, in suffering, pain, depression. While God will bring His children through the valley of the shadow of death, the New Testament does not assure a believer that his last days will provide an experience of double the prosperity he ever may have known. The multiplication of earthly possessions, and the blessing of a large family, play a greater part in the Old Testament than they do in the New, but the fundamental truths that are here abide. Before the final description of Job's abounding happiness and prosperity, we have a brief command of God to these three friends that they should prepare and offer a burnt offering upon which God's servant Job, now acceptable to God, would intercede on their behalf. "The atonement demanded of them is (verse 8) that they should recognize and confess their sin; that they should humble themselves before the very man whom they had condemned as a sinner above all men and beg him to intercede for them with the God whom they seem to have regarded as their property rather than their Lord, whom they certainly regarded as with and for them and against him. It was a terrible downfall, a bitter but wholesome humiliation, for men who were so familiar with all the secrets of Heaven; and one hardly knows with what face Zophar, who had reviled Job so loudly and harshly, could urge such a prayer as this upon him." — *Samuel Cox*. We now turn to verse 10.   10a. **And Jehovah turned the captivity of Job, when he prayed for his friends.** The phrase here translated "turned the captivity of" is a proverbial one, expressing the idea of restoration, as for example, Ezekiel 16:53; Hosea 6:11, et cetera. "Thus the future vindication of redeemed man, body and soul, at the resurrection has its earnest and adumbration in the temporal vindication of Job traced by Jehovah in person."

Spurgeon has a great sermon on this text in which he makes the following points: (1) The Lord can deliver us out of spiritual captivity and that very speedily; (2) the Lord can deliver us out of temporal captivity. "This may seem to be a very trite observation, commonplace, and such as everybody knows, but, beloved, the very things that everybody knows are those which we need to hear, if they are most suitable to our case. Those old things which we did not care about in our prosperity are most valued when we are cast down by the terrible blows of tribulation. Let me then repeat the truism, the Lord who takes away can as easily restore. 'The Lord maketh sore, *and bindeth up;* he woundeth, *and his hands make whole.* He killeth, *and he maketh alive.*' Believe that he will put forth his right hand soon if the left has been long outstretched, and, if you can believe it, it will not be long before you will be able to say, he hath regarded the low estate of his servant. He hath lifted the poor from the dunghill and set him among princes, even the princes of his people. For the Lord putteth down the mighty from their seat, but he exalteth them that are of low degree. I leave with you this simple truth. The Lord can turn the captivity of his people." — *Charles H. Spurgeon*. In conclusion the great preacher remarked: "Dear brethren, you shall never lose anything by what you suffer for God. If, for Christ's sake, you are persecuted, you shall receive in this life your reward; but if not, rejoice and be glad, for great is your reward in heaven. You shall not lose anything by God's afflicting you. You shall, for a time, be an apparent loser; but a real loser in the end you shall never be. When you get to heaven you will see that you were a priceless gainer by all the losses you endured." — *C. H. Spurgeon*.

THE LESSON IN LIFE, LITERATURE, AND ARCHAEOLOGY.

This word *leviathan* has had many usages through the centuries. From its original meaning, an aquatic animal of enormous size, it came to mean a ship of great size; as the great orator Bright used it, "your splendid river bearing the leviathan of noble architecture." Then it came to mean a man of vast power, or great wealth. Indeed, from Isaiah 27:1, it was used in the Middle Ages at times as standing for Satan, the great enemy of God. Finally, the philosopher Hobbes used this word as the title for a famous book setting forth what he thought was the organism of a political society.

A TRUTH FOR THE CLASS TO CARRY AWAY.

To know God is for light to penetrate the darkness of the experiences of life. God desires to be known. To Job, and many others, He revealed Himself through the world He has created. But His final and perfect revelation is in Jesus Christ, in whom His power, and wisdom, and love are all to be seen.

In how many ways is the natural world so much greater, as man knows it, as it was in the days of Job? How do you account for the fact that so many of our leading scientists today profess no faith in Christ? Who, in the New Testament, directed the attention of men most often to nature? (Christ.) Were Job's experiences usual or unusual?

LESSON III. — October 17.

THE WAY OF WISDOM. — Proverbs 3—4.

PRINTED TEXT, Proverbs 3:1–6, 9; 4:10–15, 18, 19.

Devotional Reading: Proverbs 4:10–20.
Beginner Topic: OUR BEST BOOK.
    Lesson Material: 2 Chronicles 34:29–33; 35:17–19.
    Memory Verse: I was glad when they said unto me, Let us go unto the house of Jehovah. Psalm 122:1.
Primary Topic: A WISE SON.
    Lesson Material: Proverbs 3.
    Memory Verse: Trust in Jehovah with all thy heart. Proverbs 3:5.
Junior Topic: GOD'S PLAN FOR WISE LIVING.
    Lesson Material: Proverbs 3.
    Memory Verse: Trust in Jehovah with all thy heart,
        And lean not upon thine own understanding:
        In all thy ways acknowledge him,
        And he will direct thy paths. Proverbs 3:5–6.
Intermediate-Senior Topic: WHICH WAY SHALL I TAKE?
    Lesson Material: Proverbs 3—4.
    Memory Verse: Trust in Jehovah with all thy heart,
        And lean not upon thine own understanding:
        In all thy ways acknowledge him,
        And he will direct thy paths. Proverbs 3:5–6.
Topic for Young People and Adults: WISDOM FOR DAILY LIVING.
    Lesson Material: Proverbs 3—4.
    Memory Verse: Trust in Jehovah with all thy heart,
        And lean not upon thine own understanding:
        In all thy ways acknowledge him,
        And he will direct thy paths. Proverbs 3:5–6.

THE TEACHER AND HIS CLASS.

The **Younger Classes** might be introduced to this lesson by an experience that anyone would have on board an ocean-liner. Though passengers almost never go up into the pilot's room, or the captain's quarters, if one did he would find in the pilot-room enormous maps, covering the entire route of the ship, with details of the coastal harbors and reefs, showing the dangerous shallows, rocks, and sandbars, which if carefully followed will keep the ship from being grounded or smashing its prow. Now the Book of Proverbs is a chart for those who fear God, which if followed will keep the craft of life from disaster, and grant to us day by day a life of infinite satisfaction.

The **Older Classes** may be introduced to this lesson by the teacher reminding his hearers of the infinite capacities of any human life for blessing and joy, for sorrow and regret, for service or shame, for failure or triumph. All of us must work, must have relationships with others. Most people, at one time or another, will have physical suffering; all will have disappointments, all will have opportunities, and all will have temptations. The question is, What will we make out of these? The Book of Proverbs contains the instructions of a father to his son, given that the son and all men of every generation might so choose that life will become increasingly rich and satisfactory.

THE LESSON IN ITS SETTING.

Time. — No definite date is assigned for the writing of these chapters. Solomon reigned about 950 B.C.

Place. — There is no geographical data in the lesson assigned to us today.

THE PLAN OF THE LESSON.

SUBJECT: Signposts Set by the Spirit of God Through the Lips of Men Who Have Travelled the Road of Life, Which If Followed Will Make Life What God Intends It To Be.

I. THE SECRET OF A LONG LIFE DIRECTED OF THE LORD, Proverbs 3:1–6.

II. THE PRIMACY OF WISDOM, Proverbs 3:7–26.

III. A LIFE OF WISDOM AS IT PERTAINS TO OUR RELATION WITH OTHERS, Proverbs 3:27–35.

IV. FURTHER INSTRUCTIONS OF THE FATHER TO HIS SON REGARDING THE SATISFACTIONS OF A LIFE OF WISDOM, Proverbs 4:1–13.

V. THE TWO DIVERGING PATHS WHICH CONFRONT EVERY MAN, Proverbs 4:14–27.

THE TEACHER'S LIBRARY.

A list of important commentaries on the Book of Proverbs will be found in the introduction to this volume. In addition, I would suggest on the subject of "wisdom," there was an interesting article by David E. Robison in the *Old Testament Commentary*, edited by Alleman and Flack, generally known as the *Lutheran Commentary*, pages 75–81; also excellent chapters in W. T. Davison, *The Wisdom Literature of the Old Testament*; H. Ranston, *The Old Testament Wisdom Books and Their Teaching*, London, 1930; and O. S. Rankin, *Israel's Wisdom Literature*, Edinburgh, 1936. Sermonic material on the passages assigned for the printed text is surprisingly scarce. On 3:6 the *Westminster Pulpit*, Vol. 4, pp. 145–152, and H. P. Liddon: *University Sermons*, First Series, 139–164. On 4:18 F. F. Shannon: *The Question of Greatness*, 32–46; and, in Alexander Maclaren: *Expositions of Holy Scripture, Esther-Ecclesiastes*, various sermons on our printed text, 84–116.

AUDIO-VISUAL AIDS.

No audio-visual aids discovered.

Before beginning the actual study of the verses of our lesson, it will help us to understand them if we remember that the principal theme of the opening chapters of this book concerns the pre-eminent value of wisdom, and the need for man to continually pursue it, if he is to be saved from disaster and bondage to sin, though I am not using the word "save" here in its Christian sense, a subject that does not occur in this Old Testament literature.

Before we proceed any further we ought to understand what the writer of the Book of Proverbs meant by wisdom. "The underlying conception of all the wisdom is that of God himself, the All-Wise. His wisdom is expressed in all His

PROVERBS 3:1. My son, forget not my law; But let thy heart keep my commandments:

2. For length of days, and years of life, And peace, will they add to thee.

works and words. Man is wise in proportion as he recognizes these truths and he knows them in the conduct of his life. The perfectly wise man is the one who in his whole being lives and thinks and acts in right relationship to the all-wise God." — *G. Campbell Morgan.* "Given that there is a Supreme Being, Creator, Sustainer, Ruler, Judge of all; then wisdom is to understand, so far as it is permitted to man's finite intelligence, the manifold adaptation and harmony, the beauty and utility, of his works and ways, and to turn our knowledge of them to practical account. Wisdom is, in all the complex relations of human life and conduct, to know and do his will." — *J. J. Perowne.* The reason why we find this particular form of wisdom in the Hebrew Scriptures alone is because the Hebrews were alone, in their day, the recipients of a true revelation of the infinitely wise and holy God. This particular part of the Wisdom Literature of the Hebrew people is as its title indicates, one that sets forth its truths in proverbs, of which there are three hundred and seventy-five down to 22:16. "A proverb presents a great truth by a very apt comparison or by a sharp and striking contrast; it is a concentrated, pithy, and pregnant saying." — *William G. Moorehead.*

I. **THE SECRET OF A LONG LIFE DIRECTED OF THE LORD,** Proverbs 3:1-6. The speaker here is the same as the one who is named at the beginning of the book, Solomon. Incidentally, the Book of Proverbs is the first book of the Bible to declare its author's name at the beginning. Solomon's authorship of three thousand proverbs is stated also in 1 Kings 4:30-32. The name of the son to whom Solomon is speaking is not given. 1. **My son, forget not my law; But let thy heart keep my commandments:** All readers will recall that the Psalter opens with this very idea of keeping the law of the Lord, "His delight is in the law of Jehovah." The Book of Deuteronomy tells us that God has given us all these laws for our good only, a passage no one ever seems to preach on (6:24, (25) In Proverbs 13:14 we read, "The law of the wise is a fountain of life." "All things are under law, for all things are in motion. The material universe is in motion, and there is the law that regulates it. The spiritual universe is in motion, and law presides over it. 'Of law,' says Hooker, 'there can be no less acknowledged, than that her seat is the bosom of God, her voice the harmony of the world. All things do her homage, the very least as feeling her care, and the greatest as not exempted from her power; both angels and men, and creatures of what condition soever, though each in different sort and manner, yet all with uniform consent, admiring her as the mother of their peace and joy.' But what is the law of the good — that which rules them in all their activities? *Supreme love to the supremely good.* It is not a written commandment, but an all-pervading, inspiring spirit, called in Scripture, 'the royal law,' the 'law of liberty,' the 'law of the Spirit.' " — *David Thomas.* The word translated "keep" here means primarily " '*to look hard at,*' and generally to *keep watch over,* as over a vineyard. The fault of men is, they can't *mind* 'what is directed,' or remember it; and, therefore, the order is very pregnant, to *watch* it, as the occasions occur in which it can be applied. . . . The difficulty of all our lives is to watch well our whole behaviour. '*Guard*' and '*watch,*' therefore, two Hebrew words, are sprinkled all over the book. . . . One Proverb (4:26) tells us that if we will watch the planting of our foot, the whole of our way will be set in order. And this thought, endlessly repeated, fills the Proverbs." — *John Miller.* We are now given a brief summary of basic blessings that will follow obedience to the law of the Lord, long life and peace. 2. **For length of days, and years of life, And peace, will they add to thee.** "The connection between obedience and physical health is clear from the three following facts: — (1) That physical health requires obedience to the divine laws of our

3. Let not kindness and truth forsake thee: Bind them about thy neck: Write them upon the tablet of thy heart.

4. So shalt thou find favor and good understanding In the sight of God and man.

5. Trust in Jehovah with all thy heart, And lean not upon thine own understanding:

6. In all thy ways acknowledge him, And he will direct thy paths.

---

being. (2) That obedience to these divine laws involves a study of them. (3) That the heartiest sympathy with the Divine author is essential to their successful study. . . . Add to this the fact that sobriety, temperance, chastity, industry, contentment, regularity, amiability, control of the temper, and the passions, which are involved in true obedience, are all conducive to corporeal health and vigour. Some people seem to regard ill-health as a mark of gentility. They are afraid to acknowledge themselves as vigorous and robust, lest they should be considered vulgar. . . . But in truth ill-health often means coarseness and crime. It grows out of the infraction of divine laws. Health of the body depends upon health of soul, and health of soul depends upon obedience to the moral laws of God. Bodily vigour depends upon moral virtue. 'Godliness is profitable unto all things, having the promise of the life that now is and of that which is to come.' " — *David Thomas*. 3. **Let not kindness and truth forsake thee: Bind them about thy neck: Write them upon the tablet of thy heart.** This passage reminds us of a similar exhortation in Deuteronomy 6:8 and 11:18. "The tablet of the heart and the Two Tables are type and anti-type. Those Moses first received are man fresh from his Creator, rock and writing all in place, and so made and so sent down together. The last were common rocks brought up to the mountain which God wrote on after the first were broken, lost humanity writ on by the finger of God (Heb. 8:10). 'I will put my laws into their mind, and write them in their hearts.' Surmounted by the mercy seat these rocks remained as a type of sanctification. They were kept perpetually in ebony as a type of their being stored forever.' " — *John Miller*. 4. **So shalt thou find favor and good understanding In the sight of God and man.** "He obtains favour in the eyes of God and man, to whom favour on both sides is shown; he obtains refined prudence, to whom it is on both sides adjudicated." — *F. Delitzsch*. 5. **Trust in Jehovah with all thy heart, And lean not upon thine own understanding: 6. In all thy ways acknowledge him, And he will direct thy paths.** I would say that this sentence is by far the most important single passage for study in our lesson, and consequently I am giving it extended space. "The first idea of the word 'acknowledge' is that of vision. It is as though the Preacher had said, In all thy ways see God. It calls us to recognition of the fact of the presence of God at every point of our lives. It reminds us that in all our ways, God is. It denies the heresy that God is in the sanctuary, and not in the market-place. It denies the heresy that God is interested in the central spiritual fact of human life, and has no relationship with the mental and the physical. The word thus calls us to a recognition of His existence, which must produce fear, not slavish fear, but that solemn awe of the soul which holds life in balance and proportion. That awe, the age lacks disastrously. . . .

"He has many ways of directing. He directs by obstacles placed across the way which I cannot overcome, and which drive me into a new way. He directs by clearing obstacles away, which I thought could not be moved. He directs by delay, keeping me waiting long after I have heard His call to service. He directs by immediateness, flinging me out into a new position wherein I must seek His guidance. He directs by opposition; the Spirit hindered Paul. He directs by encouragement; by whispers in the soul, which make a man dare, when all men tell him his daring is of no avail. He directs by disappointing, or by realising our dreams. I state these contradictory things in order to throw you back upon this

9. Honor Jehovah with thy substance, And with the first-fruits of all thine increase:

profound conviction; not from me nor from any man, must you take your rule of His direction. You must discover the rule for yourself in immediate relationship with Him. I say this now out of profound conviction, God help me to say it as it ought to be said. No youth or maiden has ever yet bared their soul to God, desiring to be led of Him and determined to follow, but that He has led, He has directed.

"I love the personality suggested by the pronoun in the text: ' *He* shall direct thy paths.' Behind the 'He' of the ancient preacher is the God of the Bible. Because that is so, the 'He' trembles with the tenderness of the Father's love. No evil can baffle if He direct the path. No enemy can prevent the final realisation of His purpose. No obstacles can hinder if He lead. No opposition can overcome if He direct. No exigencies can overwhelm the wisdom of God; no surprises prevent Him. Oh, the safety of being in the will of God. 'He shall direct thy paths.' " — *G. Campbell Morgan.*

II. **THE PRIMACY OF WISDOM,** Proverbs 3:7–26. The theme set forth in the preceding phrase, "Lean not upon thine own understanding," is now repeated in the introduction to a new section. Of course one cannot sincerely seek Divine wisdom, and determine not to act except according to the laws of God, and at the same time think that he has an understanding self-sufficient for every need. "There is a right self-reliance. In relation to our fellow men we are bound to trust our own energies, convictions, and conscience. . . . Heaven has endowed us all with faculties by which to help ourselves, if they are rightly worked. The man who is not self-reliant in this sense sinks his manhood in the parasite. But that self-trusting, to which Solomon refers, implies an exaggerated conceit of our own powers. Hence he says, 'be not wise in your own eyes.' Don't put too high an estimate on your own understanding. Thank God for your intellect. Respect it, train it, feed it with the choicest fruits on the tree of science, but don't lean on it as an infallible guide. At its best here, its eyes are very dim, its ears heavy, and its limbs feeble. . . . Self-conceit is at once offensive and pernicious; it involves *self-ignorance.* No man, who knows himself, can be vain. The hierarchs of heaven veil their faces. What is the knowledge of the most enlightened compared with what *is* to be known? What is a spark to the central fires of the universe? What compared with what he *ought* to have known? How much more the wisest on the earth might have known if they had properly employed their powers? A man 'wise in his own eyes,' is self-benighted. He is like a pauper maniac, who fancies himself a king." — *David Thomas.* As all will recognise, verses eleven and twelve are quoted in Hebrews 12:5, 6. One verse of this section is assigned for our consideration: 9. **Honor Jehovah with thy substance, And with the first-fruits of all thine increase:** The word, "substance," here means our capital or revenue. The Septuagint, without, of course, any grounds for doing so in the text, inserts the qualifying words, "on the return from thy righteous labors." "The two terms, substance and increase, exist, and are understood in all nations and all times. They correspond to capital and profit in a commercial community, or land and crop in an agricultural district. Although the direct and chief lesson of this verse be another thing, we take occasion, from the occurrence of these terms, first of all, to indicate and estimate a grievous malady that infests mercantile life in the present day. It manifests itself in these two kindred features: (1) A morbid forwardness to commence business without capital; that is, an effort to reap an increase while you have no substance to reap it from; and (2) A morbid forwardness to prosecute business to an enormous extent, upon a very limited capital; that is, an effort to reap more increase than your substance can fairly bear." — *William Arnot.* The rest of this chapter is almost entirely occupied with setting forth the infinite preciousness of wisdom which is here personified in the feminine. Let us just notice the results following the earnest pursuit of wis-

PROVERBS 4:10. Hear, O my son, and receive my sayings; And the years of thy life shall be many.

11. I have taught thee in the way of wisdom; I have led thee in paths of uprightness.

dom from day to day: happiness, length of days, honor, peace, security, preservation from stumbling, deliverance from fear.　Notice that the wisdom man is to pursue is identified with the very wisdom by which God created the world.　" 'We are raised by science,' says Lord Brougham, 'to an understanding of the infinite wisdom and goodness, which the Creator has displayed in all His works.　Not a step can we take in any direction without perceiving the most extraordinary traces of design, and the skill everywhere conspicuous is calculated in so vast a proportion of instances to promote the happiness of living creatures, and especially of ourselves, that we feel no hesitation in concluding, that if we knew the whole scheme of Providence, every part would appear in harmony with a plan of absolute benevolence." — *David Thomas*.

III. **A LIFE OF WISDOM AS IT PERTAINS TO OUR RELATION WITH OTHERS,** Proverbs 3:27–35.　We almost seem to have in the sequence of ideas in this chapter the same order as Paul observed in his great epistles, that is, first, deep, eternal truths are set forth, which in the New Testament is called "doctrine," here called "law" and "wisdom."　Then these truths are shown in their practical applications; here the king's son is shown the obligation to do good to others, just as Paul often said (Rom. 13:7; Gal. 6:10).　The words to the neighbor are like Leviticus 19:13; Deuteronomy 24:15.　Verse thirty is almost duplicated in Romans 12:18.　The second clause of verse thirty-six is repeated in 1 Peter 5:5.　There is no particular order followed in this paragraph, and the teacher will do well simply to set forth its primary truth, rather than attempting to dwell on each verse, for if he follows the latter method the half-hour will go before the lesson is half finished.

IV. **FURTHER INSTRUCTIONS OF THE FATHER TO HIS SON REGARDING THE SATISFACTIONS OF A LIFE OF WISDOM,** Proverbs 4:1–13.　The opening verses of this chapter are some of the most beautiful in all the Bible, relating to the precious privilege and obligation of parents to instruct their children in the things of the Lord.　This was first set forth in Deuteronomy 6:4–9.　If Solomon is the author of this chapter, and I am assuming he is, then he is writing here an autobiographical passage, passing on to his sons the teaching he had received from his father, which in the tests of life he had found to be so true and valuable.　Solomon was not an only son, although, as Dr. Perowne reminds us, "it may reasonably be urged that he was so in the same sense as was Isaac of whom this same word is used (Gen. 22:2, 16; Heb. 11:17), and who was not strictly an only son either, but one who stood alone in the choice of God and in the Messianic line, and therefore in the estimation of his father." — *Dr. Perowne*.　"Let a child draw his first breath in a house which possesses a sanctuary like that; let him come to know by his quick childish perceptions that there is in his home a ladder set up from earth to heaven, and that the angels of God go up and down on it; let him feel the divine atmosphere in his face, the air all suffused with heavenly light, the sweetness and the calm which prevail in a place where a constant communion is maintained, — and in after-years he will be aware of voices which call and hands which reach out to him from his childhood, connecting him with heaven, and even the most convincing negations of unbelief will be powerless to shake the faith which is deep as the springs of his life.　The first thing, then, is to give our children an atmosphere to grow up in; to cultivate their affections, and set their hearts on the things eternal; to make them associate the ideas of wealth and honor, of beauty and glory, not with material possessions, but with the treasures and rewards of Wisdom." — *R. F. Horton*.　10. **Hear, O my son, and receive my sayings; And the years of thy life shall be many.**　11. **I have taught thee in the way of wisdom;**

12. When thou goest, thy steps shall not be straitened; And if thou runnest, thou shalt not stumble.

13. Take fast hold of instruction; let her not go: Keep her; for she is thy life.

14. Enter not into the path of the wicked, And walk not in the way of evil men.

15. Avoid it, pass not by it; Turn from it, and pass on.

I have led thee in paths of uprightness. 12. When thou goest, thy steps shall not be straitened; And if thou runnest, thou shalt not stumble. 13. Take fast hold of instruction; let her not go: Keep her; for she is thy life. Inasmuch as we have seen frequently in this lesson an emphasis upon long life, which is not too often spoken of in this Christian dispensation, let us remember, for example, that the Apostle Paul himself in urging the obedience of children to their parents said, "Honor thy father and mother that it may be well with thee and that thou mayest live long on the earth." (Eph. 6:2, 3.) The words of the late Dr. Horton here are practical indeed: "We are accustomed to dwell on the promised joys of the future world as if godliness had no promise of the life which now is, and in so doing we take all life and colour from those expected blessings. The true view seems to be, The way of wisdom, the path of the upright, is so full of joy, so crowned with peace; the life of the children of the kingdom is so wisely and bountifully provided for; the inevitable pains and troubles which fall to their share are so transformed; that from this present good we can infer a future better, gathering hints and promises of what we shall be from the realized felicity of what we are.

"Yet no one thinks of measuring life only by days and years. To live long with the constant feeling that life is not worth living, or to live long with the constant apprehension of death, must be counted as a small and empty life. Now, it is the chief blessedness in the lot of the children of light that each day is a full, rich day, unmarred by recollections, unshadowed by apprehensions. Each day is distinctly worth living; it has its own exquisite lessons of cloud or sunshine, its own beautiful revelations of love, and pity, and hope. Time does not hang heavily on the hands, nor yet is its hurried flight a cause of vain regret; for it has accomplished that for which it was sent, and by staying longer could not accomplish more. And if, after all, God has appointed but a few years for His child's earthly life, that is not to be regretted; the only ground for sorrow would be to live longer than His wise love had decreed. 'If God thy death desires,' as St. Genest says to Adrien in Rotrou's tragedy, 'life has been long enow.' " — *R. F. Horton.*

V. **THE TWO DIVERGING PATHS WHICH CONFRONT EVERY MAN,** Proverbs 4:14–27. Over and over again the Bible likens the experiences of life as one walking on a road, and this road frequently is called "the path of life," for example, Psalm 16:11; 27:11; 119:35 and 105; 142:3; Isaiah 30:11; 40:14; Matthew 3:3; Hebrews 12:13. The very word, "path," is found four times in this chapter, verses 11, 14, 18, 26. Two paths are set before us here, just as our Lord did in the conclusion of the Sermon on the Mount, when He talked about the broad way that leads to destruction and the narrow way that leads unto life (Matt. 7:13, 14). Solomon first warns his son about the tragedies that will follow if one walks in the path of the wicked. 14. **Enter not into the path of the wicked, And walk not in the way of evil men. 15. Avoid it, pass not by it; Turn from it, and pass on.** The path of the wicked is "crowded with 'evil men' bent on mischief. They live *for* mischief. 'Their sleep is taken away unless they cause some to fall.' They have an infernal pleasure in doing wrong. They live *by* mischief. 'They eat the bread of wickedness, and drink the wine of violence.' What they have got to support them, they have got by dishonesty and violence. Wicked men live by falsehood, fraud, and oppression. . . . It crosses all our lines of activity. It is a very *attractive* path. The crowds are there, and there is great attraction in a crowd. . . . There is a tremendous whirlpool in the path of sin; he that comes within the circle

18. But the path of the righteous is as the dawning light, That shineth more and more unto the perfect day.

19. The way of the wicked is as darkness: They know not at what they stumble.

---

of its eddying waters is likely to be sucked down into the central gulf of irremediable ruin." — *David Thomas.* From warning concerning the path of the evil one, he promises that if one walks in the path of the righteous, he will find his way brighter and brighter unto the perfect day. 18. **But the path of the righteous is as the dawning light, That shineth more and more unto the perfect day.** 19. **The way of the wicked is as darkness: They know not at what they stumble.** It is a joy to put before my readers here a great passage from a book now seldom seen on Proverbs, which is so good that perhaps the teacher would like to read it aloud: "Light is the emblem of *intelligence, purity, and blessedness.* The march of the good is like the march of the sun — *glorious.* How glorious is the sun as it rises in the morning, tinging the distant hills with beauty, at noon flooding the earth with splendour, in evening fringing the clouds with rich purple, crimson, and gold. *Commanding.* — The sun is the ruler of the day; at his appearance the world awakes from its slumbers, the winds and waves obey him, as he moves all nature moves. *Useful.* — The sun enlightens the system and maintains harmony throughout every part. He renews the earth, quickens the seed into life, covers the landscape with beauty, ripens the harvest for man and beast. *Independent.* — Troops of black clouds may roll over the earth, but they touch not the sun, furious storms may shake the globe, but the sun is beyond their reach. He is always behind the darkest clouds, and looks calmly down upon the ocean in fury and the earth in a tempest. *Certain.* — The sun is never out of time, he is ever in his place at the right hour. In all this he is the emblem of the good man — glorious, commanding, useful, independent, and certain.

"The march of the good is A PROGRESSIVE march. 'Shineth more and more.' It has a dawn and a meridian. Godliness is progressive. We are 'to follow on to know the Lord.' We are 'to go from strength to strength.' We are to see 'greater things than these.' We are to be 'changed into the same image from glory to glory.' We are 'to press toward the mark, for the prize of the high calling of God in Jesus Christ.' The capacity of the soul for indefinite development, its eternal craving for something better, the increase both of its desire and power for further advancement as it progresses, as well as the assurances of God's Word, demonstrate that we are made for progress. 'More and more.' This is the soul's watchword — Excelsior! is its cry.

"The march of the good is A GLORIOUS march. 'Unto the perfect day.' Perfect day. What a day is that! They shall shine as the sun in the Kingdom of God. Perfect day — not one cloud of error in the sky; not one ungenial blast in the atmosphere. Perfect — knowledge free from error; love free from impurity; purpose free from selfishness; experience free from pain. The good man's progress excels even the glory of the sun. The sun does not increase in size or splendour; he is not greater in bulk or brighter in lustre now than when he shone on Adam; but growth, everlasting growth, is our destiny." — *David Thomas.*

"When God says in the Bible, 'Give me thine *heart*,' he means, 'Give me your love, your thought — in fact, *yourself.*' For your body is *yours*, but it is not *you;* your hands, your feet, your eyes, your ears, they are not you. They are part of the house in which you live. They are servants which do your work for you. But your own real self, the real boy and girl, is that in you which can hate and love and think, like and dislike, obey and disobey, be good or bad, at will. . . . Well, your heart, your mind, is the well of your life. If that is poisoned, your best life will die. And the book that bids you guard it well is not a stern book, but a kind, loving book, that wishes you well, and is your best friend. But how can we guard the *heart?* By keeping bad thoughts, bad wishes, out of it." — *J. M. Gibbon.*

THE LESSON IN LIFE, LITERATURE, AND ARCHAEOLOGY.

When Dr. Arthur T. Pierson was thirteen years of age, he left home, never to return again for any length of time. His biographer tells us that before his departure, his father gave him as a life motto the promise of Proverbs 3:6. Sixty years later the son said, "Since my father gave me that motto, no important step has been taken in my life without looking to God for His guidance, and never have I looked in vain. I have learned that if His guidance does not come at once, it is safer to wait until He sees fit to show the way."

A TRUTH FOR THE CLASS TO CARRY AWAY.

The teacher might bring this lesson to a close most profitably by reminding the pupils that we need the same guidance today that the men of old needed, but we have the advantage that there lives within us the very Spirit of God, one of Whose precious functions is this very matter of guiding those who belong to Christ, as Paul tells us in Romans 8:10–14.

Did Solomon exhibit the values of pursuing wisdom in his early life, and how do you account for the fact that he later departed from this? Did Christ himself ever have to make a choice between two paths? What is the one thing in this lesson that all people, unless in miserable health, really desire to have? (Is it not long life?) Do you think our schools ought to teach the principles of character and conduct such as set forth in this book — if not, who will? After all, if we breathe automatically and our ears listen automatically, and our eyes judge distance automatically, why do we not automatically discern and follow the right way?

LESSON IV. — October 24.

GUIDANCE FOR FAMILY LIVING. — Proverbs 4; 6:20—7:27; 17:1; 19:13–14; 31:10–31.

PRINTED TEXT, Proverbs 4:1–4; 6:20–23; 17:1; 19:13–14; 31:10–12.

Devotional Reading: 1 Corinthians 13.
Beginner Topic: My Love Gift.
    Lesson Material: Mark 12:41–44.
    Memory Verse: I will love thee, O Jehovah. Psalm 18:1.
Primary Topic: Learning from His Father.
    Lesson Material: Proverbs 4; 6:20–23.
    Memory Verse: My son, keep the commandment of thy father, And forsake not the law of thy mother. Proverbs 6:20.
Junior Topic: Wise Enough to Learn.
    Lesson Material: Proverbs 4; 6:20–23.
    Memory Verse: My son, keep the commandment of thy father, And forsake not the law of thy mother. Proverbs 6:20.
Intermediate-Senior Topic: My Home — Today and Tomorrow.
    Lesson Material: Proverbs 4; 6:20—7:27; 17:1; 19:13–14; 31:10–31.
    Memory Verse: My son, keep the commandment of thy father, And forsake not the law of thy mother. Proverbs 6:20.
Topic for Young People and Adults: Making Home Life Successful.
    Lesson Material: Proverbs 4; 6:20—7:27; 17:1; 19:13–14; 31:10–31.
    Memory Verse: My son, keep the commandment of thy father, And forsake not the law of thy mother. Proverbs 6:20.

THE TEACHER AND HIS CLASS.

The Younger Classes may be introduced to this lesson, on words spoken by a father to a son on finding the right way in life, by the following illustration: At the end of the week in which this lesson is being written, I must drive four hundred miles to Mount Hermon for a Bible conference. I have done this before, but recently heard that a friend of mine knew a shorter route, which he had been over many times. He has marked this out on a map for me. In this lesson, the father is talking to the son about a road which he himself had frequently traveled and found safe and satisfying.

The Older Classes might begin this lesson by a discussion of one of the great fundamental themes of the Bible, the relationship of father and son. Israel knew God as her Father, and God called Israel a child. In the New Testament, our Lord is called the Son of God, and we, especially in the First Epistle of John, are designated the children of God. The Lord's Prayer opens with the phrase, "Our Father, who art in heaven." These are spiritual relationships, but the same words are used for the natural relationships, of father and son in the family on earth; in fact, the family on earth should be but a replica of what the family of God is and will be.

THE LESSON IN ITS SETTING.

Time. — The writing of the Proverbs may be placed somewhere in the middle of the Tenth century B.C.

Place. — There is no geographical data here of any importance.

THE PLAN OF THE LESSON.

SUBJECT: The Disciplines and Resolutions of Life that Make for Homes of Joy, Peace, Satisfaction and Heavenliness.

I. A FATHER EXHORTS HIS SON TO DILIGENTLY KEEP THE LAWS OF LIFE THAT HAVE PROVED DEPENDABLE AND PROTECTIVE, Proverbs 4:1–4; 6:20–23; 7:1–4.

1. He had received these commandments from his own father, 4:1–4.
2. The benefactions that follow obedience to such, 6:20–23.
3. These laws are to become a part of us, 7:1–4.

II. TWO SPECIFIC AREAS IN WHICH SUCH LAWS WILL PROVE INVALUABLE, Proverbs 4:5–27; 6:24–35; 7:5–27.

1. In keeping one from a path of evil, 4:5–27.
2. In preserving one from unchaste women, 6:24–35; 7:5–27.

III. SOME CHARACTERISTICS OF THE IDEAL HOME

1. Quietness.
2. A wife of faithfulness and industry.

THE TEACHER'S LIBRARY.

For a rather full list of commentaries on the Book of Proverbs, see the bibliographies in the Introduction to this volume. For some strange reason sermonic material on the verses assigned to the printed text is almost non-existant, and I have made a very careful search of sermonic literature for this. However, on 6:22 there is a great sermon by Charles H. Spurgeon in the *Metropolitan Tabernacle Pulpit* for 1871, Vol. 17, pp. 589–600. While the passages in our lesson embracing warnings regarding unchaste women do not appear in the printed text, I would like to call my readers' attention to a most powerful sermon by Henry Ward Beecher, "The Strange Woman," in his *Twelve Lectures to Young Men*, 124–159.

AUDIO-VISUAL AIDS.

FILM: "Rim of the Wheel," Family Films, 28 min., sd., b&w. Shows how one family's difficulties are solved when a neighbor introduces family worship to the children one evening when he was baby-sitting.
FILMSTRIP: "Making Home a Happier Place," Church Screen, 72 fr., b&w, script. Takes up problems of family living, showing how each member can help to make a happy home.

I. A FATHER EXHORTS HIS SON TO DILIGENTLY KEEP THE LAWS OF LIFE THAT HAVE PROVED DEPENDABLE AND PROTECTIVE, 4:1–4; 6:20–23; 7:1–4.
1. HE HAD RECEIVED THESE COMMANDMENTS FROM HIS OWN FATHER, 4:1–4.

PROVERBS 4:1. Hear, *my* sons, the instruction of a father, And attend to know understanding:

2. For I give you good doctrine; Forsake ye not my law.

3. For I was a son unto my father, Tender and only beloved in the sight of my mother.

4. And he taught me, and said unto me: Let thy heart retain my words; Keep my commandments, and live.

---

1. **Hear, *my* sons, the instruction of a father, And attend to know understanding: 2. For I give you good doctrine; Forsake ye not my law. 3. For I was a son unto my father, Tender and only beloved in the sight of my mother. 4. And he taught me, and said unto me: Let thy heart retain my words; Keep my commandments, and live.** This beautiful passage is almost an exact autobiographical commentary on a similar exhortation in the Mosaic literature which we have often studied (Deut. 6:4–9). The phrase "only beloved" in verse three needs careful study. "Solomon was not an 'only' son, though it might reasonably be urged that he was so in the same sense as was Isaac, of whom this same word is used (Gen. 22:2, 16. Comp. Heb. 11:17), and who was not strictly an only son either, but one who stood alone in the choice of God and in the Messianic line, and therefore in the estimation of his father. See 'Solomon my son, whom alone God hath chosen,' (1 Chron. 29:1), where the word 'tender' is also applied as here to Solomon. But Solomon was from his birth specially beloved (2 Sam. 12:24, 25), and the word is used elsewhere in this derived sense, 'alone' not only in fact, but in the value set upon it (Ps. 22:20; 35:17, 'my darling')." — *T. T. Perowne.* The late Dr. Horton, in his chapters on Proverbs, is especially helpful in the passages that relate to the home, and the education of children. "If the child's heart is surrendered to God, and moulded by heavenly wisdom, the man will walk securely; a certain trend will be given to all his thoughts; a certain instinctive desire for righteousness will be engrafted in his nature; and an instinctive aversion will lead him to decline the way of the wicked.

"The first thing, then, is to give our children an atmosphere to grow up in; to cultivate their affections, and set their hearts on the things eternal; to make them associate the ideas of wealth and honour, of beauty and glory, not with material possessions, but with the treasures and rewards of Wisdom.

"But now comes the question, What is to be the definite teaching of the child? for it is an unfailing mark of the parents who themselves are holy that they are impelled to give clear and memorable instruction to their children. And this is where the great and constant difficulty emerges. If the hallowed example would suffice we might count the task comparatively easy. But some day the understanding will begin to assert itself; the desire to question, to criticise, to prove, will awake. And then, unless the truths of the heart have been applied to the conscience in such a way as to satisfy the reason, there may come the desolate time in which, while the habits of practical life remain pure, and the unconscious influence of early training continues to be effective, the mind is shaken by doubt, and the hope of the soul is shrouded in a murky cloud." — *Dr. Horton.* How wonderful it would be if every child in America could, when his children were growing up, pay a tribute like this to the religious instruction he had received from his parents. There is a verse in Paul's second letter to Timothy which most perfectly summarizes exactly the truth which we have here in this ancient volume: "Abide thou in the things which thou hast learned and hast been assured of, knowing of whom thou hast learned them; and that from a babe thou hast known the sacred writings which are able to make thee wise unto salvation" (2 Tim. 3:14, 15, with which compare 1:5–6).

2. THE BENEFACTIONS THAT FOLLOW OBEDIENCE TO SUCH, 6:20–23. Once again we have verses that take us right back to that earlier Mosaic law to which

PROVERBS 6:20. My son, keep the commandment of thy father, And forsake not the law of thy mother:

21. Bind them continually upon thy heart; Tie them about thy neck.

22. When thou walkest, it shall lead thee; When thou sleepest, it shall watch over thee; And when thou awakest, it shall talk with thee.

23. For the commandment is a lamp; and the law is light; And reproofs of instruction are the way of life.

---

we have already referred (Deut. 6:4–9). 20. **My son, keep the commandment of thy father, And forsake not the law of thy mother: 21. Bind them continually upon thy heart; Tie them about thy neck. 22. When thou walkest, it shall lead thee; When thou sleepest, it shall watch over thee; And when thou awakest, it shall talk with thee. 23. For the commandment is a lamp; and the law is light; And reproofs of instruction are the way of life.** "A FATHER'S commandment is the generic form, and is usually employed to signify parental authority; but here, in addition to the general formula, 'the law of a mother' is specifically singled out. The first feature that arrests attention in this picture is, that effects are attributed to the law of a mother which only God's law can produce. The inference is obvious and sure; it is assumed that the law which a mother instills is the word of God dwelling richly in her own heart, and that she acts as a channel to convey that word to the hearts of her children. To assume it as actually done, is the most impressive method of enjoining it. Parents are, by the constitution of things, in an important sense mediators between God and their children for a time. What you give them they receive; what you tell them they believe. This is their nature. You should weigh well what law, and what practice you impress first upon their tender hearts. First ideas and habits are to them most important. These give direction to their course, and tone to their character through life. Your children are by nature let into you, so as to drink in what you contain; the only safety is that you be by grace let into Christ, so that what they get from you, shall be, not what springs within you, but what flows into you from the Spring-head of holiness. To the children, it is the law of their mother, and therefore they receive it; but in substance it is the truth from Jesus, and to receive it is life. It is the law which converts the soul and makes wise the simple, poured through a mother's lips into infants' ears." — *William Arnot.*

There is one phrase in this paragraph which is most unique, and yet I doubt if many Bible readers know it is in the Scriptures: "When thou awakest it shall talk with thee." Spurgeon has a great sermon on this phrase, which he calls "The Talking Book." I wish I could quote the entire message, but we must content ourselves with a few lines. "To talk signifies fellowship, communion, familiarity. It does not say, 'It shall preach to thee.' Many persons have a high esteem for the book, but they look upon it as though it were some very elevated teacher speaking to them from a lofty tribunal, while they stand far below. I will not altogether condemn that reverence, but it were far better if they would understand the familiarity of God's word; it does not so much preach to us as *talk* to us. It is not, 'When thou awakest, it shall lecture thee,' or, 'it shall scold thee'; no, no, 'it shall *talk* with thee.' We sit at its feet, or rather at the feet of Jesus, in the word, and it comes down to us; it is familiar with us, as a man talketh to his friend. And here let me remind you of the delightful familiarity of Scripture in this respect, that *it speaks the language of men.* If God had written us a book of his own language, we could not have comprehended it, or what little we understood would have so alarmed us, that we should have besought that those words should not be spoken to us any more; but the Lord, in his word, often uses language which, though it be infallibly true in its meaning, is not after the knowledge of God, but according to the manner of man. . . .

"When the word of God talks with us, it influences us. All talk influences more or less. I believe there is more done in this world for good or bad by talk than there is by preaching; indeed, the preacher preaches best when he talks; there is no oratory in the word that is equal to simple talk: it is the model of eloquence; and all your rhetorician's action and verbiage are so much rubbish. The most efficient way of preaching is simply talking; the man permitting his heart to run over at his lips into other men's hearts. Now, this book, as it talks with us, influences us, and it does so in many ways.

"It soothes our sorrows, and encourages us. Many a warrior has been ready to steal away from God's battle, but the word has laid its hand on him, and said, 'Stand on thy feet, be not discouraged, be of good cheer, I will strengthen thee, I will help thee; yea, I will uphold thee with the right hand of my righteousness.' Brave saints we have read of, but we little know how often they would have been arrant cowards, only the good word came and strengthened them, and they went back to be stronger than lions and swifter than eagles." — *Charles H. Spurgeon.*

3. THESE LAWS ARE TO BECOME A PART OF US, 7:1–4. This binding of the law on the finger reminds us, of course, of verses in the preceding section: "Bind them continually upon thy heart; tie them about thy neck." The Word of God then is to be to us like a ring adorned with a precious stone, both an ornament and a memento. The most beautiful phrase here though is, "Write them upon the tablet of thy heart" (see also Prov. 3:3). We are here of course reminded of a similar exhortation in the epistles of Paul, "Let the word of Christ dwell in you richly" (Col. 3:16). If the word is written in our hearts then we can say with David, "Thy word have I laid up in my heart that I might not sin against thee" (Ps. 119:11).

II. TWO SPECIFIC AREAS IN WHICH SUCH LAWS WILL PROVE INVALUABLE, Proverbs 4:5–27, 6:24–35; 7:5–27. The paragraphs of Proverbs that I have placed under this heading do not contain any verses assigned for the printed text, but for a detailed exposition of a large portion of this fourth chapter, see the lesson for October 17th. I believe that we ought not to pass by, however, these solemn words of the father to his son concerning the tragedy that awaits any man who yields to the solicitations of women of unchaste conduct. This subject came up for consideration in the very beginning of the book (2:3–20), and is resumed here in two long passages. Dr. Horton, in a volume we have already found so helpful says, "Here is a temptation which in many varying forms has always beset human life. No small part of the danger is that this evil, above all others, grows in silence, and yet seems to be aggravated by publicity. The preacher cannot speak plainly about it, and even writers shrink from touching the subject. We can, however, be thankful that the book, which is God's book rather than man's, knows nothing of our false modesty and conventional delicacy: it speaks out not only boldly, but minutely; it is so explicit that no man who with a prayerful heart will meditate upon its teachings need fall into the pitfall — that pitfall which seems to grow even more subtle and more seductive as civilization advances, and as the great cities absorb a larger proportion of the population; or if he fall he can only admit with shame and remorse, 'I have hated instruction, and my heart despised reproof.'" — *R. F. Horton.* I must quote one paragraph from the great sermon by Henry Ward Beecher referred to above: "God did not make so much of nature with exquisite beauty, or put within us a taste for it, without object. He meant that it should delight us. He made every flower to charm us. He never made a color, nor graceful flying bird, nor silvery insect, without meaning to please our taste. When he clothes a man or woman with beauty, he confers a favor, did we know how to receive it. Beauty, *with* amiable dispositions and ripe intelligence, is more to any woman than a queen's crown. The peasant's daughter, the rustic belle, if they have woman's sound discretion, may be rightfully prouder than kings' daughters; for *God* adorns those who are both good and beautiful, man can only conceal the want of beauty by blazing jewels.

"As moths and tiny insects flutter around the bright blaze which was kindled

PROVERBS 17:1. Better is a dry morsel, and quietness therewith, Than a house full of feasting with strife.

PROVERBS 19:13. A foolish son is the calamity of his father; And the contentions of a wife are a continual dropping.

---

for no harm, so the foolish young fall down burned and destroyed by the blaze of beauty. As the flame which burns to destroy the insect is consuming itself and soon sinks into the socket, so beauty, too often, draws on itself that ruin which it inflicts upon others.

"Shame that the sweetest of all the mind's attributes should be suborned to sin! that this daughter of God should become a Ganymede to arrogant lusts, the cup-bearer to tyrants! yet so it is. Devil-tempter! will thy poison never cease? shall beauty be poisoned? shall language be charmed? shall *love* be made to defile like pitch, and burn as the living coals? Her tongue is like a bended bow, which sends the silvery shaft of flattering words. Her eyes shall cheat thee, her dress shall beguile thee; her beauty is a trap, her sighs are baits, her words are lures, her love is poisonous, her flattery is the spider's web spread for thee. O, trust not thy heart nor ear with Delilah! The locks of the mightiest Samson are soon shorn off, if he will but lay his slumbering head upon her lap. He who could slay heaps upon heaps of Philistines, and bear upon his huge shoulders the ponderous iron gate, and pull down the vast temple, was yet too weak to contend with one wicked, artful woman! Trust the sea with thy tiny boat, trust the fickle wind, trust the changing skies of April, trust the miser's generosity, the tyrant's mercy; but, ah! simple man, trust not thyself near the *artful* woman, armed in her beauty, her cunning raiment, her dimpled smiles, her sighs of sorrow, her look of love, her voice of flattery; for if thou hadst the strength of ten Ulysses, unless God help thee, Calypso shall make thee fast, and hold thee in her island." — *Henry Ward Beecher*.

III. **SOME CHARACTERISTICS OF THE IDEAL HOME,** Proverbs 17:1, 19:13–4; 31:10–31. We come, in this last division of our lesson, to what we might call the very cream of Old Testament teaching, regarding the home. Home life comes before us on the very first page of the Bible, first with Adam and Eve, and their two children, Cain and Abel, and then the terrible dark cloud of murder that fell across their threshhold. But we have a beautiful home-life revealed to us among the patriarchs, with certain gross blemishes at times, as the wife of Isaac urging Jacob to deceive his father. But there was an ideal, nevertheless, whether it was lived up to or not, which here finds its most vivid expression. I would almost think that it took the coming of Christ to make all these words possible in the family of believers.

1. QUIETNESS, 17:1. **Better is a dry morsel, and quietness therewith, Than a house full of feasting with strife.** "The word '*feasting*' refers to the practice of feasting on the flesh of slain victims when they were not holocaust to be entirely consumed on the altar. The margin gives the true idea. 'A house full of good cheer with strife — plenty with discontent.' The idea of Solomon is that domestic poverty with content is better than plenty with discontent. These things are often found in association. There is many a pauper home where the spirit of contentment reigns supreme, and many a wealthy mansion, where there is nothing but brawls and contention. And who, that knows life, will not say, that the former is the preferable condition? A contented mind is a continual feast." — *David Thomas*.

Of the next two verses, only the second strictly belongs under this heading, but I did not want to make a separate division for verse 13, so we will examine both of them now. 19:13. **A foolish son is the calamity of his father; And the contentions of a wife are a continual dropping.** "There are many things that curse a home in this sinful world. Two things are mentioned here. First: 'a foolish son.' We have had occasion more than once to refer to the foolish son. Who is he? A

14. House and riches are an inheritance from fathers; But a prudent wife is from Jehovah.

Proverbs 31:10. A worthy woman who can find? For her price is far above rubies.

11. The heart of her husband trusteth in her, And he shall have no lack of gain.

12. She doeth him good and not evil All the days of her life.

son who does not reciprocate his parents' love, does not acknowledge his parents' kindness, does not recognize his parents' rule. . . . Secondly, a contentious wife. An ill-tempered, irritable, and irritating wife is indeed a curse to a home. It is as a 'continual dropping.' You are in a house where the rain is constantly dropping from the roof into every room, there is no corner where it does not come, wherever you stand or sit irritating drops descend upon your head, damaging your clothes and furniture too. Your temper is irritated, and your goods are running to ruin. Such is the figure in which Solomon sets forth the baneful influence of a contentious wife." — *David Thomas.* 14. **House and riches are an inheritance from fathers; But a prudent wife is from Jehovah.** And who, we might ask, might truly be called a prudent wife? The word comes from a verb meaning "to be wise," and hence, by consequence to be prosperous. "The text is usually read, as meaning, *that fathers can provide wealth*, etc., but *a wife is the gift of Heaven.* The theology is not good. Wealth is eminently from God. It rather means that a wife *is* house and wealth. That is to say, it arranges them as kindred gifts. As fathers provide house and ease for themselves and their children, so God, our Highest Father, provides our own and His own intimate relations." — *John Miller.*

2. A Wife of Faithfulness and Industry, 19:13–14; 31:10–31. Throughout the Book of Proverbs we have had literally scores of verses depicting and warning young men from those types of women who would bring nothing but disaster and bitterness into their lives. It is most refreshing to come at the end of the book upon the most noble description of womanhood to be found anywhere in the Bible, either in the Old or the New Testament. **31:10. A worthy woman who can find? For her price is far above rubies. 11. The heart of her husband trusteth in her, And he shall have no lack of gain. 12. She doeth him good and not evil All the days of her life.** "We have here woman occupying and adorning her rightful place, elevated by anticipation to the high estate to which the Gospel of Christ has restored her. It is an expansion of the earlier proverb: 'Whoso findeth a wife findeth a good *thing*, and obtaineth favour of the Lord' (18:22)." — *T. T. Perowne.* "The virtuous woman of the Proverbs is a wife: and the first thing to observe is the part she plays in relation to her husband. She is his stay and confidence: 'The heart of her husband trusteth in her.' She is his natural confidante and counsellor; her advice is more valuable than that of much cleverer people, because it is so absolutely disinterested; the hearts are in such vital contact that the merely intellectual communications have a quality all their own. One may often observe in an ideal marriage, though the husband seems to be the stronger and the more self-reliant, the wife is really the pillar of strength; if death removes her, he is forlorn and bereft and helpless; the gradual work of the years has led him to depend on her more and more, to draw from her his best inspirations, and to turn instinctively to her for advice and direction." — *R. Horton.* The word translated "worthy," in verse ten, really means "virtuous," not so much as we use the word, but in the wider sense of all worthy living. The remaining verses of this description are occupied for the most part with only two aspects of the life of this remarkable companion — on the one hand, her industriousness and on the other hand the strength and dignity which her character and conduct, as it were, give to the husband and the children. Of course the form of industry here is a primitive one — the working with wool and flax, but many pictures of our Colonial ancestors

will show that the very labor emphasized here was that which could be seen in any thrifty home down to the beginning of the Industrial Revolution. As the result of all this her husband on the one hand is highly regarded (v. 23) among his fellow-citizens. "It is this strong, sweet core of life in the home which gives the man dignity and honour in public. She is a crown to her husband. His influence in the life of his town or of his country is not always directly traced to its true source. But it is that woman's noble sway over him, it is the constant spur and chastening of her love, which gives him the weighty voice and the grave authority in the counsels of the nation." — *R. Horton.* And then finally her very children rise up to call her blessed (v. 28). "In the spirit, the character and the lives of her children she meets with an ample reward for all her self-denying efforts to make them happy and good. They mark her noble life, and in the first stages of thoughtfulness they are impressed with the charms of her disinterestedness and devotion, and as they grow up under the advantages of her noble example and spiritual instruction, they love her not only as the instrumental author of their being, but as to them a ministering angel from God. Noble mother! There she sits, weakened by age, crowned with years, and beautiful to behold. Her children grown up, gather around her with a veneration the most sacred, and a love the most tender and strong. Their lives are a grateful acknowledgment of all her kindness, and in their spirit and conversation she reaps a rich harvest of delight." — *David Thomas.*

THE LESSON IN LIFE, LITERATURE, AND ARCHAEOLOGY.

"Luther applied Psalm 31 to his wife, Katherina von Bora, when he was praising her good qualities to his table companions. 'It was God's will,' he said, 'that I should take pity on the forsaken one. And the result, God be praised, has been most fortunate, for I have a pious and faithful wife.' Luther said in 1537 that his Katie had served him not only as a wife, but as a maid. He wished her to inherit everything he left behind, for he thought that the children ought to receive from the mother, and not the mother from the children."

A TRUTH FOR THE CLASS TO CARRY AWAY.

Perhaps at the close of this lesson it would be helpful if the teacher stressed not only those virtues which make for happiness within our own homes, but the atmosphere we create in our homes which is quickly apprehended by all those who visit us. I remember years ago calling upon a Presbyterian minister in Roodhouse, Illinois, whose name I have forgotten, but somehow the atmosphere in that home made a profound impression upon me as a young man, and has stayed with me for years as an ideal.

What must be true of any father before he can give instructions such as those set forth here? How is a man to know that the young woman with whom he is in love will develop into the kind of wife whose portrait is here presented? In what way are the exhortations of father to son here quite similar to those of Paul to Timothy in 1 Timothy 1 and 2 Timothy 1? When is it too late to begin practicing the principles here given?

LESSON V. — October 31.

THE DIGNITY OF WORK. — Proverbs 6:6–11; 12:24, 27; 13:11; 14:23; 15:19; 18:9; 24:30–34.

PRINTED TEXT, Proverbs 6:6–11; 18:9; 24:30–34.

Devotional Reading: Ephesians 4:11–16.
Beginners Topic: AT BABY MOSES' HOUSE.
  Lesson Material: Exodus 2:1–10.
  Memory Verse: God . . . careth for you.   1 Peter 5:7b.
Primary Topic: WORK FOR ALL OF US.
  Lesson Material: Proverbs 6:6–11; 12:24, 27; 13:11; 14:23; 15:19.
  Memory Verse: Work, for I am with you, saith Jehovah of hosts.   Haggai 2:4.
Junior Topic: WHAT WORK DOES FOR US.
  Lesson Material: Proverbs 6:6–11; 12:24, 27; 13:11; 14:23; 15:19.
  Memory Verse: Work, for I am with you, saith Jehovah of hosts.   Haggai 2:4.
Intermediate-Senior Topic: PULLING MY OWN WEIGHT.
  Lesson Material: Proverbs 6:6–11; 12:24, 27; 13:11; 14:23; 18:9; 24:30–34.
  Memory Verse: Seest thou a man diligent in his business? he shall stand before kings; he shall not stand before mean men.   Proverbs 22:29.
Topic for Young People and Adults: THE DIGNITY OF WORK.
  Lesson Material: Proverbs 6:6–11; 12:24, 27; 13:11; 14:23; 18:9; 24:30–34.
  Memory Verse: Seest thou a man diligent in his business? he shall stand before kings; he shall not stand before mean men.   Proverbs 22:29.

THE TEACHER AND HIS CLASS.

The Younger Classes may be introduced to this lesson (inasmuch as some of its truths are taken from nature) by being asked what in nature, and with man, occurs automatically and what only with labor and effort. Any piece of ground, unless a desert, will, of course, grow worthless weeds. We all breathe automatically day and night, and are not even aware of it, unless we are ill. The food we take into our mouths is digested in a marvelous way by chemicals within our body, and then redistributed to every part of it, and of this, also, we are not aware. However, to grow beautiful flowers, or fruit trees, takes effort on our part. To secure food and provide a nice home for the family involves effort. Anything worthwhile of a material nature requires labor and thought.

The Older Classes may be introduced to this lesson on work by being reminded that God gave even to unfallen man the task of tilling a garden (Gen. 2:15), which means that in the original plan of creation, God intended man to work. Fallen man, because of the perversities of nature (the ground being cursed because of sin), must work the harder (Gen. 3:17–19). It is said that even in the life to come, we will be serving the Lord (Rev. 22:3), though there will be no weariness in this. Work, then, is ordained of God and true labor is ever blessed of God.

THE LESSON IN ITS SETTING.

Time. — Most of the Proverbs were gathered together about 950 B.C.
Place. — There is no geographical data in this Book.

THE PLAN OF THE LESSON.

SUBJECT: How the Laws of Nature, the Laws of Political Economy, and Human Experience in every Land Bear Testimony to the Necessity for, the Dignity of, and the Beneficent Consequences Derived from Work of a Worthy, Honorable Nature.

I. THE ANT AS AN ILLUSTRATION OF INDUSTRIOUS HABITS, Proverbs 6:6-11.

II. THE DILIGENT AND THE SLOTHFUL MAN CONTRASTED, Proverbs 12:24, 27.
1. In relation to others, v. 24.
2. In relation to the food we eat, v. 27.

III. SOME BLESSINGS ATTENDING DILIGENCE AND EVILS ATTENDING LAZINESS, Proverbs 13:11; 14:23; 15:19.
1. In relation to the acquisition of possessions, 13:11.
2. In regard to ultimate consequences, 14:23; 15:19.

IV. THE DEEPER EVIL OF LAZINESS, Proverbs 18:9.

V. THE LESSON OF THE RUN-DOWN FARM, Proverbs 24:30-34.

THE TEACHER'S LIBRARY.

We have had one lesson on Work this year (that of September 5), but I shall try not to repeat in any way, even in the bibliography, so that some of the references to certain chapters in the bibliography of that lesson might also be consulted for this one. On the portion of the Book of Proverbs assigned to this lesson, I have found more valuable than any other work a volume by one of the most suggestive exegetes of the latter part of the 19th century, *The Practical Philosopher*, by David Thomas. I am using the 4th edition (London 1885) and because it is so rarely seen today, frequent quotations from it will appear throughout this lesson. Other helpful volumes on the Proverbs are the two great volumes by Franz Delitzsch, T. T. Perowne in *The Cambridge Bible for Schools and Colleges*, and *A Commentary on Proverbs*, by John Miller (2nd ed., Princeton, 1887). Only one chapter relates to our lesson in the notable work by William Arnot, *Laws from Heaven for Life on Earth*. R. F. Horton has a good chapter on laziness in the volume on Proverbs in *The Expositor's Bible*.

On the illustration from the life of the ant, see H. B. Tristram: *The Natural History of the Bible*, 319-321; and a sermon in Hugh Macmillan: *The Corn of Heaven*, 203-217. On 24:30-34, see a sermon by W. G. Elmslie in *The Contemporary Pulpit*, 2nd series, Vol. 1, pp. 216-230. I know of no other sermonic material on any of the verses of the printed text, with the exception of the pages on the last part of the lesson in Alexander Maclaren: *Expositions of Holy Scripture, Esther to Ecclesiastes*, 269-274.

For the various agricultural pursuits and trades in Bible times, one should consult G. M. Mackie: *Bible Manners and Customs;* Canon Tristram: *Eastern Customs in Bible Lands*, and a book most graciously presented to me last year in London by my friend the Prebendary of St. Paul's, *The Trades and Industrial Occupations of the Bible*, by W. G. Lewis. In the famous volume by C. Schmidt, *The Social Results of Early Christianity*, is a good chapter on the laboring classes, 212-236. If one wishes to study this problem further, he should consult the first volume of the monumental work by Ernst Troeltsch: *The Social Teaching of the Christian Churches*, 118 ff.

AUDIO-VISUAL AIDS.

FILMSTRIP: "Hour by Hour," Society for the Promotion of Christian Knowledge, 26 fr., b&w. This is a British filmstrip and would have to be ordered a couple of months ahead of time. It is on the week-day life of the Christian, and gives the answer to the question, "Why heat the church during the week?"

PROVERBS 6:6. Go to the ant, thou sluggard; Consider her ways, and be wise.

7. Which having no chief, Overseer, or ruler,

8. Provideth her bread in the summer, And gathereth her food in the harvest.

9. How long wilt thou sleep, O sluggard? When wilt thou arise out of thy sleep?

10. *Yet* a little sleep, a little slumber, A little folding of the hands to sleep:

11. So shall thy poverty come as a robber, And thy want as an armed man.

I. THE ANT AS AN ILLUSTRATION OF INDUSTRIOUS HABITS, Proverbs 6:6-11. 6. Go to the ant, thou sluggard; Consider her ways, and be wise. 7. Which having no chief, Overseer, or ruler, 8. Provideth her bread in the summer, And gathereth her food in the harvest. 9. How long wilt thou sleep, O sluggard? When wilt thou arise out of thy sleep? 10. *Yet* a little sleep, a little slumber, A little folding of the hands to sleep: 11. So shall thy poverty come as a robber, And thy want as an armed man. The last three verses in this section reappear in the final portion of the lesson, so here we shall confine ourselves to a study of the passage concerning the ant. "The ant is twice mentioned in the Book of Proverbs: in this passage it is held forth as a pattern of industry, and in 30:24, 25 as a model of wisdom. The natural interpretation of both these passages is that the ant proves her industry and wisdom by storing up in summer a supply for winter use. . . . The ancients were familiar with the fact that the ant stored up food for winter consumption; and who that has watched the incessant activity of these little creatures, issuing in long files from their labyrinths by a broad beaten track, and gradually dispersing in all directions by pathways that become narrower and fainter as they diverge, while a busy throng uninterruptedly conveys back by the same paths every object which they are able to drag with their powerful forceps, would not at once arrive at the same conclusion? The language of the Wise Man is in accordance not only with the universal belief of his time, but with the accurately ascertained facts of Natural History. Contrary to its habits in colder climates, the ant is not there dormant through the winter; and among the Tamarisks of the Dead Sea, it may be seen in January actively engaged in collecting the Aphides and saccharine exudations, in long files passing and repassing up and down the trunk. Two of the most common species of the Holy Land (*Atta barbara*, the black ant, and *Atta structor*, a brown ant) are strictly seed feeders and in summer lay up large stores of grain for winter use. These species are spread along the whole of the Mediterranean coasts, but are unknown in more northern climates. Hence writers who were ignorant of any ants beyond those of their own countries have been presumptuous enough to deny the accuracy of Solomon's statement."

II. **THE DILIGENT AND THE SLOTHFUL MAN CONTRASTED,** Proverbs 12:24, 27. It would have been well had those constructing these lesson assignments included all the verses in the printed text, since there are so few. At any rate, it seems wise to quote them here, so that all the needed material is immediately before us: "The hand of the diligent shall bear rule; but the slothful shall be put under taskwork" (v. 24). In this chapter we have a series of contrasts, of which the Book of Proverbs is so full Here the diligent and the slothful man are seen in their relation to others — the one ruling, the other serving. "All men desire rule, and some kind of rule every man may obtain. Social, civil, and, what is higher still, mental and spiritual. Rule over men's thoughts and hearts. Any of these dominions diligence can achieve. Diligence in study may get a knowledge that may sway an age. Diligence in business may obtain wealth that shall govern commerce. Diligence in goodness may achieve an excellence before which the soul of nations shall kneel. . . . An indolent man will never become royal in anything. He will be the mere tool of society, the mere servile attendant upon others. Men will use him, make him a rung in the ladder of their ascent. The slothful man gets neither knowledge, wealth, nor goodness. He never reaches an imperial altitude. He shall be under tribute evermore. That which he hath is ultimately taken from him; and into the outer darkness of obscurity he falls." — *David Thomas.*

"The slothful man roasteth not that which he took in hunting; but the precious substance of men is to the diligent" (v. 27). In this verse the same two types are set before us, now in relation to the food they eat. "The original word, here translated 'slothful' is in several other places rendered 'deceitful.' Slothfulness is almost necessarily connected with deceit. The idle man is a dreamer, he lives in false hopes. He makes promises that prove fallacious, because he has not the industry to work them out. Slothfulness stands almost always nearly akin to falsehood. The text means one of three things; either that the slothful man is too lazy to 'roast' and to prepare for food what he happened to strike down without much effort in the field, or, that what he 'roasts' and prepares for food he had no hand in procuring, and that he lives on the production of other men's labours. He has 'roast' meat, but that which he roasts is not what he himself took in hunting; or, what he caught in the field was so *easily* caught, caught with such little effort that he did not value it enough to prepare it for food. He did not take it up, carry it home, and prepare it for the table. The last, I think, was the idea that Solomon had in his mind when he wrote this proverb; as if he had said, the slothful man does not value sufficiently what he has, without labour, caught in the field to prepare it for food; but what the industrious man has, as the result of his work is precious to him. The general principle, therefore, contained in these words is this: — That labour enhances the relative value of a man's possessions. This principle is capable of extensive illustration; it applies to many things." — *David Thomas.*

III. SOME BLESSINGS ATTENDING DILIGENCE AND EVILS ATTENDING LAZINESS, Proverbs 13:11; 14:23; 15:19.

1. IN RELATION TO THE ACQUISITION OF POSSESSIONS, 13:11. "Wealth gotten by vanity shall be diminished; but he that gathereth by labor shall have increase." Again we have contrasts, here between two types of wealthy men — the one who has gained his possessions falsely, and the other who gained his by labor. "This verse implies three things: That worldly wealth *is a good thing*. The universal feeling of man shows this — all men strive after it. The services it can render show this. Man's physical comforts, intellectual opportunities, social resources, and the progress of his religious institutions greatly depend upon this. The Word of God shows this. 'Money,' says Solomon, 'answers all things.' The Bible does not despise wealth. It legislates for its employment and denounces its abuse. We infer — That worldly wealth may be obtained *in different ways*. There are two ways referred to in the text. The way of vanity, or wealth gotten by vanity. The word 'vanity' may represent all those tricks of trade, reckless speculations, and idle gambling, by which large fortunes are often easily gained. Within our own circle of acquaintance, there are not a few who have become millionaires by guilty hits. Secondly, the way of labour. Honest, industrious, frugal labour is the legitimate way to wealth. Honest industry is God's road to fortune. We infer — that the decrease or increase of worldly wealth *is determined by the method in which it has been obtained*. Two facts in human nature will illustrate this principle. First: What man does not highly value he is likely to squander. That which we hold cheaply we are not cautious in guarding or tenacious in holding. Second: What comes to him without labour he is not likely highly to appreciate. We generally value a thing in proportion to the difficulty in getting it." — *David Thomas.*

2. IN REGARD TO ULTIMATE CONSEQUENCES, 14:23; 15:19. In 14:23, we find an unexpected contrast: "In all labor there is profit; but the talk of the lips tendeth only to penury." "All these Proverbs might be worldly maxims, some of them actually in use; all of them with a show of wisdom; some of them utterly unsound; but all of them, when adopted by the Holy Ghost, and turned in the direction of the gospel, true, in their religious aspect. So, now, in this peculiar instance, 'all labor' might seem to promise well among the thrifty, but sometimes ruins men, even in this world, and is sure to ruin them, if worldly, in the world to come. But, now, as a religious maxim, it is without exception. 'All labor' of a pious kind is marked, and will be gloriously rewarded out of the books of the Almighty. 'All labor' of the impenitent, for their soul's salvation, has 'profit'; literally, *something over*. It brings them nearer. If continued long enough, it will bring them in; that is, if it be honest (Heb. 11:6); while 'the talk of the lips' or, possibly, 'an affair of the lips'; that is, mere intention; does 'only' mischief." — *John Miller.*

"The way of the sluggard is as a hedge of thorns; but the path of the upright is made a highway" (15:19). "The tendency of the indolent is to create difficulties. Deep in the moral nature of man is the feeling that he *ought* to work; and the slothful man endeavours to appease this feeling by making excuses. Whatever way is pointed out for him to walk in, intellectual, agricultural, mercantile, mechanical, professional, is full of difficulties. He sees thorns lie thickly everywhere before him. First: in the *commencement* he sees 'thorns.' Though his lazy limbs

PROVERBS 18:9. He also that is slack in his work Is brother to him that is a destroyer.

PROVERBS 24:30. I went by the field of the sluggard, and by the vineyard of the man void of understanding.

31. And, lo, it was all grown over with thorns, The face thereof was covered with nettles, And the stone wall thereof was broken down.

32. Then I beheld, and considered well; I saw, and received instruction:

33. *Yet* a little sleep, a little slumber, a little folding of the hands to sleep.

34. So shall thy poverty come as a robber, And thy want as an armed man.

---

are reluctant, his imagination is active in creating difficulties. It plants hedges of thorns, and they lie formidable in his prospect. Secondly: in the *pursuit* he sees 'thorns.' He has commenced, but he cannot go on. . . . The tendency of the righteous is to overcome difficulties. Honest industry plucks up the real 'thorns' from the road; it levels and paves as it proceeds. What has it not accomplished? It has literally said to mountains, 'depart,' and they have departed. And in removing these difficulties strength is gotten; the difficulties of labour are, in truth, the blessings of labor. 'Difficulty,' says Burke, 'is a severe instructor, set over us by the supreme ordinance of a parental Guardian and Legislator, Who knows us better than we know ourselves, and in their ruinous tendency. He that wrestles with us strengthens our nerves, and sharpens our skill.'" — *David Thomas*.

IV. **THE DEEPER EVIL OF LAZINESS,** Proverbs 18:9. Up to this point we have had the diligent man and the indolent man contrasted, but here the commentary is upon the indolent man only: 9. **He also that is slack in his work Is brother to him that is a destroyer.** The literal meaning of "a destroyer," to whom the indolent man is related, is "master of destruction" (Prov. 1:19), "denoting a man who has a thing or wields it; not a master in the sense of being proficient, but in the more idiomatic sense of having the thing or doing the work that the term may indicate; the meaning being that the mere 'worthless man' (see those pictures already given, 6:12; 16:27–30) or the mere discouraged unbeliever, though he may be really thoughtful, is so positively a man of sin in his holding off, that he is to be impugned as rebellious (17:11) and is 'brother of him' who is an absolute destroyer." — *John Miller*. Thomas says that "the indolent man and the waster are brothers in their self-indulgent spirit, and in their ruinous tendency. Slothfulness leads to ruin. To ruin of all sorts. To physical, intellectual, commercial ruin. The lazy man is like a tree diseased in its roots, he must rot. He who through life hides the one talent in a napkin, must ultimately be damned. Wastefulness is also ruinous. It implies a lack of that sense of individual responsibility apart from which there is no virtue. And ruin, if not in a secular, yet in a spiritual sense, is inevitable." — *David Thomas*.

V. **THE LESSON OF THE RUN-DOWN FARM,** Proverbs 24:30–34. 30. **I went by the field of the sluggard, and by the vineyard of the man void of understanding. 31. And, lo, it was all grown over with thorns, The face thereof was covered with nettles, And the stone wall thereof was broken down. 32. Then I beheld, and considered well; I saw, and received instruction: 33. *Yet* a little sleep, a little slumber, a little folding of the hands to sleep. 34. So shall thy poverty come as a robber, And thy want as an armed man.** Arnot entitles his chapter on these verses, "The Sluggard's Garden," and Maclaren takes the title for his chapter from this gifted author. "The description of the sluggard's garden brings into view two things, the abundant, because unchecked, growth of profitless weeds, and the broken down stone wall. Both of these results are but too sadly and evidently true in regard to every life where rigid and continuous control has not been exercised.   It is a familiar experience known, alas! to too many of us, that evil things, of which the seeds are in us all, grow up unchecked if there be not constant supervision and self-command.   If we do not carefully cultivate our little plot of garden ground, it will soon be overgrown by weeds.   'Ill weeds grow apace' as the homely wisdom of common experience crystallises into a significant proverb. And Jesus has taught the sadder truth that 'thorns spring up and choke the word and it becometh unfruitful.'   In the slothful man's soul evil will drive out good as surely as in the struggle for existence the thorns and nettles will cover the face of the slothful man's garden.   But not only is there this unchecked growth, but 'the stone wall thereof was broken down.'   The soul was unfenced.   The solemn imperative of duty ceases to restrain or to impel in proportion as a man yields slothfully to the baser impulses of his nature.   Nothing is hindered from going out of, nor for coming into, an unfenced soul, and he that 'hath no rule over his own spirit,' but is like a 'city broken down without walls,' is certain sooner or later to let much go forth from that spirit that should have been rigidly shut up, and to let many an enemy come in that will capture the city.   It is not yet safe to let any of the fortifications fall into disrepair, and they can only be kept in their massive strength by continuous vigilance." — *Alexander Maclaren.*   These concluding verses contain a concentrated description of the lazy man.   Here is a warning cast in almost sarcastic terms.   The teacher warns that this matter of sloth can grow upon one as a robber suddenly coming upon an unarmed man.   We can say, "Today we can take it easy and tomorrow work the harder," but when that day comes, we feel that perhaps we need work only one-half day, but will make up for it the following week.   This spirit finally takes hold of our whole being, and while our hands are folded for slumber, poverty silently steals up upon us.

While the passages of our lesson are taken exclusively from the Old Testament, the significance of work in the New Testament and the early church deserves some consideration.   Professor C. Schmidt, in his classic work of some years ago, has the following excellent comment on the place of work in the early Church: "The early Christians did not think manual labour ignominious.   They neither felt themselves to be miserable nor disgraced because they were obliged to gain their living by the sweat of their brow.   They protested against the contempt in which the pagans held them when they practised a profession.   Their doctors represented work as the common law for all men, as the condition of earthly existence.   Unless this had been the will of God, He would have made the requisites of life provide themselves spontaneously.   It is true that the Fathers speak of work as a punishment for, or rather, an expiation of, the fall of man (Gen. 3:17–19); but they also state that it received a new meaning, because it was honoured by Christ, who was the son of a workman, and by the apostles, who worked with their own hands. Work so ennobled is no longer a penalty but an honour for man; it is worthy of the highest praise.   Every profession is held to be honourable, only excepting those which destroy body and soul.   No work is thought degrading, however humble it may be, provided it can be carried on without sin.   The Church laboured to suppress only degrading or criminal industries.   The consequences of this doctrine are that work is looked upon as a duty, and idleness meets with energetic reprobation.   The suppression of slavery must also follow." — *Prof. C. Schmidt.*

THE LESSON IN LIFE, LITERATURE, AND ARCHAEOLOGY.

One of the key verses of our lesson is used by Bunyan for waking Christian out of his sleep on the hill Difficulty in *Pilgrim's Progress.*   We read that one came to him saying, "Go to the ant, thou sluggard, consider her ways and be wise," and with that Christian suddenly started up and sped on his way and went apace until he came to the top of the hill.   (Incidentally, may I add that there is no full study in the English language of Bunyan's use of the Word of God.)

A TRUTH FOR THE CLASS TO CARRY AWAY.

At the conclusion of the lesson I generally suggest that the teacher press upon the class the necessity for putting into practice the truths come upon in the study. However, it seems to me that of all the nations in the world, we are workers. Laziness is not a congenital disease in American life. Then what should we do in the study of this lesson on work? We ought to give God thanks for three things in this realm of work: First, for the work which gives us a living; secondly, for the health which we have for the performing of our tasks; and thirdly, for a land of freedom wherein we are not driven as slaves each morning to the work of the day. Recently while in the home of a friend, I witnessed on television an interview with a Scotch baron who said that at one time they had forty servants, but now they have only three in their castle in Scotland. When his father died, they had to sell twelve thousand acres to meet the inheritance tax. He came to this land because he knew there was opportunity and a future, and he wanted to become a citizen of our country. The position that he now holds could not pay him more than $60.00 a week, but he is glad to have it.

What vices may we generally expect to attend a life of habitual laziness and freedom from occupation? Do you think that every individual, if earnest, can find the kind of work for which he is best suited and which he will enjoy? What field has developed extensively in our country in the last thirty years that makes it possible for a man to more easily and quickly find the kind of work for which he is suited? (Personnel counseling.) What is meant by occupational therapy? What is the difference between the end of a day for a man who has conscientiously worked and for one who habitually does no work?

LESSON VI. — November 7.

THE SPLENDOR OF SELF-CONTROL (TEMPERANCE). —
Proverbs 14; 15:1–5; 16; 20; 23:29–35; 25.

PRINTED TEXT, Proverbs 14:29; 15:1–3; 16:32; 20:1, 22; 23:29–35.

Devotional Reading: 1 Corinthians 9:23–27.
Beginner Topic: TWO GOOD FRIENDS.
    Lesson Material: 1 Samuel 17: 55 to 18: 4; 2 Samuel 1: 23, 26; James 1: 17.
    Memory Verse: O give thanks unto Jehovah: for he is good. Psalm 136: 1.
Primary Topic: AS YOU GROW BIGGER.
    Lesson Material: Proverbs 14:9–29; 15:1–5; 16; 20; 25.
    Memory Verse: He that is slow to anger is better than the mighty. Proverbs 16:32.
Junior Topic: BETTER THAN THE MIGHTY.
    Lesson Material: Proverbs 14:9–29; 15:1–5; 16; 20; 25.
    Memory Verse: He that is slow to anger is better than the mighty; And he that ruleth his spirit, than he that taketh a city. Proverbs 16:32.
Intermediate-Senior Topic: THE SPLENDOR OF SELF-CONTROL.
    Lesson Material: Proverbs 14; 15:1–5; 16; 20; 23:29–35; 25.
    Memory Verse: He that is slow to anger is better than the mighty; And he that ruleth his spirit, than he that taketh a city. Proverbs 16:32.
Topic for Young People and Adults: THE SPLENDOR OF SELF-CONTROL.
    Lesson Material: Proverbs 14; 15:1–5; 16; 20; 23:29–35.
    Memory Verse: He that is slow to anger is better than the mighty; And he that ruleth his spirit, than he that taketh a city. Proverbs 16:32.

THE TEACHER AND HIS CLASS.

The Younger Classes may be introduced to this lesson by being reminded of a very simple fact: whenever they have been in an automobile, driving along the highway, and the car has stopped dead, everyone knows that there must be a cause for the car stopping. First, then, we look at the gasoline meter, and when we discover we have plenty of gas, and we also discover that the oil is not all gone, there is only one thing to do — get out and lift up the hood and look inside the car where the engine, fan, et cetera, are to be found. You will never find what is wrong by just walking around the car in a situation like this. Our verses today take us to the *inner* part of man's nature, telling us how to keep it wholesome, functioning, pleasing to God, bearing the results that make life rich and worthwhile. We have both the positive and the negative aspects of life here, or to put it another way, verses that guide us as to what to do, and warn us as to what not to do.

The Older Classes may begin this lesson by being reminded of a fundamental truth, which they will discover before the teaching of the lesson is concluded: namely, that the sins of today are the sins of 3,000 years ago. Everything seems to have changed except man's nature. Even our vocabulary changes, our way of travel, our means of communication, the means of making a living, except in agriculture — all change, but the human heart remains the same, with the same capacities for evil, and the same law that only the right brings joy and the approval of God. This is one of the ways in which the Word of God abides forever.

THE LESSON IN ITS SETTING.

Time. — We may place this book sometime within the Tenth Century B.C.

Place. — There is no term of geographical importance in this lesson.

THE PLAN OF THE LESSON.

SUBJECT: How to Guide Our Inner Life That It May Be Kept From Pollution, or Worse, From Abandonment to the Enemy.

I. CHARACTERISTICS OF THE WISE MAN CONTRASTED WITH THOSE OF THE FOOLISH MAN, Proverbs 14.

II. THE CAPACITIES OF THE TONGUE FOR GOOD AND EVIL, Proverbs 15:1–3.

III. THE HEART THE CITADEL OF LIFE, Proverbs 16.

IV. ALL OUR WAYS ARE KNOWN UNTO GOD, Proverbs 20:2–30.

V. THE DECEPTIONS OF DRINKING BEVERAGES THAT RESULT IN DRUNKENNESS, Proverbs 20:1; 23:29–25.

VI. A CLUSTER OF SIMILES, Proverbs 25.

THE TEACHER'S LIBRARY.

For the study of our lesson, as for that of the preceding one, a list of the more important commentaries on the Book of Proverbs will be found in the bibliographies in the Introduction to this volume. Sermonic material, for some strange reason, is amazingly scarce. However, on 16:32, one may consult the following: G. Campbell Morgan, *The Westminster Pulpit*, Vol. 8, pp. 129–136; Hugh MacMillan: *The Spring of the Day*, 104–119; W. B. Riley: *The Bible of the Expositor*, Proverbs, 209–222; Wm. S. Parry: *Life Lessons from the Book of Proverbs*, 207–224. On 23:29–35 see Alexander Maclaren: *Expositions of Holy Scripture, Esther to Ecclesiastes*, 256–263.

The entire text assigned for this lesson embraces one hundred and thirty-eight verses: of course it is absolutely impossible for any teacher to cover this many verses; if he just read them aloud the half-hour would nearly be gone. So I would suggest that the teacher concentrate on the five major themes that I have indicated in the above outline, omitting entirely, if he wishes, the sixth division, chapter twenty-five, in which there are no verses appearing in the printed text. We ought to remind the class, as we begin to teach the lesson that though it is true these are moral maxims, ethical instructions, yet such teaching belongs in the New Testament period as well as in the Old. Paul never wrote a single epistle but that he did not have many concluding ethical instructions. Our Lord's teaching is filled with it, and the Epistle of James is almost entirely occupied with just such teachings as we have in the Proverbs.

AUDIO-VISUAL AIDS.

FILM: "The Power of Decision," Religious Films, Inc., 35 min., sd., b&w. A college age boy refuses a social drink at a party honoring him and his fiancee. He explains why he makes this decision. Too long a film for the Sunday-school hour, unless a long preliminary session is planned, but can be used for a church function.

PROVERBS 14:29. He that is slow to anger is of great understanding; But he that is hasty of spirit exalteth folly.

I. **CHARACTERISTICS OF THE WISE MAN CONTRASTED WITH THOSE OF THE FOOLISH MAN,** Proverbs 14. While it is difficult to exactly outline the Book of Proverbs, still here and there we come upon a number of verses brought together that relate to one fundamental theme. In this chapter we have the wise man and the foolish man contrasted, indicated by the fact that the words "wise" and "wisdom" occur here six times, and the words "fool," "folly," and "foolish" ten times. This theme is resumed again in the twenty-sixth chapter. The phrase found at the opening of the chapter reminds one of the concluding words of our Lord in His Sermon on the Mount about a wise man and a foolish man each building a house (Matt. 7:24–27). We have already given consideration to the matter of wisdom. Now we ought to ask ourselves the question, Who is the foolish man in the Book of Proverbs? The word translated "fool" in the Hebrew refers us to "that ignorant, inconsiderate, sanguine, and self-confident temper which eschews counsel, which will have its own way, which declines to be governed by reason, which forms fond expectations and baseless hopes, and which is always sure that everything will turn out according to its wish, though it takes no means to secure the desired result. Perhaps the simplest way of describing the habit of mind and the type of character intended by the Hebrew is to use the word *infatuation*. This would not do as a translation in all the passages where it occurs, but it will serve to point out the underlying idea." — *R. F. Horton.* Another word has for its root the idea of grossness. "We have to think of moral, as well as mental, stupidity, of insensibility to all that is true and good and pure. The fool in this sense is such a dullard that he commits wickedness without perceiving it, and utters slanders almost unconsciously; he does not know when to be silent; whatever is in him quickly appears, but when it is known it is very worthless; nor has he the sense to get wisdom, even when the opportunity is in his hand; his best advantages are quickly wasted and he is none the better. Perhaps the English word which best fits the several suggestions of the Hebrew one is *senseless.*" — *R. F. Horton.* The greatest fool of all in the Bible is the one who has said, "there is no God." "The fool hath said in his heart, There is no God. They are corrupt, they have done abominable works; There is none that doeth good." (Ps. 14:1.) There are many different ways in this chapter in which the wise man and the foolish man are contrasted, of which we have one for our lesson. 29. **He that is slow to anger is of great understanding; But he that is hasty of spirit exalteth folly.** "Every man has what is called *Temper* — a kind of inner atmosphere in which he lives, breathes, and works. This atmosphere has great varieties of temperature from zero to blood heat, and great changes of weather too, severe and stormy, cloudy and sunny. This temper, however, unlike the outward atmosphere, is controllable by man. He can regulate his temperatures and weathers. He can change from the arctic to the torrid, from the tempestuous to the serene and the reverse. The passage leads us to look at temper in two aspects. . . . A sublimer sight one can scarcely have than that of a man with powerful passions majestically calm in irritating circumstances. Such a man shows a 'great understanding,' an understanding that bids the heaving billows within be calm, and they are at peace. Secondly? *It repays* the efforts of a great understanding rightly to control temper. The highest victories are the victories over temper. To raise our nature above those vexatious feelings which the annoyances and contrarieties of life are calculated to excite, is the most remunerative of labours. It gives a royalty to a man's being before which meaner spirits bow." — *David Thomas.*

II. **THE CAPACITIES OF THE TONGUE FOR GOOD AND EVIL,** Proverbs 15:1–3. The tremendous importance of the tongue interpenetrates all of Divine revelation. It was with words, that Satan deceived our first parents, and that the children of Jacob lied to their father about Joseph. Slander, false witnessing,

PROVERBS 15:1. A soft answer turneth away wrath; But a grievous word stirreth up anger.

2. The tongue of the wise uttereth knowledge aright; But the mouth of fools poureth out folly.

3. The eyes of Jehovah are in every place, Keeping watch upon the evil and the good.

---

blasphemy, evil speaking, foulness of speech — all have their source in this little member the tongue. Jesus often spoke of the capacities of the tongue for good and evil. James has a classic passage on it. Proverbs is filled with it, especially the whole of the 12th chapter, and 13:16 and 14:33. Here the opening three verses of the 15th chapter are assigned for our consideration. 1. **A soft answer turneth away wrath; But a grievous word stirreth up anger.** "We greatly need an instrument capable of turning away wrath, for there is much wrath in the world to be turned away. It is assumed here that the anger is sinful in character, or excessive in degree; but there are occasions in which a good man may do well to be angry. It is recorded of Jesus once, in the days of his flesh, that He was angry; but the explanation is immediately added, He was 'grieved for the hardness of their hearts' (Mark 3:5). It is safe for a disciple 'to follow the Lamb whithersoever He goeth.' If all our anger were grief for sin, and grief for sin our only anger, the emotion would neither displease God nor disturb men. If our love were like Christ's, our anger would be like his too. In the meantime, most of the anger that prevails is sinful and dangerous. On that side there is especial need for watching and prayer, lest we enter into temptation. . . .

"There is a contrivance to prevent the destructive collision of carriage against carriage in a railway train, which human beings might profitably imitate. On the outer extremities, where they are liable to strike against each other, there is a soft spongy covering. Within, and at the very centre, is a spring, strong, but yielding; yielding, but strong. There is both a soft surface without, and an elastic spring in the heart. If the impact of another body were met by mere hard unyielding strength, both would fly into splinters at the first shock. On the other hand, if there were in one of the carriages softness only, with no recuperative spring, the others would soon drive it from the rails, or crush it to pieces. The destroyed carriage would be lost to the owners, and its debris would cause additional mischief. These machines move in company like ourselves, and they move quickly, and jostle each other by the way. The managers have marked the danger, and made skilful provision for escaping it. They take advantage of the great pervasive law, that firmness and softness united in each is the best arrangement for the safety of all." — *W. Arnot*. 2. **The tongue of the wise uttereth knowledge aright; But the mouth of fools poureth out folly.** Knowledge is good; it is well to have the mind richly furnished with useful information, but this good thing may be, and often is, wrongly used. "There is a right use of knowledge in speech. What is that? It is to communicate it at right times, to proper persons, in suitable places, and in a becoming spirit. . . . 'Out of the abundance of the heart the mouth speaketh' (Matt. 12:34). The fool's heart is full of folly, and folly flows from his lips. Foolish words are either words without meaning, empty jargon, or words of bad meaning, the vehicles of filth, insubordination, and blasphemy. Bishop Horne well remarks that, 'Among the sources of those innumerable calamities which from age to age have overwhelmed mankind, may be reckoned as one of the principal, the abuse of words.' " — *David Thomas*. 3. **The eyes of Jehovah are in every place, Keeping watch upon the evil and the good.** For parallel passages see Job 31:4; Hebrews 4:13. "This universal inspection, this omniscience of God has an alarming, but also a comforting side." — *F. Delitzsch*. The word "beholding" here is commonly used of a watchman (1 Sam. 14:16, 2 Sam. 13:34). "There is nothing in the history of man that is not either good or evil. There is no third, no neutral

Proverbs 16:32. He that is slow to anger is better than the mighty; And he that ruleth his spirit, than he that taketh a city.

quality. He knows all the good and all the evil in the most incipient, as well as in the most developed stages. 'There is not a word on our tongue, but, O Lord, thou knowest it altogether.' This subject urges, First: *Courage for the good.* Ye men of truth and virtue, who struggle here against mighty odds, take courage under your trials and afflictions. The great Master sees you. His eyes are on you, take heart. The subject urges, Secondly: *A warning for the wicked.* 'Because sentence against an evil work is not executed speedily, therefore the hearts of the sons of men are fully set to do evil.' Because of the delay, conclude not, O sinner, that thy conduct has escaped the notice of the just God. Judgment is coming. The subject urges, Thirdly: *Circumspection for all.* Since God's eyes are always on us, let us 'walk circumspectly, not as fools, but as wise, redeeming the time, because the days are evil.'

" 'How dreadful,' says Dr. J. Todd, 'is the eye of God on him who wants to sin! Do you know about Lafayette, that great man who was the friend of Washington? He tells us that he was once shut up in a little room in a gloomy prison for a great while. In the door of his little cell was a very small hole cut. At this hole a soldier was placed day and night to watch him. All he could see was the soldier's eye, but that eye was always there. Day and night, every moment when he looked up, he always saw that eye. Oh, he says, it was dreadful! There was no escape, no hiding; when he laid down, and when he rose up, that eye was watching him. How dreadful will the eye of God be on the sinner as it watches him in the eternal world for ever!' " — *David Thomas.*

III. **THE HEART THE CITADEL OF LIFE,** Proverbs 16. In this chapter it seems that the dominating theme is the inner life of man, his heart. The word "heart" occurs five times, the word "spirit" three times, the word "soul" twice, and, in verse 22 we have the remarkable phrase, "a well-spring of life." There are marvelous verses here, each one worthy of careful study, but we must confine ourselves to the one assigned for the printed text, which might be called the key verse of the entire chapter, and almost a key verse for the whole Book of Proverbs. It is the most important single verse in our lesson and to it I would like to give more space than to any other single passage. 32. **He that is slow to anger is better than the mighty; And he that ruleth his spirit, than he that taketh a city.** "The spirit of a man is that which knows, that which discovers, that which elects and chooses. No man knows anything with his brain. His brain may be the material instrumentality which receives impressions, in order to transmit them to the spirit life, but knowledge is not of the material. It is of the spiritual. No one desires with his heart. Desire may affect that central citadel of pulsating life, which is the very organ of continued material existence, because of its sensitiveness; but desire is of the spirit. No man chooses, and here the statement is obvious, in any other way, but in his essential, mysterious, central life, which is spirit. Now, behold the man who rules his spirit. In other words, behold the man who is self-controlled. He is the man who in some inward and metaphysical mystery does reign over himself. In the realm of thought he is characterized by discrimination and reserve; he knows that knowledge grows from more to more, and therefore is never guilty of announcing the last thing of which he has become conscious as the last thing of which he or anyone else can ever be conscious. He is self-controlled in the realm of desire; he holds all desires in leash and check, and mastery; listens to their clamant cry, and then instructs them as to the true sphere in which they may seek an answer and satisfaction. His volitions are characterized at once by caution and by courage; he is courageous enough to dare not to do some things, and cautious enough to dare to do some things. . . . The ruling of the spirit is the first qualification for the taking of a city. Jerusalem is the great city of the Old Testament, and I see it thrice taken. David took it, Nebuchadnezzar took it,

PROVERBS 20:22. Say not thou, I will recompense evil: Wait for Jehovah, and he will save thee.

1. Wine is a mocker, strong drink a brawler; And whosoever erreth thereby is not wise.

Titus took it; and, within limitations, the secret of the taking of the city each time was the self-control of the man who did it.   Exclusive conquest demands intensive culture, or else it is superficial, transient.   In some great burst of passion, a man may force an entrance to a city, but he cannot take it, he cannot possess it, he cannot hold it unless he himself be under control.   Someone will presently wrest from him that which he himself has taken.   Unless he is leader and master of the empire of his own being, he cannot be leader and master within the city taken in the rush of a great passion.   And so, whatever city your eyes shall turn to, whatever campaign stretches out before you, whatever holy adventure your life is looking toward, I pray you remember the first qualification for ultimate victory is that you rule your own spirit." — *G. Campbell Morgan.*

IV. **ALL OUR WAYS ARE KNOWN UNTO GOD,** Proverbs 20:2–30.   Because I think we need to give considerable attention to the next division of our lesson I shall be exceedingly brief here in comment.   22. **Say not thou, I will recompense evil: Wait for Jehovah, and he will save thee.**   "The verse suggests two remarks at the outset.   First: That men in passing through this life are subject to injuries from their fellow men.   Through sin men, instead of being the loving brothers of each other, are become to an awful extent the deceivers, the plunderers, the oppressors, and the devils.   Hence men are everywhere found groaning under the injuries they have received from their fellow men.   Secondly: That men under a sense of injury crave for the punishment of their enemies.   There is a sense of justice placed in every human soul: injuries kindle this sense of justice into a fiery passion, and this passion is revenge, and this revenge cries for the destruction of the enemy. . . .

"Is my enemy to be allowed to perpetrate his enormities on me with impunity? No, he will be punished; punished far more effectively than I can do if I leave it in the hands of Him Who judgeth righteously.   He is Omniscient.   We know but imperfectly.   He is without passions.   We are blinded by selfishness.   He is without partiality.   We are prejudiced on our own sides.   'Vengeance is mine; I will repay, saith the Lord.'   He will avenge us of our enemies.   By the dispensations of His providence, by the compunctions of conscience, by making the injuries we have received spiritually useful to ourselves." — *David Thomas.*

V. **THE DECEPTIONS OF DRINKING BEVERAGES THAT RESULT IN DRUNKENNESS,** Proverbs 20:1; 23:29–35.   While it is true that the Bible nowhere insists that the mere drinking of wine is wrong, drunkenness is everywhere condemned as a heinous sin in the sight of God, and we should always remember this, that the first occurrence of drinking wine recorded in the Bible is accompanied at that time by drunkenness and followed at once by shameful acts (Gen. 9:20–23). I have never mentioned this before, but the word "drunk" is simply a form of the word "drink."   How close one is to the other!   20:1. **Wine is a mocker, strong drink a brawler; And whosoever erreth thereby is not wise.**   "Wine is a mocker, tempting the youth to his undoing, and deceiving him who with rashness supposes he can indulge as he pleases, and then, when he desires, set it aside. Even godly men have been deluded thereby to their shame and grief.   See Noah, and Lot (Gen. 9:20, 21; 19:30–36)." — *H. A. Ironside.*   The longer passage on the matter of drunkenness contains one of the most vivid, accurate, pathetic pictures to be found in all literature of a man who is a slave to intoxicating beverages. Each verse should be given careful study.   "The characteristic of strong drink which this text singles out is its *deceitfulness.*   In the illustration of it I shall exclusively regard our own day and our own circumstances.   The warnings of Scripture may be intensified manifold when brought to bear on the power of our in-

PROVERBS 23:29. Who hath woe? who hath sorrow? who hath contentions? Who hath complaining? who hath wounds without cause? Who hath redness of eyes?

30. They that tarry long at the wine; They that go to seek out mixed wine.

31. Look not thou upon the wine when it is red, When it sparkleth in the cup, When it goeth down smoothly:

32. At the last it biteth like a serpent, And stingeth like an adder.

33. Thine eyes shall behold strange things, And thy heart shall utter perverse things.

---

toxicants to 'mock' their victims.   If the fruit of his own vine sometimes chastised the unwary Israelite with whips, the fiery products of our distilleries chastise the nation with scorpions.   The little finger of strong drink in modern times is thicker than the loins of its father and representative in Solomon's day.   The deceits which our enemy practises are legion; and legion too are the unwise 'who are deceived thereby.'   We may mention two.

"1. A great quantity of precious food is destroyed in this country that strong drink may be extracted from the rubbish. . . .

"Perhaps, after all, the chief deception practised by strong drink on the community lies in the silent, stealthy advances which it makes upon the unsuspecting taster, followed, when the secret approaches have been carried to a certain point, by the sure spring and relentless death-grip of the raging lion who goes about amongst us seeking whom he may devour." — *W. Arnot.*

Anyone who knows city life, and who has traveled about to any extent, can write his own comment on this statement.   23:29. **Who hath woe? who hath sorrow? who hath contentions?   Who hath complaining? who hath wounds without cause? Who hath redness of eyes?   30. They that tarry long at the wine; They that go to seek out mixed wine.**   A little liquor is often inflaming, especially with the man possessing a mean disposition.   Such a one, under the influence of intoxicants, will soon look around for a quarrel, creating brawls and disturbing the peace wherever he goes — such indeed will have "wounds without cause."   There would be no reason for the beating which he received, nor for his scars, except for his own determination to quarrel — all caused by liquor.   It serves to make beasts of men.

31. **Look not thou upon the wine when it is red, When it sparkleth in the cup, When it goeth down smoothly: 32. At the last it biteth like a serpent, And stingeth like an adder.**   "The English phrase here suggests the thought of a sparkling wine, but the Hebrew word describes rather the pellucid streams flowing pleasantly from the wine skin or jug into the goblet or throat." — *E. H. Plumptre.*   " 'Look not' is a safe policy in regard to many of the snares for young lives that abound in our modern society.   It is not at all needful to 'see life,' or to know the secrets of wickedness, in order to be wise and good.   'Simple concerning evil' is a happier state than to have eaten the fruit of the tree of knowledge.   Eyes are greedy, and there is a very quick telephone from them to the desires.   'The lust of the eye' soon fans the 'lust of the flesh' into a glow.   If a man is a total abstainer he can never be a drunkard.   As much cannot be said of the moderate man.   It is childish to take a course because of a moment's gratification at the beginning, to be followed by a protracted discomfort afterwards.   To live for present satisfaction of desires cannot be the part of a sensible man, to say nothing of a religious one." — *Alexander Maclaren.*

33. **Thine eyes shall behold strange things, And thy heart shall utter perverse things.**   It is commonly understood that the first clause of this verse refers to immoral women.   The walls of our liquor depots, taverns, saloons, etc., all bear overwhelming testimony to the truthfulness of such a line as this.   The truthfulness of the second clause is likewise borne out, every day, in every place where men

34. Yea, thou shalt be as he that lieth down in the midst of the sea,
Or as he that lieth upon the top of a mast.

35. They have stricken me, *shalt thou say*, and I was not hurt; They
have beaten me, and I felt it not: When shall I awake?   I will seek it
yet again.

---

gather and drink, that they utter nonsensical words, sometimes divulging secrets
which they would not do for any price when sober.   Men under the influence of
liquor will tell stories they themselves would be ashamed to hear when normal;
they make boastful statements about their own success; they even declare how
much liquor they can drink without "getting under the table"; they may betray
secrets of some important mission on which they are engaged; they may divulge
information to competitors which will ultimately prove their own ruin.

**34. Yea, thou shalt be as he that lieth down in the midst of the sea, Or as he
that lieth upon the top of a mast.   35. They have stricken me,** *shalt thou say,* **and
I was not hurt; They have beaten me, and I felt it not: When shall I awake?   I
will seek it yet again.**   The picture here is of a man who, on a ship in the midst
of a storm at sea, climbs a mast and lies down to go to sleep.   One often sees men
who have partaken of intoxicating liquors to the point where they are utterly
helpless, stretch out on a sidewalk, or in a busy part of the city, and lie there without any sense of fear of danger.   Many a man has been killed because he has been
foolish enough to walk down a railroad track in this condition, or to drop on the
highway where fast moving automobiles are passing by, or to fall off steps as he
tries to ascend from one floor to another.   Thousands and thousands of accidents
in our country are due to this false sense of security.   We have heard it commonly
said that it is amazing how a drunken man can get around without being hit.
Well, the truth is that we may not see many of them get hit, but thousands do.
And what is worse, in their condition, if they are driving they hit those who are
innocent, and many of them have the crime of murder on their hands because of
this.

VI. **A CLUSTER OF SIMILES,** Proverbs 25.   It seems to me that the teacher
will do well not to include anything from this chapter in the teaching of the lesson
so that he might concentrate on the very important verses that are assigned for the
printed text.   The only fact we need to notice here is the opening verse, which is
significant.   "This Title is interesting as affording a proof that a revival of literary
activity accompanied the revival of religion and of national prosperity which
marked the reign of Hezekiah.   Hezekiah himself was a poet of no mean order
(Is. 38:9, ff.); and 'the men of Hezekiah' were doubtless a body of scribes engaged
under the direction of the king in literary labours.   Beside this, this brief title is
one of those 'fragments of history,' which, as Professor Sayce has shown, 'have been
illuminated by the progress of oriental research,' and 'the importance and true
significance of which can now be realised for the first time.' . . .   The 'men of
Hezekiah' who 'copied out' the proverbs of Solomon performed duties exactly
similar to the royal scribes in Nineveh.' — *T. T. Perowne.*

THE LESSON IN LIFE, LITERATURE, AND ARCHAEOLOGY.

In his correspondence with Clarinda, Robert Burns uses one of the verses of our
lesson in this way: "I am miserably stupid this morning.   Yesterday I dined with
a baronet, and sat pretty late over the bottle.   And 'who hath — who hath sorrow?
they that tarry long at the wine; they that go to seek mixed wine.'   Forgive me,
likewise, a quotation from my favourite author.   Solomon's knowledge of the
world is very great.   He may be looked on as the *Spectator* or *Adventurer* of his
day; and it is, indeed, surprising what a sameness has ever been in human nature.
The broken, but strongly characterizing hints, that the royal author gives us of
the manners of the court of Jerusalem and country of Israel are, in their great

outlines the same pictures that London and England, Versailles and France, exhibit save three thousand years later."

A TRUTH FOR THE CLASS TO CARRY AWAY.

Hardly any two words relating to the human species are at such extreme poles as *wise* and *foolish;* yet, it is a strange fact that both of these words can be true of the same man, one at one time and another at another.   With the word *wisdom* goes every worthy aspect of character, and with the word *foolish,* the opposite of each of these factors.   The glorious truth is that a man who finds himself a fool may turn to God for repentance, asking for divine help, and receive wisdom that cometh down from above.   The Bible contains warnings concerning the path of the fool, and exhortations concerning the way of the wise from beginning to end. What wondrous creatures we are, and with what enormous capacities for good and evil.

How do you account for the fact that this little member of our body, the tongue, can cause so much evil, and sorrow, and pain?   What is a good illustration from the New Testament of a man who used his tongue for evil purposes one night, and within two months the same tongue was used for bringing three thousand people to Christ in one day?   (That of Simon Peter — the night of his denial of Christ and the Day of Pentecost.)   How many sins of the tongue can you recall from the story of our Lord's crucifixion?   In what ways does man become abnormal and subnormal when under the influence of intoxicating beverages?   Why do these strange departures from controlled human conduct bring so much sorrow and tragedy?

LESSON VII. — November 14.

A STUDY IN VALUES. — Proverbs 11:24–28; 13:7; 15:13–17; 16:8, 16; 20:11–12; 22:1–5, 9; 28:6–28.

PRINTED TEXT, Proverbs 11:27–28; 15:13–17; 20:11–12; 22:1–4.

Devotional Reading: Matthew 6:24–33.
Beginner Topic: THE FRIENDLY DARK.
    Lesson Material: Psalm 4:8; 91:1–5; 121; Matthew 2:11–15.
    Memory Verse: Thou art nigh, O Jehovah.   Psalm 119:151.
Primary Topic: A GOOD NAME.
    Lesson Material: Proverbs 15:15–17; 20:11–12; 22:1–5, 9; 28:6–28.
    Memory Verse: A *good* name is rather to be chosen than great riches, *And* loving favor rather than silver and gold.   Proverbs 22:1.
Junior Topic: BETTER THAN RICHES.
    Lesson Material: Proverbs 15:15–17; 20:11–12; 22:1–5, 9; 28:6–28.
    Memory Verse: A *good* name is rather to be chosen than great riches, *And* loving favor rather than silver and gold.   Proverbs 22:1.
Intermediate-Senior Topic: CHOOSING WHAT MATTERS MOST.
    Lesson Material: Proverbs 11:24–28; 13:7; 15:13–17; 16:8, 16; 20:11–12; 22:1–4.
    Memory Verse: A *good* name is rather to be chosen than great riches, *And* loving favor rather than silver and gold.   Proverbs 22:1.
Topic for Young People and Adults: A STUDY IN VALUES.
    Lesson Material: Proverbs 11:24–28; 13:7; 15:13–17; 16:8, 16; 20:11–12; 22:1–4.
    Memory Verse: A *good* name is rather to be chosen than great riches, *And* loving favor rather than silver and gold.   Proverbs 22:1.

THE TEACHER AND HIS CLASS.

The **Younger Classes** might be introduced to this lesson on values with an illustration from the editor's own travel experiences of years ago. In early Egyptian history one of the most significant religious symbols was the beetle, and for tokens representing the protective care of their gods they carried around small carved objects in the shape of beetles, some of them made out of very precious stones. They are called "scarabs." Now there are quite a few of these scarabs, a few thousand years old, still for sale by dependable dealers in Egypt. A companion of mine, however, bought one from a guide, paying, I think, forty dollars for it. When he showed it to an expert on these things, the expert told him its real value was about two dollars, for it had been manufactured in the last two years. He had paid for it according to a value it did not have. Our lesson is concerning the proper values of the finer things of life, and how to accurately ascertain their worth.

The **Older Classes** will find here a number of moral laws laid down as axioms. Some of them will seem strange, especially about the wealthy becoming poor, et cetera. Yet those laws still prevail today in human life. Only this week I noticed in our local paper that a famous actress had arranged for an insurance policy for her young son, that there might be money enough for him when it came time for him to go to college. Someone asked why, if she was making such huge sums annually as an actress, she was worrying about matters so far ahead, and she said she had discovered that in Hollywood large incomes lasted for about ten years, and in twenty years many of the rich had become bankrupt.

THE LESSON IN ITS SETTING.

Time. — The Book of Proverbs was gathered together probably in the middle of the Tenth Century B.C.

Place. — There are no geographical data in this lesson.

THE PLAN OF THE LESSON.

SUBJECT: The Evaluation of Material, Economic, Domestic, and Spiritual Possessions Accompanied by a Proper Recognition of the Low Value a Godly Man Places on Some Things That the World Places First.

I. THE MARKS AND REWARDS OF "THE LIBERAL SOUL," Proverbs 11:24–28.

II. STRANGE LAWS RELATING TO WEALTH AND POVERTY, Proverbs 13:7.

III. THE CAPACITIES OF MAN'S HEART FOR JOY AND SORROW, Proverbs 15:13–17.

IV. WEALTH IS NOT THE GREATEST GOOD, Proverbs 16:8, 16; 22:1, 2.

V. WE ARE HIS HANDIWORK, Proverbs 20:11, 12.

VI. THE REWARDS OF PRUDENCE, HUMILITY, AND GENEROSITY, Proverbs 22:3, 4, 9.

VII. CONTRASTS IN CHARACTER AND CORRESPONDING CONTRASTS OF CONSEQUENCES, Proverbs 28:6–28.

THE TEACHER'S LIBRARY.

This lesson will have to be studied, for the most part, from the pages of the principal commentaries on the Book of Proverbs, a list of which will be found in the Introduction to this volume. The volumes by Arnot, for exposition, will be found by far the best. Sermonic material is noticeably scarce. I know of only two sermons worth considering: on 13:7 Alexander Maclaren: *Expositions of Holy Scripture, Esther-Ecclesiastes*, 163–173; and, on 20:11, Hugh Macmillan: *The Gate Beautiful*, 42–59.

AUDIO-VISUAL AIDS.

No audio-visual aids discovered.

The only theme running through the many different passages assigned for our lesson would probably be that of evaluation. What objects and objectives should we make first in our life, and to what should we assign secondary and third places? The question is, How are we going to determine what is the most valuable? Well,

PROVERBS 11:27. He that diligently seeketh good seeketh favor; But he that searcheth after evil, it shall come unto him.

28. He that trusteth in his riches shall fall; But the righteous shall flourish as the green leaf.

for one thing, the results that accrue. This is not to be an exclusive criteria, because if one goes into business to be successful, and prospers, he is said to be a wise executive, a skillful man, and a success. But what if he attains a fortune in business by deceitful methods? He has the fortune. Is he still to be looked upon with high regard and to be commended? No! So the ultimate end itself is not the only criteria. Righteousness is involved here. The laws of God come into the picture; the results upon others arising from our own activity must be considered. The teacher will be wise if he stresses, then, this one matter of the values of life and confines himself almost exclusively to the verses of the printed text.

I. **THE MARKS AND REWARDS OF "THE LIBERAL SOUL,"** Proverbs 11:24–28. I must confess that I never before noticed this phrase, "the liberal soul." It means, literally, in Hebrew and in Greek, "the soul of blessing," that is, the soul that is ready to benefit and bless in will and deed. The use of the figure of speech "water" in reference to a man's labor is one used in a very important passage in Paul's first letter to the Corinthians (1 Cor. 3:7–8). 27. **He that diligently seeketh good seeketh favor; But he that searcheth after evil, it shall come unto him.** "All men pursue one of two opposite moral objects — good or evil. The text speaks of both. . . . There are those who are industrious in the search and service of goodness, and that both for themselves and society. But some are in pursuit of *evil*. There are those who are as industrious in doing evil, as others in doing good; they are always in mischief.

"The destiny of these, the text suggests, is widely different. *The one procureth favour:* — favour with conscience, society, and God, and *The other disfavour*, i.e., mischief shall come upon him. He shall have what he deserves. The disapprobation of his own conscience — the denunciation of society — the frown of Heaven. 'Behold, he travaileth with iniquity, and hath conceived mischief, and brought forth falsehood. He made a pit, and digged it, and is fallen into the ditch which he made. His mischief shall return upon his own head, and his violent dealing shall come down upon his own pate.' " — *David Thomas*. 28. **He that trusteth in his riches shall fall; But the righteous shall flourish as the green leaf.** There is here no condemnation of wealth, but only a condemnation of trusting in wealth. This is parallel to what St. Paul refers to, at the end of his life, when he tells us that the *love* of money is a root of all kinds of evil (1 Tim. 6:10). "Here lies the secret of spiritual life among men. The righteous, — and some such there have been even in the darkest periods of the world's history, — the righteous 'flourish as a branch.' They lean not on their own stem, and live not on their own root. From the beginning the same Jesus to whom we look was made known to faith. The manner and measure of making known truth to the understanding were in those days widely different; but the nature and the source of spiritual life were the same. They stood 'afar off,' but they looked into Jesus. The medium of vision was diverse, but the object was identical. As to knowledge, the ancient disciples were children, whereas disciples now are grown men; but *life* was as true and vigorous in the Church's infancy as it is in the Church's age. There was in those ancient times a medium of union to the Redeemer: and blessed are all they that trust in Him. The branch will flourish when it is in the living tree." — *W. Arnot*. Man is often likened in the Scriptures to the leaves of a tree, as in Psalms 1:3, 92:12; 17:8.

II. **STRANGE LAWS RELATING TO WEALTH AND POVERTY,** Proverbs 13:7. With this verse compare Proverbs 11:24. "These characters abound in modern society. There are poor men who profess to be very wealthy, and they often do so not merely from vanity but from greed also. In business they hire

Proverbs 15:13. A glad heart maketh a cheerful countenance; But by sorrow of heart the spirit is broken.

14. The heart of him that hath understanding seeketh knowledge; But the mouth of fools feedeth on folly.

15. All the days of the afflicted are evil; But he that is of a cheerful heart *hath* a continual feast.

---

large warehouses, embark in extensive speculations, occupy mansions as their homes, and live in a magnificent style in order to create a false credit. Paupers put on the costume of princes, in order to swindle on a gigantic scale; sometimes they succeed, and by a pretence of large capital obtain the real one, and build up the real one — always at the expense of others. But often, on the other hand, the sparkling bubble bursts, the dazzling meteor sweeps into midnight. These characters abound in modern England, they crowd our scenes of merchandise, they create panics, they are a curse to the country. Then, also, we have amongst us a different class, men who appear to be very poor, but who are, nevertheless, very rich. These are, if not so injurious, yet as contemptible as the others; they are the wretched misers; men who are pinching themselves and families, and clutching from others, in order to gratify their wretched greed of pelf." — *David Thomas*.

III. THE CAPACITIES OF MAN'S HEART FOR JOY AND SORROW, Proverbs 15:13–17. The editor must say in studying again this year for these lessons in the Book of Proverbs that he has come to a new realization of a fact that is seldom referred to in a commentary, and a truth which I fear the editor himself was hardly aware of through the years, and that is, a great many teachings of our Lord, and of the apostles in the New Testament, are amazingly similar to the instruction in the Book of Proverbs. For example, the Book of Proverbs continually emphasizes the importance of being right in the inner man, using over and over again the word, "heart." Now this is exactly what our Lord does in the Sermon on the Mount (Matt. 5–7), where He is getting at the condition of man's heart. Here the king is giving us the secret, as it were, of how to have a glad heart, which is not far removed from the exhortation of our Lord in John, "These things have I spoken unto you that my joy might be in you and that your joy might be full." "Here are men and women around us who are unfathomable; the heart is a kind of infinite; we skim the surface, we cannot sound the depths. Here is a merry heart which makes a cheerful countenance, but here is a countenance unclouded and smiling which covers a spirit quite broken. Here is a cheerful heart which enjoys a continual feast, and finds in its own merriment a medicine for its troubles; but we cannot find the secret of the cheerfulness, or catch the tone of the merriment, any more than we can comprehend what it is which is making all the days of the afflicted evil." — *R. F. Horton*. 13. A glad heart maketh a cheerful countenance; But by sorrow of heart the spirit is broken. 14. The heart of him that hath understanding seeketh knowledge; But the mouth of fools feedeth on folly. 15. All the days of the afflicted are evil; But he that is of a cheerful heart *hath* a continual feast. "By the merry heart we shall understand the Christly cheerful heart; not the light, frivolous heart of the thoughtless and the gay. . . . Two things are said in the text of this 'merry heart.' (1) It is a radiance to the face. It maketh 'a cheerful countenance.' A man's countenance is a mirror in which you can see his soul. Emotions chisel their features on the brow. Man has an instinct to recognise this fact. We are physiognomists from childhood, judging character always from the face. This fact is a great advantage in our social life. Did men show no soul in their faces their presence would be as uninteresting as statues. Human society, if it could exist, would be oppressively monotonous. This fact suggests also the true method of beautifying the face. Beauty of countenance consisteth not in features, or complexion, so much as in expression. A genial, frank, sunny look is that which fascinates and pleases the beholder.

16. Better is little, with the fear of Jehovah, Than great treasure and trouble therewith.

17. Better is a dinner of herbs, where love is, Than a stalled ox and hatred therewith.

PROVERBS 22:1. A *good* name is rather to be chosen than great riches, *And* loving favor than silver and gold.

"The man who hath a true understanding, an unsophisticated, unbiased heart, seeketh knowledge, the highest knowledge, the knowledge of God, which is the centre and soul of all science. Such was the heart of Nicodemus, who came at night to Jesus in quest of truth. Such was the heart of Mary, who sat at the feet of the Great Teacher; such also that of the Bereans, who searched the Scriptures for themselves. *The other 'feedeth on foolishness.'* Souls, like bodies, have different tastes. Some souls have a taste — not a natural, but an acquired one — for 'foolishness.' They have a relish for things which in the sight of reason and God are foolish, they seize them with voracity, and with a zest ruminate on them afterwards." — *David Thomas.* **16. Better is little, with the fear of Jehovah, Than great treasure and trouble therewith. 17. Better is a dinner of herbs, where love is, Than a stalled ox and hatred therewith.** "A dinner of herbs and a stalled ox indicate the two extremes — humble poverty on the one side, and pampered luxury on the other. These brief expressions open for a moment the doors of the cottage and of the palace that we may obtain a glimpse of what is going on within. Look into the dwelling on this side: it is dinner time: the family, fresh from their labour, are seated round a clean uncovered table; there is no meat from the stall or the flock, no bunch of ripe grapes from the vine-yard, and even no bread from the cornfield. Some green herbs gathered in the garden have been cooked and set down as the meal of the household. The fare is poor; but this poor fare and love together make a more savoury mess than any that ever graced a royal banquet. The people thrive upon the precious mixture. Look into the lofty castle on the other side at the moment when this word throws open its doors. A rich feast is reeking in the hall. The stalled ox is there, surrounded by a labyrinth of kindred luxuries. A crowd of attendants must be in the room, observing every look, and hearing every whisper. The poor man's family dine in private; the rich man's in public. This is one point in favour of the poor. The servant at his master's back is a man with human feelings in his breast. If he has been treated unkindly, anger rankles in his heart, while the smile that is paid for plays upon his countenance. If, moreover, there be jealousy between husband and wife, rivalry between brother and brother, in this great house, their meeting at a meal is misery; their politeness before strangers is the encrusted whitewash on a sepulchre's side, cracking and falling off at every movement, and revealing the rottenness within. When love leaves the family circle, it is no longer a piece of God's own hand-work, and there is no security for safety in any of its motions." — *W. Arnot.*

IV. **WEALTH IS NOT THE GREATEST GOOD,** Proverbs 16:8, 16; 22:1, 2. The editor of this volume believes with all of his heart that the first great theme for preaching is the Lord Jesus Christ, and of Him, His atoning work. We may all say, "God forbid that we should glory save in the cross of our Lord Jesus Christ," (Gal. 6:14), but I fear that with many of us who are evangelicals we are not proclaiming to our people the whole counsel of God. By this I do not mean only that we too rarely take subjects from the Old Testament, which is probably true, but that there are many subjects in the New Testament also that we hardly ever preach on. One of them is this matter of money. Now the liberal, and those with socialistic tendencies, are always talking about the ethical teachings of Scripture, but you and I, too seldom. Our Lord says more about money and possessions than about any other one thing, apart from the Kingdom of God. Even the Apostle Paul at the end of his life, in the Pastoral Epistles, comes back to this subject of money again and again. **22:1. A *good* name is rather to be chosen**

2. The rich and the poor meet together: Jehovah is the maker of them all.

PROVERBS 20:11. Even a child maketh himself known by his doings, Whether his work be pure, and whether it be right.

12. The hearing ear, and the seeing eye, Jehovah hath made even both of them.

---

than great riches, *And* loving favor than silver and gold. "He does not say that to choose great riches is not good — the opposite is implied. Great wealth is a blessing when rightly used. Its value is more frequently denounced from envy than from conviction. Wealth increases man's sources of pleasure, and happiness is a good thing. The happy God made his universe to be happy. Wealth increases man's means of improvement. It puts at his service books, leisure, halls of science, galleries of art, and other facilities for true development. Wealth increases his power of usefulness. It enables him to mitigate poverty, to dispel ignorance, ameliorate suffering, and advance all the interests of man. With it he can rear asylums, hospitals, schools, churches, and other institutions helpful to the world. Don't despise wealth — get it if you can. In itself it is a good thing, and, rightly used, it is an immense blessing. The words suggest —

"THAT A GOOD REPUTATION IS BETTER. — 'A good name is rather to be chosen.' Why? Because a good reputation implies the possession of something more valuable than secular wealth. That cannot be a valuable reputation which is undeserved, and contrary to the facts of a man's moral life. It is a fiction — an imposture. A good reputation implies a good character — a character in harmony with the will of God. Such a character is infinitely more valuable than the wealth of millionaires — or the splendour of kingdoms. It is intrinsic, imperishable wealth. Why? Because a good reputation answers higher purposes than secular wealth. It yields higher pleasure to the possessor." — *David Thomas.*

2. **The rich and the poor meet together: Jehovah is the maker of them all.** "We should make a mistake if we supposed that the Lord recognises any class distinctions, or that He valued a man because he is poor, just as we value a man because he is rich. The truth rather is that He absolutely ignores the class distinctions, regarding the mingled mass of human beings, rich and poor, oppressor and oppressed, as on a plane of dead equality, and then distinguishing between them on a totally different principle, — on a moral, a spiritual principle; and, if there is any preference, it is on the ground of certain valuable moral effects which poverty sometimes produces that He takes the poor into His peculiar and tender care, honouring them with so close a friendship that service to them becomes service to Him." — *R. F. Horton.*

V. **WE ARE HIS HANDIWORK,** Proverbs 20:11, 12. **11. Even a child maketh himself known by his doings, Whether his work be pure, and whether it be right.** While these two verses are not exactly related to each other, I have placed the eleventh verse under the heading of that which applies more directly to the truth of verse twelve. Strange to say, every commentator with whom I have any acquaintance utterly fails to do anything with this verse, with the single exception of E. H. Plumptre: "The eye of the teacher has traced the unfolding of character from the earliest germ. The graces or the faults of children are not trifles, as they are often deemed to be. The earliest actions are prophecies of the future, whether it will be pure and right, or unclean and evil." **12. The hearing ear, and the seeing eye, Jehovah hath made even both of them.** "Two witnesses, the hearing ear and the seeing eye, are summoned forth to prove before the world that the Maker of all things is wise and good. These two palm branches, ever green plaited into a simple wreath, are chosen from the whole earth as a diadem of glory for the Sovereign's brow. These words so gently spoken, these works so wonderfully made, challenge for their Author the homage and service of all intelligent created beings. . . .

3. A prudent man seeth the evil, and hideth himself; But the simple pass on, and suffer for it.

4. The reward of humility *and* the fear of Jehovah *Is* riches, and honor, and life.

"Christian! these ears and eyes are the openings whereby light and life have reached your soul; occupy them henceforth with sounds and sights that will please Him. If I am Christ's, these ears and eyes have been bought for himself by the price of his own blood. I must not employ them to crucify him afresh, and bring him to an open shame. Let me listen to those sounds and look at those sights which I would listen to and look at if he stood beside me listening and looking too. To other sounds let me be deaf, — to other beauties blind." — *W. Arnot.*

VI. **THE REWARDS OF PRUDENCE, HUMILITY, AND GENEROSITY,** Proverbs 22:3, 4, 9. **3. A prudent man seeth the evil, and hideth himself; But the simple pass on, and suffer for it.** The word here translated "prudent" is one of the many words in the Hebrew language meaning "pious." Here there is the element of cunning. He seems to be one who recognizing the approach of calamities or the consequences of evil hides that he might escape from their blasting. But those who are simple-minded, without the capacity for discerning what is about to take place, pass on in total ignorance of impending disaster. I like the words of Arnot in drawing from this passage a warning concerning the life to come. "The greatest evils lie in the world to come, and only the eye of faith can foresee them. To be caught by death unready, and placed before the judgment-seat without a plea, and then cast out for ever, are evils so great that in their presence all others disappear like stars in the glare of day. But great though they are, the prudent may foresee, and the trustful prevent them. There is a refuge, but its gate opens into Time. If the prudent do not enter now, the simple will knock in vain at the closed door, when he has passed on into eternity without any part in Christ. If the needy are numerous, the refuge is ample. If the exposed are in danger, the admission is free. If the adversary is legion, the Saviour is God." — *W. Arnot.*

4. **The reward of humility *and* the fear of Jehovah *Is* riches, and honor, and life.** "What is humility? Not *weakness*. There are those who are sometimes considered humble who are too infertile in nature to grow ambition. They have just power enough to crawl, they have no wings to fly. Not *servility*. Those who are destitute of self-respect, who are mean and cringing in their instincts and habits, like Uriah Heep in 'David Copperfield,' are not humble, but mean and base. Not *sanctimoniousness*. There is much mock humility both in the world and in the churches: humble speeches throbbing with pride; humble dresses covering hearts beating with vanity and ambition. . . .

"The real riches, the wealth of holy thoughts, lofty sentiments, high hopes, are ever associated with genuine religion. 'Honour' is also mentioned. True spiritual excellence will always command the honour and confidence of all consciences both in this world and the world to come. It receives the honour that cometh from above. Again, 'life' is mentioned. Not, of course, mere existence, but existence in its highest and happiest developments. Existence in connection with all that can make it valuable and blessed. Such is human prosperity." — *David Thomas.*

VII. **CONTRASTS IN CHARACTER AND CORRESPONDING CONTRASTS OF CONSEQUENCES,** Proverbs 28:6–28. No part of this chapter is assigned for our printed text, and of course it is impossible even to make a running commentary on the many things that are found here. Chapters twenty-five to twenty-nine are a separate collection of proverbs made in the literary circle at the court of Hezekiah, so the text says. In this chapter Dr. Horton tells us that "We seem to have hints of the many troubled experiences through which the monarchy of Israel passed — the divided rule, the injustice, the incapacity, the oppression (vs. 2, 3, 12, 15, 16, 28)." Many of these verses in this very chapter have taken on new meaning since the two great World Wars.

THE LESSON IN LIFE, LITERATURE, AND ARCHAEOLOGY.

Athanasius, in his *Life of Saint Antony* (written about 356 A.D.), actually uses one of the verses of our lesson (Prov. 15:13), in describing the famous third-century hermit. "His countenance had a great and wonderful grace. This gift he had from the Saviour. Yet neither in height nor breadth was he conspicuous above others, but in the serenity of his manner and the purity of his soul. For as his soul was free from disturbances, his outward appearance was calm; so from the joy of his soul he possessed a cheerful countenance, and from his bodily movements could be perceived the condition of his soul, as it is written, 'When the heart is merry the countenance is cheerful, but when it is sorrowful it is cast down.' "

A TRUTH FOR THE CLASS TO CARRY AWAY.

Certainly there is one truth which we can draw from the study of any extended passage in the Book of Proverbs, and that is that what God asks of you and me is not that we should make a lot of money or become world-famous or develop a magnetic personality or go to the head of our class or become the executive head of some industry. It is that whatever we do we may do in sincerity. Whatever our acts, let them be righteous. Let us be sure that the path we are following is one on which the light of God's permissive will ever falls. Mere wealth, success, fame, have in themselves never satisfied anyone, especially as life matures and these external things become monotonous and stale. Joy is found in right doing, in Godly living, in singleness of purpose, in unselfishness of purpose. Now the grand truth is that what the Lord asks for is not beyond the attainment of men and women of just ordinary capacities. This is carried over into the New Testament when our Lord says, "Well done, thou good and faithful servant." (Matt. 25:21). Notice, He does not say, successful, or brilliant, just good and faithful.

Do you find in this lesson an actual condemnation of wealth? What are some of the things that riches in themselves cannot bestow on men? Is the kind of life set forth here for our emulation something that develops naturally in every human heart, or is it something that needs daily watching and self-discipline? What verses of our lesson would you say were especially manifested in the life of our Lord while on earth?

LESSON VIII. — November 21.

GOD'S ABUNDANCE FOR MAN'S NEED. — Psalm 104.

PRINTED TEXT, Psalm 104:1–4, 10–13, 24, 33.

Devotional Reading: Psalm 104:23–31.
Beginner Topic: BREAD FOR RUTH.
    Lesson Material: Psalm 104:1, 10–14; Genesis 8:22; Ruth 2.
    Memory Verse: O give thanks unto Jehovah: for he is good. Psalm 136:1.
Primary Topic: A SONG OF PRAISE.
    Lesson Material: Psalm 104.
    Memory Verse: The earth is full of thy riches . . . I will sing unto Jehovah. Psalm 104:24, 33.
Junior Topic: A SONG OF PRAISE.
    Lesson Material: Psalm 104.
    Memory Verse: O Jehovah, how manifold are thy works!
      In wisdom hast thou made them all: the earth is full of thy riches. Psalm 104:24.
Intermediate-Senior Topic: GOD'S GOOD GIFTS.
    Lesson Material: Psalm 104.
    Memory Verse: The earth is Jehovah's, and the fulness thereof;
      The world, and they that dwell therein. Psalm 24:1.

Topic for Young People and Adults: GOD'S PROVISION FOR HIS CREATURES.
Lesson Material: Psalm 104.
Memory Verse: The earth is Jehovah's, and the fulness thereof;
The world, and they that dwell therein. Psalm 24:1.

THE TEACHER AND HIS CLASS.

The Younger Classes, who are interested in nature study, might be introduced to this lesson by the teacher bringing in a small loaf of bread, and discussing with the class the history behind it. You could take them back to the growing wheat; to the seed that went into the ground; to the various chemicals in the ground that the seed absorbed as it began to shoot up into a stalk, and kept feeding until the wheat was ripe. Then, of course, we have to have rain for the soil, coming down from the sky, and this has to come at the right time. We also have to have sunlight, or the plant will shrivel. Now these and many other elements of nature are beautifully described for us in this nature Psalm, which talks about the food of men and beasts, and how God arranged the whole universe so that man, His last and highest creation, could comfortably and joyfully live on this earth.

The Older Classes will find here a lesson somewhat different than those we have been studying for a few years. We have here a nature Psalm, wherein God is praised as the Creator and Sustainer of this beautiful world. There was a time, especially at the end of the 18th and beginning of the 19th centuries, when the Christian church made a great deal of what we call Natural Theology, God's revelation of Himself in nature, but with the coming of evolution and the growing materialistic mood of the world the study of Natural Theology has almost passed out of modern thought. Some of our best theologians are now insisting that it is high time that we go back again into the study of nature for its marvelous revelations of the power and wisdom of God. It is this that the Apostle Paul speaks of in Romans 1:19–20.

THE LESSON IN ITS SETTING.

Time. — There is no indication when this Psalm was written.

Place. — Also there is no indication of where this Psalm was written.

THE PLAN OF THE LESSON.

SUBJECT: The Beauties, Mysteries, Orderliness, and Beneficence of Nature Lead the Soul of Man to Give Praise to God the Creator of All Nature.

  I. ELEMENTAL FORCES OF NATURE, Psalm 104:1–4.

 II. THE CREATION OF THE EARTH AND ITS SEAS, Psalm 104:5–9.

III. BIRDS AND BEASTS, Psalm 104: 10–12.

 IV. FOOD AND DRINK, Psalm 104: 13–15.

  V. TREES AND ANIMALS, Psalm 104:16–18.

 VI. TIMES AND SEASONS, Psalm 104: 19–23.

VII. THE SEA, Psalm 104:24–26.

VIII. THE RENEWAL OF NATURE, Psalm 104:27–32.

 IX. THE PRAISE OF THE LORD, Psalm 104:33–35.

THE TEACHER'S LIBRARY.

The beauties, mysteries, orderliness, and beneficence of nature lead the soul of man to give praise to God the Creator of all nature. A list of important commentaries on the Psalms will be found in the introduction to this volume. The three best commentaries that I have found for this particular Psalm are those by Delitzsch, Thomas, and, though it is very old, John Calvin. Though this Psalm has been admired and praised for centuries, sermonic material is exceedingly scarce. There is a beautiful sermon on verse 10 in Hugh MacMillan, *Two Worlds Are Ours*, 117–132.

AUDIO-VISUAL AIDS.

FILM: "Thankful Dandelion," Baptista Films, 15 min., sd., b&w. or col. A sermonette especially for children. "Teaches that we human beings ought to learn a lesson from the flowers."

There are two secular titles on Thanksgiving, which could be used: a motion picture, "Day of Thanksgiving," (Young America, 13 min., sd., b&w.), in which Bill Johnson and his family recount the blessings they enjoy as American citizens; and a filmstrip, "Thanksgiving" (also Young America, 30 fr., b&w.), which tells the story of the Pilgrims and their experiences.

PSALM 104:1. Bless Jehovah, O my soul. O Jehovah my God, thou art very great: Thou art clothed with honor and majesty.
2. Who coverest thyself with light as with a garment. Who stretches out the heavens like a curtain.

I would like to begin the study of this Psalm with a fact which I myself did not come upon until very late in life, and which I have not found really developed in any commentary I have examined. Psalm 104 introduces a remarkable consecutive series of a poetic interpretation of the whole history of God's redemptive work, as it relates to Israel. Psalm 104 concerns itself with creation; the patriarchs are reviewed in Psalm 105:1–23; the exodus and the wanderings from Psalm 105:24—106:32; the kingdom age of Israel, Psalm 106:33–39; the captivity, the last nine verses of that Psalm; and, the return of Israel from her captivity, Psalm 107. Thus we have in these four Psalms a survey of the entire Old Testament.

The author of this Psalm, whose name is not known, has been called, "the Wordsworth of the ancients." The great German naturalist, Humboldt, by no means a Christian believer, once bore this testimony to the Psalm we are about to study: "It might almost be said that one single Psalm represents the image of the whole Cosmos. . . . We are astonished to find in a lyrical poem of such limited compass the whole universe — the heavens and earth — sketched with a few bold touches. The contrast of the labour of man with the animal life of nature, and the image of the omnipresent, invisible Power, renewing the earth at will, or sweeping it of inhabitants, is a grand and solemn poetical creation." — *A. von Humboldt*. While the general order of the Psalm follows the story of creation in the first chapter of Genesis, and the beginning of the second chapter "the treatment of the subject is free and original. Sometimes the Psalmist draws a picture of the processes of creation, but for the most part it is the present order and continuous maintenance of the universe by His beneficent will which kindles the Psalmist's devout enthusiasm. God did not make the world and leave it to itself. It depends absolutely upon His will for the continuance of its existence." — *A. F. Kirkpatrick*. The first four verses are a poetic interpretation of Genesis 1:3–8; verses 5–9 of Genesis 1:9–10; verses 10–18 of Genesis 1:11–13; verses 19–30 of Genesis 1:14–31.

I. THE ELEMENTAL FORCES OF NATURE, Psalm 104:1–4. The Psalm opens with a general expression of praise. The Psalmist, it is to be noted, is speaking to his soul, as at the beginning of Psalm 103. The soul, for the Psalmist, embraces all his inner life. 1. Bless Jehovah, O my soul. O Jehovah my God, thou art very great: Thou art clothed with honor and majesty. Honor and majesty are the attributes of a king (see Ps. 96:6; 21:5, etc.). Of course we are here confronted with figurative language. God does not actually wear garments, and even if He did, honor and majesty cannot be made up into garments. This is a metaphor. While in the New Testament the love of God dominates, in the Old Testament His power and righteousness are generally the characteristics set forth most frequently. 2. Who coverest thyself with light as with a garment. Light was the first created element, being universally diffused, the source of gladness, the emblem of purity, it is a wonderfully rich expression of God's nature and is reiterated in the New Testament (1 John 1:5; 1 Tim. 6:16). Who stretches out the heavens like a curtain. "The canopy of the sky is compared to a tent-curtain, stretched out over the earth. By His simple fiat God spread out these heavens as easily as a man might pitch his tent. Their vastness is a symbol of the majesty of the King Who dwells in His royal pavilion, Whom yet 'heaven and the heaven of heavens cannot contain.' Observe the present participles, *covering thyself*, *stretching out*. The original act of creation is regarded as continued into the

. Who layeth the beams of his chambers in the waters. Who
keth the clouds his chariot. Who walketh upon the wings of the
nd;
4. Who maketh winds his messengers; Flames of fire his ministers.

---

present in the maintenance of the universe." — *A. F. Kirkpatrick.* 3. **Who layeth
the beams of his chambers in the waters.** We must grant that this is a difficult
clause. "The figures, as Calvin remarks, are all designed to teach the same truth,
viz. that we are not to pierce heaven in order to discover God, because He meets
us in His world and presents everywhere living pictures to our eyes. We must
not suppose that anything was added to Him by the creation of the world; it is
for our sakes that He puts on this garment." — *J. J. Perowne.* "Upper chambers"
here mean those built "on the flat roof of the Eastern houses. For the literal use
of the word, see for instance 2 Kings 4:10; for the figurative, as here, Amos 9:6,
and compare Jeremiah 22:13, 14." — *J. J. Perowne.* **Who maketh the clouds his
chariot.** Clouds are often used as the accompanying natural phenomena of the
advent of Christ (Ps. 18:10; Isa. 19:1; Matt. 24:30). **Who walketh upon the wings
of the wind; 4. Who maketh winds his messengers; Flames of fire his ministers.**
"God rides on the clouds, and is carried upon the wings of the wind, inasmuch as
he drives about the winds and clouds at his pleasure, and by sending them hither
and thither as swiftly as he pleases, shows thereby the signs of his presence. By
these words we are taught that the winds do not blow by chance, nor the lightnings
flash by a fortuitous impulse, but that God, in the exercise of his sovereign power,
rules and controls all the agitations and disturbances of the atmosphere. From
this doctrine a twofold advantage may be reaped. In the first place, if at any
time noxious winds arise, if the south wind corrupt the air, or if the north wind
scorch the corn, and not only tear up trees by the root, but overthrow houses,
and if other winds destroy the fruits of the earth, we ought to tremble under these
scourges of Providence. In the second place, if, on the other hand, God moderate
the excessive heat by a gentle cooling breeze, if he purify the polluted atmosphere
by the north wind, or if he moisten the parched ground by south winds; in this we
ought to contemplate his goodness." — *John Calvin.* This verse is quoted in
Hebrews 1:7.

II. **THE CREATION OF THE EARTH AND ITS SEAS,** Psalm 104:5–9.
With this passage compare Job 38:4–6. Here we have "the work of the Third Day
in its two great divisions: first, the separation of the land and water (vs. 5–9);
next, the clothing of the earth with grass, herbs, and trees (vs. 10–18). The
Poet, however, ranges beyond the first creation, and peoples the earth with the
living creatures of the Fifth Day. It is not a picture of still life like that in Genesis,
but a living, moving, animated scene. . . . The original chaos is described not
according to the heathen notion, as a confused mass, earth and water mingled
together, but the earth as already formed, yet completely enveloped in the water.
The 'earth standing out of the water, and in the water,' 2 Peter 3:5. This vast
swelling tumultuous sea hears the 'rebuke' of God, and sinks to its appointed
place; the earth appears, emerges from her watery covering, and shows her surface
diversified with mountains and valleys. So Milton writes: —

> 'The earth was form'd, but in the womb as yet
> Of waters, embryon immature involved,
> Appear'd not: over all the face of earth
> Main ocean flow'd.' " — *J. J. Perowne.*

Many thousands of pupils studying this lesson will be living in areas in our country
where they seldom see the ocean, which meant so much to the Hebrew people, so
perhaps a few facts here might not be out of place, emphasizing the importance
of these verses. The oceans cover seven-tenths of the surface of the earth. There

10. He sendeth forth springs into the valleys: They run among the mountains;
    11. They give drink to every beast of the field; The wild asses quench their thirst.
    12. By them the birds of the heavens have their habitation; They sing among the branches.
    13. He watereth the mountains from his chambers: The earth is filled with the fruit of thy works.

are five oceans, and many seas.   The largest *sea* is the Mediterranean, upon which three continents border, Europe, Asia, Africa, with an area of 813,000 square miles. Perhaps the areas of the five oceans might be interesting:

Pacific Ocean	63,634,000 square miles
Atlantic Ocean	31,530,000 square miles
Indian Ocean	28,356,000 square miles
Antarctic Ocean	5,731,000 square miles
Arctic Ocean	4,000,000 square miles

The shores of the Pacific and Indian Oceans form almost perfect circles.   The Atlantic Ocean is shaped like the letter "s" between Europe and North America, and Africa and South America.   The Pacific Ocean has an average depth of over 14,000 feet.   Off the Philippine Islands the ocean reaches its greatest depth, 35,400 feet, higher than Mt. Everest.   The shallower parts of the ocean are called the Continental Shelf, which extends outward from visible land about thirty miles.
    III. THE BIRDS AND BEASTS, Psalm 104:10–12.   10. He sendeth forth springs into the valleys: They run among the mountains; 11. They give drink to every beast of the field; The wild asses quench their thirst.   12. By them the birds of the heavens have their habitation; They sing among the branches. 13. He watereth the mountains from his chambers: The earth is filled with the fruit of thy works.   Almost all of this particular paragraph concerns the springs and valleys of the earth.   Verse 10 is similar to the description of Palestine, found in Deuteronomy 8:7.   Here we have "the loving care, the tender sympathy with which God, clothing the earth with beauty, provides at the same time for the wants of all His creatures.   Even the wild ass which shuns the approach of man, and the birds of heaven, which have no keeper, are not left unprovided for." — *J. J. Perowne.*   Calvin has a very beautiful comment here: "Rivers run even through great and desolate wildernesses, where the wild beasts enjoy some blessing of God; and no country is so barren as not to have trees growing here and there, on which birds make the air to resound with the melody of their singing.   Since even those regions where all lies waste and uncultivated, furnish manifest tokens of the Divine goodness and power, with what admiration ought we to regard that most abundant supply of all good things, which is to be seen in cultivated and favourable regions? Surely in countries where not only one river flows, or where not only grass grows for the feeding of wild beasts, or where the singing of birds is heard not only from a few trees, but where a manifold and varied abundance of good things everywhere presents itself to our view, our stupidity is more than brutish, if our minds, by such manifestations of the goodness of God, are not fixed in devout meditation on his glory." — *John Calvin.*   Spurgeon in his eloquent way remarks: "How refreshing are these words!   What happy memories they arouse of splashing waterfalls and entangled boughs, where the merry din of the falling and rushing water form a sort of solid background of music, and the sweet tuneful notes of the birds are the brighter and more flashing lights in the harmony.   Pretty birdies, sing on!   What better can ye do, and who can do it better?   When we too drink of the river of God, and eat of the fruit of the tree of life, it well becomes us to 'sing among the branches.'   Where ye dwell ye sing; and shall not we rejoice in the Lord, who has

been our dwelling-place in all generations? As ye fly from bough to bough, ye warble forth your notes, and so will we as we flit through time into eternity. It is not meet that birds of Paradise should be outdone by birds of earth." — *C. H. Spurgeon.*

IV. **FOOD AND DRINK,** Psalm 104:13–15. This section might almost be designated as belonging to the one we have just studied, concerning the streams of the earth, and yet the emphasis here is more upon the food which the earth produces than the springs of water which are basically necessary for this food. "Palestine was 'a land of mountains and valleys, drinking water of the rain of heaven' (Deut. 11:11). It is not inaccessible mountain tops which the poet is thinking of, so much as the upland corn fields (72:16), watered by the rain which God sends down from His 'upper chambers' (v. 3), as the valleys are watered by streams. . . . The 'fruit of thy works' is generally explained to mean the rain, as a product of the clouds which God has made. But this is harsh: it is much more natural to take the phrase in the simple sense of 'fruit produced by God's manifold operations.' Earth is fertilised by the rain and springs, and rejoices in its abundant produce." — *A. F. Kirkpatrick.* I must here go back to Calvin: "In these words we are taught, that God not only provides for men's necessity, and bestows upon them as much as is sufficient for the ordinary purposes of life, but that in his goodness he deals still more bountifully with them by cheering their hearts with wine and oil. Nature would certainly be satisfied with water to drink; and therefore the addition of wine is owing to God's superabundant liberality. The expression, *and oil to make his face to shine,* has been explained in different ways. As sadness spreads a gloom over the countenance, some give this exposition, That when men enjoy the commodities of wine and oil, their faces shine with gladness. Some with more refinement of interpretation, but without foundation, refer this to *lamps.*" — *John Calvin.* I cannot help but quote here only a fragment of the exquisite lines of Hugh Macmillan: "The waters long for rest, for a perpetual level. But this longing is never satisfied; for it is to this restlessness that we owe all the life and beauty and fruitfulness of the earth. Life is only compatible with mutation; and were this mutation to cease universal death would be the result. Not more certainly would life terminate in the body if the pulse ceased to beat, than would the world be locked in everlasting sleep if the pulse of the mountain spring ceased to throb. And how grand is the music of nature's rhythm as she rushes along the 'ringing grooves of change' to her unattainable repose. The mountain spring bubbles up its crystal waters in rhythmic gushes, like a happy-hearted maiden dancing to the music of her own young heart's delight. The ripples of the river are rhythmical as they flow in the quiet peace of an even and assured course; the waves of the ocean are rhythmical as they chase each other over the bosom of the deep, or break in thunder and foam on the shore. The two great forces that are incessantly employed in building up and pulling down the frame of nature, move to the sound of their own music. Water is everywhere musical as it wears down the mountains into Grecian regularity of outline; fire is everywhere musical as it piles up the mountains into rugged Gothic spires that pierce the heavens." — *Hugh Macmillan.*

V. **TREES AND ANIMALS,** Psalm 104:16–18. The phrase, "the cedars of Lebanon," is, I believe, the most frequently used expression in relation to trees to be found in all the Scriptures; e.g., 1 Kings 4:33; 2 Kings 14:9; Psalm 92:12; Ezekiel 27:5. "The word translated here '*stork*' is applied to a bird with great, wide-spreading wings (Zech. 5:9) which builds its nest upon the lofty cypresses, which has regular seasons of arriving and migrating (Jer. 8:7), and belongs to the unclean birds (Lev. 11:19; Deut. 14:18), and is perhaps mentioned in Job 39:13, along with the pelican. According to its etymology, which is assumed, it may mean either a bird of a curved neck, or of kind disposition, and is therefore supposed to be either the heron or the white dove, falcon or the stork. The word translated '*wild goat*' cannot denote the stag, but the wild or mountain goat (Job 39:1; 1 Sam. 24:3). It is mentioned in Leviticus 11:5 as an unclean ruminant,

24. O Jehovah, how manifold are thy works!   In wisdom hast thou made them all: The earth is full of thy riches.

and in Proverbs 30:26 as a sagacious animal, living in rocks, in the clefts of the rocks, and in Deuteronomy 14:7 is distinguished from the hare. The *'coney'* is scarcely meant, even if it be true that the Phoenicians gave the name Spain to the Iberian peninsula, from the number of these little animals that were found there, still less the rough and spring hedgehog. The rock-badger is most probably meant, which resembles the marmot, and is common on Lebanon and the districts about the Jordan." — *Dr. J. F. MacCurdy.*

VI. **TIMES AND SEASONS,** Psalm 104:19–23. We have here a poetic description of the fourth day of creation, in which occurs the very important statement: "And God said, Let there be lights in the firmament of heaven to divide the day from the night; and let them be for signs, and for seasons, and for days and years." "The whole picture is finely conceived, and the contrast is perfect between the restless movement and roaring of the wild beasts, and man's calm life of labour, continued in the quiet light of day from morning till evening. All the other creatures wait upon God, in simple dependence upon Him; man must *labour,* as well as gather what God gives him, if he would be satisfied with good." — *J. J. Perowne.* It is generally thought that the seasons referred to here are those religious festivals of the sacred calendar of Israel, which depended so much on the cycles of the moon, as noted in Leviticus 23:2, 4, 37.

VII. **THE SEA,** Psalm 104:24–26. Now we come back to the marvels of the sea, and the mysteries of the species that live within the waters. 24. **O Jehovah, how manifold are thy works!   In wisdom hast thou made them all: The earth is full of thy riches.** "So wisely is nature formed and governed, that its means never fail to accomplish their ends, and no change in its plans can ever be suggested for the better; and no change has been effected from the beginning, or will ever be. Nature is one complete whole. 'Every part of vegetation,' says a modern author, 'is to be regarded as the very counterpart of, and as suited to its respective tenants. The verdant field is the pasture-ground of flocks and herds, and of all the teeming armies of insect life that feed on its surface. Every forest is the roaming ground of its own wild tenants. . . . Every leaf is a playground and a pasture-ground for the numerous tribes that roam and feed and sport on its surface. Every flower, vocal with the songs of its merry tenants, is the resort or the residence of numerous families of living creatures that seek pleasure, or perfume, or nectarine sweets, or a floral shade, or shelter in its soft and quiet bosom." — *David Thomas.* One word here needs attention, "leviathan" (see Job 40:20; 41:5). "The thought required is not that the wildest and strongest of God's creatures are but as it were His tame pets, but that the sea is the playground of the mighty monsters which display His power and goodness as they disport themselves there in the enjoyment of their life. In Job 41 *leviathan* means the crocodile, but here the name is evidently used of sea-monsters generally, particularly the great cetaceans, of which there are many, and formerly were probably many more, in the Mediterranean." — *A. F. Kirkpatrick.*

VIII. **THE RENEWAL OF NATURE,** Psalm 104:27–32. The Psalmist has practically concluded his survey of the natural world, but he wants to emphasize one final truth, that not only has the whole world been created by God, but He and He alone is the sustainer of the world. I suppose that verse 29 could refer to drouth or famine or catastrophe in nature which interrupt its natural functions, and food becoming unobtainable the animals in that part of the earth die. A good illustration would be an experience I had in driving south, for a short vacation, in the late Fall, as I recall, of 1935. An unexpected heavy snow had fallen just at the time when the birds from the north were flying south. The land for hundreds of miles was blanketed so that the birds could not find nourishment in their flight, and thousands of them fell from the sky exhausted to die. On the subject of the

3. I will sing unto Jehovah as long as I live: I will sing praise to my
d while I have any being.

renewal of nature, Rotherham has an excellent passage: "God holds all life in his
own hand: all living things 'live and move and have their being in him.' If this
is true of animals, much more is it true of men. God is 'the God of the spirits
of all flesh': in every living thing save the first, concur both procreation and
creation, the parental contribution and the divine. God is the father of our
spirits. I am God's creature, as well as my parent's child. If to create is to make
a new thing — to embody an original idea — then there is something new and
distinctive in every creature which Jehovah has made. Probably no two animals
were ever perfectly alike: one may feel certain that no two men ever were. The
differentia of men should amplify as well as radiate the glory of God." — *J. B.
Rotherham.*

IX. **THE PRAISE OF THE LORD,** Psalm 104:33–35. Just as any one of us
looking upon some glorious manifestation of beauty in the natural world cries out,
"Isn't that beautiful?" or looking out in the early morning of a lovely day, says,
"It is good to be alive!" the soul of the Psalmist bursts forth in a loftier expression
than all these, giving praise to God, first, for having made such a wonderful world,
and secondly, for giving man the capacity for understanding it. 33. **I will sing
unto Jehovah as long as I live: I will sing praise to my God while I have any being.**
"As the Psalmist utters the devout wish that God may rejoice in His works, so he
utters the wish for himself that he may ever rejoice in God, that his thoughts and
words may find acceptance with Him. This is the truest, highest harmony of
creation; God finding pleasure in His creatures, His reasonable creatures finding
their joy in Him. But this harmony has been rudely broken; the sweet notes of
the vast instrument of the Universe are jangled out of tune. Sin is the discord
of the world. Sin has changed the order into disorder. Hence the prophetic hope
(35) that sinners shall be consumed, that the wicked shall be no more, that thus
the earth shall be purified, the harmony be restored, and God, once more, as at
the first, pronounce His creation 'very good.' In the prospect of such a consummation, the Poet calls upon his own soul, and upon all around him, to bless and
praise Jehovah." — *J. J. Perowne.*

THE LESSON IN LIFE, LITERATURE, AND ARCHAEOLOGY.

Instead of taking this paragraph from the use of a verse of the lesson, I think
all my readers will be grateful for the following statement, from the final page of
one of the more modern books on the subject of creation (Cambridge, 1951) *The
Origin of the Earth,* by W. M. Smart, Regius Professor of Astronomy in the
University of Glasgow, and author of a number of books on astronomical naviga-
tion: "When we study the Universe and appreciate its grandeur and orderliness,
it seems to me that we are led to the recognition of a Creative Power and Cosmic
Purpose that transcends all that our limited minds can comprehend. In one of
his essays, Lord Bacon expressed this belief picturesquely as follows: 'I had rather
believe all the Fables in the Legend and the Talmud and the Alcoran than that
this Universal Frame is without a Mind.' Today we have learned very much
more about the 'Universal Frame' than was known in Bacon's time; nevertheless,
to many of us, scientific and non-scientific alike, the belief in a Divine Creator is
as necessary now as ever it was. To one astronomer at least 'The Heavens are
telling the glory of God and the Wonder of His Work.' "

A TRUTH FOR THE CLASS TO CARRY AWAY.

Inasmuch as we are living in a day when the secret, mysterious, and deeper
truths of the world of nature are being explored as never before, it seems that mankind should be experiencing a greater reverence for God who created the world.
This does not seem to be taking place, however. My own opinion is that it would

be wise for ministers to plan once a year a series of sermons in the realm of natural theology, showing how the wisdom and power of God is revealed in this marvelous world in which we live.

Why was Palestine so well suited for the illustration of spiritual truths from the world of nature?   Where does Paul argue that the visible world leaves mankind without excuse in regard to the wisdom and power of God?   (In the first chapter of Romans.)   Why does the Church say so little about nature?   (Probably because her pre-eminent theme — as it ought to be — is the person and work of Christ.)   What does the Bible tell us about the origin of the world that science admits it cannot discover with its laws and instruments?

LESSON IX. — November 28.

IN TIME OF TROUBLE. — Psalms 46; 142.

PRINTED TEXT, Psalms 142; 46:1-3, 10-11.

Devotional Reading: Psalm 77:1-14.
Beginner Topic: A GLAD LADY.
  Lesson Material: Luke 13:10-17.
  Memory Verse: O give thanks unto Jehovah; for he is good.   Psalm 136:1.
Primary Topic: WHEN WE ARE AFRAID.
  Lesson Material: Psalm 46.
  Memory Verse: What time I am afraid, I will put my trust in thee.   Psalm 56:3.
Junior Topic: WHEN WE ARE AFRAID.
  Lesson Material: Psalm 46.
  Memory Verse: What time I am afraid, I will put my trust in thee.   Psalm 56:3.
Intermediate-Senior Topic: IN TIME OF TROUBLE.
  Lesson Material: Psalms 46; 142.
  Memory Verse: God is our refuge and strength, a very present help in trouble.   Psalm 46:1.
Topic for Young People and Adults: OUR EVER PRESENT HELP.
  Lesson Material: Psalms 46; 142.
  Memory Verse: God is our refuge and strength, a very present help in trouble.   Psalm 46:1.

THE TEACHER AND HIS CLASS.

The Younger Classes might be asked in opening this lesson, What does a boy or girl do if while outdoors playing on his bicycle, he crashes into a curbstone, skinning both of his legs? Or, what does any young child do if some older person in the neighborhood says something to him that he takes to be an insult, or tells him that he is not to come back into that particular yard, or falsely accuses him of stealing something from some other child? There is only one natural thing for a child to do — to come home at once and pour out his troubles to mother or father. A child who does not tell his troubles to his parents develops first a mood of bitterness, and later he may become an introvert, and his heart, instead of throbbing with joy, seems heavy, and life is robbed of many of its great privileges. These are very serious subjects in psychology. In these two Psalms of our lesson, one of which actually begins with the word *trouble*, we have a perfect example of what all children of God should do, and may do, in an hour of difficulty, in pouring out their heart to the Lord.

The Older Classes may be introduced to this lesson by a brief consideration of one of its principal words, *refuge*. The original meaning of the English word *refuge* is, "to flee back again," and thus, finding shelter or protection from danger or trouble, or, a place of safety or security. Adding one *e* to the word makes it *refugee*, one who has fled from trouble or persecution to some place of safety. The world has never known so many refugees as it has today, in the men and women who have fled from the terrors of totalitarianism to the shelter of some democratic country; and more millions would similarly flee if they could. Yet, it is not only those who are being persecuted in such a way that have trouble. We all have inner sorrows and disappointments, and our lesson today is an invitation to flee to God, our Father in heaven, who knows our condition and who will prove, indeed, a place of security.

THE LESSON IN ITS SETTING.

Time. — Psalm 142 was composed by David during the time he lived in a cave while in flight from the wrath of Saul, and so may be placed about 1005 B.C. If Psalm 46 was written at the time of Sennacherib's invasion, the date would be about 701 B.C.

Place. — There are no geographical terms in this lesson, but one of the caves in which David hid is elsewhere given the name Adullam (1 Sam. 22:1), located southwest of Jerusalem.

THE PLAN OF THE LESSON.

SUBJECT: God Reveals Himself and Is Truly Found to Be the Never-Failing Refuge for Those Who are His in the Days of Their Deepest Troubles.

I. A PRAYER AT THE TIME OF GREAT TROUBLE, Psalm 142.
1. He pours out his soul unto Jehovah, vs. 1, 2.
2. He is persuaded the Lord has full knowledge of his anguish, v. 3.
3. His refuge is only in God, vs. 4, 5.
4. His specific requests, vs. 6, 7.

II. THE LORD IS THE REFUGE OF HIS PEOPLE, Psalm 46.
1. The challenge of confidence, vs. 1–3.
2. The secret of confidence, vs. 4–7.
3. The vindication of confidence, vs. 8–11.

THE TEACHER'S LIBRARY.

The more important commentaries on the Book of Psalms will be found in the bibliography for the lesson of November 21. For some reason, there is almost no sermonic material on the verses assigned for our lesson. Much of what there is seems difficult to come upon, and not valuable enough for listing here. There are three exceptions: On the concluding verses of Psalm 46, see G. Campbell Morgan in *The Westminster Pulpit*, Vol. 9, pp. 177–184; Alexander Maclaren: *Expositions of Holy Scripture, Psalms 1–49*, pp. 327–350; and on Psalm 142, a page by Alexander Whyte in *The Expositor's Dictionary of Texts*, Vol. 1, p. 504, the source of which is not given. The best treatment I have found on Psalm 142, even though brief, is in Volume 5 of Calvin on the Psalms.

AUDIO-VISUAL AIDS.

No audio-visual aids discovered.

PSALM 142:1. I cry with my voice unto Jehovah; With my voice unto Jehovah do I make supplication.

2. I pour out my complaint before him; I show before him my trouble.

There is one precious invitation in the Psalter, extended to all the children of God, that might well stand as a perfect summary of the Psalm we are now about to study — "Pour out your heart before God: God is a refuge for us" (Ps. 62:8).

I. **A PRAYER AT A TIME OF GREAT TROUBLE, Psalm 142.** The title of this psalm, which was probably inserted during the kingdom age, informs us that it was composed by David either when he was in the Cave of Adullam (1 Samuel 22) or in the caves around Engedi (1 Samuel 24), fleeing from the wrath of Saul, the reigning king, who would soon meet his tragic death on Mount Gilboa in the overwhelming victory of the Philistines. Delitzsch says that this is "the last of the eight Davidic Psalms which derive from the time of the persecution of Saul."

1. HE POURS OUT HIS SOUL UNTO JEHOVAH, Psalm 142. 1. **I cry with my voice unto Jehovah; With my voice unto Jehovah do I make supplication.** 2. **I pour out my complaint before him; I show before him my trouble.** "With my

3. When my spirit was overwhelmed within me, Thou knewest my path. In the way wherein I walk Have they hidden a snare for me.

4. Look on *my* right hand, and see; For there is no man that knoweth me: Refuge hath failed me; No man careth for my soul.

5. I cried unto thee, O Jehovah; I said, Thou art my refuge, My portion in the land of the living.

---

voice" tells us that David is in such anguish that he cannot pray silently but pours out his prayer vocally, aloud, to the Lord. Of course, no one can come to God in a prayer like this unless he knows God and is on intimate terms with Him. Prayer is natural to David, for He has known God in the preceding years. It was the Lord who called him out of the shepherd life and led Samuel to anoint him as the coming king; who had preserved his life often before. There is one thing we ought to note here — that those who are walking in the will of God may often be overwhelmed with trouble. David is not in torment here because of some great sin, but because of the persecution of Saul.

2. HE IS PERSUADED THE LORD HAS FULL KNOWLEDGE OF HIS ANGUISH, v. 3. **When my spirit was overwhelmed within me, Thou knewest my path. In the way wherein I walk Have they hidden a snare for me.** "Though he owns here that he felt anxiety, yet he confirms what he had said as to the constancy of his faith. The figure which he uses of his spirit being *perplexed* aptly represents the state of the mind in alternating between various resolutions when there was no apparent outgate from danger, and increasing its distress by resorting to all kinds of devices. He adds, that though there was no apparent way of safety, God knew from the beginning in what way his deliverance should be effected. Others put a different meaning upon this clause, 'thou knowest my way,' as if David asserted God to have been witness of his integrity, but the other is the more correct, that God knew the way to deliver him, while his own mind was distracted by a variety of thoughts, and yet could not conceive any mode of extrication. The words teach us, when we have tried every remedy and know not what to do, to rest satisfied with the conviction that God is acquainted with our afflictions, and condescends to care for us, as Abraham said, 'The Lord will provide' (Gen. 22:8)." — *John Calvin.*

3. HIS REFUGE IS ONLY IN GOD, vs. 4, 5. **4. Look on *my* right hand, and see; For there is no man that knoweth me: Refuge hath failed me; No man careth for my soul. 5. I cried unto thee, O Jehovah; I said, Thou art my refuge, My portion in the land of the living.** "The prayer of the poet now becomes deep-breathed and excited, inasmuch as he goes more minutely into the details of his straitened situation. Everywhere, whithersoever he has to go (compare 143:8) the snares of craftily calculating foes threaten him. Even God's all-seeing eye will not discover any one who would right faithfully and carefully interest himself in him. The fact that David, although surrounded by a band of loyal subjects, confesses to having no true friend, is to be understood similarly to the language of Paul when he says in Philippians 2:20, 'I have no man like-minded.' All human love, since sin has taken possession of humanity, is more or less selfish, and all fellowship of faith and of love imperfect; and there are circumstances in life in which these dark sides make themselves felt overpoweringly, so that a man seems to himself to be perfectly isolated and turns all the more urgently to God, who alone is able to supply the soul's want of some object to love, whose love is absolutely unselfish, and unchangeable, and unclouded, to whom the soul can confide without reserve whatever burdens it, and who not only honestly desires its good, but is able also to compass it in spite of every obstacle. Surrounded by bloodthirsty enemies, and misunderstood, or at least not thoroughly understood, by his friends, David feels himself broken off from all created beings. On this earth every kind of refuge is for him lost. There is no one there who should ask after or care for his soul, and should right earnestly exert himself for its deliverance. Thus, then, despairing

6. Attend unto my cry; For I am brought very low: Deliver me from my persecutors; For they are stronger than I.

7. Bring my soul out of prison, That I may give thanks unto thy name: The righteous shall compass me about; For thou wilt deal bountifully with me.

---

of all visible things, he cries to the Invisible One." — *F. Delitzsch.* One cannot help but think here of Paul's own confession at the end of his Second Epistle to Timothy, "At my first defense no man took my part, but all forsook me" (4:16).

4. HIS SPECIFIC REQUESTS, vs. 6, 7.   **6. Attend unto my cry; For I am brought very low: Deliver me from my persecutors; For they are stronger than I.**   Kirkpatrick says that this might be called a mosaic of phrases which can be found elsewhere in Ps. 17:1; 79:8; 31:15, etc.   **7. Bring my soul out of prison, That I may give thanks unto thy name: The righteous shall compass me about; For thou wilt deal bountifully with me.**   "By 'prison' some suppose he alludes to the cave where he was lodged, but this is too restricted a meaning.   Of the clause, 'the righteous shall compass me,' . . . if any consider the words not to be figurative, the sense will be, That the righteous would not only congratulate him, but place a crown upon his head in token of victory.   Some explain the passage, They will assemble to congratulate me, and will stand round me on every side like a crown.   As the words literally read, 'they will crown upon me,' some supply another pronoun, and give this sense, that the righteous would construe the mercy bestowed upon David as a glory conferred upon themselves; for when God delivers any of his children he holds out the prospect of deliverance to the rest, and, as it were, gifts them with a crown.   The sense which I have adopted is the simplest, however, That the mercy vouchsafed would be shown conspicuously to all as in a theatre, proving a signal example to the righteous for establishment of their faith." — *John Calvin.* "The very fact that David contemplates his own destiny and the destiny of his foes in a not merely ideal but foreordainedly casual connection with the general end of the two powers that stand opposed to one another in the world, belongs to the characteristic impress of the Psalms of David that come from the time of Saul's persecution." — *F. Delitzsch.*

II. **THE LORD IS THE REFUGE OF HIS PEOPLE,** Psalm 46. Dr. G. Campbell Morgan says that comment on this great song of confidence seems almost unnecessary, "so beautifully has it taken hold upon the heart of humanity and so perfectly does it set forth the experience of trusting souls in all ages in circumstances of tempest shock." Though I almost invariably make my own outlines, the three-fold division used here has been suggested by Dr. G. Campbell Morgan. "The miraculous deliverance of Jerusalem from the army of Sennacherib in the reign of Hezekiah (701 B.C.) may be assigned as the occasion of these Psalms (46–48), with a probability which approaches certainty. Hezekiah had asserted his independence of Assyria and Sennacherib had come to chastise his rebellious vassal. The exact course of events is obscure, but it appears that Sennacherib, after razing Judah, compelled Hezekiah to make a humble submission and pay a heavy indemnity, without however requiring the surrender of Jerusalem (2 Kings 18:13–16). But reflection quickly convinced him that it would be imprudent to leave behind him such a strong fortress as Jerusalem in the hands of a vassal of such doubtful loyalty as Hezekiah, while he marched on into Egypt, and therefore while he was besieging Lachish with the main body of his army, he sent a force under the command of his chief officers, the Tartan and the Rabsaris and the Rab-shakeh, to demand the surrender of Jerusalem. It was an anxious moment. A refusal seemed certain to ensure condign chastisement when Sennacherib returned victorious from his Egyptian campaign. Jerusalem would share the fate which had befallen Samaria twenty-one years before. But relying upon Jehovah's promise to defend His city, communicated through the prophet Isaiah, Hezekiah refused the demand, and Sennacherib's envoys returned to their master, who was

PSALM 46:1. God is our refuge and strength, A very present help in trouble.

2. Therefore will we not fear, though the earth do change, And though the mountains be shaken into the heart of the seas.

3. Though the waters thereof roar and be troubled, Though the mountains tremble with the swelling thereof.

---

now besieging Libnah. Gladly no doubt he would have inflicted a summary vengeance on his defiant vassal. But Tirhakah's army was already on the march, and all that Sennacherib could do was to threaten. His letter to Hezekiah was a contemptuous denial of Jehovah's power to defend Jerusalem. Hezekiah took it to the Temple, and 'spread it before Jehovah,' appealing to Him to confute these blasphemies, and vindicate His claim to be the living God. Then it was that Isaiah uttered that sublime prophecy in which he declared that Sennacherib's pride was doomed to be humbled, and that Jerusalem would be preserved inviolate. And so it came to pass. A sudden and mysterious visitation destroyed Sennacherib's army. Unable to face Tirhakah, he returned to Assyria, leaving Jerusalem unharmed. A deliverance so marvelous, so strikingly verifying Isaiah's prophecy, and so visibly demonstrating the will and power of Jehovah to defend His people, could not fail to make a deep impression, and must have evoked the most heartfelt expressions of thanksgiving and praise (compare Isa. 30:29). And when we mark the numerous coincidences of thought and language between these Psalms and the prophecies of Isaiah, we can scarcely doubt that some of the noblest of these thanksgivings have been preserved to us in these Psalms." — *A. F. Kirkpatrick.*

1. THE CHALLENGE OF CONFIDENCE, Psalm 46, vs. 1–3. **1. God is our refuge and strength, A very present help in trouble. 2. Therefore will we not fear, though the earth do change, And though the mountains be shaken into the heart of the seas. 3. Though the waters thereof roar and be troubled, Though the mountains tremble with the swelling thereof.** In these three verses we have a number of figures of speech vividly setting forth the convulsiveness of times of national and international confusion, change and turmoil. A mighty empire had come up to threaten Jerusalem, but the Psalmist believed that even though the earth itself was undergoing a change, the mountains were being shaken and the waters troubled, God was the refuge of His own, and their deliverance at such a time. The convulsions of which the Psalmist speaks here are occurring in our world today, with a greater universal scope, and with more terror than the writer of the song ever knew. The secret of such confidence is in a knowledge of God. The mountains and the rivers were made by God, who alone can hold them in check. It is the Lord, as Daniel says in an hour of great crisis, who "changeth the times and the seasons; removeth and setteth up kings" (Dan. 2:21). Everything that occurs on this earth is, first of all, foreknown by God; secondly, it is permitted by God; and thirdly, it can do nothing more than fulfill the word of God. A great verse for expressing confidence in a time of universal change and confusion is Revelation 17:17.

2. THE SECRET OF CONFIDENCE, vs. 4–7. First of all, we should consider the words of Delitzsch on this great river mentioned here. "Just as, according to Genesis 2:10, a stream issued from Eden, to water the whole garden, so a stream makes Jerusalem as it were into another paradise: a river — whose streams make glad the city of Elohim. What is intended is the river of grace, which is also likened to a river of paradise in Psalm 36:9. When the city of God is threatened and encompassed by foes, still she shall not hunger and thirst, nor fear and despair; for the river of grace and of her ordinances and promises flows with its rippling waves through the holy place, where the dwelling-place or tabernacle of the Most High is pitched." — *F. Delitzsch.* "The Lord, not we, determines when the night

10. Be still, and know that I am God: I will be exalted among the nations, I will be exalted in the earth.

11. Jehovah of hosts is with us; The God of Jacob is our refuge.

---

shall thin away its blackness into morning twilight. But we may be sure that the presence which is the pledge of stability and calm even in storm and darkness will flash into energy of help at the moment when He wills. The same expression is used to mark the time of His looking from the pillar of cloud and troubling the Egyptians, and there may be an allusion to that standing instance of His help here. 'It is not for you to know the times and the seasons'; but this we may know — that the Lord of all times will always help at the right time; He will not come so quickly as to anticipate our consciousness of need, nor delay so long as to let us be irrevocably engulfed in the bog. 'Jesus loved Martha and her sister, and Lazarus. When he *heard* therefore that he was sick, He abode two days still in the same place where He was.' Yet He came in time. With what vigour the short, crashing clauses of verse 6 describe the wrath and turbulence of the nations, and the instantaneous dissolving of their strength into weakness at a word from those awful lips! The verse may be taken as hypothetical or as historical. In either case we see the sequence of events as by a succession of lightning flashes. The hurry of the style, marked by the omission of connecting particles, reflects the swiftness of incident, like *Veni, vidi, vici*. The utterance of God's will conquers all." — *Alexander Maclaren.* For the raging of the nations see also Psalm 2:1, 2 and many passages in the Book of Revelation, e.g., 11:18; 14:8; 18:3.

3. THE VINDICATION OF CONFIDENCE, vs. 8–11. In the preceding section, the Psalmist speaks of the nations of the earth raging, that is, rebelling against God, and in vs. 8 and 9, again speaking of the nations, he apparently has in mind the wars and national conflicts on earth, but is assured that the God who is his strength is also able to make wars to cease, and to destroy the very implements of military activity. While I am sure that some of the great periods of peace which the earth has known, especially that time of universal peace prevailing when our Lord was born, have been due to the overruling providence of God, the time when all wars shall cease forever upon the face of this earth has not yet occurred. The promise here is similar to that of Isaiah 2:4, but again, this will not be until the Prince of Peace himself comes to subdue the nations of the earth to his sovereign rule.

10. Be still, and know that I am God: I will be exalted among the nations, I will be exalted in the earth. 11. Jehovah of hosts is with us; The God of Jacob is our refuge. One could devote an entire lesson to verse 10. I would like to bring before my readers some marvelous words on the concluding verse of the lesson from a rare work of Dr. G. Campbell Morgan, seen by few of our generation. "The name of Jehovah was to the Jew the incommunicable name, the one name by which he knew the Deity as self-existent and eternal. Other names of God which have come to us from the Hebrew people are preceded by qualifying words, but never so with Jehovah. The Hebrew never wrote this name fully. It was the unpronounceable name, the incommunicable name, the name that stood lonely in majesty as the sign and symbol of the infinite things of God, which no man could perfectly comprehend, and therefore no man perfectly explain. Jehovah was the name which most forcefully gave expression to the facts concerning God which were beyond human comprehension — His absoluteness, without beginning, without end, without counsel taken, without forethought — for there was no thought before Him — Jehovah. The Psalmist comes very near qualifying the word, for he adds 'of hosts.' Not that the word 'of hosts' really qualifies 'Jehovah,' for, rather, the word 'Jehovah qualifies the 'of hosts.' 'Hosts.' How is that word used in the Bible? It is employed in the Old Testament Scriptures and in the New in different ways. It is used first with regard to the stars. We read in Genesis, 'And the heaven and the earth were finished, and all the *host* of them' (2:1). In the prophecy of Isaiah, 'Lift up your eyes on high, and see Who hath created these,

That bringeth out their *host* by number; He calleth them all by name; by the greatness of His might, and for that He is strong in power, not one is lacking' (40:26). This phrase, 'Jehovah of hosts,' teaches us that Jehovah is absolute, sufficient, and superior. It declares to us that God is the Lord of the heavens, and all their inhabitants. As one has beautifully expressed it, 'The universe of matter and the world of mind were not only created, but are marshalled and ordered of God.' We are now looking upon one side only of the Divine nature and being, thinking of Him as the One Who knows all hosts and marshals and controls them by His own power; and we are reminded of the wisdom of God and of the might and majesty of the Most High — Jehovah of hosts.' " — *Dr. G. Campbell Morgan.* Turning to the phrase, "the God of Jacob," Dr. Morgan reminds us of Jacob's acts of deception and his frequent disobedience toward God, but he finds here a marvelous revelation of the grace of God. "He is the 'God of Jacob.' He was his God, and loved him notwithstanding all his meanness, enwrapped him with provision, led him, told him where to rest his head, and when he had laid that head upon the stone, linked heaven and earth with a symbolic ladder to teach him His care for him, even while he was Jacob. Infinite in His majesty, 'The Lord of hosts'; infinite in His mercy, 'the God of Jacob.' Stupendous in His power, upholding all things by the word thereof, 'the Lord of Hosts'; sublime in His pity, 'the God of Jacob.' . . . 'The God of Jacob is our refuge.' Another word will convey the true meaning of this. 'The God of Jacob is our high place'; 'the name of the Lord is a strong tower, the righteous runneth into it and is set *on high.* Such is the real word: 'The God of Jacob is our high place.' What means it? We have come down from immensity to localised position, from hosts to individuality, from the magnificent outlook of the Divine movements to personal life. And what is the promise about the God of Jacob? That He will be our 'high place'; that we may be set in Him above circumstances, above enemies, above self, and so we look to the future with all confidence and security, because 'The Lord of hosts is with us; the God of Jacob is our refuge.' " — *Dr. G. Campbell Morgan.*

THE LESSON IN LIFE, LITERATURE, AND ARCHAEOLOGY.

"On Tuesday, September 16, 1656, Cromwell was reading the 85th Psalm in Whitehall. It was the day before the meeting of the second Parliament of the Protectorate. The next day, with the usual ceremonies, Parliament was opened, and the Lord Protector addressed a speech to the members. 'Yesterday,' he said, 'I did read a psalm, which truly may not unbecome both me to tell you of, and you to observe. It is the 85th Psalm; it is very instructive and significant; though I do but a little touch upon it, I desire your perusal and pleasure.' Then he expounded to them his vision of hope — God's will done on earth, and England an emblem of heaven where God's will reigns supreme. To this work he exhorted his Parliament to set their hearts. 'And,' he says, 'if you set your hearts to it, then you will sing Luther's Psalm (46). That is a rare psalm for a Christian! and if he set his heart open, and can approve it to God, we *shall* hear him say, "God is our refuge and strength, a very present help in trouble. . . . If Pope and Spaniard, and devil and all, set themselves against us — yet in the name of the Lord we should destroy them! The Lord of Hosts is with us; the God of Jacob is our refuge.' "

A TRUTH FOR THE CLASS TO CARRY AWAY.

In a most amazing way this lesson, especially Psalm 46, is one which we do well to meditate upon, and believingly embrace at a time like this. We should be comforted in the fact that nowhere in the Bible do we find any promise that the mere preaching of the Gospel will subdue the nations of the earth. Only Christ himself will be able to put enemies under His feet. So while the nations are raging today, and wars and the threat of war fill our newspapers, we have the dual promise here, which the eternal God will truly fulfil, that He will bring an end to war at the time of His ordaining, and these nations of the earth will be under His sovereign rule. How long the rebelliousness of man will continue, until Christ shall fulfil this glorious hope for us, no man knows.

What are some of the characteristics of God revealed to us in these two Psalms? What great works had God accomplished in the past which led the Psalmist to such confidence in God for the future? Could any of these petitions of the Psalmist been uttered by the Lord Jesus? What is the difference between the modern slogan we hear so often, "Just relax," and what the Psalmist does here in an hour of distress and trouble?

LESSON X. — December 5.

A CRY OUT OF THE DEPTHS. — Psalms 86; 130.

PRINTED TEXT, Psalms 130:1–8; 86:3–5, 11–13.

Devotional Reading: Psalm 51:1–13.
Beginners Topic: A HOME FOR BABY JESUS.
    Lesson Material: Matthew 1; Luke 1:26–38.
    Memory Verse: Surely God is good. Psalm 73:1.
Primary Topic: WHEN WE DO WRONG.
    Lesson Material: Psalm 86.
    Memory Verse: For Thou, Lord, art good, and ready to forgive. Psalm 86:5.
Junior Topic: WHEN A KING DID WRONG.
    Lesson Material: Psalm 86.
    Memory Verse: For Thou, Lord, art good, and ready to forgive, And abundant in lovingkindness unto all them that call upon thee. Psalm 86:5.
Intermediate-Senior Topic: A PRAYER FOR FORGIVENESS.
    Lesson Material: Psalms 86; 130.
    Memory Verse: For Thou, Lord, art good, and ready to forgive, And abundant in lovingkindness unto all them that call upon thee. Psalm 86:5.
Topic for Young People and Adults: A PRAYER FOR FORGIVENESS.
    Lesson Material: Psalms 86; 130.
    Memory Verse: For Thou, Lord, art good, and ready to forgive, And abundant in lovingkindness unto all them that call upon thee. Psalm 86:5.

THE TEACHER AND HIS CLASS.

The Younger Classes will not find this an easy lesson, and the teacher will have to prepare the more carefully. The following illustration may aid in introducing the material. A few weeks ago a well-known evangelist came to one of our local churches. One evening he was invited to dinner at the home of friends, to which the editor was also invited. In this home is a very sweet six-year-old girl, faithful in Sunday School, and who, in a most unusual way, loves to go to church. When the evangelist came into the house, he asked the little girl if she loved the Lord Jesus, and for some reason she seemed unable to answer. Later when alone, the mother asked her why she had not told the gentleman that she did love the Lord Jesus, and she replied, "I felt so naughty in my heart; I do so many things that are bad." Here was an example of even a fine little girl feeling her own insignificance and lack of perfection in the presence of the name of Jesus. There is no other name like this. The Psalmist, in our lesson today, is prostrate before God as he recalls Jehovah's infinite greatness and goodness.

The Older Classes will recognize

that the phrases and expressions of this lesson are not those found often on the lips of modern man. It is not because we in this age have outgrown the sentiments and experiences here revealed, but rather, today we have a shallow conception of God and have almost no sense of shame for sin whatever. Even in our greatest evangelistic meetings one seldom hears any great confession of sin. We need to get back to these experiences.

THE LESSON IN ITS SETTING.

Time. — There is nothing in these two Psalms that would indicate the dates they were written.

Place. — There is no geographical data here.

THE PLAN OF THE LESSON.

SUBJECT: The Confessions, Petitions, and Praises of the Soul of a Man Who is Longing for a Life of Cleansing and a Richer Spiritual Experience.

I. THE SOUL'S CRY FROM THE DEPTHS, Psalm 130.

1. He pleads with God that his prayer might be heard, vs. 1, 2.
2. His confidence that with God there is forgiveness of sin, vs. 3, 4.

3. His soul waits before the Lord, vs. 5, 6.
4. His hope of redemption, vs. 7, 8.

II. THE OUTPOURING OF THE SOUL OF A GODLY MAN LONGING FOR GREATER SPIRITUAL EXPERIENCE, Psalm 86.

1. His longing to be heard by the Lord and his assurance that he will be heard, vs. 1-7.
2. His acknowledgment of God's infinite greatness, vs. 8-10.
3. His thanksgiving for all God has done for him, vs. 11-15.
4. His final request, vs. 16, 17.

THE TEACHER'S LIBRARY.

In addition to the principal commentaries on the Psalms, the following will be found helpful: On Psalm 86, an exposition in the *Works* of that great man of God, Archbishop Robert Leighton, Vol. 2, pp. 30-48; Alexander Maclaren: *Expositions of Holy Scripture, Psalm 51-145*, pp. 159-169 (which he suggestively entitles, "A Sheath of Prayer Arrows"); John Henry Jowett, *Brooks by the Traveler's Way*, 33-40; and, if one has time for reading it, an exposition by the greatest of all the Puritan divines, John Owen, in his *Works*, Vol. 6, pp. 324-648.

On Psalm 130, see John Adams: *The Lenten Psalms*, 87-110; on verse 1, James Hastings: *Great Texts of the Bible, Psalms 119 — Song of Solomon*, 112-124; on verses 1, 2, Alexander Maclaren: The *Contemporary Pulpit*, Vol. 1, pp. 25-36; and on verse 5, Andrew Murray: *Waiting on God*, 79-82.

AUDIO-VISUAL AIDS.

No audio-visual aids discovered.

PSALM 130:1. Out of the depths have I cried unto thee, O Jehovah.

The opening words of Archbishop Leighton's rich exposition of Psalm 130 might well begin our lesson. "It is undoubtedly both a useful and a pleasant employment to observe the emotions of great and heroic minds in great and arduous affairs; but that mind only is truly great, and superior to the whole world, which does in the most placid manner subject itself to God, securely casting all its burdens and cares upon him, in all the uncertain alterations of human affairs, looking at his hand, and fixing its regard upon that alone." — *Archbishop Leighton*.

I. THE SOUL'S CRY FROM THE DEPTHS, Psalm 130. We are now about to study one of the most influential Psalms of all the Psalter, the sixth of the so-called "Penitential Psalms," frequently entitled *De Profundis*. No author is given, and I think no one can dogmatically say whose experience gave birth to this powerful and inspired prayer.

1. HE PLEADS WITH GOD THAT HIS PRAYER MIGHT BE HEARD, vs. 1, 2. 1. Out of the depths have I cried unto thee, O Jehovah. "The depths are not the depths of the soul, but the deep outward and inward distress in which the poet is sunk as in deep waters (69:3, 15). Out of these depths he cries to the God of salvation, and importunately prays Him who rules all things and can do all things

405

2. Lord, hear my voice: let thine ears be attentive To the voice of my supplications.

3. If thou, Jehovah, shouldest mark iniquities, O Lord, who could stand?

4. But there is forgiveness with thee, That thou mayest be feared.

5. I wait for Jehovah, my soul doth wait, and in his word do I hope.

---

to grant him a compliant hearing." — *F. Delitzsch.*   **2. Lord, hear my voice: let thine ears be attentive To the voice of my supplications.**   "It is certain that the greater part of men, as they babble out vain, languid, and inefficacious prayers, most unworthy the ear of the blessed God, so they seem in some degree to set a just estimate upon them, neither hoping for any success from them, nor indeed seeming to be at all solicitous about it, but committing them to the wind, as vain words, which in truth they are.   But far be it from a wise and pious man, that he should so foolishly and coldly trifle in so serious an affair: his prayer has a certain tendency and scope, at which he aims with assiduous and repeated desires, and doth not only pray that he may pray, but that he may obtain an answer: and as he firmly believes that it may be obtained, so he firmly, and constantly, and eagerly urges his petition, that he may not flatter himself with an empty hope.   For it cannot be that any pious and reasonable desire should be directed toward the throne of God in vain, since he has been pleased to assume it among his titles, that he is 'a God hearing prayer.' " — *Robert Leighton.*

2. HIS CONFIDENCE THAT WITH GOD THERE IS FORGIVENESS OF SIN, vs. 3, 4.   **3. If thou, Jehovah, shouldest mark iniquities, O Lord, who could stand?   4. But there is forgiveness with thee, That thou mayest be feared.**   " 'The forgiveness' spoken of in the law of sacrifice, such as Leviticus 4:20, 26, 31, and proclaimed at Horeb, (Ex. 34:9) and in the Temple (1 Kings 8:34, 35, 36).   This being so, the worshipper learns there 'the fear of the Lord,' and goes on his way, waiting for further light and teaching, waiting for the opening out of the Lord's hid treasures from day to day, waiting for these discoveries with intenser interest than watchman waiting for morning.   With intense desire Israel waited for Christ's coming in the flesh, and for the offering up of the 'one sacrifice for ever,' that was to make the worshipper 'perfect as pertaining to the conscience.'   Yet still he sees only a part; he waits for more of 'the Spirit of wisdom and revelation in the knowledge of Him.'   And if the Lord's Second Coming be the chief time for the unfolding of all that the worshipper desires, then the waiting for that day is not one of the least intense of his feelings." — *Andrew Bonar.*   Today, of course, we have forgiveness of sins through the shed blood of the Lord Jesus Christ.   In the Old Testament, sacrifice was offered for sin; but inasmuch as the blood of bulls and goats can never really take away sin, forgiveness was granted in the Old Testament by the Lord, knowing that the day was coming when there would be a divine sacrifice which would cancel all the accumulated debts of the faithful of the Old Testament (Heb. 9:12–14).

3. HIS SOUL WAITS BEFORE THE LORD, vs. 5, 6.   **5. I wait for Jehovah, my soul doth wait, and in his word do I hope.**   Every word in this sentence deserves extended consideration.   "Patient waiting upon God has a future.   It is an attitude of soul which is closely akin to hope.   It is deeply rooted in the soil of childlike communion with Jehovah, and will yet wave its branches and bear its fruit in the sunshine of covenant love.   The secret of the Lord is its strength.   Having turned its face towards Adonai — for without any descriptive verb he exclaims, 'my soul is *to the Lord*' — he is confident that not more surely shall they who watch for the dawn be rewarded by the glory of the sunrise, than will Adonai, the God of power, appear in His glory, and cause the night of His servant's sorrow to cease.   This sets the reality of the Psalmist's assurance of forgiveness in strongest possible light.   Once he quailed at the prospect of appearing before Adonai, but now the

6. My soul *waiteth* for the Lord More than watchmen *wait* for the morning; *Yea, more than* watchmen for the morning.

7. O Israel, hope in Jehovah; For with Jehovah there is loving-kindness, And with him is plenteous redemption.

8. And he will redeem Israel From all his iniquities.

---

advent of His Divine might is his one inspiration and hope. The same Power which might have crushed him in his state of unforgiven sin is now to appear in his favour and vindicate his confidence. He can therefore trust and not be afraid, even in the dark night of sorrow; he can stay his chastened spirit upon his God. And is this not the pressing need of the present generation? In an age when all the ephemeral playthings of the hour are duly recorded in the morning papers, and the moral energies of the race are in grave danger of being wasted on the multiplicity of trifles; and when even the Church is being tempted to accept the alluring teaching that all human suffering is an anachronism — that the natural human flight from pain is really a spiritual quality which ought to be raised to the dignity of a moral obligation; is there not an ever-growing necessity for the trumpet-call of this time-honoured psalm, emphasising, as it does, the need of a renewed deepening of thought at the centre, a firmer grasp of the value of Divine discipline, and a calm, resigned waiting upon the Lord?" — *John Adams.* Note especially the phrase, "In his word do I hope," often expressed elsewhere, both in the Old and New Testaments; see e.g., Psalm 119. There are men and women who can be trusted, upon whose word we may rest in confidence; but their word does not concern that which the Word of God reveals. God in His Word offers us forgiveness, fellowship with Him, the gift of eternal life, the resurrection of our bodies, a home in glory. 6. **My soul *waiteth* for the Lord More than watchmen *wait* for the morning; *Yea, more than* watchmen for the morning.** "More anxiously than the watchman longs for the dawn which is to release him from his duty does the devout Israelite long for the end of the night of trouble and the dawn of a happier day. The repetition of 'watchmen for the morning' gives a touch of pathetic earnestness. Most commentators suppose that military sentinels are meant by 'watchmen,' but the Targum renders, 'My soul waits for Jehovah, more than the keepers of the morning-watch which they keep in order to offer the morning sacrifice,' understanding the allusion to be to the custom that one of the Levites who kept the night-watch in the Temple was appointed to watch for the moment of the dawn, at which the daily sacrifice was to be offered. This explanation adds point to the comparison, for the Levites were watching with eager expectation for a dawn which would bring not merely release from toil but positive blessing, in the renewed assurance of God's covenant mercy." — *A. F. Kirkpatrick.*

4. HIS HOPE OF REDEMPTION, VS. 7, 8. Here we have an advancement from the personal confession of hope in verse 5 to an exhortation to the nation Israel to rest her hope in the Lord. 7. **O Israel, hope in Jehovah; For with Jehovah there is lovingkindness, And with him is plenteous redemption. 8. And he will redeem Israel From all his iniquities.** The words here are almost those of the New Testament. The phrase, "plenteous redemption" will remind any Christian of the great statement of the Apostle Paul, "the forgiveness of our trespasses according to the riches of his grace which he made to abound toward us" (Eph. 1:7, 8).

II. **THE OUTPOURING OF THE SOUL OF A GODLY MAN LONGING FOR A GREATER SPIRITUAL EXPERIENCE**, Psalm 86. Dr. Graham Scroggie points out the interesting fact that this Psalm is the only one in the Third Book of the Psalter that has the name of David prefixed to it. He continues, "The prayer is a mosaic of fragments from other Psalms and Scriptures. About twenty others Psalms are laid under contribution, and there are thoughts from Exodus, Deuteronomy, Isaiah, and Jeremiah. From this fact we may learn that the virtue

PSALM 86:3. Be merciful unto me, O Lord; For unto thee do I cry all the day long.

4. Rejoice the soul of thy servant; for unto thee, O Lord, do I lift up my soul.

5. For thou, Lord, art good, and ready to forgive, And abundant in lovingkindness unto all them that call upon thee.

---

and value of prayers do not consist necessarily in their originality, provided they are the genuine expression of the heart that offers them. And further, let us learn the value of such a knowledge of the Scriptures as shall allow of our praying in its very words. Though a string of quotations, this Psalm has an individuality all its own, a pathos and a passion which remove it far from artificiality. It is full of the Lord. Three divine titles are employed, and it is worth while noticing what they are, where they occur, and how often. There is God, *Elohim*, five times; Lord, *Jehovah*, five times; and Lord *Adonai*, six times; so that the Lord is mentioned once for every verse except one. They are the best prayers which are fullest of Him. The title *Adonai* expressed the consciousness of specially belonging to God, of standing under His immediate guidance and protection." — *Dr. Graham Scroggie.*

1. HIS LONGING TO BE HEARD BY THE LORD AND HIS ASSURANCE THAT HE WILL BE HEARD, vs. 1–7. These verses constitute a series of petitions which spring from universal need. Maclaren says that there is a specific sequence in them. "They begin with 'Bow down Thine ear,' the first of the suppliant's desires, which, as it were, clears the way for those which follow. Trusting that he will not ask in vain, the psalmist then prays that God would 'keep' his soul as a watchful guardian or sentry does, and that, as the result of such care, he may be saved from impending perils. Nor do his desires limit themselves to deliverance. They rise to more inward and select manifestations of God's heart and tenderness, for the prayer 'Be gracious' asks for such, and so goes deeper into the blessedness of the devout life than the preceding. And the crown of all these requests is 'Rejoice the soul of Thy servant,' with the joy which flows from experience of outward deliverance and of inward whispers of God's grace, heard in the silent depths of communion with Him. It matters not that every petition has parallels in other psalms, which this singer is quoting. His desires are none the less his, because they have been shared by a company of devout souls before him. His expression of them is none the less his, because his very words have been uttered by others. There is rest in thus associating oneself with an innumerable multitude who have 'cried to God and been lightened.' " — *Alexander Maclaren.* **3. Be merciful unto me, O Lord; For unto thee do I cry all the day long. 4. Rejoice the soul of thy servant; for unto thee, O Lord, do I lift up my soul. 5. For thou, Lord, art good, and ready to forgive, And abundant in lovingkindness unto all them that call upon thee.** It is worth noting that the adjective *ready* occurs only here in the Old Testament. "It is on the broad ground of God's mercy, and of that mercy as freely bestowed on *all* who seek it, that he rests. He applies the general truth (v. 5) to his own case (v. 6). In verse 7 he pleads again the need, under the pressure of which he cries to God: it is no unmanly, petulant, peevish complaint that he utters. The calamity is real, and there is but one who has power to deliver him." — *J. J. S. Perowne.* The "lovingkindness" of God is frequently found in the Old Testament; e.g., Genesis 21:23; 2 Chronicles 32:32; Psalm 42:8; and dominating throughout Psalm 136. Maclaren says that in these verses we have three petitions which may be regarded as diverse acts of deliverance or of help. " 'Preserve my soul.' The word expresses the guardianship with which a garrison keeps a fortress. It is the Hebrew equivalent of the word employed by Paul — 'The peace of God shall *keep* your hearts and minds in Christ Jesus.' The thought is that of a defenseless man or thing round which some strong pro-

11. Teach me thy way, O Jehovah; I will walk in thy truth: Unite my heart to fear thy name.

12. I will praise thee, O Lord my God, with my whole heart; And I will glorify thy name forevermore.

13. For great is thy loveingkindness toward me; And thou hast delivered my soul from the lowest Sheol.

---

tection is cast. And the desire expressed by it is that in the midst of sorrow, whatever it is, the soul may be guarded from evil. Then, the next petition 'Save Thy servant' goes a step further, and not only asks to be kept safe in the midst of sorrows, but to be delivered out of them. And then the next petition 'Be merciful unto me, O Lord!' craves that the favour which comes down to inferiors, and is bestowed upon those who might deserve something far otherwise, may manifest itself, in such acts of strengthening, or help, or deliverance, as divine wisdom may see fit. And then the last petition is 'Rejoice the soul of Thy servant.' The series begins with 'hearing,' passes through 'preserving,' 'saving,' showing 'mercy,' and comes at last to 'rejoice the soul' that has been so harassed and troubled. Gladness is God's purpose for us all; joy we all have a right to claim from Him." — *Alexander Maclaren.*

2. HIS ACKNOWLEDGMENT OF GOD'S INFINITE GREATNESS, vs. 8-10. Dean Perowne summarizes these three verses excellently. "There are two kinds of doubt which are wont in the hour of temptation to assail the soul; the doubt as to God's *willingness*, and the doubt as to God's *power* to succour. The first of these the Psalmist has already put from him: he now shows that he has overcome the second. God is able as well as willing to help, and every being on the face of the earth who receives help, receives it from the hand of Him who is the only God, and who shall one day be recognized (so speaks the prophetic hope within him, v. 9) as the only God. This hope rests on the fact that God has created all men ('all nations whom *Thou hast made*') and nothing can be imagined more self-contradictory than that the spirit which has come from God should remain for ever unmindful of its source. In verse 8 it might seem as if God were merely compared with the gods of the nations. In verse 10 they are plainly said to be 'no gods,' though they 'be called gods.' There is but one God: 'Thou art God alone.' " — *Dean Perowne.* The first half of verse 8 is borrowed from Exodus 15:11, and verse 9 is found, almost in its entirety, in Psalm 22:27.

3. HIS THANKSGIVING FOR ALL GOD HAS DONE FOR HIM, vs. 11-13. 11. Teach me thy way, O Jehovah; I will walk in thy truth: Unite my heart to fear thy name. This verse recalls to mind the fact that Jesus Christ came as a *teacher;* that one of the early gifts of the Holy Spirit to the Church was that of *teaching;* and that Paul's Pastoral Epistles, especially, are filled with the words *teaching, teach, taught.* On the beautiful phrase, "Unite my heart," Perowne says, "Suffer it no longer to scatter itself upon a multiplicity of objects, to be drawn hither and thither by a thousand different aims, but turn all its power, all its affections in one direction, collect them in one focus, make them all one in Thee. The prayer derives a special force from the resolution immediately preceding: 'I will walk in Thy truth.' The same integrity of heart which made the resolve could alone utter the prayer. The nearest Old Testament parallels are: the 'one heart,' (Jer. 32:39); 'And I will give them one heart and one way, that they may fear me for ever': and the 'whole heart' of love to God (Deut. 6:5; 10:12). Our Lord teaches us how needful the prayer of this verse is. Compare what He says of 'the single eye,' the impossibility of serving two masters, the folly and the wearisomeness of those anxious cares by which men suffer themselves to be hampered and distracted, and in contrast with all this, the exhortation, 'Seek ye first the kingdom of God' (Matt. 6:19-34)." 12. I will praise thee, O Lord my God, with my whole heart; And I will glorify thy name forevermore. 13. For great is thy lovingkind-

ness toward me; And thou hast delivered my soul from the lowest Sheol. "The psalmist asks for a heart made one with itself in the fear of God, and then vows that, with that united heart, he will praise his delivering God. As in many other psalms, he anticipates the answers to his prayers, and in verse 13 speaks of God's lovingkindness as freshly manifested to him, and of deliverance from the dismal depths of the unseen world, which threatened to swallow him up. It seems more in accordance with the usage in similar psalms to regard verse 13 as thus recounting, with prophetic certainty, the coming deliverance as if it were accomplished, than to suppose that in it the psalmist is falling back on former instances of God's rescuing grace." — *Alexander Maclaren.* The vow "to praise the Lord and glorify His name" springs from an experience of the Psalmist. He has known the love of God which has been manifested to him in the assurance that he has been delivered from the power of spiritual death. We do not know much about the beliefs of the Hebrew people at this time concerning the life to come, but sentences like this persuade us that the deeper hope of their hearts, the longings and expectation of their soul, were never limited by the things of this earth. All of this is consummated and made perfect for us in the great deliverance of the Lord Jesus Christ from the power of sin now, from the fear of death here, and from eternal death, granting to us an abundant entrance into the very presence of God. No human being, no mere religious leader, no philosophical discussion, no laws of nature can bring this about — only God can do these things.

4. HIS FINAL REQUESTS, vs. 16, 17. "The psalm ends with prayer for present help. If God is, as the psalmist has seen Him to be, 'full of compassion and gracious,' it is no presumptuous petition that the streams of these perfections should be made to flow towards a needy suppliant. 'Be gracious to *me*' asks that the light, which pours through the universe, may fall on one heart, which is surrounded by earth-born darkness. As in the introductory verses, so in the closing petitions, the psalmist grounds his prayer principally on God's manifested character, and secondarily on his own relation to God. Thus in verse 16 he pleads that he is God's servant, and 'the son of Thy handmaid' (compare Psalm 116:16). That expression does not imply any special piety in the psalmist's mother, but pleads his hereditary relation as servant to God, or, in other words, his belonging by birth to Israel, as a reason for his prayers being heard. His last petition for 'a sign' does not necessarily mean a miracle, but a clear manifestation of God's favour, which might be as unmistakably shown by an every-day event as by a supernatural intervention. To the devout heart, all common things are from God, and bear witness for Him. Even blind eyes and hard hearts may be led to see and feel that God is the helper and comforter of humble souls who trust in Him. A heart that is made at peace with itself by the fear of God, and has but one dominant purpose and desire, will long for God's mercies, not only because they have a bearing on its own outward well-being, but because they will demonstrate that it is no vain thing to wait on the Lord, and may lead some, who cherished enmity to God's servant and alienation from Himself, to learn the sweetness of His Name and the security of trust in Him." — *Alexander Maclaren.*

THE LESSON IN LIFE, LITERATURE, AND ARCHAEOLOGY.

"When Luther, in the year 1530, was in the fortress of Coburg on four occasions during the night there seemed to pass before his eyes burning torches and this was followed by a severe headache. One night he saw three blazing torches come in at the window of his room, and he swooned away. His servant, coming to his assistance, poured oil of almonds into his ear, and rubbed his feet with hot napkins. As soon as he recovered, he bade him read to him a portion of the Epistle to the Galatians, and during the reading fell asleep. The danger was over, and when he awoke, he cried out joyfully: 'Come, to spite the devil, let us sing the Psalm *De profundis*, in four parts.' Being asked on one occasion which were the best Psalms, he replied, 'The Pauline Psalms,' and being pressed to say which they were, he answered: 'The 32d, the 51st, the 130th, and the 143rd. For they teach us that the forgiveness of sins is vouchsafed to them that believe without the law and without works; therefore they are Pauline Psalms; and when David sings, "With Thee is forgiveness, that Thou mayest be feared," so Paul likewise saith, "God hath concluded all under sin, that He may have mercy on all." Therefore none can boast of his own righteousness, but the words, "That Thou mayest be feared," thrust away all self-merit, teach us to take off our hat before God, and confess, it is all forgiveness, and no merit.' "

A TRUTH FOR THE CLASS TO CARRY AWAY.

One phrase seems to stand out in this lesson, "a man of God." Paul says at the end of the third chapter of his Second Epistle to Timothy that all who are in Christ are men of God; but how seldom do we hear it said of anyone, "He is a true man of God." We might say that he is a great preacher, or a great evangelist, or expositor, or wonderfully liberal with his money, or is a hard worker, but how tragically infrequent is the comment, "He is a man of God." None of the things just listed may be true of us, but anyone has the privilege of being a man of God. If we cannot pray like the Psalmist, let us open our Bible on our knees and pray with the Psalmist, and thus grow in grace. Never shall I forget hearing Dr. Sangster for the first time in Westminster Hall in London during the summer of 1952. When that man opened his lips to pray, I felt lifted to heaven itself. Seldom in years have I so felt that a public prayer was coming from a soul that had lived that week with God.

Do you think that any of these experiences of the Psalmist were those of the Lord Jesus? From what source do you think the Psalmist derived such a rich knowledge of God? Can prayers like these be offered to anyone but God himself? Why are these petitions possible only with a mature servant of the Lord, and not with one just beginning the Christian life? What one truth about God set forth in this lesson do we too rarely consider in these days, especially as we approach God in prayer? (I would say His infinite greatness.)

LESSON XI. — December 12.

YEARNING FOR THE LIVING GOD. — Psalms 42; 84; 102:25-27.

PRINTED TEXT, Psalms 42:1-8a; 84:4, 5, 10, 11; 102:25-27.

Devotional Reading: Psalm 63:1-8.
Beginner Topic: IN BETHLEHEM.
    Lesson Material: Micah 5:2; Luke 2:1-7.
    Memory Verse: God . . . loved us, and sent his Son. 1 John 4:10.
Primary Topic: THE DOORKEEPER'S SONG.
    Lesson Material: Psalm 84.
    Memory Verse: Blessed are they that dwell in thy house. Psalm 84:4.
Junior Topic: THE DOORKEEPER'S SONG.
    Lesson Material: Psalm 84.
    Memory Verse: Blessed are they that dwell in thy house: They will be still praising thee. Psalm 84:4.
Intermediate-Senior Topic: LIFE'S DEEPEST LONGING.
    Lesson Material: Psalms 42; 84; 102:25-27.
    Memory Verse: For this God is our God for ever and ever. Psalm 48:14.
Topic for Young People and Adults: YEARNING FOR THE LIVING GOD.
    Lesson Material: Psalms 42; 84; 102:25-27.
    Memory Verse: For this God is our God for ever and ever. Psalms 48:14.

THE TEACHER AND HIS CLASS.

The Younger Classes may be introduced to this lesson by a brief discussion of a phrase that all have heard about at least one person in their church, maybe more — almost every church has one such individual about whom it is said — "She is the first one here in the morning, and the last one to leave at night." This is a compliment to the person referred to, for the statement implies that this individual loves to be in the house of the Lord. Of course our church buildings can never mean to us what the Temple in Jerusalem meant; and yet, they can become, by regular habits of worship, a place in which we truly love to be. This desire for fellowship with God in His house is especially set forth in Psalm 84.

The Older Classes may be introduced to this lesson by being reminded of a fundamental truth, manifested in all the higher aspects of life, namely, that what we get out of anything is determined, in large part, by what we bring to it. At a concert of the Chicago Symphony Orchestra one evening, I watched a listener, seated near me, following the score of a symphony being played, his fingers moving rapidly across the page as the music proceeded. He seemed almost to be quivering with excitement. When the symphony was finished, he leaped to his feet and applauded. I could not do that, because I could not bring to that concert the knowledge of music which this man possessed. So also in reading a great book, like Dante, or Milton, or Homer, and even the Bible — the more we know of early Greece, the more we get out of Homer; the more we know of history, the more we get out of Dante; the more we know of biblical times, and the deeper our own experience, the more we get out of the Bible. It is so as we go into the house of God. If we go up with a heart of joy, thanksgiving, and love, the service will be so much the richer. If we go up listlessly and indifferently, we come away generally with little blessing. It is in the Psalms of our lesson that we discover those conditions of the human heart which will make an hour of worship so rich and satisfying.

THE LESSON IN ITS SETTING.

Time. — There are no clear indications of time in our lesson.

Place. — Of course, the Temple here referred to, was in Jerusalem. For Mount Mizar see the lesson notes.

THE PLAN OF THE LESSON.

SUBJECT: The Deepest Longings of the Human Heart Find Perfect Satisfaction in God and Only in Him.

I. The Soul's Thirst for God, Psalm 42.

  1. The opening exclamation, vs. 1, 2.
  2. The contrast with others, vs. 3, 4.
  3. He interrogates his own soul, vs. 5–7.
  4. His unshaken confidence in God, vs. 8–11.

II. The Psalmist's Longing for the Temple, Psalm 84.

  1. The fact proclaimed, vs. 1–3.
  2. The blessedness of those who often worship in Zion, vs. 4–8.
  3. The gifts of God to those who trust Him, vs. 9–12.

III. The Eternal Unchangeableness of God, Psalm 102:25–27.

THE TEACHER'S LIBRARY.

In addition to the commentaries on the Psalms, to which we have often referred in the lessons for this quarter, contrary to many of our studies in the Psalms, the one for today has considerable sermonic material. On 42:1, see John A. Hutton: *The Weapons of Our Warfare*, 103–118; verses 4–6, J. Stuart Holden: *Life's Flood-Tide*, 120–133; verse 5, J. Stuart Holden: *Supposition and Certainty*, 89–100; verse 8, J. Stuart Holden: *The Confidence of Faith*, 33–40. On 84:11, see G. H. Morrison: *The Unlighted Lustre*, 65 ff.; Hugh Macmillan: *The Corn of Heaven*, 102–116; James Hastings: *Great Texts of the Bible, Psalms 24–119*, pp. 196–207; and two sermons in a volume I have not been able to consult — R. S. Candlish: *The Sonship and Brotherhood of Believers*, 66–99.

AUDIO-VISUAL AIDS.

No audio-visual aids discovered.

PSALM 42:1. As the hart panteth after the water brooks, So panteth my soul after thee, O God.

2. My soul thirsteth for God, for the living God: When shall I come and appear before God?

3. My tears have been my food day and night, While they continually say unto me, Where is thy God?

4. These things I remember, and pour out my soul within me, How I went with the throng and led them to the house of God, With the voice of joy and praise, a multitude keeping holyday.

I. **THE SOUL'S THIRST FOR GOD,** Psalm 42. We do not know, with any exactness, the historical background for this Psalm. Professor A. F. Kirkpatrick has summarized all that is necessary in the following note: "The author of these Psalms was one who had been wont to conduct processions of pilgrims to the Temple for the great festivals with joyous songs of praise. But now he is forcibly debarred from going up to the worship of the sanctuary. He describes the locality where he is detained as 'the land of Jordan and the range of Hermon,' the district in which the Jordan takes its rise from the roots of Hermon. 'Mount Mizar' was doubtless some hill in the neighbourhood, though it cannot now be identified. He is surrounded by inhuman heathen enemies (43:1) who continually taunt him with being deserted by his God (42:3, 10; 43:2). His faith is sorely tried; but he is confident that he will soon be allowed once more to go up to Jerusalem, and join in the services of the sanctuary." — *Prof. A. F. Kirkpatrick.*

1. THE OPENING EXCLAMATION, vs. 1, 2. 1. **As the hart panteth after the water brooks, So panteth my soul after thee, O God.** As usual, Delitzsch here enters into the very depths of the meaning of this verse. "The soul's longing is as a thirsting hart seeking the water — brooks, a symbol of flowing grace which never dries up and stills the thirst of the soul." "The longing of the Psalmist is described as directed towards God himself, not towards the place of his worship." — *E. W. Hengstenberg.* 2. **My soul thirsteth for God, for the living God: When shall I come and appear before God?** "The addition: 'after the *living* God,' draws attention to what the Psalmist had lost in God, and indicates the ground of his fervent desire and his painful longing after him. His God is not a phantom, which, itself dead, is also capable of imparting life; he is the living, and consequently the life-giving God." — *E. W. Hengstenberg.*

2. THE CONTRAST WITH OTHERS, vs. 3, 4. 3. **My tears have been my food day and night, While they continually say unto me, Where is thy God?** The words here are put on the lips of those who would mock the Psalmist, for, when finding him weeping, they mockingly ask if his God has forsaken him, assuming that if God was with him, his soul would rejoice. But to all of the saints of God, trouble comes at times, and there is nothing in the Scriptures to imply that weeping is unbecoming a servant of the Lord; even our Lord wept when approaching the tomb of Lazarus. 4. **These things I remember, and pour out my soul within me, How I went with the throng and led them to the house of God, With the voice of joy and praise, a multitude keeping holyday.** Deliverance from utter depression is in remembering what God had done for him in the days gone by, his experiences as he went up to the Temple, rejoicing, with a multitude. Dr. J. Stuart Holden has very beautifully said, "What a mysterious thing memory is! It works spontaneously without any apparent stimulus, annihilating time and space, showing no regard for any circumstances — hence the invasion of holiest moments by unworthiest thoughts — and is entirely unresponsive to anything in the nature of control or restraint. It exercises its strange and often awful power unbidden and unchecked; and, perhaps, its strongest fact of all is that it becomes both despotic and reproductive. By that I mean that what a man's memory dictates has a very large influence on what he does. If his prevailing memories are unholy his

5. Why art thou cast down, O my soul? And *why* art thou disquieted within me? Hope thou in God; for I shall yet praise him *For* the help of his countenance.

6. O my God, my soul is cast down within me: Therefore do I remember thee from the land of the Jordan, And the Hermons, from the hill Mizar.

---

present life will inevitably tend toward unholiness, too. But, thank God! the converse is grandly true. If his most frequent remembrance is of the highest and noblest and worthiest things, so, too, will his life tend toward acquiring and achieving them. . . . To remember all this is to make faith's conquest certain, for it is to be in the close following of our Lord Christ Himself. He is our Forerunner and Example in this as in all things else. Think of the memories which must have crowded in upon Him day by day, the causes of depression which had been quite reasonable. And think, too, of the memory which for Him outweighed them all — 'I am not alone; the Father is with Me' (John 16:32). Remember that even your loneliest pathway is not trackless. There are footprints for your guidance; and they are His. Remember Him! This is the answer to the condemnation of the unfulfilled responsibilities, missed opportunities, misused endowments, and misdirected capacities."

3. HE INTERROGATES HIS OWN SOUL, vs. 5–7. In this desperate experience of depression and sorrow, the Psalmist addresses his own soul, asking *why* there seems to be such a heaviness resting upon his inner life, where joy was once bursting forth. **5. Why art thou cast down, O my soul? And *why* art thou disquieted within me?** In a remarkable sermon on this text, Dr. J. Stuart Holden asks, what are some of the causes for a soul's being cast down? He replies, "Well, perhaps one of the most potent is the seeming lack of progress in life. I know that there are those who have met the Lord face to face, and have registered eternal vows of consecration, and have gone back to the home, to the sphere of ordinary life, to the parish, to duty, with a conviction that the power of God was going to be manifested in their lives as never before. And yet, as they sum up the results of it all, they are dissatisfied. . . . And then there are souls cast down because of the nature of their temporal circumstances, circumstances known only to themselves and to God, and circumstances which have succeeded in mastering them. Oh, how many Christians there are who are mastered by circumstances, mastered by their circumstances of poverty, of sickness, of loneliness, and of all those experiences incident upon life in such a world as this! May I say that in allowing your circumstances to master you, you have completely misconceived their divinely-ordered purpose? That poverty, that uncongeniality of companionship, or whatsoever it be that oppresses you, is God's way of blessing you. . . . Many believers are cast down, because of the consequences of honestly attempted obedience to the will of God. You have honestly tried to apply the principles of the kingdom of God, but you have had nothing but conflict and fight, and your soul is cast down within you. Or another has sought to obey God, and has had in consequence to walk in a solitary pathway. Friendships have been broken, human love has been withdrawn and withheld, and you are distressed because of the solitariness of the way. . . . Lastly, there are those who are cast down because of the smart and sting of wilfully committed sin. There are those who are cast down because the awful tyranny of memory has got us in its grip; dread thoughts of deeds of unholiness, of impurity, of unworthiness, rise up before us to condemn us! How can we be otherwise than cast down? Neglected duties, unfulfilled responsibilities, perverted relationships, missed opportunities, misdirected capacities — God knows how guilty we are!" — *Dr. J. Stuart Holden.* **Hope thou in God; for I shall yet praise him *For* the help of his countenance. 6. O my God, my soul is cast down within me: Therefore do I remember thee from the land of the Jordan,**

7. Deep calleth unto deep at the noise of thy waterfalls: All thy waves and thy billows are gone over me.

8a. *Yet* Jehovah will command his loveingkindness in the day-time; And in the night his song shall be with me.

And the Hermons, from the hill Mizar. "Take the word of the Psalmist again: 'Therefore will I remember thee.' I will remember that Thou art working, though the progress in my life seems to be slow. I will remember that Thou hast arranged my circumstances, and that I am here for Thy glory and for my own highest good. I will remember, O my God, that in all these untoward circumstances which press upon me, Thou art disciplining my life and shaping me for Thine own ends. And I remember, O my God, that Thou hast said if I confess my sin, Thou art faithful and just to forgive it, and to cleanse me from all unrighteousness. I say to you, 'Hope thou in God,' the Unchangeable, the Immutable. Leave thy burden with Him, and carry away the son of His praise and of His faithfulness." — *J. Stuart Holden.* **7. Deep calleth unto deep at the noise of thy waterfalls: All thy waves and thy billows are gone over me.** "The floods are the roaring sea-billows of suffering and pain. Flood calls to flood, one invites, as it were, another to pour itself forth upon the Psalmist. The Psalmist points to the origin of these floods: a new opening again of the windows of heaven has brought this new deluge upon him, by which he is already well nigh drowned. This language is descriptive of a great temptation. For just as on the sea, when there is storm or tempest, wind and sea roar, and the waves and billows mount the ship, now high aloft, now into a great deep, so that one sees on all sides nothing but one abyss calling, in a manner, to another, and one thinks the abyss will swallow all up, and the mighty waves will fall upon the ship and cover her; so happens it invariably with the heart in heavy trials. But God has the floods in his hand and power, can soon alter and assuage them, and by his word still them, as the Lord Christ commands the wind and sea and it becomes a great calm. — *E. W. Hengstenberg.*

4. His Unshaken Confidence in God, vs. 8–11. **8a. *Yet* Jehovah will command his lovingkindness in the day-time; And in the night his song shall be with me.** The remaining verses of this Psalm record the resurgence of the Psalmist's absolute confidence in the lovingkindness and unmoveableness of God. David Thomas, in a helpful brief exposition, which he calls "Soul Reliefs," says that here the Psalmist is experiencing four ways by which he escapes from the depression upon him: first, memory; secondly, hope; thirdly, prayer, and finally, self-fellowship. "The Psalmist here does two things — (1) Inquires of his own soul the cause of his own sorrows; and (2) Exhorts it to trust in God. 'Hope thou in God.' God is the 'health of my countenance'; that is, the salvation of my countenance. This means, He will clear away all the gloom that hangs over my face, and make it bright with the sunshine of His love. The soul can relieve itself often by self-communion. A power which it has, and which distinguishes it from all other mundane existences. It can withdraw itself from the outer world, retire into the chambers of its own nature, and there work in order to relieve its own burden, invigorate its energies, and brighten its hopes." — *David Thomas.*

II. THE PSALMIST'S LONGING FOR THE TEMPLE, Psalm 84. Andrew Bonar, the great Scotch divine and song-writer, in his fine, but now seldom-seen work on the Psalms, begins his exposition of these verses as follows: "That pilgrimage of Israel, to the place where the Lord had put his name, was significant of more than met the eye. It told of other pilgrims who should in after ages travel through the world with their heart toward the Lord, and their hope fixed on seeing him revealed at the end of their pilgrimage in another manner than they knew him by the way. It included, too, the journey of him who, as Chief of Pilgrims, was to take the same road, share the same hardships, feel the same longings, hope for the same resting-place, and enter on the same full enjoyment of the Father's grace and glory." — *Andrew Bonar.* We have here, says Delitzsch, "a thoroughly

PSALM 84:4. Blessed are they that dwell in thy house: They will be still praising thee.

5. Blessed is the man whose strength is in thee; In whose heart are the highways to *Zion.*

10. For a day in thy courts is better than a thousand. I had rather be a doorkeeper in the house of my God, Than to dwell in the tents of wickedness.

---

heartfelt and intelligent expression of the love to the sanctuary of Jahve which yearns towards it out of the distance, and calls all those happy who have the like good fortune to have their home there. The prayer takes the form of an intercession for God's anointed; for the poet is among the followers of David, the banished one. He does not pray, as it were, out of his soul, but for him; for loving Jahve of Hosts, the heavenly King, he also loves His inviolably chosen one. And wherefore should he not do so, since with him a new era for the neglected sanctuary had dawned, and the delightful services of the Lord had taken a new start, and one so rich in song? With him he shares both joy and grief. With his future he indissolubly united his own." — *F. Delitzsch.* **4. Blessed are they that dwell in thy house: They will be still praising thee. 5. Blessed is the man whose strength is in thee; In whose heart are the highways to *Zion.*** Maclaren reminds us that there are three extremes of blessedness in this Psalm; the first begins at verse 4, the second with verse 5, while the third concludes the Psalm. May we dwell for a moment on the first. "We can see gleaming through all their words, though only gleaming through them, the same truth which Jesus Christ couched in the immortal phrase — the charter of the Church's emancipation from all externalisms — 'neither in this mountain, nor yet in Jerusalem, shall men worship the Father.' To 'dwell in the house of the Lord' is not only to be present in bodily form in the Temple — the Psalmist did not think that it was *only* that — but to possess communion with Him, of which the external presence is but the symbol, the shadow, and the means." — *Alexander Maclaren.* **10. For a day in thy courts is better than a thousand. I had rather be a doorkeeper in the house of my God, Than to dwell in the tents of wickedness.** The finest comment I know of on this verse is that by David Thomas, upon whom we have depended much in this quarter. "The doctrine we raise from these words is, that time spent in worship is time best spent. Time spent in secular engagements, scientific research, social fellowships, innocent recreations, is worthless to man, compared with time spent in genuine worship. (1) There is no time like it for the development of the highest thoughts. Mind quickens mind. The greater the mind with which we are in conscious contact, the more power it has to rouse the intellect and set the wheels of thought agoing. Conscious contact with God's mind is the strongest impulse to thought, and to thought of the highest kind. Thought upon Him, His attributes, operations, laws, claims, etc. Hence no engagement like that of genuine worship can evoke and develop the wonderful powers of human thought. It is by thought alone that a man rises. (2) There is no time like it for the excitation of the sublimest emotions. As our physical life is in the flowing blood, so our happiness is in the current of our emotions. (3) There is no time like it for the promotion of soul growth. Our well-being consists in the healthy growth of all the wonderful germs of thought and feeling and faculty which are embedded in our spiritual natures. As there were in the earth, when first it came from the hands of Almighty God, the germs of all the vegetable and sentient life that have appeared during the untold ages that have gone, so with the human soul. All the germs of power, greatness, and blessedness that a man will ever become, are slumbering as embryonic germs in his soul. His paradise consists in their development. Now genuine worship is the means, the only means, that can bring

11. For Jehovah God is a sun and a shield: Jehovah will give grace and glory; No good thing will he withhold from them that walk uprightly.

PSALM 102:25. Of old didst thou lay the foundation of the earth; And the heavens are the work of thy hands.

these powers out.   It is only as the earth turns its face to the sun that its seeds of life are quickened, and it is only as the soul turns itself into *conscious* contact with God, that its unbounded potentialities are quickened into vitality and stimulate to growth.   Say not then that time spent in worship is lost time; it is the only well-spent time.   In sooth, all time should be worship, in order to make all time valuable.   God should be worshipped in everything; the whole of life, with all its multifarious engagements, should be one unbroken psalm of devotion.   Like Enoch, we should always walk with God." — *David Thomas.*   11. **For Jehovah God is a sun and a shield: Jehovah will give grace and glory; No good thing will he withhold from them that walk uprightly.**   Almost every word in this verse deserves extended comment, for which of course we do not have time; but I must here place before my readers some of the lines of the great sermon by George H. Morrison, on "The Lord God is a sun," which he calls, "The Glorious Lamp of Heaven."   "I question if the strongest language could exaggerate the indebtedness of the earth to the great luminary.   We owe so much to it, and we are so dependent on it for every thought we think and every breath we draw, that no one can be much surprised at sun-worship.   Without the sun our corn would never ripen, we should have no harvest in our autumn fields.   Without the sun no rose would ever blush, no blade of grass would be green in any meadow, no mantle of royal purple would be cast over the passion-flower at the gate.   Without the sun there would be no dew at day break, no glory of clouds, never one shower of rain.   What lights our coal?   The power of the sun.   What drives our engines?   The power of the sun.   What alone makes physical life a possibility to the millions of the human race?   There is a very literal sense in which it is true that in the sun we live and move and have our being.   Yet the sun is an extraordinary distance from the earth — the sun is ninety-two million miles away. Once more I was greatly impressed by this, that without the atmosphere the sun could never bless us.   Without the envelope of closely clinging air that engirdles this globe like some diaphanous garment, the heat of the sun and all the light of it would fall quite ineffectually on the earth. . . .   When the sun is invisible we still see its reflected light; for we all know that the light which gilds the moon, and which gives such a lustre of brilliance to the planets, is not the light of their own burning hearts but the light of the sun which to our eyes has set.   Now in the spiritual world are there not also times when the sun seems to have set?   There is such evil in the state and such quarrelling in the church, that men are tempted to cry, There is no God.   In such hours, urgent and paramount becomes the duty of personal religion.   In such hours Christian character is called for, with an appeal that no other time can match.   For the Lord God is a sun, and when He seems to sink out of the national or ecclesiastical horizon, then lives that still glow with His light amid the dark are the unanswerable argument for Him." — *George H. Morrison.*

III. **THE ETERNAL UNCHANGEABLENESS OF GOD,** Psalm 102:25–27. These three verses span the eternal ages.   In verse 25, we are taken back to the very creation of the world.   This is followed by a striking expression concerning the transitory nature of this earth.   But with the eternity and unchangeableness of God being reaffirmed, the Psalmist draws the comforting conclusion that the children of God will be established forever.   25. **Of old didst thou lay the founda-**

417

26. They shall perish, but thou shalt endure; Yea, all of them shall wax old like a garment; As a vesture shalt thou change them, and they shall be changed.

27. But thou art the same, And thy years shall have no end.

tion of the earth; And the heavens are the work of thy hands. **26. They shall perish, but thou shalt endure; Yea, all of them shall wax old like a garment; As a vesture shalt thou change them, and they shall be changed.** "The fact that God will create heaven and earth anew is a revelation that is indicated even in Isaiah 34:4, but is first of all expressed more fully and in many ways in 51:6, 16; 65:17; 66:22." — *Franz Delitzsch.* Compare also Isaiah 34:4; Matthew 24:35; 2 Peter 3:10; Revelation 20:11 — a remarkable illustration of the certainty of Biblical truth through the various periods of divine revelation. Bonar points out that the Hebrew word here translated *change* means *something succeeding to another,* having in it the idea of substitution. "If the Lord has created the heavens and the earth by the exercise of his omnipotence, he not only *can* but will change them when they no longer fulfil their destination." — *E. W. Hengstenberg.* **27. But thou art the same, And thy years shall have no end.** With this compare Deuteronomy 32:39; Isaiah 43:10; 48:12; Malachi 3:6 and James 1:17. In an excellent summary of divine immutability, Thomas says that God's unchangeableness means that His being changes not, His thoughts do not change, His love does not change — all this being clear first from reason, and secondly, from the Bible. "Change in a being must occur either on account of something *in* himself, or of some *external* force acting upon him, or both. Men change for these two reasons. But to suppose that there is a principle in God to change Him in any respect, or any power in the universe that can in any way affect Him, is to contradict all our notions of a God. Immutability enters into the essence of our idea of Deity." — *David Thomas.*

THE LESSON IN LIFE, LITERATURE, AND ARCHAEOLOGY.

From the life of David Brainerd we take the following paragraph: "On the evening of Tuesday, September 29, as he lay on his bed, he seemed to be in an extraordinary frame; his mind greatly engaged in sweet meditations concerning the prosperity of Zion. There being present here at that time two young gentlemen of his acquaintance that were candidates for the ministry, he desired us all to unite in singing a Psalm on that subject, even Zion's prosperity. And on his desire we sang a part of the One Hundred Second Psalm. This seemed much to refresh and revive him, and gave him new strength; so that, though before he could scarcely speak at all, now he proceeded, with some freedom of speech, to give his dying counsels to those two young gentlemen before mentioned, relating to their preparation for and prosecution of that great work of the ministry they were designed for."

A TRUTH FOR THE CLASS TO CARRY AWAY.

All the passages of our lesson unfold one great primary aspect of man — his hunger and thirst for God and the house of the Lord. There is something to do about these longings, and that is to recognize them, and then to seek for their satisfaction, for the quenching of this thirst. At the conclusion of this lesson I believe a warning is in order, namely, that if these longings are not responded to, they will ultimately die out. In the New Testament we are told not to quench the Holy Spirit. These longings will not remain in the heart of a man if he does not respond to them. God sends the movement of His Spirit to awaken us to our spiritual needs, but the Spirit does not always strive with man.

Do you think all men have a real thirst for God? (*My reply would be in the negative.*) *Do you think that men without God are, in their deeper nature, dissatisfied?* (*Yes.*) *What are the primary differences between the relation of a*

Christian to the house of God today, and that of an Israelite of old to the Temple in Jerusalem? What verses in our lesson would you say Christ himself often experienced? Who else, or what else in the universe is unchangeable and eternal, apart from the triune God? (Nothing and no one.)

LESSON XII. — December 19.

GLORY TO GOD IN THE HIGHEST. — Psalm 148;
Matthew 1:18–25; Luke 2:1–20.

PRINTED TEXT, Psalm 148:1–3, 11–13; Matthew 1:18–25.

Devotional Reading: Luke 2:8–20.
Beginner Topic: THE FIRST CHRISTMAS.
　　Lesson Material: Luke 2:1–20.
　　Memory Verse: God . . . loved us and sent his Son.　1 John 4:10.
Primary Topic: THE FIRST CHRISTMAS.
　　Lesson Material: Matthew 1:18–25; Luke 2:1–20.
　　Memory Verse: Thou shalt call his name JESUS; for it is he that shall save his people from their sins.　Matthew 1:21.
Junior Topic: THE FIRST CHRISTMAS.
　　Lesson Material: Matthew 1:18–25; Luke 2:1–20.
　　Memory Verse: Thou shalt call his name JESUS; for it is he that shall save his people from their sins.　Matthew 1:21.
Intermediate-Senior Topic: GLORY TO GOD IN THE HIGHEST.
　　Lesson Material: Psalm 148; Matthew 1:18–25.
　　Memory Verse: Oh come, let us worship and bow down; Let us kneel before Jehovah our Maker.　Psalm 95:6.
Topic for Young People and Adults: PRAISE FOR GOD'S GIFT.
　　Lesson Material: Psalm 148; Matthew 1:18–25.
　　Memory Verse: Oh come, let us worship and bow down; Let us kneel before Jehovah our Maker.　Psalm 95:6.

THE TEACHER AND HIS CLASS.

The Younger Classes will not be too young to know the great joy that fills any home when a little baby is born, even though they do not know the *reasons* why there is so much abounding joy. In our lesson concerning the birth of Jesus, everyone is rejoicing, and singing, and praising God, but there is something else that makes this joy more universal and deeper than could ever be true with the birth of any other babe. Mothers and fathers never know when their babe is born what he is going to do in the years to come, but the angels announced to Joseph and to Mary and to the shepherds what this Babe would do, which no one else had ever been able to do and no one since can do — He will save us from our sins.

The Older Classes, it seems to me, should have emphasized the deeper meanings and the significance of the glorious news declared to Joseph in this lesson, and it is this that I shall give especial attention to in our Christmas lesson. There is a danger that in our fascination with the stories of the Magi, the shepherds, the angels, and all the characters that appear in the Christmas story, we sometimes fail to give our supreme attention to Him Who makes the Christmas story what it is.

THE LESSON IN ITS SETTING.

Time. — The 148th Psalm was, no doubt, composed after the return from the Exile, perhaps in the 5th century B.C. Our Lord's birth took place sometime between 4 B.C. and 6 B.C.

Place. — Nazareth, the residence of Joseph and Mary, was about ninety

419

miles north of Jerusalem, and Bethlehem, about five miles south of the capitol.

THE PLAN OF THE LESSON.

SUBJECT: Some Occasions When Men and Angels Both Are Compelled to Offer The Highest Praise to God for His Infinite Goodness and Mercy.

I. ALL THE UNIVERSE IS CALLED UPON TO PRAISE JEHOVAH, Psalm 148.

   1. The Heavenly Host, vs. 1, 2.
   2. Nature, vs. 3–10.
   3. All Degrees of Mankind, vs. 11–13.
   4. Israel, vs. 14.

II. THE ANNUNCIATION TO JOSEPH CONCERNING THE COMING BIRTH OF JESUS, Matthew 1: 18–25.

III. THE BIRTH OF JESUS IN BETHLEHEM, Luke 2:1–20.

   1. The Journey of the Holy Family, vs. 1–7.
   2. The Angels' Announcement to the Shepherds and Their Visit to Bethlehem, vs. 8–20.

THE TEACHER'S LIBRARY.

It is difficult to know what to recommend for the study of the Christmas lesson, so vast is the literature. On Psalm 148, any of the volumes on the Psalms referred to, for example, in the bibliography of the lesson for Nov. 21, will be adequate for the study of the introductory part of our lesson. My readers may wish to consult a very extensive bibliography on the birth of Christ, by the editor, which appears in the *Moody Monthly*, for December, 1952. Bibliographies will also be found in *Peloubet's Notes* for 1952, for December 1st and December 28th. I think here I will eliminate references to material on the cities of Nazareth and Bethlehem, and concentrate, rather, on that relating to the babe, Jesus. First of all, may I suggest the

glorious articles in James Hastings' *Dictionary of Christ and the Gospels* on such subjects as the birth of Christ, Joseph, Mary, the nativity, the shepherds, et cetera. Of course, all lives of Christ will have rich material. See also relevant chapters in Alexander Whyte: *Bible Characters, Joseph and Mary to James the Lord's Brother*, and in H. P. Liddon: *Christmastide Sermons*. On the names and titles of our Lord, much material is of a trivial nature, but there are magnificent sermons in Charles H. Spurgeon's *Sermons on the Names and Titles of Our Lord*. On the Gospel of Matthew, I have found, for this lesson, that the best commentaries are those by John R. Broadus, R. C. H. Lenski, and a work I have not previously used for the Christmas lesson, Dean Mansel, in the *Bible Commentary*. There are also some very vivacious chapters in Samuel M. Zwemer: *The Glory of the Manger*, especially chapters 4, 5, 6, and 8. If one wishes to *study* Matthew's account of the Virgin Birth, there is nothing better than the chapter in J. Gresham Machen: *The Virgin Birth of Christ*, 169–187. Maclaren has a great deal of material on the verses taken from Matthew.

AUDIO-VISUAL AIDS.

There are now a considerable number of Christmas films and filmstrips available. Brief descriptions of them can be found in the *Educational Film Guide* and *Filmstrip Guide* (available in most public libraries) under the classification number 394.26. Since the emphasis in the printed text this year emphasizes the annunciation, the following aids are listed here:

SLIDE SET: "Annunciation to Mary," Church-Craft, 6 sl., col.

SLIDE SET: "The Christmas Story," Visserslides, 17 s. col. A survey of the whole Christmas story including a hymnslide, "O Come, All Ye Faithful." Beautiful coloring.

FILM: "Holy Night," Cathedral, 30 min., sd., b&w or col. This film emphasizes the prophetic aspect of the birth of Christ, beginning with the prophecy of Isaiah. The siege of Jerusalem and the slaying of the 185,000 is shown, followed by the annunciation to Mary and her response and subsequent events in the nativity story. Not recommended for the youngest groups on account of the fighting scenes. Requires some background preparation for the prophetic material.

Inasmuch as our entire lesson is concerned with the subject of praise, it might be well to give some consideration to the exact meaning of the word itself. The finest discussion of the word I have come upon is in a volume published years ago by W. H. Griffith Thomas, *The Christian Life:* "The genealogy and history of praise are contained in six well-known words. They are all associated etymologically and when placed in order they tell their own story. The six words are: 'price,' 'appraise,' 'appreciate,' 'prize,' 'precious,' 'praise.' Praise may therefore be defined as the expression of appreciation. Praising is the result of prizing. We can easily see from this that the praise of God is the expression of our appreciation of God. We prize Him, therefore we praise Him. He is precious, and is therefore to be praised. This appreciation of God refers both to what He is and what He gives, for Scripture uses praise in connection with both ideas. The true spirit of praise will thus be the true expression of our appreciation. In so far as

PSALM 148:1. Praise ye Jehovah. Praise ye Jehovah from the heavens: Praise him in the heights.

2. Praise ye him, all his angels: Praise ye him, all his host.

3. Praise ye him, sun and moon: Praise him, all ye stars of light.

God is real and realized in our life we shall find Him precious, and the result will be praise. But the question at once arises, What is the true spirit of praise? How may we know that this is ours? There is at least one sure test and certain proof: the possession by us of the spirit of joy. When we know what the joy of the Lord is, when we understand what it is to rejoice in the Lord, we shall have the guarantee of the true spirit of praise. What is joy? Joy is a condition of soul, an attitude of soul, an emotion of soul, which is the direct result of our being right with God. It is due to our accepting, maintaining, and realizing a right position before God. It cannot be too strongly emphasized or too constantly remembered that joy is the immediate and necessary outcome of a heart that is right and a life that is straight with God." — *W. H. Griffith Thomas.*

I. **ALL THE UNIVERSE IS CALLED UPON TO PRAISE JEHOVAH,** Psalm 148. We would have all the material we need for any one lesson period without using this remarkable Psalm. It was placed here no doubt as an expression of the joy and gratitude of Old Testament saints over God's returning them to their land, though the Psalm has a greater sweep than a mere recognition of this Divine event. "In this splendid Anthem the Psalmist calls upon the whole creation, in its two great divisions (according to the Hebrew conception) of heaven and earth, to praise Jehovah. Things with and things without life, beings rational and irrational, are summoned to join the mighty chorus. The Psalm is an expression of the loftiest devotion, and embraces at the same time the most comprehensive view of the relation of the creature to the Creator. Whether it is exclusively the utterance of a heart filled to the full with the thought of the infinite majesty of God, or whether it is also an anticipation, a prophetic forecast, of the final glory of creation, when, at the manifestation of the sons of God, the creation itself also shall be redeemed from the bondage of corruption (Rom. 8:18-23), and the homage of praise shall indeed be rendered by all things that are in heaven and earth and under the earth, is a question into which we need not enter. The former seems to my mind the more probable view.

"Isaac Taylor says: 'It is but faintly and afar off that the ancient liturgies (except so far as they merely copied their originals) come up to the majesty and the wide compass of the Hebrew worship such as it is indicated in the 148th Psalm. Neither Ambrose, nor Gregory, nor the Greeks, have reached or approached this level; and in tempering the boldness of their originals by admixtures of what is more Christianlike and spiritual, the added elements sustain an injury which is not compensated by what they bring forward of a purer or less earthly kind: feeble, indeed, is the tone of these anthems of the ancient Church!'" — *J. J. Perowne.* 1. **Praise ye Jehovah. Praise ye Jehovah from the heavens: Praise him in the heights. 2. Praise ye him, all his angels: Praise ye him, all his host. 3. Praise ye him, sun and moon: Praise him, all ye stars of light.** Hengstenberg suggests that the first source of the praise, "in the heights," which would be in heaven, "primarily determines only the place from whence the praise must issue; the persons celebrating the praise are first described more nearly afterwards. 'The hosts of God, in verse 2, are the sun, moon, and stars, which in verse 3 are individually named; compare Psalm 103:21. The only thing peculiar here is the call to praise God. But this merely expresses the satisfaction of the Psalmist regarding that which is done at any rate." — *E. W. Hengstenberg.*

The next seven verses express the Psalmist's call to nature to praise her Creator. Of course this is figurative. Nature cannot be conscious of her Creator, and yet the heavens do declare the glory of God and the firmament showeth His handi-

11. Kings of the earth and all people; Princes and all judges of the earth;

12. Both young men and virgins; Old men and children:

13. Let them praise the name of Jehovah; For his name alone is exalted: His glory is above the earth and the heavens.

work. 11. **Kings of the earth and all peoples; Princes and all judges of the earth; 12. Both young men and virgins; Old men and children: 13. Let them praise the name of Jehovah; For his name alone is exalted: His glory is above the earth and the heavens.** Dr. Andrew Bonar suggestively closes his chapter on this Psalm as follows: "Surely the 'great voice of much people in heaven, saying, *Hallelujah!*' (Rev. 19:1) will present an appropriate response to the call in verses 1–6. And not less does their summons to men on earth (Rev. 19:5, 6) accord with the call in verses 7–13." — *Dr. Andrew Bonar.*

"LET THEM PRAISE, exactly as at the close of the first great division of the anthem, verse 5; and in the same way as there, the reason for the exhortation follows in the next clause. But it is a different reason. It is no longer because He has given them a decree, bound them as passive unconscious creatures by a law which they cannot transgress. (It is the fearful mystery of the reasonable will that it can transgress the law.) It is because His Name is exalted, so that the eyes of men can see and the hearts and tongues of men confess it; it is because He has graciously revealed Himself to, and mightily succoured, the people whom He loves, the nation that is near to Him. If it be said, that what was designed to be a Universal Anthem is thus narrowed at its close, it must be remembered that, however largely the glory of God was written on the visible creation, it was only to the Jew that any direct revelation of His character had been made." — *J. J. Perowne.*

Before beginning the next portion of the lesson I feel lead to place before my readers for their information not only in the study of this lesson, but in all studies of the birth of Christ the principal words and phrases current in our language arising from the exquisite records in Matthew and Luke of the advent of our Lord, which just in the listing will give one a new conception of the inestimable treasures that are here: Advent, Angels, Anna, Annunciation, Apostle's Creed, Benedictus, Bethlehem, Birth of Christ; Christ, Birth of; Christ, Incarnation; Christ, Infancy; Christ, Nativity; Christmas; Conception, the Divine; David, Christ, the seed of; Elizabeth, Emmanuel, Epiphany, Feast of the Nativity, Flight into Egypt, Gabriel, Genealogy, Gloria in Excelsis, Herod, Holy Spirit, Incarnation, Infancy, Inn; Innocents, Massacre of; Jesus, Joseph; King, Christ as; Luke's account of the Nativity, Magi, Magnificat; Mary, Virgin; Matthew's account of the Nativity, Messianic Prophecies, Nativity, Nativity narratives, Nazareth, Nunc Dimittis; Old Testament, Christ in; Presentation, Purification, Quirinius, Shepherds, Simeon, Soldiers, Star, Temple, Virgin Birth, Zacharias. Of course no other character in history, even if the entire life is considered, would ever justly allow for the use of most of these names, which belong to one person only.

II. THE ANNUNCIATION TO JOSEPH CONCERNING THE COMING BIRTH OF JESUS, Matthew 1:18–25. Whether I have ever done this before or not, I would like here, before we actually begin the study of this Christmas narrative, to combine the stories of Matthew and Luke and give the approximate order of the events from the announcement of the birth of John the Baptist to the flight into Egypt. (1) The Announcement of the Birth of John, Luke 1:5–25; (2) The Annunciation to Mary, Luke 1:26–38; (3) The Annunciation to Joseph, Matthew 1:18–25; (4) The Three-months' Visit of Mary to Elizabeth, Luke 1:39–56, in which the *Magnificat* is sung; (5) The Birth of John the Baptist, Luke 1:57–80, in which is sung the *Benedictus;* (6) The Journey of the Holy Family to Bethlehem and the Birth of Jesus, Luke 2:1–7; (7) The Annunciation to Shep-

MATTHEW 1:18. Now the birth of Jesus Christ was on this wise: When his mother Mary had been betrothed to Joseph, before they came together she was found with child of the Holy Spirit.

herds and Their Visit to Bethlehem, Luke 2:8–20, including the *Gloria in Excelsis;* (8) The *Circumcision in Bethlehem,* Luke 2:21; (9) The Presentation of Jesus in the Temple in Jerusalem, Luke 2:22–38, including the Nunc Dimittis; (10) The Visit of the Wise Men, Matthew 2:1–12; (11) The Flight into Egypt and the Return to Nazareth, Matthew 2:13–23. 18. **Now the birth of Jesus Christ was on this wise: When his mother Mary had been betrothed to Joseph, before they came together she was found with child of the Holy Spirit.** We will notice at once that the verbs here are in the past tense. Some great things have happened to Mary that Matthew assumes his readers know, the conception of Jesus in the womb of the Virgin Mary by the Holy Spirit, a Divine event which is described only by one New Testament writer, St. Luke (1:26–38). I think perhaps we ought, before we proceed another step, to give some consideration to the Virgin Mary. I notice in the new monumental one-volume commentary just published by the Roman Catholic Church that they have an entire separate article on, "Our Lady in the Scriptures," in which they acknowledge that the Bible does not say very much about the Virgin Mary, but that what it does say is important, and that is true. "Six Marys are mentioned in the New Testament: Mary the wife of Cleopas, Mary of Magdalene, Mary of Bethany, Mary the mother of Mark, and the unknown Mary of Romans 16:6. But *Mary the Mother of Jesus* is the greatest of them all. Some sixty Marys are found on the pages of secular history. Good Marys, bad Marys, bloody Marys and peaceful Marys, but none approach the Virgin mother in purity or in faith and devotion. No other Mary ever had, or can have, such unique and holy office as the Virgin Mother of our Lord. . . .

"If we turn to the Scriptures as the only rule of faith, Mary is revealed in the gospels as a woman of deep piety, poetic imagination, constant faith, and spiritual insight. She is above all this, and because of all this, the chosen mother of our Lord and Saviour. We hail her today, as the angel did 1900 years ago. She was present at Bethlehem's manger, at the marriage in Cana, in the temple at Jerusalem, beside the cross on Calvary, in the upper room before Pentecost and on the crest of Olivet. Because she treasured all these experiences in her mother-heart, she may well teach us to honor all motherhood. . . .

"The sinlessness of Christ and His headship of believers imply a miracle in his origin. He is the second Adam. The doctrines of the incarnation and pre-existence of the Son demand a miracle in Christ's human origin. It would be incongruous if otherwise. We must not forget that most of those who deny the Virgin Birth of our Lord are not positive about His sinlessness and his Deity. Some have even sought a parallel to the story of the gospel in Greek or Buddhist mythology. . . .

"We honor Mary also because of her character. She was mother in the first Christian home and gave us the first Christian song. Although not mentioned in any of the Epistles and once only in the Acts, we learn much of her character from the gospels. What purity of soul, what delicate reserve, what inspired exultation, what lowly obedience, what simple faith are revealed in the chapters of the nativity." — *Samuel Zwemer.* Our verse tells us that Mary was with child before Joseph and Mary entered into the marriage relationship, though she was betrothed to Joseph. "It appears to have been a custom among the Jews for a betrothed maiden to remain still for some time in her father's house before the marriage was consummated." — *John R. Broadus.* The text would seem to indicate that Mary had not told Joseph of the Divine act which she had experienced and when he discovered that she was great with child, of course inevitably he drew the conclusion that she had been unfaithful to the vows of betrothal.

19. And Joseph her husband, being a righteous man, and not willing to make her a public example, was minded to put her away privily.

20. But when he thought on these things, behold, an angel of the Lord appeared unto him in a dream, saying, Joseph, thou son of David, fear not to take unto thee Mary thy wife: for that which is conceived in her is of the Holy Spirit.

21. And she shall bring forth a son; and thou shalt call his name JESUS; for it is he that shall save his people from their sins.

---

19. **And Joseph her husband, being a righteous man, and not willing to make her a public example, was minded to put her away privily.** Undoubtedly the two talked this over, but it would seem as though he could not believe (and this we can understand) the event which Luke records and which Mary must have unfolded to him. Joseph was one who "could not tolerate an erring wife, but also could not bear to expose her to unnecessary shame. His righteousness is shown not so much in putting her away as it is in doing it privately and not with the formality of the law (Deut. 24:1)." 20. **But when he thought on these things, behold, an angel of the Lord appeared unto him in a dream, saying, Joseph, thou son of David, fear not to take unto thee Mary thy wife: for that which is conceived in her is of the Holy Spirit.** "Divine communications by means of *dreams* are mentioned by Matthew in 1:20; 2:12, 13, 19; 27:19; and referred to in Acts 2:17; not elsewhere in New Testament. Edersheim shows that the Jews attached great importance to dreams. There was probably something connected with such dreams as really gave divine guidance to distinguish them from ordinary dreams. Joseph is addressed as son of David, and thereby somewhat prepared for the remarkable disclosure about to be made. He probably knew that his was a leading branch of the royal family." — *John Broadus.* The late Professor David Smith has a very interesting comment here: "A wise man is never hasty and ere proceeding in the matter Joseph would 'take council with his pillow.' He lay down that night with a troubled heart and as he slept an angel indicated to him the wonderful truth of his betrothed's condition." — *Prof. David Smith.* 21. **And she shall bring forth a son; and thou shalt call his name JESUS; for it is he that shall save his people from their sins.** The word, *Jesus*, is the Greek form of the word, *Joshua*, and the word Joshua, is an abbreviation of a longer word, *Jehoshua*, meaning *Jehovah saves*. The first syllable is the abbreviated form of Jehovah, and the terminating part of the word is the verb, *yasha*. I have always discovered that the first use of any great word in the Bible embryonically contains all the great truths that will gather around that word in subsequent centuries. Now this word, *yasha, to save,* first occurs in the Bible, most significantly, and appropriately, at the conclusion of Israel's exodus out of Egypt, when she has come down to the Red Sea and found the great Egyptian army about to overwhelm her and destroy her. When the Lord allowed the Israelites to pass through the sea on dry land, and then by bringing back the waters and swallowing up the Egyptian hosts we read, "Thus Jehovah saved Israel that day out of the hand of the Egyptians; and Israel saw the Egyptians dead upon the seashore" (Ex. 14:30). "God took hold of a name previously familiar which set the new-born Child among the children of men, rather than separated from them. Jehovah and salvation are here woven into one name. So far as God was concerned it was an affirmation of faith, of absolute assurance and certainty. When heaven spoke to Joseph it was a prophecy, an indication, a hope. The full meaning of the word Paul unfolds in Philippians 2:6–9, where he tells us that in that name of Jesus every knee shall bow. The Babe bore that name and carried it through the simplicity of childhood and the Boy passed out into youth and bore the same name, Jesus, in purity and in resistance to all evil, and he bore it on through the years of

22. Now all this is come to pass, that it might be fulfilled which was spoken by the Lord through the prophet, saying,

23. Behold, the virgin shall be with child, and shall bring forth a son, And they shall call his name Immanuel; which is, being interpreted, God with us.

24. And Joseph arose from his sleep, and did as the angel of the Lord commanded him, and took unto him his wife;

25. and knew her not till she had brought forth a son: and he called his name JESUS.

---

public ministry and he bore it on the cross, and never so unfairly as there. Who is this upon the cross? The Babe whose name is Jesus — Joshua, Jehovah, Salvation." — *Campbell Morgan.* Around this name some of the most wonderful hymns of the church have been written, as for example, Charles Wesley's "Jesus, Lover of My Soul"; Edward Hopper's "Jesus, Savior, Pilot Me"; "Jesus, the Very Thought of Thee" by Bernard of Clairvoux; and the song, "Jesus Thou Joy of Loving Hearts." 22. **Now all this is come to pass, that it might be fulfilled which was spoken by the Lord through the prophet, saying, 23. Behold, the virgin shall be with child, and shall bring forth a son, And they shall call his name Immanuel; which is, being interpreted, God with us.** In the first two verses of our lesson Joseph is prominent; in the next two verses we have the message of the angel; in these two verses we have an inspired comment of Matthew. The quotation used by Matthew is taken from the Septuagint form of Isaiah 7:14. Around this passage in Isaiah a vast literature has arisen, especially since the appearance of the Revised Standard Version. It is probably true, as Broadus and others suggest, that Isaiah did have in mind, in a preliminary way, the fact that Ahaz would be delivered from the dreaded kings of Syria and Israel by the coming of the Assyrians. But as T. R. Birks remarked years ago, "The birth of a child in the usual course of nature would hardly be a sign. . . . Isaiah's prophecy can refer to no wife of the prophet, since this was to be a royal child; nor of Ahaz of whom no younger son came to the throne; nor of Hezekiah, still a mere child." — *T. R. Birks.* Therefore, undoubtedly the Holy Spirit through Isaiah was predicting the coming of the Great Deliverer. This word *Immanuel*, is one of the grandest titles of Christ in either the Old or New Testament. It is a Hebrew word and if we break it up in its three parts we have "Imm" equal with "God"; "anu" equal with "us"; "El" is the word for "God," as in Elijah, "God the Mighty One"; Bethel, "House of God"; Daniel, "God Is Judge"; and here, "God With Us." Now God had already promised to be present with His people, as to Moses (Ex. 3:12), to Joshua (Joshua 1:5), to Isaiah (Isa. 43:2), to Jeremiah (Jer. 1:8), but this name only finds its full, final, and glorious fulfillment in Jesus, Who by being born of a woman is truly God with us, and thus we have a Mediator and a High Priest Who can succor us (Heb. 2:18), and the assurance of our resurrection. A. B. Simpson has some wonderful words on this: "In Jesus God has bestowed Himself on a sinful world. He has given us His Babe and permitted us to do what we would with the tender, sacred gift. Henceforth, Christ belongs to sinful men, and in Him God in all His fulness has been made over as the portion and property of every soul who would accept Him. . . .

"Mystery of mysteries, to the latest ages as aft as from some distant world a new inhabitant will come to gaze upon the glories of the metropolis of this universe; seated upon the throne amid its dazzling glory, He will behold the face of a Man. How transcendently has God honoured humanity by the incarnation of Emmanuel." — *A. B. Simpson.* 24. **And Joseph arose from his sleep, and did as the angel of the Lord commanded him, and took unto him his wife; 25. and**

knew her not till she had brought forth a son: and he called his name JESUS. The Roman Catholics insist upon what they term the perpetual virginity of the Virgin Mary, but surely the word "till" in this passage would indicate that after the birth of Jesus, Joseph and Mary lived together normally as husband and wife, and we believe that such passages as Matthew 13:55 and others imply that later other children were born.   As we conclude this portion of our lesson we should remind ourself of what Dr. Machen justly emphasizes, that throughout this story of the birth of Jesus in the first two chapters of Matthew, "Joseph is never designated as the father of Jesus, though Mary is designated as His mother, and Jesus is never designated as Joseph's son.   Instead, Joseph is told by the angel to take 'the young child and his mother,' but the angel does not use the word 'wife,' though such a word occurs frequently in preceding verses.   The manner in which the relationship of Joseph to Mary and the child is treated throughout the story of the Magi, is natural only if there is something unique in that relationship; Joseph is represented as the guardian of the mother of the child." — *Dr. Gresham Machen.*

III. **THE BIRTH OF JESUS IN BETHLEHEM,** Luke 2:1–20.   It seems to me that the teacher will do well to concentrate on the Matthew passage, and we will have time only for the briefest reference to this marvelously rich material in Luke.   Luke is known as "the Gospel of Womanhood," and many women of the Gospel narratives are mentioned only in Luke, as for instance the woman with the lost coin, the widow casting in a mite into the treasury, and Elizabeth and Anna.   It is thus natural that Luke should give such an elaborate account of Mary and of the birth of her first child.   How perfect the timing, that the decree from Rome regarding taxing should reach Nazareth just in the last days of Mary's pregnancy, so that they would find themselves in Bethlehem, the homestead of the ancestors of Joseph and Mary, just at the time when the Babe was born, thus fulfilling the prophecy of Micah 5:1–3, that there He would be born.   The second paragraph of this chapter is confined to the beautiful account of the visit of the shepherds to Bethlehem.   In Matthew the Gentiles, the learned, the rich, come to the manger of Bethlehem, in the Magi, but in Luke it is the Hebrew, and the poor, and the unlearned that come to the manger.   It is the stars that guide the Magi, but it is the angels from heaven who make an announcement to the shepherds.

Inasmuch as our lesson opens with praise, we should note that this last section embraces a double exclamation of praise to God in prophecy on the part of the angel and in the very experience of the shepherds.   The angels said, "I bring you good tidings of great joy which shall be to all the people," for as Bishop Ryle says, "The spiritual darkness which had covered the earth for four thousand years, was about to be rolled away.   The way to pardon and peace with God was about to be thrown open to all mankind.   The head of Satan was about to be bruised. Liberty was about to be proclaimed to the captives, and recovering of sight to the blind.   The mighty truth was about to be proclaimed that God could be just, and yet for Christ's sake justify the ungodly.   Salvation was no longer to be seen through types and figures, but openly, and face to face.   The knowledge of God was no longer to be confined to the Jews, but to be offered to the whole Gentile world.   The days of heathenism were numbered.   The first stone of God's kingdom was about to be set up." — *Bishop Ryle.*   Now when the shepherds had gone to Bethlehem and seen with their own eyes what the angels had announced, we read "the shepherds returned, glorifying and praising God for all the things that they had heard and seen, even as it was spoken unto them" (v. 20).

THE LESSON IN LIFE, LITERATURE, AND ARCHAEOLOGY.

Psalm 148 was the basis for one of the most famous hymns composed in the Middle Ages, "The Canticle of the Sun," by St. Francis of Assisi, which begins,

426

O most high, almighty, good Lord God, to
thee belong praise, glory, honor and all blessing!
Praised be my Lord God with all his creatures, and specially our brother the sun, who
brings us the day and who brings us the light;
fair is he and shines with a very great splendor:
O Lord, he signifies to us thee!
Praised be my Lord for our sister the moon,
and for the stars, the which he has set clear and
lovely in heaven.
Praised be my Lord for our brother the wind,
and for air and cloud, calms and all weather by
the which thou upholdest life in all creatures.

A TRUTH FOR THE CLASS TO CARRY AWAY.

Thinking back upon this lesson, I believe all of us will agree that praise to God
occupies too small a place in our lives.   No doubt there are many who go from
Monday morning to Saturday night without uttering a word of praise to the
Lord, and then only joining in the congregational singing of hymns of praise on
the Lord's Day.   We may not all have gifts for singing, but all can begin the day
with reading a hymn of praise aloud.   Only those can praise God who know Him,
and the more we know Him, the more such praise spontaneously arises from our
hearts.

*What is the difference between the praise of men in the Old Testament and that
which arises from those who know Christ?   How many different factors make
Christmas the greatest time of joy of any season of the year?   Inasmuch as praise
to men for their achievements is a part of human experience, and justly so, what
is the difference between our praise of men and praise to God?   In what part
of the lesson do we have an illustration of Psalm 148:1, 2?   Why did not the
angels appear to some royal personage in Palestine instead of to the shepherds?*

LESSON XIII. — December 26.

THINKING REALISTICALLY ABOUT LIFE. —
Ecclesiastes 1—5; 12.

**PRINTED TEXT, Ecclesiastes 1:2, 3, 13; 2:1, 18; 3:16; 4:1;
5:10–12; 12:1, 2, 13, 14.**

Devotional Reading: Job 28:20–28.
Beginner Topic: GIFTS FOR LITTLE JESUS.
   Lesson Material: Matthew 2:1–12.
   Memory Verse: God . . . loved us and sent his Son.   1 John 4:10.
Primary Topic: THINKING ABOUT GOD.
   Lesson Material: Ecclesiastes 12.
   Memory Verse: Remember also thy Creator in the days of thy youth.
      Ecclesiastes 12:1.
Junior Topic: THINKING ABOUT GOD.
   Lesson Material: Ecclesiastes 12.
   Memory Verse: Remember also thy Creator in the days of thy youth.
      Ecclesiastes 12:1.
Intermediate-Senior Topic: WHAT IS LIFE ALL ABOUT?
   Lesson Material: Ecclesiastes 1—5; 12.
   Memory Verse: *This is* the end of the matter; all hath been heard: Fear
      God, and keep his commandments; for this is the whole *duty* of man.
      Ecclesiastes 12:13.

427

Topic for Young People and Adults: THE WHOLE DUTY OF MAN.
Lesson Material: Ecclesiastes 1—5; 12.
Memory Verse: *This is* the end of the matter; all hath been heard: Fear
God, and keep his commandments; for this is the whole *duty* of man.
Ecclesiastes 12:13.

THE TEACHER AND HIS CLASS.

The Younger Classes may be introduced to this lesson by a simple illustration. Some years ago it was the editor's privilege to take a trip to Panama. The stokers of the ship were Chinese coolies. The work was exhausting, of course, and especially so as we got near the equator. Some of them fainted, and I understand at times some died from the heat. The tragedy was that most of them, as soon as they got off the boat, would gamble away in one night all the cash that the purser of the boat would give them. It was their pay, and the work was honorable — far better to work than to beg — but how foolish it was to work for days and days in terrific heat in front of the furnaces of a great ship and then throw away all wages for such labor in a couple of hours. And yet, often we do things just as foolish, and our lesson is made up, for the most part, of the confession of a man who was foolish in that he tried to find satisfaction for his inner life by achievements and pleasures without, only to discover that his search for satisfaction in this way failed, and all of his expenditures in these directions were wasted.

The Older Classes may be reminded at the beginning of the lesson that man, though made up of many parts, is nevertheless a unit; that is, he is one single individual, and his physical life cannot be lived apart from his mental life, and what he thinks and does cannot be separated from his spiritual experiences. Each influences the other. The Book of Ecclesiastes is not the record of a man at the end of years of sinful indulgence, but rather, his discovery that no experiences or achievements in the realm of natural life, with all that the earth can give, can permanently satisfy his entire nature. This man was not a loafer; he was not a deceiver; he had committed no great crimes; he was not an unbeliever nor an idolator. He was a man of great ability, of a capacity for deeper things; but nothing brought him satisfaction apart from a knowledge of God. Most of the experiences mentioned here are not sinful in themselves, but they simply do not satisfy.

THE LESSON IN ITS SETTING.

Time. — The time element in this book is not important. Solomon flourished in the middle of the Tenth century B.C.

Place. — Geographical terms are likewise not important. The only city of significance mentioned in the book is Jerusalem.

THE PLAN OF THE LESSON.

SUBJECT: **How a Man High in a Nation's Life, with Wide Experience and Great Achievements Finds No Final Satisfaction in Life Except in the Recognition of God and Obedience to His Will.**

I. THE THEME ANNOUNCED, Ecclesiastes 1:1–3.

II. THE THEME PROVED FROM THE AUTHOR'S OWN EXPERIENCES, Ecclesiastes 1:4—4:16.

III. VARIOUS EXHORTATIONS ARISING OUT OF SUCH EXPERIENCES, Ecclesiastes 5.

IV. THE CONCLUSIONS OF THE WHOLE MATTER, Ecclesiastes 12.

THE TEACHER'S LIBRARY.

The best material for the study of this lesson will be found not in sermons on the texts assigned, because many of them became quite fanciful, but in the commentaries on this book. The following, in chronological order, are the better commentaries: Ralph Wardlaw: *Lectures, Expository and Practical, on the Book of Ecclesiastes* (1868); E. H. Plumptre in the *Cambridge Bible for Schools and Colleges* (1881); C. H. H. Wright: *The Book of Koheleth* (London, 1883) a learned work of over 500 pages); G. G. Bradley: *Lectures on Ecclesiastes Delivered in Westminster Abbey* (Oxford, 1885); T. C. Finlayson: *The Meditations and Maxims of Koheleth* (1887); John F. Genung: *Words of Koheleth* (Boston, 1904); Oswald Chambers: *Shade of His Hand* (Oxford, 1924); see also a superb article on Ecclesiastes in *The Evangelical Quarterly*, January, 1946, pp. 18–34. The older work by E. W. Hengstenberg (1860) is still of great value.

For sermonic material, on 1:13, see Alexander Maclaren: *Expositions of Holy Scripture, Esther to Ecclesiastes*, 317–322; on chapter 12, the same, 402–409; and on 12:1, Hugh Macmillan: *The Daisies of Nazareth*, 69–74.

AUDIO-VISUAL AIDS.

No audio-visual aids discovered.

ECCLESIASTES 1:2. Vanity of vanities, saith the Preacher; vanity of vanities, all is vanity.

3. What profit hath man of all his labor wherein he laboreth under the sun?

The title of this book in our Bible is a Greek word, and though it is named in every recitation of the books of the Bible, I think very few see in it our Greek word for church, *ecclesia*, meaning, a group of people called together. This book is entitled Ecclesiastes, being the meditations of "The Preacher," which in Hebrew is called the *Koheleth*, a word that occurs in no other book of the Old Testament, meaning, probably, one who gathers together an assembly. Certain phrases in the book are repeated over and over again — "under the sun," 28 times; "under the heaven," 3 times; "upon the earth," 7 times. The word most frequently found is *vanity*, called "the watchword of the book, the keynote of its melancholy music," occurring here 39 times. Incidentally, the Book of Ecclesiastes is never quoted in the New Testament. The opening verse tells us that the author was Solomon, the son of David, and while many modern writers deny its Solomonic origin, no one else has ever been suggested to satisfactorily meet all the requirements of authorship that this book demands.

Some years ago Professor Salmon wrote in the preface to his work on Ecclesiastes in the *Bible Commentary for English Readers*, "If to the reader it seem strange that the Bible should contain a detailed record of perplexities which a later revelation has removed, let him remember that the Bible contains an inspired account of the external history of God's people, including the story of the sins and follies of many of them, and that we have all cause to own that this history contains valuable lessons for our learning. In an age when the trials of many are from speculative difficulties more than from the allurements of vice, can we pronounce it unfitting that the sacred volume should also contain for our instruction an inspired account of the internal history of a pious man of old, should make known to us his doubts and difficulties, and let us see how, apparently without being in possession of any such satisfactory solution of his difficulties as could content his intellect, his heart taught him that surely it shall be well with them that fear God, and that the conclusion of the whole matter is that to fear God and keep His commandments is the whole duty of man." — *Professor Salmon.*

I. **THE THEME ANNOUNCED,** Ecclesiastes 1:1–3. 2. **Vanity of vanities, saith the Preacher; vanity of vanities, all is vanity.** Our word *vanity* today means *vain*, but that is not its meaning in this Book of Ecclesiastes. "In its primary meaning the word denotes breath or vapour, and is so translated here in some of the Greek versions (compare James 4:14; so in Isaiah 57:13. It is frequently applied in Scripture to the follies of heathenism (Jer. 14:22, etc.) and also to the whole estate of men (Ps. 39:5, 6; 62:9; 144:4). The translation 'vanity' is that of the LXX. We may reasonably believe that St. Paul (Rom. 8:20) had this keynote of Ecclesiastes in his mind." — *G. Salmon.* 3. **What profit hath man of all his labor wherein he laboreth under the sun?** "The word translated *profit* — meaning basally surplusage, residuum, what is left over — is, rather than the word *vanity*, the controlling term of Koheleth's thought; he is concerned, whether nega-

13. And I applied my heart to seek and to search out by wisdom concerning all that is done under heaven: it is a sore travail that God hath given to the sons of men to be exercised therewith.

ECCLESIASTES 2:1. I said in my heart, Come now, I will prove thee with mirth; therefore enjoy pleasure: and, behold, this also was vanity.

tively or interrogatively, with the question of profit, rather than trying to make all issue finally in vanity. The idea of profit is used in a pregnant, expansible application. It begins as the plain commercial term denoting the wage or reward which, as the thing of final and supreme value, the laborer seeks beyond the work itself; it is the thing which the work exists to produce." — *J. F. Genung.*

II. THE THEME PROVED FROM THE AUTHOR'S OWN EXPERIENCES, Ecclesiastes 1:4—4:16. Before entering upon a study of the text proper, we ought to have before us the major areas of experience which the author calls upon in defense of his statement that life is nothing but vanity: (1) the monotonous sameness of life (1:4–11); (2) the acquisition of wisdom does not satisfy (1:12–18); (3) nor indulgence in pleasure (2:1–3); (4) nor the successful accomplishment of great works (2:4–11); (5) wise men are often no better than the foolish (2:16–26); (6) human life is ruled by inexorable laws (chap. 3); and in conclusion the writer enumerates many of the vicissitudes of national and individual life (chap. 4).

13. And I applied my heart to seek and to search out by wisdom concerning all that is done under heaven: it is a sore travail that God hath given to the sons of men to be exercised therewith. "Wisdom is the instrument employed in carrying out the investigation. The object of the investigation is all that is done or happens under the sun. We are not to suppose, however, that it refers predominantly, much less exclusively, to the moral aspects of human action, but rather, as appears from a comparison of verse 15 with chapter 7, verse 13, mainly to the results thereof. All that takes place beneath the sun belongs to the sphere which had its origin in the fall of man, is tainted with sin, and is attended by sin's fell train of suffering and punishment. Everywhere the earth shows itself to be a scene of vanity. Thus much may be regarded as settled — that inasmuch as wisdom yields so melancholy a result, it cannot be the highest good, it cannot be that good which will satisfy the wretched heart of man. Earthly things must be far other than they are, before wisdom can quicken and refresh the soul." — *E. W. Hengstenberg.* The very nature of man leads him to carry on an investigation of this and that phenomenon, but a mere acquisition of knowledge, however deep and accurate, does not satisfy one's soul.

The second chapter of this book has been helpfully divided by Oswald Chambers as follows: The culture of revolt (vs. 1–11); the culture of restraint (vs. 12–23); the culture of religion (vs. 24–26). 2:1. I said in my heart, Come now, I will prove thee with mirth; therefore enjoy pleasure: and, behold, this also was vanity. "From wisdom Koheleth turns to the pursuit of mirth, in order to see whether the true good is to be found in it, but here again he finds not what he sought, he finds nothing to still the cravings of his heart. . . . Taking the coarsest first, Koheleth tries what wine drinking will do (v. 3). Then he seeks pleasure in great works and improvements (vs. 4–6), in rich possessions, brilliant connections, and in the manifold enjoyments of love (vs. 7, 8) at the same time not renouncing wisdom, but keeping it as his companion in all his undertakings, and letting it be their very life and soul (v. 9). He follows after mirth with all eagerness, intending thus to obtain a recompense for the great trouble caused him by the procuring of the material of pleasure (v. 10). On a closer examination, however, this pleasure also evades his grasp, and so all his pains and efforts appear to him vain (v. 11). The one thought alone that all that which he has effected by his wisdom will be inherited, to judge from the usual course of things in this world, by an evil successor, mixes gall with the satisfaction with which he regards his creations (v. 12). . . . The heart is to be proved, whether perchance it feels itself contented and

18. And I hated all my labor wherein I labored under the sun, seeing that I must leave it unto the man that shall be after me.

ECCLESIASTES 3:16. And moreover I saw under the sun, in the place of justice, that wickedness was there; and in the place of righteousness, that wickedness was there.

---

fully satisfied by this new object presented to it.   The mirth is that which springs from possessions and pleasures. . . .   The laughter mentioned in verse 2 is that which accompanies common sensual gratification: 'mirth' or 'joy' is not identical with laughter, but has a more comprehensive signification, as is clear from verse 10. Extravagant mirth, the intoxication of the senses, at once shows itself to be vanity (v. 3).   But even the joy taken in earthly projects and possessions does not stand the test." — *E. W. Hengstenberg.*   It is not possible to discuss the intervening verses of this chapter here; some of them, as verses 8 and 9, will appear later for consideration.   18. **And I hated all my labor wherein I labored under the sun, seeing that I must leave it unto the man that shall be after me.**   "Alas! to the worldling, who seeks his portion in the present life, as Solomon was now doing, even the simple thought that all must be left, cannot but be, in the extreme, galling and disheartening.   But there is something more here.   They must not only be left, and left to another: the character of the successor, and the use he is to make of them, are matters of vexatious uncertainty: — 'And who knoweth, whether he shall be wise man or a fool? yet shall he have rule over all my labor wherein I have labored, and wherein I have showed myself wise under the sun. This is also vanity.'   If a man has a son to succeed to his wealth and honors, he may be a foolish son, without principle, and destitute of discretion and common sense; or, if there be about him promising symptoms of wisdom, the very succession to riches and splendor may work, as experience shows it to have many a time done, a fatal change; may frustrate a father's partial anticipations; may intoxicate the youthful heart, and effectually make a fool of the hopeful heir.   If a man have no son, and fixes the succession to his estate on one whom he esteems wise and prudent, capable of keeping them together and of using them to advantage, he may have been deceived by specious appearances, assumed for the purpose of obtaining his good graces; or, the same change of character may be produced by actual change of condition, which we have supposed in the case of the son; — and whosoever be the heir, sudden death may prevent his entering on his new inheritance, or may very soon transmit it again to other hands — and these may be the hands of a fool." — *Ralph Wardlaw.*

Professor Hengstenberg has an excellent introduction to the third chapter. "In chapters 1 and 2, the author developed the thought that on earth, the scene of vanity, men may not seek true happiness, that times which seem most fortunate and happy are not so different from wretched ones as a superifical examination might lead us to think, and finally, that all earthly happiness is but glittering misery.   In the present chapter, Koheleth seeks to comfort his suffering fellow countrymen by directing their thoughts to the all-ruling providence of God.   The theme of his discourse is the words of Jeremiah 10:23, 'I know, O Lord, that the way of man is not in himself; it is not in man that walketh to direct his steps. He labours to impress upon them the truth, that all prosperity and misfortune comes from God alone, and admonishes them to humble themselves beneath his mighty hand, that in his own good time he may exalt them.   Everything has its season, and there is a time ordained by God, when every desire of the faithful shall be satisfied.   Here then our duty is not to be careful and murmuring, and to harass ourselves, but to surrender and submit ourselves to, and patiently wait on God (vs. 1-8)." — *E. W. Hengstenberg.*   3:16.   **And moreover I saw under the sun, in the place of justice, that wickedness was there; and in the place of righteousness, that wickedness was there.**   It is in verses such as this appearing in the Book of Ecclesiastes that we have ample proof that the one here recording his

ECCLESIASTES 4:1. Then I returned, and saw all the oppressions that are done under the sun: and behold, the tears of such as were oppressed, and they had no comforter; and on the side of their oppressors there was power; but they had no comforter.

---

experiences was not ignorant of the great spiritual truths of divine revelation. He knows God; he knows God as Creator; he knows there is a judgment to come. "In the Bible there is this conviction, that the basis of human life is in the hand of God, not in the hand of human reason; and that exalted positions — moral, physical, mental or spiritual — make a man either more God-like or more devil-like, by the decree of God and not by chance. If a man has mounted high and has the satisfaction of fulfiling his ambition, he is compelled to be either a great humble man or a diabolical fiend. Solomon is pointing out that when a man has realized his ambition he may pervert it and become tyrannical. Unless kings and rulers are God-fearing men, they may become tyrants of the wildest order." — *Oswald Chambers.* "The judgment of the wicked may be looked for with the greater confidence when they are found occupying the seat of law and justice, thence practising wickedness and misusing their authority for injustice. The tribunal of justice is of God (Deut. 1:17); whoever appears there appears before God (Ex. 21:6; 22:7, 8). For this reason it is impossible that God should leave unpunished the misuse of authority; a thought which is further carried out in Psalm 82. Our duty is to wait patiently for this judgment of God's. The more shamelessly and wantonly their heathen rulers abuse their authority the more certain may we be that it will come, and the more cheerfully may we wait." — *E. W. Hengstenberg.*

In the fourth chapter of this book, Solomon considers the more tragic aspects of normal life on this earth. We recall here other autobiographical passages in the Old Testament, such as Job 35:9. **4:1. Then I returned, and saw all the oppressions that are done under the sun: and behold, the tears of such as were oppressed, and they had no comforter; and on the side of their oppressors there was power; but they had no comforter.** "Koheleth has seen all the labors; now by a similar large outlook he sees the world over, the heartlessness of those who have the upper hand, and its cruel results. There must needs be high and low, stupid and clever, controller and controlled; and the evil that besets these relations is lack of sympathy, the man brutally doing what he has might and opportunity to do, regardless of the misery he makes, or the law he transgresses. This fact touches the very heart of that lack which Koheleth dimly discerns in his world and dispensation — the lack of the free outflow of human love. . . . Outrage is the violence that passes all bounds of decency or expediency. The fact is portrayed in strong enough terms to include the extreme; there is a kind of overflow, or superfluity, even in human heartlessness, which evinces the greatness of man's nature. 'And they had no comforter' is the pathos of the situation put into a repeat, a kind of refrain." — *J. F. Genung.* Of course Solomon did not know as large a world as we know, and the population of the earth at that time was only a fragment of what it now is; and the oppressions of the earth in the last few years have developed into an awfulness and universality that Solomon never dreamed of.

III. **VARIOUS EXHORTATIONS ARISING OUT OF SUCH EXPERIENCES,** Ecclesiastes 5. Up to this point, Solomon has simply been recording his own experiences, and confessing that none of them brought the deep satisfaction for which he was seeking. In the remaining part of the book we have, for the most part, exhortations to his son, and to mankind in general, arising from the experiences he has been describing. The opening words of the chapter refer to the tongue. Notice how the words resulting from bitter experience are multiplied here: In this one chapter we find the words evil (four times), sorrow, oppression, sore trial; and in later chapters, grief, misery, sadness, mourning, etc. Solomon now turns to the

ECCLESIASTES 5:10. He that loveth silver shall not be satisfied with silver; nor he that loveth abundance, with increase; this also is vanity.

11. When goods increase, they are increased that eat them; and what advantage is there to the owner thereof, save the beholding *of them* with his eyes?

12. The sleep of a laboring man is sweet, whether he eat little or much; but the fulness of the rich will not suffer him to sleep.

---

subject of the accumulation of wealth.   **10. He that loveth silver shall not be satisfied with silver; nor he that loveth abundance, with increase; this also is vanity.   11. When goods increase, they are increased that eat them; and what advantage is there to the owner thereof, save the beholding** *of them* **with his eyes?** With this compare Psalm 37:16. "To make treasure is different to making profit. Treasure means that the thing is esteemed for itself, not for what it brings.   What the Bible tirades against is possession for possessions's sake.   'Where your treasure is, there will your heart be also.'   If your treasure is in gold or land or possessions of earth, that is where your heart will be, and when wars and rumours of war arise, your heart will fail you for fear.   If a man has his treasure vested in bonds, and a war strikes, how can he keep his mind and heart at rest?   Panic and devastation and ruin are the result — profitless in every degree." — *Oswald Chambers*.   " 'He that loveth silver' is the man that sets his heart upon riches and places his happiness in the attainment of them; and 'he that loveth abundance' is only another form of the same designation.   He 'shall not be satisfied with silver': that is, when he has gotten it, he will find himself disappointed in his expectations from the acquisition; he will find himself the possessor, indeed, of abundance, but not on that account the possessor of happiness.   A man's ideas and desires enlarge as he advances.   His notions of poverty and riches, where are to so great a degree relative terms, undergo change with his changing circumstances.   What seemed to him riches at the outset of his career, soon comes to be accounted poverty. That which, from a lower point in the scale, was the height of his ambition, becomes, when he has reached it, only a point from which to look higher.   He never says, 'It is enough'; but what he gets is still but the means of getting more.   The thirst of gain, instead of being quenched, becomes more and more ardent and insatiable.   And if a man has not a satisfied and contented mind, he is in want of the very essence of happiness.   He carries about within him a source of disquietude and 'vexation of spirit,' which will make him unhappy amidst the most superfluous abundance.   A contented spirit is the very first requisite of true enjoyment; and the poor man who has but 'food and raiment' and both, it may be, scantily, is more really and substantially happy if he possesses it, than the richest man on earth can ever be without it.   Even when a man has so far appeared to be satisfied with what he has got, as to retire from the pursuit of more, he will still feel a void to a greater degree sometimes, than when the bustle of business kept his mind engaged." — *Ralph Wardlaw*.   12. **The sleep of a laboring man is sweet, whether he eat little or much; but the fulness of the rich will not suffer him to sleep.**   "It appears to be of the anxiety produced by wealth, in the bosom of the covetous, the man who 'loveth silver,' that Solomon here speaks, as adding nights of sleeplessness to days of solicitude and 'vexation of spirit.'   Innumerable are the apprehensions and disquieting jealousies and alarms, some well-founded and others groundless, that haunt the bosom of the rich man whose wealth is his idol and his all; — apprehensions, and jealousies, and alarms, from which the man of moderate possessions is comparatively free.   The full meals of the rich and luxurious may be envied by the poor and hard-toiled laborer; yet they frequently have no other effect than to add to the restlessness of anxiety, harassing even the little sleep they can obtain." — *Ralph Wardlaw*.

ECCLESIASTES 12:1. Remember also thy Creator in the days of thy youth, before the evil days come, and the years draw nigh, when thou shalt say, I have no pleasure in them;

2. before the sun, and the light, and the moon, and the stars, are darkened, and the clouds returned after the rain.

IV. **THE CONCLUSION OF THE WHOLE MATTER,** Ecclesiastes 12. As the Book of Psalms contains many chapters that speak of captivity, oppression, the prosperity of the wicked, the restlessness that follows unforgiven sin, and yet ends with a great series of psalms of praise to God; and as the Book of Job, after a long, moving, pathetic description of the tragic experiences of this sore-tried man, concludes with a great confession of God's infinite greatness; so this Book of Ecclesiastes is brought to a close on a high level, with the solution of the problem — we are to remember our Creator, to fear God, to keep His commandments, knowing that a judgment is yet to come. 1. **Remember also thy Creator in the days of thy youth, before the evil days come, and the years draw nigh, when thou shalt say, I have no pleasure in them;** 2. **before the sun, and the light, and the moon, and the stars, are darkened, and the clouds return after the rain.** Only here and twice in Isaiah, 40:28 and 43:15, do we have the word Creator as a name for God. "Remember him, as the great Author of your being; and spend not the existence which he has given and which he every moment sustains, in forgetfulness of him and rebellion against him. Remember your unceasing dependence upon him for 'life, and breath, and all things,' and cherish the humility that becomes dependent creatures. Remember him, as your all-bountiful Benefactor, both in providence and in redemption; the Father of mercies, the God of salvation. Remember him in all the characters in which he has been pleased to make himself known to his creatures, especially that in which it is the principal design of the Bible to reveal him, as 'by Jesus Christ reconciling the world unto himself'; just in justifying the ungodly; displaying, in the redemption of sinners by the work of his Son, his infinite wisdom, his spotless purity, his inviolable righteousness, and his unbounded mercy, in that inseparable harmony in which, by the necessity of his nature, they exist in his perfect character. . . . The youngest amongst you, and the healthiest and most vigorous, is not sure of a day. If you do not wish, therefore, to die in forgetfulness of God, your safest way is to remember him now: — because he is supremely entitled to the choicest and best, nay to the whole, of your days. He has a paramount claim upon all your time. Every day of your life is misspent, that is spent without God. . . . When every other spring has run dry, or its streams have become vapid or nauseous, the 'wells of salvation' will continue in all their fulness, and freshness, and sweetness. The blessed truths of God will yield to the soul consolation and peace, and tranquil gladness and animating hope. Instead of bitter and unavailing regrets for pleasures that are past and can never return, you will experience, amidst the felt exhaustion of nature; amidst the 'labor and sorrow' of fourscore years, a 'joy with which a stranger cannot intermeddle.' Leaning on the arm of Divine love and power, you will pass without fear through the 'valley of the shadow of death,' and be 'gathered to the grave, as a shock of corn, fully ripe, is brought in in his season." — *Ralph Wardlaw.*

Between the first and the last two verses of our chapter are some remarkable figures of speech which have been given a number of different interpretations. "A variety of analogies have been suggested; the two principal ones being, that here is described the oncoming of a storm, with its various perturbations so much greater in the East, where storms are rare, than with us; and that here is described, in a kind of story, the progressive decay coming upon the bodily members. The latter is the more likely one, if a single basis of imagery is sought; but the effect of crowding each detail into one preconceived picture is to force and belittle the idea. If we read the passage rather as a collection of the natural images of oncoming feebleness and decay, and think of each as an independent metaphor,

434

13. *This is* the end of the matter; all hath been heard: fear God, and keep his commandments; for this is the whole *duty* of man.

14. For God will bring every work into judgment, with every hidden thing, whether it be good, or whether it be evil.

rather than as a constituent of a larger allegory, the portrayal will yield more dignity as well as significance." — *J. F. Genung.*

13. *This is* **the end of the matter; all hath been heard: fear God, and keep his commandments; for this is the whole** *duty* **of man.** "Here Solomon gets above the sun and things begin at once to disentangle and straighten. The 'fear of God' is the Old Testament description of the New Testament 'love of God.' Love God, obey Him, trust Him and all will be well with you, for the judgment approaches in which all wrongs will be righted, and all mysteries cleared up, and you will be made glad with a joy unspeakable. This is the key of the book. Live under the sun, rise no higher and doubt and unbelief will ensue. Live above the sun, spend the days with God, and light and peace you shall have. Dr. McCook imagines a conversation between a bird and a mole which has pushed its head out of the ground: 'What are you making such a noise about?' he asked the bird as it was swinging and singing on a branch of the tree. 'O, the sunshine, the trees, the grasses, the shining stream yonder, and the white clouds on the mountain side. The world is full of beauty.' 'Nonsense!' said Mr. Mole. 'I have lived longer in the world than you have and I have gone deeper into it; I have traversed it and tunneled it, and I know what I am talking about, and I tell you there is nothing in it but fishing worms.' Let a man live 'under the sun,' let him burrow in the earth and strive to get satisfaction for his soul out of it and he will have the experience of the mole. There will come the time, the bitter hour, when he will say with splash of tears and sobs of secret longing, 'My soul hath no pleasure in it.' 'I hate my life.' But let him rise above the sun and bask in the splendor of God's light and presence and he will sing." — *W. G. Moorehead.* 14. **For God will bring every work into judgment, with every hidden thing, whether it be good, or whether it be evil.** "The certainty of this event is ascertained by all the evidence that establishes the divine authority of the Bible; it is confirmed by the secret intentions of conscience; and by all the present irregularities, otherwise so unaccountable in the divine administrations towards the children of men. Every work and every secret thing shall then be brought into judgment — all the doings of men, however private, however anxiously concealed from their fellow-creatures, performed in the dead of night, and far from any human eye, and all their thoughts and desires and purposes, though studiously kept within their bosoms and never whispered to human ear. Nothing shall escape detection and disclosure, the Eye of Omnipotence having witnessed all, and the Mind that embraces present, past, and future, with equal minuteness and equal certainty having retailed all; the sentence pronounced on each individual will be founded in a complete and unerring knowledge of all that he has been and all that he has done." — *Ralph Wardlaw.*

THE LESSON IN LIFE, LITERATURE, AND ARCHAEOLOGY.

The Five Scrolls of the Old Testament as used in Judaism are read aloud in the synagogue as follows: The Song of Songs on Pesah, Ruth on Shavuot, Lamentations on the Ninth of Ab, Ecclesiastes on Succot, and Esther on Purim.

A TRUTH FOR THE CLASS TO CARRY AWAY.

Inasmuch as this entire book deals with the problem of what is, and what is not profitable in life, we as Christians would do well to remind ourselves here of the three things which Paul found most profitable: godliness (1 Tim. 4:8); the Scriptures (2 Tim. 3:16); and good works (Titus 3:8).

What do you think is the least profitable pursuit named in this book? Does a man of lesser gifts than Solomon had have the same experiences as he had? In what ways do our newspapers confirm the conclusions of this teacher? Do you think that in the life of Christ or in the life of Paul there were ever such gloomy verdicts? In what ways does the Book of Ecclesiastes differ from the Book of Job?

INDEX.

The titles of the lessons are printed in SMALL CAPITALS.

437

INDEX.

INDEX.

439